HOMER

THE ODYSSEY

I

104

TO
MY WIFE

HOMER
THE ODYSSEY

WITH AN ENGLISH TRANSLATION BY
A. T. MURRAY
PROFESSOR OF GREEK, STANFORD UNIVERSITY, CALIFORNIA

IN TWO VOLUMES

I

CAMBRIDGE, MASSACHUSETTS
HARVARD UNIVERSITY PRESS
LONDON
WILLIAM HEINEMANN LTD
MCMLXXXIV

American ISBN 0–674–99116–8
British ISBN 0 434 99104 X

First Printed 1919
Reprinted 1924, 1927, 1930, 1938, 1945, 1953, 1960,
1966, 1974, 1976, 1984

Printed Offset Litho and bound in Great Britain by
Fletcher & Son Ltd, Norwich

CONTENTS

INTRODUCTION

THE name "Homer" brings before the mind a definite picture of the blind minstrel, roaming from city to city and singing or chanting portions of the great poems that are traditionally ascribed to him. Such a type is splendidly represented by the bust of Homer in the Naples Museum, and almost all that tradition tells of the poet, save in so far as it is made up of statements regarding his date—which in turn rest upon combinations often demonstrably false—groups itself about such a typical figure, and is plainly without historic worth.

The ancient "lives" of Homer which have come down to us are all later than the beginning of the Christian era, and from them we can gather little that has any claim to attention except the two statements that Homer was an Ionian—Chios and Smyrna being the cities most uniformly given as his birthplace; and that in Chios there was a guild or clan of Homeridae—that is, "sons of Homer." The first mention of the Chian Homeridae occurs in the geographer Strabo (about 18 A.D.). Pindar

uses the term apparently of those devoted to
Homeric poetry without any reference to the Chian
clan, and the word is similarly used by Plato.

As for the name "Homer" itself it is most
naturally taken as that of a real individual—a poet
to whom by the middle of the sixth century B.C.
the great mass of epic poetry which survived from
the early age of Greece had come to be attri-
buted; although as time went on all poems save
the *Iliad* and *Odyssey* were rejected, and in later
antiquity there were those who referred these to
separate authors. The earliest author to mention
Homer is Callinus of Ephesus (about 660 B.C.) and
the earliest quotation from the Homeric poems is
found in Simonides of Amorgos, of the same date,
unless it is possibly to be attributed to the later
Simonides of Ceos (about 480 B.C.). Modern scholars
have, however, made many attempts—all uncon-
vincing—to interpret the word "Homer" in other
ways than as the name of an actual person. The
word itself means "hostage." It has been thought
that the Homeridae may have been "sons of
hostages"—not trusted to fight but allowed to
serve as custodians of traditional poetry—and that
"Homer" is merely their imaginary ancestor;
others, seeking a different etymology for the word,

have held that it denotes merely the legendary
fitter-together or harmonizer ($\delta\mu\hat{\eta}$ + $\dot{\alpha}\rho$) of tradi-
tional poetical material. That the word means
"blind" was assumed in antiquity, but is believed
by no one.

If the personality of the poet, under whose name
the *Odyssey* has come down to us, is thus vague
and shadowy—even the most familiar elements
being drawn perhaps from his own portrayal of the
blind bard, Demodocus—so too there has seemed
to many scholars to be a like obscurity regarding
the early history of the poem itself. Regarding
this the evidence is as follows:

The oldest manuscripts of the *Odyssey* date from
the tenth and eleventh centuries A.D. Papyrus
fragments whose dates range from the third cen-
tury B.C. to the fourth century A.D. carry our know-
ledge still further back, and the evidence afforded
by our acquaintance with the work of the Alexan-
drian grammarians is invaluable in tracing the
history of the text; while, finally, we have quota-
tions from Homer in classical authors, and some-
what vague and not wholly convincing evidence of
the constitution of an authoritative text at Athens
in the sixth century B.C. Certain facts stand out
prominently. First, our modern text is remarkably

well established—far better established than is, for example, the text of Shakespeare. Secondly, this text seems to have been fixed as the result of a purging or pruning process. We know, for example, that the critical work of the Alexandrians was concerned largely with the rejection of lines held on one ground or another to be spurious, that the text of the papyri differs widely from our vulgate text, and that the quotations in ancient authors show many lines not found in our Homer.

From this evidence the conclusion has been drawn that in antiquity "Homer" meant the whole mass of epic poetry—for this there is definite evidence—and that our *Iliad* and *Odyssey*, both as regards text and content, were in a more or less fluid state until they gradually crystallized into the forms familiar to us. On this view it is impossible to speak of a poet, Homer, as the author either of *Iliad* or *Odyssey*. It should be stated, however, that while much of modern Homeric criticism has been analytic and destructive, in many important respects recent studies have shown that both the methods and the results of destructive criticism are misleading, and have given stronger and more convincing grounds for a belief in the essential integrity of both poems, each as the work of one supreme artist.

INTRODUCTION

The most notable Homeric critics of antiquity were Zenodotus of Ephesus, librarian of the great library at Alexandria under Ptolemy Philadelphus (who reigned 285–247 B.C.), Aristophanes of Byzantium, a pupil of Zenodotus, and like him, librarian at Alexandria (about 200 B.C.), and Aristarchus of Samothrace, pupil of Aristophanes and his successor as librarian (about 160 B.C.). Other scholars cited in the critical notes are Rhianus (about 225 B.C.), the poet, Onomacritus (about 550 B.C.), and Callistratus, a follower of Aristophanes.

The aim of the translator has been to give a faithful rendering of the *Odyssey* that preserves in so far as possible certain traits of the style of the original. Such a rendering should be smooth and flowing and should be given in elevated but not in stilted language. In particular the recurrent lines and phrases which are so noticeable in the original should be preserved. Hence even when in a given context a varying phrase would seem preferable, the translator has felt bound to use the traditional formula. This has in some instances necessitated the use of a more or less colourless phrase, adapted to various contexts. In the case of doubtful renderings, alternatives are sometimes given in a footnote.

INTRODUCTION

The Greek text of this edition is in all essentials the modern vulgate. The notes under the text give occasionally the name of the ancient critic whose reading is adopted and note the lines rejected by the Alexandrians. Variants, if cited, are marked off by colons.

BIBLIOGRAPHY

Manuscripts

The manuscripts of the *Odyssey* have been most carefully studied and classified by Mr. T. W. Allen, the results of whose studies are given in the *Papers of the British School at Rome*, vol v., pp. 1–85, and briefly in his Oxford text of the *Odyssey*. Chief among the manuscripts are:–

Laur. 32, 24 and Laur. 52, both of the tenth century, in the Laurentian Library at Florence.

Harl. 5674, of the thirteenth century, in the British Museum.

B. 99 sup., of the thirteenth century, in the Ambrosian Library at Milan.

Marc. 613, of the thirteenth century, in the Library of St. Mark's in Venice.

Pal. 45, written in 1201, in the Palatine Library at Heidelberg.

[For Papyri, see now Stephanie West, *The Ptolemaic Papyri of Homer*, Köln, 1967; R. A. Pack, *Greek and Latin Literary Texts from Greco-Roman Egypt*, Ann Arbor, 1965. The editions of the Scholia (especially on the *Odyssey*. W. Dindorf, Oxford, 1855; on the *Iliad*, W. Dindorf and E. Maass, Oxford, 1875–1888) are being replaced by that of H. Erbse (vol. i, Berlin 1969).]

History of the Text of Homer

T. W. Allen, *Homer: The Origins and Transmission,* Oxford, 1924.

G. S. Kirk, *The Songs of Homer,* Cambridge, 1962, pp. 301 ff.

A. J. B. Wace and F. H. Stubbings, *A Companion to Homer*, London, 1962, pp. 215 ff. (by J. A. Davison).

BIBLIOGRAPHY

M. H. A. L. H. van der Valk, *Researches on the Text and Scholia of the Iliad*, Leiden, 1963: *Textual Criticism of the Odyssey*, Leiden, 1949.

TEXT, EDITIONS

Iliad. D. B. Munro and T. W. Allen, Oxford, 3rd ed., 1920; T. W. Allen, Oxford, 1931; P. Mazon (with French translation), Association G. Budé, Paris, 1947–1949; E. Schwarz, ed. Br. Snell, Berlin-Darmstadt, 1956.

Odyssey. T. W. Allen, Oxford, 2nd ed., 1917–1919; V. Bérard (with French translation), Association G. Budé, Paris, 2nd ed., 1933; P. von der Muhll (Basel, 1946); E. Schwarz, ed. Br. Snell, Berlin-Darmstadt, 1956.

TRANSLATIONS INTO ENGLISH

Of the many which exist, we mention the following only. The quasi-biblical English prose-renderings of the *Iliad* by A. Lang, W. Leaf and E. Myers (1883) and of the *Odyssey* by S. A. Butcher and A. Lang (1889) must give way to the much more acceptable prose of E. V. Rieu (*Iliad*, Penguin Books, 1950; and a superior *Odyssey*, Penguin Books, 1946) and the excellent free verse of R. Lattimore (*Iliad*, Chicago, 1951; *Odyssey*, New York, 1967).

COMMENTARIES IN ENGLISH

On the *Iliad* we must still use that of D. B. Munro, Oxford, 1884, and that of W. Leaf and M. A. Bayfield, London, 1895–1898; but a commentary is in progress by M. M. Wilcock—books 1–6 appeared in 1970 (London); on the *Odyssey* there is now W. B. Stanford, *Odyssey*, London, 2nd ed., 1958.

LEXICA AND GRAMMARS

For English readers R. J. Cunliffe, *A Lexicon of the Homeric Dialect*, London, 1924, is useful; as is also A. Gehring, *Index Homericus*, Leipzig, 1891. Invaluable is H. Ebeling (ed.), *Lexicon Homericum*, Leipzig, 1880–1885; Olms, 1963—a

BIBLIOGRAPHY

reprint. In progress is the great *Lexicon des frühgriechischen Epos* under the care of Br. Snell, H. J. Mette, and others (Göttingen, 1955–). The best grammar is that of P. Chantraine, *Grammaire homérique*, Paris, 2nd ed., 1953, 2 vols.

The modern literature about Homer is now very extensive, and readers should consult the surveys of it which have been made: F. M. Combellack in *Classical Weekly*, xlix, 1955, pp. 17 ff. E. R. Dodds, L. R. Palmer, and D. H. F. Gray in *Fifty Years of Classical Scholarship*, ed. M. Platnauer, Oxford, 1954, 1968. In *Lustrum*, I, 1956, H. J. Mette, "Homer 1930–1956," pp. 7 ff., 319; and in II, 1957, IV, 1959, V, 1960, XI, 1966, pp. 33 ff.; in I again T. B. L. Webster, "Greek Archaeology and Literature 1950–1955," pp. 87 ff. and in VI, 1961, pp. 5 ff., XI, 1966, pp. 5 ff. A. Lesky, "Homeros," in Pauly-Wissowa, *Realencyclopädie*, Suppl. xi, 1968, cols. 687–846; and in his *History of Greek Literature* as translated by Willis and De Heer, London, 1966. G. S. Kirk in *The Songs of Homer*, Cambridge, 1962. J. B. Hainsworth. *Homer*, "Greece and Rome," New Surveys in the Classics, No. 3, Oxford, 1969.

Lastly, details appear yearly in *L'Année Philologique* (J. Marouzeau). For general background G. S. Kirk, *Songs of Homer* (see above; also abridged as *Homer and the Epic*, 1964) and A. J. B. Wace and F. H. Stubbings (editors), *A Companion to Homer*, London, 1962. For archaeology: Mrs. H. L. Lorimer, *Homer and the Monuments*, London, 1905; Emily Vermeule, *Greece in the Bronze Age*, Chicago, 1956. *Archaeologia Homerica* (edited by Matz and Buchholz, Göttingen, 1967–) is in progress. Social life: M. I. Finley, *The World of Odysseus*, London, 1956. For the "Homeric Question": in F. M. Combellack and E. R. Dodds and G. S. Kirk and Hainsworth as cited above; J. L. Myres, *Homer and his Critics* (continued by D. H. F. Gray, London, 1958); D. L. Page, *History and the Homeric Iliad*, Berkeley and Los Angeles, 1959; and *The Homeric Odyssey*, Oxford, 1955; Agatha Thornton's *People and Themes in Homer's Odyssey*, London 1970; A. Dihle, *Homer-Problème*, Opladen, 1970.

xiv

HOMER'S ODYSSEY

ΟΔΥΣΣΕΙΑ

Α

Ἄνδρα μοι ἔννεπε, μοῦσα, πολύτροπον, ὃς μάλα πολλὰ
πλάγχθη, ἐπεὶ Τροίης ἱερὸν πτολίεθρον ἔπερσεν·
πολλῶν δ' ἀνθρώπων ἴδεν ἄστεα καὶ νόον [1] ἔγνω,
πολλὰ δ' ὅ γ' ἐν πόντῳ πάθεν ἄλγεα ὃν κατὰ θυμόν,
ἀρνύμενος ἥν τε ψυχὴν καὶ νόστον ἑταίρων.
ἀλλ' οὐδ' ὣς ἑτάρους ἐρρύσατο, ἱέμενός περ·
αὐτῶν γὰρ σφετέρῃσιν ἀτασθαλίῃσιν ὄλοντο,
νήπιοι, οἳ κατὰ βοῦς Ὑπερίονος Ἠελίοιο
ἤσθιον· αὐτὰρ ὁ τοῖσιν ἀφείλετο νόστιμον ἦμαρ.
τῶν ἁμόθεν γε, θεά, θύγατερ Διός, εἰπὲ καὶ ἡμῖν.
   Ἔνθ' ἄλλοι μὲν πάντες, ὅσοι φύγον αἰπὺν ὄλεθρον,
οἴκοι ἔσαν, πόλεμόν τε πεφευγότες ἠδὲ θάλασσαν·
τὸν δ' οἶον νόστου κεχρημένον ἠδὲ γυναικὸς
νύμφη πότνι' ἔρυκε Καλυψὼ δῖα θεάων
ἐν σπέσσι γλαφυροῖσι, λιλαιομένη πόσιν εἶναι.
ἀλλ' ὅτε δὴ ἔτος ἦλθε περιπλομένων ἐνιαυτῶν,
τῷ οἱ ἐπεκλώσαντο θεοὶ οἰκόνδε νέεσθαι
εἰς Ἰθάκην, οὐδ' ἔνθα πεφυγμένος ἦεν ἀέθλων
καὶ μετὰ οἷσι φίλοισι.   θεοὶ δ' ἐλέαιρον ἅπαντες

---

[1] νόον : νόμον Zenodotus.

2

THE ODYSSEY

BOOK I

TELL me, O Muse, of the man of many devices, who wandered full many ways after he had sacked the sacred citadel of Troy. Many were the men whose cities he saw and whose mind he learned, aye, and many the woes he suffered in his heart upon the sea, seeking to win his own life and the return of his comrades. Yet even so he saved not his comrades, though he desired it sore, for through their own blind folly they perished—fools, who devoured the kine of Helios Hyperion; but he took from them the day of their returning. Of these things, goddess, daughter of Zeus, beginning where thou wilt, tell thou even unto us.

Now all the rest, as many as had escaped sheer destruction, were at home, safe from both war and sea, but Odysseus alone, filled with longing for his return and for his wife, did the queenly nymph Calypso, that bright goddess, keep back in her hollow caves, yearning that he should be her husband. But when, as the seasons revolved, the year came in which the gods had ordained that he should return home to Ithaca, not even there was he free from toils, even among his own folk. And all the gods

νόσφι Ποσειδάωνος· ὁ δ' ἀσπερχὲς μενέαινεν   20
ἀντιθέῳ Ὀδυσῆι πάρος ἣν γαῖαν ἱκέσθαι.

'Αλλ' ὁ μὲν Αἰθίοπας μετεκίαθε τηλόθ' ἐόντας,
Αἰθίοπας τοὶ διχθὰ δεδαίαται, ἔσχατοι ἀνδρῶν,
οἱ μὲν δυσομένου Ὑπερίονος οἱ δ' ἀνιόντος,
ἀντιόων ταύρων τε καὶ ἀρνειῶν ἑκατόμβης.   25
ἔνθ' ὅ γ' ἐτέρπετο δαιτὶ παρήμενος· οἱ δὲ δὴ ἄλλοι
Ζηνὸς ἐνὶ μεγάροισιν Ὀλυμπίου ἀθρόοι ἦσαν.
τοῖσι δὲ μύθων ἦρχε πατὴρ ἀνδρῶν τε θεῶν τε·
μνήσατο γὰρ κατὰ θυμὸν ἀμύμονος Αἰγίσθοιο,
τόν ῥ' Ἀγαμεμνονίδης τηλεκλυτὸς ἔκταν' Ὀρέστης·   30
τοῦ ὅ γ' ἐπιμνησθεὶς ἔπε' ἀθανάτοισι μετηύδα·

"Ὦ πόποι, οἷον δή νυ θεοὺς βροτοὶ αἰτιόωνται·
ἐξ ἡμέων γάρ φασι κάκ' ἔμμεναι, οἱ δὲ καὶ αὐτοὶ
σφῇσιν ἀτασθαλίῃσιν ὑπὲρ μόρον ἄλγε' ἔχουσιν,
ὡς καὶ νῦν Αἴγισθος ὑπὲρ μόρον Ἀτρεΐδαο   35
γῆμ' ἄλοχον μνηστήν, τὸν δ' ἔκτανε νοστήσαντα,
εἰδὼς αἰπὺν ὄλεθρον, ἐπεὶ πρό οἱ εἴπομεν ἡμεῖς,
Ἑρμείαν πέμψαντες, ἐύσκοπον ἀργεϊφόντην,
μήτ' αὐτὸν κτείνειν μήτε μνάασθαι ἄκοιτιν·
ἐκ γὰρ Ὀρέσταο τίσις ἔσσεται Ἀτρεΐδαο,   40
ὁππότ' ἂν ἡβήσῃ τε καὶ ἧς ἱμείρεται [1] αἴης.
ὣς ἔφαθ' Ἑρμείας, ἀλλ' οὐ φρένας Αἰγίσθοιο
πεῖθ' ἀγαθὰ φρονέων· νῦν δ' ἀθρόα πάντ' ἀπέτισεν."

[1] ἱμείρεται : ἐπιβήσεται.

---

[1] It seems best to regard this epithet, for purposes of translation, as a proper name. The word doubtless means

4

pitied him save Poseidon; but he continued to rage unceasingly against godlike Odysseus until at length he reached his own land.

Howbeit Poseidon had gone among the far-off Ethiopians—the Ethiopians who dwell sundered in twain, the farthermost of men, some where Hyperion sets and some where he rises, there to receive a hecatomb of bulls and rams, and there he was taking his joy, sitting at the feast; but the other gods were gathered together in the halls of Olympian Zeus. Among them the father of gods and men was first to speak, for in his heart he thought of noble Aegisthus, whom far-famed Orestes, Agamemnon's son, had slain. Thinking on him he spoke among the immortals, and said:

"Look you now, how ready mortals are to blame the gods. It is from us, they say, that evils come, but they even of themselves, through their own blind folly, have sorrows beyond that which is ordained. Even as now Aegisthus, beyond that which was ordained, took to himself the wedded wife of the son of Atreus, and slew him on his return, though well he knew of sheer destruction, seeing that we spake to him before, sending Hermes, the keen-sighted Argeïphontes,[1] that he should neither slay the man nor woo his wife; for from Orestes shall come vengeance for the son of Atreus when once he has come to manhood and longs for his own land. So Hermes spoke, but for all his good intent he prevailed not upon the heart of Aegisthus; and now he has paid the full price of all."

---

[1] "the swift appearer" (root φαν). The rendering "slayer of Argus" (root φεν) is inadmissible, as there is no trace of the Argus-myth in Homer.

Τὸν δ' ἠμείβετ' ἔπειτα θεά, γλαυκῶπις Ἀθήνη·
"Ὦ πάτερ ἡμέτερε Κρονίδη, ὕπατε κρειόντων,
καὶ λίην κεῖνός γε ἐοικότι κεῖται ὀλέθρῳ·
ὡς ἀπόλοιτο καὶ ἄλλος, ὅτις τοιαῦτά γε ῥέζοι·
ἀλλά μοι ἀμφ' Ὀδυσῆι δαΐφρονι δαίεται ἦτορ,
δυσμόρῳ, ὃς δὴ δηθὰ φίλων ἄπο πήματα πάσχει
νήσῳ ἐν ἀμφιρύτῃ, ὅθι τ' ὀμφαλός ἐστι θαλάσσης.
νῆσος δενδρήεσσα, θεὰ δ' ἐν δώματα ναίει,
Ἄτλαντος θυγάτηρ ὀλοόφρονος, ὅς τε θαλάσσης
πάσης βένθεα οἶδεν, ἔχει δέ τε κίονας αὐτὸς
μακράς, αἳ γαῖάν τε καὶ οὐρανὸν ἀμφὶς ἔχουσιν·
τοῦ θυγάτηρ δύστηνον ὀδυρόμενον κατερύκει,
αἰεὶ δὲ μαλακοῖσι καὶ αἱμυλίοισι λόγοισιν
θέλγει, ὅπως Ἰθάκης ἐπιλήσεται· αὐτὰρ Ὀδυσσεύς,
ἱέμενος καὶ καπνὸν ἀποθρῴσκοντα νοῆσαι
ἧς γαίης, θανέειν ἱμείρεται.   οὐδέ νυ σοί περ
ἐντρέπεται φίλον ἦτορ, Ὀλύμπιε. οὔ νύ τ' Ὀδυσσεὺς
Ἀργείων παρὰ νηυσὶ χαρίζετο ἱερὰ ῥέζων
Τροίῃ ἐν εὐρείῃ; τί νύ οἱ τόσον ὠδύσαο, Ζεῦ;"
   Τὴν δ' ἀπαμειβόμενος προσέφη νεφεληγερέτα Ζεύς·
"Τέκνον ἐμόν, ποῖόν σε ἔπος φύγεν ἕρκος ὀδόντων.
πῶς ἂν ἔπειτ' Ὀδυσῆος ἐγὼ θείοιο λαθοίμην,
ὃς περὶ μὲν νόον ἐστὶ βροτῶν, περὶ δ' ἱρὰ θεοῖσιν
ἀθανάτοισιν ἔδωκε, τοὶ οὐρανὸν εὐρὺν ἔχουσιν;
ἀλλὰ Ποσειδάων γαιήοχος ἀσκελὲς αἰεὶ
Κύκλωπος κεχόλωται, ὃν ὀφθαλμοῦ ἀλάωσεν,

---

[1] Others, "grey-eyed"; but if colour is meant it is almost certainly *blue*. The meaning given above is strongly supported by *Il.* xx. 172 and *Il.* i. 200.

Then the goddess, flashing-eyed[1] Athene, answered him: "Father of us all, thou son of Cronos, high above all lords, aye, verily that man lies low in a destruction that is his due; so, too, may any other also be destroyed who does such deeds. But my heart is torn for wise Odysseus, hapless man, who far from his friends has long been suffering woes in a sea-girt isle, where is the navel of the sea. 'Tis a wooded isle, and therein dwells a goddess, daughter of Atlas of baneful mind, who knows the depths of every sea, and himself holds the tall pillars which keep earth and heaven apart. His daughter it is that keeps back that wretched, sorrowing man; and ever with soft and wheedling words she beguiles him that he may forget Ithaca. But Odysseus, in his longing to see were it but the smoke leaping up from his own land, yearns to die. Yet thy heart doth not regard it, Olympian. Did not Odysseus beside the ships of the Argives offer thee sacrifice without stint in the broad land of Troy? Wherefore then didst thou conceive such wrath[2] against him, O Zeus?"

Then Zeus, the cloud-gatherer, answered her and said: "My child, what a word has escaped the barrier of thy teeth? How should I, then, forget godlike Odysseus, who is beyond all mortals in wisdom, and beyond all has paid sacrifice to the immortal gods, who hold broad heaven? Nay, it is Poseidon, the earth-enfolder, who is ever filled with stubborn wrath because of the Cyclops, whom Odysseus blinded of

[2] In the Greek there is a play upon the verb ὠδύσαο and the name Ὀδυσεύς, the latter suggesting the meaning "man of wrath." See xix. 409.

ἀντίθεον Πολύφημον, ὅου κράτος ἐστὶ μέγιστον
πᾶσιν Κυκλώπεσσι· Θόωσα δέ μιν τέκε νύμφη,
Φόρκυνος θυγάτηρ ἁλὸς ἀτρυγέτοιο μέδοντος,
ἐν σπέσσι γλαφυροῖσι Ποσειδάωνι μιγεῖσα.
ἐκ τοῦ δὴ Ὀδυσῆα Ποσειδάων ἐνοσίχθων
οὔ τι κατακτείνει, πλάζει δ' ἀπὸ πατρίδος αἴης.
ἀλλ' ἄγεθ', ἡμεῖς οἵδε περιφραζώμεθα πάντες
νόστον, ὅπως ἔλθῃσι· Ποσειδάων δὲ μεθήσει
ὃν χόλον· οὐ μὲν γάρ τι δυνήσεται ἀντία πάντων
ἀθανάτων ἀέκητι θεῶν ἐριδαινέμεν οἶος."

Τὸν δ' ἠμείβετ' ἔπειτα θεά, γλαυκῶπις Ἀθήνη·
"Ὦ πάτερ ἡμέτερε Κρονίδη, ὕπατε κρειόντων,
εἰ μὲν δὴ νῦν τοῦτο φίλον μακάρεσσι θεοῖσιν,
νοστῆσαι Ὀδυσῆα πολύφρονα[1] ὅνδε δόμονδε,
Ἑρμείαν μὲν ἔπειτα διάκτορον ἀργεϊφόντην
νῆσον ἐς Ὠγυγίην ὀτρύνομεν, ὄφρα τάχιστα
νύμφῃ ἐϋπλοκάμῳ εἴπῃ νημερτέα βουλήν,
νόστον Ὀδυσσῆος ταλασίφρονος, ὥς κε νέηται·
αὐτὰρ ἐγὼν Ἰθάκηνδ' ἐσελεύσομαι, ὄφρα οἱ υἱὸν
μᾶλλον ἐποτρύνω καί οἱ μένος ἐν φρεσὶ θείω,
εἰς ἀγορὴν καλέσαντα κάρη κομόωντας Ἀχαιοὺς
πᾶσι μνηστήρεσσιν ἀπειπέμεν, οἵ τέ οἱ αἰεὶ
μῆλ' ἀδινὰ σφάζουσι καὶ εἰλίποδας ἕλικας βοῦς.
πέμψω δ' ἐς Σπάρτην[2] τε καὶ ἐς Πύλον ἠμαθόεντα
νόστον πευσόμενον πατρὸς φίλου, ἤν που ἀκούσῃ,
ἠδ' ἵνα μιν κλέος ἐσθλὸν ἐν ἀνθρώποισιν ἔχῃσιν."

---

[1] πολύφρονα : δαΐφρονα.
[2] Σπάρτην : Κρήτην Zenodotus; cf. 285.

---

[1] Others render "unvintaged" or "unharvested" (τρυγάω),
but it seems better to connect the word with the root τρυ,
"rub," "wear out."

his eye—even the godlike Polyphemus, whose might is greatest among all the Cyclopes; and the nymph Thoosa bore him, daughter of Phorcys who rules over the unresting[1] sea; for in the hollow caves she lay with Poseidon. From that time forth Poseidon, the earth-shaker, does not indeed slay Odysseus, but makes him a wanderer from his native land. But come, let us who are here all take thought of his return, that he may come home; and Poseidon will let go his anger, for he will in no wise be able, against all the immortal gods and in their despite, to contend alone."

Then the goddess, flashing-eyed Athene, answered him: "Father of us all, thou son of Cronos, high above all lords, if indeed this is now well pleasing to the blessed gods, that the wise Odysseus should return to his own home, let us send forth Hermes, the messenger, Argeïphontes, to the isle Ogygia, that with all speed he may declare to the fair-tressed nymph our fixed resolve, even the return of Odysseus of the steadfast heart, that he may come home. But, as for me, I will go to Ithaca, that I may the more arouse his son, and set courage in his heart to call to an assembly the long-haired Achaeans, and speak out his word to all the wooers, who are ever slaying his thronging sheep and his sleek[2] kine of shambling gait. And I will guide him to Sparta and to sandy Pylos, to seek tidings of the return of his dear father, if haply he may hear of it, that good report may be his among men."

[2] ἕλικας is a word of uncertain etymology. The rendering given above connects it with σέλας. Others understand it as referring to the "crumpled" horns of cattle, or treat it as virtually equivalent to εἰλίποδας. The ancients took the word to mean "black."

Ὡς εἰποῦσ' ὑπὸ ποσσὶν ἐδήσατο καλὰ πέδιλα,
ἀμβρόσια χρύσεια, τά μιν φέρον ἠμὲν ἐφ' ὑγρὴν [1]
ἠδ' ἐπ' ἀπείρονα γαῖαν ἅμα πνοιῇς ἀνέμοιο·
εἵλετο δ' ἄλκιμον ἔγχος, ἀκαχμένον ὀξέι χαλκῷ,
βριθὺ μέγα στιβαρόν, τῷ δάμνησι στίχας ἀνδρῶν   100
ἡρώων, τοῖσίν τε κοτέσσεται ὀβριμοπάτρη.
βῆ δὲ κατ' Οὐλύμποιο καρήνων ἀίξασα,
στῆ δ' Ἰθάκης ἐνὶ δήμῳ ἐπὶ προθύροις Ὀδυσῆος,
οὐδοῦ ἐπ' αὐλείου· παλάμῃ δ' ἔχε χάλκεον ἔγχος,
εἰδομένη ξείνῳ, Ταφίων ἡγήτορι Μέντῃ.   105
εὗρε δ' ἄρα μνηστῆρας ἀγήνορας. οἱ μὲν ἔπειτα
πεσσοῖσι προπάροιθε θυράων θυμὸν ἔτερπον
ἥμενοι ἐν ῥινοῖσι βοῶν, οὓς ἔκτανον αὐτοί·
κήρυκες δ' αὐτοῖσι καὶ ὀτρηροὶ θεράποντες
οἱ μὲν οἶνον ἔμισγον ἐνὶ κρητῆρσι καὶ ὕδωρ,   110
οἱ δ' αὖτε σπόγγοισι πολυτρήτοισι τραπέζας
νίζον καὶ πρότιθεν, τοὶ δὲ κρέα πολλὰ δατεῦντο.
  Τὴν δὲ πολὺ πρῶτος ἴδε Τηλέμαχος θεοειδής,
ἧστο γὰρ ἐν μνηστῆρσι φίλον τετιημένος ἦτορ,
ὀσσόμενος πατέρ' ἐσθλὸν ἐνὶ φρεσίν, εἴ ποθεν ἐλθὼν 115
μνηστήρων τῶν μὲν σκέδασιν κατὰ δώματα θείη,
τιμὴν δ' αὐτὸς ἔχοι καὶ δώμασιν [2] οἷσιν ἀνάσσοι.
τὰ φρονέων, μνηστῆρσι μεθήμενος, εἴσιδ' Ἀθήνην.
βῆ δ' ἰθὺς προθύροιο, νεμεσσήθη δ' ἐνὶ θυμῷ

---

[1] Aristarchus rejected lines 97–101.
[2] δώμασιν : κτήμασιν.

---

[1] ἀμβρόσιος, like ἄμβροτος, ἄφθιτος, and even ἀθάνατος (iv.
79), may be used of inanimate things. Some assume that
the word has properly no connection with βροτός, and means
merely "fragrant" (see xviii. 193).

So she spoke, and bound beneath her feet her beautiful sandals, immortal,[1] golden, which were wont to bear her both over the waters of the sea and over the boundless land swift as the blasts of the wind. And she took her mighty spear, tipped with sharp bronze, heavy and huge and strong, wherewith she vanquishes the ranks of men—of warriors, with whom she is wroth, she, the daughter of the mighty sire. Then she went darting down from the heights of Olympus, and took her stand in the land of Ithaca at the outer gate of Odysseus, on the threshold of the court. In her hand she held the spear of bronze, and she was in the likeness of a stranger, Mentes, the leader of the Taphians. There she found the proud wooers. They were taking their pleasure at draughts in front of the doors, sitting on the hides of oxen which they themselves had slain; and of the heralds[2] and busy squires, some were mixing wine and water for them in bowls, others again were washing the tables with porous sponges and setting them forth, while still others were portioning out meats in abundance.

Her the godlike Telemachus was far the first to see, for he was sitting among the wooers, sad at heart, seeing in thought his noble father, should he perchance come from somewhere and make a scattering of the wooers in the palace, and himself win honour and rule over his own house. As he thought of these things, sitting among the wooers, he beheld Athene, and he went straight to the outer door; for in his heart he counted it shame that a stranger

[2] It has seemed better to render the word κῆρυξ uniformly by "herald," although the meanings range from "herald" in battle scenes to "page" or "henchman" in scenes portraying life in the palace.

HOMER

ξεῖνον δηθὰ θύρῃσιν ἐφεστάμεν· ἐγγύθι δὲ στὰς
χεῖρ' ἕλε δεξιτερὴν καὶ ἐδέξατο χάλκεον ἔγχος,
καί μιν φωνήσας ἔπεα πτερόεντα προσηύδα·
   "Χαῖρε, ξεῖνε, παρ' ἄμμι φιλήσεαι· αὐτὰρ ἔπειτα
δείπνου πασσάμενος μυθήσεαι ὅττεό σε χρή."
   Ὣς εἰπὼν ἡγεῖθ', ἡ δ' ἕσπετο Παλλὰς Ἀθήνη.
οἱ δ' ὅτε δή ῥ' ἔντοσθεν ἔσαν δόμου ὑψηλοῖο,
ἔγχος μέν ῥ' ἔστησε φέρων πρὸς κίονα μακρὴν
δουροδόκης ἔντοσθεν ἐυξόου, ἔνθα περ ἄλλα
ἔγχε' Ὀδυσσῆος ταλασίφρονος ἵστατο πολλά,
αὐτὴν δ' ἐς θρόνον εἷσεν ἄγων, ὑπὸ λῖτα πετάσσας,
καλὸν δαιδάλεον· ὑπὸ δὲ θρῆνυς ποσὶν ἦεν.
πὰρ δ' αὐτὸς κλισμὸν θέτο ποικίλον, ἔκτοθεν ἄλλων
μνηστήρων, μὴ ξεῖνος ἀνιηθεὶς ὀρυμαγδῷ
δείπνῳ ἀδήσειεν, ὑπερφιάλοισι μετελθών,
ἠδ' ἵνα μιν περὶ πατρὸς ἀποιχομένοιο ἔροιτο.
χέρνιβα δ' ἀμφίπολος προχόῳ ἐπέχευε φέρουσα
καλῇ χρυσείῃ, ὑπὲρ ἀργυρέοιο λέβητος,
νίψασθαι· παρὰ δὲ ξεστὴν ἐτάνυσσε τράπεζαν.
σῖτον δ' αἰδοίη ταμίη παρέθηκε φέρουσα,
εἴδατα πόλλ' ἐπιθεῖσα, χαριζομένη παρεόντων·
δαιτρὸς δὲ κρειῶν πίνακας παρέθηκεν ἀείρας
παντοίων, παρὰ δέ σφι τίθει χρύσεια κύπελλα·
κῆρυξ δ' αὐτοῖσιν θάμ' ἐπῴχετο οἰνοχοεύων.
   Ἐς δ' ἦλθον μνηστῆρες ἀγήνορες. οἱ μὲν ἔπειτα
ἑξείης ἕζοντο κατὰ κλισμούς τε θρόνους τε,
τοῖσι δὲ κήρυκες μὲν ὕδωρ ἐπὶ χεῖρας ἔχευαν,

---

[1] The words are picturesquely thought of as winging their way from the speaker to the person addressed; cf. ἄπτερος, of an unspoken word, in xvii. 57, and elsewhere.

should stand long at the gates. So, drawing near, he clasped her right hand, and took from her the spear of bronze; and he spoke, and addressed her with winged words:[1]

"Hail, stranger; in our house thou shalt find entertainment, and then, when thou hast tasted food, thou shalt tell of what thou hast need."

So saying, he led the way, and Pallas Athene followed. And when they were within the lofty house, he bore the spear and set it against a tall pillar in a polished spear-rack, where were set many spears besides, even those of Odysseus of the steadfast heart. Athene herself he led and seated on a chair, spreading a linen cloth beneath—a beautiful chair, richly-wrought,[2] and below was a footstool for the feet. Beside it he placed for himself an inlaid seat, apart from the others, the wooers, lest the stranger, vexed by their din, should loathe the meal, seeing that he was in the company of overweening men; and also that he might ask him about his father that was gone. Then a handmaid brought water for the hands in a fair pitcher of gold, and poured it over a silver basin for them to wash, and beside them drew up a polished table. And the grave housewife brought and set before them bread, and therewith dainties in abundance, giving freely of her store. And a carver lifted up and placed before them platters of all manner of meats, and set by them golden goblets, while a herald ever walked to and fro pouring them wine.

Then in came the proud wooers, and thereafter sat them down in rows on chairs and high seats. Heralds poured water over their hands, and maid-

[2] Perhaps "carven."

σῖτον δὲ δμῳαὶ παρενήνεον ἐν κανέοισιν,
κοῦροι δὲ κρητῆρας ἐπεστέψαντο ποτοῖο.
οἱ δ' ἐπ' ὀνείαθ' ἑτοῖμα προκείμενα χεῖρας ἴαλλον.
αὐτὰρ ἐπεὶ πόσιος καὶ ἐδητύος ἐξ ἔρον ἔντο   150
μνηστῆρες, τοῖσιν μὲν ἐνὶ φρεσὶν ἄλλα μεμήλει,
μολπῇ τ' ὀρχηστύς τε· τὰ γάρ τ' ἀναθήματα δαιτός·
κῆρυξ δ' ἐν χερσὶν κίθαριν περικαλλέα θῆκεν
Φημίῳ, ὅς ῥ' ἤειδε παρὰ μνηστῆρσιν ἀνάγκῃ.
ἦ τοι ὁ φορμίζων ἀνεβάλλετο καλὸν ἀείδειν.   155

Αὐτὰρ Τηλέμαχος προσέφη γλαυκῶπιν Ἀθήνην,
ἄγχι σχὼν κεφαλήν, ἵνα μὴ πευθοίαθ' οἱ ἄλλοι·
"Ξεῖνε φίλ', ἦ καί μοι νεμεσήσεαι ὅττι κεν εἴπω;
τούτοισιν μὲν ταῦτα μέλει, κίθαρις καὶ ἀοιδή,
ῥεῖ', ἐπεὶ ἀλλότριον βίοτον νήποινον ἔδουσιν,   160
ἀνέρος, οὗ δή που λεύκ' ὀστέα πύθεται ὄμβρῳ
κείμεν' ἐπ' ἠπείρου, ἢ εἰν ἁλὶ κῦμα κυλίνδει.
εἰ κεῖνόν γ' Ἰθάκηνδε ἰδοίατο νοστήσαντα,
πάντες κ' ἀρησαίατ' ἐλαφρότεροι πόδας εἶναι
ἢ ἀφνειότεροι χρυσοῖό τε ἐσθῆτός τε.   165
νῦν δ' ὁ μὲν ὣς ἀπόλωλε κακὸν μόρον, οὐδέ τις ἡμῖν
θαλπωρή,[1] εἴ πέρ τις ἐπιχθονίων ἀνθρώπων
φῇσιν ἐλεύσεσθαι· τοῦ δ' ὤλετο νόστιμον ἦμαρ.
ἀλλ' ἄγε μοι τόδε εἰπὲ καὶ ἀτρεκέως κατάλεξον·
τίς, πόθεν εἰς ἀνδρῶν; πόθι τοι πόλις ἠδὲ τοκῆες;   170
ὁπποίης τ' ἐπὶ νηὸς ἀφίκεο· πῶς δέ σε ναῦται
ἤγαγον εἰς Ἰθάκην; τίνες ἔμμεναι εὐχετόωντο;
οὐ μὲν γάρ τί σε πεζὸν ὀίομαι ἐνθάδ' ἱκέσθαι.
καί μοι τοῦτ' ἀγόρευσον ἐτήτυμον, ὄφρ' ἐὺ εἰδῶ,
ἠὲ νέον μεθέπεις ἢ καὶ πατρώιός ἐσσι   175

---

[1] θαλπωρή : ἐλπωρή.

14

servants heaped by them bread in baskets, and youths
filled the bowls brim full of drink; and they put
forth their hands to the good cheer lying ready
before them. Now after the wooers had put from
them the desire of food and drink, their hearts
turned to other things, to song and to dance; for
these things are the crown of a feast. And a herald
put the beautiful lyre in the hands of Phemius, who
sang perforce among the wooers; and he struck the
chords in prelude [1] to his sweet lay.

But Telemachus spoke to flashing-eyed Athene,
holding his head close, that the others might not
hear: "Dear stranger, wilt thou be wroth with me
for the word that I shall say? These men care for
things like these, the lyre and song, full easily, seeing
that without atonement they devour the livelihood
of another, of a man whose white bones, it may be,
rot in the rain as they lie upon the mainland, or the
wave rolls them in the sea. Were they to see him
returned to Ithaca, they would all pray to be swifter
of foot, rather than richer in gold and in raiment.
But now he has thus perished by an evil doom, nor
for us is there any comfort, no, not though any one
of men upon the earth should say that he will come;
gone is the day of his returning. But come, tell me
this, and declare it truly. Who art thou among
men, and from whence? Where is thy city and
where thy parents? On what manner of ship didst
thou come, and how did sailors bring thee to Ithaca?
Who did they declare themselves to be? For nowise,
methinks, didst thou come hither on foot. And tell
me this also truly, that I may know full well, whether
this is thy first coming hither, or whether thou art

[1] Or ἀνεβάλλετο may be used of the voice: "so he struck
the chords, and lifted up his voice in sweet song."

ξεῖνος, ἐπεὶ πολλοὶ ἴσαν ἀνέρες ἡμέτερον δῶ
ἄλλοι, ἐπεὶ καὶ κεῖνος ἐπίστροφος ἦν ἀνθρώπων."

Τὸν δ' αὖτε προσέειπε θεά, γλαυκῶπις Ἀθήνη·
"Τοιγὰρ ἐγώ τοι ταῦτα μάλ' ἀτρεκέως ἀγορεύσω.
Μέντης Ἀγχιάλοιο δαΐφρονος εὔχομαι εἶναι   180
υἱός, ἀτὰρ Ταφίοισι φιληρέτμοισιν ἀνάσσω.
νῦν δ' ὧδε ξὺν νηὶ κατήλυθον ἠδ' ἑτάροισιν
πλέων ἐπὶ οἴνοπα πόντον ἐπ' ἀλλοθρόους ἀνθρώπους,
ἐς Τεμέσην μετὰ χαλκόν, ἄγω δ' αἴθωνα σίδηρον.
νηῦς δέ μοι ἥδ' ἕστηκεν ἐπ' ἀγροῦ νόσφι πόληος,   185
ἐν λιμένι Ῥείθρῳ ὑπὸ Νηΐῳ ὑλήεντι.
ξεῖνοι δ' ἀλλήλων πατρώιοι εὐχόμεθ' εἶναι
ἐξ ἀρχῆς, εἴ πέρ τε γέροντ' εἴρηαι ἐπελθὼν
Λαέρτην ἥρωα, τὸν οὐκέτι φασὶ πόλινδε
ἔρχεσθ', ἀλλ' ἀπάνευθεν ἐπ' ἀγροῦ πήματα πάσχειν   190
γρηὶ σὺν ἀμφιπόλῳ, ἥ οἱ βρῶσίν τε πόσιν τε
παρτιθεῖ, εὖτ' ἄν μιν κάματος κατὰ γυῖα λάβῃσιν
ἑρπύζοντ' ἀνὰ γουνὸν ἀλωῆς οἰνοπέδοιο.
νῦν δ' ἦλθον· δὴ γάρ μιν ἔφαντ' ἐπιδήμιον εἶναι,
σὸν πατέρ'· ἀλλά νυ τόν γε θεοὶ βλάπτουσι κελεύθου.
οὐ γάρ πω τέθνηκεν ἐπὶ χθονὶ δῖος Ὀδυσσεύς,   196
ἀλλ' ἔτι που ζωὸς κατερύκεται εὐρέι πόντῳ
νήσῳ ἐν ἀμφιρύτῃ, χαλεποὶ δέ μιν ἄνδρες ἔχουσιν
ἄγριοι, οἵ που κεῖνον ἐρυκανόωσ' ἀέκοντα.
αὐτὰρ νῦν τοι ἐγὼ μαντεύσομαι, ὡς ἐνὶ θυμῷ   200
ἀθάνατοι βάλλουσι καὶ ὡς τελέεσθαι ὀίω,
οὔτε τι μάντις ἐὼν οὔτ' οἰωνῶν σάφα εἰδώς.

16

indeed a friend of my father's house. For many were the men who came to our house as strangers, since he, too, had gone to and fro[1] among men."

Then the goddess, flashing-eyed Athene, answered him: "Therefore of a truth will I frankly tell thee all. I declare that I am Mentes, the son of wise Anchialus, and I am lord over the oar-loving Taphians. And now have I put in here, as thou seest, with ship and crew, while sailing over the wine-dark sea to men of strange speech, on my way to Temese for copper; and I bear with me shining iron. My ship lies yonder beside the fields away from the city, in the harbour of Rheithron, under woody Neion. Friends of one another do we declare ourselves to be, even as our fathers were, friends from of old. Nay, if thou wilt, go and ask the old warrior Laertes, who, they say, comes no more to the city, but afar in the fields suffers woes attended by an aged woman as his handmaid, who sets before him food and drink, after weariness has laid hold of his limbs, as he creeps along the slope of his vineyard plot. And now am I come, for of a truth men said that he, thy father, was among his people; but lo, the gods are thwarting him of his return. For not yet has goodly Odysseus perished on the earth, but still, I ween, he lives and is held back on the broad sea in a sea-girt isle, and cruel men keep him, a savage folk, that constrain him, haply sore against his will. Nay, I will now prophesy to thee, as the immortals put it in my heart, and as I think it shall be brought to pass, though I am in no wise a soothsayer, nor one versed in the

---

[1] Or ἐπίστροφος may mean, as the scholiast took it, ἐπιστροφὴν καὶ ἐπιμέλειαν ποιούμενος τῶν ἀνθρώπων, "one that shewed care and attention to men." Yet see xvii. 486.

οὔ τοι ἔτι δηρόν γε φίλης ἀπὸ πατρίδος αἴης
ἔσσεται, οὐδ' εἴ πέρ τε σιδήρεα δέσματ' ἔχῃσιν·
φράσσεται ὥς κε νέηται, ἐπεὶ πολυμήχανός ἐστιν. 2
ἀλλ' ἄγε μοι τόδε εἰπὲ καὶ ἀτρεκέως κατάλεξον,
εἰ δὴ ἐξ αὐτοῖο τόσος πάις εἰς Ὀδυσῆος.
αἰνῶς μὲν κεφαλήν τε καὶ ὄμματα καλὰ ἔοικας
κείνῳ, ἐπεὶ θαμὰ τοῖον ἐμισγόμεθ' ἀλλήλοισιν,
πρίν γε τὸν ἐς Τροίην ἀναβήμεναι, ἔνθα περ ἄλλοι 2
Ἀργείων οἱ ἄριστοι ἔβαν κοίλῃς ἐνὶ νηυσίν·
ἐκ τοῦ δ' οὔτ' Ὀδυσῆα ἐγὼν ἴδον οὔτ' ἔμ' ἐκεῖνος."

    Τὴν δ' αὖ Τηλέμαχος πεπνυμένος ἀντίον ηὔδα·
"Τοιγὰρ ἐγώ τοι, ξεῖνε, μάλ' ἀτρεκέως ἀγορεύσω.
μήτηρ μέν τέ μέ φησι τοῦ ἔμμεναι, αὐτὰρ ἐγώ γε 2
οὐκ οἶδ'· οὐ γάρ πώ τις ἑὸν γόνον αὐτὸς ἀνέγνω.
ὡς δὴ ἐγώ γ' ὄφελον μάκαρός νύ τευ ἔμμεναι υἱὸς
ἀνέρος, ὃν κτεάτεσσιν ἑοῖς ἔπι γῆρας ἔτετμε.
νῦν δ' ὃς ἀποτμότατος γένετο θνητῶν ἀνθρώπων,
τοῦ μ' ἔκ φασι γενέσθαι, ἐπεὶ σύ με τοῦτ' ἐρεείνεις." 2

    Τὸν δ' αὖτε προσέειπε θεά, γλαυκῶπις Ἀθήνη·
"Οὐ μέν τοι γενεήν γε θεοὶ νώνυμνον ὀπίσσω
θῆκαν, ἐπεὶ σέ γε τοῖον ἐγείνατο Πηνελόπεια.
ἀλλ' ἄγε μοι τόδε εἰπὲ καὶ ἀτρεκέως κατάλεξον·
τίς δαίς, τίς δὲ ὅμιλος ὅδ' ἔπλετο; τίπτε δέ σε χρεώ; 2
εἰλαπίνη ἠὲ γάμος; ἐπεὶ οὐκ ἔρανος τάδε γ' ἐστίν·
ὥς τέ μοι ὑβρίζοντες ὑπερφιάλως δοκέουσι
δαίνυσθαι κατὰ δῶμα. νεμεσσήσαιτό κεν ἀνὴρ
αἴσχεα πόλλ' ὁρόων, ὅς τις πινυτός γε μετέλθοι."

    Τὴν δ' αὖ Τηλέμαχος πεπνυμένος ἀντίον ηὔδα· 2

signs of birds. Not much longer shall he be absent
from his dear native land, no, not though bonds of
iron hold him. He will contrive a way to return,
for he is a man of many devices. But come, tell me
this and declare it truly, whether indeed, tall as
thou art, thou art the son of Odysseus himself.
Wondrously like his are thy head and beautiful
eyes; for full often did we consort with one an-
other before he embarked for the land of Troy,
whither others, too, the bravest of the Argives, went
in their hollow ships. But since that day neither
have I seen Odysseus, nor he me."

Then wise Telemachus answered her: "Therefore
of a truth, stranger, will I frankly tell thee all. My
mother says that I am his child; but I know not,
for never yet did any man of himself know his own
parentage. Ah, would that I had been the son of
some blest man, whom old age overtook among his
own possessions. But now of him who was the most
ill-fated of mortal men they say that I am sprung,
since thou askest me of this."

Then the goddess, flashing-eyed Athene, answered
him: "Surely, then, no nameless lineage have the
gods appointed for thee in time to come, seeing that
Penelope bore thee such as thou art. But come,
tell me this and declare it truly. What feast, what
throng is this? What need hast thou of it? Is it
a drinking bout, or a wedding feast? For this plainly
is no meal to which each brings his portion, with
such outrage and overweening do they seem to me
to be feasting in thy halls. Angered would a man
be at seeing all these shameful acts, any man of
sense who should come among them."

Then wise Telemachus answered her: "Stranger,

" Ξεῖν', ἐπεὶ ἂρ δὴ ταῦτά μ' ἀνείρεαι ἠδὲ μεταλλᾷς,
μέλλεν μέν ποτε οἶκος ὅδ' ἀφνειὸς καὶ ἀμύμων
ἔμμεναι, ὄφρ' ἔτι κεῖνος ἀνὴρ ἐπιδήμιος ἦεν·
νῦν δ' ἑτέρως ἐβόλοντο θεοὶ κακὰ μητιόωντες,
οἳ κεῖνον μὲν ἄιστον ἐποίησαν περὶ πάντων   235
ἀνθρώπων, ἐπεὶ οὔ κε θανόντι περ ὧδ' ἀκαχοίμην,
εἰ μετὰ οἷς ἑτάροισι δάμη Τρώων ἐνὶ δήμῳ,
ἠὲ φίλων ἐν χερσίν, ἐπεὶ πόλεμον τολύπευσεν.
τῷ κέν οἱ τύμβον μὲν ἐποίησαν Παναχαιοί,
ἠδέ κε καὶ ᾧ παιδὶ μέγα κλέος ἦρατ' ὀπίσσω.   240
νῦν δέ μιν ἀκλειῶς ἅρπυιαι ἀνηρείψαντο·
οἴχετ' ἄιστος ἄπυστος, ἐμοὶ δ' ὀδύνας τε γόους τε
κάλλιπεν. οὐδέ τι κεῖνον ὀδυρόμενος στεναχίζω
οἶον, ἐπεί νύ μοι ἄλλα θεοὶ κακὰ κήδε' ἔτευξαν.
ὅσσοι γὰρ νήσοισιν ἐπικρατέουσιν ἄριστοι,   245
Δουλιχίῳ τε Σάμῃ τε καὶ ὑλήεντι Ζακύνθῳ,
ἠδ' ὅσσοι κραναὴν Ἰθάκην κάτα κοιρανέουσιν,
τόσσοι μητέρ' ἐμὴν μνῶνται, τρύχουσι δὲ οἶκον.
ἡ δ' οὔτ' ἀρνεῖται στυγερὸν γάμον οὔτε τελευτὴν
ποιῆσαι δύναται· τοὶ δὲ φθινύθουσιν ἔδοντες   250
οἶκον ἐμόν· τάχα δή με διαρραίσουσι καὶ αὐτόν."

    Τὸν δ' ἐπαλαστήσασα προσηύδα Παλλὰς Ἀθήνη·
" Ὦ πόποι, ἦ δὴ πολλὸν ἀποιχομένου Ὀδυσῆος
δεύῃ, ὅ κε μνηστῆρσιν ἀναιδέσι χεῖρας ἐφείη.
εἰ γὰρ νῦν ἐλθὼν δόμου ἐν πρώτῃσι θύρῃσι   255
σταίη, ἔχων πήληκα καὶ ἀσπίδα καὶ δύο δοῦρε,

since indeed thou dost ask and question me of this,
our house once bade fair to be rich and honourable,
so long as that man was still among his people. But
now the gods have willed otherwise in their evil
devising, seeing that they have caused him to pass
from sight as they have no other man. For I should
not so grieve for his death, if he had been slain
among his comrades in the land of the Trojans, or
had died in the arms of his friends, when he had
wound up the skein of war. Then would the whole
host of the Achaeans have made him a tomb, and
for his son, too, he would have won great glory in
days to come. But as it is, the spirits of the storm[1]
have swept him away and left no tidings: he is gone
out of sight, out of hearing, and for me he has left
anguish and weeping; nor do I in any wise mourn
and wail for him alone, seeing that the gods have
brought upon me other sore troubles. For all the
princes who hold sway over the islands—Dulichium
and Same and wooded Zacynthus—and those who
lord it over rocky Ithaca, all these woo my mother
and lay waste my house. And she neither refuses
the hateful marriage, nor is she able to make an
end; but they with feasting consume my substance:
ere long they will bring me, too, to ruin."

Then, stirred to anger, Pallas Athene spoke to him:
"Out on it! Thou hast of a truth sore need of
Odysseus that is gone, that he might put forth his
hands upon the shameless wooers. Would that he
might come now and take his stand at the outer gate
of the house, with helmet and shield and two spears,

[1] The ἅρπυιαι, or "snatchers," are in Homer personified
storm-winds; see xiv. 371; xx. 61–82; and *Iliad*, vi. 346.
They have nothing in common with Virgil's Harpies (*Aen.* iii.
211 ff.).

τοῖος ἐὼν οἷόν μιν ἐγὼ τὰ πρῶτ' ἐνόησα
οἴκῳ ἐν ἡμετέρῳ πίνοντά τε τερπόμενόν τε,
ἐξ Ἐφύρης ἀνιόντα παρ' Ἴλου Μερμερίδαο—
ᾤχετο γὰρ καὶ κεῖσε θοῆς ἐπὶ νηὸς Ὀδυσσεὺς   2
φάρμακον ἀνδροφόνον διζήμενος, ὄφρα οἱ εἴη
ἰοὺς χρίεσθαι χαλκήρεας· ἀλλ' ὁ μὲν οὔ οἱ
δῶκεν, ἐπεί ῥα θεοὺς νεμεσίζετο αἰὲν ἐόντας,
ἀλλὰ πατήρ οἱ δῶκεν ἐμός· φιλέεσκε γὰρ αἰνῶς—
τοῖος ἐὼν μνηστήρσιν ὁμιλήσειεν Ὀδυσσεύς·   2
πάντες κ' ὠκύμοροί τε γενοίατο πικρόγαμοί τε.
ἀλλ' ἦ τοι μὲν ταῦτα θεῶν ἐν γούνασι κεῖται,
ἦ κεν νοστήσας ἀποτίσεται, ἦε καὶ οὐκί,
οἷσιν ἐνὶ μεγάροισι· σὲ δὲ φράζεσθαι ἄνωγα,
ὅππως κε μνηστῆρας ἀπώσεαι ἐκ μεγάροιο.   2
εἰ δ' ἄγε νῦν ξυνίει καὶ ἐμῶν ἐμπάζεο μύθων·
αὔριον εἰς ἀγορὴν καλέσας ἥρωας Ἀχαιοὺς
μῦθον πέφραδε πᾶσι, θεοὶ δ' ἐπὶ μάρτυροι ἔστων.
μνηστῆρας μὲν ἐπὶ σφέτερα σκίδνασθαι ἄνωχθι,
μητέρα δ', εἴ οἱ θυμὸς ἐφορμᾶται γαμέεσθαι,   2
ἂψ ἴτω ἐς μέγαρον πατρὸς μέγα δυναμένοιο·
οἱ δὲ γάμον τεύξουσι καὶ ἀρτυνέουσιν ἔεδνα
πολλὰ μάλ', ὅσσα ἔοικε φίλης ἐπὶ παιδὸς ἕπεσθαι.[1]
σοὶ δ' αὐτῷ πυκινῶς ὑποθήσομαι, αἴ κε πίθηαι·
νῆ' ἄρσας ἐρέτῃσιν ἐείκοσιν, ἥ τις ἀρίστη,   2
ἔρχεο πευσόμενος πατρὸς δὴν οἰχομένοιο,
ἤν τίς τοι εἴπῃσι βροτῶν, ἢ ὄσσαν ἀκούσῃς

---

[1] Line 278, rejected by Rhianus, is bracketed by many editors; cf. ii. 197.

---

[1] The ἔεδνα are regularly gifts brought by a woman's wooers to her parents. In the present passage and in ii. 196 the context seems rather to suggest the meaning "dowry,"

such a man as he was when I first saw him in our
house drinking and making merry, on his way back
from Ephyre, from the house of Ilus, son of Mermerus.
For thither, too, went Odysseus in his swift ship in
search of a deadly drug, that he might have where-
with to smear his bronze-tipped arrows; yet Ilus
gave it not to him, for he stood in awe of the gods
that are forever; but my father gave it, for he held
him strangely dear. Would, I say, that in such
strength Odysseus might come amongst the wooers;
then should they all find swift destruction and bit-
terness in their wooing. Yet these things verily lie
on the knees of the gods, whether he shall return
and wreak vengeance in his halls, or whether he
shall not; but for thyself, I bid thee take thought
how thou mayest thrust forth the wooers from the
hall. Come now, give ear, and hearken to my words.
On the morrow call to an assembly the Achaean
lords, and speak out thy word to all, and let the gods
be thy witnesses. As for the wooers, bid them scatter,
each to his own; and for thy mother, if her heart
bids her marry, let her go back to the hall of her
mighty father, and there they will prepare a wedding
feast, and make ready the gifts[1] full many — aye, all
that should follow after a well-loved daughter. And
to thyself will I give wise counsel, if thou wilt
hearken. Man with twenty rowers the best ship
thou hast, and go to seek tidings of thy father, that
has long been gone, if haply any mortal may tell

---

but we must still think of the gifts as brought by the wooers,
even though they were subsequently given to the bride by
her parents. Owing to this difficulty many scholars reject
line 278 (and ii. 197), and take οἱ δὲ of the wooers, not of the
kinsfolk of Penelope.

ἐκ Διός, ᾗ τε μάλιστα φέρει κλέος ἀνθρώποισι.
πρῶτα μὲν ἐς Πύλον ἐλθὲ καὶ εἴρεο Νέστορα δῖον,
κεῖθεν δὲ Σπάρτηνδε παρὰ ξανθὸν Μενέλαον·[1]
ὃς γὰρ δεύτατος ἦλθεν Ἀχαιῶν χαλκοχιτώνων.
εἰ μέν κεν πατρὸς βίοτον καὶ νόστον ἀκούσῃς,
ἦ τ' ἂν τρυχόμενός περ ἔτι τλαίης ἐνιαυτόν·
εἰ δέ κε τεθνηῶτος ἀκούσῃς μηδ' ἔτ' ἐόντος,
νοστήσας δὴ ἔπειτα φίλην ἐς πατρίδα γαῖαν
σῆμά τέ οἱ χεῦαι καὶ ἐπὶ κτέρεα κτερεΐξαι
πολλὰ μάλ', ὅσσα ἔοικε, καὶ ἀνέρι μητέρα δοῦναι.
αὐτὰρ ἐπὴν δὴ ταῦτα τελευτήσῃς τε καὶ ἔρξῃς,
φράζεσθαι δὴ ἔπειτα κατὰ φρένα καὶ κατὰ θυμὸν
ὅππως κε μνηστῆρας ἐνὶ μεγάροισι τεοῖσι
κτείνῃς ἠὲ δόλῳ ἢ ἀμφαδόν· οὐδέ τί σε χρὴ
νηπιάας ὀχέειν, ἐπεὶ οὐκέτι τηλίκος ἐσσι.
ἦ οὐκ ἀίεις οἷον κλέος ἔλλαβε δῖος Ὀρέστης
πάντας ἐπ' ἀνθρώπους, ἐπεὶ ἔκτανε πατροφονῆα,
Αἴγισθον δολόμητιν, ὅ οἱ πατέρα κλυτὸν ἔκτα;
καὶ σύ, φίλος, μάλα γάρ σ' ὁρόω καλόν τε μέγαν τε,
ἄλκιμος ἔσσ', ἵνα τίς σε καὶ ὀψιγόνων ἐὺ εἴπῃ.
αὐτὰρ ἐγὼν ἐπὶ νῆα θοὴν κατελεύσομαι ἤδη
ἠδ' ἑτάρους, οἵ πού με μάλ' ἀσχαλόωσι μένοντες·
σοὶ δ' αὐτῷ μελέτω, καὶ ἐμῶν ἐμπάζεο μύθων."
   Τὴν δ' αὖ Τηλέμαχος πεπνυμένος ἀντίον ηὔδα·
"Ξεῖν', ἦ τοι μὲν ταῦτα φίλα φρονέων ἀγορεύεις,
ὥς τε πατὴρ ᾧ παιδί, καὶ οὔ ποτε λήσομαι αὐτῶν.
ἀλλ' ἄγε νῦν ἐπίμεινον, ἐπειγόμενός περ ὁδοῖο,
ὄφρα λοεσσάμενός τε τεταρπόμενός τε φίλον κῆρ,
δῶρον ἔχων ἐπὶ νῆα κίῃς, χαίρων ἐνὶ θυμῷ,

----

[1] κεῖθεν δὲ Σπάρτηνδε κ.τ.λ. : κεῖθεν δ' ἐς Κρήτην τε παρ' Ἰδομενῆα ἄνακτα, "and thence to Crete to the lord Idomeneus," Zenodotus.

thee, or thou mayest hear a voice from Zeus, which oftenest brings tidings to men. First go to Pylos and question goodly Nestor, and from thence to Sparta to fair-haired Menelaus; for he was the last to reach home of the brazen-coated Achaeans. If so be thou shalt hear that thy father is alive and coming home, then verily, though thou art sore afflicted, thou couldst endure for yet a year. But if thou shalt hear that he is dead and gone, then return to thy dear native land and heap up a mound for him, and over it pay funeral rites, full many as is due, and give thy mother to a husband. Then when thou hast done all this and brought it to an end, thereafter take thought in mind and heart how thou mayest slay the wooers in thy halls whether by guile or openly; for it beseems thee not to practise childish ways, since thou art no longer of such an age. Or hast thou not heard what fame the goodly Orestes won among all mankind when he slew his father's murderer, the guileful Aegisthus, for that he slew his glorious father? Thou too, my friend, for I see that thou art comely and tall, be thou valiant, that many an one of men yet to be born may praise thee. But now I will go down to my swift ship and my comrades, who, methinks, are chafing much at waiting for me. For thyself, give heed and have regard to my words."

Then wise Telemachus answered her: "Stranger, in truth thou speakest these things with kindly thought, as a father to his son, and never will I forget them. But come now, tarry, eager though thou art to be gone, in order that when thou hast bathed and satisfied thy heart to the full, thou mayest go to thy ship glad in spirit, and bearing a gift costly

τιμῆεν, μάλα καλόν, ὅ τοι κειμήλιον ἔσται
ἐξ ἐμεῦ, οἷα φίλοι ξεῖνοι ξείνοισι διδοῦσι."

Τὸν δ' ἠμείβετ' ἔπειτα θεά, γλαυκῶπις Ἀθήνη·
"Μή μ' ἔτι νῦν κατέρυκε, λιλαιόμενόν περ ὁδοῖο.   31
δῶρον δ' ὅττι κέ μοι δοῦναι φίλον ἦτορ ἀνώγῃ,
αὖτις ἀνερχομένῳ δόμεναι οἶκόνδε φέρεσθαι,
καὶ μάλα καλὸν ἑλών· σοὶ δ' ἄξιον ἔσται ἀμοιβῆς."

Ἡ μὲν ἄρ' ὣς εἰποῦσ' ἀπέβη γλαυκῶπις Ἀθήνη,
ὄρνις δ' ὣς ἀνόπαια διέπτατο· τῷ δ' ἐνὶ θυμῷ   32
θῆκε μένος καὶ θάρσος, ὑπέμνησέν τέ ἑ πατρὸς
μᾶλλον ἔτ' ἢ τὸ πάροιθεν. ὁ δὲ φρεσὶν ᾗσι νοήσας
θάμβησεν κατὰ θυμόν· ὀίσατο γὰρ θεὸν εἶναι.
αὐτίκα δὲ μνηστῆρας ἐπῴχετο ἰσόθεος φώς.

Τοῖσι δ' ἀοιδὸς ἄειδε περικλυτός, οἱ δὲ σιωπῇ   32
ἥατ' ἀκούοντες· ὁ δ' Ἀχαιῶν νόστον ἄειδε
λυγρόν, ὃν ἐκ Τροίης ἐπετείλατο Παλλὰς Ἀθήνη.
τοῦ δ' ὑπερωιόθεν φρεσὶ σύνθετο θέσπιν ἀοιδὴν
κούρη Ἰκαρίοιο, περίφρων Πηνελόπεια·
κλίμακα δ' ὑψηλὴν κατεβήσετο οἷο δόμοιο,   33
οὐκ οἴη, ἅμα τῇ γε καὶ ἀμφίπολοι δύ' ἕποντο.
ἡ δ' ὅτε δὴ μνηστῆρας ἀφίκετο δῖα γυναικῶν,
στῆ ῥα παρὰ σταθμὸν τέγεος πύκα ποιητοῖο,
ἄντα παρειάων σχομένη λιπαρὰ κρήδεμνα·
ἀμφίπολος δ' ἄρα οἱ κεδνὴ ἑκάτερθε παρέστη.   33
δακρύσασα δ' ἔπειτα προσηύδα θεῖον ἀοιδόν·

"Φήμιε, πολλὰ γὰρ ἄλλα βροτῶν θελκτήρια οἶδας,
ἔργ' ἀνδρῶν τε θεῶν τε, τά τε κλείουσιν ἀοιδοί·

---

¹ ἀνόπαια is probably a neut. pl. with the force of an
adverb, and means simply "upward." Aristarchus took it

and very beautiful, which shall be to thee an heir-
loom from me, even such a gift as dear friends give
to friends."

Then the goddess, flashing-eyed Athene, answered
him : "Stay me now no longer, when I am eager to
be gone, and whatsoever gift thy heart bids thee
give me, give it when I come back, to bear to my
home, choosing a right beautiful one ; it shall bring
thee its worth in return."

So spoke the goddess, flashing-eyed Athene, and
departed, flying upward[1] as a bird ; and in his heart
she put strength and courage, and made him think
of his father even more than aforetime. And in his
mind he marked her and marvelled, for he deemed
that she was a god ; and straightway he went among
the wooers, a godlike man.

For them the famous minstrel was singing, and
they sat in silence listening ; and he sang of the
return of the Achaeans—the woeful return from
Troy which Pallas Athene laid upon them. And
from her upper chamber the daughter of Icarius,
wise Penelope, heard his wondrous song, and she
went down the high stairway from her chamber, not
alone, for two handmaids attended her. Now when
the fair lady had come to the wooers, she stood by
the doorpost of the well-built hall, holding before
her face her shining veil ; and a faithful handmaid
stood on either side of her. Then she burst into
tears, and spoke to the divine minstrel :

"Phemius, many other things thou knowest to
charm mortals, deeds of men and gods which min-

---

to be the name of a bird. Others give it the meaning
"invisibly," and still others render "through the openings
(ὀπαί) in the roof."

τῶν ἕν γέ σφιν ἄειδε παρήμενος, οἱ δὲ σιωπῇ
οἶνον πινόντων· ταύτης δ᾽ ἀποπαύε᾽ ἀοιδῆς
λυγρῆς, ἥ τέ μοι αἰεὶ ἐνὶ στήθεσσι φίλον κῆρ
τείρει, ἐπεί με μάλιστα καθίκετο πένθος ἄλαστον.
τοίην γὰρ κεφαλὴν ποθέω μεμνημένη αἰεί,
ἀνδρός, τοῦ κλέος εὐρὺ καθ᾽ Ἑλλάδα καὶ μέσον
    Ἄργος." [1]
    Τὴν δ᾽ αὖ Τηλέμαχος πεπνυμένος ἀντίον ηὔδα·
"Μῆτερ ἐμή, τί τ᾽ ἄρα φθονέεις ἐρίηρον ἀοιδὸν
τέρπειν ὅππῃ οἱ νόος ὄρνυται; οὐ νύ τ᾽ ἀοιδοὶ
αἴτιοι, ἀλλά ποθι Ζεὺς αἴτιος, ὅς τε δίδωσιν
ἀνδράσιν ἀλφηστῇσιν, ὅπως ἐθέλῃσιν, ἑκάστῳ.
τούτῳ δ᾽ οὐ νέμεσις Δαναῶν κακὸν οἶτον ἀείδειν·
τὴν γὰρ ἀοιδὴν μᾶλλον ἐπικλείουσ᾽ ἄνθρωποι,
ἥ τις ἀκουόντεσσι νεωτάτη ἀμφιπέληται.
σοὶ δ᾽ ἐπιτολμάτω κραδίη καὶ θυμὸς ἀκούειν·
οὐ γὰρ Ὀδυσσεὺς οἶος ἀπώλεσε νόστιμον ἦμαρ
ἐν Τροίῃ, πολλοὶ δὲ καὶ ἄλλοι φῶτες ὄλοντο.
ἀλλ᾽ εἰς οἶκον ἰοῦσα τὰ σ᾽ αὐτῆς ἔργα κόμιζε,[2]
ἱστόν τ᾽ ἠλακάτην τε, καὶ ἀμφιπόλοισι κέλευε
ἔργον ἐποίχεσθαι· μῦθος δ᾽ ἄνδρεσσι μελήσει
πᾶσι, μάλιστα δ᾽ ἐμοί· τοῦ γὰρ κράτος ἔστ᾽ ἐνὶ οἴκῳ."
    Ἡ μὲν θαμβήσασα πάλιν οἶκόνδε βεβήκει·
παιδὸς γὰρ μῦθον πεπνυμένον ἔνθετο θυμῷ.
ἐς δ᾽ ὑπερῷ᾽ ἀναβᾶσα σὺν ἀμφιπόλοισι γυναιξὶ
κλαῖεν ἔπειτ᾽ Ὀδυσῆα φίλον πόσιν, ὄφρα οἱ ὕπνον
ἡδὺν ἐπὶ βλεφάροισι βάλε γλαυκῶπις Ἀθήνη.

---

[1] Line 344 was rejected by Aristarchus ; cf. iv. 726, 816, xv. 80.

[2] Lines 356-9, rejected by Aristarchus, are bracketed by many editors.

strels make famous. Sing them one of these, as thou sittest here, and let them drink their wine in silence. But cease from this woeful song which ever harrows the heart in my breast, for upon me above all women has come a sorrow not to be forgotten. So dear a head do I ever remember with longing, even my husband, whose fame is wide through Hellas and mid-Argos." [1]

Then wise Telemachus answered her: "My mother, why dost thou begrudge the good minstrel to give pleasure in whatever way his heart is moved? It is not minstrels that are to blame, but Zeus, I ween, is to blame, who gives to men that live by toil,[2] to each one as he will. With this man no one can be wroth if he sings of the evil doom of the Danaans; for men praise that song the most which comes the newest to their ears. For thyself, let thy heart and soul endure to listen; for not Odysseus alone lost in Troy the day of his return, but many others likewise perished. Nay, go to thy chamber, and busy thyself with thine own tasks, the loom and the distaff, and bid thy handmaids ply their tasks; but speech shall be for men, for all, but most of all for me; since mine is the authority in the house."

She then, seized with wonder, went back to her chamber, for she laid to heart the wise saying of her son. Up to her upper chamber she went with her handmaids, and then bewailed Odysseus, her dear husband, until flashing-eyed Athene cast sweet sleep upon her eyelids.

---

[1] The phrase probably means no more than "throughout the length and breadth of Greece."

[2] Others render "that live by bread," and still others "gain-getting."

Μνηστῆρες δ᾽ ὁμάδησαν ἀνὰ μέγαρα σκιόεντα,　365
πάντες δ᾽ ἠρήσαντο παραὶ λεχέεσσι κλιθῆναι.
τοῖσι δὲ Τηλέμαχος πεπνυμένος ἤρχετο μύθων·
" Μητρὸς ἐμῆς μνηστῆρες ὑπέρβιον ὕβριν ἔχοντες,
νῦν μὲν δαινύμενοι τερπώμεθα, μηδὲ βοητὺς
ἔστω, ἐπεὶ τόδε καλὸν ἀκουέμεν ἐστὶν ἀοιδοῦ　370
τοιοῦδ᾽ οἷος ὅδ᾽ ἐστί, θεοῖς ἐναλίγκιος αὐδήν.
ἠῶθεν δ᾽ ἀγορήνδε καθεζώμεσθα κιόντες
πάντες, ἵν᾽ ὑμῖν μῦθον ἀπηλεγέως ἀποείπω,
ἐξιέναι μεγάρων· ἄλλας δ᾽ ἀλεγύνετε δαῖτας,
ὑμὰ κτήματ᾽ ἔδοντες, ἀμειβόμενοι κατὰ οἴκους.　375
εἰ δ᾽ ὑμῖν δοκέει τόδε λωΐτερον καὶ ἄμεινον
ἔμμεναι, ἀνδρὸς ἑνὸς βίοτον νήποινον ὀλέσθαι,
κείρετ᾽· ἐγὼ δὲ θεοὺς ἐπιβώσομαι αἰὲν ἐόντας,
αἴ κέ ποθι Ζεὺς δῷσι παλίντιτα ἔργα γενέσθαι·
νήποινοί κεν ἔπειτα δόμων ἔντοσθεν ὄλοισθε."　380
Ὣς ἔφαθ᾽, οἱ δ᾽ ἄρα πάντες ὀδὰξ ἐν χείλεσι φύντες
Τηλέμαχον θαύμαζον, ὃ θαρσαλέως ἀγόρευεν.
Τὸν δ᾽ αὖτ᾽ Ἀντίνοος προσέφη, Εὐπείθεος υἱός·
"Τηλέμαχ᾽, ἦ μάλα δή σε διδάσκουσιν θεοὶ αὐτοὶ
ὑψαγόρην τ᾽ ἔμεναι καὶ θαρσαλέως ἀγορεύειν·　385
μὴ σέ γ᾽ ἐν ἀμφιάλῳ Ἰθάκῃ βασιλῆα Κρονίων
ποιήσειεν, ὅ τοι γενεῇ πατρώϊόν ἐστιν."
Τὸν δ᾽ αὖ Τηλέμαχος πεπνυμένος ἀντίον ηὔδα·
"Ἀντίνο᾽, ἦ καί μοι νεμεσήσεαι[1] ὅττι κεν εἴπω;
καί κεν τοῦτ᾽ ἐθέλοιμι Διός γε διδόντος ἀρέσθαι.　390
ἦ φὴς τοῦτο κάκιστον ἐν ἀνθρώποισι τετύχθαι;
οὐ μὲν γάρ τι κακὸν βασιλευέμεν· αἶψά τέ οἱ δῶ

[1] ἦ καί μοι νεμεσήσεαι: εἴ πέρ μοι καὶ ἀγάσσεαι, "even though
thou be angry."

30

But the wooers broke into uproar throughout the shadowy halls, and all prayed, each that he might lie by her side. And among them wise Telemachus was the first to speak:

"Wooers of my mother, overweening in your insolence, for the present let us make merry with feasting, but let there be no brawling; for this is a goodly thing, to listen to a minstrel such as this man is, like to the gods in voice. But in the morning let us go to the assembly and take our seats, one and all, that I may declare my word to you outright that you depart from these halls. Prepare you other feasts, eating your own substance and changing from house to house. But if this seems in your eyes to be a better and more profitable thing, that one man's livelihood should be ruined without atonement, waste ye it. But I will call upon the gods that are forever, if haply Zeus may grant that deeds of requital may be wrought. Without atonement, then, should ye perish within my halls."

So he spoke, and they all bit their lips and marvelled at Telemachus, for that he spoke boldly.

Then Antinous, son of Eupeithes, answered him: "Telemachus, verily the gods themselves are teaching thee to be a man of vaunting tongue, and to speak with boldness. May the son of Cronos never make thee king in sea-girt Ithaca, which thing is by birth thy heritage."

Then wise Telemachus answered him: "Antinous, wilt thou be wroth with me for the word that I shall say? Even this should I be glad to accept from the hand of Zeus. Thinkest thou indeed that this is the worst fate among men? Nay, it is no bad thing to be a king. Straightway one's house grows rich and

31

ἀφνειὸν πέλεται καὶ τιμηέστερος αὐτός.
ἀλλ' ἦ τοι βασιλῆες Ἀχαιῶν εἰσὶ καὶ ἄλλοι
πολλοὶ ἐν ἀμφιάλῳ Ἰθάκῃ, νέοι ἠδὲ παλαιοί,   395
τῶν κέν τις τόδ' ἔχῃσιν, ἐπεὶ θάνε δῖος Ὀδυσσεύς·
αὐτὰρ ἐγὼν οἴκοιο ἄναξ ἔσομ' ἡμετέροιο
καὶ δμώων, οὕς μοι ληΐσσατο δῖος Ὀδυσσεύς."

Τὸν δ' αὖτ' Εὐρύμαχος Πολύβου πάϊς ἀντίον ηὔδα·
" Τηλέμαχ', ἦ τοι ταῦτα θεῶν ἐν γούνασι κεῖται,   400
ὅς τις ἐν ἀμφιάλῳ Ἰθάκῃ βασιλεύσει Ἀχαιῶν·
κτήματα δ' αὐτὸς ἔχοις καὶ δώμασιν οἷσιν ἀνάσσοις.
μὴ γὰρ ὅ γ' ἔλθοι ἀνὴρ ὅς τίς σ' ἀέκοντα βίηφιν
κτήματ' ἀπορραίσει, Ἰθάκης ἔτι ναιετοώσης.
ἀλλ' ἐθέλω σε, φέριστε, περὶ ξείνοιο ἐρέσθαι,   405
ὁππόθεν οὗτος ἀνήρ, ποίης δ' ἐξ εὔχεται εἶναι
γαίης, ποῦ δέ νύ οἱ γενεὴ καὶ πατρὶς ἄρουρα.
ἠέ τιν' ἀγγελίην πατρὸς φέρει ἐρχομένοιο,
ἦ ἑὸν αὐτοῦ χρεῖος ἐελδόμενος τόδ' ἱκάνει;
οἷον ἀναΐξας ἄφαρ οἴχεται, οὐδ' ὑπέμεινε   410
γνώμεναι· οὐ μὲν γάρ τι κακῷ εἰς ὦπα ἐῴκει."

Τὸν δ' αὖ Τηλέμαχος πεπνυμένος ἀντίον ηὔδα·
" Εὐρύμαχ', ἦ τοι νόστος ἀπώλετο πατρὸς ἐμοῖο·
οὔτ' οὖν ἀγγελίῃ ἔτι πείθομαι, εἴ ποθεν ἔλθοι,
οὔτε θεοπροπίης ἐμπάζομαι, ἥν τινα μήτηρ   415
ἐς μέγαρον καλέσασα θεοπρόπον ἐξερέηται.
ξεῖνος δ' οὗτος ἐμὸς πατρώϊος ἐκ Τάφου ἐστίν,
Μέντης δ' Ἀγχιάλοιο δαΐφρονος εὔχεται εἶναι
υἱός, ἀτὰρ Ταφίοισι φιληρέτμοισιν ἀνάσσει."

Ὣς φάτο Τηλέμαχος, φρεσὶ δ' ἀθανάτην θεὸν ἔγνω.
Οἱ δ' εἰς ὀρχηστύν τε καὶ ἱμερόεσσαν ἀοιδὴν   421

32

oneself is held in greater honour. However, there are other kings of the Achaeans full many in sea-girt Ithaca, both young and old. One of these haply may have this place, since goodly Odysseus is dead. But I will be lord of our own house and of the slaves that goodly Odysseus won for me."

Then Eurymachus, son of Polybus, answered him: "Telemachus, this matter verily lies on the knees of the gods, who of the Achaeans shall be king in sea-girt Ithaca; but as for thy possessions, thou mayest keep them thyself, and be lord in thine own house. Never may that man come who by violence and against thy will shall wrest thy possessions from thee, while men yet live in Ithaca. But I am fain, good sir, to ask thee of the stranger, whence this man comes. Of what land does he declare himself to be? Where are his kinsmen and his native fields? Does he bring some tidings of thy father's coming, or came he hither in furtherance of some matter of his own? How he started up, and was straightway gone! Nor did he wait to be known; and yet he seemed no base man to look upon."

Then wise Telemachus answered him: "Eury-machus, surely my father's home-coming is lost and gone. No longer do I put trust in tidings, whence-soever they may come, nor reck I of any prophecy which my mother haply may learn of a seer, when she has called him to the hall. But this stranger is a friend of my father's house from Taphos. He declares that he is Mentes, son of wise Anchialus, and he is lord over the oar-loving Taphians."

So spoke Telemachus, but in his heart he knew the immortal goddess.

Now the wooers turned to the dance and to glad-

33

τρεψάμενοι τέρποντο, μένον δ' ἐπὶ ἕσπερον ἐλθεῖν.
τοῖσι δὲ τερπομένοισι μέλας ἐπὶ ἕσπερος ἦλθε·
δὴ τότε κακκείοντες ἔβαν οἶκόνδε ἕκαστος.
Τηλέμαχος δ', ὅθι οἱ θάλαμος περικαλλέος αὐλῆς   4
ὑψηλὸς δέδμητο περισκέπτῳ ἐνὶ χώρῳ,
ἔνθ' ἔβη εἰς εὐνὴν πολλὰ φρεσὶ μερμηρίζων.
τῷ δ' ἄρ' ἅμ' αἰθομένας δαΐδας φέρε κεδνὰ ἰδυῖα
Εὐρύκλει', Ὦπος θυγάτηρ Πεισηνορίδαο,
τήν ποτε Λαέρτης πρίατο κτεάτεσσιν ἑοῖσιν   4
πρωθήβην ἔτ' ἐοῦσαν, ἐεικοσάβοια δ' ἔδωκεν,
ἶσα δέ μιν κεδνῇ ἀλόχῳ τίεν ἐν μεγάροισιν,
εὐνῇ δ' οὔ ποτ' ἔμικτο, χόλον δ' ἀλέεινε γυναικός·
ἥ οἱ ἅμ' αἰθομένας δαΐδας φέρε, καί ἑ μάλιστα
δμῳάων φιλέεσκε, καὶ ἔτρεφε τυτθὸν ἐόντα.   4
ὤιξεν δὲ θύρας θαλάμου πύκα ποιητοῖο,
ἕζετο δ' ἐν λέκτρῳ, μαλακὸν δ' ἔκδυνε χιτῶνα·
καὶ τὸν μὲν γραίης πυκιμηδέος ἔμβαλε χερσίν.
ἡ μὲν τὸν πτύξασα καὶ ἀσκήσασα χιτῶνα,
πασσάλῳ ἀγκρεμάσασα παρὰ τρητοῖσι λέχεσσι   4
βῆ ῥ' ἴμεν ἐκ θαλάμοιο, θύρην δ' ἐπέρυσσε κορώνη
ἀργυρέῃ, ἐπὶ δὲ κληῖδ' ἐτάνυσσεν ἱμάντι.
ἔνθ' ὅ γε παννύχιος, κεκαλυμμένος οἰὸς ἀώτῳ,
βούλευε φρεσὶν ᾗσιν ὁδὸν τὴν πέφραδ' Ἀθήνη.

34

some song, and made them merry, and waited till
evening should come; and as they made merry dark
evening came upon them. Then they went, each
man to his house, to take their rest. But Telemachus,
where his chamber was built in the beautiful court,
high, in a place of wide outlook, thither went to his
bed, pondering many things in mind; and with him,
bearing blazing torches, went true-hearted Eurycleia,
daughter of Ops, son of Peisenor. Her long ago
Laertes had bought with his wealth, when she was
in her first youth, and gave for her the price of
twenty oxen; and he honoured her even as he
honoured his faithful wife in his halls, but he never
lay with her in love, for he shunned the wrath of
his wife. She it was who bore for Telemachus the
blazing torches; for she of all the handmaids loved
him most, and had nursed him when he was a child.
He opened the doors of the well-built chamber, sat
down on the bed, and took off his soft tunic and laid
it in the wise old woman's hands. And she folded
and smoothed the tunic and hung it on a peg beside
the corded [1] bedstead, and then went forth from the
chamber, drawing the door to by its silver handle,
and driving the bolt home with the thong. So there,
the night through, wrapped in a fleece of wool, he
pondered in his mind upon the journey which Athene
had shewn him.

[1] Possibly "mortised"; yet see xxiii. 201.

B

Ἦμος δ᾿ ἠριγένεια φάνη ῥοδοδάκτυλος Ἠώς,
ὤρνυτ᾿ ἄρ᾿ ἐξ εὐνῆφιν Ὀδυσσῆος φίλος υἱὸς
εἵματα ἑσσάμενος, περὶ δὲ ξίφος ὀξὺ θέτ᾿ ὤμῳ,
ποσσὶ δ᾿ ὑπὸ λιπαροῖσιν ἐδήσατο καλὰ πέδιλα,
βῆ δ᾿ ἴμεν ἐκ θαλάμοιο θεῷ ἐναλίγκιος ἄντην.
αἶψα δὲ κηρύκεσσι λιγυφθόγγοισι κέλευσε
κηρύσσειν ἀγορήνδε κάρη κομόωντας Ἀχαιούς.
οἱ μὲν ἐκήρυσσον, τοὶ δ᾿ ἠγείροντο μάλ᾿ ὦκα.
αὐτὰρ ἐπεί ῥ᾿ ἤγερθεν ὁμηγερέες τ᾿ ἐγένοντο,
βῆ ῥ᾿ ἴμεν εἰς ἀγορήν, παλάμῃ δ᾿ ἔχε χάλκεον ἔγχος, [10]
οὐκ οἶος, ἅμα τῷ γε δύω κύνες [1] ἀργοὶ ἕποντο.
θεσπεσίην δ᾿ ἄρα τῷ γε χάριν κατέχευεν Ἀθήνη.
τὸν δ᾿ ἄρα πάντες λαοὶ ἐπερχόμενον θηεῦντο·
ἕζετο δ᾿ ἐν πατρὸς θώκῳ, εἶξαν δὲ γέροντες.
    Τοῖσι δ᾿ ἔπειθ᾿ ἥρως Αἰγύπτιος ἦρχ᾿ ἀγορεύειν, [15]
ὃς δὴ γήραϊ κυφὸς ἔην καὶ μυρία ᾔδη.
καὶ γὰρ τοῦ φίλος υἱὸς ἅμ᾿ ἀντιθέῳ Ὀδυσῆι
Ἴλιον εἰς ἐύπωλον ἔβη κοίλης ἐνὶ νηυσίν,
Ἄντιφος αἰχμητής· τὸν δ᾿ ἄγριος ἔκτανε Κύκλωψ
ἐν σπῆι γλαφυρῷ, πύματον δ᾿ ὡπλίσσατο δόρπον. [20]
τρεῖς δέ οἱ ἄλλοι ἔσαν, καὶ ὁ μὲν μνηστῆρσιν ὁμίλει,
Εὐρύνομος, δύο δ᾿ αἰὲν [2] ἔχον πατρώια ἔργα.

---

[1] δύω κύνες : κύνες πόδας.
[2] δύο δ᾿ αἰὲν : δύο δ᾿ ἄλλοι.

BOOK II

Soon as early Dawn appeared, the rosy-fingered,
up from his bed arose the dear son of Odysseus and
put on his clothing. About his shoulder he slung
his sharp sword, and beneath his shining feet bound
his fair sandals, and went forth from his chamber
like a god to look upon. Straightway he bade the
clear-voiced heralds to summon to the assembly the
long-haired Achaeans. And the heralds made the
summons, and the Achaeans assembled full quickly.
Now when they were assembled and met together,
Telemachus went his way to the place of assembly,
holding in his hand a spear of bronze—not alone,
for along with him two swift hounds followed; and
wondrous was the grace that Athene shed upon him,
and all the people marvelled at him as he came. But
he sat down in his father's seat, and the elders gave
place.

Then among them the lord Aegyptius was the
first to speak, a man bowed with age and wise with
wisdom untold. Now he spoke, because his dear son
had gone in the hollow ships to Ilius, famed for its
horses, in the company of godlike Odysseus, even
the warrior Antiphus. But him the savage Cyclops
had slain in his hollow cave, and made of him his
latest meal. Three others there were; one, Eury-
nomus, consorted with the wooers, and two ever kept

ἀλλ' οὐδ' ὣς τοῦ λήθετ' ὀδυρόμενος καὶ ἀχεύων.
τοῦ ὅ γε δάκρυ χέων ἀγορήσατο καὶ μετέειπε·
  "Κέκλυτε δὴ νῦν μευ, Ἰθακήσιοι, ὅττι κεν εἴπω·
οὔτε ποθ' ἡμετέρη ἀγορὴ γένετ' οὔτε θόωκος
ἐξ οὗ Ὀδυσσεὺς δῖος ἔβη κοίλης ἐνὶ νηυσί.
νῦν δὲ τίς ὧδ' ἤγειρε; τίνα χρειὼ τόσον ἵκει
ἠὲ νέων ἀνδρῶν ἢ οἳ προγενέστεροί εἰσιν;
ἠέ τιν' ἀγγελίην στρατοῦ ἔκλυεν ἐρχομένοιο,
ἥν χ' ἡμῖν σάφα εἴποι, ὅτε πρότερός γε πύθοιτο;
ἠέ τι δήμιον ἄλλο πιφαύσκεται ἠδ' ἀγορεύει;
ἐσθλός μοι δοκεῖ εἶναι, ὀνήμενος. εἴθε οἱ αὐτῷ
Ζεὺς ἀγαθὸν τελέσειεν, ὅτι φρεσὶν ᾗσι μενοινᾷ."
  Ὣς φάτο, χαῖρε δὲ φήμῃ Ὀδυσσῆος φίλος υἱός,
οὐδ' ἄρ' ἔτι δὴν ἧστο, μενοίνησεν δ' ἀγορεύειν,
στῆ δὲ μέσῃ ἀγορῇ· σκῆπτρον δέ οἱ ἔμβαλε χειρὶ
κῆρυξ Πεισήνωρ πεπνυμένα μήδεα εἰδώς.
πρῶτον ἔπειτα γέροντα καθαπτόμενος προσέειπεν·
  "Ὦ γέρον, οὐχ ἑκὰς οὗτος ἀνήρ, τάχα δ' εἴσεαι αὐτό
ὃς λαὸν ἤγειρα· μάλιστα δέ μ' ἄλγος ἱκάνει.
οὔτε τιν' ἀγγελίην στρατοῦ ἔκλυον ἐρχομένοιο,
ἥν χ' ὑμῖν σάφα εἴπω, ὅτε πρότερός γε πυθοίμην,
οὔτε τι δήμιον ἄλλο πιφαύσκομαι οὐδ' ἀγορεύω,
ἀλλ' ἐμὸν αὐτοῦ χρεῖος, ὅ μοι κακὰ ἔμπεσεν οἴκῳ
δοιά· τὸ μὲν πατέρ' ἐσθλὸν ἀπώλεσα, ὅς ποτ' ἐν ὑμῖν

their father's farm. Yet, even so, he could not forget
that other, mourning and sorrowing; and weeping
for him he addressed the assembly, and spoke among
them:

"Hearken now to me, men of Ithaca, to the word
that I shall say. Never have we held assembly or
session since the day when goodly Odysseus departed
in the hollow ships. And now who has called us
together? On whom has such need come either of
the young men or of those who are older? Has he
heard some tidings of the army's return,[1] which he
might tell us plainly, seeing that he has first learned
of it himself? Or is there some other public matter
on which he is to speak and address us? A good
man he seems in my eyes, a blessed man. May Zeus
fulfil unto him himself some good, even whatsoever
he desires in his heart."

So he spoke, and the dear son of Odysseus re-
joiced at the word of omen; nor did he thereafter
remain seated, but was fain to speak. So he took
his stand in the midst of the assembly, and the staff
was placed in his hands by the herald Peisenor, wise
in counsel. Then he spoke, addressing first the old
man:

"Old man, not far off, as thou shalt soon learn thy-
self, is that man who has called the host together—
even I; for on me above all others has sorrow come.
I have neither heard any tidings of the army's re-
turn, which I might tell you plainly, seeing that I
had first learned of it myself, nor is there any other
public matter on which I am to speak and address
you. Nay, it is mine own need, for that evil has
fallen upon my house in two-fold wise. First, I have
lost my noble sire who was once king among you

---

[1] Or, possibly, "regarding an invading host."

τοῖσδεσσιν βασίλευε, πατὴρ δ' ὡς ἤπιος ἦεν·
νῦν δ' αὖ καὶ πολὺ μεῖζον, ὃ δὴ τάχα οἶκον ἅπαντα
πάγχυ διαρραίσει, βίοτον δ' ἀπὸ πάμπαν ὀλέσσει.
μητέρι μοι μνηστῆρες ἐπέχραον οὐκ ἐθελούσῃ,
τῶν ἀνδρῶν φίλοι υἷες, οἳ ἐνθάδε γ' εἰσὶν ἄριστοι,
οἳ πατρὸς μὲν ἐς οἶκον ἀπερρίγασι νέεσθαι
Ἰκαρίου, ὥς κ' αὐτὸς ἐεδνώσαιτο θύγατρα,
δοίη δ' ᾧ κ' ἐθέλοι καί οἱ κεχαρισμένος ἔλθοι·
οἳ δ' εἰς ἡμέτερον πωλεύμενοι ἤματα πάντα,
βοῦς ἱερεύοντες καὶ ὄις καὶ πίονας αἶγας
εἰλαπινάζουσιν πίνουσί τε αἴθοπα οἶνον
μαψιδίως· τὰ δὲ πολλὰ κατάνεται. οὐ γὰρ ἔπ' ἀνήρ,
οἷος Ὀδυσσεὺς ἔσκεν, ἀρὴν ἀπὸ οἴκου ἀμῦναι.
ἡμεῖς δ' οὔ νύ τι τοῖοι ἀμυνέμεν· ἦ καὶ ἔπειτα
λευγαλέοι τ' ἐσόμεσθα καὶ οὐ δεδαηκότες ἀλκήν.
ἦ τ' ἂν ἀμυναίμην, εἴ μοι δύναμίς γε παρείη.
οὐ γὰρ ἔτ' ἀνσχετὰ ἔργα τετεύχαται, οὐδ' ἔτι καλῶς
οἶκος ἐμὸς διόλωλε. νεμεσσήθητε καὶ αὐτοί,
ἄλλους τ' αἰδέσθητε περικτίονας ἀνθρώπους,
οἳ περιναιετάουσι· θεῶν δ' ὑποδείσατε μῆνιν,
μή τι μεταστρέψωσιν ἀγασσάμενοι κακὰ ἔργα.
λίσσομαι ἠμὲν Ζηνὸς Ὀλυμπίου ἠδὲ Θέμιστος,
ἥ τ' ἀνδρῶν ἀγορὰς ἠμὲν λύει ἠδὲ καθίζει·
σχέσθε, φίλοι, καί μ' οἶον ἐάσατε πένθεϊ λυγρῷ
τείρεσθ', εἰ μή πού τι πατὴρ ἐμὸς ἐσθλὸς Ὀδυσσεὺς
δυσμενέων κάκ' ἔρεξεν ἐυκνήμιδας Ἀχαιούς,
τῶν μ' ἀποτινύμενοι κακὰ ῥέζετε δυσμενέοντες,
τούτους ὀτρύνοντες.   ἐμοὶ δέ κε κέρδιον εἴη

here, and was gentle as a father; and now there is
come an evil yet greater far, which will presently
altogether destroy my house and ruin all my liveli-
hood. My mother have wooers beset against her will,
the sons of those men who are here the noblest.
They shrink from going to the house of her father,
Icarius, that he may himself exact the bride-gifts for
his daughter, and give her to whom he will, even
to him who meets his favour, but thronging our
house day after day they slay our oxen and sheep
and fat goats, and keep revel, and drink the sparkling
wine recklessly; and havoc is made of all this wealth.
For there is no man here, such as Odysseus was, to
ward off ruin from the house. As for me, I am no wise
such as he to ward it off. Nay verily, even if I try I
shall be found a weakling and one knowing naught of
valour. Yet truly I would defend myself, if I had
but the power; for now deeds past all enduring have
been wrought, and past all that is seemly has my
house been destroyed. Take shame upon yourselves,
and have regard to your neighbours who dwell round
about, and fear the wrath of the gods, lest haply
they turn against you in anger at your evil deeds.[1] I
pray you by Olympian Zeus, and by Themis who
looses and gathers the assemblies of men, forbear,
my friends,[2] and leave me alone to pine in bitter
grief—unless indeed my father, goodly Odysseus,
despitefully wrought the well-greaved Achaeans woe,
in requital whereof ye work me woe despitefully by
urging these men on. For me it were better that

[1] Or, possibly, "Lest in wrath they bring your evil deeds
upon your own heads." Against this, however, are xiv. 284
and xxiii. 64.
[2] These words are addressed apparently to the whole body
of the men of Ithaca, not to the wooers alone.

ὑμέας ἐσθέμεναι κειμήλιά τε πρόβασίν τε. 75
εἴ χ' ὑμεῖς γε φάγοιτε, τάχ' ἄν ποτε καὶ τίσις εἴη·
τόφρα γὰρ ἂν κατὰ ἄστυ ποτιπτυσσοίμεθα μύθῳ
χρήματ' ἀπαιτίζοντες, ἕως κ' ἀπὸ πάντα δοθείη·
νῦν δέ μοι ἀπρήκτους ὀδύνας ἐμβάλλετε θυμῷ."
   Ὣς φάτο χωόμενος, ποτὶ δὲ σκῆπτρον βάλε γαίῃ 80
δάκρυ' ἀναπρήσας· οἶκτος δ' ἕλε λαὸν ἅπαντα.
ἔνθ' ἄλλοι μὲν πάντες ἀκὴν ἔσαν, οὐδέ τις ἔτλη
Τηλέμαχον μύθοισιν ἀμείψασθαι χαλεποῖσιν·
Ἀντίνοος δέ μιν οἶος ἀμειβόμενος προσέειπε·
   "Τηλέμαχ' ὑψαγόρη, μένος ἄσχετε, ποῖον ἔειπες 85
ἡμέας αἰσχύνων· ἐθέλοις δέ κε μῶμον ἀνάψαι.
σοὶ δ' οὔ τι μνηστῆρες Ἀχαιῶν αἴτιοί εἰσιν,
ἀλλὰ φίλη μήτηρ, ἥ τοι πέρι κέρδεα οἶδεν.
ἤδη γὰρ τρίτον ἐστὶν ἔτος, τάχα δ' εἶσι τέταρτον,
ἐξ οὗ ἀτέμβει θυμὸν ἐνὶ στήθεσσιν Ἀχαιῶν. 90
πάντας μέν ῥ' ἔλπει καὶ ὑπίσχεται ἀνδρὶ ἑκάστῳ
ἀγγελίας προϊεῖσα, νόος δέ οἱ ἄλλα μενοινᾷ.
ἡ δὲ δόλον τόνδ' ἄλλον ἐνὶ φρεσὶ μερμήριξε·
στησαμένη μέγαν ἱστὸν ἐνὶ μεγάροισιν ὕφαινε,
λεπτὸν καὶ περίμετρον· ἄφαρ δ' ἡμῖν μετέειπε· 95
   "'Κοῦροι ἐμοὶ μνηστῆρες, ἐπεὶ θάνε δῖος Ὀδυσσεύς,
μίμνετ' ἐπειγόμενοι τὸν ἐμὸν γάμον, εἰς ὅ κε φᾶρος
ἐκτελέσω, μή μοι μεταμώνια νήματ' ὄληται,
Λαέρτῃ ἥρωι ταφήιον, εἰς ὅτε κέν μιν
μοῖρ' ὀλοὴ καθέλῃσι τανηλεγέος θανάτοιο, 100

---

[1] The verb would more naturally be rendered " will soon
come "; but this would be in glaring contradiction to 107.

42

ye should yourselves eat up my treasures and my flocks. If ye were to devour them, recompense would haply be made some day; for just so long should we go up and down the city, pressing our suit and asking back our goods, until all was given back. But now past cure are the woes ye put upon my heart."

Thus he spoke in wrath, and dashed the staff down upon the ground, bursting into tears; and pity fell upon all the people. Then all the others kept silent, and no man had the heart to answer Telemachus with angry words. Antinous alone answered him, and said:

"Telemachus, thou braggart, unrestrained in daring, what a thing hast thou said, putting us to shame, and wouldest fain fasten reproach upon us! Nay, I tell thee, it is not the Achaean wooers who are anywise at fault, but thine own mother, for she is crafty above all women. For it is now the third year and the fourth will soon pass,[1] since she has been deceiving the hearts of the Achaeans in their breasts. To all she offers hopes, and has promises for each man, sending them messages, but her mind is set on other things. And she devised in her heart this guileful thing also: she set up in her halls a great web, and fell to weaving—fine of thread was the web and very wide; and straightway she spoke among us:

"'Young men, my wooers, since goodly Odysseus is dead, be patient, though eager for my marriage, until I finish this robe—I would not that my spinning should come to naught—a shroud for the lord Laertes, against the time when the fell fate of grievous [2] death shall strike him down; lest any of the Achaean

---

[2] Others render "that lays men at their length."

μή τίς μοι κατὰ δῆμον Ἀχαιιάδων νεμεσήσῃ,
αἴ κεν ἄτερ σπείρου κεῖται πολλὰ κτεατίσσας.'
   "ˊΩς ἔφαθ᾽, ἡμῖν δ᾽ αὖτ᾽ ἐπεπείθετο θυμὸς ἀγήνωρ.
ἔνθα καὶ ἠματίη μὲν ὑφαίνεσκεν μέγαν ἱστόν,
νύκτας δ᾽ ἀλλύεσκεν, ἐπεὶ δαΐδας παραθεῖτο.
ὡς τρίετες μὲν ἔληθε δόλῳ καὶ ἔπειθεν Ἀχαιούς·
ἀλλ᾽ ὅτε τέτρατον ἦλθεν ἔτος καὶ ἐπήλυθον ὧραι,
καὶ τότε δή τις ἔειπε γυναικῶν, ἣ σάφα ᾔδη,
καὶ τήν γ᾽ ἀλλύουσαν ἐφεύρομεν ἀγλαὸν ἱστόν.
ὡς τὸ μὲν ἐξετέλεσσε καὶ οὐκ ἐθέλουσ᾽ ὑπ᾽ ἀνάγκης·
σοὶ δ᾽ ὧδε μνηστῆρες ὑποκρίνονται, ἵν᾽ εἰδῇς
αὐτὸς σῷ θυμῷ, εἰδῶσι δὲ πάντες Ἀχαιοί·
μητέρα σὴν ἀπόπεμψον, ἄνωχθι δέ μιν γαμέεσθαι
τῷ ὅτεῴ τε πατὴρ κέλεται καὶ ἁνδάνει αὐτῇ.
εἰ δ᾽ ἔτ᾽ ἀνιήσει γε πολὺν χρόνον υἷας Ἀχαιῶν,
τὰ φρονέουσ᾽ ἀνὰ θυμόν, ὅ οἱ πέρι δῶκεν Ἀθήνη
ἔργα τ᾽ ἐπίστασθαι περικαλλέα καὶ φρένας ἐσθλὰς
κέρδεά θ᾽, οἷ᾽ οὔ πώ τιν᾽ ἀκούομεν οὐδὲ παλαιῶν,
τάων αἳ πάρος ἦσαν ἐϋπλοκαμῖδες Ἀχαιαί,
Τυρώ τ᾽ Ἀλκμήνη τε ἐϋστέφανός τε Μυκήνη·
τάων οὔ τις ὁμοῖα νοήματα Πηνελοπείῃ
ᾔδη· ἀτὰρ μὲν τοῦτό γ᾽ ἐναίσιμον οὐκ ἐνόησε.
τόφρα γὰρ οὖν βίοτόν τε τεὸν καὶ κτήματ᾽ ἔδονται,
ὄφρα κε κείνη τοῦτον ἔχῃ νόον, ὅν τινά οἱ νῦν
ἐν στήθεσσι τιθεῖσι θεοί. μέγα μὲν κλέος αὐτῇ
ποιεῖτ᾽, αὐτὰρ σοί γε ποθὴν πολέος βιότοιο.
ἡμεῖς δ᾽ οὔτ᾽ ἐπὶ ἔργα πάρος γ᾽ ἴμεν οὔτε πη ἄλλη,
πρίν γ᾽ αὐτὴν γήμασθαι Ἀχαιῶν ᾧ κ᾽ ἐθέλῃσι."

women in the land should be wroth with me, if he, who had won great possessions, were to lie without a shroud.'

"So she spoke, and our proud hearts consented. Then day by day she would weave at the great web, but by night would unravel it, when she had let place torches by her. Thus for three years she by her craft kept the Achaeans from knowing, and beguiled them; but when the fourth year came as the seasons rolled on, even then one of her women who knew all told us, and we caught her unravelling the splendid web. So she finished it against her will, perforce. Therefore to thee the wooers make answer thus, that thou mayest thyself know it in thine heart, and that all the Achaeans may know. Send away thy mother, and command her to wed whomsoever her father bids, and whoso is pleasing to her. But if she shall continue long time to vex the sons of the Achaeans, mindful in her heart of this, that Athene has endowed her above other women with knowledge of fair handiwork and an understanding heart, and wiles, such as we have never yet heard that any even of the women of old knew, of those who long ago were fair-tressed Achaean women—Tyro and Alcmene and Mycene of the fair crown—of whom not one was like Penelope in shrewd device; yet this at least she devised not aright. For so long shall men devour thy livelihood and thy possessions, even as long as she shall keep the counsel which the gods now put in her heart. Great fame she brings on herself, but on thee regret for thy much substance. For us, we will go neither to our lands nor elsewhither, until she marries that one of the Achaeans whom she will."

45

Τὸν δ' αὖ Τηλέμαχος πεπνυμένος ἀντίον ηὔδα·
"'Αντίνο', οὔ πως ἔστι δόμων ἀέκουσαν ἀπῶσαι   13(
ἥ μ' ἔτεχ', ἥ μ' ἔθρεψε· πατὴρ δ' ἐμὸς ἄλλοθι γαίης,
ζώει ὅ γ' ἦ τέθνηκε· κακὸν δέ με πόλλ' ἀποτίνειν
'Ικαρίῳ, αἴ κ' αὐτὸς ἑκὼν ἀπὸ μητέρα πέμψω.
ἐκ γὰρ τοῦ πατρὸς κακὰ πείσομαι, ἄλλα δὲ δαίμων
δώσει, ἐπεὶ μήτηρ στυγερὰς ἀρήσετ' ἐρινῦς   13:
οἴκου ἀπερχομένη· νέμεσις δέ μοι ἐξ ἀνθρώπων
ἔσσεται· ὣς οὐ τοῦτον ἐγώ ποτε μῦθον ἐνίψω.
ὑμέτερος δ' εἰ μὲν θυμὸς νεμεσίζεται αὐτῶν,
ἔξιτέ μοι μεγάρων, ἄλλας δ' ἀλεγύνετε δαῖτας
ὑμὰ κτήματ' ἔδοντες ἀμειβόμενοι κατὰ οἴκους.   14(
εἰ δ' ὑμῖν δοκέει τόδε λωίτερον καὶ ἄμεινον
ἔμμεναι, ἀνδρὸς ἑνὸς βίοτον νήποινον ὀλέσθαι,
κείρετ'· ἐγὼ δὲ θεοὺς ἐπιβώσομαι αἰὲν ἐόντας,
αἴ κέ ποθι Ζεὺς δῷσι παλίντιτα ἔργα γενέσθαι.
νήποινοί κεν ἔπειτα δόμων ἔντοσθεν ὄλοισθε."   14:

Ὣς φάτο Τηλέμαχος, τῷ δ' αἰετὼ εὐρύοπα Ζεὺς
ὑψόθεν ἐκ κορυφῆς ὄρεος προέηκε πέτεσθαι.
τὼ δ' ἕως μέν ῥ' ἐπέτοντο μετὰ πνοιῇς ἀνέμοιο
πλησίω ἀλλήλοισι τιταινομένω πτερύγεσσιν·
ἀλλ' ὅτε δὴ μέσσην ἀγορὴν πολύφημον ἱκέσθην,   15(
ἔνθ' ἐπιδινηθέντε τιναξάσθην πτερὰ πυκνά,
ἐς δ' ἰδέτην πάντων κεφαλάς, ὄσσοντο δ' ὄλεθρον·
δρυψαμένω δ' ὀνύχεσσι παρειὰς ἀμφί τε δειρὰς
δεξιὼ ἤιξαν διά τ' οἰκία καὶ πόλιν αὐτῶν.

Then wise Telemachus answered him, and said : " Antinous, in no wise may I thrust forth from the house against her will her that bore me and reared me ; and, as for my father, he is in some other land, whether he be alive or dead. An evil thing it were for me to pay back a great price to Icarius, as I must, if of my own will I send my mother away. For from her father's hand shall I suffer evil, and heaven will send other ills besides, for my mother as she leaves the house will invoke the dread Avengers ; and I shall have blame, too, from men. Therefore will I never speak this word. And for you, if your own heart is wroth hereat, get you forth from my halls and prepare you other feasts, eating your own substance and changing from house to house. But if this seems in your eyes to be a better and more profitable thing, that one man's livelihood should be ruined without atonement, waste ye it. But I will call upon the gods that are forever, if haply Zeus may grant that deeds of requital may be wrought. Without atonement then should ye perish within my halls."

So spoke Telemachus, and in answer Zeus, whose voice is borne afar,[1] sent forth two eagles, flying from on high, from a mountain peak. For a time they flew swift as the blasts of the wind side by side with wings outspread ; but when they reached the middle of the many-voiced assembly, then they wheeled about, flapping their wings rapidly, and down on the heads of all they looked, and death was in their glare. Then they tore with their talons one another's cheeks and necks on either side, and darted away to the right across the houses and the city of the men.

---

[1] The adjective is sometimes rendered " far-seeing."

θάμβησαν δ' ὄρνιθας, ἐπεὶ ἴδον ὀφθαλμοῖσιν· 155
ὥρμηναν δ' ἀνὰ θυμὸν ἅ περ τελέεσθαι ἔμελλον.
τοῖσι δὲ καὶ μετέειπε γέρων ἥρως Ἁλιθέρσης
Μαστορίδης· ὁ γὰρ οἶος ὁμηλικίην ἐκέκαστο
ὄρνιθας γνῶναι καὶ ἐναίσιμα μυθήσασθαι·
ὅ σφιν ἐῢ φρονέων ἀγορήσατο καὶ μετέειπε· 160
   "Κέκλυτε δὴ νῦν μευ, Ἰθακήσιοι, ὅττι κεν εἴπω·
μνηστῆρσιν δὲ μάλιστα πιφαυσκόμενος τάδε εἴρω·
τοῖσιν γὰρ μέγα πῆμα κυλίνδεται· οὐ γὰρ Ὀδυσσεὺς
δὴν ἀπάνευθε φίλων ὧν ἔσσεται, ἀλλά που ἤδη
ἐγγὺς ἐὼν τοῖσδεσσι φόνον καὶ κῆρα φυτεύει 165
πάντεσσιν· πολέσιν δὲ καὶ ἄλλοισιν κακὸν ἔσται,
οἳ νεμόμεσθ' Ἰθάκην ἐυδείελον. ἀλλὰ πολὺ πρὶν
φραζώμεσθ', ὥς κεν καταπαύσομεν· οἱ δὲ καὶ αὐτοὶ
παυέσθων· καὶ γάρ σφιν ἄφαρ τόδε λώιόν ἐστιν.
οὐ γὰρ ἀπείρητος μαντεύομαι, ἀλλ' ἐῢ εἰδώς· 170
καὶ γὰρ κείνῳ φημὶ τελευτηθῆναι ἅπαντα,
ὥς οἱ ἐμυθεόμην, ὅτε Ἴλιον εἰσανέβαινον
Ἀργεῖοι, μετὰ δέ σφιν ἔβη πολύμητις Ὀδυσσεύς.
φῆν κακὰ πολλὰ παθόντ', ὀλέσαντ' ἄπο πάντας
   ἑταίρους,
ἄγνωστον πάντεσσιν ἐεικοστῷ ἐνιαυτῷ 175
οἴκαδ' ἐλεύσεσθαι· τὰ δὲ δὴ νῦν πάντα τελεῖται."
   Τὸν δ' αὖτ' Εὐρύμαχος Πολύβου πάις ἀντίον ηὔδα·
"Ὦ γέρον, εἰ δ' ἄγε νῦν μαντεύεο σοῖσι τέκεσσιν
οἴκαδ' ἰών, μή πού τι κακὸν πάσχωσιν ὀπίσσω·
ταῦτα δ' ἐγὼ σέο πολλὸν ἀμείνων μαντεύεσθαι. 180
ὄρνιθες δέ τε πολλοὶ ὑπ' αὐγὰς ἠελίοιο
φοιτῶσ', οὐδέ τε πάντες ἐναίσιμοι· αὐτὰρ Ὀδυσσεὺς

But they were seized with wonder at the birds when their eyes beheld them, and pondered in their hearts on what was to come to pass. Then among them spoke the old lord Halitherses, son of Mastor, for he surpassed all men of his day in knowledge of birds and in uttering words of fate. He with good intent addressed their assembly, and spoke among them:

"Hearken now to me, men of Ithaca, to the word that I shall say; and to the wooers especially do I declare and announce these things, since on them a great woe is rolling. For Odysseus shall not long be away from his friends, but even now, methinks, he is near, and is sowing death and fate for these men, one and all. Aye, and to many others of us also who dwell in clear-seen Ithaca will he be a bane. But long ere that let us take thought how we may make an end of this—or rather let them of themselves make an end, for this is straightway the better course for them. Not as one untried do I prophesy, but with sure knowledge. For unto Odysseus I declare that all things are fulfilled even as I told him, when the Argives embarked for Ilios and with them went Odysseus of many wiles. I declared that after suffering many ills and losing all his comrades he would come home in the twentieth year unknown to all; and lo, all this is now being brought to pass."

Then Eurymachus, son of Polybus, answered him, and said: "Old man, up now, get thee home and prophesy to thy children, lest haply in days to come they suffer ill. In this matter I am better far than thou to prophesy. Many birds there are that fare to and fro under the rays of the sun, and not all are fateful. As for Odysseus, he has perished far away,

ὤλετο τῆλ’, ὡς καὶ σὺ καταφθίσθαι σὺν ἐκείνῳ
ὤφελες. οὐκ ἂν τόσσα θεοπροπέων ἀγόρευες,
οὐδέ κε Τηλέμαχον κεχολωμένον ὧδ’ ἀνιείης,   1[ ]
σῷ οἴκῳ δῶρον ποτιδέγμενος, αἴ κε πόρῃσιν.
ἀλλ’ ἔκ τοι ἐρέω, τὸ δὲ καὶ τετελεσμένον ἔσται·
αἴ κε νεώτερον ἄνδρα παλαιά τε πολλά τε εἰδὼς
παρφάμενος ἐπέεσσιν ἐποτρύνῃς χαλεπαίνειν,
αὐτῷ μέν οἱ πρῶτον ἀνιηρέστερον ἔσται,   1[ ]
πρῆξαι δ’ ἔμπης οὔ τι δυνήσεται εἵνεκα τῶνδε· [1]
σοὶ δέ, γέρον, θωὴν ἐπιθήσομεν, ἥν κ’ ἐνὶ θυμῷ
τίνων ἀσχάλλῃς· χαλεπὸν δέ τοι ἔσσεται ἄλγος.
Τηλεμάχῳ δ’ ἐν πᾶσιν ἐγὼν ὑποθήσομαι αὐτός·
μητέρα ἣν ἐς πατρὸς ἀνωγέτω ἀπονέεσθαι·   1[ ]
οἱ δὲ γάμον τεύξουσι καὶ ἀρτυνέουσιν ἔεδνα
πολλὰ μάλ’, ὅσσα ἔοικε φίλης ἐπὶ παιδὸς ἕπεσθαι.
οὐ γὰρ πρὶν παύσεσθαι ὀίομαι υἷας Ἀχαιῶν
μνηστύος ἀργαλέης, ἐπεὶ οὔ τινα δείδιμεν ἔμπης,
οὔτ’ οὖν Τηλέμαχον μάλα περ πολύμυθον ἐόντα,   20
οὔτε θεοπροπίης ἐμπαζόμεθ’, ἣν σύ, γεραιέ,
μυθέαι ἀκράαντον, ἀπεχθάνεαι δ’ ἔτι μᾶλλον.
χρήματα δ’ αὖτε κακῶς βεβρώσεται, οὐδέ ποτ’ ἶσα
ἔσσεται, ὄφρα κεν ἥ γε διατρίβῃσιν Ἀχαιοὺς
ὃν γάμον· ἡμεῖς δ’ αὖ ποτιδέγμενοι ἤματα πάντα 20
εἵνεκα τῆς ἀρετῆς ἐριδαίνομεν, οὐδὲ μετ’ ἄλλας
ἐρχόμεθ’, ἃς ἐπιεικὲς ὀπυιέμεν ἐστὶν ἑκάστῳ.
    Τὸν δ’ αὖ Τηλέμαχος πεπνυμένος ἀντίον ηὔδα·
“Εὐρύμαχ’ ἠδὲ καὶ ἄλλοι, ὅσοι μνηστῆρες ἀγαυοί,
ταῦτα μὲν οὐχ ὑμέας ἔτι λίσσομαι οὐδ’ ἀγορεύω· 21
ἤδη γὰρ τὰ ἴσασι θεοὶ καὶ πάντες Ἀχαιοί.

---

[1] Line 191 is omitted in most MSS. Some of those which
retain it have οἷος ἀπ’ ἄλλων instead of εἵνεκα τῶνδε.

as I would that thou hadst likewise perished with him. Then wouldst thou not prate so much in thy reading of signs, or be urging Telemachus on in his wrath, hoping for some gift for thy house, if haply he shall give it. But I will speak out to thee, and this word shall verily be brought to pass. If thou, wise in the wisdom of old, shalt beguile with thy talk a younger man, and set him on to be wroth, for him in the first place it shall be the more grievous, and he will in no case be able to do aught because of these men here, and on thee, old man, will we lay a fine which it will grieve thy soul to pay, and bitter shall be thy sorrow. And to Telemachus I myself, here among all, will offer this counsel. His mother let him bid to go back to the house of her father, and they will prepare a wedding feast and make ready the gifts full many,—aye, all that should follow after a well-loved daughter. For ere that, methinks, the sons of the Achaeans will not cease from their grievous wooing, since in any case we fear no man,— no, not Telemachus for all his many words,—nor do we reck of any soothsaying which thou, old man, mayest declare; it will fail of fulfilment, and thou shalt be hated the more. Aye, and his possessions shall be devoured in evil wise, nor shall requital ever be made, so long as she shall put off the Achaeans in the matter of her marriage. And we on our part waiting here day after day are rivals by reason of her excellence, and go not after other women, whom each one might fitly wed."

Then wise Telemachus answered him: " Eury-machus and all ye other lordly wooers, in this matter I entreat you no longer nor speak thereof, for now the gods know it, and all the Achaeans. But come,

51

ἀλλ' ἄγε μοι δότε νῆα θοὴν καὶ εἴκοσ' ἑταίρους,
οἵ κέ μοι ἔνθα καὶ ἔνθα διαπρήσσωσι κέλευθον.
εἶμι γὰρ ἐς Σπάρτην[1] τε καὶ ἐς Πύλον ἠμαθόεντα
νόστον πευσόμενος πατρὸς δὴν οἰχομένοιο,   20
ἤν τίς μοι εἴπῃσι βροτῶν ἢ ὄσσαν ἀκούσω
ἐκ Διός, ἥ τε μάλιστα φέρει κλέος ἀνθρώποισιν·
εἰ μέν κεν πατρὸς βίοτον καὶ νόστον ἀκούσω,
ἦ τ' ἂν, τρυχόμενός περ, ἔτι τλαίην ἐνιαυτόν·
εἰ δέ κε τεθνηῶτος ἀκούσω μηδ' ἔτ' ἐόντος,   22
νοστήσας δὴ ἔπειτα φίλην ἐς πατρίδα γαῖαν
σῆμά τέ οἱ χεύω καὶ ἐπὶ κτέρεα κτερεΐξω
πολλὰ μάλ', ὅσσα ἔοικε, καὶ ἀνέρι μητέρα δώσω."
    Ἦ τοι ὅ γ' ὣς εἰπὼν κατ' ἄρ' ἕζετο, τοῖσι δ' ἀνέστη
Μέντωρ, ὅς ῥ' Ὀδυσῆος ἀμύμονος ἦεν ἑταῖρος,   22
καί οἱ ἰὼν ἐν νηυσὶν ἐπέτρεπεν οἶκον ἅπαντα,
πείθεσθαί τε γέροντι καὶ ἔμπεδα πάντα φυλάσσειν·
ὅ σφιν ἐὺ φρονέων ἀγορήσατο καὶ μετέειπεν·
    "Κέκλυτε δὴ νῦν μευ, Ἰθακήσιοι, ὅττι κεν εἴπω·
μή τις ἔτι πρόφρων ἀγανὸς καὶ ἤπιος ἔστω   23
σκηπτοῦχος βασιλεύς, μηδὲ φρεσὶν αἴσιμα εἰδώς,
ἀλλ' αἰεὶ χαλεπός τ' εἴη καὶ αἴσυλα ῥέζοι·
ὡς οὔ τις μέμνηται Ὀδυσσῆος θείοιο
λαῶν οἷσιν ἄνασσε, πατὴρ δ' ὣς ἤπιος ἦεν.
ἀλλ' ἦ τοι μνηστῆρας ἀγήνορας οὔ τι μεγαίρω   23
ἔρδειν ἔργα βίαια κακορραφίῃσι νόοιο·
σφὰς γὰρ παρθέμενοι κεφαλὰς κατέδουσι βιαίως
οἶκον Ὀδυσσῆος, τὸν δ' οὐκέτι φασὶ νέεσθαι.
νῦν δ' ἄλλῳ δήμῳ νεμεσίζομαι, οἷον ἅπαντες

---

[1] Σπάρτην : Κρήτην Zenodotus ; cf. i. 93.

give me a swift ship and twenty comrades who will accomplish my journey for me to and fro. For I shall go to Sparta and to sandy Pylos to seek tidings of the return of my father that has long been gone, if haply any mortal man may tell me, or I may hear a voice from Zeus, which oftenest brings tidings to men. If so be I shall hear that my father is alive and coming home, then verily, though I am sore afflicted, I could endure for yet a year. But if I shall hear that he is dead and gone, then I will return to my dear native land and heap up a mound for him, and over it pay funeral rites, full many, as is due, and give my mother to a husband."

So saying he sat down, and among them rose Mentor, who was a comrade of noble Odysseus. To him, on departing with his ships, Odysseus had given all his house in charge, that it should obey the old man and that he should keep all things safe. He with good intent addressed their assembly, and spoke among them :

" Hearken now to me, men of Ithaca, to the word that I shall say. Never henceforth let sceptred king with a ready heart be kind and gentle, nor let him heed righteousness in his heart, but let him ever be harsh and work unrighteousness, seeing that no one remembers divine Odysseus of the people whose lord he was; yet gentle was he as a father. But of a truth I begrudge not the proud wooers that they work deeds of violence in the evil contrivings of their minds, for it is at the hazard of their own lives that they violently devour the house of Odysseus, who, they say, will no more return. Nay, rather it is with the rest of the folk that I am wroth,

ἦσθ' ἄνεω, ἀτὰρ οὔ τι καθαπτόμενοι ἐπέεσσι
παύρους μνηστῆρας καταπαύετε¹ πολλοὶ ἐόντες."

Τὸν δ' Εὐηνορίδης Λειώκριτος ἀντίον ηὔδα·
" Μέντορ ἀταρτηρέ, φρένας ἠλεέ, ποῖον ἔειπες
ἡμέας ὀτρύνων καταπαυέμεν. ἀργαλέον δὲ
ἀνδράσι καὶ πλεόνεσσι μαχήσασθαι περὶ δαιτί.
εἴ περ γάρ κ' Ὀδυσεὺς Ἰθακήσιος αὐτὸς ἐπελθὼν
δαινυμένους κατὰ δῶμα ἑὸν μνηστῆρας ἀγαυοὺς
ἐξελάσαι μεγάροιο μενοινήσει' ἐνὶ θυμῷ,
οὔ κέν οἱ κεχάροιτο γυνή, μάλα περ χατέουσα,
ἐλθόντ', ἀλλά κεν αὐτοῦ ἀεικέα πότμον ἐπίσποι,
εἰ πλεόνεσσι μάχοιτο·² σὺ δ' οὐ κατὰ μοῖραν ἔειπες.
ἀλλ' ἄγε, λαοὶ μὲν σκίδνασθ' ἐπὶ ἔργα ἕκαστος,
τούτῳ δ' ὀτρυνέει Μέντωρ ὁδὸν ἠδ' Ἁλιθέρσης,
οἵ τέ οἱ ἐξ ἀρχῆς πατρώιοί εἰσιν ἑταῖροι.
ἀλλ' ὀίω, καὶ δηθὰ καθήμενος ἀγγελιάων
πεύσεται εἰν Ἰθάκῃ, τελέει δ' ὁδὸν οὔ ποτε ταύτην."

Ὣς ἄρ' ἐφώνησεν, λῦσεν δ' ἀγορὴν αἰψηρήν.
οἱ μὲν ἄρ' ἐσκίδναντο ἑὰ πρὸς δώμαθ' ἕκαστος,
μνηστῆρες δ' ἐς δώματ' ἴσαν θείου Ὀδυσῆος.

Τηλέμαχος δ' ἀπάνευθε κιὼν ἐπὶ θῖνα θαλάσσης,
χεῖρας νιψάμενος πολιῆς ἁλὸς εὔχετ' Ἀθήνῃ·
" Κλῦθί μευ, ὃ χθιζὸς θεὸς ἤλυθες ἡμέτερον δῶ
καί μ' ἐν νηὶ κέλευσας ἐπ' ἠεροειδέα πόντον
νόστον πευσόμενον πατρὸς δὴν οἰχομένοιο

---

¹ καταπαύετε Rhianus : κατερύκετε.
² πλεόνεσσι μάχοιτο : πλέονές οἱ ἕποιντο the scholia (Aristarchus?).

---

[1] So the word was understood in antiquity. Modern scholars connect it with τείρω, and make it mean " hard," " insolent."
[2] So the text, as it stands, must be interpreted. The scholiast read in 251, εἰ πλέονές οἱ ἕποιντο, " even though he

that ye all sit thus in silence, and utter no word of rebuke to make the wooers cease, though ye are many and they but few."

Then Leocritus, son of Euenor, answered him: "Mentor, thou mischief-maker,[1] thou wanderer in thy wits, what hast thou said, bidding men make us cease? Nay, it were a hard thing to fight about a feast with men that moreover outnumber you. For if Ithacan Odysseus himself were to come and be eager at heart to drive out from his hall the lordly wooers who are feasting in his house, then should his wife have no joy at his coming, though sorely she longed for him, but right here would he meet a shameful death, if he fought with men that outnumbered him.[2] Thou hast not spoken aright. But come now, ye people, scatter, each one of you to his own lands. As for this fellow, Mentor and Halitherses will speed his journey, for they are friends of his father's house from of old. But methinks he will long abide here and get his tidings in Ithaca, and never accomplish this journey."

So he spoke, and hastily broke up the assembly. They then scattered, each one to his own house; and the wooers went to the house of divine Odysseus.

But Telemachus went apart to the shore of the sea, and having washed his hands in the grey seawater, prayed to Athene: "Hear me, thou who didst come yesterday as a god to our house, and didst bid me go in a ship over the misty deep to seek tidings of the return of my father, that has

had the larger following." If this be adopted, the πλεόνεσσι in 245 may be construed with ἀργαλέον, "Hard would it be for you, though you are more in number than we." As it is, Leocritus speaks defiantly, and denies that Mentor's party is the more numerous.

ἔρχεσθαι· τὰ δὲ πάντα διατρίβουσιν Ἀχαιοί,
μνηστῆρες δὲ μάλιστα κακῶς ὑπερηνορέοντες."
  Ὣς ἔφατ' εὐχόμενος, σχεδόθεν δέ οἱ ἦλθεν Ἀθήνη,
Μέντορι εἰδομένη ἠμὲν δέμας ἠδὲ καὶ αὐδήν,
καί μιν φωνήσασ' ἔπεα πτερόεντα προσηύδα·
  "Τηλέμαχ', οὐδ' ὄπιθεν κακὸς ἔσσεαι οὐδ' ἀνοήμω
εἰ δή τοι σοῦ πατρὸς ἐνέστακται μένος ἠύ,
οἷος κεῖνος ἔην τελέσαι ἔργον τε ἔπος τε·
οὔ τοι ἔπειθ' ἁλίη ὁδὸς ἔσσεται οὐδ' ἀτέλεστος.
εἰ δ' οὐ κείνου γ' ἐσσὶ γόνος καὶ Πηνελοπείης,
οὐ σέ γ' ἔπειτα ἔολπα τελευτήσειν, ἃ μενοινᾷς.
παῦροι γάρ τοι παῖδες ὁμοῖοι πατρὶ πέλονται,
οἱ πλέονες κακίους, παῦροι δέ τε πατρὸς ἀρείους.
ἀλλ' ἐπεὶ οὐδ' ὄπιθεν κακὸς ἔσσεαι οὐδ' ἀνοήμων,
οὐδέ σε πάγχυ γε μῆτις Ὀδυσσῆος προλέλοιπεν,
ἐλπωρή τοι ἔπειτα τελευτῆσαι τάδε ἔργα.
τῶ νῦν μνηστήρων μὲν ἔα βουλήν τε νόον τε
ἀφραδέων, ἐπεὶ οὔ τι νοήμονες οὐδὲ δίκαιοι·
οὐδέ τι ἴσασιν θάνατον καὶ κῆρα μέλαιναν,
ὃς δή σφι σχεδόν ἐστιν, ἐπ' ἤματι πάντας ὀλέσθαι.
σοὶ δ' ὁδὸς οὐκέτι δηρὸν ἀπέσσεται ἢν σὺ μενοινᾷς·
τοῖος γάρ τοι ἑταῖρος ἐγὼ πατρώιός εἰμι,
ὅς τοι νῆα θοὴν στελέω καὶ ἅμ' ἕψομαι αὐτός.
ἀλλὰ σὺ μὲν πρὸς δώματ' ἰὼν μνηστήρσιν ὁμίλει,
ὅπλισσόν τ' ἤια καὶ ἄγγεσιν ἄρσον ἅπαντα,
οἶνον ἐν ἀμφιφορεῦσι, καὶ ἄλφιτα, μυελὸν ἀνδρῶν,
δέρμασιν ἐν πυκινοῖσιν· ἐγὼ δ' ἀνὰ δῆμον ἑταίρους
αἶψ' ἐθελοντῆρας συλλέξομαι. εἰσὶ δὲ νῆες
πολλαὶ ἐν ἀμφιάλῳ Ἰθάκῃ, νέαι ἠδὲ παλαιαί·
τάων μέν τοι ἐγὼν ἐπιόψομαι ἥ τις ἀρίστη,
ὦκα δ' ἐφοπλίσσαντες ἐνήσομεν εὐρέι πόντῳ."

long been gone.   Lo, all this the Achaeans hinder,
but the wooers most of all in their evil insolence."

So he spoke in prayer, and Athene drew near to
him in the likeness of Mentor, both in form and in
voice; and she spoke, and addressed him with winged
words:

"Telemachus, neither hereafter shalt thou be a
base man or a witless, if aught of thy father's goodly
spirit has been instilled into thee, such a man was
he to fulfil both deed and word.   So then shall this
journey of thine be neither vain nor unfulfilled.   But
if thou art not the son of him and of Penelope, then
I have no hope that thou wilt accomplish thy desire.
Few sons indeed are like their fathers; most are
worse, few better than their fathers.   But since neither
hereafter shalt thou be a base man or a witless, nor
has the wisdom of Odysseus wholly failed thee, there
is therefore hope that thou wilt accomplish this work.
Now then let be the will and counsel of the wooers—
fools, for they are in no wise either prudent or just,
nor do they know aught of death or black fate, which
verily is near at hand for them, that they shall all
perish in a day.   But for thyself, the journey on
which thy heart is set shall not be long delayed, so
true a friend of thy father's house am I, who will
equip for thee a swift ship, and myself go with thee.
But go thou now to the house and join the company
of the wooers ; make ready stores, and bestow all in
vessels—wine in jars, and barley meal, the marrow
of men, in stout skins;—but I, going through the
town, will quickly gather comrades that go willingly.
And ships there are full many in sea-girt Ithaca,
both new and old; of these will I choose out for
thee the one that is best, and quickly will we make
her ready and launch her on the broad deep."

Ὣς φάτ' Ἀθηναίη κούρη Διός· οὐδ' ἄρ' ἔτι δὴν
Τηλέμαχος παρέμιμνεν, ἐπεὶ θεοῦ ἔκλυεν αὐδήν.
βῆ δ' ἰέναι πρὸς δῶμα, φίλον τετιημένος ἦτορ,
εὗρε δ' ἄρα μνηστῆρας ἀγήνορας ἐν μεγάροισιν,
αἶγας ἀνιεμένους σιάλους θ' εὕοντας ἐν αὐλῇ.   30
Ἀντίνοος δ' ἰθὺς γελάσας κίε Τηλεμάχοιο,
ἔν τ' ἄρα οἱ φῦ χειρί, ἔπος τ' ἔφατ' ἔκ τ' ὀνόμαζε·

"Τηλέμαχ' ὑψαγόρη, μένος ἄσχετε, μή τί τοι ἄλλο
ἐν στήθεσσι κακὸν μελέτω ἔργον τε ἔπος τε,
ἀλλά μοι[1] ἐσθιέμεν καὶ πινέμεν, ὡς τὸ πάρος περ.   30
ταῦτα δέ τοι μάλα πάντα τελευτήσουσιν Ἀχαιοί,
νῆα καὶ ἐξαίτους ἐρέτας, ἵνα θᾶσσον ἵκηαι
ἐς Πύλον ἠγαθέην μετ' ἀγαυοῦ πατρὸς ἀκουήν."

Τὸν δ' αὖ Τηλέμαχος πεπνυμένος ἀντίον ηὔδα·
"Ἀντίνο', οὔ πως ἔστιν ὑπερφιάλοισι μεθ' ὑμῖν   31
δαίνυσθαί τ' ἀκέοντα[2] καὶ εὐφραίνεσθαι ἔκηλον.
ἦ οὐχ ἅλις ὡς τὸ πάροιθεν ἐκείρετε πολλὰ καὶ ἐσθλὰ
κτήματ' ἐμά, μνηστῆρες, ἐγὼ δ' ἔτι νήπιος ἦα;
νῦν δ' ὅτε δὴ μέγας εἰμὶ καὶ ἄλλων μῦθον ἀκούων
πυνθάνομαι, καὶ δή μοι ἀέξεται ἔνδοθι θυμός,   31
πειρήσω, ὥς κ' ὔμμι κακὰς ἐπὶ κῆρας ἰήλω,
ἠὲ Πύλονδ' ἐλθών, ἢ αὐτοῦ τῷδ' ἐνὶ δήμῳ.
εἶμι μέν, οὐδ' ἁλίη ὁδὸς ἔσσεται ἣν ἀγορεύω,
ἔμπορος· οὐ γὰρ νηὸς ἐπήβολος οὐδ' ἐρετάων
γίγνομαι· ὥς νύ που ὔμμιν ἐείσατο κέρδιον εἶναι."   32

Ἦ ῥα, καὶ ἐκ χειρὸς χεῖρα σπάσατ' Ἀντινόοιο
ῥεῖα· μνηστῆρες δὲ δόμον κάτα δαῖτα πένοντο.[3]

---

[1] μοι : μάλ'.   [2] ἀκέοντα : ἀέκοντα Rhianus.
[3] Line 322 was rejected by Aristophanes and Aristarchus.

---

[1] The verb ὀνομάζειν is most commonly, as here, followed
by the name of the person addressed, or by something

So spoke Athene, daughter of Zeus, nor did Telemachus tarry long after he had heard the voice of the goddess, but went his way to the house, his heart heavy within him. He found there the proud wooers in the halls, flaying goats and singeing swine in the court. And Antinous with a laugh came straight to Telemachus, and clasped his hand, and spoke, and addressed [1] him :

"Telemachus, thou braggart, unrestrained in daring, let no more any evil deed or word be in thy heart. Nay, I bid thee, eat and drink even as before. All these things the Achaeans will surely provide for thee—the ship and chosen oarsmen— that with speed thou mayest go to sacred Pylos to seek for tidings of thy noble father."

Then wise Telemachus answered him : "Antinous, in no wise is it possible for me in your overweening company to sit at meat quietly and to make merry with an easy mind. Is it not enough, ye wooers, that in time past ye wasted many goodly possessions of mine, while I was still a child ? But now that I am grown, and gain knowledge by hearing the words of others, yea and my spirit waxes within me, I will try how I may hurl forth upon you evil fates, either going to Pylos or here in this land. For go I will, nor shall the journey be in vain whereof I speak, though I voyage in another's ship, since I may not be master of ship or oarsmen. So, I ween, it seemed to you to be more to your profit."

He spoke, and snatched his hand from the hand of Antinous without more ado, and the wooers were busy with the feast throughout the hall. They

equivalent to it. In a number of passages, however, the word is freely used, and it has seemed best to adopt a rendering which suits all, or nearly all, cases.

οἱ δ' ἐπελώβευον καὶ ἐκερτόμεον ἐπέεσσιν.
ὧδε δέ τις εἴπεσκε νέων ὑπερηνορεόντων·
    "Ἦ μάλα Τηλέμαχος φόνον ἧμιν μερμηρίζει.
ἤ τινας ἐκ Πύλου ἄξει ἀμύντορας ἠμαθόεντος
ἢ ὅ γε καὶ Σπάρτηθεν, ἐπεί νύ περ ἵεται αἰνῶς·
ἠὲ καὶ εἰς Ἐφύρην ἐθέλει, πίειραν ἄρουραν,
ἐλθεῖν, ὄφρ' ἔνθεν θυμοφθόρα φάρμακ' ἐνείκη,
ἐν δὲ βάλῃ κρητῆρι καὶ ἡμέας πάντας ὀλέσσῃ."
    Ἄλλος δ' αὖτ' εἴπεσκε νέων ὑπερηνορεόντων·
"Τίς δ' οἶδ', εἴ κε καὶ αὐτὸς ἰὼν κοίλης ἐπὶ νηὸς
τῆλε φίλων ἀπόληται ἀλώμενος ὥς περ Ὀδυσσεύς;
οὕτω κεν καὶ μᾶλλον ὀφέλλειεν πόνον ἄμμιν·
κτήματα γάρ κεν πάντα δασαίμεθα, οἰκία δ' αὖτε
τούτου μητέρι δοῖμεν ἔχειν ἠδ' ὅς τις ὀπυίοι."
    Ὣς φάν, ὁ δ' ὑψόροφον θάλαμον κατεβήσετο πατρὸ
εὐρύν, ὅθι νητὸς χρυσὸς καὶ χαλκὸς ἔκειτο
ἐσθής τ' ἐν χηλοῖσιν ἅλις τ' εὐῶδες ἔλαιον·
ἐν δὲ πίθοι οἴνοιο παλαιοῦ ἡδυπότοιο
ἕστασαν, ἄκρητον θεῖον ποτὸν ἐντὸς ἔχοντες,
ἑξείης ποτὶ τοῖχον ἀρηρότες, εἴ ποτ' Ὀδυσσεὺς
οἴκαδε νοστήσειε καὶ ἄλγεα πολλὰ μογήσας.
κληισταὶ δ' ἔπεσαν σανίδες πυκινῶς ἀραρυῖαι,
δικλίδες· ἐν δὲ γυνὴ ταμίη νύκτας τε καὶ ἧμαρ
ἔσχ', ἣ πάντ' ἐφύλασσε νόου πολυϊδρείῃσιν,
Εὐρύκλει', Ὦπος θυγάτηρ Πεισηνορίδαο.
τὴν τότε Τηλέμαχος προσέφη θαλαμόνδε καλέσας·
    "Μαῖ', ἄγε δή μοι οἶνον ἐν ἀμφιφορεῦσιν ἄφυσσο
ἡδύν, ὅτις μετὰ τὸν λαρώτατος ὃν σὺ φυλάσσεις
κεῖνον ὀιομένη τὸν κάμμορον, εἴ ποθεν ἔλθοι

mocked and jeered at him in their talk; and thus
would one of the proud youths speak:

"Aye, verily Telemachus is planning our murder.
He will bring men to aid him from sandy Pylos or
even from Sparta, so terribly is he set upon it. Or
he means to go to Ephyre, that rich land, to bring
from thence deadly drugs, that he may cast them in
the wine-bowl, and destroy us all."

And again another of the proud youths would
say: "Who knows but he himself as he goes on
the hollow ship may perish wandering far from his
friends, even as Odysseus did? So would he cause
us yet more labour; for we should have to divide
all his possessions, and his house we should give
to his mother to possess, and to him who should
wed her."

So they spoke, but Telemachus went down to the
high-roofed treasure-chamber of his father, a wide
room where gold and bronze lay piled, and raiment
in chests, and stores of fragrant oil. There, too,
stood great jars of wine, old and sweet, holding with-
in them an unmixed divine drink, and ranged in
order along the wall, if ever Odysseus should return
home even after many grievous toils. Shut were
the double doors, close-fitted; and there both night
and day a stewardess abode, who guarded all in
wisdom of mind, Eurycleia, daughter of Ops, son of
Peisenor. To her now Telemachus, when he had
called her to the treasure-chamber, spoke, and
said:

"Nurse, draw me off wine in jars, sweet wine that
is the choicest next to that which thou guardest ever
thinking upon that ill-fated one, if haply Zeus-born
Odysseus may come I know not whence, having

διογενὴς Ὀδυσεὺς θάνατον καὶ κῆρας ἀλύξας.
δώδεκα δ' ἔμπλησον καὶ πώμασιν ἄρσον ἅπαντας.
ἐν δέ μοι ἄλφιτα χεῦον ἐυρραφέεσσι δοροῖσιν·
εἴκοσι δ' ἔστω μέτρα μυληφάτου ἀλφίτου ἀκτῆς.   3
αὐτὴ δ' οἴη ἴσθι· τὰ δ' ἀθρόα πάντα τετύχθω·
ἑσπέριος γὰρ ἐγὼν αἱρήσομαι, ὁππότε κεν δὴ
μήτηρ εἰς ὑπερῷ' ἀναβῇ κοίτου τε μέδηται.
εἶμι γὰρ ἐς Σπάρτην τε καὶ ἐς Πύλον ἠμαθόεντα
νόστον πευσόμενος πατρὸς φίλου, ἤν που ἀκούσω." 3

Ὣς φάτο, κώκυσεν δὲ φίλη τροφὸς Εὐρύκλεια,
καί ῥ' ὀλοφυρομένη ἔπεα πτερόεντα προσηύδα·
"Τίπτε δέ τοι, φίλε τέκνον, ἐνὶ φρεσὶ τοῦτο νόημα
ἔπλετο; πῇ δ' ἐθέλεις ἰέναι πολλὴν ἐπὶ γαῖαν
μοῦνος ἐὼν ἀγαπητός; ὁ δ' ὤλετο τηλόθι πάτρης   3
διογενὴς Ὀδυσεὺς ἀλλογνώτῳ ἐνὶ δήμῳ.
οἱ δέ τοι αὐτίκ' ἰόντι κακὰ φράσσονται ὀπίσσω,
ὥς κε δόλῳ φθίῃς, τάδε δ' αὐτοὶ πάντα δάσονται.
ἀλλὰ μέν' αὖθ' ἐπὶ σοῖσι καθήμενος· οὐδέ τί σε χρὴ
πόντον ἐπ' ἀτρύγετον κακὰ πάσχειν οὐδ' ἀλάλησθαι.

Τὴν δ' αὖ Τηλέμαχος πεπνυμένος ἀντίον ηὔδα·   3
"Θάρσει, μαῖ', ἐπεὶ οὔ τοι ἄνευ θεοῦ ἥδε γε βουλή.
ἀλλ' ὄμοσον μὴ μητρὶ φίλῃ τάδε μυθήσασθαι,
πρίν γ' ὅτ' ἂν ἑνδεκάτη τε δυωδεκάτη τε γένηται,
ἢ αὐτὴν ποθέσαι καὶ ἀφορμηθέντος ἀκοῦσαι,   3
ὡς ἂν μὴ κλαίουσα κατὰ χρόα καλὸν ἰάπτῃ."

Ὣς ἄρ' ἔφη, γρῆυς δὲ θεῶν μέγαν ὅρκον ἀπώμνυ.
αὐτὰρ ἐπεί ῥ' ὄμοσέν τε τελεύτησέν τε τὸν ὅρκον,
αὐτίκ' ἔπειτά οἱ οἶνον ἐν ἀμφιφορεῦσιν ἄφυσσεν,

escaped from death and the fates. Fill twelve jars and fit them all with covers, and pour me barley meal into well-sewn skins, and let there be twenty measures of ground barley meal. But keep knowledge hereof to thyself, and have all these things brought together; for at evening I will fetch them, when my mother goes to her upper chamber and bethinks her of her rest. For I am going to Sparta and to sandy Pylos to seek tidings of the return of my dear father, if haply I may hear any."

So he spoke, and the dear nurse, Eurycleia, uttered a shrill cry, and weeping spoke to him winged words: "Ah, dear child, how has this thought come into thy mind? Whither art thou minded to go over the wide earth, thou who art an only son and well-beloved? But he hath perished far from his country, the Zeus-born Odysseus, in a strange land; and these men, so soon as thou art gone, will devise evil for thee hereafter, that thou mayest perish by guile, and themselves divide all these possessions. Nay, abide here in charge of what is thine; thou hast no need to suffer ills and go a wanderer over the unresting sea."

Then wise Telemachus answered her: "Take heart, nurse, for not without a god's warrant is this my plan. But swear to tell naught of this to my dear mother until the eleventh or twelfth day shall come, or until she shall herself miss me and hear that I am gone, that she may not mar her fair flesh with weeping."

So he spoke, and the old woman swore a great oath by the gods to say naught. But when she had sworn and made an end of the oath, straightway she drew for him wine in jars, and poured barley meal

ἐν δέ οἱ ἄλφιτα χεῦεν ἐυρραφέεσσι δοροῖσι.　　　3⋮
Τηλέμαχος δ' ἐς δώματ' ἰὼν μνηστῆρσιν ὁμίλει.

Ἔνθ' αὖτ' ἄλλ' ἐνόησε θεά, γλαυκῶπις Ἀθήνη.
Τηλεμάχῳ ἐικυῖα κατὰ πτόλιν ᾤχετο πάντῃ,
καί ῥα ἑκάστῳ φωτὶ παρισταμένη φάτο μῦθον,
ἑσπερίους δ' ἐπὶ νῆα θοὴν ἀγέρεσθαι ἀνώγει.　　3⋮
ἡ δ' αὖτε Φρονίοιο Νοήμονα φαίδιμον υἱὸν
ᾔτεε νῆα θοήν· ὁ δέ οἱ πρόφρων ὑπέδεκτο.

Δύσετό τ' ἠέλιος σκιόωντό τε πᾶσαι ἀγυιαί,
καὶ τότε νῆα θοὴν ἅλαδ' εἴρυσε, πάντα δ' ἐν αὐτῇ
ὅπλ' ἐτίθει, τά τε νῆες ἐύσσελμοι φορέουσι.　　3⋮
στῆσε δ' ἐπ' ἐσχατιῇ λιμένος, περὶ δ' ἐσθλοὶ ἑταῖροι
ἀθρόοι ἠγερέθοντο· θεὰ δ' ὤτρυνεν ἕκαστον.

Ἔνθ' αὖτ' ἄλλ' ἐνόησε θεά, γλαυκῶπις Ἀθήνη.
βῆ ῥ' ἰέναι πρὸς δώματ' Ὀδυσσῆος θείοιο·
ἔνθα μνηστήρεσσιν ἐπὶ γλυκὺν ὕπνον ἔχευε,　　3⋮
πλάζε δὲ πίνοντας, χειρῶν δ' ἔκβαλλε κύπελλα.
οἱ δ' εὕδειν ὤρνυντο κατὰ πτόλιν, οὐδ' ἄρ' ἔτι δὴν
ἥατ', ἐπεί σφισιν ὕπνος ἐπὶ βλεφάροισιν ἔπιπτεν.
αὐτὰρ Τηλέμαχον προσέφη γλαυκῶπις Ἀθήνη
ἐκπροκαλεσσαμένη μεγάρων ἐὺ ναιεταόντων,　　4⋮
Μέντορι εἰδομένη ἠμὲν δέμας ἠδὲ καὶ αὐδήν·

"Τηλέμαχ', ἤδη μέν τοι ἐυκνήμιδες ἑταῖροι
ἥατ' ἐπήρετμοι τὴν σὴν ποτιδέγμενοι ὁρμήν·
ἀλλ' ἴομεν, μὴ δηθὰ διατρίβωμεν ὁδοῖο."

Ὣς ἄρα φωνήσας' ἡγήσατο Παλλὰς Ἀθήνη　　4⋮
καρπαλίμως· ὁ δ' ἔπειτα μετ' ἴχνια βαῖνε θεοῖο.
αὐτὰρ ἐπεί ῥ' ἐπὶ νῆα κατήλυθον ἠδὲ θάλασσαν,

into well-sewn skins; and Telemachus went to the hall and joined the company of the wooers.

Then the goddess, flashing-eyed Athene, took other counsel. In the likeness of Telemachus she went everywhere throughout the city, and to each of the men she drew near and spoke her word, bidding them gather at even beside the swift ship. Furthermore, of Noemon, the glorious son of Phronius, she asked a swift ship, and he promised it to her with a ready heart.

Now the sun set and all the ways grew dark. Then she drew the swift ship to the sea and put in it all the gear that well-benched ships carry. And she moored it at the mouth of the harbour, and round about it the goodly company was gathered together, and the goddess heartened each man.

Then again the goddess, flashing-eyed Athene, took other counsel. She went her way to the house of divine Odysseus, and there began to shed sweet sleep upon the wooers and made them to wander in their drinking, and from their hands she cast the cups. But they rose to go to their rest throughout the city, and remained no long time seated, for sleep was falling upon their eyelids. But to Telemachus spoke flashing-eyed Athene, calling him forth before the stately hall, having likened herself to Mentor both in form and in voice:

"Telemachus, already thy well-greaved comrades sit at the oar and await thy setting out. Come, let us go, that we may not long delay their journey."

So saying, Pallas Athene led the way quickly, and he followed in the footsteps of the goddess. Now when they had come down to the ship and to

εὗρον ἔπειτ' ἐπὶ θινὶ κάρη κομόωντας ἑταίρους.
τοῖσι δὲ καὶ μετέειφ' ἱερὴ ἲς Τηλεμάχοιο·
   " Δεῦτε, φίλοι, ἦια φερώμεθα· πάντα γὰρ ἤδη
ἀθρό' ἐνὶ μεγάρῳ. μήτηρ δ' ἐμὴ οὔ τι πέπυσται,
οὐδ' ἄλλαι δμωαί, μία δ' οἴη μῦθον ἄκουσεν."
   Ὣς ἄρα φωνήσας ἡγήσατο, τοὶ δ' ἅμ' ἕποντο.
οἱ δ' ἄρα πάντα φέροντες ἐυσσέλμῳ ἐπὶ νηὶ
κάτθεσαν, ὡς ἐκέλευσεν Ὀδυσσῆος φίλος υἱός.
ἂν δ' ἄρα Τηλέμαχος νηὸς βαῖν', ἦρχε δ' Ἀθήνη,
νηὶ δ' ἐνὶ πρυμνῇ κατ' ἄρ' ἕζετο· ἄγχι δ' ἄρ' αὐτῆς
ἕζετο Τηλέμαχος. τοὶ δὲ πρυμνῆσι' ἔλυσαν,
ἂν δὲ καὶ αὐτοὶ βάντες ἐπὶ κληῖσι καθῖζον.
τοῖσιν δ' ἴκμενον οὖρον ἵει γλαυκῶπις Ἀθήνη,
ἀκραῆ Ζέφυρον, κελάδοντ' ἐπὶ οἴνοπα πόντον.
Τηλέμαχος δ' ἑτάροισιν ἐποτρύνας ἐκέλευσεν
ὅπλων ἅπτεσθαι· τοὶ δ' ὀτρύνοντος ἄκουσαν.
ἱστὸν δ' εἰλάτινον κοίλης ἔντοσθε μεσόδμης
στῆσαν ἀείραντες, κατὰ δὲ προτόνοισιν ἔδησαν,
ἕλκον δ' ἱστία λευκὰ ἐυστρέπτοισι βοεῦσιν.
ἔπρησεν δ' ἄνεμος μέσον ἱστίον, ἀμφὶ δὲ κῦμα
στείρῃ πορφύρεον μεγάλ' ἴαχε νηὸς ἰούσης·
ἡ δ' ἔθεεν κατὰ κῦμα διαπρήσσουσα κέλευθον.
δησάμενοι δ' ἄρα ὅπλα θοὴν ἀνὰ νῆα μέλαιναν
στήσαντο κρητῆρας ἐπιστεφέας οἴνοιο,
λεῖβον δ' ἀθανάτοισι θεοῖς αἰειγενέτῃσιν,
ἐκ πάντων δὲ μάλιστα Διὸς γλαυκώπιδι κούρῃ.
παννυχίη μέν ῥ' ἥ γε καὶ ἠῶ πεῖρε κέλευθον.

---

[1] It is hard to determine with exactness to what extent
the original meaning " strong " survives in the uses of ἱερός.

the sea, they found on the shore their long-haired
comrades, and the strong and mighty[1] Telemachus
spoke among them :

"Come, friends, let us fetch the stores, for all are
now gathered together in the hall. My mother
knows naught hereof, nor the handmaids either :
one only heard my word."

Thus saying, he led the way, and they went along
with him. So they brought and stowed everything
in the well-benched ship, as the dear son of Odysseus
bade. Then on board the ship stepped Telemachus,
and Athene went before him and sat down in the
stern of the ship, and near her sat Telemachus,
while the men loosed the stern cables and them-
selves stepped on board, and sat down upon the
benches. And flashing-eyed Athene sent them a
favourable wind, a strong-blowing West wind that
sang over the wine-dark sea. And Telemachus
called to his men, and bade them lay hold of the
tackling, and they hearkened to his call. The mast
of fir they raised and set in the hollow socket, and
made it fast with fore-stays, and hauled up the white
sail with twisted thongs of ox-hide. So the wind
filled the belly of the sail, and the dark wave sang
loudly about the stem of the ship as she went, and
she sped over the wave accomplishing her way.
Then, when they had made the tackling fast in the
swift black ship, they set forth bowls brim full of
wine, and poured libations to the immortal gods
that are forever, and chiefest of all to the flashing-
eyed daughter of Zeus. So all night long and through
the dawn the ship cleft her way.

It may be that in ἱερὴ ἴς and ἱερὸν μένος (vii. 167) we should
see a reference to the sanctity attaching to royal station.

Γ

Ἠέλιος δ' ἀνόρουσε, λιπὼν περικαλλέα λίμνην,
οὐρανὸν ἐς πολύχαλκον, ἵν' ἀθανάτοισι φαείνοι
καὶ θνητοῖσι βροτοῖσιν ἐπὶ ζείδωρον ἄρουραν·
οἱ δὲ Πύλον, Νηλῆος ἐυκτίμενον πτολίεθρον,
ἷξον· τοὶ δ' ἐπὶ θινὶ θαλάσσης ἱερὰ ῥέζον,   5
ταύρους παμμέλανας, ἐνοσίχθονι κυανοχαίτῃ.
ἐννέα δ' ἕδραι ἔσαν, πεντακόσιοι δ' ἐν ἑκάστῃ
ἥατο καὶ προύχοντο ἑκάστοθι ἐννέα ταύρους.
εὖθ' οἱ σπλάγχνα πάσαντο, θεῷ δ' ἐπὶ μηρί' ἔκαιον,
οἱ δ' ἰθὺς κατάγοντο ἰδ' ἱστία νηὸς ἐίσης   10
στεῖλαν ἀείραντες, τὴν δ' ὥρμισαν, ἐκ δ' ἔβαν αὐτοί·
ἐκ δ' ἄρα Τηλέμαχος νηὸς βαῖν', ἦρχε δ' Ἀθήνη.
τὸν προτέρη προσέειπε θεά, γλαυκῶπις Ἀθήνη·

   "Τηλέμαχ', οὐ μέν σε χρὴ ἔτ' αἰδοῦς, οὐδ' ἠβαιόν·
τούνεκα γὰρ καὶ πόντον ἐπέπλως, ὄφρα πύθηαι   15
πατρός, ὅπου κύθε γαῖα καὶ ὅν τινα πότμον ἐπέσπεν.
ἀλλ' ἄγε νῦν ἰθὺς κίε Νέστορος ἱπποδάμοιο·
εἴδομεν ἥν τινα μῆτιν ἐνὶ στήθεσσι κέκευθε.
λίσσεσθαι δέ μιν αὐτός, ὅπως νημερτέα εἴπῃ·
ψεῦδος δ' οὐκ ἐρέει· μάλα γὰρ πεπνυμένος ἐστί."   20

BOOK III

AND now the sun, leaving the beauteous mere, sprang up into the brazen heaven to give light to the immortals and to mortal men on the earth, the giver of grain; and they came to Pylos, the well-built citadel of Neleus. Here the townsfolk on the shore of the sea were offering sacrifice of black bulls to the dark-haired Earth-shaker. Nine companies there were, and five hundred men sat in each, and in each they held nine bulls ready for sacrifice. Now when they had tasted the inner parts and were burning the thigh-pieces to the god, the others put straight in to the shore, and hauled up and furled the sail of the shapely ship, and moored her, and themselves stepped forth. Forth too from the ship stepped Telemachus, and Athene led the way. And the goddess, flashing-eyed Athene, spake first to him, and said:

"Telemachus, no longer hast thou need to feel shame, no, not a whit. For to this end hast thou sailed over the sea, that thou mightest seek tidings of thy father,—where the earth covered him, and what fate he met. But come now, go straightway to Nestor, tamer of horses; let us learn what counsel he keepeth hid in his breast. And do thou beseech him thyself that he may tell thee the very truth. A lie will he not utter, for he is wise indeed."

Τὴν δ' αὖ Τηλέμαχος πεπνυμένος ἀντίον ηὔδα·
"Μέντορ, πῶς τ' ἄρ' ἴω; πῶς τ' ἂρ προσπτύξομαι
    αὐτόν;
οὐδέ τί πω μύθοισι πεπείρημαι πυκινοῖσιν·
αἰδὼς δ' αὖ νέον ἄνδρα γεραίτερον ἐξερέεσθαι."
Τὸν δ' αὖτε προσέειπε θεά, γλαυκῶπις Ἀθήνη·   2
"Τηλέμαχ', ἄλλα μὲν αὐτὸς ἐνὶ φρεσὶ σῇσι νοήσεις,
ἄλλα δὲ καὶ δαίμων ὑποθήσεται· οὐ γὰρ ὀίω
οὔ σε θεῶν ἀέκητι γενέσθαι τε τραφέμεν τε."
Ὣς ἄρα φωνήσασ' ἡγήσατο Παλλὰς Ἀθήνη
καρπαλίμως· ὁ δ' ἔπειτα μετ' ἴχνια βαῖνε θεοῖο.   3
ἷξον δ' ἐς Πυλίων ἀνδρῶν ἄγυρίν τε καὶ ἕδρας,
ἔνθ' ἄρα Νέστωρ ἧστο σὺν υἱάσιν, ἀμφὶ δ' ἑταῖροι
δαῖτ' ἐντυνόμενοι κρέα τ' ὤπτων ἄλλα τ' ἔπειρον.
οἱ δ' ὡς οὖν ξείνους ἴδον, ἀθρόοι ἦλθον ἅπαντες,
χερσίν τ' ἠσπάζοντο καὶ ἑδριάασθαι ἄνωγον.   3
πρῶτος Νεστορίδης Πεισίστρατος ἐγγύθεν ἐλθὼν
ἀμφοτέρων ἕλε χεῖρα καὶ ἵδρυσεν παρὰ δαιτὶ
κώεσιν ἐν μαλακοῖσιν ἐπὶ ψαμάθοις ἁλίῃσιν
πάρ τε κασιγνήτῳ Θρασυμήδεϊ καὶ πατέρι ᾧ·
δῶκε δ' ἄρα σπλάγχνων μοίρας, ἐν δ' οἶνον ἔχευεν   4
χρυσείῳ δέπαϊ· δειδισκόμενος δὲ προσηύδα
Παλλάδ' Ἀθηναίην κούρην Διὸς αἰγιόχοιο·
"Εὔχεο νῦν, ὦ ξεῖνε, Ποσειδάωνι ἄνακτι·
τοῦ γὰρ καὶ δαίτης ἠντήσατε δεῦρο μολόντες.
αὐτὰρ ἐπὴν σπείσῃς τε καὶ εὔξεαι, ἣ θέμις ἐστί,   4
δὸς καὶ τούτῳ ἔπειτα δέπας μελιηδέος οἴνου
σπεῖσαι, ἐπεὶ καὶ τοῦτον ὀίομαι ἀθανάτοισιν
εὔχεσθαι· πάντες δὲ θεῶν χατέουσ' ἄνθρωποι.
ἀλλὰ νεώτερός ἐστιν, ὁμηλικίη δ' ἐμοὶ αὐτῷ·
τούνεκα σοὶ προτέρῳ δώσω χρύσειον ἄλεισον."   5

Then wise Telemachus answered her: "Mentor, how shall I go, and how shall I greet him? I am as yet all unversed in subtle speech, and moreover a young man has shame to question an elder."

Then the goddess, flashing-eyed Athene, answered him: "Telemachus, somewhat thou wilt of thyself devise in thy breast, and somewhat heaven too will prompt thee. For, methinks, not without the favour of the gods hast thou been born and reared."

So spake Pallas Athene, and led the way quickly; but he followed in the footsteps of the goddess; and they came to the gathering and the companies of the men of Pylos. There Nestor sat with his sons, and round about his people, making ready the feast, were roasting some of the meat and putting other pieces on spits. But when they saw the strangers they all came thronging about them, and clasped their hands in welcome, and bade them sit down. First Nestor's son Peisistratus came near and took both by the hand, and made them to sit down at the feast on soft fleeces upon the sand of the sea, beside his brother Thrasymedes and his father. Thereupon he gave them portions of the inner meat and poured wine in a golden cup, and, pledging her, he spoke to Pallas Athene, daughter of Zeus who bears the aegis:

"Pray now, stranger, to the lord Poseidon, for his is the feast whereon you have chanced in coming hither. And when thou hast poured libations and hast prayed, as is fitting, then give thy friend also the cup of honey-sweet wine that he may pour, since he too, I ween, prays to the immortals; for all men have need of the gods. Howbeit he is the younger, of like age with myself, wherefore to thee first will I give the golden cup."

Ὣς εἰπὼν ἐν χειρὶ τίθει δέπας ἡδέος οἴνου·
χαῖρε δ' Ἀθηναίη πεπνυμένῳ ἀνδρὶ δικαίῳ,
οὕνεκα οἱ προτέρῃ δῶκε χρύσειον ἄλεισον·
αὐτίκα δ' εὔχετο πολλὰ Ποσειδάωνι ἄνακτι·

"Κλῦθι, Ποσείδαον γαιήοχε, μηδὲ μεγήρῃς   5
ἡμῖν εὐχομένοισι τελευτῆσαι τάδε ἔργα.
Νέστορι μὲν πρώτιστα καὶ υἱάσι κῦδος ὄπαζε,
αὐτὰρ ἔπειτ' ἄλλοισι δίδου χαρίεσσαν ἀμοιβὴν
σύμπασιν Πυλίοισιν ἀγακλειτῆς ἑκατόμβης.
δὸς δ' ἔτι Τηλέμαχον καὶ ἐμὲ πρήξαντα νέεσθαι,   6
οὕνεκα δεῦρ' ἱκόμεσθα θοῇ σὺν νηὶ μελαίνῃ."

Ὣς ἄρ' ἔπειτ' ἠρᾶτο καὶ αὐτὴ πάντα τελεύτα.
δῶκε δὲ Τηλεμάχῳ καλὸν δέπας ἀμφικύπελλον·
ὣς δ' αὔτως ἠρᾶτο Ὀδυσσῆος φίλος υἱός.
οἱ δ' ἐπεὶ ὤπτησαν κρέ' ὑπέρτερα καὶ ἐρύσαντο,   6
μοίρας δασσάμενοι δαίνυντ' ἐρικυδέα δαῖτα.
αὐτὰρ ἐπεὶ πόσιος καὶ ἐδητύος ἐξ ἔρον ἕντο,
τοῖς ἄρα μύθων ἦρχε Γερήνιος ἱππότα Νέστωρ·

"Νῦν δὴ κάλλιόν ἐστι μεταλλῆσαι καὶ ἐρέσθαι
ξείνους, οἵ τινές εἰσιν, ἐπεὶ τάρπησαν ἐδωδῆς.   7
ὦ ξεῖνοι, τίνες ἐστέ; πόθεν πλεῖθ' ὑγρὰ κέλευθα;
ἦ τι κατὰ πρῆξιν ἦ μαψιδίως ἀλάλησθε
οἷά τε ληιστῆρες ὑπεὶρ ἅλα, τοί τ' ἀλόωνται
ψυχὰς παρθέμενοι κακὸν ἀλλοδαποῖσι φέροντες;"

Τὸν δ' αὖ Τηλέμαχος πεπνυμένος ἀντίον ηὔδα   7
θαρσήσας· αὐτὴ γὰρ ἐνὶ φρεσὶ θάρσος Ἀθήνη

So he spake, and placed in her hand the cup of sweet wine. But Pallas Athene rejoiced at the man's wisdom and judgment, in that to her first he gave the golden cup; and straightway she prayed earnestly to the lord Poseidon:

"Hear me, Poseidon, thou Earth-enfolder, and grudge not in answer to our prayer to bring these deeds to fulfilment. To Nestor, first of all, and to his sons vouchsafe renown, and then do thou grant to the rest gracious requital for this glorious hecatomb, even to all the men of Pylos; and grant furthermore that Telemachus and I may return when we have accomplished all that for which we came hither with our swift black ship."

Thus she prayed, and was herself fulfilling all. Then she gave Telemachus the fair two-handled [1] cup, and in like manner the dear son of Odysseus prayed. Then when they had roasted the outer flesh and drawn it off the spits, they divided the portions and feasted a glorious feast. But when they had put from them the desire of food and drink, the horseman, Nestor of Gerenia,[2] spoke first among them:

"Now verily is it seemlier to ask and enquire of the strangers who they are, since now they have had their joy of food. Strangers, who are ye? Whence do ye sail over the watery ways? Is it on some business, or do ye wander at random over the sea, even as pirates, who wander hazarding their lives and bringing evil to men of other lands?"

Then wise Telemachus took courage, and made answer, for Athene herself put courage in his heart,

---

[1] Others, "double cup," *i.e.* shaped like an hour-glass.
[2] The precise meaning of this epithet is quite unknown.

θῆχ', ἵνα μιν περὶ πατρὸς ἀποιχομένοιο ἔροιτο
ἠδ' ἵνα μιν κλέος ἐσθλὸν ἐν ἀνθρώποισιν ἔχῃσιν·[1]
   "Ὦ Νέστορ Νηληϊάδη, μέγα κῦδος Ἀχαιῶν,
εἴρεαι ὁππόθεν εἰμέν· ἐγὼ δέ κέ τοι καταλέξω.   8
ἡμεῖς ἐξ Ἰθάκης ὑπονηίου εἰλήλουθμεν·
πρῆξις δ' ἥδ' ἰδίη, οὐ δήμιος, ἣν ἀγορεύω.
πατρὸς ἐμοῦ κλέος εὐρὺ μετέρχομαι, ἤν που ἀκούσω,
δίου Ὀδυσσῆος ταλασίφρονος, ὅν ποτέ φασι
σὺν σοὶ μαρνάμενον Τρώων πόλιν ἐξαλαπάξαι.   8
ἄλλους μὲν γὰρ πάντας, ὅσοι Τρωσὶν πολέμιζον,
πευθόμεθ', ἧχι ἕκαστος ἀπώλετο λυγρῷ ὀλέθρῳ,
κείνου δ' αὖ καὶ ὄλεθρον ἀπευθέα θῆκε Κρονίων.
οὐ γάρ τις δύναται σάφα εἰπέμεν ὁππόθ' ὄλωλεν,
εἴθ' ὅ γ' ἐπ' ἠπείρου δάμη ἀνδράσι δυσμενέεσσιν,   9
εἴτε καὶ ἐν πελάγει μετὰ κύμασιν Ἀμφιτρίτης.
τούνεκα νῦν τὰ σὰ γούναθ' ἱκάνομαι, αἴ κ' ἐθέλῃσθα
κείνου λυγρὸν ὄλεθρον ἐνισπεῖν, εἴ που ὄπωπας
ὀφθαλμοῖσι τεοῖσιν ἢ ἄλλου μῦθον ἄκουσας
πλαζομένου· πέρι γάρ μιν ὀιζυρὸν τέκε μήτηρ.   9
μηδέ τί μ' αἰδόμενος μειλίσσεο μηδ' ἐλεαίρων,
ἀλλ' εὖ μοι κατάλεξον ὅπως ἤντησας ὀπωπῆς.
λίσσομαι, εἴ ποτέ τοί τι πατὴρ ἐμός, ἐσθλὸς Ὀδυσσεύς,
ἢ ἔπος ἠέ τι ἔργον ὑποστὰς ἐξετέλεσσε
δήμῳ ἔνι Τρώων, ὅθι πάσχετε πήματ' Ἀχαιοί,   10
τῶν νῦν μοι μνῆσαι, καί μοι νημερτὲς ἐνίσπες."
   Τὸν δ' ἠμείβετ' ἔπειτα Γερήνιος ἱππότα Νέστωρ·
   "Ὦ φίλ', ἐπεί μ' ἔμνησας ὀιζύος, ἣν ἐν ἐκείνῳ
δήμῳ ἀνέτλημεν μένος ἄσχετοι υἷες Ἀχαιῶν,

---

[1] Line 78 (=i. 95) is omitted in the best MSS.

that he might ask about his father that was gone, and that good report might be his among men:

"Nestor, son of Neleus, great glory of the Achaeans, thou askest whence we are, and I will surely tell thee. We have come from Ithaca that is below Neion; but this business whereof I speak is mine own, and concerns not the people. I come after the wide-spread rumour of my father, if haply I may hear of it, even of goodly Odysseus of the steadfast heart, who once, men say, fought by thy side and sacked the city of the Trojans. For of all men else, as many as warred with the Trojans, we learn where each man died a woeful death, but of him the son of Cronos has made even the death to be past learning; for no man can tell surely where he hath died,—whether he was overcome by foes on the mainland, or on the deep among the waves of Amphitrite. Therefore am I now come to thy knees, if perchance thou wilt be willing to tell me of his woeful death, whether thou sawest it haply with thine own eyes, or didst hear from some other the story of his wanderings;[1] for beyond all men did his mother bear him to sorrow. And do thou nowise out of ruth or pity for me speak soothing words, but tell me truly how thou didst come to behold him. I beseech thee, if ever my father, noble Odysseus, promised aught to thee of word or deed and fulfilled it in the land of the Trojans, where you Achaeans suffered woes, be mindful of it now, I pray thee, and tell me the very truth."

Then the horseman, Nestor of Gerenia, answered him: "My friend, since thou hast recalled to my mind the sorrow which we endured in that land, we

---

[1] Or, "from some other wanderer."

ἠμὲν ὅσα ξὺν νηυσὶν ἐπ᾽ ἠεροειδέα πόντον
πλαζόμενοι κατὰ ληίδ᾽, ὅπῃ ἄρξειεν Ἀχιλλεύς,
ἠδ᾽ ὅσα καὶ περὶ ἄστυ μέγα Πριάμοιο ἄνακτος
μαρνάμεθ᾽· ἔνθα δ᾽ ἔπειτα κατέκταθεν ὅσσοι ἄριστοι.
ἔνθα μὲν Αἴας κεῖται ἀρήιος, ἔνθα δ᾽ Ἀχιλλεύς,
ἔνθα δὲ Πάτροκλος, θεόφιν μήστωρ ἀτάλαντος,
ἔνθα δ᾽ ἐμὸς φίλος υἱός, ἅμα κρατερὸς καὶ ἀμύμων,
Ἀντίλοχος, πέρι μὲν θείειν ταχὺς ἠδὲ μαχητής·
ἄλλα τε πόλλ᾽ ἐπὶ τοῖς πάθομεν κακά· τίς κεν ἐκεῖνα
πάντα γε μυθήσαιτο καταθνητῶν ἀνθρώπων;
οὐδ᾽ εἰ πεντάετές γε καὶ ἑξάετες παραμίμνων
ἐξερέοις ὅσα κεῖθι πάθον κακὰ δῖοι Ἀχαιοί·
πρίν κεν ἀνιηθεὶς σὴν πατρίδα γαῖαν ἵκοιο.
εἰνάετες γάρ σφιν κακὰ ῥάπτομεν ἀμφιέποντες
παντοίοισι δόλοισι, μόγις δ᾽ ἐτέλεσσε Κρονίων.
ἔνθ᾽ οὔ τίς ποτε μῆτιν ὁμοιωθήμεναι ἄντην
ἤθελ᾽, ἐπεὶ μάλα πολλὸν ἐνίκα δῖος Ὀδυσσεὺς
παντοίοισι δόλοισι, πατὴρ τεός, εἰ ἐτεόν γε
κείνου ἔκγονός ἐσσι· σέβας μ᾽ ἔχει εἰσορόωντα.
ἦ τοι γὰρ μῦθοί γε ἐοικότες, οὐδέ κε φαίης
ἄνδρα νεώτερον ὧδε ἐοικότα μυθήσασθαι.
ἔνθ᾽ ἦ τοι ἧος μὲν ἐγὼ καὶ δῖος Ὀδυσσεὺς
οὔτε ποτ᾽ εἰν ἀγορῇ δίχ᾽ ἐβάζομεν οὔτ᾽ ἐνὶ βουλῇ,
ἀλλ᾽ ἕνα θυμὸν ἔχοντε νόῳ καὶ ἐπίφρονι βουλῇ
φραζόμεθ᾽ Ἀργείοισιν ὅπως ὄχ᾽ ἄριστα γένοιτο.
αὐτὰρ ἐπεὶ Πριάμοιο πόλιν διεπέρσαμεν αἰπήν,
βῆμεν δ᾽ ἐν νήεσσι, θεὸς δ᾽ ἐκέδασσεν Ἀχαιούς,[1]
καὶ τότε δὴ Ζεὺς λυγρὸν ἐνὶ φρεσὶ μήδετο νόστον
Ἀργείοις, ἐπεὶ οὔ τι νοήμονες οὐδὲ δίκαιοι

---

[1] Line 131, though found in the MSS., is out of harmony with what follows. It may have been interpolated from xiii. 317, where it is in place.

sons of the Achaeans, unrestrained in daring,—all that we endured on shipboard, as we roamed after booty over the misty deep whithersoever Achilles led ; and all our fightings around the great city of king Priam ;—lo, there all our best were slain. There lies warlike Aias, there Achilles, there Patroclus, the peer of the gods in counsel ; and there my own dear son, strong alike and peerless, Antilochus, pre-eminent in speed of foot and as a warrior. Aye, and many other ills we suffered besides these ; who of mortal men could tell them all ? Nay, if for five years' space or six years' space thou wert to abide here, and ask of all the woes which the goodly Achaeans endured there, thou wouldest grow weary ere the end and get thee back to thy native land. For nine years' space were we busied plotting their ruin with all manner of wiles ; and hardly did the son of Cronos bring it to pass. There no man ventured to vie with him in counsel, since goodly Odysseus far excelled in all manner of wiles,—thy father, if indeed thou art his son. Amazement holds me as I look on thee, for verily thy speech is like his ; nor would one think that a younger man would speak so like him. Now all the time that we were there goodly Odysseus and I never spoke at variance either in the assembly or in the council, but being of one mind advised the Argives with wisdom and shrewd counsel how all might be for the best. But when we had sacked the lofty city of Priam, and had gone away in our ships, and a god had scattered the Achaeans, then, even then, Zeus planned in his heart a woeful return for the Argives, for in no wise prudent or just were all.

πάντες ἔσαν· τῶ σφεων πολέες κακὸν οἶτον ἐπέσπον
μήνιος ἐξ ὀλοῆς γλαυκώπιδος ὀβριμοπάτρης,　　13
ἥ τ' ἔριν Ἀτρεΐδησι μετ' ἀμφοτέροισιν ἔθηκε.
τὼ δὲ καλεσσαμένω ἀγορὴν ἐς πάντας Ἀχαιούς,
μάψ, ἀτὰρ οὐ κατὰ κόσμον, ἐς ἠέλιον καταδύντα,
οἱ δ' ἦλθον οἴνῳ βεβαρηότες υἶες Ἀχαιῶν,
μῦθον μυθείσθην, τοῦ εἵνεκα λαὸν ἄγειραν.　　14
ἔνθ' ἦ τοι Μενέλαος ἀνώγει πάντας Ἀχαιοὺς
νόστου μιμνήσκεσθαι ἐπ' εὐρέα νῶτα θαλάσσης,
οὐδ' Ἀγαμέμνονι πάμπαν ἑήνδανε· βούλετο γάρ ῥα
λαὸν ἐρυκακέειν ῥέξαι θ' ἱερὰς ἑκατόμβας,
ὡς τὸν Ἀθηναίης δεινὸν χόλον ἐξακέσαιτο,　　14
νήπιος, οὐδὲ τὸ ἤδη, ὃ οὐ πείσεσθαι ἔμελλεν·
οὐ γάρ τ' αἶψα θεῶν τρέπεται νόος αἰὲν ἐόντων.
ὣς τὼ μὲν χαλεποῖσιν ἀμειβομένω ἐπέεσσιν
ἔστασαν· οἱ δ' ἀνόρουσαν ἐϋκνήμιδες Ἀχαιοὶ
ἠχῇ θεσπεσίῃ, δίχα δέ σφισιν ἥνδανε βουλή.　　15
νύκτα μὲν ἀέσαμεν χαλεπὰ φρεσὶν ὁρμαίνοντες
ἀλλήλοις· ἐπὶ γὰρ Ζεὺς ἤρτυε πῆμα κακοῖο·
ἠῶθεν δ' οἱ μὲν νέας ἕλκομεν εἰς ἅλα δῖαν
κτήματά τ' ἐντιθέμεσθα βαθυζώνους τε γυναῖκας.
ἡμίσεες δ' ἄρα λαοὶ ἐρητύοντο μένοντες　　15
αὖθι παρ' Ἀτρεΐδῃ Ἀγαμέμνονι, ποιμένι λαῶν·
ἡμίσεες δ' ἀναβάντες ἐλαύνομεν· αἱ δὲ μάλ' ὦκα
ἔπλεον, ἐστόρεσεν δὲ θεὸς μεγακήτεα πόντον.
ἐς Τένεδον δ' ἐλθόντες ἐρέξαμεν ἱρὰ θεοῖσιν,
οἴκαδε ἱέμενοι· Ζεὺς δ' οὔ πω μήδετο νόστον,　　16
σχέτλιος, ὅς ῥ' ἔριν ὦρσε κακὴν ἔπι δεύτερον αὖτις.
οἱ μὲν ἀποστρέψαντες ἔβαν νέας ἀμφιελίσσας

Wherefore many of them met an evil fate through the fell wrath of the flashing-eyed goddess, the daughter of the mighty sire, for she caused strife between the two sons of Atreus. Now these two called to an assembly all the Achaeans, recklessly and in no due order, at set of sun—and they came heavy with wine, the sons of the Achaeans,—and they spoke their word, and told wherefore they had gathered the host together. Then in truth Menelaus bade all the Achaeans think of their return over the broad back of the sea, but in no wise did he please Agamemnon, for he was fain to hold back the host and to offer holy hecatombs, that he might appease the dread wrath of Athene,—fool! nor knew he this, that with her was to be no hearkening; for the mind of the gods that are forever is not quickly turned. So these two stood bandying harsh words; but the well-greaved Achaeans sprang up with a wondrous din, and two-fold plans found favour with them. That night we rested, each side pondering hard thoughts against the other, for Zeus was bringing upon us an evil doom, but in the morning some of us launched our ships upon the bright sea, and put on board our goods and the low-girdled women. Half, indeed, of the host held back and remained there with Agamemnon, son of Atreus, shepherd of the host, but half of us embarked and rowed away; and swiftly the ships sailed, for a god made smooth the cavernous sea. But when we came to Tenedos, we offered sacrifice to the gods, being eager to reach our homes, howbeit Zeus did not yet purpose our return, stubborn god, who roused evil strife again a second time. Then some turned back their curved ships

ἀμφ' Ὀδυσῆα ἄνακτα δαΐφρονα, ποικιλομήτην,
αὖτις ἐπ' Ἀτρεΐδῃ Ἀγαμέμνονι ἦρα φέροντες·
αὐτὰρ ἐγὼ σὺν νηυσὶν ἀολλέσιν, αἵ μοι ἕποντο,   165
φεῦγον, ἐπεὶ γίγνωσκον, ὃ δὴ κακὰ μήδετο δαίμων.
φεῦγε δὲ Τυδέος υἱὸς ἀρήιος, ὦρσε δ' ἑταίρους.
ὀψὲ δὲ δὴ μετὰ νῶι κίε ξανθὸς Μενέλαος,
ἐν Λέσβῳ δ' ἔκιχεν δολιχὸν πλόον ὁρμαίνοντας,
ἢ καθύπερθε Χίοιο νεοίμεθα παιπαλοέσσης,   170
νήσου ἔπι Ψυρίης, αὐτὴν ἐπ' ἀριστέρ' ἔχοντες,
ἢ ὑπένερθε Χίοιο, παρ' ἠνεμόεντα Μίμαντα.
ᾐτέομεν δὲ θεὸν φῆναι τέρας· αὐτὰρ ὅ γ' ἥμιν
δεῖξε, καὶ ἠνώγει πέλαγος μέσον εἰς Εὔβοιαν
τέμνειν, ὄφρα τάχιστα ὑπὲκ κακότητα φύγοιμεν.   175
ὦρτο δ' ἐπὶ λιγὺς οὖρος ἀήμεναι· αἱ δὲ μάλ' ὦκα
ἰχθυόεντα κέλευθα διέδραμον, ἐς δὲ Γεραιστὸν
ἐννύχιαι κατάγοντο· Ποσειδάωνι δὲ ταύρων
πόλλ' ἐπὶ μῆρ' ἔθεμεν, πέλαγος μέγα μετρήσαντες.
τέτρατον ἦμαρ ἔην, ὅτ' ἐν Ἄργεϊ νῆας ἐΐσας   180
Τυδεΐδεω ἕταροι Διομήδεος ἱπποδάμοιο
ἵστασαν· αὐτὰρ ἐγώ γε Πύλονδ' ἔχον, οὐδέ ποτ' ἔσβη
οὖρος, ἐπεὶ δὴ πρῶτα θεὸς προέηκεν ἀῆναι.

"Ὣς ἦλθον, φίλε τέκνον, ἀπευθής, οὐδέ τι οἶδα
κείνων, οἵ τ' ἐσάωθεν Ἀχαιῶν οἵ τ' ἀπόλοντο.   185
ὅσσα δ' ἐνὶ μεγάροισι καθήμενος ἡμετέροισι
πεύθομαι, ἣ θέμις ἐστί, δαήσεαι, οὐδέ σε κεύσω.
εὖ μὲν Μυρμιδόνας φάσ' ἐλθέμεν ἐγχεσιμώρους,
οὓς ἄγ' Ἀχιλλῆος μεγαθύμου φαίδιμος υἱός,
εὖ δὲ Φιλοκτήτην, Ποιάντιον ἀγλαὸν υἱόν·   190
πάντας δ' Ἰδομενεὺς Κρήτην εἰσήγαγ' ἑταίρους,

and departed, even the lord Odysseus, the wise and crafty-minded, with his company, once more showing favour to Agamemnon, son of Atreus; but I with the full company of ships that followed me fled on, for I knew that the god was devising evil. And the war-like son of Tydeus fled and urged on his men; and late upon our track came fair-haired Menelaus, and overtook us in Lesbos, as we were debating the long voyage, whether we should sail to sea-ward of rugged Chios, toward the isle Psyria, keeping Chios itself[1] on our left, or to land-ward of Chios past windy Mimas. So we asked the god to shew us a sign, and he shewed it us, and bade us cleave through the midst of the sea to Euboea, that we might the soonest escape from misery. And a shrill wind sprang up to blow, and the ships ran swiftly over the teeming ways, and at night put in to Geraestus. There on the altar of Poseidon we laid many thighs of bulls, thankful to have traversed the great sea. It was the fourth day when in Argos the company of Diomedes, son of Tydeus, tamer of horses, stayed their shapely ships; but I held on toward Pylos, and the wind was not once quenched from the time when the god first sent it forth to blow.

"Thus I came, dear child, without tidings, nor know I aught of those others, who of the Achaeans were saved, and who were lost. But what tidings I have heard as I abide in our halls thou shalt hear, as is right, nor will I hide it from thee. Safely, they say, came the Myrmidons that rage with the spear, whom the famous son of great-hearted Achilles led; and safely Philoctetes, the glorious son of Poias. All his company, too, did Idomeneus bring to Crete,

---

[1] Possibly, " keeping the isle (Psyria) on our left."

οἳ φύγον ἐκ πολέμου, πόντος δέ οἱ οὔ τιν' ἀπηύρα.
'Ατρεΐδην δὲ καὶ αὐτοὶ ἀκούετε, νόσφιν ἐόντες,
ὥς τ' ἦλθ', ὥς τ' Αἴγισθος ἐμήσατο λυγρὸν ὄλεθρον.
ἀλλ' ἦ τοι κεῖνος μὲν ἐπισμυγερῶς ἀπέτισεν·   1
ὡς ἀγαθὸν καὶ παῖδα καταφθιμένοιο λιπέσθαι
ἀνδρός, ἐπεὶ καὶ κεῖνος ἐτίσατο πατροφονῆα,
Αἴγισθον δολόμητιν, ὅ οἱ πατέρα κλυτὸν ἔκτα.
καὶ σὺ φίλος, μάλα γάρ σ' ὁρόω καλόν τε μέγαν τε,
ἄλκιμος ἔσσ', ἵνα τίς σε καὶ ὀψιγόνων ἐὺ εἴπῃ." [1]   2

Τὸν δ' αὖ Τηλέμαχος πεπνυμένος ἀντίον ηὔδα·
"'Ω Νέστορ Νηληϊάδη, μέγα κῦδος 'Αχαιῶν,
καὶ λίην κεῖνος μὲν ἐτίσατο, καί οἱ 'Αχαιοὶ
οἴσουσι κλέος εὐρὺ καὶ ἐσσομένοισι πυθέσθαι· [2]
αἱ γὰρ ἐμοὶ τοσσήνδε θεοὶ δύναμιν περιθεῖεν,   2
τίσασθαι μνηστῆρας ὑπερβασίης ἀλεγεινῆς,
οἵ τέ μοι ὑβρίζοντες ἀτάσθαλα μηχανόωνται.
ἀλλ' οὔ μοι τοιοῦτον ἐπέκλωσαν θεοὶ ὄλβον,
πατρί τ' ἐμῷ καὶ ἐμοί· νῦν δὲ χρὴ τετλάμεν ἔμπης."

Τὸν δ' ἠμείβετ' ἔπειτα Γερήνιος ἱππότα Νέστωρ· 2
"'Ω φίλ', ἐπεὶ δὴ ταῦτά μ' ἀνέμνησας καὶ ἔειπες,
φασὶ μνηστῆρας σῆς μητέρος εἵνεκα πολλοὺς
ἐν μεγάροις ἀέκητι σέθεν κακὰ μηχανάασθαι·
εἰπέ μοι, ἠὲ ἑκὼν ὑποδάμνασαι, ἦ σέ γε λαοὶ
ἐχθαίρουσ' ἀνὰ δῆμον, ἐπισπόμενοι θεοῦ ὀμφῇ.   2
τίς δ' οἶδ' εἴ κέ ποτέ σφι βίας ἀποτίσεται ἐλθών,
ἦ ὅ γε μοῦνος ἐὼν ἦ καὶ σύμπαντες 'Αχαιοί;
εἰ γάρ σ' ὡς ἐθέλοι φιλέειν γλαυκῶπις 'Αθήνη,

---

[1] Lines 199 f. (=i. 301 f.) were rejected by Aristophanes and Aristarchus.   [2] πυθέσθαι: ἀοιδήν.

all who escaped the war, and the sea robbed him of none. But of the son of Atreus you have yourselves heard, far off though you are, how he came, and how Aegisthus devised for him a woeful doom. Yet verily he paid the reckoning therefor in terrible wise, so good a thing is it that a son be left behind a man at his death, since that son took vengeance on his father's slayer, the guileful Aegisthus, for that he slew his glorious father. Thou, too, friend, for I see thou art a comely man and tall, be thou valiant, that many an one among men yet to be born may praise thee."

Then wise Telemachus answered him : " Nestor, son of Neleus, great glory of the Achaeans, yea verily that son took vengeance, and the Achaeans shall spread his fame abroad, that men who are yet to be may hear thereof. O that the gods would clothe me with such strength, that I might take vengeance on the wooers for their grievous sin, who in wantonness devise mischief against me. But lo, the gods have spun for me no such happiness, for me or for my father ; and now I must in any case endure."

Then the horseman, Nestor of Gerenia, answered him : " Friend, since thou calledst this to my mind and didst speak of it, they say that many wooers for the hand of thy mother devise evils in thy halls in thy despite. Tell me, art thou willingly thus oppressed, or do the people throughout the land hate thee, following the voice of a god ? Who knows but Odysseus may some day come and take vengeance on them for their violent deeds,—he alone, it may be, or even all the host of the Achaeans ? Ah, would that flashing-eyed Athene

ὡς τότ' Ὀδυσσῆος περικήδετο κυδαλίμοιο
δήμῳ ἔνι Τρώων, ὅθι πάσχομεν ἄλγε' Ἀχαιοί— 220
οὐ γάρ πω ἴδον ὧδε θεοὺς ἀναφανδὰ φιλεῦντας,
ὡς κείνῳ ἀναφανδὰ παρίστατο Παλλὰς Ἀθήνη—
εἴ σ' οὕτως ἐθέλοι φιλέειν κήδοιτό τε θυμῷ,
τῶ κέν τις κείνων γε καὶ ἐκλελάθοιτο γάμοιο."

Τὸν δ' αὖ Τηλέμαχος πεπνυμένος ἀντίον ηὔδα· 225
"Ὦ γέρον, οὔ πω τοῦτο ἔπος τελέεσθαι ὀίω·
λίην γὰρ μέγα εἶπες· ἄγη μ' ἔχει. οὐκ ἂν ἐμοί γε
ἐλπομένῳ τὰ γένοιτ', οὐδ' εἰ θεοὶ ὣς ἐθέλοιεν."

Τὸν δ' αὖτε προσέειπε θεά, γλαυκῶπις Ἀθήνη·
"Τηλέμαχε, ποῖόν σε ἔπος φύγεν ἕρκος ὀδόντων. 230
ῥεῖα θεός γ' ἐθέλων καὶ τηλόθεν ἄνδρα σαῶσαι.
βουλοίμην δ' ἂν ἐγώ γε καὶ ἄλγεα πολλὰ μογήσας
οἴκαδέ τ' ἐλθέμεναι καὶ νόστιμον ἦμαρ ἰδέσθαι,
ἢ ἐλθὼν ἀπολέσθαι ἐφέστιος, ὡς Ἀγαμέμνων
ὤλεθ' ὑπ' Αἰγίσθοιο δόλῳ καὶ ἧς ἀλόχοιο. 235
ἀλλ' ἦ τοι θάνατον μὲν ὁμοίιον οὐδὲ θεοί περ
καὶ φίλῳ ἀνδρὶ δύνανται ἀλαλκέμεν, ὁππότε κεν δὴ
μοῖρ' ὀλοὴ καθέλῃσι τανηλεγέος θανάτοιο."

Τὴν δ' αὖ Τηλέμαχος πεπνυμένος ἀντίον ηὔδα·
"Μέντορ, μηκέτι ταῦτα λεγώμεθα κηδόμενοί περ· 240
κείνῳ δ' οὐκέτι νόστος ἐτήτυμος, ἀλλά οἱ ἤδη
φράσσαντ' ἀθάνατοι θάνατον καὶ κῆρα μέλαιναν.
νῦν δ' ἐθέλω ἔπος ἄλλο μεταλλῆσαι καὶ ἐρέσθαι

---

[1] The word is a dubious one and connection with ὁμοῖος is very uncertain. Save for this passage, ὁμοίιος is only used of

might choose to love thee even as then she cared exceedingly for glorious Odysseus in the land of the Trojans, where we Achaeans suffered woes. For never yet have I seen the gods so manifestly shewing love, as Pallas Athene did to him, standing manifest by his side. If she would be pleased to love thee in such wise and would care for thee at heart, then would many an one of them utterly forget marriage."

Then wise Telemachus answered him: "Old man, in no wise do I deem that this word will be brought to pass. Too great is what thou sayest; amazement holds me. No hope have I that this will come to pass, no, not though the gods should so will it."

Then the goddess, flashing-eyed Athene, spoke to him, and said: "Telemachus, what a word has escaped the barrier of thy teeth! Easily might a god who willed it bring a man safe home, even from afar. But for myself, I had rather endure many grievous toils ere I reached home and saw the day of my returning, than after my return be slain at my hearth, as Agamemnon was slain by the guile of Aegisthus and of his own wife. But of a truth death that is common to all[1] the gods themselves cannot ward from a man they love, when the fell fate of grievous death shall strike him down."

Then wise Telemachus answered her: "Mentor, no longer let us tell of these things despite our grief. For him no return can ever more be brought to pass; nay, ere this the immortals have devised for him death and black fate. But now I would make enquiry and ask Nestor regarding another matter,

war or strife. Some would read ὀλοίιος, "baneful, destructive."

85

Νέστορ', ἐπεὶ περὶ οἶδε δίκας ἠδὲ φρόνιν ἄλλων·
τρὶς γὰρ δή μίν φασιν ἀνάξασθαι γένε' ἀνδρῶν·   24
ὥς τέ μοι ἀθάνατος ἰνδάλλεται εἰσοράασθαι.
ὦ Νέστορ Νηληιάδη, σὺ δ' ἀληθὲς ἐνίσπες·
πῶς ἔθαν' Ἀτρείδης εὐρὺ κρείων Ἀγαμέμνων;
ποῦ Μενέλαος ἔην; τίνα δ' αὐτῷ μήσατ' ὄλεθρον
Αἴγισθος δολόμητις, ἐπεὶ κτάνε πολλὸν ἀρείω;   25
ἦ οὐκ Ἄργεος ἦεν Ἀχαιικοῦ, ἀλλά πη ἄλλη
πλάζετ' ἐπ' ἀνθρώπους, ὁ δὲ θαρσήσας κατέπεφνε;"
    Τὸν δ' ἠμείβετ' ἔπειτα Γερήνιος ἱππότα Νέστωρ·
"Τοιγὰρ ἐγώ τοι, τέκνον, ἀληθέα πάντ' ἀγορεύσω.
ἦ τοι μὲν τάδε καὐτὸς ὀίεαι, ὥς κεν ἐτύχθη,[1]   25
εἰ ζωόν γ' Αἴγισθον ἐνὶ μεγάροισιν ἔτετμεν
Ἀτρείδης Τροίηθεν ἰών, ξανθὸς Μενέλαος·
τῷ κέ οἱ οὐδὲ θανόντι χυτὴν ἐπὶ γαῖαν ἔχευαν,
ἀλλ' ἄρα τόν γε κύνες τε καὶ οἰωνοὶ κατέδαψαν
κείμενον ἐν πεδίῳ ἑκὰς ἄστεος,[2] οὐδέ κέ τίς μιν   26
κλαῦσεν Ἀχαιιάδων· μάλα γὰρ μέγα μήσατο ἔργον.
ἡμεῖς μὲν γὰρ κεῖθι πολέας τελέοντες ἀέθλους
ἥμεθ'· ὁ δ' εὔκηλος μυχῷ Ἄργεος ἱπποβότοιο
πόλλ' Ἀγαμεμνονέην ἄλοχον θέλγεσκ' ἐπέεσσιν.
ἡ δ' ἦ τοι τὸ πρὶν μὲν ἀναίνετο ἔργον ἀεικὲς   26
δῖα Κλυταιμνήστρη· φρεσὶ γὰρ κέχρητ' ἀγαθῇσι·
πὰρ δ' ἄρ' ἔην καὶ ἀοιδὸς ἀνήρ, ᾧ πόλλ' ἐπέτελλεν
Ἀτρείδης Τροίηνδε κιὼν εἴρυσθαι ἄκοιτιν.
ἀλλ' ὅτε δή μιν μοῖρα θεῶν ἐπέδησε δαμῆναι,
δὴ τότε τὸν μὲν ἀοιδὸν ἄγων ἐς νῆσον ἐρήμην   27

---

[1] ὥς κεν ἐτύχθη : ὥς περ ἐτύχθη, followed by a colon.
[2] ἄστεος : Ἄργεος.

since beyond all others he knows judgments and wisdom; for thrice, men say, has he been king for a generation of men, and like unto an immortal he seems to me to look upon. Nestor, son of Neleus, do thou tell me truly: how was the son of Atreus, wide-ruling Agamemnon, slain? Where was Menelaus? What death did guileful Aegisthus plan for the king, since he slew a man mightier far than himself? Was Menelaus not in Achaean Argos, but wandering elsewhere among men, so that Aegisthus took heart and did the murderous deed?"

Then the horseman, Nestor of Gerenia, answered him: "Then verily, my child, will I tell thee all the truth. Lo, of thine own self thou dost guess how this matter would have fallen out, if the son of Atreus, fair-haired Menelaus, on his return from Troy had found Aegisthus in his halls alive. Then for him not even in death would they have piled the up-piled earth, but the dogs and birds would have torn him as he lay on the plain far from the city, nor would any of the Achaean women have bewailed him; for monstrous was the deed he devised. We on our part abode there in Troy fulfilling our many toils; but he, at ease in a nook of horse-pasturing Argos, ever sought to beguile with words the wife of Agamemnon. Now at the first she put from her the unseemly deed, the beautiful Clytemnestra, for she had an understanding heart; and with her was furthermore a minstrel whom the son of Atreus straitly charged, when he set forth for the land of Troy, to guard his wife. But when at length the doom of the gods bound her that she should be overcome, then verily Aegisthus took

κάλλιπεν οἰωνοῖσιν ἕλωρ καὶ κύρμα γενέσθαι,
τὴν δ' ἐθέλων ἐθέλουσαν ἀνήγαγεν ὅνδε δόμονδε.
πολλὰ δὲ μηρί' ἔκηε θεῶν ἱεροῖς ἐπὶ βωμοῖς,
πολλὰ δ' ἀγάλματ' ἀνῆψεν, ὑφάσματά τε χρυσόν τε,
ἐκτελέσας μέγα ἔργον, ὃ οὔ ποτε ἔλπετο θυμῷ.   2

   "'Ημεῖς μὲν γὰρ ἅμα πλέομεν Τροίηθεν ἰόντες,
'Ατρεΐδης καὶ ἐγώ, φίλα εἰδότες ἀλλήλοισιν·
ἀλλ' ὅτε Σούνιον ἱρὸν ἀφικόμεθ', ἄκρον 'Αθηνέων,
ἔνθα κυβερνήτην Μενελάου Φοῖβος 'Απόλλων
οἷς ἀγανοῖς βελέεσσιν ἐποιχόμενος κατέπεφνε,   2
πηδάλιον μετὰ χερσὶ θεούσης νηὸς ἔχοντα,
Φρόντιν 'Ονητορίδην, ὃς ἐκαίνυτο φῦλ' ἀνθρώπων
νῆα κυβερνῆσαι, ὁπότε σπέρχοιεν ἄελλαι.
ὣς ὁ μὲν ἔνθα κατέσχετ', ἐπειγόμενός περ ὁδοῖο,
ὄφρ' ἕταρον θάπτοι καὶ ἐπὶ κτέρεα κτερίσειεν.   2
ἀλλ' ὅτε δὴ καὶ κεῖνος ἰὼν ἐπὶ οἴνοπα πόντον
ἐν νηυσὶ γλαφυρῇσι Μαλειάων ὄρος αἰπὺ
ἷξε θέων, τότε δὴ στυγερὴν ὁδὸν εὐρύοπα Ζεὺς
ἐφράσατο, λιγέων δ' ἀνέμων ἐπ' αὐτμένα χεῦε,
κύματά τε τροφέοντο [1] πελώρια, ἶσα ὄρεσσιν.   2
ἔνθα διατμήξας τὰς μὲν Κρήτῃ ἐπέλασσεν,
ἧχι Κύδωνες ἔναιον 'Ιαρδάνου ἀμφὶ ῥέεθρα.
ἔστι δέ τις λισσὴ αἰπεῖά τε εἰς ἅλα πέτρη
ἐσχατιῇ Γόρτυνος ἐν ἠεροειδέι πόντῳ·
ἔνθα Νότος μέγα κῦμα ποτὶ σκαιὸν ῥίον ὠθεῖ,   2
ἐς Φαιστόν, μικρὸς δὲ λίθος μέγα κῦμ' ἀποέργει.
αἱ μὲν ἄρ' ἔνθ' ἦλθον, σπουδῇ δ' ἤλυξαν ὄλεθρον

---

[1] τροφέοντο Aristarchus : τροφόεντα.

the minstrel to a desert isle and left him to be the prey and spoil of birds ; and her, willing as he was willing, he led to his own house. And many thigh-pieces he burned upon the holy altars of the gods, and many offerings he hung up, woven stuffs and gold, since he had accomplished a mighty deed beyond all his heart had hoped.

"Now we were sailing together on our way from Troy, the son of Atreus and I, in all friendship ; but when we came to holy Sunium, the cape of Athens, there Phoebus Apollo assailed with his gentle[1] shafts and slew the helmsman of Menelaus, as he held in his hands the steering-oar of the speeding ship, even Phrontis, son of Onetor, who excelled the tribes of men in piloting a ship when the storm winds blow strong. So Menelaus tarried there, though eager for his journey, that he might bury his comrade and over him pay funeral rites. But when he in his turn, as he passed over the wine-dark sea in the hollow ships, reached in swift course the steep height of Malea, then verily Zeus, whose voice is borne afar, planned for him a hateful path and poured upon him the blasts of shrill winds, and the waves were swollen to huge size, like unto mountains. Then, parting his ships in twain, he brought some to Crete, where the Cydonians dwelt about the streams of Iardanus. Now there is a smooth cliff, sheer towards the sea, on the border of Gortyn in the misty deep, where the South-west Wind drives the great wave against the head-land on the left toward Phaestus, and a little rock holds back a great wave. Thither came some of his ships, and the men with much ado escaped

---

[1] A gentle, painless death was thought to be due to Apollo's shafts.

ἄνδρες, ἀτὰρ νῆάς γε ποτὶ σπιλάδεσσιν ἔαξαν
κύματ'· ἀτὰρ τὰς πέντε νέας κυανοπρωρείους
Αἰγύπτῳ ἐπέλασσε φέρων ἄνεμός τε καὶ ὕδωρ.   30
ὡς ὁ μὲν ἔνθα πολὺν βίοτον καὶ χρυσὸν ἀγείρων
ἠλᾶτο ξὺν νηυσὶ κατ' ἀλλοθρόους ἀνθρώπους·
τόφρα δὲ ταῦτ' Αἴγισθος ἐμήσατο οἴκοθι λυγρά.
ἑπτάετες δ' ἤνασσε πολυχρύσοιο Μυκήνης,   30
κτείνας Ἀτρείδην, δέδμητο δὲ λαὸς ὑπ' αὐτῷ.   30
τῷ δέ οἱ ὀγδοάτῳ κακὸν ἤλυθε δῖος Ὀρέστης
ἂψ ἀπ' Ἀθηνάων,[1] κατὰ δ' ἔκτανε πατροφονῆα,
Αἴγισθον δολόμητιν, ὅ οἱ πατέρα κλυτὸν ἔκτα.
ἦ τοι ὁ τὸν κτείνας δαίνυ τάφον Ἀργείοισιν
μητρός τε στυγερῆς καὶ ἀνάλκιδος Αἰγίσθοιο·
αὐτῆμαρ δέ οἱ ἦλθε βοὴν ἀγαθὸς Μενέλαος   31
πολλὰ κτήματ' ἄγων, ὅσα οἱ νέες ἄχθος ἄειραν.

"Καὶ σύ, φίλος, μὴ δηθὰ δόμων ἄπο τῆλ' ἀλάλησο,
κτήματά τε προλιπὼν ἄνδρας τ' ἐν σοῖσι δόμοισιν
οὕτω ὑπερφιάλους, μή τοι κατὰ πάντα φάγωσιν   3
κτήματα δασσάμενοι, σὺ δὲ τηϋσίην ὁδὸν ἔλθῃς.
ἀλλ' ἐς μὲν Μενέλαον ἐγὼ κέλομαι καὶ ἄνωγα
ἐλθεῖν· κεῖνος γὰρ νέον ἄλλοθεν εἰλήλουθεν,
ἐκ τῶν ἀνθρώπων, ὅθεν οὐκ ἔλποιτό γε θυμῷ
ἐλθέμεν, ὅν τινα πρῶτον ἀποσφήλωσιν ἄελλαι   3
ἐς πέλαγος μέγα τοῖον, ὅθεν τέ περ οὐδ' οἰωνοὶ
αὐτόετες οἰχνεῦσιν, ἐπεὶ μέγα τε δεινόν τε.
ἀλλ' ἴθι νῦν σὺν νηΐ τε σῇ καὶ σοῖς ἑτάροισιν·
εἰ δ' ἐθέλεις πεζός, πάρα τοι δίφρος τε καὶ ἵπποι,
πὰρ δέ τοι υἷες ἐμοί, οἵ τοι πομπῆες ἔσονται   3

---

[1] Ἀθηνάων: Ἀθηναίης Aristarchus, Φωκήων Zenodotus.

destruction, howbeit the ships the waves dashed to pieces against the reef. But the five other dark-prowed ships the wind, as it bore them, and the wave brought to Egypt. So he was wandering there with his ships among men of strange speech, gathering much livelihood and gold; but meanwhile Aegisthus devised this woeful work at home. Seven years he reigned over Mycenae, rich in gold, after slaying the son of Atreus, and the people were subdued under him; but in the eighth came as his bane the goodly Orestes back from Athens, and slew his father's murderer, the guileful Aegisthus, for that he had slain his glorious father. Now when he had slain him, he made a funeral feast for the Argives over his hateful mother and the craven Aegisthus; and on the self-same day there came to him Menelaus, good at the war-cry, bringing much treasure, even all the burden that his ships could bear.

"So do not thou, my friend, wander long far from home, leaving thy wealth behind thee and men in thy house so insolent, lest they divide and devour all thy wealth, and thou shalt have gone on a fruitless journey. But to Menelaus I bid and command thee to go, for he has but lately come from a strange land, from a folk whence no one would hope in his heart to return, whom the storms had once driven astray into a sea so great, whence the very birds do not fare in the space of a year, so great is it and terrible. But now go thy way with thy ship and thy comrades, or, if thou wilt go by land, here are chariot and horses at hand for thee, and here at thy service are my sons, who will be thy guides to goodly

ἐς Λακεδαίμονα δῖαν, ὅθι ξανθὸς Μενέλαος.
λίσσεσθαι δέ μιν αὐτός, ἵνα νημερτὲς ἐνίσπῃ·
ψεῦδος δ' οὐκ ἐρέει· μάλα γὰρ πεπνυμένος ἐστίν."
   "Ὡς ἔφατ', ἠέλιος δ' ἄρ' ἔδυ καὶ ἐπὶ κνέφας ἦλθε.
τοῖσι δὲ καὶ μετέειπε θεά, γλαυκῶπις Ἀθήνη·   3
"Ὦ γέρον, ἦ τοι ταῦτα κατὰ μοῖραν κατέλεξας·
ἀλλ' ἄγε τάμνετε μὲν γλώσσας, κεράασθε δὲ οἶνον,
ὄφρα Ποσειδάωνι καὶ ἄλλοις ἀθανάτοισιν
σπείσαντες κοίτοιο μεδώμεθα· τοῖο γὰρ ὥρη.
ἤδη γὰρ φάος οἴχεθ' ὑπὸ ζόφον, οὐδὲ ἔοικεν·   3
δηθὰ θεῶν ἐν δαιτὶ θαασσέμεν, ἀλλὰ νέεσθαι."
   Ἦ ῥα Διὸς θυγάτηρ, οἱ δ' ἔκλυον αὐδησάσης.
τοῖσι δὲ κήρυκες μὲν ὕδωρ ἐπὶ χεῖρας ἔχευαν,
κοῦροι δὲ κρητῆρας ἐπεστέψαντο ποτοῖο,
νώμησαν δ' ἄρα πᾶσιν ἐπαρξάμενοι δεπάεσσι·   3
γλώσσας δ' ἐν πυρὶ βάλλον, ἀνιστάμενοι δ' ἐπέλειβο
αὐτὰρ ἐπεὶ σπεῖσάν τ' ἔπιον θ', ὅσον ἤθελε θυμός,
δὴ τότ' Ἀθηναίη καὶ Τηλέμαχος θεοειδὴς
ἄμφω ἱέσθην κοίλην ἐπὶ νῆα νέεσθαι.
Νέστωρ δ' αὖ κατέρυκε καθαπτόμενος ἐπέεσσιν·   3
   "Ζεὺς τό γ' ἀλεξήσειε καὶ ἀθάνατοι θεοὶ ἄλλοι,
ὡς ὑμεῖς παρ' ἐμεῖο θοὴν ἐπὶ νῆα κίοιτε
ὥς τέ τευ ἦ παρὰ πάμπαν ἀνείμονος ἠδὲ πενιχροῦ,
ᾧ οὔ τι χλαῖναι καὶ ῥήγεα πόλλ' ἐνὶ οἴκῳ,
οὔτ' αὐτῷ μαλακῶς οὔτε ξείνοισιν ἐνεύδειν.   3
αὐτὰρ ἐμοὶ πάρα μὲν χλαῖναι καὶ ῥήγεα καλά.
οὔ θην δὴ τοῦδ' ἀνδρὸς Ὀδυσσῆος φίλος υἱὸς
νηὸς ἐπ' ἰκριόφιν καταλέξεται, ὄφρ' ἂν ἐγώ γε
92

Lacedaemon, where lives fair-haired Menelaus. And do thou beseech him thyself that he may tell thee the very truth. A lie will he not utter, for he is wise indeed."

So he spoke, and the sun set, and darkness came on. Then among them spoke the goddess, flashing-eyed Athene: "Old man, of a truth thou hast told this tale aright. But come, cut out the tongues of the victims and mix the wine, that when we have poured libations to Poseidon and the other immortals, we may bethink us of sleep; for it is the time thereto. Even now has the light gone down beneath the darkness, and it is not fitting to sit long at the feast of the gods, but to go our way."

So spoke the daughter of Zeus, and they hearkened to her voice. Heralds poured water over their hands, and youths filled the bowls brim full of drink, and served out to all, pouring first drops for libation into the cups. Then they cast the tongues upon the fire, and, rising up, poured libations upon them. But when they had poured libations and had drunk to their heart's content, then verily Athene and godlike Telemachus were both fain to return to the hollow ship; but Nestor on his part sought to stay them, and he spoke to them, saying:

"This may Zeus forbid, and the other immortal gods, that ye should go from my house to your swift ship as from one utterly without raiment and poor, who has not cloaks and blankets in plenty in his house, whereon both he and his guests may sleep softly. Nay, in my house there are cloaks and fair blankets. Never surely shall the dear son of this man Odysseus lie down upon the deck of a ship,

ζώω, ἔπειτα δὲ παῖδες ἐνὶ μεγάροισι λίπωνται,
ξείνους ξεινίζειν, ὅς τίς κ' ἐμὰ δώμαθ' ἵκηται."

Τὸν δ' αὖτε προσέειπε θεά, γλαυκῶπις Ἀθήνη·
" Εὖ δὴ ταῦτά γ' ἔφησθα, γέρον φίλε· σοὶ δὲ ἔοικεν
Τηλέμαχον πείθεσθαι, ἐπεὶ πολὺ κάλλιον οὕτως.
ἀλλ' οὗτος μὲν νῦν σοὶ ἅμ' ἔψεται, ὄφρα κεν εὕδῃ
σοῖσιν ἐνὶ μεγάροισιν· ἐγὼ δ' ἐπὶ νῆα μέλαιναν
εἶμ', ἵνα θαρσύνω θ' ἑτάρους εἴπω τε ἕκαστα.
οἶος γὰρ μετὰ τοῖσι γεραίτερος εὔχομαι εἶναι·
οἱ δ' ἄλλοι φιλότητι νεώτεροι ἄνδρες ἕπονται,
πάντες ὁμηλικίη μεγαθύμου Τηλεμάχοιο.
ἔνθα κε λεξαίμην κοίλῃ παρὰ νηὶ μελαίνῃ
νῦν· ἀτὰρ ἠῶθεν μετὰ Καύκωνας μεγαθύμους
εἶμ' ἔνθα χρεῖός μοι ὀφέλλεται, οὔ τι νέον γε
οὐδ' ὀλίγον. σὺ δὲ τοῦτον, ἐπεὶ τεὸν ἵκετο δῶμα,
πέμψον σὺν δίφρῳ τε καὶ υἱέι· δὸς δέ οἱ ἵππους,
οἵ τοι ἐλαφρότατοι θείειν καὶ κάρτος ἄριστοι."

Ὣς ἄρα φωνήσασ' ἀπέβη γλαυκῶπις Ἀθήνη
φήνῃ εἰδομένη· θάμβος δ' ἕλε πάντας ἰδόντας.[1]
θαύμαζεν δ' ὁ γεραιός, ὅπως ἴδεν ὀφθαλμοῖσι·
Τηλεμάχου δ' ἕλε χεῖρα, ἔπος τ' ἔφατ' ἔκ τ' ὀνόμαζε·
"Ὦ φίλος, οὔ σε ἔολπα κακὸν καὶ ἄναλκιν ἔσεσθ'
εἰ δή τοι νέῳ ὧδε θεοὶ πομπῆες ἕπονται.
οὐ μὲν γάρ τις ὅδ' ἄλλος Ὀλύμπια δώματ' ἐχόντων,
ἀλλὰ Διὸς θυγάτηρ, κυδίστη [2] τριτογένεια,

---

[1] ἰδόντας : Ἀχαιούς.   [2] κυδίστη Zenodotus : ἀγελείη.

[1] The precise meaning of the word is uncertain, as is the
case with so many epithets of the gods. It perhaps means

while I yet live and children after me are left in my halls to entertain strangers, even whosoever shall come to my house."

Then the goddess, flashing-eyed Athene, answered him: "Well indeed hast thou spoken in this, old friend, and it were fitting for Telemachus to hearken to thee, since it is far better thus. But while he shall now follow with thee, that he may sleep in thy halls, I for my part will go to the black ship, that I may hearten my comrades and tell them all. For alone among them I declare that I am an older man; the others are younger who follow in friendship, all of them of like age with great-hearted Telemachus. There will I lay me down by the hollow black ship this night, but in the morning I will go to the great-hearted Cauconians, where a debt is owing to me, in no wise new or small. But do thou send this man on his way with a chariot and with thy son, since he has come to thy house, and give him horses, the fleetest thou hast in running and the best in strength."

So spoke the goddess, flashing-eyed Athene, and she departed in the likeness of a sea-eagle; and amazement fell upon all at the sight, and the old man marvelled, when his eyes beheld it. And he grasped the hand of Telemachus, and spoke, and addressed him:

"Friend, in no wise do I think that thou wilt prove a base man or a craven, if verily when thou art so young the gods follow thee to be thy guides. For truly this is none other of those that have their dwellings on Olympus but the daughter of Zeus, Tritogeneia,[1] the maid most glorious, she that

"Triton-born," possibly with reference to an actual stream of that name (in Boeotia or Thessaly).

ἤ τοι καὶ πατέρ' ἐσθλὸν ἐν Ἀργείοισιν ἐτίμα.
ἀλλὰ ἄνασσ' ἵληθι, δίδωθι δέ μοι κλέος ἐσθλόν,
αὐτῷ καὶ παίδεσσι καὶ αἰδοίῃ παρακοίτι·
σοὶ δ' αὖ ἐγὼ ῥέξω βοῦν ἦνιν εὐρυμέτωπον
ἀδμήτην, ἣν οὔ πω ὑπὸ ζυγὸν ἤγαγεν ἀνήρ·
τήν τοι ἐγὼ ῥέξω χρυσὸν κέρασιν περιχεύας."

Ὣς ἔφατ' εὐχόμενος, τοῦ δ' ἔκλυε Παλλὰς Ἀθήνη,
τοῖσιν δ' ἡγεμόνευε Γερήνιος ἱππότα Νέστωρ,
υἱάσι καὶ γαμβροῖσιν, ἑὰ πρὸς δώματα καλά.
ἀλλ' ὅτε δώμαθ' ἵκοντο ἀγακλυτὰ τοῖο ἄνακτος,
ἑξείης ἕζοντο κατὰ κλισμούς τε θρόνους τε·
τοῖς δ' ὁ γέρων ἐλθοῦσιν ἀνὰ κρητῆρα κέρασσεν
οἴνου ἡδυπότοιο, τὸν ἑνδεκάτῳ ἐνιαυτῷ
ὦιξεν ταμίη καὶ ἀπὸ κρήδεμνον ἔλυσε·
τοῦ ὁ γέρων κρητῆρα κεράσσατο, πολλὰ δ' Ἀθήνῃ
εὔχετ' ἀποσπένδων, κούρῃ Διὸς αἰγιόχοιο.

Αὐτὰρ ἐπεὶ σπεῖσάν τ' ἔπιον θ', ὅσον ἤθελε θυμός,
οἱ μὲν κακκείοντες ἔβαν οἰκόνδε ἕκαστος,
τὸν δ' αὐτοῦ κοίμησε Γερήνιος ἱππότα Νέστωρ,
Τηλέμαχον, φίλον υἱὸν Ὀδυσσῆος θείοιο,
τρητοῖς ἐν λεχέεσσιν ὑπ' αἰθούσῃ ἐριδούπῳ,
πὰρ δ' ἄρ' ἐϋμμελίην Πεισίστρατον, ὄρχαμον ἀνδρῶν
ὅς οἱ ἔτ' ἠίθεος παίδων ἦν ἐν μεγάροισιν·
αὐτὸς δ' αὖτε καθεῦδε μυχῷ δόμου ὑψηλοῖο,
τῷ δ' ἄλοχος δέσποινα λέχος πόρσυνε καὶ εὐνήν.

Ἦμος δ' ἠριγένεια φάνη ῥοδοδάκτυλος Ἠώς,.

honoured also thy noble father among the Argives. Nay, O Queen, be gracious, and grant to me fair renown, to me and to my sons and to my revered wife ; and to thee in return will I sacrifice a sleek [1] heifer, broad of brow, unbroken, which no man hath yet led beneath the yoke. Her will I sacrifice, and I will overlay her horns with gold.''

So he spoke in prayer, and Pallas Athene heard him. Then the horseman, Nestor of Gerenia, led them, his sons and the husbands of his daughters, to his beautiful palace. And when they reached the glorious palace of the king, they sat down in rows on the chairs and high seats ; and on their coming the old man mixed for them a bowl of sweet wine, which now in the eleventh year the housewife opened, when she had loosed the string that held the lid. Thereof the old man bade mix a bowl, and earnestly he prayed, as he poured libations, to Athene, the daughter of Zeus who bears the aegis.

But when they had poured libations, and had drunk to their heart's content, they went, each to his home, to take their rest. But the horseman, Nestor of Gerenia, bade Telemachus, the dear son of divine Odysseus, to sleep there on a corded bedstead under the echoing portico, and by him Peisistratus, of the good ashen spear, a leader of men, who among his sons was still unwed in the palace. But he himself slept in the inmost chamber of the lofty house, and beside him lay the lady his wife, who had strewn the couch.

Soon as early Dawn appeared, the rosy-fingered,

---

[1] Scholars generally follow the ancient commentators, and render ἧνιν '' one year old.'' The meaning ''sleek'' was suggested by Goebel, whom Ameis follows.

ὤρνυτ' ἄρ' ἐξ εὐνῆφι Γερήνιος ἱππότα Νέστωρ,
ἐκ δ' ἐλθὼν κατ' ἄρ' ἔζετ' ἐπὶ ξεστοῖσι λίθοισιν,
οἵ οἱ ἔσαν προπάροιθε θυράων ὑψηλάων
λευκοί, ἀποστίλβοντες ἀλείφατος· οἷς ἔπι μὲν πρὶν
Νηλεὺς ἵζεσκεν, θεόφιν μήστωρ ἀτάλαντος·
ἀλλ' ὁ μὲν ἤδη κηρὶ δαμεὶς Ἀϊδόσδε βεβήκει,
Νέστωρ αὖ τότ' ἐφῖζε Γερήνιος, οὖρος Ἀχαιῶν,
σκῆπτρον ἔχων.   περὶ δ' υἷες ἀολλέες ἠγερέθοντο
ἐκ θαλάμων ἐλθόντες, Ἐχέφρων τε Στρατίος τε
Περσεύς τ' Ἄρητός τε καὶ ἀντίθεος Θρασυμήδης.
τοῖσι δ' ἔπειθ' ἕκτος Πεισίστρατος ἤλυθεν ἥρως,
πὰρ δ' ἄρα Τηλέμαχον θεοείκελον εἷσαν ἄγοντες.
τοῖσι δὲ μύθων ἦρχε Γερήνιος ἱππότα Νέστωρ·

"Καρπαλίμως μοι, τέκνα φίλα, κρηήνατ' ἐέλδωρ,
ὄφρ' ἦ τοι πρώτιστα θεῶν ἱλάσσομ' Ἀθήνην,
ἥ μοι ἐναργὴς ἦλθε θεοῦ ἐς δαῖτα θάλειαν.
ἀλλ' ἄγ' ὁ μὲν πεδίονδ' ἐπὶ βοῦν ἴτω, ὄφρα τάχιστα
ἔλθησιν, ἐλάσῃ δὲ βοῶν ἐπιβουκόλος ἀνήρ·
εἷς δ' ἐπὶ Τηλεμάχου μεγαθύμου νῆα μέλαιναν
πάντας ἰὼν ἑτάρους ἀγέτω, λιπέτω δὲ δύ' οἴους·
εἷς δ' αὖ χρυσοχόον Λαέρκεα δεῦρο κελέσθω
ἐλθεῖν, ὄφρα βοὸς χρυσὸν κέρασιν περιχεύῃ.
οἱ δ' ἄλλοι μένετ' αὐτοῦ ἀολλέες, εἴπατε δ' εἴσω
δμῳῆσιν κατὰ δώματ' ἀγακλυτὰ δαῖτα πένεσθαι,
ἕδρας τε ξύλα τ' ἀμφὶ καὶ ἀγλαὸν οἰσέμεν ὕδωρ."

up from his bed rose the horseman, Nestor of
Gerenia, and went forth and sat down on the
polished stones which were before his lofty doors,
white and glistening as with oil.[1] On these of old
was wont to sit Neleus, the peer of the gods in
counsel; but he ere this had been stricken by fate
and had gone to the house of Hades, and now there
sat upon them in his turn Nestor of Gerenia, the
warder of the Achaeans, holding a sceptre in his
hands. About him his sons gathered in a throng
as they came forth from their chambers, Echephron
and Stratius and Perseus and Aretus and godlike
Thrasymedes; and to these thereafter came as the
sixth the lord Peisistratus. And they led godlike
Telemachus and made him sit beside them; and
the horseman, Nestor of Gerenia, was first to speak
among them:

"Quickly, my dear children, fulfil my desire, that
first of all the gods I may propitiate Athene, who
came to me in manifest presence to the rich feast of
the god. Come now, let one go to the plain for a
heifer, that she may come speedily, and that the
neatherd may drive her; and let one go to the
black ship of great-hearted Telemachus and bring
all his comrades, and let him leave two men only;
and let one again bid the goldsmith Laërces come
hither, that he may overlay the heifer's horns with
gold. And do ye others abide here together; and
bid the handmaids within to make ready a feast
throughout our glorious halls, to fetch seats, and
logs to set on either side of the altar, and to bring
clear water."

[1] So Eustathius and the scholia. Others think of a wash
or stucco, covering the stones.

ὫΩς ἔφαθ', οἱ δ' ἄρα πάντες ἐποίπνυον. ἦλθε
    μὲν ἂρ βοῦς 4
ἐκ πεδίου, ἦλθον δὲ θοῆς παρὰ νηὸς ἐίσης
Τηλεμάχου ἔταροι μεγαλήτορος, ἦλθε δὲ χαλκεὺς
ὅπλ' ἐν χερσὶν ἔχων χαλκήια, πείρατα τέχνης,
ἄκμονά τε σφῦράν τ' ἐυποίητόν τε πυράγρην,
οἷσίν τε χρυσὸν εἰργάζετο· ἦλθε δ' Ἀθήνη 4
ἱρῶν ἀντιόωσα. γέρων δ' ἱππηλάτα Νέστωρ
χρυσὸν ἔδωχ'· ὁ δ' ἔπειτα βοὸς κέρασιν περίχευεν
ἀσκήσας, ἵν' ἄγαλμα θεὰ κεχάροιτο ἰδοῦσα.
βοῦν δ' ἀγέτην κεράων Στρατίος καὶ δῖος Ἐχέφρων.
χέρνιβα δέ σφ' Ἄρητος ἐν ἀνθεμόεντι λέβητι 4
ἤλυθεν ἐκ θαλάμοιο φέρων, ἑτέρῃ δ' ἔχεν οὐλὰς
ἐν κανέῳ· πέλεκυν δὲ μενεπτόλεμος Θρασυμήδης
ὀξὺν ἔχων ἐν χειρὶ παρίστατο βοῦν ἐπικόψων.
Περσεὺς δ' ἀμνίον εἶχε· γέρων δ' ἱππηλάτα Νέστωρ
χέρνιβά τ' οὐλοχύτας τε κατήρχετο, πολλὰ δ' Ἀθήνῃ
εὔχετ' ἀπαρχόμενος, κεφαλῆς τρίχας ἐν πυρὶ βάλ-
    λων. 4

Αὐτὰρ ἐπεὶ ῥ' εὔξαντο καὶ οὐλοχύτας προβάλοντο,
αὐτίκα Νέστορος υἱὸς ὑπέρθυμος Θρασυμήδης
ἤλασεν ἄγχι στάς· πέλεκυς δ' ἀπέκοψε τένοντας
αὐχενίους, λῦσεν δὲ βοὸς μένος. αἱ δ' ὀλόλυξαν 4
θυγατέρες τε νυοί τε καὶ αἰδοίη παράκοιτις
Νέστορος, Εὐρυδίκη, πρέσβα Κλυμένοιο θυγατρῶν.
οἱ μὲν ἔπειτ' ἀνελόντες ἀπὸ χθονὸς εὐρυοδείης
ἔσχον· ἀτὰρ σφάξεν Πεισίστρατος, ὄρχαμος ἀνδρῶν.

So he spoke, and they all set busily to work. The heifer came from the plain, and from the swift, shapely ship came the comrades of great-hearted Telemachus; the smith came, bearing in his hands his tools of bronze, the implements of his craft, anvil and hammer and well-made tongs, wherewith he wrought the gold; and Athene came to accept the sacrifice. Then the old man, Nestor, the driver of chariots, gave gold, and the smith prepared it, and overlaid therewith the horns of the heifer, that the goddess might rejoice when she beheld the offering. And Stratius and goodly Echephron led the heifer by the horns, and Aretus came from the chamber, bringing them water for the hands in a basin embossed with flowers, and in the other hand he held barley grains in a basket; and Thrasymedes, steadfast in fight, stood by, holding in his hands a sharp axe, to fell the heifer; and Perseus held the bowl for the blood. Then the old man, Nestor, driver of chariots, began the opening rite of hand-washing and sprinkling with barley grains, and earnestly he prayed to Athene, cutting off as first offering the hair from the head, and casting it into the fire.

Now when they had prayed, and had strewn the barley grains, straightway the son of Nestor, Thrasymedes, high of heart, came near and dealt the blow; and the axe cut through the sinews of the neck, and loosened the strength of the heifer. Then the women raised the sacred cry, the daughters and the sons' wives and the revered wife of Nestor, Eurydice, the eldest of the daughters of Clymenus, and the men raised the heifer's head from the broad-wayed earth and held it, and Peisistratus,

τῆς δ' ἐπεὶ ἐκ μέλαν αἷμα ῥύη, λίπε δ' ὀστέα θυμός, 45
αἶψ' ἄρα μιν διέχευαν, ἄφαρ δ' ἐκ μηρία τάμνον
πάντα κατὰ μοῖραν, κατά τε κνίσῃ ἐκάλυψαν
δίπτυχα ποιήσαντες, ἐπ' αὐτῶν δ' ὠμοθέτησαν.
καῖε δ' ἐπὶ σχίζῃς ὁ γέρων, ἐπὶ δ' αἴθοπα οἶνον
λεῖβε· νέοι δὲ παρ' αὐτὸν ἔχον πεμπώβολα χερσίν. 46
αὐτὰρ ἐπεὶ κατὰ μῆρ' ἐκάη καὶ σπλάγχνα πάσαντο,
μίστυλλόν τ' ἄρα τἆλλα καὶ ἀμφ' ὀβελοῖσιν ἔπειραν,
ὤπτων δ' ἀκροπόρους ὀβελοὺς ἐν χερσὶν ἔχοντες.

Τόφρα δὲ Τηλέμαχον λοῦσεν καλὴ Πολυκάστη,
Νέστορος ὁπλοτάτη θυγάτηρ Νηληιάδαο. 46
αὐτὰρ ἐπεὶ λοῦσέν τε καὶ ἔχρισεν λίπ' ἐλαίῳ,
ἀμφὶ δέ μιν φᾶρος καλὸν βάλεν ἠδὲ χιτῶνα,
ἔκ ῥ' ἀσαμίνθου βῆ δέμας ἀθανάτοισιν ὁμοῖος·
πὰρ δ' ὅ γε Νέστορ' ἰὼν κατ' ἄρ' ἕζετο, ποιμένα λαῶν.

Οἱ δ' ἐπεὶ ὤπτησαν κρέ' ὑπέρτερα καὶ ἐρύσαντο, 47
δαίνυνθ' ἑζόμενοι· ἐπὶ δ' ἀνέρες ἐσθλοὶ ὄροντο
οἶνον οἰνοχοεῦντες ἐνὶ χρυσέοις δεπάεσσιν.
αὐτὰρ ἐπεὶ πόσιος καὶ ἐδητύος ἐξ ἔρον ἕντο,
τοῖσι δὲ μύθων ἦρχε Γερήνιος ἱππότα Νέστωρ·

" Παῖδες ἐμοί, ἄγε Τηλεμάχῳ καλλίτριχας ἵππους 47
ζεύξαθ' ὑφ' ἅρματ' ἄγοντες, ἵνα πρήσσῃσιν ὁδοῖο."

Ὣς ἔφαθ', οἱ δ' ἄρα τοῦ μάλα μὲν κλύον ἠδ' ἐπίθοντο,
καρπαλίμως δ' ἔζευξαν ὑφ' ἅρμασιν ὠκέας ἵππους.
ἐν δὲ γυνὴ ταμίη σῖτον καὶ οἶνον ἔθηκεν
ὄψα τε, οἷα ἔδουσι διοτρεφέες βασιλῆες. 48

leader of men, cut the throat. And when the black blood had flowed from her and the life had left the bones, at once they cut up the body and straightway cut out the thigh-pieces all in due order, and covered them with a double layer of fat, and laid raw flesh upon them. Then the old man burned them on billets of wood, and poured over them sparkling wine, and beside him the young men held in their hands the five-pronged forks. But when the thigh-pieces were wholly burned, and they had tasted the inner parts, they cut up the rest and spitted and roasted it, holding the pointed spits in their hands.

Meanwhile the fair Polycaste, the youngest daughter of Nestor, son of Neleus, bathed Telemachus. And when she had bathed him and anointed him richly [1] with oil, and had cast about him a fair cloak and a tunic, forth from the bath he came in form like unto the immortals ; and he went and sat down by Nestor, the shepherd of the people.

Now when they had roasted the outer flesh and had drawn it off the spits, they sat down and feasted, and worthy men waited on them, pouring wine [2] into golden cups. But when they had put from them the desire of food and drink, the horseman, Nestor of Gerenia, was first to speak, saying :

" My sons, up, yoke for Telemachus horses with beautiful mane beneath the car, that he may get forward on his journey."

So he spoke, and they readily hearkened and obeyed ; and quickly they yoked beneath the car the swift horses. And the housewife placed in the car bread and wine and dainties, such as kings,

---

[1] Others simply " with olive oil."
[2] Or possibly " uprose to pour them wine."

ἂν δ' ἄρα Τηλέμαχος περικαλλέα βήσετο δίφρον·
πὰρ δ' ἄρα Νεστορίδης Πεισίστρατος, ὄρχαμος ἀνδρῶ
ἐς δίφρον τ' ἀνέβαινε καὶ ἡνία λάζετο χερσί,
μάστιξεν δ' ἐλάαν, τὼ δ' οὐκ ἀέκοντε πετέσθην
ἐς πεδίον, λιπέτην δὲ Πύλου αἰπὺ πτολίεθρον.   48
οἱ δὲ πανημέριοι σεῖον ζυγὸν ἀμφὶς ἔχοντες.

Δύσετό τ' ἠέλιος σκιόωντό τε πᾶσαι ἀγυιαί,
ἐς Φηρὰς δ' ἵκοντο Διοκλῆος ποτὶ δῶμα,
υἱέος Ὀρτιλόχοιο, τὸν Ἀλφειὸς τέκε παῖδα.
ἔνθα δὲ νύκτ' ἄεσαν, ὁ δὲ τοῖς πὰρ ξείνια θῆκεν.   49

Ἦμος δ' ἠριγένεια φάνη ῥοδοδάκτυλος Ἠώς,
ἵππους τε ζεύγνυντ' ἀνά θ' ἅρματα ποικίλ' ἔβαινον·
ἐκ δ' ἔλασαν προθύροιο καὶ αἰθούσης ἐριδούπου· [1]
μάστιξεν δ' ἐλάαν, τὼ δ' οὐκ ἀέκοντε πετέσθην.
ἷξον δ' ἐς πεδίον πυρηφόρον, ἔνθα δ' ἔπειτα   49
ἦνον ὁδόν· τοῖον γὰρ ὑπέκφερον ὠκέες ἵπποι.
δύσετό τ' ἠέλιος σκιόωντό τε πᾶσαι ἀγυιαί.

[1] Line 493 is omitted in most MSS.

fostered of Zeus, are wont to eat. Then Telemachus mounted the beautiful car, and Peisistratus, son of Nestor, a leader of men, mounted beside him, and took the reins in his hands. He touched the horses with the whip to start them, and nothing loath the pair sped on to the plain, and left the steep citadel of Pylos. So all day long they shook the yoke which they bore about their necks.

Now the sun set and all the ways grew dark. And they came to Pherae, to the house of Diocles, son of Ortilochus, whom Alpheus begot. There they spent the night, and before them he set the entertainment due to strangers.

So soon as early Dawn appeared, the rosy-fingered, they yoked the horses and mounted the inlaid car, and drove forth from the gateway and the echoing portico. Then Peisistratus touched the horses with the whip to start them, and nothing loath the pair sped onward. So they came to the wheat-bearing plain, and thereafter pressed on toward their journey's end, so well did their swift horses bear them on. And the sun set and all the ways grew dark.

Δ

Οἱ δ' ἷξον κοίλην Λακεδαίμονα κητώεσσαν,
πρὸς δ' ἄρα δώματ' ἔλων Μενελάου κυδαλίμοιο.
τὸν δ' εὗρον δαινύντα γάμον πολλοῖσιν ἔτῃσιν
υἱέος ἠδὲ θυγατρὸς ἀμύμονος ᾧ ἐνὶ οἴκῳ.
τὴν μὲν Ἀχιλλῆος ῥηξήνορος υἱέι πέμπεν·
ἐν Τροίῃ γὰρ πρῶτον ὑπέσχετο καὶ κατένευσε
δωσέμεναι, τοῖσιν δὲ θεοὶ γάμον ἐξετέλειον.
τὴν ἄρ' ὅ γ' ἔνθ' ἵπποισι καὶ ἅρμασι πέμπε νέεσθαι
Μυρμιδόνων προτὶ ἄστυ περικλυτόν, οἷσιν ἄνασσεν.
υἱέι δὲ Σπάρτηθεν Ἀλέκτορος ἤγετο κούρην,
ὅς οἱ τηλύγετος γένετο κρατερὸς Μεγαπένθης
ἐκ δούλης· Ἑλένῃ δὲ θεοὶ γόνον οὐκέτ' ἔφαινον,
ἐπεὶ δὴ τὸ πρῶτον ἐγείνατο παῖδ' ἐρατεινήν,
Ἑρμιόνην, ἣ εἶδος ἔχε χρυσέης Ἀφροδίτης.
ὣς οἱ μὲν δαίνυντο καθ' ὑψερεφὲς μέγα δῶμα
γείτονες ἠδὲ ἔται Μενελάου κυδαλίμοιο,
τερπόμενοι· μετὰ δέ σφιν ἐμέλπετο θεῖος ἀοιδὸς
φορμίζων, δοιὼ δὲ κυβιστητῆρε κατ' αὐτούς,
μολπῆς ἐξάρχοντος,[1] ἐδίνευον κατὰ μέσσους.

[1] ἐξάρχοντος : ἐξάρχοντες.

BOOK IV

AND they came to the hollow land of Lacedaemon
with its many ravines, and drove to the palace of
glorious Menelaus. Him they found giving a mar-
riage feast to his many kinsfolk for his noble son and
daughter within his house. His daughter he was
sending to the son of Achilles, breaker of the ranks
of men, for in the land of Troy he first had promised
and pledged that he would give her, and now the
gods were bringing their marriage to pass. Her then
he was sending forth with horses and chariots to go
her way to the glorious city of the Myrmidons, over
whom her lord was king; but for his son he was
bringing to his home from Sparta the daughter of
Alector, even for the stalwart Megapenthes, who
was his son well-beloved,[1] born of a slave woman;
for to Helen the gods vouchsafed issue no more after
that she had at the first borne her lovely child,
Hermione, who had the beauty of golden Aphrodite.
So they were feasting in the great high-roofed hall,
the neighbours and kinsfolk of glorious Menelaus,
and making merry; and among them a divine min-
strel was singing to the lyre, and two tumblers
whirled up and down through the midst of them,
as he began his song.

[1] I follow Buttmann in the rendering of this doubtful
word. Suggested etymologies are not convincing. Others
take the word to mean " grown big."

Τὼ δ' αὖτ' ἐν προθύροισι δόμων αὐτώ τε καὶ ἵππω,
Τηλέμαχός θ' ἥρως καὶ Νέστορος ἀγλαὸς υἱός,
στῆσαν· ὁ δὲ προμολὼν ἴδετο κρείων Ἐτεωνεύς,
ὀτρηρὸς θεράπων Μενελάου κυδαλίμοιο,
βῆ δ' ἴμεν ἀγγελέων διὰ δώματα ποιμένι λαῶν,
ἀγχοῦ δ' ἱστάμενος ἔπεα πτερόεντα προσηύδα·
  " Ξείνω δή τινε τώδε, διοτρεφὲς ὦ Μενέλαε,
ἄνδρε δύω, γενεῇ δὲ Διὸς μεγάλοιο ἔικτον.
ἀλλ' εἴπ', ἤ σφωιν καταλύσομεν ὠκέας ἵππους,
ἦ ἄλλον πέμπωμεν ἱκανέμεν, ὅς κε φιλήσῃ."
  Τὸν δὲ μέγ' ὀχθήσας προσέφη ξανθὸς Μενέλαος·
"Οὐ μὲν νήπιος ἦσθα, Βοηθοΐδη Ἐτεωνεῦ,
τὸ πρίν· ἀτὰρ μὲν νῦν γε πάις ὣς νήπια βάζεις.
ἦ μὲν δὴ νῶι ξεινήια πολλὰ φαγόντε
ἄλλων ἀνθρώπων δεῦρ' ἱκόμεθ', αἴ κέ ποθι Ζεὺς
ἐξοπίσω περ παύσῃ ὀιζύος. ἀλλὰ λύ' ἵππους
ξείνων, ἐς δ' αὐτοὺς προτέρω ἄγε θοινηθῆναι."
  Ὣς φάθ', ὁ δὲ μεγάροιο διέσσυτο, κέκλετο δ' ἄλλους
ὀτρηροὺς θεράποντας ἅμα σπέσθαι ἑοῖ αὐτῷ.
οἱ δ' ἵππους μὲν λῦσαν ὑπὸ ζυγοῦ ἱδρώοντας,
καὶ τοὺς μὲν κατέδησαν ἐφ' ἱππείῃσι κάπῃσι,
πὰρ δ' ἔβαλον ζειάς, ἀνὰ δὲ κρῖ λευκὸν ἔμιξαν,
ἅρματα δ' ἔκλιναν πρὸς ἐνώπια παμφανόωντα,
αὐτοὺς δ' εἰσῆγον θεῖον δόμον. οἱ δὲ ἰδόντες
θαύμαζον κατὰ δῶμα διοτρεφέος βασιλῆος·
ὥς τε γὰρ ἠελίου αἴγλη πέλεν ἠὲ σελήνης
δῶμα καθ' ὑψερεφὲς Μενελάου κυδαλίμοιο.
αὐτὰρ ἐπεὶ τάρπησαν ὁρώμενοι ὀφθαλμοῖσιν,
ἔς ῥ' ἀσαμίνθους βάντες ἐυξέστας λούσαντο.

Then the two, the prince Telemachus and the glorious son of Nestor, halted at the gateway of the palace, they and their two horses. And the lord Eteoneus came forth and saw them, the busy squire of glorious Menelaus; and he went through the hall to bear the tidings to the shepherd of the people. So he came near and spoke to him winged words:

"Here are two strangers, Menelaus, fostered of Zeus, two men that are like the seed of great Zeus. But tell me, shall we unyoke for them their swift horses, or send them on their way to some other host, who will give them entertainment?"

Then, stirred to sore displeasure, fair-haired Menelaus spoke to him: "Aforetime thou wast not wont to be a fool, Eteoneus, son of Boethous, but now like a child thou talkest folly. Surely we two ate full often hospitable cheer of other men, ere we came hither in the hope that Zeus would hereafter grant us respite from sorrow. Nay, unyoke the strangers' horses, and lead the men forward into the house, that they may feast."

So he spoke, and the other hastened through the hall, and called to the other busy squires to follow along with him. They loosed the sweating horses from beneath the yoke and tied them at the stalls of the horses, and flung before them spelt, and mixed therewith white barley. Then they tilted the chariot against the bright entrance walls, and led the men into the divine palace. But at the sight they marvelled as they passed through the palace of the king, fostered of Zeus; for there was a gleam as of sun or moon over the high-roofed house of glorious Menelaus. But when they had satisfied their eyes with gazing they went into the polished baths and bathed.

τοὺς δ' ἐπεὶ οὖν δμῳαὶ λοῦσαν καὶ χρῖσαν ἐλαίῳ,
ἀμφὶ δ' ἄρα χλαίνας οὔλας βάλον ἠδὲ χιτῶνας,
ἕς ῥα θρόνους ἕζοντο παρ' Ἀτρεΐδην Μενέλαον.
χέρνιβα δ' ἀμφίπολος προχόῳ ἐπέχευε φέρουσα
καλῇ χρυσείῃ ὑπὲρ ἀργυρέοιο λέβητος,
νίψασθαι· παρὰ δὲ ξεστὴν ἐτάνυσσε τράπεζαν.
σῖτον δ' αἰδοίη ταμίη παρέθηκε φέρουσα,
εἴδατα πόλλ' ἐπιθεῖσα, χαριζομένη παρεόντων.
δαιτρὸς δὲ κρειῶν πίνακας παρέθηκεν ἀείρας
παντοίων, παρὰ δέ σφι τίθει χρύσεια κύπελλα.[1]
τὼ καὶ δεικνύμενος προσέφη ξανθὸς Μενέλαος·

"Σίτου θ' ἅπτεσθον καὶ χαίρετον. αὐτὰρ ἔπειτα
δείπνου πασσαμένω εἰρησόμεθ', οἵ τινές ἐστον
ἀνδρῶν· οὐ γὰρ σφῷν γε γένος ἀπόλωλε τοκήων,
ἀλλ' ἀνδρῶν γένος ἐστὲ διοτρεφέων βασιλήων
σκηπτούχων, ἐπεὶ οὔ κε κακοὶ τοιούσδε τέκοιεν." [2]

Ὣς φάτο, καί σφιν νῶτα βοὸς παρὰ πίονα θῆκεν
ὄπτ' ἐν χερσὶν ἑλών, τά ῥά οἱ γέρα πάρθεσαν αὐτῷ.
οἱ δ' ἐπ' ὀνείαθ' ἑτοῖμα προκείμενα χεῖρας ἴαλλον.
αὐτὰρ ἐπεὶ πόσιος καὶ ἐδητύος ἐξ ἔρον ἕντο,
δὴ τότε Τηλέμαχος προσεφώνεε Νέστορος υἱόν,
ἄγχι σχὼν κεφαλήν, ἵνα μὴ πευθοίαθ' οἱ ἄλλοι·

"Φράζεο, Νεστορίδη, τῷ ἐμῷ κεχαρισμένε θυμῷ,
χαλκοῦ τε στεροπὴν κὰδ δώματα ἠχήεντα
χρυσοῦ τ' ἠλέκτρου τε καὶ ἀργύρου ἠδ' ἐλέφαντος.

---

[1] Lines 57 and 58 are omitted in many MSS.
[2] Lines 62-4, rejected by Zenodotus, Aristophanes, and
Aristarchus, are bracketed by many editors.

And when the maids had bathed them and anointed them with oil, and had cast about them fleecy cloaks and tunics, they sat down on chairs beside Menelaus, son of Atreus. Then a handmaid brought water for the hands in a fair pitcher of gold, and poured it over a silver basin for them to wash, and beside them drew up a polished table. And the grave housewife brought and set before them bread, and therewith dainties in abundance, giving freely of her store. And a carver lifted up and placed before them platters of all manner of meats, and set by them golden goblets. Then fair-haired Menelaus greeted the two and said:

"Take of the food, and be glad, and then when you have supped, we will ask you who among men you are; for in you two the breed of your sires is not lost, but ye are of the breed of men that are sceptred kings, fostered of Zeus; for base churls could not beget such sons as you."

So saying he took in his hands roast meat and set it before them, even the fat ox-chine which they had set before himself as a mess of honour. So they put forth their hands to the good cheer lying ready before them. But when they had put from them the desire of food and drink, lo, then Telemachus spoke to the son of Nestor, holding his head close to him, that the others might not hear:

"Son of Nestor, dear to this heart of mine, mark the flashing of bronze throughout the echoing halls, and the flashing of gold, of electrum,[1] of silver, and

---

[1] Probably here the metal is meant, an alloy of gold and silver. In xv. 460 and xviii. 296 the word, in the plural, means "amber beads."

Ζηνός που τοιήδε γ' Ὀλυμπίου ἔνδοθεν αὐλή,
ὅσσα τάδ' ἄσπετα πολλά· σέβας μ' ἔχει εἰσορόωντα."
　Τοῦ δ' ἀγορεύοντος ξύνετο ξανθὸς Μενέλαος,
καί σφεας φωνήσας ἔπεα πτερόεντα προσηύδα·
　"Τέκνα φίλ', ἦ τοι Ζηνὶ βροτῶν οὐκ ἄν τις ἐρίζοι·
ἀθάνατοι γὰρ τοῦ γε δόμοι καὶ κτήματ' ἔασιν·
ἀνδρῶν δ' ἤ κέν τίς μοι ἐρίσσεται, ἠὲ καὶ οὐκί,
κτήμασιν. ἦ γὰρ πολλὰ παθὼν καὶ πόλλ' ἐπαληθεὶς
ἠγαγόμην ἐν νηυσὶ καὶ ὀγδοάτῳ ἔτει ἦλθον,
Κύπρον Φοινίκην τε καὶ Αἰγυπτίους ἐπαληθείς,
Αἰθίοπάς θ' ἱκόμην καὶ Σιδονίους καὶ Ἐρεμβοὺς
καὶ Λιβύην, ἵνα τ' ἄρνες ἄφαρ κεραοὶ τελέθουσι.
τρὶς γὰρ τίκτει μῆλα τελεσφόρον εἰς ἐνιαυτόν.
ἔνθα μὲν οὔτε ἄναξ ἐπιδευὴς οὔτε τι ποιμὴν
τυροῦ καὶ κρειῶν οὐδὲ γλυκεροῖο γάλακτος,
ἀλλ' αἰεὶ παρέχουσιν ἐπηετανὸν γάλα θῆσθαι.
ἧος ἐγὼ περὶ κεῖνα πολὺν βίοτον συναγείρων
ἠλώμην, τῆός μοι ἀδελφεὸν ἄλλος ἔπεφνεν
λάθρῃ, ἀνωιστί, δόλῳ οὐλομένης ἀλόχοιο·
ὡς οὔ τοι χαίρων τοῖσδε κτεάτεσσιν ἀνάσσω.
καὶ πατέρων τάδε μέλλετ' ἀκουέμεν, οἵ τινες ὑμῖν
εἰσίν, ἐπεὶ μάλα πολλὰ πάθον, καὶ ἀπώλεσα οἶκον
εὖ μάλα ναιετάοντα, κεχανδότα πολλὰ καὶ ἐσθλά.
ὧν ὄφελον τριτάτην περ ἔχων ἐν δώμασι μοῖραν
ναίειν, οἱ δ' ἄνδρες σόοι ἔμμεναι, οἳ τότ' ὄλοντο
Τροίῃ ἐν εὐρείῃ ἑκὰς Ἄργεος ἱπποβότοιο.

of ivory. Of such sort, methinks, is the court of Olympian Zeus within, such untold wealth is here; amazement holds me as I look."

Now as he spoke fair-haired Menelaus heard him, and he spoke and addressed them with winged words:

"Dear children, with Zeus verily no mortal man could vie, for everlasting are his halls and his possessions; but of men another might vie with me in wealth or haply might not. For of a truth after many woes and wide wanderings I brought my wealth home in my ships and came in the eighth year. Over Cyprus and Phoenicia I wandered, and Egypt, and I came to the Ethiopians and the Sidonians and the Erembi, and to Libya, where the lambs are horned from their birth.[1] For there the ewes bear their young thrice within the full course of the year; there neither master nor shepherd has any lack of cheese or of meat or of sweet milk, but the flocks ever yield milk to the milking the year through. While I wandered in those lands gathering much livelihood, meanwhile another slew my brother by stealth and at unawares, by the guile of his accursed wife. Thus, thou mayest see, I have no joy in being lord of this wealth; and you may well have heard of this from your fathers, whosoever they may be, for full much did I suffer, and let fall into ruin a stately house and one stored with much goodly treasure. Would that I dwelt in my halls with but a third part of this wealth, and that those men were safe who then perished in the broad land of Troy far from horse-pasturing Argos.

[1] So Aristotle understood the passage (*H.A.* viii. 28); Herodotus, on the contrary, took the meaning to be "begin at once to become horned" (iv. 29). Eustathius agrees with Herodotus.

ἀλλ' ἔμπης πάντας μὲν ὀδυρόμενος καὶ ἀχεύων   1
πολλάκις ἐν μεγάροισι καθήμενος ἡμετέροισιν
ἄλλοτε μέν τε γόῳ φρένα τέρπομαι, ἄλλοτε δ' αὖτε
παύομαι· αἰψηρὸς δὲ κόρος κρυεροῖο γόοιο.
τῶν πάντων οὐ τόσσον ὀδύρομαι, ἀχνύμενός περ,
ὡς ἑνός, ὅς τέ μοι ὕπνον ἀπεχθαίρει καὶ ἐδωδὴν   1
μνωομένῳ, ἐπεὶ οὔ τις Ἀχαιῶν τόσσ' ἐμόγησεν,
ὅσσ' Ὀδυσεὺς ἐμόγησε καὶ ἤρατο. τῷ δ' ἄρ' ἔμελλεν
αὐτῷ κήδε' ἔσεσθαι, ἐμοὶ δ' ἄχος αἰὲν ἄλαστον
κείνου, ὅπως δὴ δηρὸν ἀποίχεται, οὐδέ τι ἴδμεν,
ζώει ὅ γ' ἦ τέθνηκεν. ὀδύρονταί νύ που αὐτὸν   1
Λαέρτης θ' ὁ γέρων καὶ ἐχέφρων Πηνελόπεια
Τηλέμαχός θ', ὃν ἔλειπε νέον γεγαῶτ' ἐνὶ οἴκῳ."

Ὣς φάτο, τῷ δ' ἄρα πατρὸς ὑφ' ἵμερον ὦρσε γόοιο.
δάκρυ δ' ἀπὸ βλεφάρων χαμάδις βάλε πατρὸς ἀκούσ
χλαῖναν πορφυρέην ἄντ' ὀφθαλμοῖιν ἀνασχὼν   1
ἀμφοτέρῃσιν χερσί. νόησε δέ μιν Μενέλαος,
μερμήριξε δ' ἔπειτα κατὰ φρένα καὶ κατὰ θυμόν,
ἠέ μιν αὐτὸν πατρὸς ἐάσειε μνησθῆναι
ἦ πρῶτ' ἐξερέοιτο ἕκαστά τε πειρήσαιτο.

Ἧος ὁ ταῦθ' ὥρμαινε κατὰ φρένα καὶ κατὰ θυμόν,
ἐκ δ' Ἑλένη θαλάμοιο θυώδεος ὑψορόφοιο
ἤλυθεν Ἀρτέμιδι χρυσηλακάτῳ εἰκυῖα.
τῇ δ' ἄρ' ἅμ' Ἀδρήστη κλισίην εὔτυκτον ἔθηκεν,
Ἀλκίππη δὲ τάπητα φέρεν μαλακοῦ ἐρίοιο,
Φυλὼ δ' ἀργύρεον τάλαρον φέρε, τόν οἱ ἔδωκεν
Ἀλκάνδρη, Πολύβοιο δάμαρ, ὃς ἔναι' ἐνὶ Θήβῃς

And yet, though I often sit in my halls weeping
and sorrowing for them all—one moment indeed I
ease my heart with weeping, and then again I
cease, for men soon have surfeit of chill lament—
yet for them all I mourn not so much, despite my
grief, as for òne only, who makes me to loathe both
sleep and food, when I think of him; for no one
of the Achaeans toiled so much as Odysseus toiled
and endured.   But to himself, as it seems, his
portion was to be but woe, and for me there is
sorrow never to be forgotten for him, in that he
is gone so long, nor do we know aught whether
he be alive or dead.   Mourned is he, I ween, by the
old man Laertes, and by constant Penelope, and by
Telemachus, whom he left a new-born child in his
house.''

So he spoke, and in Telemachus he roused the
desire to weep for his father.   Tears from his eye-
lids he let fall upon the ground, when he heard his
father's name, and with both hands held up his
purple cloak before his eyes.   And Menelaus noted
him, and debated in mind and heart whether he
should leave him to speak of his father himself, or
whether he should first question him and prove him
in each thing.

While he pondered thus in mind and heart, forth
then from her fragrant high-roofed chamber came
Helen, like Artemis of the golden arrows;[1] and with
her came Adraste, and placed for her a chair, beau-
tifully wrought, and Alcippe brought a rug of soft
wool and Phylo a silver basket, which Alcandre had
given her, the wife of Polybus, who dwelt in Thebes

[1] The common meaning of ἠλακάτη is "distaff," but
Hesychius glosses χρυσηλάκατος by καλλίτοξος· ἠλακάτη γὰρ ὁ
τοξικὸς κάλαμος.

Αἰγυπτίης, ὅθι πλεῖστα δόμοις ἐν κτήματα κεῖται·
ὃς Μενελάῳ δῶκε δύ' ἀργυρέας ἀσαμίνθους,
δοιοὺς δὲ τρίποδας, δέκα δὲ χρυσοῖο τάλαντα.
χωρὶς δ' αὖθ' Ἑλένη ἄλοχος πόρε κάλλιμα δῶρα·   13
χρυσέην τ' ἠλακάτην τάλαρόν θ' ὑπόκυκλον ὄπασσεν
ἀργύρεον, χρυσῷ δ' ἐπὶ χείλεα κεκράαντο.
τόν ῥά οἱ ἀμφίπολος Φυλὼ παρέθηκε φέρουσα
νήματος ἀσκητοῖο βεβυσμένον· αὐτὰρ ἐπ' αὐτῷ
ἠλακάτη τετάννυστο ἰοδνεφὲς εἶρος ἔχουσα.   13
ἕζετο δ' ἐν κλισμῷ, ὑπὸ δὲ θρῆνυς ποσὶν ἦεν.
αὐτίκα δ' ἥ γ' ἐπέεσσι πόσιν ἐρέεινεν ἕκαστα·

    "'Ἴδμεν δή, Μενέλαε διοτρεφές, οἵ τινες οἵδε
ἀνδρῶν εὐχετόωνται ἱκανέμεν ἡμέτερον δῶ;
ψεύσομαι ἦ ἔτυμον ἐρέω; κέλεται δέ με θυμός.   14
οὐ γάρ πώ τινά φημι ἐοικότα ὧδε ἰδέσθαι
οὔτ' ἄνδρ' οὔτε γυναῖκα, σέβας μ' ἔχει εἰσορόωσαν,
ὡς ὅδ' Ὀδυσσῆος μεγαλήτορος υἷι ἔοικε,
Τηλεμάχῳ, τὸν ἔλειπε νέον γεγαῶτ' ἐνὶ οἴκῳ
κεῖνος ἀνήρ, ὅτ' ἐμεῖο κυνώπιδος εἵνεκ' Ἀχαιοὶ   14
ἤλθεθ' ὑπὸ Τροίην πόλεμον θρασὺν ὁρμαίνοντες."

    Τὴν δ' ἀπαμειβόμενος προσέφη ξανθὸς Μενέλαος·
" Οὕτω νῦν καὶ ἐγὼ νοέω, γύναι, ὡς σὺ ἐΐσκεις·
κείνου γὰρ τοιοίδε πόδες τοιαίδε τε χεῖρες
ὀφθαλμῶν τε βολαὶ κεφαλή τ' ἐφύπερθέ τε χαῖται.   15
καὶ νῦν ἦ τοι ἐγὼ μεμνημένος ἀμφ' Ὀδυσῆι
μυθεόμην, ὅσα κεῖνος ὀϊζύσας ἐμόγησεν
ἀμφ' ἐμοί, αὐτὰρ ὁ πικρὸν[1] ὑπ' ὀφρύσι δάκρυον εἶβε,
χλαῖναν πορφυρέην ἄντ' ὀφθαλμοῖιν ἀνασχών."

***

[1] πικρὸν : πυκνὸν.

of Egypt, where greatest store of wealth is laid up in men's houses. He gave to Menelaus two silver baths and two tripods and ten talents of gold. And besides these, his wife gave to Helen also beautiful gifts,—a golden distaff and a basket with wheels beneath did she give, a basket of silver, and with gold were the rims thereof gilded.[1] This then the handmaid, Phylo, brought and placed beside her, filled with finely-spun yarn, and across it was laid the distaff laden with violet-dark wool. So Helen sat down upon the chair, and below was a footstool for the feet; and at once she questioned her husband on each matter, and said:

"Do we know, Menelaus, fostered of Zeus, who these men declare themselves to be who have come to our house? Shall I disguise my thought, or speak the truth? Nay, my heart bids me speak. For never yet, I declare, saw I one so like another, whether man or woman—amazement holds me, as I look—as this man is like the son of great-hearted Odysseus, even Telemachus, whom that warrior left a new-born child in his house, when for the sake of shameless me ye Achaeans came up under the walls of Troy, pondering in your hearts fierce war."

Then fair-haired Menelaus answered her: "Even so do I myself now note it, wife, as thou markest the likeness. Such were his feet, such his hands, and the glances of his eyes, and his head and hair above. And verily but now, as I made mention of Odysseus and was telling of all the woe and toil he endured for my sake, this youth let fall a bitter tear from beneath his brows, holding up his purple cloak before his eyes."

[1] Others render, "were finished."

Τὸν δ' αὖ Νεστορίδης Πεισίστρατος ἀντίον ηὔδα· 15
"'Ατρεΐδη Μενέλαε διοτρεφές, ὄρχαμε λαῶν,
κείνου μέν τοι ὅδ' υἱὸς ἐτήτυμον, ὡς ἀγορεύεις·
ἀλλὰ σαόφρων ἐστί, νεμεσσᾶται δ' ἐνὶ θυμῷ
ὧδ' ἐλθὼν τὸ πρῶτον ἐπεσβολίας ἀναφαίνειν
ἄντα σέθεν, τοῦ νῶϊ θεοῦ ὡς τερπόμεθ' αὐδῇ.   16
αὐτὰρ ἐμὲ προέηκε Γερήνιος ἱππότα Νέστωρ
τῷ ἅμα πομπὸν ἕπεσθαι· ἐέλδετο γάρ σε ἰδέσθαι,
ὄφρα οἱ ἤ τι ἔπος ὑποθήσεαι ἠέ τι ἔργον.
πολλὰ γὰρ ἄλγε' ἔχει πατρὸς πάϊς οἰχομένοιο
ἐν μεγάροις, ᾧ μὴ ἄλλοι ἀοσσητῆρες ἔωσιν,   16
ὡς νῦν Τηλεμάχῳ ὁ μὲν οἴχεται, οὐδέ οἱ ἄλλοι
εἴσ' οἵ κεν κατὰ δῆμον ἀλάλκοιεν κακότητα."

Τὸν δ' ἀπαμειβόμενος προσέφη ξανθὸς Μενέλαος·
"Ὢ πόποι, ἦ μάλα δὴ φίλου ἀνέρος υἱὸς ἐμὸν δῶ
ἵκεθ', ὃς εἵνεκ' ἐμεῖο πολέας ἐμόγησεν ἀέθλους·   17
καί μιν ἔφην ἐλθόντα φιλησέμεν ἔξοχον ἄλλων
'Αργείων, εἰ νῶϊν ὑπεὶρ ἅλα νόστον ἔδωκε
νηυσὶ θοῇσι γενέσθαι 'Ολύμπιος εὐρύοπα Ζεύς.
καί κέ οἱ Ἄργεϊ νάσσα πόλιν καὶ δώματ' ἔτευξα,
ἐξ Ἰθάκης ἀγαγὼν σὺν κτήμασι καὶ τέκεϊ ᾧ   17
καὶ πᾶσιν λαοῖσι, μίαν πόλιν ἐξαλαπάξας,
αἳ περιναιετάουσιν, ἀνάσσονται δ' ἐμοὶ αὐτῷ.
καί κε θάμ' ἐνθάδ' ἐόντες ἐμισγόμεθ'· οὐδέ κεν ἡμέας
ἄλλο διέκρινεν φιλέοντέ τε τερπομένω τε,
πρίν γ' ὅτε δὴ θανάτοιο μέλαν νέφος ἀμφεκάλυψεν.   18
ἀλλὰ τὰ μέν που μέλλεν ἀγάσσεσθαι θεὸς αὐτός,
ὃς κεῖνον δύστηνον ἀνόστιμον οἶον ἔθηκεν."

Then Peisistratus, son of Nestor, answered him:
"Menelaus, son of Atreus, fostered of Zeus, leader
of hosts, his son indeed this youth is, as thou sayest.
But he is of prudent mind and feels shame at heart
thus on his first coming to make a show of forward
words in the presence of thee, in whose voice we
both take delight as in a god's. But the horseman,
Nestor of Gerenia, sent me forth to go with him as
his guide, for he was eager to see thee, that thou
mightest put in his heart some word or some deed.
For many sorrows has a son in his halls when his
father is gone, when there are none other to be his
helpers, even as it is now with Telemachus; his
father is gone, and there are no others among the
people who might ward off ruin."

Then fair-haired Menelaus answered him and
said: "Lo now, verily is there come to my house
the son of a man well-beloved, who for my sake
endured many toils. And I thought that if he came
back I should give him welcome beyond all the
other Argives, if Olympian Zeus, whose voice is
borne afar, had granted to us two a return in our
swift ships over the sea. And in Argos I would
have given him a city to dwell in, and would have
built him a house, when I had brought him from
Ithaca with his goods and his son and all his people,
driving out the dwellers of some one city among
those that lie round about and obey me myself as
their lord. Then, living here, should we ofttimes
have met together, nor would aught have parted us,
loving and joying in one another, until the black
cloud of death enfolded us. Howbeit of this, me-
thinks, the god himself must have been jealous, who
to that hapless man alone vouchsafed no return."

Ὣς φάτο, τοῖσι δὲ πᾶσιν ὑφ' ἵμερον ὦρσε γόοιο.
κλαῖε μὲν Ἀργείη Ἑλένη, Διὸς ἐκγεγαυῖα,
κλαῖε δὲ Τηλέμαχός τε καὶ Ἀτρεΐδης Μενέλαος,   18
οὐδ' ἄρα Νέστορος υἱὸς ἀδακρύτω ἔχεν ὄσσε·
μνήσατο γὰρ κατὰ θυμὸν ἀμύμονος Ἀντιλόχοιο,
τόν ῥ' Ἠοῦς ἔκτεινε φαεινῆς ἀγλαὸς υἱός·
τοῦ ὅ γ' ἐπιμνησθεὶς ἔπεα πτερόεντ' ἀγόρευεν·

"Ἀτρεΐδη, περὶ μέν σε βροτῶν πεπνυμένον εἶναι 19
Νέστωρ φάσχ' ὁ γέρων, ὅτ' ἐπιμνησαίμεθα σεῖο
οἷσιν ἐνὶ μεγάροισι, καὶ ἀλλήλους ἐρέοιμεν.
καὶ νῦν, εἴ τί που ἔστι, πίθοιό μοι· οὐ γὰρ ἐγώ γε
τέρπομ' ὀδυρόμενος μεταδόρπιος, ἀλλὰ καὶ ἠὼς
ἔσσεται ἠριγένεια· νεμεσσῶμαί γε μὲν οὐδὲν 19
κλαίειν ὅς κε θάνῃσι βροτῶν καὶ πότμον ἐπίσπῃ.
τοῦτό νυ καὶ γέρας οἶον ὀιζυροῖσι βροτοῖσιν,
κείρασθαί τε κόμην βαλέειν τ' ἀπὸ δάκρυ παρειῶν.
καὶ γὰρ ἐμὸς τέθνηκεν ἀδελφεός, οὔ τι κάκιστος
Ἀργείων· μέλλεις δὲ σὺ ἴδμεναι· οὐ γὰρ ἐγώ γε 20
ἤντησ' οὐδὲ ἴδον· περὶ δ' ἄλλων φασὶ γενέσθαι
Ἀντίλοχον, πέρι μὲν θείειν ταχὺν ἠδὲ μαχητήν."

Τὸν δ' ἀπαμειβόμενος προσέφη ξανθὸς Μενέλαος·
"Ὦ φίλ', ἐπεὶ τόσα εἶπες, ὅσ' ἂν πεπνυμένος ἀνὴρ
εἴποι καὶ ῥέξειε, καὶ ὃς προγενέστερος εἴη· 20
τοίου γὰρ καὶ πατρός, ὃ καὶ πεπνυμένα βάζεις,
ῥεῖα δ' ἀρίγνωτος γόνος ἀνέρος ᾧ τε Κρονίων
ὄλβον ἐπικλώσῃ γαμέοντί τε γεινομένῳ τε,
ὡς νῦν Νέστορι δῶκε διαμπερὲς ἤματα πάντα

So he spoke, and in them all aroused the desire of
lament. Argive Helen wept, the daughter of Zeus,
Telemachus wept, and Menelaus, son of Atreus, nor
could the son of Nestor keep his eyes tearless. For
he thought in his heart of peerless Antilochus, whom
the glorious son of the bright Dawn [1] had slain.
Thinking of him, he spoke winged words :

" Son of Atreus, old Nestor used ever to say that
thou wast wise above all men, whenever we made
mention of thee in his halls and questioned one
another. And now, if it may in any wise be,
hearken to me, for I take no joy in weeping at
supper time,[2]—and moreover early dawn will soon
be here.[3] I count it indeed no blame to weep for
any mortal who has died and met his fate. Yea,
this is the only due we pay to miserable mortals, to
cut the hair and let a tear fall from the cheeks.
For a brother of mine, too, is dead, nowise the
meanest of the Argives, and thou mayest well have
known him. As for me, I never met him nor saw him ;
but men say that Antilochus was above all others
pre-eminent in speed of foot and as a warrior."

Then fair-haired Menelaus answered him and
said : " My friend, truly thou hast said all that a
wise man might say or do, even one that was older
than thou ; for from such a father art thou sprung,
wherefore thou dost even speak wisely. Easily
known is the seed of that man for whom the son of
Cronos spins the thread of good fortune at marriage
and at birth, even as now he has granted to Nestor
throughout all his days continually that he should

---

[1] *i.e.* Memnon, leader of the Ethiopians.
[2] Others render, "after supper" ; but see 213.
[3] Possibly, " shall serve for that" (Merry), with which *cf.*
214 ; but see xv. 50.

αὐτὸν μὲν λιπαρῶς γηρασκέμεν ἐν μεγάροισιν,   2
υἱέας αὖ πινυτούς τε καὶ ἔγχεσιν εἶναι ἀρίστους.
ἡμεῖς δὲ κλαυθμὸν μὲν ἐάσομεν, ὃς πρὶν ἐτύχθη,
δόρπου δ' ἐξαῦτις μνησώμεθα, χερσὶ δ' ἐφ' ὕδωρ
χευάντων.   μῦθοι δὲ καὶ ἠῶθέν περ ἔσονται
Τηλεμάχῳ καὶ ἐμοὶ διαειπέμεν ἀλλήλοισιν."   2
    Ὣς ἔφατ', Ἀσφαλίων δ' ἄρ' ὕδωρ ἐπὶ χεῖρας ἔχευεν
ὀτρηρὸς θεράπων Μενελάου κυδαλίμοιο.
οἱ δ' ἐπ' ὀνείαθ' ἑτοῖμα προκείμενα χεῖρας ἴαλλον.
    Ἔνθ' αὖτ' ἄλλ' ἐνόησ' Ἑλένη Διὸς ἐκγεγαυῖα·
αὐτίκ' ἄρ' εἰς οἶνον βάλε φάρμακον, ἔνθεν ἔπινον,   2
νηπενθές τ' ἄχολόν τε, κακῶν ἐπίληθον ἁπάντων.
ὃς τὸ καταβρόξειεν, ἐπὴν κρητῆρι μιγείη,
οὔ κεν ἐφημέριός γε βάλοι κατὰ δάκρυ παρειῶν,
οὐδ' εἴ οἱ κατατεθναίη μήτηρ τε πατήρ τε,
οὐδ' εἴ οἱ προπάροιθεν ἀδελφεὸν ἢ φίλον υἱὸν   2
χαλκῷ δηιόωεν, ὁ δ' ὀφθαλμοῖσιν ὁρῶτο.
τοῖα Διὸς θυγάτηρ ἔχε φάρμακα μητιόεντα,
ἐσθλά, τά οἱ Πολύδαμνα πόρεν, Θῶνος παράκοιτις
Αἰγυπτίη, τῇ πλεῖστα φέρει ζείδωρος ἄρουρα
φάρμακα, πολλὰ μὲν ἐσθλὰ μεμιγμένα πολλὰ δὲ
        λυγρά·   2
ἰητρὸς δὲ ἕκαστος ἐπιστάμενος περὶ πάντων
ἀνθρώπων· ἦ γὰρ Παιήονός εἰσι γενέθλης.
αὐτὰρ ἐπεί ῥ' ἐνέηκε κέλευσέ τε οἰνοχοῆσαι,
ἐξαῦτις μύθοισιν ἀμειβομένη προσέειπεν·
    "Ἀτρεΐδη Μενέλαε διοτρεφὲς ἠδὲ καὶ οἵδε   2
ἀνδρῶν ἐσθλῶν παῖδες· ἀτὰρ θεὸς ἄλλοτε ἄλλῳ

himself reach a sleek old age in his halls, and that his sons in their turn should be wise and most valiant with the spear. But we will cease the weeping which but now was made, and let us once more think of our supper, and let them pour water over our hands. Tales there will be in the morning also for Telemachus and me to tell to one another to the full."

So he spoke, and Asphalion poured water over their hands, the busy squire of glorious Menelaus. And they put forth their hands to the good cheer lying ready before them.

Then Helen, daughter of Zeus, took other counsel. Straightway she cast into the wine of which they were drinking a drug to quiet all pain and strife, and bring forgetfulness of every ill. Whoso should drink this down, when it is mingled in the bowl, would not in the course of that day let a tear fall down over his cheeks, no, not though his mother and father should lie there dead, or though before his face men should slay with the sword his brother or dear son, and his own eyes beheld it. Such cunning drugs had the daughter of Zeus, drugs of healing, which Polydamna, the wife of Thon, had given her, a woman of Egypt, for there the earth, the giver of grain, bears greatest store of drugs, many that are healing when mixed, and many that are baneful; there every man is a physician, wise above human kind; for they are of the race of Paeëon. Now when she had cast in the drug, and had bidden pour forth the wine, again she made answer, and said :

"Menelaus, son of Atreus, fostered of Zeus, and ye that are here, sons of noble men—though now to

HOMER

Ζεὺς ἀγαθόν τε κακόν τε διδοῖ· δύναται γὰρ ἅπαντα
ἦ τοι νῦν δαίνυσθε καθήμενοι ἐν μεγάροισι
καὶ μύθοις τέρπεσθε· ἐοικότα γὰρ καταλέξω.
πάντα μὲν οὐκ ἂν ἐγὼ μυθήσομαι οὐδ' ὀνομήνω,
ὅσσοι Ὀδυσσῆος ταλασίφρονός εἰσιν ἄεθλοι·
ἀλλ' οἷον τόδ' ἔρεξε καὶ ἔτλη καρτερὸς ἀνὴρ
δήμῳ ἔνι Τρώων, ὅθι πάσχετε πήματ' Ἀχαιοί.
αὐτόν μιν πληγῇσιν ἀεικελίῃσι δαμάσσας,
σπεῖρα κάκ' ἀμφ' ὤμοισι βαλών, οἰκῆι ἐοικώς,
ἀνδρῶν δυσμενέων κατέδυ πόλιν εὐρυάγυιαν·
ἄλλῳ δ' αὐτὸν φωτὶ κατακρύπτων ἤισκε,
δέκτῃ, ὃς οὐδὲν τοῖος ἔην ἐπὶ νηυσὶν Ἀχαιῶν.
τῷ ἴκελος κατέδυ Τρώων πόλιν, οἱ δ' ἀβάκησαν
πάντες· ἐγὼ δέ μιν οἴη ἀνέγνων τοῖον ἐόντα,
καί μιν ἀνηρώτων· ὁ δὲ κερδοσύνῃ ἀλέεινεν.
ἀλλ' ὅτε δή μιν ἐγὼ λόεον καὶ χρῖον ἐλαίῳ,
ἀμφὶ δὲ εἵματα ἕσσα καὶ ὤμοσα καρτερὸν ὅρκον
μὴ μὲν πρὶν Ὀδυσῆα μετὰ Τρώεσσ' ἀναφῆναι,
πρίν γε τὸν ἐς νῆάς τε θοὰς κλισίας τ' ἀφικέσθαι,
καὶ τότε δή μοι πάντα νόον κατέλεξεν Ἀχαιῶν.
πολλοὺς δὲ Τρώων κτείνας ταναήκεϊ χαλκῷ
ἦλθε μετ' Ἀργείους, κατὰ δὲ φρόνιν ἤγαγε πολλήν.
ἔνθ' ἄλλαι Τρωαὶ λίγ' ἐκώκυον· αὐτὰρ ἐμὸν κῆρ
χαῖρ', ἐπεὶ ἤδη μοι κραδίη τέτραπτο νέεσθαι
ἂψ οἰκόνδ', ἄτην δὲ μετέστενον, ἣν Ἀφροδίτη
δῶχ', ὅτε μ' ἤγαγε κεῖσε φίλης ἀπὸ πατρίδος αἴης,

one and now to another Zeus gives good and ill, for
he can do all things,—now verily sit ye in the halls
and feast, and take ye joy in telling tales, for I will
tell what fitteth the time. All things I cannot tell
or recount, even all the labours of Odysseus of the
steadfast heart; but what a thing was this which
that mighty man wrought and endured in the land
of the Trojans, where you Achaeans suffered woes!
Marring his own body with cruel blows, and flinging
a wretched garment about his shoulders, in the
fashion of a slave he entered the broad-wayed city
of the foe, and he hid himself under the likeness of
another, a beggar, he who was in no wise such an
one at the ships of the Achaeans. In this likeness
he entered the city of the Trojans, and all of them
were but as babes.[1] I alone recognised him in this
disguise, and questioned him, but he in his cunning
sought to avoid me. Howbeit when I was bathing
him and anointing him with oil, and had put on him
raiment, and sworn a mighty oath not to make him
known among the Trojans as Odysseus before that
he reached the swift ships and the huts, then at
length he told me all the purpose of the Achaeans.
And when he had slain many of the Trojans with
the long sword, he returned to the company of
the Argives and brought back plentiful tidings.
Then the other Trojan women wailed aloud, but my
soul was glad, for already my heart was turned to
go back to my home, and I groaned for the blind-
ness that Aphrodite gave me, when she led me
thither from my dear native land, forsaking my

---

[1] The rare word ἀβάκησαν seems literally to mean " could
say naught "; cf. νηπιάζω.

παῖδά τ' ἐμὴν νοσφισσαμένην θάλαμόν τε πόσιν τε
οὔ τευ δευόμενον, οὔτ' ἂρ φρένας οὔτε τι εἶδος."
   Τὴν δ' ἀπαμειβόμενος προσέφη ξανθὸς Μενέλαος· 2[?]
"Ναὶ δὴ ταῦτά γε πάντα, γύναι, κατὰ μοῖραν ἔειπες.
ἤδη μὲν πολέων ἐδάην βουλήν τε νόον τε
ἀνδρῶν ἡρώων, πολλὴν δ' ἐπελήλυθα γαῖαν·
ἀλλ' οὔ πω τοιοῦτον ἐγὼν ἴδον ὀφθαλμοῖσιν,
οἷον Ὀδυσσῆος ταλασίφρονος ἔσκε φίλον κῆρ.   2[?]
οἷον καὶ τόδ' ἔρεξε καὶ ἔτλη καρτερὸς ἀνὴρ
ἵππῳ ἔνι ξεστῷ, ἵν' ἐνήμεθα πάντες ἄριστοι
Ἀργείων Τρώεσσι φόνον καὶ κῆρα φέροντες.
ἦλθες ἔπειτα σὺ κεῖσε· κελευσέμεναι δέ σ' ἔμελλε
δαίμων, ὃς Τρώεσσιν ἐβούλετο κῦδος ὀρέξαι·   2[?]
καί τοι Δηΐφοβος θεοείκελος ἕσπετ' ἰούσῃ.
τρὶς δὲ περίστειξας κοῖλον λόχον ἀμφαφόωσα,
ἐκ δ' ὀνομακλήδην Δαναῶν ὀνόμαζες ἀρίστους,
πάντων Ἀργείων φωνὴν ἴσκουσ' ἀλόχοισιν.
αὐτὰρ ἐγὼ καὶ Τυδεΐδης καὶ δῖος Ὀδυσσεὺς   2[?]
ἥμενοι ἐν μέσσοισιν ἀκούσαμεν ὡς ἐβόησας.
νῶϊ μὲν ἀμφοτέρω μενεήναμεν ὁρμηθέντε
ἢ ἐξελθέμεναι, ἢ ἔνδοθεν αἶψ' ὑπακοῦσαι·
ἀλλ' Ὀδυσεὺς κατέρυκε καὶ ἔσχεθεν ἱεμένω περ.
ἔνθ' ἄλλοι μὲν πάντες ἀκὴν ἔσαν υἷες Ἀχαιῶν,   2[?]
Ἄντικλος δὲ σέ γ' οἶος ἀμείψασθαι ἐπέεσσιν
ἤθελεν.   ἀλλ' Ὀδυσεὺς ἐπὶ μάστακα χερσὶ πίεζεν
νωλεμέως κρατερῇσι, σάωσε δὲ πάντας Ἀχαιούς·
τόφρα δ' ἔχ', ὄφρα σε νόσφιν ἀπήγαγε Παλλὰς
   Ἀθήνη.''
   Τὸν δ' αὖ Τηλέμαχος πεπνυμένος ἀντίον ηὔδα·   2[?]
"Ἀτρεΐδη Μενέλαε διοτρεφές, ὄρχαμε λαῶν,
ἄλγιον· οὐ γάρ οἵ τι τάδ' ἤρκεσε λυγρὸν ὄλεθρον,

child and my bridal chamber, and my husband, a man who lacked nothing, whether in wisdom or in comeliness."

Then fair-haired Menelaus answered her and said: "Aye verily, all this, wife, hast thou spoken aright. Ere now have I come to know the counsel and the mind of many warriors, and have travelled over the wide earth, but never yet have mine eyes beheld such an one as was Odysseus of the steadfast heart. What a thing was this, too, which that mighty man wrought and endured in the carven horse, wherein all we chiefs of the Argives were sitting, bearing to the Trojans death and fate! Then thou camest thither, and it must be that thou wast bidden by some god, who wished to grant glory to the Trojans, and godlike Deiphobus followed thee on thy way. Thrice didst thou go about the hollow ambush, trying it with thy touch, and thou didst name aloud the chieftains of the Danaans by their names, likening thy voice to the voices of the wives of all the Argives. Now I and the son of Tydeus and goodly Odysseus sat there in the midst and heard how thou didst call, and we two were eager to rise up and come forth, or else to answer straightway from within, but Odysseus held us back and stayed us, despite our eagerness. Then all the other sons of the Achaeans held their peace, but Anticlus alone was fain to speak and answer thee; but Odysseus firmly closed his mouth with strong hands, and saved all the Achaeans, and held him thus until Pallas Athene led thee away."

Then wise Telemachus answered him: "Menelaus, son of Atreus, fostered of Zeus, leader of hosts, all the more grievous is it; for in no wise did this ward

οὐδ' εἴ οἱ κραδίη γε σιδηρέη ἔνδοθεν ἦεν.
ἀλλ' ἄγετ' εἰς εὐνὴν τράπεθ' ἡμέας, ὄφρα καὶ ἤδη
ὕπνῳ ὕπο γλυκερῷ ταρπώμεθα κοιμηθέντες."   29

Ὣς ἔφατ', Ἀργείη δ' Ἑλένη δμῳῇσι κέλευσεν
δέμνι' ὑπ' αἰθούσῃ θέμεναι καὶ ῥήγεα καλὰ
πορφύρε' ἐμβαλέειν στορέσαι τ' ἐφύπερθε τάπητας,
χλαίνας τ' ἐνθέμεναι οὔλας καθύπερθεν ἕσασθαι.
αἱ δ' ἴσαν ἐκ μεγάροιο δάος μετὰ χερσὶν ἔχουσαι,   30
δέμνια δὲ στόρεσαν· ἐκ δὲ ξείνους ἄγε κῆρυξ.
οἱ μὲν ἄρ' ἐν προδόμῳ δόμου αὐτόθι κοιμήσαντο,
Τηλέμαχός θ' ἥρως καὶ Νέστορος ἀγλαὸς υἱός·
Ἀτρεΐδης δὲ καθεῦδε μυχῷ δόμου ὑψηλοῖο,
πὰρ δ' Ἑλένη τανύπεπλος ἐλέξατο, δῖα γυναικῶν.   30

Ἦμος δ' ἠριγένεια φάνη ῥοδοδάκτυλος Ἠώς,
ὤρνυτ' ἄρ' ἐξ εὐνῆφι βοὴν ἀγαθὸς Μενέλαος
εἵματα ἑσσάμενος, περὶ δὲ ξίφος ὀξὺ θέτ' ὤμῳ,
ποσσὶ δ' ὑπὸ λιπαροῖσιν ἐδήσατο καλὰ πέδιλα,
βῆ δ' ἴμεν ἐκ θαλάμοιο θεῷ ἐναλίγκιος ἄντην,   31
Τηλεμάχῳ δὲ παρῖζεν, ἔπος τ' ἔφατ' ἔκ τ' ὀνόμαζεν·

"Τίπτε δέ σε χρειὼ δεῦρ' ἤγαγε, Τηλέμαχ' ἥρως,
ἐς Λακεδαίμονα δῖαν, ἐπ' εὐρέα νῶτα θαλάσσης;
δήμιον ἦ ἴδιον; τόδε μοι νημερτὲς ἐνίσπες."

Τὸν δ' αὖ Τηλέμαχος πεπνυμένος ἀντίον ηὔδα·   31
"Ἀτρεΐδη Μενέλαε διοτρεφές, ὄρχαμε λαῶν,
ἤλυθον, εἴ τινά μοι κληηδόνα πατρὸς ἐνίσποις.
ἐσθίεταί μοι οἶκος, ὄλωλε δὲ πίονα ἔργα,
δυσμενέων δ' ἀνδρῶν πλεῖος δόμος, οἵ τέ μοι αἰεὶ

off from him woeful destruction, nay, not though the heart within him had been of iron. But come, send us to bed, that lulled now by sweet sleep we may rest and take our joy."

Thus he spoke, and Argive Helen bade her hand-maids place bedsteads beneath the portico, and to lay on them fair purple blankets, and to spread thereover coverlets, and on these to put fleecy cloaks for clothing. But the maids went forth from the hall with torches in their hands and strewed the couch, and a herald led forth the guests. So they slept there in the fore-hall of the palace, the prince Telemachus and the glorious son of Nestor; but the son of Atreus slept in the inmost chamber of the lofty house, and beside him lay long-robed Helen, peerless among women.

So soon as early Dawn appeared, the rosy-fingered, up from his bed arose Menelaus, good at the war-cry, and put on his clothing. About his shoulders he slung his sharp sword, and beneath his shining feet bound his fair sandals, and went forth from his chamber like unto a god to look upon. Then he sat down beside Telemachus, and spoke, and addressed him:

"What need has brought thee hither, prince Telemachus, to goodly Lacedaemon over the broad back of the sea? Is it a public matter, or thine own? Tell me the truth of this."

Then wise Telemachus answered him: "Menelaus, son of Atreus, fostered of Zeus, leader of hosts, I came if haply thou mightest tell me some tidings of my father. My home is being devoured and my rich lands are ruined; with men that are foes my house is filled, who are ever slaying my thronging

μῆλ' ἀδινὰ σφάζουσι καὶ εἰλίποδας ἕλικας βοῦς,　3
μητρὸς ἐμῆς μνηστῆρες ὑπέρβιον ὕβριν ἔχοντες.
τούνεκα νῦν τὰ σὰ γούναθ' ἱκάνομαι, αἴ κ' ἐθέλησθα
κείνου λυγρὸν ὄλεθρον ἐνισπεῖν, εἴ που ὄπωπας
ὀφθαλμοῖσι τεοῖσιν ἢ ἄλλου μῦθον ἄκουσας
πλαζομένου· περὶ γάρ μιν ὀιζυρὸν τέκε μήτηρ.　3
μηδέ τί μ' αἰδόμενος μειλίσσεο μηδ' ἐλεαίρων,
ἀλλ' εὖ μοι κατάλεξον ὅπως ἤντησας ὀπωπῆς.
λίσσομαι, εἴ ποτέ τοί τι πατὴρ ἐμός, ἐσθλὸς Ὀδυσσεὺ
ἢ ἔπος ἠέ τι ἔργον ὑποστὰς ἐξετέλεσσε
δήμῳ ἔνι Τρώων, ὅθι πάσχετε πήματ' Ἀχαιοί,　3
τῶν νῦν μοι μνῆσαι, καί μοι νημερτὲς ἐνίσπες."

　　Τὸν δὲ μέγ' ὀχθήσας προσέφη ξανθὸς Μενέλαος·
"Ὦ πόποι, ἦ μάλα δὴ κρατερόφρονος ἀνδρὸς ἐν εὐνῇ
ἤθελον εὐνηθῆναι ἀνάλκιδες αὐτοὶ ἐόντες.
ὡς δ' ὁπότ' ἐν ξυλόχῳ ἔλαφος κρατεροῖο λέοντος　3
νεβροὺς κοιμήσασα νεηγενέας γαλαθηνοὺς
κνημοὺς ἐξερέῃσι καὶ ἄγκεα ποιήεντα
βοσκομένη, ὁ δ' ἔπειτα ἑὴν εἰσήλυθεν εὐνήν,
ἀμφοτέροισι δὲ τοῖσιν ἀεικέα πότμον ἐφῆκεν,
ὣς Ὀδυσεὺς κείνοισιν ἀεικέα πότμον ἐφήσει.　3
αἲ γάρ, Ζεῦ τε πάτερ καὶ Ἀθηναίη καὶ Ἄπολλον,
τοῖος ἐών, οἷός ποτ' ἐυκτιμένῃ ἐνὶ Λέσβῳ
ἐξ ἔριδος Φιλομηλεΐδῃ ἐπάλαισεν ἀναστάς,
κὰδ δ' ἔβαλε κρατερῶς, κεχάροντο δὲ πάντες Ἀχαιοί,
τοῖος ἐὼν μνηστῆρσιν ὁμιλήσειεν Ὀδυσσεύς·　3

sheep and my sleek kine of shambling gait, even the wooers of my mother, overweening in their insolence. Therefore am I now come to thy knees, if perchance thou wilt be willing to tell me of his woeful death, whether thou sawest it haply with thine own eyes, or didst hear from some other the story of his wanderings; for beyond all men did his mother bear him to sorrow. And do thou no wise out of ruth or pity for me speak soothing words, but tell me truly how thou didst come to behold him. I beseech thee, if ever my father, noble Odysseus, promised aught to thee of word or deed and fulfilled it in the land of the Trojans, where you Achaeans suffered woes, be mindful of it now, I pray thee, and tell me the truth."

Then, stirred to sore displeasure, fair-haired Menelaus spoke to him: "Out upon them, for verily in the bed of a man of valiant heart were they fain to lie, who are themselves cravens. Even as when in the thicket-lair of a mighty lion a hind has laid to sleep her new-born suckling fawns, and roams over the mountain slopes and grassy vales seeking pasture, and then the lion comes to his lair and upon the two [1] lets loose a cruel doom, so will Odysseus let loose a cruel doom upon these men. I would, O father Zeus and Athene and Apollo, that in such strength as when once in fair-stablished Lesbos he rose up and wrestled a match with Philomeleides and threw him mightily, and all the Achaeans rejoiced, even in such strength Odysseus might come among the wooers; then

---

[1] The Greek seems to denote a pair of fawns, the slaying taking place in the absence of the hind; *cf. Iliad*, xi. 113 ff. Others assume that the dual means "both hind and fawns."

πάντες κ' ὠκύμοροί τε γενοίατο πικρόγαμοί τε.
ταῦτα δ' ἅ μ' εἰρωτᾷς καὶ λίσσεαι, οὐκ ἂν ἐγώ γε
ἄλλα παρὲξ εἴποιμι παρακλιδόν, οὐδ' ἀπατήσω,
ἀλλὰ τὰ μέν μοι ἔειπε γέρων ἅλιος νημερτής,
τῶν οὐδέν τοι ἐγὼ κρύψω ἔπος οὐδ' ἐπικεύσω.   3[

  " Αἰγύπτῳ μ' ἔτι δεῦρο θεοὶ μεμαῶτα νέεσθαι
ἔσχον, ἐπεὶ οὔ σφιν ἔρεξα τεληέσσας ἑκατόμβας.
οἱ δ' αἰεὶ βούλοντο θεοὶ μεμνῆσθαι ἐφετμέων.[1]
νῆσος ἔπειτά τις ἔστι πολυκλύστῳ ἐνὶ πόντῳ
Αἰγύπτου προπάροιθε, Φάρον δέ ἑ κικλήσκουσι,   35
τόσσον ἄνευθ' ὅσσον τε πανημερίη γλαφυρὴ νηῦς
ἤνυσεν, ᾗ λιγὺς οὖρος ἐπιπνείῃσιν ὄπισθεν·
ἐν δὲ λιμὴν ἐύορμος, ὅθεν τ' ἀπὸ νῆας ἐίσας
ἐς πόντον βάλλουσιν, ἀφυσσάμενοι μέλαν ὕδωρ.
ἔνθα μ' ἐείκοσιν ἤματ' ἔχον θεοί, οὐδέ ποτ' οὖροι   36
πνείοντες φαίνονθ' ἁλιαέες, οἵ ῥά τε νηῶν
πομπῆες γίγνονται ἐπ' εὐρέα νῶτα θαλάσσης.
καί νύ κεν ἤια πάντα κατέφθιτο καὶ μένε' ἀνδρῶν,
εἰ μή τίς με θεῶν ὀλοφύρατο καί μ' ἐσάωσε,[2]
Πρωτέος ἰφθίμου θυγάτηρ ἁλίοιο γέροντος,   36[
Εἰδοθέη· τῇ γάρ ῥα μάλιστά γε θυμὸν ὄρινα.
ἥ μ' οἴῳ ἔρροντι συνήντετο νόσφιν ἑταίρων·
αἰεὶ γὰρ περὶ νῆσον ἀλώμενοι ἰχθυάασκον
γναμπτοῖς ἀγκίστροισιν, ἔτειρε δὲ γαστέρα λιμός.
ἡ δέ μευ ἄγχι στᾶσα ἔπος φάτο φώνησέν τε·   37[

---

[1] Line 353, rejected by Zenodotus, is bracketed by many
editors.   [2] μ' ἐσάωσε : μ' ἐλέησε.

---

[1] Or possibly " the river Aegyptus " (cf. line 477).   Homer
has no other name for the Nile.

should they all find swift destruction and bitterness in their wooing. But in this matter of which thou dost ask and beseech me, verily I will not swerve aside to speak of other things, nor will I deceive thee; but of all that the unerring old man of the sea told me not one thing will I hide from thee or conceal.

"In Egypt,[1] eager though I was to journey hither, the gods still held me back, because I offered not to them hecatombs that bring fulfilment, and the gods ever wished that men should be mindful of their commands. Now there is an island in the surging sea in front of Egypt, and men call it Pharos, distant as far as a hollow ship runs in a whole day when the shrill wind blows fair behind her. Therein is a harbour with good anchorage, whence men launch the shapely ships into the sea, when they have drawn supplies of black[2] water. There for twenty days the gods kept me, nor ever did the winds that blow over the deep spring up, which speed men's ships over the broad back of the sea. And now would all my stores have been spent and the strength of my men, had not one of the gods taken pity on me and saved me, even Eidothea, daughter of mighty Proteus, the old man of the sea; for her heart above all others had I moved. She met me as I wandered alone apart from my comrades, who were ever roaming about the island, fishing with bent hooks, for hunger pinched their bellies; and she came close to me, and spoke, and said:

---

[2] The epithet "black" is applied to water in deep places, where the light cannot reach it, and to water trickling down the face of a rock covered with lichens (*Iliad*, xvi. 4 ff.).

"'Νήπιός εἰς, ὦ ξεῖνε, λίην τόσον ἠδὲ χαλίφρων,
ἦε ἑκὼν μεθίεις καὶ τέρπεαι ἄλγεα πάσχων;
ὡς δὴ δήθ' ἐνὶ νήσῳ ἐρύκεαι, οὐδέ τι τέκμωρ
εὑρέμεναι δύνασαι, μινύθει δέ τοι ἦτορ ἑταίρων.'

"Ὣς ἔφατ', αὐτὰρ ἐγώ μιν ἀμειβόμενος προσέειπ
'Ἐκ μέν τοι ἐρέω, ἥ τις σύ πέρ ἐσσι θεάων,
ὡς ἐγὼ οὔ τι ἑκὼν κατερύκομαι, ἀλλά νυ μέλλω
ἀθανάτους ἀλιτέσθαι, οἳ οὐρανὸν εὐρὺν ἔχουσιν.
ἀλλὰ σύ πέρ μοι εἰπέ, θεοὶ δέ τε πάντα ἴσασιν,
ὅς τίς μ' ἀθανάτων πεδάᾳ καὶ ἔδησε κελεύθου,
νόστον θ', ὡς ἐπὶ πόντον ἐλεύσομαι ἰχθυόεντα.'

"Ὣς ἐφάμην, ἡ δ' αὐτίκ' ἀμείβετο δῖα θεάων·
'Τοιγὰρ ἐγώ τοι, ξεῖνε, μάλ' ἀτρεκέως ἀγορεύσω.
πωλεῖταί τις δεῦρο γέρων ἅλιος νημερτὴς
ἀθάνατος Πρωτεὺς Αἰγύπτιος, ὅς τε θαλάσσης
πάσης βένθεα οἶδε, Ποσειδάωνος ὑποδμώς·
τὸν δέ τ' ἐμόν φασιν πατέρ' ἔμμεναι ἠδὲ τεκέσθαι.
τόν γ' εἴ πως σὺ δύναιο λοχησάμενος λελαβέσθαι,
ὅς κέν τοι εἴπῃσιν ὁδὸν καὶ μέτρα κελεύθου
νόστον θ', ὡς ἐπὶ πόντον ἐλεύσεαι ἰχθυόεντα.
καὶ δέ κέ τοι εἴπῃσι, διοτρεφές, αἴ κ' ἐθέλῃσθα,
ὅττι τοι ἐν μεγάροισι κακόν τ' ἀγαθόν τε τέτυκται
οἰχομένοιο σέθεν δολιχὴν ὁδὸν ἀργαλέην τε.'

"Ὣς ἔφατ', αὐτὰρ ἐγώ μιν ἀμειβόμενος προσέειπ
'Αὐτὴ νῦν φράζευ σὺ λόχον θείοιο γέροντος,
μή πώς με προϊδὼν ἠὲ προδαεὶς ἀλέηται·
ἀργαλέος γάρ τ' ἐστὶ θεὸς βροτῷ ἀνδρὶ δαμῆναι.'

134

"'Art thou so very foolish, stranger, and slack of wit, or art thou of thine own will remiss, and hast pleasure in suffering woes? So long art thou pent in the isle and canst find no sign of deliverance.[1] and the heart of thy comrades grows faint.'

"So she spoke, and I made answer and said : 'I will speak out and tell thee, whosoever among goddesses thou art, that in no wise am I pent here of mine own will, but it must be that I have sinned against the immortals, who hold broad heaven. But do thou tell me—for the gods know all things—who of the immortals fetters me here, and has hindered me from my path, and tell me of my return, how I may go over the teeming deep.'

"So I spoke, and the beautiful goddess straightway made answer : 'Then verily, stranger, will I frankly tell thee all. There is wont to come hither the unerring old man of the sea, immortal Proteus of Egypt, who knows the depths of every sea, and is the servant of Poseidon. He, they say, is my father that begat me. If thou couldst in any wise lie in wait and catch him, he will tell thee thy way and the measure of thy path, and of thy return, how thou mayest go over the teeming deep. Aye, and he will tell thee, thou fostered of Zeus, if so thou wilt, what evil and what good has been wrought in thy halls, while thou hast been gone on thy long and grievous way.'

"So she spoke, and I made answer and said : 'Do thou thyself now devise a means of lying in wait for the divine old man, lest haply he see me beforehand and being ware of my purpose avoid me. For hard is a god for a mortal man to master.'

[1] Lit. "appointed end."

"Ὣς ἐφάμην, ἡ δ' αὐτίκ' ἀμείβετο δῖα θεάων·
'Τοιγὰρ ἐγώ τοι, ξεῖνε,[1] μάλ' ἀτρεκέως ἀγορεύσω.
ἦμος δ' ἠέλιος μέσον οὐρανὸν ἀμφιβεβήκῃ,   4
τῆμος ἄρ' ἐξ ἁλὸς εἶσι γέρων ἅλιος νημερτὴς
πνοιῇ ὕπο Ζεφύροιο μελαίνῃ φρικὶ καλυφθείς,
ἐκ δ' ἐλθὼν κοιμᾶται ὑπὸ σπέσσι γλαφυροῖσιν·
ἀμφὶ δέ μιν φῶκαι νέποδες καλῆς ἁλοσύδνης
ἀθρόαι εὕδουσιν, πολιῆς ἁλὸς ἐξαναδῦσαι,   4
πικρὸν ἀποπνείουσαι ἁλὸς πολυβενθέος ὀδμήν.
ἔνθα σ' ἐγὼν ἀγαγοῦσα ἅμ' ἠοῖ φαινομένηφιν
εὐνάσω ἑξείης· σὺ δ' ἐῢ κρίνασθαι ἑταίρους
τρεῖς, οἵ τοι παρὰ νηυσὶν ἐϋσσέλμοισιν ἄριστοι.
πάντα δέ τοι ἐρέω ὀλοφώϊα τοῖο γέροντος.   4
φώκας μέν τοι πρῶτον ἀριθμήσει καὶ ἔπεισιν·
αὐτὰρ ἐπὴν πάσας πεμπάσσεται ἠδὲ ἴδηται,
λέξεται ἐν μέσσῃσι νομεὺς ὣς πώεσι μήλων.
τὸν μὲν ἐπὴν δὴ πρῶτα κατευνηθέντα ἴδησθε,
καὶ τότ' ἔπειθ' ὑμῖν μελέτω κάρτος τε βίη τε,   4
αὖθι δ' ἔχειν μεμαῶτα καὶ ἐσσύμενόν περ ἀλύξαι.
πάντα δὲ γιγνόμενος πειρήσεται, ὅσσ' ἐπὶ γαῖαν
ἑρπετὰ γίγνονται, καὶ ὕδωρ καὶ θεσπιδαὲς πῦρ·
ὑμεῖς δ' ἀστεμφέως ἐχέμεν μᾶλλόν τε πιέζειν.
ἀλλ' ὅτε κεν δή σ' αὐτὸς ἀνείρηται ἐπέεσσι,   42
τοῖος ἐὼν οἷόν κε κατευνηθέντα ἴδησθε,
καὶ τότε δὴ σχέσθαι τε βίης λῦσαί τε γέροντα,
ἥρως, εἴρεσθαι δέ, θεῶν ὅς τίς σε χαλέπτει,
νόστον θ', ὡς ἐπὶ πόντον ἐλεύσεαι ἰχθυόεντα.'

[1] ξεῖνε : ταῦτα.

" So I spoke, and the beautiful goddess straightway made answer : ' Then verily, stranger, will I frankly tell thee all. When the sun hath reached mid heaven, the unerring old man of the sea is wont to come forth from the brine at the breath of the West Wind, hidden by the dark ripple. And when he is come forth, he lies down to sleep in the hollow caves; and around him the seals, the brood of the fair daughter of the sea, sleep in a herd, coming forth from the gray water, and bitter is the smell they breathe of the depths of the sea. Thither will I lead thee at break of day and lay you all in a row ; for do thou choose carefully three of thy companions, who are the best thou hast in thy well-benched ships. And I will tell thee all the wizard wiles of that old man. First he will count the seals, and go over them ; but when he has told them all off by fives, and beheld them, he will lay himself down in their midst, as a shepherd among his flocks of sheep. Now so soon as you see him laid to rest, thereafter let your hearts be filled with strength and courage, and do you hold him there despite his striving and struggling to escape. For try he will, and will assume all manner of shapes of all things that move upon the earth, and of water, and of wondrous blazing fire. Yet do ye hold him unflinchingly and grip him yet the more. But when at length of his own will he speaks and questions thee in that shape in which you saw him laid to rest, then, hero, stay thy might, and set the old man free, and ask him who of the gods is wroth with thee, and of thy return, how thou mayest go over the teeming deep.'

"'Ὡς εἰποῦσ' ὑπὸ πόντον ἐδύσετο κυμαίνοντα.   4[

αὐτὰρ ἐγὼν ἐπὶ νῆας, ὅθ' ἕστασαν ἐν ψαμάθοισιν,

ἦια· πολλὰ δέ μοι κραδίη πόρφυρε κιόντι.

αὐτὰρ ἐπεί ῥ' ἐπὶ νῆα κατήλυθον ἠδὲ θάλασσαν,

δόρπον θ' ὁπλισάμεσθ', ἐπί τ' ἤλυθεν ἀμβροσίη νύξ·

δὴ τότε κοιμήθημεν ἐπὶ ῥηγμῖνι θαλάσσης.   4[

ἦμος δ' ἠριγένεια φάνη ῥοδοδάκτυλος Ἠώς,

καὶ τότε δὴ παρὰ θῖνα θαλάσσης εὐρυπόροιο

ἦια πολλὰ θεοὺς γουνούμενος· αὐτὰρ ἑταίρους

τρεῖς ἄγον, οἷσι μάλιστα πεποίθεα πᾶσαν ἐπ' ἰθύν.

"Τόφρα δ' ἄρ' ἥ γ' ὑποδῦσα θαλάσσης εὐρέα κόλπ[

τέσσαρα φωκάων ἐκ πόντου δέρματ' ἔνεικε·   4[

πάντα δ' ἔσαν νεόδαρτα· δόλον δ' ἐπεμήδετο πατρί.

εὐνὰς δ' ἐν ψαμάθοισι διαγλάψασ' ἁλίῃσιν

ἧστο μένουσ'· ἡμεῖς δὲ μάλα σχεδὸν ἤλθομεν αὐτῆς·

ἑξείης δ' εὔνησε, βάλεν δ' ἐπὶ δέρμα ἑκάστῳ.   4[

ἔνθα κεν [1] αἰνότατος λόχος ἔπλετο· τεῖρε γὰρ αἰνῶς

φωκάων ἁλιοτρεφέων ὀλοώτατος ὀδμή·

τίς γάρ κ' εἰναλίῳ παρὰ κήτεϊ κοιμηθείη;

ἀλλ' αὐτὴ ἐσάωσε καὶ ἐφράσατο μέγ' ὄνειαρ·

ἀμβροσίην ὑπὸ ῥῖνα ἑκάστῳ θῆκε φέρουσα   4[

ἡδὺ μάλα πνείουσαν, ὄλεσσε δὲ κήτεος ὀδμή.

πᾶσαν δ' ἠοίην μένομεν τετληότι θυμῷ·

φῶκαι δ' ἐξ ἁλὸς ἦλθον ἀολλέες. αἱ μὲν ἔπειτα

ἑξῆς εὐνάζοντο παρὰ ῥηγμῖνι θαλάσσης·

ἔνδιος δ' ὁ γέρων ἦλθ' ἐξ ἁλός, εὗρε δὲ φώκας   4[

ζατρεφέας, πάσας δ' ἄρ' ἐπῴχετο, λέκτο δ' ἀριθμόν·

ἐν δ' ἡμέας πρώτους λέγε κήτεσιν, οὐδέ τι θυμῷ

---

[1] ἔνθα κεν : κεῖθι δή.

"So saying she plunged beneath the surging sea, but I went to my ships, where they stood on the sand, and many things did my heart darkly ponder as I went. But when I had come down to the ship and to the sea, and we had made ready our supper, and immortal night had come on, then we lay down to rest on the shore of the sea. And as soon as early Dawn appeared, the rosy-fingered, I went along the shore of the broad-wayed sea, praying earnestly to the gods; and I took with me three of my comrades, in whom I trusted most for every adventure.

"She meanwhile had plunged beneath the broad bosom of the sea, and had brought forth from the deep the skins of four seals, and all were newly flayed; and she devised a plot against her father. She had scooped out lairs in the sand of the sea, and sat waiting; and we came very near to her, and she made us to lie down in a row, and cast a skin over each. Then would our ambush have proved most terrible, for terribly did the deadly stench of the brine-bred seals distress us—who would lay him down by a beast of the sea?—but she of herself delivered us, and devised a great boon; she brought and placed ambrosia of a very sweet fragrance beneath each man's nose, and destroyed the stench of the beast. So all the morning we waited with steadfast heart, and the seals came forth from the sea in throngs. These then laid them down in rows along the shore of the sea, and at noon the old man came forth from the sea and found the fatted seals; and he went over all, and counted their number. Among the creatures he counted us first, nor did his heart guess that there was guile; and

ὠίσθη δόλον εἶναι· ἔπειτα δὲ λέκτο καὶ αὐτός.
ἡμεῖς δὲ ἰάχοντες ἐπεσσύμεθ᾽, ἀμφὶ δὲ χεῖρας
βάλλομεν· οὐδ᾽ ὁ γέρων δολίης ἐπελήθετο τέχνης,
ἀλλ᾽ ἦ τοι πρώτιστα λέων γένετ᾽ ἠυγένειος,
αὐτὰρ ἔπειτα δράκων καὶ πάρδαλις ἠδὲ μέγας σῦς·
γίγνετο δ᾽ ὑγρὸν ὕδωρ καὶ δένδρεον ὑψιπέτηλον·
ἡμεῖς δ᾽ ἀστεμφέως ἔχομεν τετληότι θυμῷ.
ἀλλ᾽ ὅτε δή ῥ᾽ ἀνίαζ᾽ ὁ γέρων ὀλοφώια εἰδώς,
καὶ τότε δή μ᾽ ἐπέεσσιν ἀνειρόμενος προσέειπε·

"'Τίς νύ τοι, Ἀτρέος υἱέ, θεῶν συμφράσσατο βουλ
ὄφρα μ᾽ ἕλοις ἀέκοντα λοχησάμενος; τέο σε χρή;'

"Ὣς ἔφατ᾽, αὐτὰρ ἐγώ μιν ἀμειβόμενος προσέειπε
'Οἶσθα, γέρον, τί με ταῦτα παρατροπέων ἐρεείνεις;[1]
ὡς δὴ δήθ᾽ ἐνὶ νήσῳ ἐρύκομαι, οὐδέ τι τέκμωρ
εὑρέμεναι δύναμαι, μινύθει δέ μοι ἔνδοθεν ἦτορ.
ἀλλὰ σύ πέρ μοι εἰπέ, θεοὶ δέ τε πάντα ἴσασιν,
ὅς τίς μ᾽ ἀθανάτων πεδάᾳ καὶ ἔδησε κελεύθου,
νόστον θ᾽, ὡς ἐπὶ πόντον ἐλεύσομαι ἰχθυόεντα.'

"Ὣς ἐφάμην, ὁ δέ μ᾽ αὐτίκ᾽ ἀμειβόμενος προσέειπ
'Ἀλλὰ μάλ᾽ ὤφελλες Διί τ᾽ ἄλλοισίν τε θεοῖσι
ῥέξας ἱερὰ κάλ᾽ ἀναβαινέμεν, ὄφρα τάχιστα
σὴν ἐς πατρίδ᾽ ἵκοιο πλέων ἐπὶ οἴνοπα πόντον.
οὐ γάρ τοι πρὶν μοῖρα φίλους τ᾽ ἰδέειν καὶ ἱκέσθαι
οἶκον ἐυκτίμενον καὶ σὴν ἐς πατρίδα γαῖαν,
πρίν γ᾽ ὅτ᾽ ἂν Αἰγύπτοιο, διιπετέος ποταμοῖο,
αὖτις ὕδωρ ἔλθῃς ῥέξῃς θ᾽ ἱερὰς ἑκατόμβας
ἀθανάτοισι θεοῖσι, τοὶ οὐρανὸν εὐρὺν ἔχουσι·
καὶ τότε τοι δώσουσιν ὁδὸν θεοί, ἣν σὺ μενοινᾷς.'

---

[1] ἐρεείνεις Aristarchus : ἀγορεύεις.

then he too laid him down. Thereat we rushed upon him with a shout, and threw our arms about him, nor did that old man forget his crafty wiles. Nay, at the first he turned into a bearded lion, and then into a serpent, and a leopard, and a huge boar; then he turned into flowing water, and into a tree, high and leafy; but we held on unflinchingly with steadfast heart. But when at last that old man, skilled in wizard arts, grew weary, then he questioned me, and spoke, and said:

"'Who of the gods, son of Atreus, took counsel with thee that thou mightest lie in wait for me, and take me against my will? Of what hast thou need?'

"So he spoke, and I made answer, and said: 'Thou knowest, old man—why dost thou seek to put me off with this question?—how long a time I am pent in this isle, and can find no sign of deliverance, and my heart grows faint within me. But do thou tell me—for the gods know all things— who of the immortals fetters me here, and has hindered me from my path, and tell me of my return, how I may go over the teeming deep.'

"So I spoke, and he straightway made answer, and said: 'Nay, surely thou oughtest to have made fair offerings to Zeus and the other gods before embarking, that with greatest speed thou mightest have come to thy country, sailing over the wine-dark sea. For it is not thy fate to see thy friends, and reach thy well-built house and thy native land, before that thou hast once more gone to the waters of Aegyptus, the heaven-fed river, and hast offered holy hecatombs to the immortal gods who hold broad heaven. Then at length shall the gods grant thee the journey thou desirest.'

141

"Ὣς ἔφατ', αὐτὰρ ἐμοί γε κατεκλάσθη φίλον ἦτορ
οὕνεκά μ' αὖτις ἄνωγεν ἐπ' ἠεροειδέα πόντον
Αἰγυπτόνδ' ἰέναι, δολιχὴν ὁδὸν ἀργαλέην τε.
ἀλλὰ καὶ ὣς μύθοισιν[1] ἀμειβόμενος προσέειπον·

"'Ταῦτα μὲν οὕτω δὴ τελέω, γέρον, ὡς σὺ κελεύεις
ἀλλ' ἄγε μοι τόδε εἰπὲ καὶ ἀτρεκέως κατάλεξον,   48
ἠ πάντες σὺν νηυσὶν ἀπήμονες ἦλθον Ἀχαιοί,
οὓς Νέστωρ καὶ ἐγὼ λίπομεν Τροίηθεν ἰόντες,
ἠέ τις ὤλετ' ὀλέθρῳ ἀδευκέι ἧς ἐπὶ νηὸς
ἠὲ φίλων ἐν χερσίν, ἐπεὶ πόλεμον τολύπευσεν.'   49

"Ὣς ἐφάμην, ὁ δέ μ' αὐτίκ' ἀμειβόμενος προσέειπ‹
'Ἀτρεΐδη, τί με ταῦτα διείρεαι; οὐδέ τί σε χρὴ
ἴδμεναι, οὐδὲ δαῆναι ἐμὸν νόον· οὐδέ σέ φημι
δὴν ἄκλαυτον ἔσεσθαι, ἐπὴν εὖ πάντα πύθηαι.
πολλοὶ μὲν γὰρ τῶν γε δάμεν, πολλοὶ δὲ λίποντο   49
ἀρχοὶ δ' αὖ δύο μοῦνοι Ἀχαιῶν χαλκοχιτώνων
ἐν νόστῳ ἀπόλοντο· μάχῃ δέ τε καὶ σὺ παρῆσθα.
εἷς δ' ἔτι που ζωὸς κατερύκεται εὐρέι πόντῳ.

"'Αἴας μὲν μετὰ νηυσὶ δάμη δολιχηρέτμοισι.
Γυρῇσίν μιν πρῶτα Ποσειδάων ἐπέλασσεν   5‹
πέτρῃσιν μεγάλῃσι καὶ ἐξεσάωσε θαλάσσης·
καί νύ κεν ἔκφυγε κῆρα καὶ ἐχθόμενός περ Ἀθήνῃ,
εἰ μὴ ὑπερφίαλον ἔπος ἔκβαλε καὶ μέγ' ἀάσθη·
φῆ ῥ' ἀέκητι θεῶν φυγέειν μέγα λαῖτμα θαλάσσης.
τοῦ δὲ Ποσειδάων μεγάλ' ἔκλυεν αὐδήσαντος·   5‹
αὐτίκ' ἔπειτα τρίαιναν ἑλὼν χερσὶ στιβαρῇσιν
ἤλασε Γυραίην πέτρην, ἀπὸ δ' ἔσχισεν αὐτήν·
καὶ τὸ μὲν αὐτόθι μεῖνε, τὸ δὲ τρύφος ἔμπεσε πόντῳ,

[1] μύθοισιν : μιν ἔπεσσιν.

" So he spoke, and my spirit was broken within me, for that he bade me go again over the misty deep to Aegyptus, a long and weary way. Yet even so I made answer, and said :

" ' All this will I perform, old man, even as thou dost bid. But come now, tell me this, and declare it truly. Did all the Achaeans return unscathed in their ships, all those whom Nestor and I left, as we set out from Troy ? Or did any perish by a cruel death on board his ship, or in the arms of his friends, when he had wound up the skein of war ? '

" So I spoke, and he straightway made answer, and said : ' Son of Atreus, why dost thou question me of this ? In no wise does it behove thee to know, or to learn my mind ; nor, methinks, wilt thou long be free from tears, when thou hast heard all aright. For many of them were slain, and many were left ; but two chieftains alone of the brazen-coated Achaeans perished on their homeward way (as for the fighting, thou thyself wast there), and one, I ween, still lives, and is held back on the broad deep.

" ' Aias truly was lost amid his long-oared ships. Upon the great rocks of Gyrae Poseidon at first drove him, but saved him from the sea ; and he would have escaped his doom, hated of Athene though he was, had he not uttered a boastful word in great blindness of heart. He declared that it was in spite of the gods that he had escaped the great gulf of the sea ; and Poseidon heard his boastful speech, and straightway took his trident in his mighty hands, and smote the rock of Gyrae and clove it in sunder. And one part abode in its place, but the sundered part fell into the sea, even that on

τῷ ῥ' Αἴας τὸ πρῶτον ἐφεζόμενος μέγ' ἀάσθη·
τὸν δ' ἐφόρει κατὰ πόντον ἀπείρονα κυμαίνοντα.   5
ὣς ὁ μὲν ἔνθ' ἀπόλωλεν, ἐπεὶ πίεν ἁλμυρὸν ὕδωρ.

  "' Σὸς δέ που ἔκφυγε κῆρας ἀδελφεὸς ἠδ' ὑπάλυξεν
ἐν νηυσὶ γλαφυρῇσι· σάωσε δὲ πότνια Ἥρη.
ἀλλ' ὅτε δὴ τάχ' ἔμελλε Μαλειάων ὄρος αἰπὺ
ἵξεσθαι, τότε δή μιν ἀναρπάξασα θύελλα   5
πόντον ἐπ' ἰχθυόεντα φέρεν βαρέα στενάχοντα,
ἀγροῦ ἐπ' ἐσχατιήν, ὅθι δώματα ναῖε Θυέστης
τὸ πρίν, ἀτὰρ τότ' ἔναιε Θυεστιάδης Αἴγισθος.
ἀλλ' ὅτε δὴ καὶ κεῖθεν ἐφαίνετο νόστος ἀπήμων,
ἂψ δὲ θεοὶ οὖρον στρέψαν, καὶ οἴκαδ' ἵκοντο,   52
ἦ τοι ὁ μὲν χαίρων ἐπεβήσετο πατρίδος αἴης
καὶ κύνει ἁπτόμενος ἣν πατρίδα· πολλὰ δ' ἀπ' αὐτοῦ
δάκρυα θερμὰ χέοντ', ἐπεὶ ἀσπασίως ἴδε γαῖαν.
τὸν δ' ἄρ' ἀπὸ σκοπιῆς εἶδε σκοπός, ὅν ῥα καθεῖσεν
Αἴγισθος δολόμητις ἄγων, ὑπὸ δ' ἔσχετο μισθὸν   52
χρυσοῦ δοιὰ τάλαντα· φύλασσε δ' ὅ γ' εἰς ἐνιαυτόν,
μή ἑ λάθοι παριών, μνήσαιτο δὲ θούριδος ἀλκῆς.
βῆ δ' ἴμεν ἀγγελέων πρὸς δώματα ποιμένι λαῶν.
αὐτίκα δ' Αἴγισθος δολίην ἐφράσσατο τέχνην·
κρινάμενος κατὰ δῆμον ἐείκοσι φῶτας ἀρίστους   53
εἷσε λόχον, ἑτέρωθι δ' ἀνώγει δαῖτα πένεσθαι.
αὐτὰρ ὁ βῆ καλέων Ἀγαμέμνονα, ποιμένα λαῶν
ἵπποισιν καὶ ὄχεσφιν, ἀεικέα μερμηρίζων.

---

¹ Unless we accept the tradition which places the home of
Thyestes (and Aegisthus) in Cythera (though Aegisthus was

which Aias sat at the first when his heart was greatly
blinded, and it bore him down into the boundless
surging deep.   So there he perished, when he had
drunk the salt water.

"'But thy brother escaped, indeed, the fates and
shunned them with his hollow ships, for queenly
Hera saved him.   But when he was now about to
reach the steep height of Malea, then the storm-
wind caught him up and bore him over the teeming
deep, groaning heavily, to the border of the land,[1]
where aforetime Thyestes dwelt, but where now
dwelt Thyestes' son Aegisthus.   But when from
hence too a safe return was shewed him, and the
gods changed the course of the wind that it blew
fair, and they reached home, then verily with
rejoicing did Agamemnon set foot on his native
land, and he clasped his land and kissed it, and
many were the hot tears that streamed from his
eyes, for welcome to him was the sight of his land.
Now from his place of watch a watchman saw
him, whom guileful Aegisthus took and set there,
promising him as a reward two talents of gold ; and
he had been keeping guard for a year, lest Agamemnon
should pass by him unseen, and be mindful of his
furious might.   So he went to the palace to bear the
tidings to the shepherd of the people, and Aegisthus
straightway planned a treacherous device.   He chose
out twenty men, the best in the land, and set them
to lie in wait, but on the further side of the hall he
bade prepare a feast.   Then he went with chariot
and horses to summon Agamemnon, shepherd of the
people, his mind pondering a dastardly deed.   So

at this time in Mycenae), we must understand this phrase to
mean the Argolic promontory.

τὸν δ' οὐκ εἰδότ' ὄλεθρον ἀνήγαγε καὶ κατέπεφνεν
δειπνίσσας, ὥς τίς τε κατέκτανε βοῦν ἐπὶ φάτνῃ.   5
οὐδέ τις Ἀτρεΐδεω ἑτάρων λίπεθ' οἵ οἱ ἕποντο,
οὐδέ τις Αἰγίσθου, ἀλλ' ἔκταθεν ἐν μεγάροισιν.'

"'Ὣς ἔφατ', αὐτὰρ ἐμοί γε κατεκλάσθη φίλον ἦτορ·
κλαῖον δ' ἐν ψαμάθοισι καθήμενος, οὐδέ νύ μοι κῆρ
ἤθελ' ἔτι ζώειν καὶ ὁρᾶν φάος ἠελίοιο.   5
αὐτὰρ ἐπεὶ κλαίων τε κυλινδόμενός τε κορέσθην,
δὴ τότε με προσέειπε γέρων ἅλιος νημερτής·

" ' Μηκέτι, Ἀτρέος υἱέ, πολὺν χρόνον ἀσκελὲς οὕτω
κλαῖ', ἐπεὶ οὐκ ἄνυσίν τινα δήομεν· ἀλλὰ τάχιστα
πείρα ὅπως κεν δὴ σὴν πατρίδα γαῖαν ἵκηαι.   5
ἢ γάρ μιν ζωόν γε κιχήσεαι, ἤ κεν Ὀρέστης
κτεῖνεν ὑποφθάμενος, σὺ δέ κεν τάφου ἀντιβολήσαις.'

"'Ὣς ἔφατ', αὐτὰρ ἐμοὶ κραδίη καὶ θυμὸς ἀγήνωρ
αὖτις ἐνὶ στήθεσσι καὶ ἀχνυμένῳ περ ἰάνθη,
καί μιν φωνήσας ἔπεα πτερόεντα προσηύδων·   5

" ' Τούτους μὲν δὴ οἶδα· σὺ δὲ τρίτον ἄνδρ' ὀνόμαζ'
ὅς τις ἔτι ζωὸς κατερύκεται εὐρέι πόντῳ
ἠὲ θανών· ἐθέλω δὲ καὶ ἀχνύμενός περ ἀκοῦσαι.'[1]

"'Ὣς ἐφάμην, ὁ δέ μ' αὐτίκ' ἀμειβόμενος προσέειπε·
'Υἱὸς Λαέρτεω, Ἰθάκῃ ἔνι οἰκία ναίων·   5
τὸν δ' ἴδον ἐν νήσῳ θαλερὸν κατὰ δάκρυ χέοντα,
νύμφης ἐν μεγάροισι Καλυψοῦς, ἥ μιν ἀνάγκῃ
ἴσχει· ὁ δ' οὐ δύναται ἣν πατρίδα γαῖαν ἱκέσθαι·
οὐ γάρ οἱ πάρα νῆες ἐπήρετμοι καὶ ἑταῖροι,
οἵ κέν μιν πέμποιεν ἐπ' εὐρέα νῶτα θαλάσσης.   5

<hr />

[1] Line 553 was rejected by all ancient critics.

he brought him up all unaware of his doom, and when he had feasted him he slew him, as one slays an ox at the stall. And not one of the comrades of the son of Atreus was left, of all that followed him, nor one of the men of Aegisthus, but they were all slain in the halls.'

"So he spoke, and my spirit was broken within me, and I wept, as I sat on the sands, nor had my heart any longer desire to live and to behold the light of the sun. But when I had had my fill of weeping and writhing, then the unerring old man of the sea said to me:

"'No more, son of Atreus, do thou weep long time thus without ceasing, for in it we shall find no help. Nay, rather, with all the speed thou canst, strive that thou mayest come to thy native land, for either thou wilt find Aegisthus alive, or haply Orestes may have forestalled thee and slain him, and thou mayest chance upon his funeral feast.'

"So he spoke, and my heart and spirit were again warmed with comfort in my breast despite my grief, and I spoke, and addressed him with winged words:

"'Of these men now I know, but do thou name the third, who he is that still lives, and is held back upon the broad sea, or is haply dead. Fain would I hear, despite my grief.'

"So I spoke, and he straightway made answer, and said: 'It is the son of Laertes, whose home is in Ithaca. Him I saw in an island, shedding big tears, in the halls of the nymph Calypso, who keeps him there perforce, and he cannot come to his native land, for he has at hand no ships with oars and no comrades to send him on his way over the broad

σοὶ δ' οὐ θέσφατόν ἐστι, διοτρεφὲς ὦ Μενέλαε,
Ἄργει ἐν ἱπποβότῳ θανέειν καὶ πότμον ἐπισπεῖν,
ἀλλά σ' ἐς Ἠλύσιον πεδίον καὶ πείρατα γαίης
ἀθάνατοι πέμψουσιν, ὅθι ξανθὸς Ῥαδάμανθυς,
τῇ περ ῥηίστη βιοτὴ πέλει ἀνθρώποισιν·   56
οὐ νιφετός, οὔτ' ἂρ χειμὼν πολὺς οὔτε ποτ' ὄμβρος,
ἀλλ' αἰεὶ Ζεφύροιο λιγὺ πνείοντος ἀήτας
Ὠκεανὸς ἀνίησιν ἀναψύχειν ἀνθρώπους·
οὕνεκ' ἔχεις Ἑλένην καί σφιν γαμβρὸς Διός ἐσσι.'

"Ὣς εἰπὼν ὑπὸ πόντον ἐδύσετο κυμαίνοντα.   57
αὐτὰρ ἐγὼν ἐπὶ νῆας ἅμ' ἀντιθέοις ἑτάροισιν
ἤια, πολλὰ δέ μοι κραδίη πόρφυρε κιόντι.
αὐτὰρ ἐπεί ῥ' ἐπὶ νῆα κατήλθομεν ἠδὲ θάλασσαν,
δόρπον θ' ὁπλισάμεσθ', ἐπί τ' ἤλυθεν ἀμβροσίη νύξ,
δὴ τότε κοιμήθημεν ἐπὶ ῥηγμῖνι θαλάσσης.   57
ἦμος δ' ἠριγένεια φάνη ῥοδοδάκτυλος Ἠώς,
νῆας μὲν πάμπρωτον ἐρύσσαμεν εἰς ἅλα δῖαν,
ἐν δ' ἱστοὺς τιθέμεσθα καὶ ἱστία νηυσὶν ἐίσης,
ἂν δὲ καὶ αὐτοὶ βάντες ἐπὶ κληῖσι καθῖζον·
ἑξῆς δ' ἑζόμενοι πολιὴν ἅλα τύπτον ἐρετμοῖς.   58
ἂψ δ' εἰς Αἰγύπτοιο διιπετέος ποταμοῖο
στῆσα νέας, καὶ ἔρεξα τεληέσσας ἑκατόμβας.
αὐτὰρ ἐπεὶ κατέπαυσα θεῶν χόλον αἰὲν ἐόντων,
χεῦ' Ἀγαμέμνονι τύμβον, ἵν' ἄσβεστον κλέος εἴη.
ταῦτα τελευτήσας νεόμην, ἔδοσαν δέ μοι οὖρον   58
ἀθάνατοι, τοί μ' ὦκα φίλην ἐς πατρίδ' ἔπεμψαν.
ἀλλ' ἄγε νῦν ἐπίμεινον ἐνὶ μεγάροισιν ἐμοῖσιν,
ὄφρα κεν ἑνδεκάτη τε δυωδεκάτη τε γένηται·
καὶ τότε σ' εὖ πέμψω, δώσω δέ τοι ἀγλαὰ δῶρα,

back of the sea.   But for thyself, Menelaus, fostered of Zeus, it is not ordained that thou shouldst die and meet thy fate in horse-pasturing Argos, but to the Elysian plain and the bounds of the earth will the immortals convey thee, where dwells fair-haired Rhadamanthus, and where life is easiest for men. No snow is there, nor heavy storm, nor ever rain, but ever does Ocean send up blasts of the shrill-blowing West Wind that they may give cooling to men; for thou hast Helen to wife, and art in their eyes the husband of the daughter of Zeus.'

"So saying he plunged beneath the surging sea, but I went to my ships with my godlike comrades, and many things did my heart darkly ponder as I went.   But when I had come down to the ship and to the sea, and we had made ready our supper, and immortal night had come on, then we lay down to rest on the shore of the sea.   And as soon as early Dawn appeared, the rosy-fingered, our ships first of all we drew down to the bright sea, and set the masts and the sails in the shapely ships, and the men, too, went on board and sat down upon the benches, and sitting well in order smote the grey sea with their oars.   So back again to the waters of Aegyptus, the heaven-fed river, I sailed, and there moored my ships and offered hecatombs that bring fulfilment. But when I had stayed the wrath of the gods that are forever, I heaped up a mound to Agamemnon, that his fame might be unquenchable.   Then, when I had made an end of this, I set out for home, and the immortals gave me a fair wind, and brought me swiftly to my dear native land.   But come now, tarry in my halls until the eleventh or the twelfth day be come.   Then will I send thee forth with honour and

τρεῖς ἵππους καὶ δίφρον ἐΰξοον· αὐτὰρ ἔπειτα　5
δώσω καλὸν ἄλεισον, ἵνα σπένδῃσθα θεοῖσιν
ἀθανάτοις ἐμέθεν μεμνημένος ἤματα πάντα."

　Τὸν δ' αὖ Τηλέμαχος πεπνυμένος ἀντίον ηὔδα·
"'Ατρεΐδη, μὴ δή με πολὺν χρόνον ἐνθάδ' ἔρυκε.
καὶ γάρ κ' εἰς ἐνιαυτὸν ἐγὼ παρὰ σοί γ' ἀνεχοίμην　5
ἥμενος, οὐδέ κέ μ' οἴκου ἕλοι πόθος οὐδὲ τοκήων·
αἰνῶς γὰρ μύθοισιν ἔπεσσί τε σοῖσιν ἀκούων
τέρπομαι. ἀλλ' ἤδη μοι ἀνιάζουσιν ἑταῖροι
ἐν Πύλῳ ἠγαθέῃ· σὺ δέ με χρόνον ἐνθάδ' ἐρύκεις.
δῶρον δ' ὅττι κέ μοι δοίης, κειμήλιον ἔστω·　　6
ἵππους δ' εἰς 'Ιθάκην οὐκ ἄξομαι, ἀλλὰ σοὶ αὐτῷ
ἐνθάδε λείψω ἄγαλμα· σὺ γὰρ πεδίοιο ἀνάσσεις
εὐρέος, ᾧ ἔνι μὲν λωτὸς πολύς, ἐν δὲ κύπειρον
πυροί τε ζειαί τε ἰδ' εὐρυφυὲς κρῖ λευκόν.
ἐν δ' 'Ιθάκῃ οὔτ' ἂρ δρόμοι εὐρέες οὔτε τι λειμών·　6
αἰγίβοτος, καὶ μᾶλλον ἐπήρατος ἱπποβότοιο.
οὐ γάρ τις νήσων ἱππήλατος οὐδ' εὐλείμων,
αἵ θ' ἁλὶ κεκλίαται· 'Ιθάκη δέ τε καὶ περὶ πασέων."

　Ὣς φάτο, μείδησεν δὲ βοὴν ἀγαθὸς Μενέλαος,
χειρί τέ μιν κατέρεξεν ἔπος τ' ἔφατ' ἔκ τ' ὀνόμαζεν·　6
　"Αἵματός εἰς ἀγαθοῖο, φίλον τέκος, οἷ' ἀγορεύεις·
τοιγὰρ ἐγώ τοι ταῦτα μεταστήσω· δύναμαι γάρ.
δώρων δ' ὅσσ' ἐν ἐμῷ οἴκῳ κειμήλια κεῖται,
δώσω ὃ κάλλιστον καὶ τιμηέστατόν ἐστιν·
δώσω τοι κρητῆρα τετυγμένον· ἀργύρεος δὲ　　6
ἔστιν ἅπας, χρυσῷ δ' ἐπὶ χείλεα κεκράανται,
ἔργον δ' 'Ηφαίστοιο. πόρεν δέ ἑ Φαίδιμος ἥρως,

give thee splendid gifts, three horses and a well-polished car; and besides I will give thee a beautiful cup, that thou mayest pour libations to the immortal gods, and remember me all thy days."

Then wise Telemachus answered him: "Son of Atreus, keep me no long time here, for verily for a year would I be content to sit in thy house, nor would desire for home or parents come upon me; for wondrous is the pleasure I take in listening to thy tales and thy speech. But even now my comrades are chafing in sacred Pylos, and thou art keeping me long time here. And whatsoever gift thou wouldest give me, let it be some treasure; but horses will I not take to Ithaca, but will leave them here for thyself to delight in, for thou art lord of a wide plain, wherein is lotus in abundance, and galingale and wheat and spelt, and broad-eared white barley. But in Ithaca there are no widespread courses nor aught of meadow-land. It is a pasture-land of goats and pleasanter than one that pastures horses. For not one of the islands that lean upon the sea is fit for driving horses, or rich in meadows, and Ithaca least of all."

So he spoke, and Menelaus, good at the war-cry, smiled, and stroked him with his hand, and spoke, and addressed him:

"Thou art of noble blood, dear child, that thou speakest thus. Therefore will I change these gifts, for well I may. Of all the gifts that lie stored as treasures in my house, I will give thee that one which is fairest and costliest. I will give thee a well-wrought mixing bowl. All of silver it is, and with gold are the rims thereof gilded, the work of Hephaestus; and the warrior Phaedimus, king of the

Σιδονίων βασιλεύς, ὅθ' ἑὸς δόμος ἀμφεκάλυψε
κεῖσέ με νοστήσαντα· τεῖν δ' ἐθέλω τόδ' ὀπάσσαι."
    Ὣς οἱ μὲν τοιαῦτα πρὸς ἀλλήλους ἀγόρευον,
δαιτυμόνες δ' ἐς δώματ' ἴσαν θείου βασιλῆος.
οἱ δ' ἦγον μὲν μῆλα, φέρον δ' εὐήνορα οἶνον·
σῖτον δέ σφ' ἄλοχοι καλλικρήδεμνοι ἔπεμπον.[1]
ὣς οἱ μὲν περὶ δεῖπνον ἐνὶ μεγάροισι πένοντο.
    Μνηστῆρες δὲ πάροιθεν Ὀδυσσῆος μεγάροιο
δίσκοισιν τέρποντο καὶ αἰγανέῃσιν ἱέντες
ἐν τυκτῷ δαπέδῳ, ὅθι περ πάρος, ὕβριν ἔχοντες.[2]
Ἀντίνοος δὲ καθῆστο καὶ Εὐρύμαχος θεοειδής,
ἀρχοὶ μνηστήρων, ἀρετῇ δ' ἔσαν ἔξοχ' ἄριστοι.
τοῖς δ' υἱὸς Φρονίοιο Νοήμων ἐγγύθεν ἐλθὼν
Ἀντίνοον μύθοισιν ἀνειρόμενος προσέειπεν·
    "'Ἀντίνο', ἦ ῥά τι ἴδμεν ἐνὶ φρεσίν, ἦε καὶ οὐκί,
ὁππότε Τηλέμαχος νεῖτ' ἐκ Πύλου ἠμαθόεντος;
νῆά μοι οἴχετ' ἄγων· ἐμὲ δὲ χρεὼ γίγνεται αὐτῆς
Ἤλιδ' ἐς εὐρύχορον διαβήμεναι, ἔνθα μοι ἵπποι
δώδεκα θήλειαι, ὑπὸ δ' ἡμίονοι ταλαεργοὶ
ἀδμῆτες· τῶν κέν τιν' ἐλασσάμενος δαμασαίμην."
    Ὣς ἔφαθ', οἱ δ' ἀνὰ θυμὸν ἐθάμβεον· οὐ γὰρ ἔφαν
ἐς Πύλον οἴχεσθαι Νηλήιον, ἀλλά που αὐτοῦ
ἀγρῶν ἢ μήλοισι παρέμμεναι ἠὲ συβώτῃ.
    Τὸν δ' αὖτ' Ἀντίνοος προσέφη Εὐπείθεος υἱός·
" Νημερτές μοι ἔνισπε, πότ' ᾤχετο καὶ τίνες αὐτῷ
κοῦροι ἕποντ'; Ἰθάκης ἐξαίρετοι, ἦ ἑοὶ αὐτοῦ
θῆτές τε δμῶές τε; δύναιτό κε καὶ τὸ τελέσσαι.
καί μοι τοῦτ' ἀγόρευσον ἐτήτυμον, ὄφρ' ἐὺ εἰδῶ,

----

[1] ἔπεμπον : ἔνεικαν.   [2] ἔχοντες Aristarchus : ἔχεσκον.

Sidonians, gave it me, when his house sheltered me as I came thither, and now I am minded to give it to thee."

Thus they spoke to one another, and meanwhile the banqueters came to the palace of the divine king. They drove up sheep, and brought strengthening wine, and their wives with beautiful veils sent them bread. Thus they were busied about the feast in the halls.

But the wooers in front of the palace of Odysseus were making merry, throwing the discus and the javelin in a levelled place, as their wont was, in insolence of heart; and Antinous and godlike Eurymachus were sitting there, the leaders of the wooers, who in valiance were far the best of all. To them Noemon, son of Phronius, drew near, and he questioned Antinous, and spoke, and said:

"Antinous, know we at all in our hearts, or know we not, when Telemachus will return from sandy Pylos? He is gone, taking a ship of mine, and I have need of her to cross over to spacious Elis, where I have twelve brood mares, and at the teat sturdy mules as yet unbroken. Of these I would fain drive one off and break him in."

So he spoke, and they marvelled at heart, for they did not deem that Telemachus had gone to Neleian Pylos, but that he was somewhere there on his lands, among the flocks or with the swineherd.

Then Antinous, son of Eupeithes, spoke to him, saying: "Tell me the truth; when did he go, and what youths went with him? Were they chosen youths of Ithaca, or hirelings and slaves of his own? Able would he be to accomplish even that. And tell me this truly, that I may know full well. Was it

HOMER

ἤ σε βίῃ ἀέκοντος ἀπηύρα νῆα μέλαιναν,
ἦε ἑκών οἱ δῶκας, ἐπεὶ προσπτύξατο μύθῳ."

Τὸν δ' υἱὸς Φρονίοιο Νοήμων ἀντίον ηὔδα·
" Αὐτὸς ἑκών οἱ δῶκα· τί κεν ῥέξειε καὶ ἄλλος,
ὁππότ' ἀνὴρ τοιοῦτος ἔχων μελεδήματα θυμῷ
αἰτίζῃ; χαλεπόν κεν ἀνήνασθαι δόσιν εἴη.
κοῦροι δ', οἳ κατὰ δῆμον ἀριστεύουσι μεθ' ἡμέας,
οἵ οἱ ἔποντ'· ἐν δ' ἀρχὸν ἐγὼ βαίνοντ' ἐνόησα
Μέντορα, ἠὲ θεόν, τῷ δ' αὐτῷ πάντα ἐῴκει.
ἀλλὰ τὸ θαυμάζω· ἴδον ἐνθάδε Μέντορα δῖον
χθιζὸν ὑπηοῖον, τότε δ' ἔμβη νηὶ Πύλονδε."

Ὥς ἄρα φωνήσας ἀπέβη πρὸς δώματα πατρός,
τοῖσιν δ' ἀμφοτέροισιν ἀγάσσατο θυμὸς ἀγήνωρ.
μνηστῆρας δ' ἄμυδις κάθισαν καὶ παῦσαν ἀέθλων.
τοῖσιν δ' Ἀντίνοος μετέφη Εὐπείθεος υἱός,
ἀχνύμενος· μένεος δὲ μέγα φρένες ἀμφιμέλαιναι
πίμπλαντ', ὄσσε δέ οἱ πυρὶ λαμπετόωντι ἐίκτην· [1]

" Ὢ πόποι, ἦ μέγα ἔργον ὑπερφιάλως ἐτελέσθη
Τηλεμάχῳ ὁδὸς ἥδε· φάμεν δέ οἱ οὐ τελέεσθαι.
ἐκ τοσσῶνδ' ἀέκητι νέος πάις οἴχεται αὔτως
νῆα ἐρυσσάμενος, κρίνας τ' ἀνὰ δῆμον ἀρίστους.
ἄρξει καὶ προτέρω κακὸν ἔμμεναι· ἀλλά οἱ αὐτῷ
Ζεὺς ὀλέσειε βίην, πρὶν ἥβης μέτρον ἱκέσθαι.[2]
ἀλλ' ἄγε μοι δότε νῆα θοὴν καὶ εἴκοσ' ἑταίρους,
ὄφρα μιν αὐτὸν ἰόντα λοχήσομαι ἠδὲ φυλάξω
ἐν πορθμῷ Ἰθάκης τε Σάμοιό τε παιπαλοέσσης,
ὡς ἂν ἐπισμυγερῶς ναυτίλλεται εἵνεκα πατρός."

[1] Lines 661 and 662 were rejected by Aristarchus, as borrowed from *Il.* i. 103 f.
[2] ἥβης μέτρον ἱκέσθαι Aristarchus : ἡμῖν πῆμα γενέσθαι.

154

perforce and against thy will that he took from thee the black ship? or didst thou give it him freely of thine own will, because he besought thee?"

Then Noemon, son of Phronius, answered him: "I myself freely gave it him. What else could any man do, when a man like him, his heart laden with care, makes entreaty? Hard it were to deny the gift. The youths that are the noblest in the land after ourselves, even these have gone with him; and among them I noted one going on board as their leader, Mentor, or a god, who was in all things like unto Mentor. But at this I marvel. I saw goodly Mentor here yesterday at early dawn; but at that time he embarked for Pylos."

So saying he departed to his father's house, but of those two the proud hearts were angered. The wooers they straightway made to sit down and cease from their games; and among them spoke Antinous, son of Eupeithes, in displeasure; and with rage was his black heart wholly filled, and his eyes were like blazing fire.

"Out upon him, verily a proud deed has been insolently brought to pass by Telemachus, even this journey, and we deemed that he would never see it accomplished. Forth in despite of all of us here the lad is gone without more ado, launching a ship, and choosing the best men in the land. He will begin by and by to be our bane; but to his own undoing may Zeus destroy his might before ever he reaches the measure of manhood. But come, give me a swift ship and twenty men, that I may watch in ambush for him as he passes in the strait between Ithaca and rugged Samos. Thus shall his voyaging in search of his father come to a sorry end."

Ὣς ἔφαθ', οἱ δ' ἄρα πάντες ἐπήνεον ἠδ' ἐκέλευον.
αὐτίκ' ἔπειτ' ἀνστάντες ἔβαν δόμον εἰς Ὀδυσῆος.
    Οὐδ' ἄρα Πηνελόπεια πολὺν χρόνον ἦεν ἄπυστος
μύθων, οὓς μνηστῆρες ἐνὶ φρεσὶ βυσσοδόμευον·
κῆρυξ γάρ οἱ ἔειπε Μέδων, ὃς ἐπεύθετο βουλὰς
αὐλῆς ἐκτὸς ἐών· οἱ δ' ἔνδοθι μῆτιν ὕφαινον.
βῆ δ' ἴμεν ἀγγελέων διὰ δώματα Πηνελοπείῃ·
τὸν δὲ κατ' οὐδοῦ βάντα προσηύδα Πηνελόπεια·
    "Κῆρυξ, τίπτε δέ σε πρόεσαν μνηστῆρες ἀγαυοί;
ἦ εἰπέμεναι δμῳῆσιν Ὀδυσσῆος θείοιο
ἔργων παύσασθαι, σφίσι δ' αὐτοῖς δαῖτα πένεσθαι;
μὴ μνηστεύσαντες μηδ' ἄλλοθ' ὁμιλήσαντες
ὕστατα καὶ πύματα νῦν ἐνθάδε δειπνήσειαν·
οἳ θάμ' ἀγειρόμενοι βίοτον κατακείρετε πολλόν,
κτῆσιν Τηλεμάχοιο δαΐφρονος· οὐδέ τι πατρῶν
ὑμετέρων τὸ πρόσθεν ἀκούετε, παῖδες ἐόντες,
οἷος Ὀδυσσεὺς ἔσκε μεθ' ὑμετέροισι τοκεῦσιν,
οὔτε τινὰ ῥέξας ἐξαίσιον οὔτε τι εἰπὼν
ἐν δήμῳ, ἥ τ' ἐστὶ δίκη θείων βασιλήων·
ἄλλον κ' ἐχθαίρῃσι βροτῶν, ἄλλον κε φιλοίη.
κεῖνος δ' οὔ ποτε πάμπαν ἀτάσθαλον ἄνδρα ἐώργει.
ἀλλ' ὁ μὲν ὑμέτερος θυμὸς καὶ ἀεικέα ἔργα
φαίνεται, οὐδέ τίς ἐστι χάρις μετόπισθ' ἐνεργέων."
    Τὴν δ' αὖτε προσέειπε Μέδων πεπνυμένα εἰδώς·
"Αἲ γὰρ δή, βασίλεια, τόδε πλεῖστον κακὸν εἴη.
ἀλλὰ πολὺ μεῖζόν τε καὶ ἀργαλεώτερον ἄλλο
μνηστῆρες φράζονται, ὃ μὴ τελέσειε Κρονίων·

So he spoke, and they all praised his words, and bade him act. And straightway they rose up and went to the house of Odysseus.

Now Penelope was no long time without knowledge of the plans which the wooers were plotting in the deep of their hearts; for the herald Medon told her, who heard their counsel as he stood without the court and they within were weaving their plot. So he went through the hall to bear the tidings to Penelope; and as he stepped across the threshold Penelope spoke to him and said:

" Herald, why have the lordly wooers sent thee forth? Was it to tell the handmaids of divine Odysseus to cease from their tasks, and make ready a feast for them? Never wooing[1] any more, nor consorting together elsewhere, may they now feast here their latest and their last—even ye who are ever thronging here and wasting much livelihood, the wealth of wise Telemachus. Surely ye hearkened not at all in olden days, when ye were children, when your fathers told what manner of man Odysseus was among them that begat you, in that he wrought no wrong in deed or word to any man in the land, as the wont is of divine kings—one man they hate and another they love. Yet he never wrought iniquity at all to any man. But your mind and your unseemly deeds are plain to see, nor is there in after days any gratitude for good deeds done."

Then Medon, wise of heart, answered her: " I would, O queen, that this were the greatest evil. But another greater far and more grievous are the wooers planning, which I pray that the son of Cronos

---

[1] In the interpretation of this vexed passage I follow Agar, *Homerica*, pp. 59 ff.

Τηλέμαχον μεμάασι κατακτάμεν ὀξέι χαλκῷ   7
οἴκαδε νισόμενον· ὁ δ' ἔβη μετὰ πατρὸς ἀκουὴν
ἐς Πύλον ἠγαθέην ἠδ' ἐς Λακεδαίμονα δῖαν."

Ὣς φάτο, τῆς δ' αὐτοῦ λύτο γούνατα καὶ φίλον ἦτ
δὴν δέ μιν ἀμφασίη ἐπέων λάβε· τὼ δέ οἱ ὄσσε
δακρυόφι πλῆσθεν, θαλερὴ δέ οἱ ἔσχετο φωνή.   7
ὀψὲ δὲ δή μιν ἔπεσσιν ἀμειβομένη προσέειπε·

" Κῆρυξ, τίπτε δέ μοι πάις οἴχεται; οὐδέ τί μιν χρ
νηῶν ὠκυπόρων ἐπιβαινέμεν, αἵ θ' ἁλὸς ἵπποι
ἀνδράσι γίγνονται, περόωσι δὲ πουλὺν ἐφ' ὑγρήν.
ἦ ἵνα μηδ' ὄνομ' αὐτοῦ ἐν ἀνθρώποισι λίπηται;"   7

Τὴν δ' ἠμείβετ' ἔπειτα Μέδων πεπνυμένα εἰδώς·
" Οὐκ οἶδ' ἤ τίς μιν θεὸς ὤρορεν, ἦε καὶ αὐτοῦ
θυμὸς ἐφωρμήθη ἵμεν ἐς Πύλον, ὄφρα πύθηται
πατρὸς ἑοῦ ἢ νόστον ἢ ὅν τινα πότμον ἐπέσπεν."

Ὣς ἄρα φωνήσας ἀπέβη κατὰ δῶμ' Ὀδυσῆος.   7
τὴν δ' ἄχος ἀμφεχύθη θυμοφθόρον, οὐδ' ἄρ' ἔτ' ἔτλη
δίφρῳ ἐφέζεσθαι πολλῶν κατὰ οἶκον ἐόντων,
ἀλλ' ἄρ' ἐπ' οὐδοῦ ἷζε πολυκμήτου θαλάμοιο
οἴκτρ' ὀλοφυρομένη· περὶ δὲ δμῳαὶ μινύριζον
πᾶσαι, ὅσαι κατὰ δώματ' ἔσαν νέαι ἠδὲ παλαιαί.   7
τῆς δ' ἁδινὸν γοόωσα μετηύδα Πηνελόπεια·

"Κλῦτε, φίλαι· πέρι γάρ μοι Ὀλύμπιος ἄλγε' ἔδω
ἐκ πασέων, ὅσσαι μοι ὁμοῦ τράφεν ἠδ' ἐγένοντο·
ἢ πρὶν μὲν πόσιν ἐσθλὸν ἀπώλεσα θυμολέοντα,
παντοίῃς ἀρετῇσι κεκασμένον ἐν Δαναοῖσιν,   7
ἐσθλόν, τοῦ κλέος εὐρὺ καθ' Ἑλλάδα καὶ μέσον Ἄργε

---

¹ Line 726 was rejected by Aristarchus; cf. i. 344 and, below, 816.

may never bring to pass. They are minded to slay
Telemachus with the sharp sword on his homeward
way; for he went in quest of tidings of his father
to sacred Pylos and to goodly Lacedaemon."

So he spoke, and her knees were loosened where
she sat, and her heart melted. Long time she was
speechless, and both her eyes were filled with tears,
and the flow of her voice was checked. But at last
she made answer, and said to him:

"Herald, why is my son gone? He had no need
to go on board swift-faring ships, which serve men
as horses of the deep, and cross over the wide waters
of the sea. Was it that not even his name should
be left among men?"

Then Medon, wise of heart, answered her: "I
know not whether some god impelled him, or whether
his own heart was moved to go to Pylos, that he
might learn either of his father's return or what fate
he had met."

So he spoke, and departed through the house of
Odysseus, and on her fell a cloud of soul-consuming
grief, and she had no more the heart to sit upon one
of the many seats that were in the room, but down
upon the threshold of her fair-wrought chamber she
sank, moaning piteously, and round about her wailed
her handmaids, even all that were in the house, both
young and old. Among these with sobs of lament-
ation spoke Penelope:

"Hear me, my friends, for to me the Olympian
has given sorrow above all the women who were
bred and born with me. For long since I lost my
noble husband of the lion heart, pre-eminent in all
manner of worth among the Danaans, my noble
husband, whose fame is wide through Hellas and

νῦν αὖ παῖδ' ἀγαπητὸν ἀνηρείψαντο θύελλαι
ἀκλέα ἐκ μεγάρων, οὐδ' ὁρμηθέντος ἄκουσα.
σχέτλιαι, οὐδ' ὑμεῖς περ ἐνὶ φρεσὶ θέσθε ἑκάστη
ἐκ λεχέων μ' ἀνεγεῖραι, ἐπιστάμεναι σάφα θυμῷ,   73
ὁππότ' ἐκεῖνος ἔβη κοίλην ἐπὶ νῆα μέλαιναν.
εἰ γὰρ ἐγὼ πυθόμην ταύτην ὁδὸν ὁρμαίνοντα,
τῷ κε μάλ' ἤ κεν ἔμεινε καὶ ἐσσύμενός περ ὁδοῖο,
ἤ κέ με τεθνηκυῖαν ἐνὶ μεγάροισιν ἔλειπεν.
ἀλλά τις ὀτρηρῶς Δολίον καλέσειε γέροντα,   73
δμῶ' ἐμόν, ὅν μοι δῶκε πατὴρ ἔτι δεῦρο κιούσῃ,
καί μοι κῆπον ἔχει πολυδένδρεον, ὄφρα τάχιστα
Λαέρτῃ τάδε πάντα παρεζόμενος καταλέξῃ,
εἰ δή πού τινα κεῖνος ἐνὶ φρεσὶ μῆτιν ὑφήνας
ἐξελθὼν λαοῖσιν ὀδύρεται, οἳ μεμάασιν   74
ὃν καὶ Ὀδυσσῆος φθῖσαι γόνον ἀντιθέοιο."

  Τὴν δ' αὖτε προσέειπε φίλη τροφὸς Εὐρύκλεια·
"Νύμφα φίλη, σὺ μὲν ἄρ με κατάκτανε νηλέϊ χαλκῷ
ἤ ἔα ἐν μεγάρῳ· μῦθον δέ τοι οὐκ ἐπικεύσω.
ᾔδε' ἐγὼ τάδε πάντα, πόρον δέ οἱ ὅσσ' ἐκέλευε,   74
σῖτον καὶ μέθυ ἡδύ· ἐμεῦ δ' ἕλετο μέγαν ὅρκον
μὴ πρὶν σοὶ ἐρέειν, πρὶν δωδεκάτην γε γενέσθαι
ἤ σ' αὐτὴν ποθέσαι καὶ ἀφορμηθέντος ἀκοῦσαι,
ὡς ἂν μὴ κλαίουσα κατὰ χρόα καλὸν ἰάπτῃς.
ἀλλ' ὑδρηναμένη, καθαρὰ χροΐ εἵμαθ' ἑλοῦσα,   75
εἰς ὑπερῷ' ἀναβᾶσα σὺν ἀμφιπόλοισι γυναιξὶν
εὔχε' Ἀθηναίῃ κούρῃ Διὸς αἰγιόχοιο·
ἤ γάρ κέν μιν ἔπειτα καὶ ἐκ θανάτοιο σαώσαι.
μηδὲ γέροντα κάκου κεκακωμένον· οὐ γὰρ ὀΐω
πάγχυ θεοῖς μακάρεσσι γονὴν Ἀρκεισιάδαο   75

mid-Argos. And now again my well-loved son have the storm-winds swept away from our halls without tidings, nor did I hear of his setting forth. Cruel, that ye are! Not even you took thought, any one of you, to rouse me from my couch, though in your hearts ye knew full well when he went on board the hollow black ship. For had I learned that he was pondering this journey, he should verily have stayed here, how eager soever to be gone, or he should have left me dead in the halls. But now let one hasten to call hither the aged Dolius, my servant, whom my father gave me or ever I came hither, and who keeps my garden of many trees, that he may straightway go and sit by Laertes, and tell him of all these things. So haply may Laertes weave some plan in his heart, and go forth and with weeping make his plea to the people, who are minded to destroy his race and that of godlike Odysseus."

Then the good nurse Eurycleia answered her: "Dear lady, thou mayest verily slay me with the pitiless sword or let me abide in the house, yet will I not hide my word from thee. I knew all this, and gave him whatever he bade me, bread and sweet wine. But he took from me a mighty oath not to tell thee until at least the twelfth day should come, or thou shouldst thyself miss him and hear that he was gone, that thou mightest not mar thy fair flesh with weeping. But now bathe thyself, and take clean raiment for thy body, and then go up to thy upper chamber with thy handmaids and pray to Athene, the daughter of Zeus who bears the aegis; for she may then save him even from death. And trouble not a troubled old man; for the race of the son of Arceisius is not, methinks, utterly hated by the blessed gods,

ἔχθεσθ᾽, ἀλλ᾽ ἔτι πού τις ἐπέσσεται ὅς κεν ἔχῃσι
δώματά θ᾽ ὑψερεφέα καὶ ἀπόπροθι πίονας ἀγρούς."

Ὣς φάτο, τῆς δ᾽ εὔνησε γόον, σχέθε δ᾽ ὄσσε γόοιο.
ἡ δ᾽ ὑδρηναμένη, καθαρὰ χροῒ εἵμαθ᾽ ἑλοῦσα
εἰς ὑπερῷ᾽ ἀνέβαινε σὺν ἀμφιπόλοισι γυναιξίν,   7
ἐν δ᾽ ἔθετ᾽ οὐλοχύτας κανέῳ, ἠρᾶτο δ᾽ Ἀθήνῃ·

" Κλῦθί μευ, αἰγιόχοιο Διὸς τέκος, ἀτρυτώνη,
εἴ ποτέ τοι πολύμητις ἐνὶ μεγάροισιν Ὀδυσσεὺς
ἢ βοὸς ἢ ὄιος κατὰ πίονα μηρί᾽ ἔκηε,
τῶν νῦν μοι μνῆσαι, καί μοι φίλον υἷα σάωσον,   7
μνηστῆρας δ᾽ ἀπάλαλκε κακῶς ὑπερηνορέοντας."

Ὣς εἰποῦσ᾽ ὀλόλυξε, θεὰ δέ οἱ ἔκλυεν ἀρῆς.
μνηστῆρες δ᾽ ὁμάδησαν ἀνὰ μέγαρα σκιόεντα·
ὧδε δέ τις εἴπεσκε νέων ὑπερηνορεόντων·

"Ἦ μάλα δὴ γάμον ἄμμι πολυμνήστη βασίλεια 7
ἀρτύει, οὐδέ τι οἶδεν ὅ οἱ φόνος υἷι τέτυκται."

Ὣς ἄρα τις εἴπεσκε, τὰ δ᾽ οὐκ ἴσαν ὡς ἐτέτυκτο.
τοῖσιν δ᾽ Ἀντίνοος ἀγορήσατο καὶ μετέειπε·

" Δαιμόνιοι, μύθους μὲν ὑπερφιάλους ἀλέασθε
πάντας ὁμῶς, μή πού τις ἀπαγγείλῃσι[1] καὶ εἴσω,   7
ἀλλ᾽ ἄγε σιγῇ τοῖον ἀναστάντες τελέωμεν
μῦθον, ὃ δὴ καὶ πᾶσιν ἐνὶ φρεσὶν ἤραρεν ἡμῖν."

Ὣς εἰπὼν ἐκρίνατ᾽ ἐείκοσι φῶτας ἀρίστους,
βὰν δ᾽ ἴεναι ἐπὶ νῆα θοὴν καὶ θῖνα θαλάσσης.

[1] ἀπαγγείλῃσι: ἐπαγγείλῃσι.

---

[1] The word δαιμόνιος properly means "under the influence
of a δαίμων." It is used in the vocative in cases where the

but there shall still be one, I ween, to hold the high-roofed halls and the rich fields far away."

So she spoke, and lulled Penelope's laments, and made her eyes to cease from weeping. She then bathed, and took clean raiment for her body, and went up to her upper chamber with her handmaids, and placing barley grains in a basket prayed to Athene:

"Hear me, child of Zeus who bears the aegis, unwearied one. If ever Odysseus, of many wiles, burnt to thee in his halls fat thigh-pieces of heifer or ewe, remember these things now, I pray thee, and save my dear son, and ward off from him the wooers in their evil insolence."

So saying she raised the sacred cry, and the goddess heard her prayer. But the wooers broke into uproar throughout the shadowy halls, and thus would one of the proud youths speak:

"Aye, verily the queen, wooed of many, is preparing our marriage, nor does she know at all that death has been made ready for her son."

So would one of them speak; but they knew not how these things were to be. And Antinous addressed their company, and said:

"Good sirs,[1] shun haughty speech of every kind alike, lest someone report your speech even within the house. Nay come, in silence thus let us arise and put into effect our plan which pleased us one and all at heart."

So he spoke, and chose twenty men that were best, and they went their way to the swift ship and the

person addressed is acting in some unaccountable or ill-omened way. Hence the tone varies from angry remonstrance to gentle expostulation, or even pity.

νῆα μὲν οὖν πάμπρωτον ἁλὸς βένθοσδε ἔρυσσαν,   7⸱
ἐν δ' ἱστόν τ' ἐτίθεντο καὶ ἱστία νηὶ μελαίνῃ,
ἠρτύναντο δ' ἐρετμὰ τροποῖς ἐν δερματίνοισιν,
πάντα κατὰ μοῖραν, ἀνά θ' ἱστία λευκὰ πέτασσαν[1]
τεύχεα δέ σφ' ἤνεικαν ὑπέρθυμοι θεράποντες.
ὑψοῦ δ' ἐν νοτίῳ τήν γ' ὥρμισαν, ἐκ δ' ἔβαν αὐτοί·   7⸱
ἔνθα δὲ δόρπον ἕλοντο, μένον δ' ἐπὶ ἕσπερον ἐλθεῖν.

  Ἡ δ' ὑπερωίῳ αὖθι περίφρων Πηνελόπεια
κεῖτ' ἄρ' ἄσιτος, ἄπαστος ἐδητύος ἠδὲ ποτῆτος,
ὁρμαίνουσ' ἤ οἱ θάνατον φύγοι υἱὸς ἀμύμων,
ἦ ὅ γ' ὑπὸ μνηστῆρσιν ὑπερφιάλοισι δαμείη.   7⸱
ὅσσα δὲ μερμήριξε λέων ἀνδρῶν ἐν ὁμίλῳ
δείσας, ὁππότε μιν δόλιον περὶ κύκλον ἄγωσι,
τόσσα μιν ὁρμαίνουσαν ἐπήλυθε νήδυμος ὕπνος·
εὗδε δ' ἀνακλινθεῖσα, λύθεν δέ οἱ ἅψεα πάντα.

  Ἔνθ' αὖτ' ἄλλ' ἐνόησε θεά, γλαυκῶπις Ἀθήνη·   7⸱
εἴδωλον ποίησε, δέμας δ' ἤικτο γυναικί,
Ἰφθίμῃ, κούρῃ μεγαλήτορος Ἰκαρίοιο,
τὴν Εὔμηλος ὄπυιε Φερῇς ἔνι οἰκία ναίων.
πέμπε δέ μιν πρὸς δώματ' Ὀδυσσῆος θείοιο,
ἠος Πηνελόπειαν ὀδυρομένην γοόωσαν   8⸱
παύσειε κλαυθμοῖο γόοιό τε δακρυόεντος.
ἐς θάλαμον δ' εἰσῆλθε παρὰ κληῖδος ἱμάντα,
στῆ δ' ἄρ' ὑπὲρ κεφαλῆς, καί μιν πρὸς μῦθον ἔειπεν·

  "Εὕδεις, Πηνελόπεια, φίλον τετιημένη ἦτορ;
οὐ μέν σ' οὐδὲ ἐῶσι θεοὶ ῥεῖα ζώοντες   8⸱
κλαίειν οὐδ' ἀκάχησθαι, ἐπεί ῥ' ἔτι νόστιμός ἐστι
σὸς παῖς· οὐ μὲν γάρ τι θεοῖς ἀλιτήμενός ἐστι."

---

[1] Line 783 (= viii. 54) is omitted in many MSS.

shore of the sea. The ship first of all they drew down to the deep water, and set the mast and sail in the black ship, and fitted the oars in the leathern thole-straps, all in due order, and spread the white sail. And proud squires brought them their weapons. Well out in the roadstead they moored the ship, and themselves disembarked. There then they took supper, and waited till evening should come.

But she, the wise Penelope, lay there in her upper chamber, touching no food, tasting neither meat nor drink, pondering whether her peerless son would escape death, or be slain by the insolent wooers. And even as a lion is seized with fear and broods amid a throng of men, when they draw their crafty ring about him, so was she pondering when sweet[1] sleep came upon her. And she sank back and slept, and all her joints relaxed.

Then the goddess, flashing-eyed Athene, took other counsel. She made a phantom, and likened it in form to a woman, Iphthime, daughter of great-hearted Icarius, whom Eumelus wedded, whose home was in Pherae. And she sent it to the house of divine Odysseus, to Penelope in the midst of her wailing and lamenting, to bid her cease from weeping and tearful lamentation. So into the chamber it passed by the thong of the bolt, and stood above her head, and spoke to her, and said:

"Sleepest thou, Penelope, thy heart sore stricken? Nay, the gods that live at ease suffer thee not to weep or be distressed, seeing that thy son is yet to return; for in no wise is he a sinner in the eyes of the gods."

---

[1] It seems certain that νήδυμος has in all cases supplanted an original Fήδυμος = ἡδύς. See Buttmann, *Lexilogus*, i. p. 179, and Merry's note here.

Τὴν δ' ἠμείβετ' ἔπειτα περίφρων Πηνελόπεια,
ἡδὺ μάλα κνώσσουσ' ἐν ὀνειρείῃσι πύλῃσιν·
" Τίπτε, κασιγνήτη, δεῦρ' ἤλυθες; οὔ τι πάρος γε 8
πωλέ', ἐπεὶ μάλα πολλὸν ἀπόπροθι δώματα ναίεις·
καί με κέλεαι παύσασθαι οἰζύος ἠδ' ὀδυνάων
πολλέων, αἴ μ' ἐρέθουσι κατὰ φρένα καὶ κατὰ θυμόν,
ἣ πρὶν μὲν πόσιν ἐσθλὸν ἀπώλεσα θυμολέοντα,
παντοίῃς ἀρετῇσι κεκασμένον ἐν Δαναοῖσιν, 8
ἐσθλόν, τοῦ κλέος εὐρὺ καθ' Ἑλλάδα καὶ μέσον
Ἄργος· [1]
νῦν αὖ παῖς ἀγαπητὸς ἔβη κοίλης ἐπὶ νηός,
νήπιος, οὔτε πόνων ἐῢ εἰδὼς οὔτ' ἀγοράων.
τοῦ δὴ ἐγὼ καὶ μᾶλλον ὀδύρομαι ἤ περ ἐκείνου·
τοῦ δ' ἀμφιτρομέω καὶ δείδια, μή τι πάθῃσιν, 8
ἢ ὅ γε τῶν ἐνὶ δήμῳ, ἵν' οἴχεται, ἢ ἐνὶ πόντῳ·
δυσμενέες γὰρ πολλοὶ ἐπ' αὐτῷ μηχανόωνται,
ἱέμενοι κτεῖναι πρὶν πατρίδα γαῖαν ἱκέσθαι."
Τὴν δ' ἀπαμειβόμενον προσέφη εἴδωλον ἀμαυρόν·
" Θάρσει, μηδέ τι πάγχυ μετὰ φρεσὶ δείδιθι λίην·
τοίη γάρ οἱ πομπὸς ἅμ' ἔρχεται, ἥν τε καὶ ἄλλοι
ἀνέρες ἠρήσαντο παρεστάμεναι, δύναται γάρ,
Παλλὰς Ἀθηναίη· σὲ δ' ὀδυρομένην ἐλεαίρει·
ἣ νῦν με προέηκε τεῒν τάδε μυθήσασθαι."
Τὴν δ' αὖτε προσέειπε περίφρων Πηνελόπεια· 8
" Εἰ μὲν δὴ θεός ἐσσι θεοῖό τε ἔκλυες αὐδῆς,
εἰ δ' ἄγε μοι καὶ κεῖνον οἰζυρὸν κατάλεξον,
ἤ που ἔτι ζώει καὶ ὁρᾷ φάος ἠελίοιο,
ἢ ἤδη τέθνηκε καὶ εἰν Ἀΐδαο δόμοισι."
Τὴν δ' ἀπαμειβόμενον προσέφη εἴδωλον ἀμαυρόν·
" Οὐ μέν τοι κεῖνόν γε διηνεκέως ἀγορεύσω,
ζώει ὅ γ' ἢ τέθνηκε· κακὸν δ' ἀνεμώλια βάζειν."

[1] Line 816 was rejected by Aristarchus ; cf. 726 and i. 344.

Then wise Penelope answered her, as she slumbered very sweetly at the gates of dreams:

"Why, sister, art thou come hither? Thou hast not heretofore been wont to come, for thou dwellest in a home far away. And thou biddest me cease from my grief and the many pains that distress me in mind and heart. Long since I lost my noble husband of the lion heart, pre-eminent in all manner of worth among the Danaans, my noble husband whose fame is wide in Hellas and mid-Argos. And now again my well-loved son is gone forth in a hollow ship, a mere child, knowing naught of toils and the gatherings of men. For him I sorrow even more than for that other, and tremble for him, and fear lest aught befall him, whether it be in the land of the men to whom he is gone, or on the sea. For many foes are plotting against him, eager to slay him before he comes back to his native land."

Then the dim phantom answered her, and said: "Take heart, and be not in thy mind too sore afraid; since such a guide goes with him as men have full often besought to stand by their side, for she has power,—even Pallas Athene. And she pities thee in thy sorrow, for she it is that has sent me forth to tell thee this."

Then again wise Penelope answered her: "If thou art indeed a god, and hast listened to the voice of a god, come, tell me, I pray thee, also of that hapless one, whether he still lives and beholds the light of the sun, or whether he is already dead and in the house of Hades."

And the dim phantom answered her, and said: "Nay, of him I may not speak at length, whether he be alive or dead; it is an ill thing to speak words vain as wind."

Ὣς εἰπὸν σταθμοῖο παρὰ κληῖδα λιάσθη
ἐς πνοιὰς ἀνέμων. ἡ δ' ἐξ ὕπνου ἀνόρουσε
κούρη Ἰκαρίοιο· φίλον δέ οἱ ἦτορ ἰάνθη,
ὥς οἱ ἐναργὲς ὄνειρον ἐπέσσυτο νυκτὸς ἀμολγῷ.

Μνηστῆρες δ' ἀναβάντες ἐπέπλεον ὑγρὰ κέλευθα
Τηλεμάχῳ φόνον αἰπὺν ἐνὶ φρεσὶν ὁρμαίνοντες.
ἔστι δέ τις νῆσος μέσσῃ ἁλὶ πετρήεσσα,
μεσσηγὺς Ἰθάκης τε Σάμοιό τε παιπαλοέσσης,
Ἀστερίς, οὐ μεγάλη· λιμένες δ' ἔνι ναύλοχοι αὐτῇ
ἀμφίδυμοι· τῇ τόν γε μένον λοχόωντες Ἀχαιοί.

So saying the phantom glided away by the bolt of the door into the breath of the winds. And the daughter of Icarius started up from sleep, and her heart was warmed with comfort, that so clear a vision had sped to her in the darkness [1] of night.

But the wooers embarked, and sailed over the watery ways, pondering in their hearts utter murder for Telemachus. There is a rocky isle in the midst of the sea, midway between Ithaca and rugged Samos, Asteris, of no great size, but therein is a harbour where ships may lie, with an entrance on either side. There it was that the Achaeans tarried, lying in wait for Telemachus.

[1] The word is of uncertain etymology, and its precise significance is doubtful.

E

Ἠὼς δ’ ἐκ λεχέων παρ’ ἀγαυοῦ Τιθωνοῖο
ὤρνυθ’, ἵν’ ἀθανάτοισι φόως φέροι ἠδὲ βροτοῖσιν·
οἱ δὲ θεοὶ θῶκόνδε καθίζανον, ἐν δ’ ἄρα τοῖσι
Ζεὺς ὑψιβρεμέτης, οὗ τε κράτος ἐστὶ μέγιστον.
τοῖσι δ’ Ἀθηναίη λέγε κήδεα πόλλ’ Ὀδυσῆος
μνησαμένη· μέλε γάρ οἱ ἐὼν ἐν δώμασι νύμφης·

"Ζεῦ πάτερ ἠδ’ ἄλλοι μάκαρες θεοὶ αἰὲν ἐόντες,
μή τις ἔτι πρόφρων ἀγανὸς καὶ ἤπιος ἔστω
σκηπτοῦχος βασιλεύς, μηδὲ φρεσὶν αἴσιμα εἰδώς,
ἀλλ’ αἰεὶ χαλεπός τ’ εἴη καὶ αἴσυλα ῥέζοι·
ὡς οὔ τις μέμνηται Ὀδυσσῆος θείοιο
λαῶν οἷσιν ἄνασσε, πατὴρ δ’ ὡς ἤπιος ἦεν.
ἀλλ’ ὁ μὲν ἐν νήσῳ κεῖται κρατέρ’ ἄλγεα πάσχων
νύμφης ἐν μεγάροισι Καλυψοῦς, ἥ μιν ἀνάγκη
ἴσχει· ὁ δ’ οὐ δύναται ἣν πατρίδα γαῖαν ἱκέσθαι·
οὐ γάρ οἱ πάρα νῆες ἐπήρετμοι καὶ ἑταῖροι,
οἵ κέν μιν πέμποιεν ἐπ’ εὐρέα νῶτα θαλάσσης.
νῦν αὖ παῖδ’ ἀγαπητὸν ἀποκτεῖναι μεμάασιν
οἴκαδε νισόμενον· ὁ δ’ ἔβη μετὰ πατρὸς ἀκουὴν
ἐς Πύλον ἠγαθέην ἠδ’ ἐς Λακεδαίμονα δῖαν."

Τὴν δ’ ἀπαμειβόμενος προσέφη νεφεληγερέτα Ζεύς·
"Τέκνον ἐμόν, ποῖόν σε ἔπος φύγεν ἕρκος ὀδόντων.

BOOK V

Now Dawn arose from her couch from beside
lordly Tithonus, to bear light to the immortals and
to mortal men. And the gods were sitting down to
council, and among them Zeus, who thunders on
high, whose might is supreme. To them Athene
was recounting the many woes of Odysseus, as she
called them to mind; for it troubled her that he
abode in the dwelling of the nymph:

"Father Zeus, and ye other blessed gods that are
forever, never henceforward let sceptred king with
a ready heart be kind and gentle, nor let him heed
righteousness in his mind; but let him ever be
harsh, and work unrighteousness, seeing that no
one remembers divine Odysseus of the people
whose lord he was; yet gentle was he as a father.
He verily abides in an island suffering grievous
pains, in the halls of the nymph Calypso, who keeps
him perforce; and he cannot return to his own land,
for he has at hand no ships with oars and no com-
rades to send him on his way over the broad back of
the sea. And now again they are minded to slay
his well-loved son on his homeward way; for he
went in quest of tidings of his father to sacred
Pylos and to goodly Lacedaemon."

Then Zeus, the cloud-gatherer, answered her,
and said: "My child, what a word has escaped

οὐ γὰρ δὴ τοῦτον μὲν ἐβούλευσας νόον αὐτή,
ὡς ἦ τοι κείνους Ὀδυσεὺς ἀποτίσεται ἐλθών;
Τηλέμαχον δὲ σὺ πέμψον ἐπισταμένως, δύνασαι γάρ,
ὥς κε μάλ' ἀσκηθὴς ἣν πατρίδα γαῖαν ἵκηται,
μνηστῆρες δ' ἐν νηὶ·παλιμπετὲς ἀπονέωνται."
    Ἦ ῥα καὶ Ἑρμείαν, υἱὸν φίλον, ἀντίον ηὔδα·
"Ἑρμεία, σὺ γὰρ αὖτε τά τ' ἄλλα περ ἄγγελός ἐσσι,
νύμφῃ ἐυπλοκάμῳ εἰπεῖν νημερτέα βουλήν,
νόστον Ὀδυσσῆος ταλασίφρονος, ὥς κε νέηται
οὔτε θεῶν πομπῇ οὔτε θνητῶν ἀνθρώπων·
ἀλλ' ὅ γ' ἐπὶ σχεδίης πολυδέσμου πήματα πάσχων
ἤματί κ' εἰκοστῷ Σχερίην ἐρίβωλον ἵκοιτο,
Φαιήκων ἐς γαῖαν, οἳ ἀγχίθεοι γεγάασιν,
οἵ κέν μιν περὶ κῆρι θεὸν ὣς τιμήσουσιν,
πέμψουσιν δ' ἐν νηὶ φίλην ἐς πατρίδα γαῖαν,
χαλκόν τε χρυσόν τε ἅλις ἐσθῆτά τε δόντες,
πόλλ', ὅσ' ἂν οὐδέ ποτε Τροίης ἐξήρατ' Ὀδυσσεύς,
εἴ περ ἀπήμων ἦλθε, λαχὼν ἀπὸ ληίδος αἶσαν.
ὣς γάρ οἱ μοῖρ' ἐστὶ φίλους τ' ἰδέειν καὶ ἱκέσθαι
οἶκον ἐς ὑψόροφον καὶ ἑὴν ἐς πατρίδα γαῖαν."
    Ὣς ἔφατ', οὐδ' ἀπίθησε διάκτορος ἀργεϊφόντης.
αὐτίκ' ἔπειθ' ὑπὸ ποσσὶν ἐδήσατο καλὰ πέδιλα,
ἀμβρόσια χρύσεια, τά μιν φέρον ἠμὲν ἐφ' ὑγρὴν
ἠδ' ἐπ' ἀπείρονα γαῖαν ἅμα πνοιῇς ἀνέμοιο.
εἵλετο δὲ ῥάβδον, τῇ τ' ἀνδρῶν ὄμματα θέλγει,
ὧν ἐθέλει, τοὺς δ' αὖτε καὶ ὑπνώοντας ἐγείρει.
τὴν μετὰ χερσὶν ἔχων πέτετο κρατὺς ἀργεϊφόντης.

the barrier of thy teeth! Didst thou not thyself devise this plan, that verily Odysseus might take vengeance on these men at his coming? But concerning Telemachus, do thou guide him in thy wisdom, for thou canst, that all unscathed he may reach his native land, and the wooers may come back in their ship baffled in their purpose."

He spoke, and said to Hermes, his dear son: "Hermes, do thou now, seeing that thou art at other times our messenger, declare to the fair-tressed nymph our fixed resolve, even the return of Odysseus of the steadfast heart, that he may return with guidance neither of gods nor of mortal men, but that on a stoutly-bound raft, suffering woes, he may come on the twentieth day to deep-soiled Scheria, the land of the Phaeacians, who are near of kin to the gods. These shall heartily shew him all honour, as if he were a god, and shall send him in a ship to his dear native land, after giving him stores of bronze and gold and raiment, more than Odysseus would ever have won for himself from Troy, if he had returned unscathed with his due share of the spoil. For in this wise it is his fate to see his friends, and reach his high-roofed house and his native land."

So he spoke, and the messenger, Argeïphontes, failed not to hearken. Straightway he bound beneath his feet his beautiful sandals, immortal, golden, which were wont to bear him over the waters of the sea and over the boundless land swift as the blasts of the wind. And he took the wand wherewith he lulls to sleep the eyes of whom he will, while others again he awakens even out of slumber. With this in his hand the strong Argeïphontes flew. On to

Πιερίην δ' ἐπιβὰς ἐξ αἰθέρος ἔμπεσε πόντῳ·
σεύατ' ἔπειτ' ἐπὶ κῦμα λάρῳ ὄρνιθι ἐοικώς,
ὅς τε κατὰ δεινοὺς κόλπους ἁλὸς ἀτρυγέτοιο
ἰχθῦς ἀγρώσσων πυκινὰ πτερὰ δεύεται ἅλμῃ·
τῷ ἴκελος πολέεσσιν ὀχήσατο κύμασιν Ἑρμῆς.
ἀλλ' ὅτε δὴ τὴν νῆσον ἀφίκετο τηλόθ' ἐοῦσαν,
ἔνθ' ἐκ πόντου βὰς ἰοειδέος ἤπειρόνδε
ἤιεν, ὄφρα μέγα σπέος ἵκετο, τῷ ἔνι νύμφη
ναῖεν ἐυπλόκαμος· τὴν δ' ἔνδοθι τέτμεν ἐοῦσαν.
πῦρ μὲν ἐπ' ἐσχαρόφιν μέγα καίετο, τηλόσε δ' ὀδμὴ
κέδρου τ' εὐκεάτοιο θύου τ' ἀνὰ νῆσον ὀδώδει
δαιομένων· ἡ δ' ἔνδον ἀοιδιάουσ' ὀπὶ καλῇ
ἱστὸν ἐποιχομένη χρυσείῃ κερκίδ' ὕφαινεν.
ὕλη δὲ σπέος ἀμφὶ πεφύκει τηλεθόωσα,
κλήθρη τ' αἴγειρός τε καὶ εὐώδης κυπάρισσος.
ἔνθα δέ τ' ὄρνιθες τανυσίπτεροι εὐνάζοντο,
σκῶπές τ' ἴρηκές τε τανύγλωσσοί τε κορῶναι
εἰνάλιαι, τῇσίν τε θαλάσσια ἔργα μέμηλεν.
ἡ δ' αὐτοῦ τετάνυστο περὶ σπείους γλαφυροῖο
ἡμερὶς ἡβώωσα, τεθήλει δὲ σταφυλῇσι.
κρῆναι δ' ἑξείης πίσυρες ῥέον ὕδατι λευκῷ,
πλησίαι ἀλλήλων τετραμμέναι ἄλλυδις ἄλλη.
ἀμφὶ δὲ λειμῶνες μαλακοὶ ἴου ἠδὲ σελίνου
θήλεον. ἔνθα κ' ἔπειτα καὶ ἀθάνατός περ ἐπελθὼν
θηήσαιτο ἰδὼν καὶ τερφθείη φρεσὶν ᾗσιν.
ἔνθα στὰς θηεῖτο διάκτορος ἀργεϊφόντης.
αὐτὰρ ἐπεὶ δὴ πάντα ἑῷ θηήσατο θυμῷ,
αὐτίκ' ἄρ' εἰς εὐρὺ σπέος ἤλυθεν. οὐδέ μιν ἄντην
ἠγνοίησεν ἰδοῦσα Καλυψώ, δῖα θεάων·
οὐ γάρ τ' ἀγνῶτες θεοὶ ἀλλήλοισι πέλονται
ἀθάνατοι, οὐδ' εἴ τις ἀπόπροθι δώματα ναίει.

Pieria he stepped from the upper air, and swooped
down upon the sea, and then sped over the wave
like a bird, the cormorant, which in quest of fish
over the dread gulfs of the unresting sea wets its
thick plumage in the brine.   In such wise did
Hermes ride upon the multitudinous waves.   But
when he had reached the island which lay afar,
then forth from the violet sea he came to land, and
went his way until he came to a great cave, wherein
dwelt the fair-tressed nymph ; and he found her
within.   A great fire was burning on the hearth,
and from afar over the isle there was a fragrance
of cleft cedar and juniper, as they burned ; but
she within was singing with a sweet voice as she
went to and fro before the loom, weaving with a
golden shuttle.   Round about the cave grew a
luxuriant wood, alder and poplar and sweet-smelling
cypress, wherein birds long of wing were wont to
nest, owls and falcons and sea-crows with chattering
tongues, who ply their business on the sea.   And
right there about the hollow cave ran trailing a
garden vine, in pride of its prime, richly laden with
clusters.   And fountains four in a row were flowing
with bright water hard by one another, turned one
this way, one that.   And round about soft meadows
of violets and parsley were blooming.   There even
an immortal, who chanced to come, might gaze and
marvel, and delight his soul ; and there the messenger
Argeïphontes stood and marvelled.   But when he
had marvelled in his heart at all things, straightway
he went into the wide cave ; nor did Calypso, the
beautiful goddess, fail to know him, when she saw
him face to face ; for not unknown are the immortal
gods to one another, even though one dwells in a

οὐδ' ἄρ' Ὀδυσσῆα μεγαλήτορα ἔνδον ἔτετμεν,
ἀλλ' ὅ γ' ἐπ' ἀκτῆς κλαῖε καθήμενος, ἔνθα πάρος περ,
δάκρυσι καὶ στοναχῇσι καὶ ἄλγεσι θυμὸν ἐρέχθων.
πόντον ἐπ' ἀτρύγετον δερκέσκετο δάκρυα λείβων.[1]
Ἑρμείαν δ' ἐρέεινε Καλυψώ, δῖα θεάων,   85
ἐν θρόνῳ ἱδρύσασα φαεινῷ σιγαλόεντι·

  "Τίπτε μοι, Ἑρμεία χρυσόρραπι, εἰλήλουθας
αἰδοῖός τε φίλος τε; πάρος γε μὲν οὔ τι θαμίζεις.
αὔδα ὅ τι φρονέεις· τελέσαι δέ με θυμὸς ἄνωγεν,
εἰ δύναμαι τελέσαι γε καὶ εἰ τετελεσμένον ἐστίν.   90
ἀλλ' ἕπεο προτέρω, ἵνα τοι πὰρ ξείνια θείω." [2]

  Ὣς ἄρα φωνήσασα θεὰ παρέθηκε τράπεζαν
ἀμβροσίης πλήσασα, κέρασσε δὲ νέκταρ ἐρυθρόν.
αὐτὰρ ὁ πῖνε καὶ ἦσθε διάκτορος ἀργεϊφόντης.
αὐτὰρ ἐπεὶ δείπνησε καὶ ἤραρε θυμὸν ἐδωδῇ,   95
καὶ τότε δή μιν ἔπεσσιν ἀμειβόμενος προσέειπεν·

  "Εἰρωτᾷς μ' ἐλθόντα θεὰ θεόν· αὐτὰρ ἐγώ τοι
νημερτέως τὸν μῦθον ἐνισπήσω· κέλεαι γάρ.
Ζεὺς ἐμέ γ' ἠνώγει δεῦρ' ἐλθέμεν οὐκ ἐθέλοντα·
τίς δ' ἂν ἑκὼν τοσσόνδε διαδράμοι ἁλμυρὸν ὕδωρ   100
ἄσπετον; οὐδέ τις ἄγχι βροτῶν πόλις, οἵ τε θεοῖσιν
ἱερά τε ῥέζουσι καὶ ἐξαίτους ἑκατόμβας.
ἀλλὰ μάλ' οὔ πως ἔστι Διὸς νόον αἰγιόχοιο
οὔτε παρεξελθεῖν ἄλλον θεὸν οὔθ' ἁλιῶσαι.
φησί τοι ἄνδρα παρεῖναι ὀιζυρώτατον ἄλλων,   105
τῶν ἀνδρῶν, οἳ ἄστυ πέρι Πριάμοιο μάχοντο
ἰνάετες, δεκάτῳ δὲ πόλιν πέρσαντες ἔβησαν
οἴκαδ'· ἀτὰρ ἐν νόστῳ Ἀθηναίην ἀλίτοντο,
σφιν ἐπῶρσ' ἄνεμόν τε κακὸν καὶ κύματα μακρά.

---

[1] Line 84 (=158) was rejected by Aristarchus.
[2] Line 91 is omitted in the best MSS.

home far away. But the great-hearted Odysseus he found not within; for he sat weeping on the shore, as his wont had been, racking his soul with tears and groans and griefs, and he would look over the unresting sea, shedding tears. And Calypso, the beautiful goddess, questioned Hermes, when she had made him sit on a bright shining chair:

"Why, pray, Hermes of the golden wand, hast thou come, an honourable guest and welcome? Heretofore thou hast not been wont to come. Speak what is in thy mind; my heart bids me fulfil it, if fulfil it I can, and it is a thing that hath fulfilment. But follow me further, that I may set before thee entertainment."

So saying, the goddess set before him a table laden with ambrosia, and mixed the ruddy nectar. So he drank and ate, the messenger Argeïphontes. But when he had dined and satisfied his soul with food, then he made answer, and addressed her, saying:

"Thou, a goddess, dost question me, a god, upon my coming, and I will speak my word truly, since thou biddest me. It was Zeus who bade me come hither against my will. Who of his own will would speed over so great space of salt sea-water, great past telling? Nor is there at hand any city of mortals who offer to the gods sacrifice and choice hecatombs. But it is in no wise possible for any other god to evade or make void the will of Zeus, who bears the aegis. He says that there is here with thee a man most wretched above all those warriors who around the city of Priam fought for nine years, and in the tenth year sacked the city and departed homeward. But on the way they sinned against Athene, and she sent upon them an evil wind and long waves. There

ἔνθ᾽ ἄλλοι μὲν πάντες ἀπέφθιθεν ἐσθλοὶ ἑταῖροι,　11
τὸν δ᾽ ἄρα δεῦρ᾽ ἄνεμός τε φέρων καὶ κῦμα πέλασσε.¹
τὸν νῦν σ᾽ ἠνώγειν ἀποπεμπέμεν ὅττι τάχιστα·
οὐ γάρ οἱ τῇδ᾽ αἶσα φίλων ἀπονόσφιν ὀλέσθαι,
ἀλλ᾽ ἔτι οἱ μοῖρ᾽ ἐστὶ φίλους τ᾽ ἰδέειν καὶ ἱκέσθαι
οἶκον ἐς ὑψόροφον καὶ ἐὴν ἐς πατρίδα γαῖαν.”　11

῾Ὼς φάτο, ῥίγησεν δὲ Καλυψώ, δῖα θεάων,
καί μιν φωνήσασ᾽ ἔπεα πτερόεντα προσηύδα·
“ Σχέτλιοί ἐστε, θεοί, ζηλήμονες ἔξοχον ἄλλων,
οἵ τε θεαῖς ἀγάασθε παρ᾽ ἀνδράσιν εὐνάζεσθαι
ἀμφαδίην, ἤν τίς τε φίλον ποιήσετ᾽ ἀκοίτην.　12
ὡς μὲν ὅτ᾽ Ὠρίων᾽ ἕλετο ῥοδοδάκτυλος Ἠώς,
τόφρα οἱ ἠγάασθε θεοὶ ῥεῖα ζώοντες,
ἧος ἐν Ὀρτυγίῃ χρυσόθρονος Ἄρτεμις ἁγνὴ
οἷς ἀγανοῖς βελέεσσιν ἐποιχομένη κατέπεφνεν.
ὡς δ᾽ ὁπότ᾽ Ἰασίωνι ἐυπλόκαμος Δημήτηρ,　12
ᾧ θυμῷ εἴξασα, μίγη φιλότητι καὶ εὐνῇ
νειῷ ἔνι τριπόλῳ· οὐδὲ δὴν ἦεν ἄπυστος
Ζεύς, ὅς μιν κατέπεφνε βαλὼν ἀργῆτι κεραυνῷ.
ὡς δ᾽ αὖ νῦν μοι ἄγασθε, θεοί, βροτὸν ἄνδρα παρεῖναι.
τὸν μὲν ἐγὼν ἐσάωσα περὶ τρόπιος βεβαῶτα　1
οἶον, ἐπεί οἱ νῆα θοὴν ἀργῆτι κεραυνῷ
Ζεὺς ἔλσας ² ἐκέασσε μέσῳ ἐνὶ οἴνοπι πόντῳ.
ἔνθ᾽ ἄλλοι μὲν πάντες ἀπέφθιθεν ἐσθλοὶ ἑταῖροι,
τὸν δ᾽ ἄρα δεῦρ᾽ ἄνεμός τε φέρων καὶ κῦμα πέλασσε.
τὸν μὲν ἐγὼ φίλεόν τε καὶ ἔτρεφον, ἠδὲ ἔφασκον　1

¹ Lines 110 f. (=133 f.) cannot be genuine in this place.
Aristarchus rejected the whole passage 105 (107 ?)–111.
² ἔλσας : ἐλάσας Zenodotus ; cf. vii. 250.

all the rest of his goodly comrades perished, but as for him, the wind and the wave, as they bore him, brought him hither. Him now Zeus bids thee to send on his way with all speed, for it is not his fate to perish here far from his friends, but it is still his lot to see his friends and reach his high-roofed house and his native land."

So he spoke, and Calypso, the beautiful goddess, shuddered, and she spoke, and addressed him with winged words: "Cruel are ye, O ye gods, and quick to envy above all others, seeing that ye begrudge goddesses that they should mate with men openly, if any takes a mortal as her dear bed-fellow. Thus, when rosy-fingered Dawn took to herself Orion, ye gods that live at ease begrudged her, till in Ortygia chaste Artemis of the golden throne assailed him with her gentle[1] shafts and slew him. Thus too, when fair-tressed Demeter, yielding to her passion, lay in love with Iasion in the thrice-ploughed fallow land, Zeus was not long without knowledge thereof, but smote him with his bright thunder-bolt and slew him. And even so again do ye now begrudge me, O ye gods, that a mortal man should abide with me. Him I saved when he was bestriding the keel and all alone, for Zeus had smitten his swift ship with his bright thunder-bolt, and had shattered[2] it in the midst of the wine-dark sea. There all the rest of his goodly comrades perished, but as for him, the wind and the wave, as they bore him, brought him hither. Him I welcomed kindly and gave him food,

---

[1] The phrase commonly denotes a painless death (so in iii. 280). It is only here used of death sent by a wrathful god or goddess.

[2] Possibly "submerged"; cf. vii. 250.

θήσειν ἀθάνατον καὶ ἀγήραον ἤματα πάντα.
ἀλλ' ἐπεὶ οὔ πως ἔστι Διὸς νόον αἰγιόχοιο
οὔτε παρεξελθεῖν ἄλλον θεὸν οὔθ' ἁλιῶσαι,
ἐρρέτω, εἴ μιν κεῖνος ἐποτρύνει καὶ ἀνώγει,
πόντον ἐπ' ἀτρύγετον· πέμψω δέ μιν οὔ πῃ ἐγώ γε· 14
οὐ γάρ μοι πάρα νῆες ἐπήρετμοι καὶ ἑταῖροι,
οἵ κέν μιν πέμποιεν ἐπ' εὐρέα νῶτα θαλάσσης.
αὐτάρ οἱ πρόφρων ὑποθήσομαι, οὐδ' ἐπικεύσω,
ὥς κε μάλ' ἀσκηθὴς ἦν πατρίδα γαῖαν ἵκηται."

Τὴν δ' αὖτε προσέειπε διάκτορος ἀργεϊφόντης· 14
"Οὕτω νῦν ἀπόπεμπε, Διὸς δ' ἐποπίζεο μῆνιν,
μή πώς τοι μετόπισθε κοτεσσάμενος χαλεπήνῃ."

Ὣς ἄρα φωνήσας ἀπέβη κρατὺς ἀργεϊφόντης·
ἡ δ' ἐπ' Ὀδυσσῆα μεγαλήτορα πότνια νύμφη
ἤι', ἐπεὶ δὴ Ζηνὸς ἐπέκλυεν ἀγγελιάων. 15
τὸν δ' ἄρ' ἐπ' ἀκτῆς εὗρε καθήμενον· οὐδέ ποτ' ὄσσε
δακρυόφιν τέρσοντο, κατείβετο δὲ γλυκὺς αἰὼν
νόστον ὀδυρομένῳ, ἐπεὶ οὐκέτι ἥνδανε νύμφη.
ἀλλ' ἦ τοι νύκτας μὲν ἰαύεσκεν καὶ ἀνάγκῃ
ἐν σπέσσι γλαφυροῖσι παρ' οὐκ ἐθέλων ἐθελούσῃ· 15
ἤματα δ' ἂμ πέτρῃσι καὶ ἠιόνεσσι καθίζων
δάκρυσι καὶ στοναχῇσι καὶ ἄλγεσι θυμὸν ἐρέχθων [1]
πόντον ἐπ' ἀτρύγετον δερκέσκετο δάκρυα λείβων.
ἀγχοῦ δ' ἱσταμένη προσεφώνεε δῖα θεάων·

"Κάμμορε, μή μοι ἔτ' ἐνθάδ' ὀδύρεο, μηδέ τοι αἰὼν 16
φθινέτω· ἤδη γάρ σε μάλα πρόφρασσ' ἀποπέμψω.
ἀλλ' ἄγε δούρατα μακρὰ ταμὼν ἁρμόζεο χαλκῷ

---

[1] Line 157 (=83), omitted in many MSS., seems to have been unknown to Aristarchus.

and said that I would make him immortal and age-
less all his days. But since it is in no wise possible
for any other god to evade or make void the will of
Zeus who bears the aegis, let him go his way, if Zeus
thus orders and commands, over the unresting sea.
But it is not I that shall give him convoy, for I have
at hand no ships with oars and no men to send him
on his way over the broad back of the sea. But with
a ready heart will I give him counsel, and will hide
naught, that all unscathed he may return to his
native land."

Then again the messenger Argeïphontes answered
her: "Even so send him forth now, and beware of
the wrath of Zeus, lest haply he wax wroth and visit
his anger upon thee hereafter."

So saying, the strong Argeïphontes departed, and
the queenly nymph went to the great-hearted Odys-
seus, when she had heard the message of Zeus.
Him she found sitting on the shore, and his eyes
were never dry of tears, and his sweet life was
ebbing away, as he longed mournfully for his return,
for the nymph was no longer pleasing in his sight.
By night indeed he would sleep by her side perforce
in the hollow caves, unwilling beside the willing
nymph, but by day he would sit on the rocks and
the sands, racking his soul with tears and groans and
griefs, and he would look over the unresting sea,
shedding tears. Then coming close to him, the
beautiful goddess addressed him:

"Unhappy man, sorrow no longer here, I pray
thee, nor let thy life pine away; for even now with
a ready heart will I send thee on thy way. Nay,
come, hew with the axe long beams, and make a

εὐρεῖαν σχεδίην· ἀτὰρ ἴκρια πῆξαι ἐπ' αὐτῆς
ὑψοῦ, ὥς σε φέρῃσιν ἐπ' ἠεροειδέα πόντον.
αὐτὰρ ἐγὼ σῖτον καὶ ὕδωρ καὶ οἶνον ἐρυθρὸν
ἐνθήσω μενοεικέ', ἅ κέν τοι λιμὸν ἐρύκοι,
εἵματά τ' ἀμφιέσω· πέμψω δέ τοι οὖρον ὄπισθεν,
ὥς κε μάλ' ἀσκηθὴς σὴν πατρίδα γαῖαν ἵκηαι,
αἴ κε θεοί γ' ἐθέλωσι, τοὶ οὐρανὸν εὐρὺν ἔχουσιν,
οἵ μευ φέρτεροί εἰσι νοῆσαί τε κρῆναί τε,"
    Ὣς φάτο, ῥίγησεν δὲ πολύτλας δῖος Ὀδυσσεύς,
καί μιν φωνήσας ἔπεα πτερόεντα προσηύδα·
"Ἄλλο τι δὴ σύ, θεά, τόδε μήδεαι, οὐδέ τι πομπήν,
ἥ με κέλεαι σχεδίῃ περάαν μέγα λαῖτμα θαλάσσης,
δεινόν τ' ἀργαλέον τε· τὸ δ' οὐδ' ἐπὶ νῆες ἐΐσαι
ὠκύποροι περόωσιν, ἀγαλλόμεναι Διὸς οὔρῳ.
οὐδ' ἂν ἐγὼν ἀέκητι σέθεν σχεδίης ἐπιβαίην,
εἰ μή μοι τλαίης γε, θεά, μέγαν ὅρκον ὀμόσσαι
μή τί μοι αὐτῷ πῆμα κακὸν βουλευσέμεν ἄλλο."
    Ὣς φάτο, μείδησεν δὲ Καλυψὼ δῖα θεάων,
χειρί τέ μιν κατέρεξεν ἔπος τ' ἔφατ' ἔκ τ' ὀνόμαζεν·
"Ἦ δὴ ἀλιτρός γ' ἐσσὶ καὶ οὐκ ἀποφώλια εἰδώς,
οἷον δὴ τὸν μῦθον ἐπεφράσθης ἀγορεῦσαι.
ἴστω νῦν τόδε γαῖα καὶ οὐρανὸς εὐρὺς ὕπερθε
καὶ τὸ κατειβόμενον Στυγὸς ὕδωρ, ὅς τε μέγιστος
ὅρκος δεινότατός τε πέλει μακάρεσσι θεοῖσι,
μή τί τοι αὐτῷ πῆμα κακὸν βουλευσέμεν ἄλλο.
ἀλλὰ τὰ μὲν νοέω καὶ φράσσομαι, ἅσσ' ἂν ἐμοί περ
αὐτῇ μηδοίμην, ὅτε με χρειὼ τόσον ἵκοι·
καὶ γὰρ ἐμοὶ νόος ἐστὶν ἐναίσιμος, οὐδέ μοι αὐτῇ
θυμὸς ἐνὶ στήθεσσι σιδήρεος, ἀλλ' ἐλεήμων."

broad raft, and fasten upon it cross-planks for a deck well above it, that it may bear thee over the misty deep. And I will place therein bread and water and red wine to satisfy thy heart, to keep hunger from thee. And I will clothe thee with raiment, and will send a fair wind behind thee, that all unscathed thou mayest return to thy native land, if it be the will of the gods who hold broad heaven; for they are mightier than I both to purpose and to fulfil."

So she spoke, and much-enduring goodly Odysseus shuddered, and he spoke, and addressed her with winged words: "Some other thing, goddess, art thou planning in this, and not my sending, seeing that thou biddest me cross on a raft the great gulf of the sea, dread and grievous, over which not even the shapely, swift-faring ships pass, rejoicing in the wind of Zeus. But I will not set foot on a raft in thy despite, unless thou, goddess, wilt bring thyself to swear a mighty oath that thou wilt not plot against me any fresh mischief to my hurt."

So he spoke, but Calypso, the beautiful goddess, smiled, and stroked him with her hand, and spoke, and addressed him: "Verily thou art a knave, and not stunted in wit, that thou hast bethought thee to utter such a word. Now therefore let earth be witness to this, and the broad heaven above, and the down-flowing water of the Styx, which is the greatest and most dread oath for the blessed gods, that I will not plot against thee any fresh mischief to thy hurt. Nay, I have such thoughts in mind, and will give such counsel, as I should devise for mine own self, if such need should come on me. For I too have a mind that is righteous, and the heart in this breast of mine is not of iron, but hath compassion."

Ὣς ἄρα φωνήσασ' ἡγήσατο δῖα θεάων
καρπαλίμως· ὁ δ' ἔπειτα μετ' ἴχνια βαῖνε θεοῖο.
ἷξον δὲ σπεῖος γλαφυρὸν θεὸς ἠδὲ καὶ ἀνήρ,
καί ῥ' ὁ μὲν ἔνθα καθέζετ' ἐπὶ θρόνου ἔνθεν ἀνέστη   1
Ἑρμείας, νύμφη δ' ἐτίθει πάρα πᾶσαν ἐδωδήν,
ἔσθειν καὶ πίνειν, οἷα βροτοὶ ἄνδρες ἔδουσιν·
αὐτὴ δ' ἀντίον ἷζεν Ὀδυσσῆος θείοιο,
τῇ δὲ παρ' ἀμβροσίην δμῳαὶ καὶ νέκταρ ἔθηκαν.
οἱ δ' ἐπ' ὀνείαθ' ἑτοῖμα προκείμενα χεῖρας ἴαλλον.   1
αὐτὰρ ἐπεὶ τάρπησαν ἐδητύος ἠδὲ ποτῆτος,
τοῖς ἄρα μύθων ἦρχε Καλυψώ, δῖα θεάων·
   " Διογενὲς Λαερτιάδη, πολυμήχαν' Ὀδυσσεῦ,
οὕτω δὴ οἶκόνδε φίλην ἐς πατρίδα γαῖαν
αὐτίκα νῦν ἐθέλεις ἰέναι; σὺ δὲ χαῖρε καὶ ἔμπης.   1
εἴ γε μὲν εἰδείης σῇσι φρεσὶν ὅσσα τοι αἶσα
κήδε' ἀναπλῆσαι, πρὶν πατρίδα γαῖαν ἱκέσθαι,
ἐνθάδε κ' αὖθι μένων σὺν ἐμοὶ τόδε δῶμα φυλάσσοις
ἀθάνατός τ' εἴης, ἱμειρόμενός περ ἰδέσθαι
σὴν ἄλοχον, τῆς τ' αἰὲν ἐέλδεαι ἤματα πάντα.   2
οὐ μέν θην κείνης γε χερείων εὔχομαι εἶναι,
οὐ δέμας οὐδὲ φυήν, ἐπεὶ οὔ πως οὐδὲ ἔοικεν
θνητὰς ἀθανάτῃσι δέμας καὶ εἶδος ἐρίζειν."
   Τὴν δ' ἀπαμειβόμενος προσέφη πολύμητις Ὀδυσσ
   " Πότνα θεά, μή μοι τόδε χώεο· οἶδα καὶ αὐτὸς   2
πάντα μάλ', οὕνεκα σεῖο περίφρων Πηνελόπεια
εἶδος ἀκιδνοτέρη μέγεθός τ' εἰσάντα ἰδέσθαι·
ἡ μὲν γὰρ βροτός ἐστι, σὺ δ' ἀθάνατος καὶ ἀγήρως.
ἀλλὰ καὶ ὣς ἐθέλω καὶ ἐέλδομαι ἤματα πάντα
οἴκαδέ τ' ἐλθέμεναι καὶ νόστιμον ἦμαρ ἰδέσθαι.
εἰ δ' αὖ τις ῥαίῃσι θεῶν ἐνὶ οἴνοπι πόντῳ,
τλήσομαι ἐν στήθεσσιν ἔχων ταλαπενθέα θυμόν·

So saying, the beautiful goddess led the way quickly, and he followed in the footsteps of the goddess. And they came to the hollow cave, the goddess and the man, and he sat down upon the chair from which Hermes had arisen, and the nymph set before him all manner of food to eat and drink, of such sort as mortal men eat. But she herself sat over against divine Odysseus, and before her the handmaids set ambrosia and nectar. So they put forth their hands to the good cheer lying ready before them. But when they had had their fill of food and drink, Calypso, the beautiful goddess, was the first to speak, and said:

"Son of Laertes, sprung from Zeus, Odysseus of many devices, would'st thou then fare now forthwith home to thy dear native land! Yet, even so fare thee well. Howbeit if in thy heart thou knewest all the measure of woe it is thy fate to fulfil before thou comest to thy native land thou wouldest abide here and keep this house with me, and wouldest be immortal, for all thy desire to see thy wife for whom thou longest day by day. Surely not inferior to her do I declare myself to be either in form or stature, for in no wise is it seemly that mortal women should vie with immortals in form or comeliness."

Then Odysseus of many wiles answered her, and said: "Mighty goddess, be not wroth with me for this. I know full well of myself that wise Penelope is meaner to look upon than thou in comeliness and in stature, for she is a mortal, while thou art immortal and ageless. But even so I wish and long day by day to reach my home, and to see the day of my return. And if again some god shall smite me on the wine-dark sea, I will endure it, having in my breast a

ἤδη γὰρ μάλα πολλὰ πάθον καὶ πολλὰ μόγησα
κύμασι καὶ πολέμῳ· μετὰ καὶ τόδε τοῖσι γενέσθω."
  Ὣς ἔφατ', ἠέλιος δ' ἄρ' ἔδυ καὶ ἐπὶ κνέφας ἦλθεν·
ἐλθόντες δ' ἄρα τώ γε μυχῷ σπείους γλαφυροῖο   2
τερπέσθην φιλότητι, παρ' ἀλλήλοισι μένοντες.
  Ἦμος δ' ἠριγένεια φάνη ῥοδοδάκτυλος Ἠώς,
αὐτίχ' ὁ μὲν χλαῖνάν τε χιτῶνά τε ἔννυτ' Ὀδυσσεύς,
αὐτὴ δ' ἀργύφεον φᾶρος μέγα ἔννυτο νύμφη,   2
λεπτὸν καὶ χαρίεν, περὶ δὲ ζώνην βάλετ' ἰξυῖ
καλὴν χρυσείην, κεφαλῇ δ' ἐφύπερθε[1] καλύπτρην.
καὶ τότ' Ὀδυσσῆι μεγαλήτορι μήδετο πομπήν·
δῶκέν οἱ πέλεκυν μέγαν, ἄρμενον ἐν παλάμῃσι,
χάλκεον, ἀμφοτέρωθεν ἀκαχμένον· αὐτὰρ ἐν αὐτῷ   2
στειλειὸν περικαλλὲς ἐλάινον, εὖ ἐναρηρός·
δῶκε δ' ἔπειτα σκέπαρνον ἐύξοον· ἦρχε δ' ὁδοῖο
νήσου ἐπ' ἐσχατιῆς, ὅθι δένδρεα μακρὰ πεφύκει,
κλήθρη τ' αἴγειρός τ', ἐλάτη τ' ἦν οὐρανομήκης,
αὖα πάλαι, περίκηλα, τά οἱ πλώοιεν ἐλαφρῶς.   2
αὐτὰρ ἐπεὶ δὴ δεῖξ', ὅθι δένδρεα μακρὰ πεφύκει,
ἡ μὲν ἔβη πρὸς δῶμα Καλυψώ, δῖα θεάων,
αὐτὰρ ὁ τάμνετο δοῦρα· θοῶς δέ οἱ ἤνυτο ἔργον.
εἴκοσι δ' ἔκβαλε πάντα, πελέκκησεν δ' ἄρα χαλκῷ,
ξέσσε δ' ἐπισταμένως καὶ ἐπὶ στάθμην ἴθυνεν.   2
τόφρα δ' ἔνεικε τέρετρα Καλυψώ, δῖα θεάων·
τέτρηνεν δ' ἄρα πάντα καὶ ἥρμοσεν ἀλλήλοισιν,
γόμφοισιν δ' ἄρα τήν γε καὶ ἁρμονίῃσιν ἄρασσεν.
ὅσσον τίς τ' ἔδαφος νηὸς τορνώσεται ἀνὴρ
φορτίδος εὐρείης, ἐὺ εἰδὼς τεκτοσυνάων,   2
τόσσον ἐπ' εὐρεῖαν σχεδίην ποιήσατ' Ὀδυσσεύς.

---

[1] ἐφύπερθε Aristarchus : ἐπέθηκε.

heart that endures affliction. For ere this I have suffered much and toiled much amid the waves and in war; let this also be added unto that."

So he spoke, and the sun set and darkness came on. And the two went into the innermost recess of the hollow cave, and took their joy of love, abiding each by the other's side.

As soon as early Dawn appeared, the rosy-fingered, straightway Odysseus put on a cloak and a tunic, and the nymph clothed herself in a long white robe, finely woven and beautiful, and about her waist she cast a fair girdle of gold, and on her head a veil above. Then she set herself to plan the sending of the great-hearted Odysseus. She gave him a great axe, well fitted to his hands, an axe of bronze, sharpened on both sides; and in it was a beautiful handle of olive wood, securely fastened; and thereafter she gave him a polished adze. Then she led the way to the borders of the island where tall trees were standing, alder and poplar and fir, reaching to the skies, long dry and well-seasoned, which would float for him lightly. But when she had shewn him where the tall trees grew, Calypso, the beautiful goddess, returned homewards, but he fell to cutting timbers, and his work went forward apace. Twenty trees in all did he fell, and trimmed them with the axe; then he cunningly smoothed them all and made them straight to the line. Meanwhile Calypso, the beautiful goddess, brought him augers; and he bored all the pieces and fitted them to one another, and with pegs and morticings did he hammer it together. Wide as a man well-skilled in carpentry marks out the curve of the hull of a freight-ship, broad of beam, even so wide did Odysseus make his

ἴκρια δὲ στήσας, ἀραρὼν θαμέσι σταμίνεσσι,
ποίει· ἀτὰρ μακρῆσιν ἐπηγκενίδεσσι τελεύτα.
ἐν δ' ἱστὸν ποίει καὶ ἐπίκριον ἄρμενον αὐτῷ·
πρὸς δ' ἄρα πηδάλιον ποιήσατο, ὄφρ' ἰθύνοι.   2
φράξε δέ μιν ῥίπεσσι διαμπερὲς οἰσυΐνῃσι
κύματος εἶλαρ ἔμεν· πολλὴν δ' ἐπεχεύατο ὕλην.
τόφρα δὲ φάρε' ἔνεικε Καλυψώ, δῖα θεάων,
ἱστία ποιήσασθαι· ὁ δ' εὖ τεχνήσατο καὶ τά.
ἐν δ' ὑπέρας τε κάλους τε πόδας τ' ἐνέδησεν ἐν αὐτῇ,   2
μοχλοῖσιν δ' ἄρα τήν γε κατείρυσεν εἰς ἅλα δῖαν.

Τέτρατον ἦμαρ ἔην, καὶ τῷ τετέλεστο ἅπαντα·
τῷ δ' ἄρα πέμπτῳ πέμπ' ἀπὸ νήσου δῖα Καλυψώ,
εἵματά τ' ἀμφιέσασα θυώδεα καὶ λούσασα.
ἐν δέ οἱ ἀσκὸν ἔθηκε θεὰ μέλανος οἴνοιο   2
τὸν ἕτερον, ἕτερον δ' ὕδατος μέγαν, ἐν δὲ καὶ ἦα
κωρύκῳ· ἐν δέ οἱ ὄψα τίθει μενοεικέα πολλά·
οὖρον δὲ προέηκεν ἀπήμονά τε λιαρόν τε.
γηθόσυνος δ' οὔρῳ πέτασ' ἱστία δῖος Ὀδυσσεύς.
αὐτὰρ ὁ πηδαλίῳ ἰθύνετο τεχνηέντως   2
ἥμενος, οὐδέ οἱ ὕπνος ἐπὶ βλεφάροισιν ἔπιπτεν
Πληιάδας τ' ἐσορῶντι καὶ ὀψὲ δύοντα Βοώτην
Ἄρκτον θ', ἣν καὶ Ἄμαξαν ἐπίκλησιν καλέουσιν,
ἥ τ' αὐτοῦ στρέφεται καί τ' Ὠρίωνα δοκεύει,
οἴη δ' ἄμμορός ἐστι λοετρῶν Ὠκεανοῖο·   2
τὴν γὰρ δή μιν ἄνωγε Καλυψώ, δῖα θεάων,
ποντοπορευέμεναι ἐπ' ἀριστερὰ χειρὸς ἔχοντα.
ἑπτὰ δὲ καὶ δέκα μὲν πλέεν ἤματα ποντοπορεύων,

raft. And he set up the deck-beams, bolting them to the close set ribs, and laboured on; and he finished the raft with long gunwales. In it he set a mast and a yard-arm, fitted to it, and furthermore made him a steering-oar, wherewith to steer. Then he fenced in the whole from stem to stern with willow withes to be a defence against the wave, and strewed much brush thereon.[1] Meanwhile Calypso, the beautiful goddess, brought him cloth to make him a sail, and he fashioned that too with skill. And he made fast in the raft braces and halyards and sheets, and then with levers[2] forced it down into the bright sea.

Now the fourth day came and all his work was done. And on the fifth the beautiful Calypso sent him on his way from the island after she had bathed him and clothed him in fragrant raiment. On the raft the goddess put a skin of dark wine, and another, a great one, of water, and provisions, too, in a wallet. Therein she put abundance of dainties to satisfy his heart, and she sent forth a gentle wind and warm. Gladly then did goodly Odysseus spread his sail to the breeze; and he sat and guided his raft skilfully with the steering-oar, nor did sleep fall upon his eyelids, as he watched the Pleiads, and late-setting Bootes, and the Bear, which men also call the Wain, which ever circles where it is and watches Orion, and alone has no part in the baths of Ocean. For this star Calypso, the beautiful goddess, had bidden him to keep on the left hand as he sailed over the sea. For seventeen days then he sailed over the

---

[1] The precise meaning of the phrase is uncertain. The scholiast assumed that it meant " threw in much ballast," but this seems impossible. Ameis thinks that the ὕλη was to afford Odysseus a comfortable bed.   [2] Possibly "rollers."

ὀκτωκαιδεκάτῃ δ' ἐφάνη ὄρεα σκιόεντα
γαίης Φαιήκων, ὅθι τ' ἄγχιστον πέλεν αὐτῷ·⠀⠀2
εἴσατο δ' ὡς ὅτε ῥινὸν¹ ἐν ἠεροειδέι πόντῳ.

⠀⠀Τὸν δ' ἐξ Αἰθιόπων ἀνιὼν κρείων ἐνοσίχθων
τηλόθεν ἐκ Σολύμων ὀρέων ἴδεν· εἴσατο γάρ οἱ
πόντον ἐπιπλώων. ὁ δ' ἐχώσατο κηρόθι μᾶλλον,
κινήσας δὲ κάρη προτὶ ὃν μυθήσατο θυμόν·⠀⠀2

⠀⠀"Ὢ πόποι, ἦ μάλα δὴ μετεβούλευσαν θεοὶ ἄλλως
ἀμφ' Ὀδυσῆι ἐμεῖο μετ' Αἰθιόπεσσιν ἐόντος,
καὶ δὴ Φαιήκων γαίης σχεδόν, ἔνθα οἱ αἶσα
ἐκφυγέειν μέγα πεῖραρ ὀιζύος, ἥ μιν ἱκάνει.
ἀλλ' ἔτι μέν μίν φημι ἄδην ἐλάαν κακότητος."⠀⠀2

⠀⠀Ὣς εἰπὼν σύναγεν νεφέλας, ἐτάραξε δὲ πόντον
χερσὶ τρίαιναν ἑλών· πάσας δ' ὀρόθυνεν ἀέλλας
παντοίων ἀνέμων, σὺν δὲ νεφέεσσι κάλυψε
γαῖαν ὁμοῦ καὶ πόντον· ὀρώρει δ' οὐρανόθεν νύξ.
σὺν δ' Εὖρός τε Νότος τ' ἔπεσον Ζέφυρός τε δυσαὴς⠀⠀2
καὶ Βορέης αἰθρηγενέτης, μέγα κῦμα κυλίνδων.
καὶ τότ' Ὀδυσσῆος λύτο γούνατα καὶ φίλον ἦτορ,
ὀχθήσας δ' ἄρα εἶπε πρὸς ὃν μεγαλήτορα θυμόν·

⠀⠀"Ὤ μοι ἐγὼ δειλός, τί νύ μοι μήκιστα γένηται;
δείδω μὴ δὴ πάντα θεὰ νημερτέα εἶπεν,⠀⠀3
ἥ μ' ἔφατ' ἐν πόντῳ, πρὶν πατρίδα γαῖαν ἱκέσθαι,
ἄλγε' ἀναπλήσειν· τὰ δὲ δὴ νῦν πάντα τελεῖται.
οἵοισιν νεφέεσσι περιστέφει οὐρανὸν εὐρὺν

_____
¹ ὅτε ῥινὸν MSS.: ὅτ' ἐρινὸν Aristarchus.

sea, and on the eighteenth appeared the shadowy mountains of the land of the Phaeacians, where it lay nearest to him; and it shewed like unto a shield in the misty deep.

But the glorious Earth-shaker, as he came back from the Ethiopians,[1] beheld him from afar, from the mountains of the Solymi: for Odysseus was seen of him sailing over the sea; and he waxed the more wroth in spirit, and shook his head, and thus he spoke to his own heart:

"Out on it! Surely the gods have changed their purpose regarding Odysseus, while I was among the Ethiopians. And lo, he is near to the land of the Phaeacians, where it is his fate to escape from the great bonds of the woe which has come upon him. Aye, but even yet, methinks, I shall drive him to surfeit of evil."

So saying, he gathered the clouds, and seizing his trident in his hands troubled the sea, and roused all blasts of all manner of winds, and hid with clouds land and sea alike; and night rushed down from heaven. Together the East Wind and the South Wind dashed, and the fierce-blowing West Wind and the North Wind, born in the bright heaven, rolling before him a mighty wave. Then were the knees of Odysseus loosened and his heart melted, and deeply moved he spoke to his own mighty spirit:

"Ah me, wretched that I am! What is to befall me at the last? I fear me that verily all that the goddess said was true, when she declared that on the sea, before ever I came to my native land, I should fill up my measure of woes; and lo, all this now is being brought to pass. In such wise does Zeus overcast the broad heaven with clouds, and has stirred

[1] See i. 21 f.

Ζεύς, ἐτάραξε δὲ πόντον, ἐπισπέρχουσι δ᾽ ἄελλαι
παντοίων ἀνέμων. νῦν μοι σῶς αἰπὺς ὄλεθρος. 30
τρὶς μάκαρες Δαναοὶ καὶ τετράκις, οἳ τότ᾽ ὄλοντο
Τροίῃ ἐν εὐρείῃ χάριν Ἀτρείδῃσι φέροντες.
ὡς[1] δὴ ἐγώ γ᾽ ὄφελον θανέειν καὶ πότμον ἐπισπεῖν
ἤματι τῷ ὅτε μοι πλεῖστοι χαλκήρεα δοῦρα
Τρῶες ἐπέρριψαν περὶ Πηλεΐωνι θανόντι. 31
τῷ κ᾽ ἔλαχον κτερέων, καί μευ κλέος ἦγον Ἀχαιοί·
νῦν δέ με λευγαλέῳ θανάτῳ εἵμαρτο ἁλῶναι."

    "Ὣς ἄρα μιν εἰπόντ᾽ ἔλασεν μέγα κῦμα κατ᾽ ἄκρης
δεινὸν ἐπεσσύμενον, περὶ δὲ σχεδίην ἐλέλιξε.·
τῆλε δ᾽ ἀπὸ σχεδίης αὐτὸς πέσε, πηδάλιον δὲ 3
ἐκ χειρῶν προέηκε· μέσον δέ οἱ ἱστὸν ἔαξεν
δεινὴ μισγομένων ἀνέμων ἐλθοῦσα θύελλα,
τηλοῦ δὲ σπεῖρον καὶ ἐπίκριον ἔμπεσε πόντῳ.
τὸν δ᾽ ἄρ᾽ ὑπόβρυχα θῆκε πολὺν χρόνον, οὐδ᾽ ἐδυνάσθη
αἶψα μάλ᾽ ἀνσχεθέειν μεγάλου ὑπὸ κύματος ὁρμῆς· 3
εἵματα γάρ ῥ᾽ ἐβάρυνε, τά οἱ πόρε δῖα Καλυψώ.
ὀψὲ δὲ δή ῥ᾽ ἀνέδυ, στόματος δ᾽ ἐξέπτυσεν ἅλμην
πικρήν, ἥ οἱ πολλὴ ἀπὸ κρατὸς κελάρυζεν.
ἀλλ᾽ οὐδ᾽ ὣς σχεδίης ἐπελήθετο, τειρόμενός περ,
ἀλλὰ μεθορμηθεὶς ἐνὶ κύμασιν ἐλλάβετ᾽ αὐτῆς, 3
ἐν μέσσῃ δὲ καθῖζε τέλος θανάτου ἀλεείνων.
τὴν δ᾽ ἐφόρει μέγα κῦμα κατὰ ῥόον ἔνθα καὶ ἔνθα.
ὡς δ᾽ ὅτ᾽ ὀπωρινὸς Βορέης φορέῃσιν ἀκάνθας
ἂμ πεδίον, πυκιναὶ δὲ πρὸς ἀλλήλῃσιν ἔχονται,
ὣς τὴν ἂμ πέλαγος ἄνεμοι φέρον ἔνθα καὶ ἔνθα· 3

        [1] ὡς : καί.

up the sea, and the blasts of all manner of winds sweep upon me; now is my utter destruction sure. Thrice blessed those Danaans, aye, four times blessed, who of old perished in the wide land of Troy, doing the pleasure of the sons of Atreus. Even so would that I had died and met my fate on that day when the throngs of the Trojans hurled upon me bronze-tipped spears, fighting around the body of the dead son of Peleus. Then should I have got funeral rites, and the Achaeans would have spread my fame, but now by a miserable death was it appointed me to be cut off."

Even as thus he spoke the great wave smote him from on high, rushing upon him with terrible might, and around it whirled his raft. Far from the raft he fell, and let fall the steering-oar from his hand; but his mast was broken in the midst by the fierce blast of tumultuous winds that came upon it, and far in the sea sail and yardarm fell. As for him, long time did the wave hold him in the depths, nor could he rise at once from beneath the onrush of the mighty wave, for the garments which beautiful Calypso had given him weighed him down. At length, however, he came up, and spat forth from his mouth the bitter brine which flowed in streams from his head. Yet even so he did not forget his raft, in evil case though he was, but sprang after it amid the waves, and laid hold of it, and sat down in the midst of it, seeking to escape the doom of death; and a great wave ever bore him this way and that along its course. As when in autumn the North Wind bears the thistle-tufts over the plain, and close they cling to one another, so did the winds bear the raft this

ἄλλοτε μέν τε Νότος Βορέῃ προβάλεσκε φέρεσθαι,
ἄλλοτε δ' αὖτ' Εὖρος Ζεφύρῳ εἴξασκε διώκειν.

Τὸν δὲ ἴδεν Κάδμου θυγάτηρ, καλλίσφυρος Ἰνώ,
Λευκοθέη, ἣ πρὶν μὲν ἔην βροτὸς αὐδήεσσα,
νῦν δ' ἁλὸς ἐν πελάγεσσι θεῶν ἐξ ἔμμορε τιμῆς.   3
ἥ ῥ' Ὀδυσῆ' ἐλέησεν ἀλώμενον, ἄλγε' ἔχοντα,
αἰθυίῃ δ' εἰκυῖα ποτῇ ἀνεδύσετο λίμνης,
ἷζε δ' ἐπὶ σχεδίης πολυδέσμου εἶπέ τε μῦθον·[1]

"Κάμμορε, τίπτε τοι ὧδε Ποσειδάων ἐνοσίχθων
ὠδύσατ' ἐκπάγλως, ὅτι τοι κακὰ πολλὰ φυτεύει;   3
οὐ μὲν δή σε καταφθίσει μάλα περ μενεαίνων.
ἀλλὰ μάλ' ὧδ' ἔρξαι, δοκέεις δέ μοι οὐκ ἀπινύσσειν·
εἵματα ταῦτ' ἀποδὺς σχεδίην ἀνέμοισι φέρεσθαι
κάλλιπ', ἀτὰρ χείρεσσι νέων ἐπιμαίεο νόστου
γαίης Φαιήκων, ὅθι τοι μοῖρ' ἐστὶν ἀλύξαι.   3
τῇ δέ, τόδε κρήδεμνον ὑπὸ στέρνοιο τανύσσαι
ἄμβροτον· οὐδέ τί τοι παθέειν δέος οὐδ' ἀπολέσθαι.
αὐτὰρ ἐπὴν χείρεσσιν ἐφάψεαι ἠπείροιο,
ἂψ ἀπολυσάμενος βαλέειν εἰς οἴνοπα πόντον
πολλὸν ἀπ' ἠπείρου, αὐτὸς δ' ἀπονόσφι τραπέσθαι."

Ὣς ἄρα φωνήσασα θεὰ κρήδεμνον ἔδωκεν,
αὐτὴ δ' ἂψ ἐς πόντον ἐδύσετο κυμαίνοντα
αἰθυίῃ εἰκυῖα· μέλαν δέ ἑ κῦμα κάλυψεν.
αὐτὰρ ὁ μερμήριξε πολύτλας δῖος Ὀδυσσεύς,
ὀχθήσας δ' ἄρα εἶπε πρὸς ὃν μεγαλήτορα θυμόν·   3

"Ὤ μοι ἐγώ, μή τίς μοι ὑφαίνῃσιν δόλον αὖτε
ἀθανάτων, ὅ τέ με σχεδίης ἀποβῆναι ἀνώγει.

---

[1] πολυδέσμου εἶπέ τε μῦθον : καί μιν πρὸς μῦθον ἔειπε.

way and that over the sea. Now the South Wind
would fling it to the North Wind to be driven on,
and now again the East Wind would yield it to the
West Wind to drive.

But the daughter of Cadmus, Ino of the fair
ankles, saw him, even Leucothea, who of old was a
mortal of human speech, but now in the deeps of the
sea has won a share of honour from the gods. She
was touched with pity for Odysseus, as he wandered
and was in sore travail, and she rose up from the
deep like a sea-mew on the wing, and sat on the
stoutly-bound raft, and spoke, saying:

"Unhappy man, how is it that Poseidon, the earth-
shaker, has conceived such furious wrath against
thee, that he is sowing for thee the seeds of many
evils? Yet verily he shall not utterly destroy thee
for all his rage. Nay, do thou thus; and methinks
thou dost not lack understanding. Strip off these
garments, and leave thy raft to be driven by the
winds, but do thou swim with thy hands and so
strive to reach the land of the Phaeacians, where it is
thy fate to escape. Come, take this veil, and stretch
it beneath thy breast. It is immortal; there is no
fear that thou shalt suffer aught or perish. But
when with thy hands thou hast laid hold of the land,
loose it from thee, and cast it into the wine-dark sea
far from the land, and thyself turn away."

So saying, the goddess gave him the veil, and
herself plunged again into the surging deep, like a
sea-mew; and the dark wave hid her. Then the
much-enduring, goodly Odysseus pondered, and
deeply moved he spoke to his own mighty spirit:

"Woe is me! Let it not be that some one of the
immortals is again weaving a snare for me, that she

195

ἀλλὰ μάλ' οὔ πω πείσομ', ἐπεὶ ἑκὰς ὀφθαλμοῖσιν
γαῖαν ἐγὼν ἰδόμην, ὅθι μοι φάτο φύξιμον εἶναι.
ἀλλὰ μάλ' ὧδ' ἔρξω, δοκέει δέ μοι εἶναι ἄριστον·   30
ὄφρ' ἂν μέν κεν δούρατ' ἐν ἁρμονίῃσιν ἀρήρῃ,
τόφρ' αὐτοῦ μενέω καὶ τλήσομαι ἄλγεα πάσχων·
αὐτὰρ ἐπὴν δή μοι σχεδίην διὰ κῦμα τινάξῃ,
νήξομ', ἐπεὶ οὐ μέν τι πάρα προνοῆσαι ἄμεινον."
    Ἧος ὁ ταῦθ' ὥρμαινε κατὰ φρένα καὶ κατὰ θυμόν,
ὦρσε δ' ἐπὶ μέγα κῦμα Ποσειδάων ἐνοσίχθων,   35
δεινόν τ' ἀργαλέον τε, κατηρεφές, ἤλασε δ' αὐτόν.
ὡς δ' ἄνεμος ζαὴς ἠίων θημῶνα τινάξῃ
καρφαλέων· τὰ μὲν ἄρ τε διεσκέδασ' ἄλλυδις ἄλλῃ·
ὡς τῆς δούρατα μακρὰ διεσκέδασ'. αὐτὰρ Ὀδυσσεὺς   37
ἀμφ' ἑνὶ δούρατι βαῖνε, κέληθ' ὡς ἵππον ἐλαύνων,
εἵματα δ' ἐξαπέδυνε, τά οἱ πόρε δῖα Καλυψώ.
αὐτίκα δὲ κρήδεμνον ὑπὸ στέρνοιο τάνυσσεν,
αὐτὸς δὲ πρηνὴς ἁλὶ κάππεσε, χεῖρε πετάσσας,
νηχέμεναι μεμαώς. ἴδε δὲ κρείων ἐνοσίχθων,   37
κινήσας δὲ κάρη προτὶ ὃν μυθήσατο θυμόν·
    "Οὕτω νῦν κακὰ πολλὰ παθὼν ἀλόω κατὰ πόντον,
εἰς ὅ κεν ἀνθρώποισι διοτρεφέεσσι μιγήῃς.
ἀλλ' οὐδ' ὥς σε ἔολπα ὀνόσσεσθαι κακότητος."
    Ὣς ἄρα φωνήσας ἵμασεν καλλίτριχας ἵππους,   38
ἵκετο δ' εἰς Αἰγάς, ὅθι οἱ κλυτὰ δώματ' ἔασιν.
    Αὐτὰρ Ἀθηναίη κούρη Διὸς ἄλλ' ἐνόησεν.
ἤ τοι τῶν ἄλλων ἀνέμων κατέδησε κελεύθους,
παύσασθαι δ' ἐκέλευσε καὶ εὐνηθῆναι ἅπαντας·
ὦρσε δ' ἐπὶ κραιπνὸν Βορέην, πρὸ δὲ κύματ' ἔαξεν,   38
196

bids me leave my raft. Nay, but verily I will not yet obey, for afar off mine eyes beheld the land, where she said I was to escape. But this will I do, and meseems that this is best: as long as the timbers hold firm in their fastenings, so long will I remain here and endure to suffer affliction; but when the wave shall have shattered the raft to pieces, I will swim, seeing that there is naught better to devise."

While he pondered thus in mind and heart, Poseidon, the earth-shaker, made to rise up a great wave, dread and grievous, arching over from above, and drove it upon him. And as when a strong wind tosses a heap of straw that is dry, and some it scatters here, some there, even so the wave scattered the long timbers of the raft. But Odysseus bestrode one plank, as though he were riding a horse, and stripped off the garments which beautiful Calypso had given him. Then straightway he stretched the veil beneath his breast, and flung himself headlong into the sea with hands outstretched, ready to swim. And the lord, the earth-shaker, saw him, and he shook his head, and thus he spoke to his own heart:

"So now, after thou hast suffered many ills, go wandering over the deep, till thou comest among the folk fostered of Zeus. Yet even so, methinks, thou shalt not make any mock at thy suffering."

So saying, he lashed his fair-maned horses, and came to Aegae, where is his glorious palace.

But Athene, daughter of Zeus, took other counsel. She stayed the paths of the other winds, and bade them all cease and be lulled to rest; but she roused the swift North Wind, and broke the waves before

ἧος ὃ Φαιήκεσσι φιληρέτμοισι μιγείη
διογενὴς Ὀδυσεὺς θάνατον καὶ κῆρας ἀλύξας.
    Ἔνθα δύω νύκτας δύο τ' ἤματα κύματι πηγῷ
πλάζετο, πολλὰ δέ οἱ κραδίη προτιόσσετ' ὄλεθρον.
ἀλλ' ὅτε δὴ τρίτον ἦμαρ ἐυπλόκαμος τέλεσ' Ἠώς,   3
καὶ τότ' ἔπειτ' ἄνεμος μὲν ἐπαύσατο ἠδὲ γαλήνη
ἔπλετο νηνεμίη· ὁ δ' ἄρα σχεδὸν εἴσιδε γαῖαν
ὀξὺ μάλα προϊδών, μεγάλου ὑπὸ κύματος ἀρθείς.
ὡς δ' ὅτ' ἂν ἀσπάσιος βίοτος παίδεσσι φανήῃ
πατρός, ὃς ἐν νούσῳ κῆται κρατέρ' ἄλγεα πάσχων,   3
δηρὸν τηκόμενος, στυγερὸς δέ οἱ ἔχραε δαίμων,
ἀσπάσιον δ' ἄρα τόν γε θεοὶ κακότητος ἔλυσαν,
ὣς Ὀδυσεῖ ἀσπαστὸν ἐείσατο γαῖα καὶ ὕλη,
νῆχε δ' ἐπειγόμενος ποσὶν ἠπείρου ἐπιβῆναι.
ἀλλ' ὅτε τόσσον ἀπῆν ὅσσον τε γέγωνε βοήσας,   4
καὶ δὴ δοῦπον ἄκουσε ποτὶ σπιλάδεσσι θαλάσσης·
ῥόχθει γὰρ μέγα κῦμα ποτὶ ξερὸν ἠπείροιο
δεινὸν ἐρευγόμενον, εἴλυτο δὲ πάνθ' ἁλὸς ἄχνῃ·
οὐ γὰρ ἔσαν λιμένες νηῶν ὄχοι, οὐδ' ἐπιωγαί·
ἀλλ' ἀκταὶ προβλῆτες ἔσαν σπιλάδες τε πάγοι τε·   4
καὶ τότ' Ὀδυσσῆος λύτο γούνατα καὶ φίλον ἦτορ,
ὀχθήσας δ' ἄρα εἶπε πρὸς ὃν μεγαλήτορα θυμόν·
    " Ὤ μοι, ἐπεὶ δὴ γαῖαν ἀελπέα δῶκεν ἰδέσθαι
Ζεύς, καὶ δὴ τόδε λαῖτμα διατμήξας ἐπέρησα,[1]
ἔκβασις οὔ πῃ φαίνεθ' ἁλὸς πολιοῖο θύραζε·   4
ἔκτοσθεν μὲν γὰρ πάγοι ὀξέες, ἀμφὶ δὲ κῦμα
βέβρυχεν ῥόθιον, λισσὴ δ' ἀναδέδρομε πέτρη,
ἀγχιβαθὴς δὲ θάλασσα, καὶ οὔ πως ἔστι πόδεσσι

---

[1] ἐπέρησα : ἐτέλεσσα

him, to the end that Zeus-born Odysseus might come among the Phaeacians, lovers of the oar, escaping from death and the fates.

Then for two nights and two days he was driven about over the swollen waves, and full often his heart forboded destruction. But when fair-tressed Dawn brought to its birth the third day, then the wind ceased and there was a windless calm, and he caught sight of the shore close at hand, casting a quick glance forward, as he was raised up by a great wave. And even as when most welcome to his children appears the life of a father who lies in sickness, bearing grievous pains, long while wasting away, and some cruel god assails him, but then to their joy the gods free him from his woe, so to Odysseus did the land and the wood seem welcome; and he swam on, eager to set foot on the land. But when he was as far away as a man's voice carries when he shouts, and heard the boom of the sea upon the reefs—for the great wave thundered against the dry land, belching upon it in terrible fashion, and all things were wrapped in the foam of the sea; for there were neither harbours where ships might ride, nor road-steads, but projecting headlands, and reefs, and cliffs —then the knees of Odysseus were loosened and his heart melted, and deeply moved he spoke to his own mighty spirit:

"Ah me, when Zeus has at length granted me to see the land beyond my hopes, and lo, I have prevailed to cleave my way and to cross this gulf, nowhere doth there appear a way to come forth from the grey sea. For without are sharp crags, and around them the wave roars foaming, and the rock runs up sheer, and the water is deep close in shore, so that in no

στήμεναι ἀμφοτέροισι καὶ ἐκφυγέειν κακότητα·
μή πώς μ' ἐκβαίνοντα βάλῃ λίθακι ποτὶ πέτρῃ   4)
κῦμα μέγ' ἁρπάξαν· μελέη δέ μοι ἔσσεται ὁρμή.
εἰ δέ κ' ἔτι προτέρω παρανήξομαι, ἤν που ἐφεύρω
ἠιόνας τε παραπλῆγας λιμένας τε θαλάσσης,
δείδω μή μ' ἐξαῦτις ἀναρπάξασα θύελλα
πόντον ἐπ' ἰχθυόεντα φέρῃ βαρέα στενάχοντα,   4ς
ἠέ τί μοι καὶ κῆτος ἐπισσεύῃ μέγα δαίμων
ἐξ ἁλός, οἷά τε πολλὰ τρέφει κλυτὸς Ἀμφιτρίτη·
οἶδα γάρ, ὥς μοι ὀδώδυσται κλυτὸς ἐννοσίγαιος."

Ὣς ὁ ταῦθ' ὥρμαινε κατὰ φρένα καὶ κατὰ θυμόν,
τόφρα δέ μιν μέγα κῦμα φέρε τρηχεῖαν ἐπ' ἀκτήν.   4ς
ἔνθα κ' ἀπὸ ῥινοὺς δρύφθη, σὺν δ' ὀστέ' ἀράχθη,
εἰ μὴ ἐπὶ φρεσὶ θῆκε θεά, γλαυκῶπις Ἀθήνη·
ἀμφοτέρῃσι δὲ χερσὶν ἐπεσσύμενος λάβε πέτρης,
τῆς ἔχετο στενάχων, ἧος μέγα κῦμα παρῆλθε.
καὶ τὸ μὲν ὣς ὑπάλυξε, παλιρρόθιον δέ μιν αὖτις   4)
πλῆξεν ἐπεσσύμενον, τηλοῦ δέ μιν ἔμβαλε πόντῳ.
ὡς δ' ὅτε πουλύποδος θαλάμης ἐξελκομένοιο
πρὸς κοτυληδονόφιν πυκιναὶ λάιγγες ἔχονται,
ὣς τοῦ πρὸς πέτρῃσι θρασειάων ἀπὸ χειρῶν
ῥινοὶ ἀπέδρυφθεν· τὸν δὲ μέγα κῦμα κάλυψεν.   4ς
ἔνθα κε δὴ δύστηνος ὑπὲρ μόρον ὤλετ' Ὀδυσσεύς,
εἰ μὴ ἐπιφροσύνην δῶκε γλαυκῶπις Ἀθήνη.
κύματος ἐξαναδύς, τά τ' ἐρεύγεται ἠπειρόνδε,
νῆχε παρέξ, ἐς γαῖαν ὁρώμενος, εἴ που ἐφεύροι
ἠιόνας τε παραπλῆγας λιμένας τε θαλάσσης.   4)
ἀλλ' ὅτε δὴ ποταμοῖο κατὰ στόμα καλλιρόοιο

wise is it possible to plant both feet firmly and escape ruin. Haply were I to seek to land, a great wave may seize me and dash me against the jagged rock, and so shall my striving be in vain. But if I swim on yet further in hope to find shelving beaches [1] and harbours of the sea, I fear me lest the storm-wind may catch me up again, and bear me, groaning heavily, over the teeming deep; or lest some god may even send forth upon me some great monster from out the sea—and many such does glorious Amphitrite breed. For I know that the glorious Earth-shaker is filled with wrath against me."

While he pondered thus in mind and heart, a great wave bore him against the rugged shore. There would his skin have been stripped off and his bones broken, had not the goddess, flashing-eyed Athene, put a thought in his mind. On he rushed and seized the rock with both hands, and clung to it, groaning, until the great wave went by. Thus then did he escape this wave, but in its backward flow it once more rushed upon him and smote him, and flung him far out in the sea. And just as, when a cuttlefish is dragged from its hole, many pebbles cling to its suckers, even so from his strong hands were bits of skin stripped off against the rocks; and the great wave covered him. Then verily would hapless Odysseus have perished beyond his fate, had not flashing-eyed Athene given him prudence. Making his way forth from the surge where it belched upon the shore, he swam outside, looking ever toward the land in hope to find shelving beaches and harbours of the sea. But when, as he swam, he came to the mouth of a fair-flowing river, where seemed to him

---

[1] Possibly "shores that take the waves aslant."

ἷξε νέων, τῇ δή οἱ ἐείσατο χῶρος ἄριστος,
λεῖος πετράων, καὶ ἐπὶ σκέπας ἦν ἀνέμοιο,
ἔγνω δὲ προρέοντα καὶ εὔξατο ὃν κατὰ θυμόν·
  "Κλῦθι, ἄναξ, ὅτις ἐσσί· πολύλλιστον δέ σ' ἱκάνω, 44
φεύγων ἐκ πόντοιο Ποσειδάωνος ἐνιπάς.
αἰδοῖος μέν τ' ἐστὶ καὶ ἀθανάτοισι θεοῖσιν
ἀνδρῶν ὅς τις ἵκηται ἀλώμενος, ὡς καὶ ἐγὼ νῦν
σόν τε ῥόον σά τε γούναθ' ἱκάνω πολλὰ μογήσας.
ἀλλ' ἐλέαιρε, ἄναξ· ἱκέτης δέ τοι εὔχομαι εἶναι." 45
  Ὣς φάθ', ὁ δ' αὐτίκα παῦσεν ἐὸν ῥόον, ἔσχε δὲ κῦμ,
πρόσθε δέ οἱ ποίησε γαλήνην, τὸν δ' ἐσάωσεν
ἐς ποταμοῦ προχοάς. ὁ δ' ἄρ' ἄμφω γούνατ' ἔκαμψε
χεῖράς τε στιβαράς· ἁλὶ γὰρ δέδμητο φίλον κῆρ.
ᾤδεε δὲ χρόα πάντα, θάλασσα δὲ κήκιε πολλὴ 45
ἂν στόμα τε ῥῖνάς θ'· ὁ δ' ἄρ' ἄπνευστος καὶ ἄναυδος
κεῖτ' ὀλιγηπελέων, κάματος δέ μιν αἰνὸς ἵκανεν.
ἀλλ' ὅτε δή ῥ' ἄμπνυτο καὶ ἐς φρένα θυμὸς ἀγέρθη,
καὶ τότε δὴ κρήδεμνον ἀπὸ ἕο λῦσε θεοῖο.
καὶ τὸ μὲν ἐς ποταμὸν ἁλιμυρήεντα μεθῆκεν, 46
ἂψ δ' ἔφερεν μέγα κῦμα κατὰ ῥόον, αἶψα δ' ἄρ' Ἰνὼ
δέξατο χερσὶ φίλῃσιν· ὁ δ' ἐκ ποταμοῖο λιασθεὶς
σχοίνῳ ὑπεκλίνθη, κύσε δὲ ζείδωρον ἄρουραν.
ὀχθήσας δ' ἄρα εἶπε πρὸς ὃν μεγαλήτορα θυμόν·
  "Ὤ μοι ἐγώ, τί πάθω; τί νύ μοι μήκιστα γένηται; 4
εἰ μέν κ' ἐν ποταμῷ δυσκηδέα νύκτα φυλάσσω,

the best place, since it was smooth of stones, and besides there was shelter from the wind, he knew the river as he flowed forth, and prayed to him in his heart:

"Hear me, O king, whosoever thou art. As to one greatly longed-for[1] do I come to thee, seeking to escape from out the sea from the threats of Poseidon. Reverend even in the eyes of the immortal gods is that man who comes as a wanderer, even as I have now come to thy stream and to thy knees, after many toils. Nay, pity me, O king, for I declare that I am thy suppliant."

So he spoke, and the god straightway stayed his stream, and checked the waves, and made a calm before him, and brought him safely to the mouth of the river. And he let his two knees bend and his strong hands fall, for his spirit was crushed by the sea. And all his flesh was swollen, and sea water flowed in streams up through his mouth and nostrils. So he lay breathless and speechless, with scarce strength to move; for terrible weariness had come upon him. But when he revived, and his spirit returned again into his breast, then he loosed from him the veil of the goddess and let it fall into the river that murmured seaward; and the great wave bore it back down the stream, and straightway Ino received it in her hands. But Odysseus, going back from the river, sank down in the reeds and kissed the earth, the giver of grain; and deeply moved he spoke to his own mighty spirit:

"Ah, woe is me! what is to befall me? What will happen to me at the last? If here in the river bed I keep watch throughout the weary night, I fear

[1] Or, "to whom many prayers are made."

μή μ' ἄμυδις στίβη τε κακὴ καὶ θῆλυς ἐέρση
ἐξ ὀλιγηπελίης δαμάσῃ κεκαφηότα θυμόν·
αὔρη δ' ἐκ ποταμοῦ ψυχρὴ πνέει ἠῶθι πρό.
εἰ δέ κεν ἐς κλιτὺν ἀναβὰς καὶ δάσκιον ὕλην   4
θάμνοις ἐν πυκινοῖσι καταδράθω, εἴ με μεθείη
ῥῖγος καὶ κάματος, γλυκερὸς δέ μοι ὕπνος ἐπέλθῃ,
δείδω, μὴ θήρεσσιν ἕλωρ καὶ κύρμα γένωμαι."
    Ὣς ἄρα οἱ φρονέοντι δοάσσατο κέρδιον εἶναι·
βῆ ῥ' ἴμεν εἰς ὕλην· τὴν δὲ σχεδὸν ὕδατος εὗρεν   4
ἐν περιφαινομένῳ· δοιοὺς δ' ἄρ' ὑπήλυθε θάμνους,
ἐξ ὁμόθεν πεφυῶτας· ὁ μὲν φυλίης, ὁ δ' ἐλαίης.
τοὺς μὲν ἄρ' οὔτ' ἀνέμων διάη μένος ὑγρὸν ἀέντων,
οὔτε ποτ' ἠέλιος φαέθων ἀκτῖσιν ἔβαλλεν,
οὔτ' ὄμβρος περάασκε διαμπερές· ὣς ἄρα πυκνοὶ   4
ἀλλήλοισιν ἔφυν ἐπαμοιβαδίς· οὓς ὑπ' Ὀδυσσεὺς
δύσετ'.   ἄφαρ δ' εὐνὴν ἐπαμήσατο χερσὶ φίλῃσιν
εὐρεῖαν· φύλλων γὰρ ἔην χύσις ἤλιθα πολλή,
ὅσσον τ' ἠὲ δύω ἠὲ τρεῖς ἄνδρας ἔρυσθαι
ὥρῃ χειμερίῃ, εἰ καὶ μάλα περ χαλεπαίνοι.   4
τὴν μὲν ἰδὼν γήθησε πολύτλας δῖος Ὀδυσσεύς,
ἐν δ' ἄρα μέσσῃ λέκτο, χύσιν δ' ἐπεχεύατο φύλλων.
ὡς δ' ὅτε τις δαλὸν σποδιῇ ἐνέκρυψε μελαίνῃ
ἀγροῦ ἐπ' ἐσχατιῆς, ᾧ μὴ πάρα γείτονες ἄλλοι,
σπέρμα πυρὸς σώζων, ἵνα μή ποθεν ἄλλοθεν αὔοι,   4
ὣς Ὀδυσεὺς φύλλοισι καλύψατο· τῷ δ' ἄρ' Ἀθήνη
ὕπνον ἐπ' ὄμμασι χεῦ', ἵνα μιν παύσειε τάχιστα
δυσπονέος καμάτοιο φίλα βλέφαρ' ἀμφικαλύψας.

that together the bitter frost and the fresh dew may overcome me, when from feebleness I have breathed forth my spirit; and the breeze from the river blows cold in the early morning. But if I climb up the slope to the shady wood and lie down to rest in the thick brushwood, in the hope that the cold and weariness might leave me, and if sweet sleep comes over me, I fear me lest I become a prey and spoil to wild beasts."

Then, as he pondered, this thing seemed to him the better: he went his way to the wood and found it near the water in a clear space; and he crept beneath two bushes that grew from the same spot, one of thorn and one of olive. Through these the strength of the wet winds could never blow, nor the rays of the bright sun beat, nor could the rain pierce through them, so closely did they grow, intertwining one with the other. Beneath these Odysseus crept and straightway gathered with his hands a broad bed, for fallen leaves were there in plenty, enough to shelter two men or three in winter time, however bitter the weather. And the much-enduring goodly Odysseus saw it, and was glad, and he lay down in the midst, and heaped over him the fallen leaves. And as a man hides a brand beneath the dark embers in an outlying farm, a man who has no neighbours, and so saves a seed of fire, that he may not have to kindle it from some other source, so Odysseus covered himself with leaves. And Athene shed sleep upon his eyes, that it might enfold his lids and speedily free him from toilsome weariness.

Z

Ὣς ὁ μὲν ἔνθα καθεῦδε πολύτλας δῖος Ὀδυσσεὺς
ὕπνῳ καὶ καμάτῳ ἀρημένος· αὐτὰρ Ἀθήνη
βῆ ῥ᾽ ἐς Φαιήκων ἀνδρῶν δῆμόν τε πόλιν τε,
οἳ πρὶν μέν ποτ᾽ ἔναιον ἐν εὐρυχόρῳ Ὑπερείῃ,
ἀγχοῦ Κυκλώπων ἀνδρῶν ὑπερηνορεόντων,
οἵ σφεας σινέσκοντο, βίηφι δὲ φέρτεροι ἦσαν.
ἔνθεν ἀναστήσας ἄγε Ναυσίθοος θεοειδής,
εἷσεν δὲ Σχερίῃ, ἑκὰς ἀνδρῶν ἀλφηστάων,
ἀμφὶ δὲ τεῖχος ἔλασσε πόλει, καὶ ἐδείματο οἴκους,
καὶ νηοὺς ποίησε θεῶν, καὶ ἐδάσσατ᾽ ἀρούρας.
ἀλλ᾽ ὁ μὲν ἤδη κηρὶ δαμεὶς Ἀιδόσδε βεβήκει,
Ἀλκίνοος δὲ τότ᾽ ἦρχε, θεῶν ἄπο μήδεα εἰδώς.
τοῦ μὲν ἔβη πρὸς δῶμα θεά, γλαυκῶπις Ἀθήνη,
νόστον Ὀδυσσῆι μεγαλήτορι· μητιόωσα.
βῆ δ᾽ ἴμεν ἐς θάλαμον πολυδαίδαλον, ᾧ ἔνι κούρη
κοιμᾶτ᾽ ἀθανάτῃσι φυὴν καὶ εἶδος ὁμοίη,
Ναυσικάα, θυγάτηρ μεγαλήτορος Ἀλκινόοιο,
πὰρ δὲ δύ᾽ ἀμφίπολοι, Χαρίτων ἄπο κάλλος ἔχουσαι,
σταθμοῖιν ἑκάτερθε· θύραι δ᾽ ἐπέκειντο φαειναί.
Ἡ δ᾽ ἀνέμου ὡς πνοιὴ ἐπέσσυτο δέμνια κούρης,
στῆ δ᾽ ἄρ᾽ ὑπὲρ κεφαλῆς, καί μιν πρὸς μῦθον ἔειπεν,
εἰδομένη κούρῃ ναυσικλειτοῖο Δύμαντος,

BOOK VI

So he lay there asleep, the much-enduring goodly
Odysseus, overcome with sleep and weariness; but
Athene went to the land and city of the Phaeacians.
These dwelt of old in spacious Hypereia hard by the
Cyclopes, men overweening in pride who plundered
them continually and were mightier than they.
From thence Nausithous, the godlike, had removed
them, and led and settled them in Scheria far from
men that live by toil.   About the city he had drawn
a wall, he had built houses and made temples for
the gods, and divided the ploughlands; but he, ere
now, had been stricken by fate and had gone to the
house of Hades, and Alcinous was now king, made
wise in counsel by the gods.   To his house went
the goddess, flashing-eyed Athene, to contrive the
return of great-hearted Odysseus.   She went to a
chamber, richly wrought, wherein slept a maiden
like the immortal goddesses in form and comeliness,
Nausicaa, the daughter of great-hearted Alcinous;
hard by slept two hand-maidens, gifted with beauty
by the Graces, one on either side of the door-posts,
and the bright doors were shut.
But like a breath of air the goddess sped to the
couch of the maiden, and stood above her head, and
spoke to her, taking the form of the daughter of
Dymas, famed for his ships, a girl who was of like

ἥ οἱ ὁμηλικίη μὲν ἔην, κεχάριστο δὲ θυμῷ.
τῇ μιν ἐεισαμένη προσέφη γλαυκῶπις Ἀθήνη·
   "Ναυσικάα, τί νύ σ' ὧδε μεθήμονα γείνατο μήτηρ;
εἵματα μέν τοι κεῖται ἀκηδέα σιγαλόεντα,
σοὶ δὲ γάμος σχεδόν ἐστιν, ἵνα χρὴ καλὰ μὲν αὐτὴν
ἕννυσθαι, τὰ δὲ τοῖσι παρασχεῖν, οἵ κέ σ' ἄγωνται.
ἐκ γάρ τοι τούτων φάτις ἀνθρώπους ἀναβαίνει
ἐσθλή, χαίρουσιν δὲ πατὴρ καὶ πότνια μήτηρ.   3
ἀλλ' ἴομεν πλυνέουσαι ἅμ' ἠοῖ φαινομένηφι·
καί τοι ἐγὼ συνέριθος ἅμ' ἕψομαι, ὄφρα τάχιστα
ἐντύνεαι, ἐπεὶ οὔ τοι ἔτι δὴν παρθένος ἔσσεαι·
ἤδη γάρ σε μνῶνται ἀριστῆες κατὰ δῆμον
πάντων Φαιήκων, ὅθι τοι γένος ἐστὶ καὶ αὐτῇ.   3
ἀλλ' ἄγ' ἐπότρυνον πατέρα κλυτὸν ἠῶθι πρὸ
ἡμιόνους καὶ ἄμαξαν ἐφοπλίσαι, ἥ κεν ἄγῃσι
ζῶστρά τε καὶ πέπλους καὶ ῥήγεα σιγαλόεντα.
καὶ δὲ σοὶ ὧδ' αὐτῇ πολὺ κάλλιον ἠὲ πόδεσσιν
ἔρχεσθαι· πολλὸν γὰρ ἀπὸ πλυνοί εἰσι πόληος."   4
   Ἡ μὲν ἄρ' ὣς εἰποῦσ' ἀπέβη γλαυκῶπις Ἀθήνη
Οὔλυμπόνδ', ὅθι φασὶ θεῶν ἕδος ἀσφαλὲς αἰεὶ
ἔμμεναι.   οὔτ' ἀνέμοισι τινάσσεται οὔτε ποτ' ὄμβρῳ
δεύεται οὔτε χιὼν ἐπιπίλναται, ἀλλὰ μάλ' αἴθρη
πέπταται ἀνέφελος, λευκὴ δ' ἐπιδέδρομεν αἴγλη·   4
τῷ ἔνι τέρπονται μάκαρες θεοὶ ἤματα πάντα.
ἔνθ' ἀπέβη γλαυκῶπις, ἐπεὶ διεπέφραδε κούρῃ.
   Αὐτίκα δ' Ἠὼς ἦλθεν ἐύθρονος, ἥ μιν ἔγειρε
Ναυσικάαν ἐύπεπλον· ἄφαρ δ' ἀπεθαύμασ' ὄνειρον,
βῆ δ' ἰέναι διὰ δώμαθ', ἵν' ἀγγείλειε τοκεῦσιν,   5

age with Nausicaa, and was dear to her heart.
Likening herself to her, the flashing-eyed Athene
spoke and said :

" Nausicaa, how comes it that thy mother bore
thee so heedless ? Thy bright raiment is lying un-
cared for ; yet thy marriage is near at hand, when
thou must needs thyself be clad in fair garments,
and give other such to those who escort thee. It is
from things like these, thou knowest, that good
report goeth up among men, and the father and
honoured mother rejoice. Nay, come, let us go to
wash them at break of day, for I will follow with
thee to aid thee, that thou mayest with speed make
thee ready ; for thou shalt not long remain a maiden.
Even now thou hast suitors in the land, the noblest
of all the Phaeacians, from whom is thine own line-
age. Nay, come, bestir thy noble father early this
morning that he make ready mules and a waggon
for thee, to bear the girdles and robes and bright
coverlets. And for thyself, too, it is far more seemly
to go thus than on foot, for the washing tanks are
far from the city."

So saying, the goddess, flashing-eyed Athene,
departed to Olympus, where, they say, is the abode
of the gods that stands fast forever. Neither is it
shaken by winds nor ever wet with rain, nor does
snow fall upon it, but the air is outspread clear and
cloudless, and over it hovers a radiant whiteness.
Therein the blessed gods are glad all their days, and
thither went the flashing-eyed one, when she had
spoken all her word to the maiden.

At once then came fair-throned Dawn and awakened
Nausicaa of the beautiful robes, and straightway she
marvelled at her dream, and went through the house

πατρὶ φίλῳ καὶ μητρί· κιχήσατο δ' ἔνδον ἐόντας·
ἡ μὲν ἐπ' ἐσχάρῃ ἧστο σὺν ἀμφιπόλοισι γυναιξὶν
ἠλάκατα στρωφῶσ' ἁλιπόρφυρα· τῷ δὲ θύραζε
ἐρχομένῳ ξύμβλητο μετὰ κλειτοὺς βασιλῆας
ἐς βουλήν, ἵνα μιν κάλεον Φαίηκες ἀγαυοί.
ἡ δὲ μάλ' ἄγχι στᾶσα φίλον πατέρα προσέειπε·

"Πάππα φίλ', οὐκ ἂν δή μοι ἐφοπλίσσειας ἀπήνην
ὑψηλὴν ἐύκυκλον, ἵνα κλυτὰ εἵματ' ἄγωμαι
ἐς ποταμὸν πλυνέουσα, τά μοι ῥερυπωμένα κεῖται;
καὶ δὲ σοὶ αὐτῷ ἔοικε μετὰ πρώτοισιν ἐόντα
βουλὰς βουλεύειν καθαρὰ χροΐ εἵματ' ἔχοντα.
πέντε δέ τοι φίλοι υἷες ἐνὶ μεγάροις γεγάασιν,
οἱ δύ' ὀπυίοντες, τρεῖς δ' ἠίθεοι θαλέθοντες·
οἱ δ' αἰεὶ ἐθέλουσι νεόπλυτα εἵματ' ἔχοντες
ἐς χορὸν ἔρχεσθαι· τὰ δ' ἐμῇ φρενὶ πάντα μέμηλεν."

Ὣς ἔφατ'· αἴδετο γὰρ θαλερὸν γάμον ἐξονομῆναι
πατρὶ φίλῳ.   ὁ δὲ πάντα νόει καὶ ἀμείβετο μύθῳ·
"Οὔτε τοι ἡμιόνων φθονέω, τέκος, οὔτε τευ ἄλλου.
ἔρχευ· ἀτάρ τοι δμῶες ἐφοπλίσσουσιν ἀπήνην
ὑψηλὴν ἐύκυκλον, ὑπερτερίῃ ἀραρυῖαν."

Ὣς εἰπὼν δμώεσσιν ἐκέκλετο, τοὶ δ' ἐπίθοντο.
οἱ μὲν ἄρ' ἐκτὸς ἄμαξαν ἐύτροχον ἡμιονείην
ὥπλεον, ἡμιόνους θ' ὕπαγον ζεῦξάν θ' ὑπ' ἀπήνῃ·
κούρη δ' ἐκ θαλάμοιο φέρεν ἐσθῆτα φαεινήν.
καὶ τὴν μὲν κατέθηκεν ἐυξέστῳ ἐπ' ἀπήνῃ,
μήτηρ δ' ἐν κίστῃ ἐτίθει μενοεικέ' ἐδωδὴν

to tell her parents, her father dear and her mother;
and she found them both within. The mother sat
at the hearth with her handmaidens, spinning the
yarn of purple dye, and her father she met as he was
going forth to join the glorious kings in the place of
council, to which the lordly Phaeacians called him.
But she came up close to her dear father, and said:

"Papa dear, wilt thou not make ready for me a
waggon, high and stout of wheel, that I may take to
the river for washing the goodly raiment of mine
which is lying here soiled? Moreover for thyself it
is seemly that when thou art at council with the
princes thou shouldst have clean raiment upon thee;
and thou hast five sons living in thy halls—two are
wedded, but three are sturdy bachelors—and these
ever wish to put on them freshly-washed raiment,
when they go to the dance. Of all this must I take
thought."

So she spoke, for she was ashamed to name glad-
some [1] marriage to her father; but he understood all,
and answered, saying: "Neither the mules do I be-
grudge thee, my child, nor aught beside. Go thy
way; the slaves shall make ready for thee the
waggon, high and stout of wheel and fitted with a
box above." [2]

With this he called to the slaves, and they
hearkened. Outside the palace they made ready the
light-running mule waggon, and led up the mules and
yoked them to it; and the maiden brought from her
chamber the bright raiment, and placed it upon the
polished car, while her mother put in a chest food of

---

[1] Possibly "fruitful"; cf. xx. 74; Il. ii. 53.
[2] Presumably with a body above the running-gear, not
a mere δίφρος. Others assume that ὑπερτερίη denotes an
"awning."

παντοίην, ἐν δ᾽ ὄψα τίθει, ἐν δ᾽ οἶνον ἔχευεν
ἀσκῷ ἐν αἰγείῳ· κούρη δ᾽ ἐπεβήσετ᾽ ἀπήνης.
δῶκεν δὲ χρυσέῃ ἐν ληκύθῳ ὑγρὸν ἔλαιον,
ἧος χυτλώσαιτο σὺν ἀμφιπόλοισι γυναιξίν.   8

ἡ δ᾽ ἔλαβεν μάστιγα καὶ ἡνία σιγαλόεντα,
μάστιξεν δ᾽ ἐλάαν· καναχὴ δ᾽ ἦν ἡμιόνοιιν.
αἱ δ᾽ ἄμοτον τανύοντο, φέρον δ᾽ ἐσθῆτα καὶ αὐτήν,
οὐκ οἴην, ἅμα τῇ γε καὶ ἀμφίπολοι κίον ἄλλαι.

Αἱ δ᾽ ὅτε δὴ ποταμοῖο ῥόον περικαλλέ᾽ ἵκοντο,   8
ἔνθ᾽ ἦ τοι πλυνοὶ ἦσαν ἐπηετανοί, πολὺ δ᾽ ὕδωρ
καλὸν ὑπεκπρόρεεν [1] μάλα περ ῥυπόωντα καθῆραι,
ἔνθ᾽ αἵ γ᾽ ἡμιόνους μὲν ὑπεκπροέλυσαν ἀπήνης.
καὶ τὰς μὲν σεῦαν ποταμὸν πάρα δινήεντα
τρώγειν ἄγρωστιν μελιηδέα· ταὶ δ᾽ ἀπ᾽ ἀπήνης   9
εἵματα χερσὶν ἕλοντο καὶ ἐσφόρεον μέλαν ὕδωρ,
στεῖβον δ᾽ ἐν βόθροισι θοῶς ἔριδα προφέρουσαι.
αὐτὰρ ἐπεὶ πλῦνάν τε κάθηράν τε ῥύπα πάντα,
ἑξείης πέτασαν παρὰ θῖν᾽ ἁλός, ἧχι μάλιστα
λάιγγας ποτὶ χέρσον ἀποπλύνεσκε [2] θάλασσα.   9
αἱ δὲ λοεσσάμεναι καὶ χρισάμεναι λίπ᾽ ἐλαίῳ
δεῖπνον ἔπειθ᾽ εἵλοντο παρ᾽ ὄχθῃσιν ποταμοῖο,
εἵματα δ᾽ ἠελίοιο μένον τερσήμεναι αὐγῇ.
αὐτὰρ ἐπεὶ σίτου τάρφθεν δμῳαί τε καὶ αὐτή,
σφαίρῃ ταὶ δ᾽ ἄρ᾽ ἔπαιζον, ἀπὸ κρήδεμνα βαλοῦσαι·   10
τῇσι δὲ Ναυσικάα λευκώλενος ἤρχετο μολπῆς.
οἵη δ᾽ Ἄρτεμις εἶσι κατ᾽ οὔρεα [3] ἰοχέαιρα,
ἢ κατὰ Τηΰγετον περιμήκετον ἢ Ἐρύμανθον,
τερπομένη κάπροισι καὶ ὠκείῃς ἐλάφοισι·

---

[1] ὑπεκπρόρεεν : ὑπεκπρορέει MSS.
[2] ἀποπλύνεσκε : ἀποπτύεσκε.
[3] οὔρεα : οὔρεος.

all sorts to satisfy the heart. Therein she put dainties, and poured wine in a goat-skin flask; and the maiden mounted upon the waggon. Her mother gave her also soft olive oil in a flask of gold, that she and her maidens might have it for the bath. Then Nausicaa took the whip and the bright reins, and smote the mules to start them; and there was a clatter of the mules as they sped on amain, bearing the raiment and the maiden; neither went she alone, for with her went her handmaids as well.

Now when they came to the beautiful streams of the river, where were the washing tanks that never failed —for abundant clear water welled up from beneath and flowed over, to cleanse garments however soiled —there they loosed the mules from under the waggon and drove them along the eddying river to graze on the honey-sweet water-grass, and themselves took in their arms the raiment from the waggon, and bore it into the dark water, and trampled it in the trenches, busily vying each with each. Now when they had washed the garments, and had cleansed them of all the stains, they spread them out in rows on the shore of the sea where the waves dashing against the land washed the pebbles cleanest; and they, after they had bathed and anointed themselves richly with oil, took their meal on the river's banks, and waited for the clothing to dry in the bright sunshine. Then when they had had their joy of food, she and her handmaids, they threw off their head-gear and fell to playing at ball, and white-armed Nausicaa was leader in the song.[1] And even as Artemis, the archer, roves over the mountains, along the ridges of lofty Taÿgetus or Erymanthus, joying in the pursuit of boars and

---

[1] They sing while tossing the ball to one another.

τῇ δέ θ᾽ ἅμα νύμφαι, κοῦραι Διὸς αἰγιόχοιο, 1
ἀγρονόμοι παίζουσι, γέγηθε δέ τε φρένα Λητώ·
πασάων δ᾽ ὑπὲρ ἥ γε κάρη ἔχει ἠδὲ μέτωπα,
ῥεῖά τ᾽ ἀριγνώτη πέλεται, καλαὶ δέ τε πᾶσαι·
ὡς ἥ γ᾽ ἀμφιπόλοισι μετέπρεπε παρθένος ἀδμής.
   Ἀλλ᾽ ὅτε δὴ ἄρ᾽ ἔμελλε πάλιν οἶκόνδε νέεσθαι 1
ζεύξασ᾽ ἡμιόνους πτύξασά τε εἵματα καλά,
ἔνθ᾽ αὖτ᾽ ἀλλ᾽ ἐνόησε θεά, γλαυκῶπις Ἀθήνη,
ὡς Ὀδυσεὺς ἔγροιτο, ἴδοι τ᾽ εὐώπιδα κούρην,
ἥ οἱ Φαιήκων ἀνδρῶν πόλιν ἡγήσαιτο.
σφαῖραν ἔπειτ᾽ ἔρριψε μετ᾽ ἀμφίπολον βασίλεια· 1
ἀμφιπόλου μὲν ἅμαρτε, βαθείῃ δ᾽ ἔμβαλε δίνῃ·
αἱ δ᾽ ἐπὶ μακρὸν ἄυσαν· ὁ δ᾽ ἔγρετο δῖος Ὀδυσσεύς,
ἑζόμενος δ᾽ ὥρμαινε κατὰ φρένα καὶ κατὰ θυμόν·
   "Ὤ μοι ἐγώ, τέων αὖτε βροτῶν ἐς γαῖαν ἱκάνω;
ἦ ῥ᾽ οἵ γ᾽ ὑβρισταί τε καὶ ἄγριοι οὐδὲ δίκαιοι, 1
ἦε φιλόξεινοι καί σφιν νόος ἐστὶ θεουδής;
ὥς τέ με κουράων ἀμφήλυθε θῆλυς ἀυτή·
νυμφάων, αἳ ἔχουσ᾽ ὀρέων αἰπεινὰ κάρηνα
καὶ πηγὰς ποταμῶν καὶ πίσεα ποιήεντα.
ἦ νύ που ἀνθρώπων εἰμὶ σχεδὸν αὐδηέντων; 1
ἀλλ᾽ ἄγ᾽ ἐγὼν αὐτὸς πειρήσομαι ἠδὲ ἴδωμαι."
   Ὡς εἰπὼν θάμνων ὑπεδύσετο δῖος Ὀδυσσεύς,
ἐκ πυκινῆς δ᾽ ὕλης πτόρθον κλάσε χειρὶ παχείῃ
φύλλων, ὡς ῥύσαιτο περὶ χροῒ μήδεα φωτός.
βῆ δ᾽ ἴμεν ὥς τε λέων ὀρεσίτροφος ἀλκὶ πεποιθώς, 1
ὅς τ᾽ εἶσ᾽ ὑόμενος καὶ ἀήμενος, ἐν δέ οἱ ὄσσε
δαίεται· αὐτὰρ ὁ βουσὶ μετέρχεται ἢ οἴεσσιν
ἠὲ μετ᾽ ἀγροτέρας ἐλάφους· κέλεται δέ ἑ γαστὴρ

swift deer, and with her sport the wood-nymphs, the daughters of Zeus who bears the aegis, and Leto is glad at heart—high above them all Artemis holds her head and brows, and easily may she be known, though all are fair—so amid her handmaidens shone the maid unwed.

But when she was about to yoke the mules, and fold the fair raiment, in order to return homeward, then the goddess, flashing-eyed Athene, took other counsel, that Odysseus might awake and see the fair-faced maid, who should lead him to the city of the Phaeacians. So then the princess tossed the ball to one of her maidens; the maiden indeed she missed, but cast it into a deep eddy, and thereat they cried aloud, and goodly Odysseus awoke, and sat up, and thus he pondered in mind and heart:

"Woe is me! to the land of what mortals am I now come? Are they cruel, and wild, and unjust? or do they love strangers and fear the gods in their thoughts? There rang in my ears a cry as of maidens, of nymphs who haunt the towering peaks of the mountains, the springs that feed the rivers, and the grassy meadows! Can it be that I am some-where near men of human speech? Nay, I will myself make trial and see."

So saying the goodly Odysseus came forth from beneath the bushes, and with his stout hand he broke from the thick wood a leafy branch, that he might hold it about him and hide therewith his nakedness. Forth he came like a mountain-nurtured lion trusting in his might, who goes forth, beaten with rain and wind, but his two eyes are ablaze: into the midst of the kine he goes, or of the sheep, or on the track of the wild deer, and his belly bids

HOMER

μήλων πειρήσοντα καὶ ἐς πυκινὸν δόμον ἐλθεῖν·
ὡς Ὀδυσεὺς κούρῃσιν ἐυπλοκάμοισιν ἔμελλε
μίξεσθαι, γυμνός περ ἐών· χρειὼ γὰρ ἵκανε.
σμερδαλέος δ' αὐτῇσι φάνη κεκακωμένος ἅλμῃ,
τρέσσαν δ' ἄλλυδις ἄλλη ἐπ' ἠιόνας προὐχούσας·
οἴη δ' Ἀλκινόου θυγάτηρ μένε· τῇ γὰρ Ἀθήνη
θάρσος ἐνὶ φρεσὶ θῆκε καὶ ἐκ δέος εἵλετο γυίων.
στῆ δ' ἄντα σχομένη· ὁ δὲ μερμήριξεν Ὀδυσσεύς,
ἢ γούνων λίσσοιτο λαβὼν ἐυώπιδα κούρην,
ἢ αὔτως ἐπέεσσιν ἀποσταδὰ μειλιχίοισι
λίσσοιτ', εἰ δείξειε πόλιν καὶ εἵματα δοίη.
ὣς ἄρα οἱ φρονέοντι δοάσσατο κέρδιον εἶναι,
λίσσεσθαι ἐπέεσσιν ἀποσταδὰ μειλιχίοισι,
μή οἱ γοῦνα λαβόντι χολώσαιτο φρένα κούρη.
αὐτίκα μειλίχιον καὶ κερδαλέον φάτο μῦθον.

" Γουνοῦμαί σε, ἄνασσα· θεός νύ τις, ἦ βροτός ἐσ;
εἰ μέν τις θεός ἐσσι, τοὶ οὐρανὸν εὐρὺν ἔχουσιν,
Ἀρτέμιδί σε ἐγώ γε, Διὸς κούρῃ μεγάλοιο,
εἶδός τε μέγεθός τε φυήν τ' ἄγχιστα ἐίσκω·
εἰ δέ τίς ἐσσι βροτῶν, τοὶ ἐπὶ χθονὶ ναιετάουσιν,
τρὶς μάκαρες μὲν σοί γε πατὴρ καὶ πότνια μήτηρ,
τρὶς μάκαρες δὲ κασίγνητοι· μάλα πού σφισι θυμὸς
αἰὲν ἐυφροσύνῃσιν ἰαίνεται εἵνεκα σεῖο,
λευσσόντων τοιόνδε θάλος χορὸν εἰσοιχνεῦσαν.
κεῖνος δ' αὖ περὶ κῆρι μακάρτατος ἔξοχον ἄλλων,
ὅς κέ σ' ἐέδνοισι βρίσας οἶκόνδ' ἀγάγηται.

---

¹ This metaphorical use of θάλος and, e.g., ἔρνος is very common : see *Il.* xxii. 87 ; xviii. 56, and *cf. Psalms* cxliv. 12.

him go even into the close-built fold, to make an
attack upon the flocks.   Even so Odysseus was about
to enter the company of the fair-tressed maidens,
naked though he was, for need had come upon him.
But terrible did he seem to them, all befouled with
brine, and they shrank in fear, one here, one there,
along the jutting sand-spits.   Alone the daughter of
Alcinous kept her place, for in her heart Athene put
courage, and took fear from her limbs.   She fled not,
but stood and faced him; and Odysseus pondered
whether he should clasp the knees of the fair-faced
maid, and make his prayer, or whether, standing
apart as he was, he should beseech her with gentle
words, in hope that she might show him the city
and give him raiment.   And, as he pondered, it
seemed to him better to stand apart and beseech her
with gentle words, lest the maiden's heart should be
wroth with him if he clasped her knees; so straight-
way he spoke a gentle word and crafty:

"I beseech thee, O queen,—a goddess art thou,
or art thou mortal?   If thou art a goddess, one
of those who hold broad heaven, to Artemis, the
daughter of great Zeus, do I liken thee most nearly
in comeliness and in stature and in form.   But if
thou art one of mortals who dwell upon the earth,
thrice-blessed then are thy father and thy honoured
mother, and thrice-blessed thy brethren.   Full well,
I ween, are their hearts ever warmed with joy
because of thee, as they see thee entering the
dance, a plant[1] so fair.   But he again is blessed in
heart above all others, who shall prevail with his
gifts of wooing and lead thee to his home.   For

"That our sons may be as plants"; and *Isaiah* v. 7, "For
the vineyard of the Lord of Hosts is the house of Israel, and
the men of Judah his pleasant plant."

οὐ γάρ πω τοιοῦτον ἴδον βροτὸν[1] ὀφθαλμοῖσιν,
οὔτ᾽ ἄνδρ᾽ οὔτε γυναῖκα· σέβας μ᾽ ἔχει εἰσορόωντα.
Δήλῳ δή ποτε τοῖον Ἀπόλλωνος παρὰ βωμῷ
φοίνικος νέον ἔρνος ἀνερχόμενον ἐνόησα·
ἦλθον γὰρ καὶ κεῖσε, πολὺς δέ μοι ἕσπετο λαός,
τὴν ὁδὸν ᾗ δὴ μέλλεν ἐμοὶ κακὰ κήδε᾽ ἔσεσθαι.
ὣς δ᾽ αὔτως καὶ κεῖνο ἰδὼν ἐτεθήπεα θυμῷ
δήν, ἐπεὶ οὔ πω τοῖον ἀνήλυθεν ἐκ δόρυ γαίης,
ὡς σέ, γύναι, ἄγαμαί τε τέθηπά τε, δείδια δ᾽ αἰνῶς
γούνων ἅψασθαι· χαλεπὸν δέ με πένθος ἱκάνει.
χθιζὸς ἐεικοστῷ φύγον ἤματι οἴνοπα πόντον·
τόφρα δέ μ᾽ αἰεὶ κῦμ᾽ ἐφόρει κραιπναί τε θύελλαι
νήσου ἀπ᾽ Ὠγυγίης. νῦν δ᾽ ἐνθάδε κάββαλε δαίμων,
ὄφρ᾽ ἔτι που καὶ τῇδε πάθω κακόν· οὐ γὰρ ὀίω
παύσεσθ᾽, ἀλλ᾽ ἔτι πολλὰ θεοὶ τελέουσι πάροιθεν.
ἀλλά, ἄνασσ᾽, ἐλέαιρε· σὲ γὰρ κακὰ πολλὰ μογήσας
ἐς πρώτην ἱκόμην, τῶν δ᾽ ἄλλων οὔ τινα οἶδα
ἀνθρώπων, οἳ τήνδε πόλιν καὶ γαῖαν ἔχουσιν.
ἄστυ δέ μοι δεῖξον, δὸς δὲ ῥάκος ἀμφιβαλέσθαι,
εἴ τί που εἴλυμα σπείρων ἔχες ἐνθάδ᾽ ἰοῦσα.
σοὶ δὲ θεοὶ τόσα δοῖεν ὅσα φρεσὶ σῇσι μενοινᾷς,
ἄνδρα τε καὶ οἶκον, καὶ ὁμοφροσύνην ὀπάσειαν
ἐσθλήν· οὐ μὲν γὰρ τοῦ γε κρεῖσσον καὶ ἄρειον,
ἢ ὅθ᾽ ὁμοφρονέοντε νοήμασιν οἶκον ἔχητον
ἀνὴρ ἠδὲ γυνή· πόλλ᾽ ἄλγεα δυσμενέεσσι,
χάρματα δ᾽ εὐμενέτῃσι, μάλιστα δέ τ᾽ ἔκλυον αὐτοί."

[1] ἴδον βροτὸν : ἐγὼν ἴδον.

never yet have mine eyes looked upon a mortal such as thou, whether man or woman; amazement holds me as I look on thee. Of a truth in Delos once I saw such a thing, a young shoot of a palm springing up beside the altar of Apollo—for thither, too, I went, and much people followed with me, on that journey on which evil woes were to be my portion;—even so, when I saw that, I marvelled long at heart, for never yet did such a tree spring up from the earth. And in like manner, lady, do I marvel at thee, and am amazed, and fear greatly to touch thy knees; but sore grief has come upon me. Yesterday, on the twentieth day, I escaped from the wine-dark sea, but ever until then the wave and the swift winds bore me from the island of Ogygia; and now fate has cast me ashore here, that here too, haply, I may suffer some ill. For not yet, methinks, will my troubles cease, but the gods ere that will bring many to pass. Nay, O queen, have pity; for it is to thee first that I am come after many grievous toils, and of the others who possess this city and land I know not one. Shew me the city, and give me some rag to throw about me, if thou hadst any wrapping for the clothes when thou camest hither. And for thyself, may the gods grant thee all that thy heart desires; a husband and a home may they grant thee, and oneness of heart—a goodly gift. For nothing is greater or better than this, when man and wife dwell in a home in one accord, a great grief to their foes and a joy to their friends; but they know it[1] best themselves."

---

[1] Lit. "they hear." This use of κλύω is quite without parallel.

Τὸν δ' αὖ Ναυσικάα λευκώλενος ἀντίον ηὔδα·
"Ξεῖν', ἐπεὶ οὔτε κακῷ οὔτ' ἄφρονι φωτὶ ἔοικας·
Ζεὺς δ' αὐτὸς νέμει ὄλβον Ὀλύμπιος ἀνθρώποισιν,
ἐσθλοῖς ἠδὲ κακοῖσιν, ὅπως ἐθέλησιν, ἑκάστῳ·
καί που σοὶ τάδ' ἔδωκε, σὲ δὲ χρὴ τετλάμεν ἔμπης. 19
νῦν δ', ἐπεὶ ἡμετέρην τε πόλιν καὶ γαῖαν ἱκάνεις,
οὔτ' οὖν ἐσθῆτος δευήσεαι οὔτε τευ ἄλλου,
ὧν ἐπέοιχ' ἱκέτην ταλαπείριον ἀντιάσαντα.
ἄστυ δέ τοι δείξω, ἐρέω δέ τοι οὔνομα λαῶν.
Φαίηκες μὲν τήνδε πόλιν καὶ γαῖαν ἔχουσιν,   19
εἰμὶ δ' ἐγὼ θυγάτηρ μεγαλήτορος Ἀλκινόοιο,
τοῦ δ' ἐκ Φαιήκων ἔχεται κάρτος τε βίη τε."
   Ἦ ῥα καὶ ἀμφιπόλοισιν ἐυπλοκάμοισι κέλευσε·
"Στῆτέ μοι, ἀμφίπολοι· πόσε φεύγετε φῶτα ἰδοῦσαι
ἦ μή πού τινα δυσμενέων φάσθ' ἔμμεναι ἀνδρῶν;   2(
οὐκ ἔσθ' οὗτος ἀνὴρ διερὸς βροτὸς οὐδὲ γένηται,
ὅς κεν Φαιήκων ἀνδρῶν ἐς γαῖαν ἵκηται
δηιοτῆτα φέρων· μάλα γὰρ φίλοι ἀθανάτοισιν.
οἰκέομεν δ' ἀπάνευθε πολυκλύστῳ ἐνὶ πόντῳ,
ἔσχατοι, οὐδέ τις ἄμμι βροτῶν ἐπιμίσγεται ἄλλος. 2(
ἀλλ' ὅδε τις δύστηνος ἀλώμενος ἐνθάδ' ἱκάνει,
τὸν νῦν χρὴ κομέειν· πρὸς γὰρ Διός εἰσιν ἅπαντες
ξεῖνοί τε πτωχοί τε, δόσις δ' ὀλίγη τε φίλη τε.
ἀλλὰ δότ', ἀμφίπολοι, ξείνῳ βρῶσίν τε πόσιν τε,
λούσατέ τ' ἐν ποταμῷ, ὅθ' ἐπὶ σκέπας ἔστ' ἀνέμοιο." 2
   Ὣς ἔφαθ', αἱ δ' ἔσταν τε καὶ ἀλλήλῃσι κέλευσαν,
κὰδ δ' ἄρ' Ὀδυσσῆ' εἶσαν ἐπὶ σκέπας, ὡς ἐκέλευσεν

Then white-armed Nausicaa answered him : "Stranger, since thou seemest to be neither an evil man nor a witless, and it is Zeus himself, the Olympian, that gives happy fortune to men, both to the good and the evil, to each man as he will; so to thee, I ween, he has given this lot, and thou must in any case endure it. But now, since thou hast come to our city and land, thou shalt not lack clothing or aught else of those things which befit a sore-tried suppliant when he cometh in the way. The city will I shew thee, and will tell thee the name of the people. The Phaeacians possess this city and land, and I am the daughter of great-hearted Alcinous, upon whom depend the might and power of the Phaeacians."

She spoke, and called to her fair-tressed hand-maids : "Stand, my maidens. Whither do ye flee at the sight of a man? Ye do not think, surely, that he is an enemy? That mortal man lives not, or exists [1] nor shall ever be born who shall come to the land of the Phaeacians as a foeman, for we are very dear to the immortals. Far off we dwell in the surging sea, the furthermost of men, and no other mortals have dealings with us. Nay, this is some hapless wanderer that has come hither. Him must we now tend; for from Zeus are all strangers and beggars, and a gift, though small, is welcome. Come, then, my maidens, give to the stranger food and drink, and bathe him in the river in a spot where there is shelter from the wind."

So she spoke, and they halted and called to each other. Then they set Odysseus in a sheltered

---

[1] The doubtful word διερός is here taken to mean "living" (Aristarchus, ὁ ζῶν). In ix. 43 διερῷ must be a different word.

Ναυσικάα θυγάτηρ μεγαλήτορος Ἀλκινόοιο·
πὰρ δ' ἄρα οἱ φᾶρός τε χιτῶνά τε εἵματ' ἔθηκαν,
δῶκαν δὲ χρυσέῃ ἐν ληκύθῳ ὑγρὸν ἔλαιον,
ἤνωγον δ' ἄρα μιν λοῦσθαι ποταμοῖο ῥοῇσιν.
δὴ ῥα τότ' ἀμφιπόλοισι μετηύδα δῖος Ὀδυσσεύς·
"'Ἀμφίπολοι, στῆθ' οὕτω ἀπόπροθεν, ὄφρ' ἐγὼ αὐτὸ
ἅλμην ὤμοιιν ἀπολούσομαι, ἀμφὶ δ' ἐλαίῳ
χρίσομαι· ἦ γὰρ δηρὸν ἀπὸ χροός ἐστιν ἀλοιφή.
ἄντην δ' οὐκ ἂν ἐγώ γε λοέσσομαι· αἰδέομαι γὰρ
γυμνοῦσθαι κούρῃσιν ἐυπλοκάμοισι μετελθών."
    ῍Ως ἔφαθ', αἱ δ' ἀπάνευθεν ἴσαν, εἶπον δ' ἄρα κούρ
αὐτὰρ ὁ ἐκ ποταμοῦ χρόα νίζετο δῖος Ὀδυσσεὺς
ἅλμην, ἥ οἱ νῶτα καὶ εὐρέας ἄμπεχεν ὤμους,
ἐκ κεφαλῆς δ' ἔσμηχεν ἁλὸς χνόον ἀτρυγέτοιο.
αὐτὰρ ἐπεὶ δὴ πάντα λοέσσατο καὶ λίπ' ἄλειψεν,
ἀμφὶ δὲ εἵματα ἔσσαθ' ἅ οἱ πόρε παρθένος ἀδμής,
τὸν μὲν Ἀθηναίη θῆκεν Διὸς ἐκγεγαυῖα
μείζονά τ' εἰσιδέειν καὶ πάσσονα, κὰδ δὲ κάρητος
οὔλας ἧκε κόμας, ὑακινθίνῳ ἄνθει ὁμοίας.
ὡς δ' ὅτε τις χρυσὸν περιχεύεται ἀργύρῳ ἀνὴρ
ἴδρις, ὃν Ἥφαιστος δέδαεν καὶ Παλλὰς Ἀθήνη
τέχνην παντοίην, χαρίεντα δὲ ἔργα τελείει,
ὣς ἄρα τῷ κατέχευε χάριν κεφαλῇ τε καὶ ὤμοις.
ἕζετ' ἔπειτ' ἀπάνευθε κιὼν ἐπὶ θῖνα θαλάσσης,
κάλλεϊ καὶ χάρισι στίλβων· θηεῖτο δὲ κούρη.
δὴ ῥα τότ' ἀμφιπόλοισιν ἐυπλοκάμοισι μετηύδα·
    "Κλῦτέ μευ, ἀμφίπολοι λευκώλενοι, ὄφρα τι εἴπ
οὐ πάντων ἀέκητι θεῶν, οἳ Ὄλυμπον ἔχουσιν,

place, as Nausicaa, the daughter of great-hearted Alcinous, bade, and beside him they put a cloak and a tunic for raiment, and gave him soft olive oil in the flask of gold, and bade him bathe in the streams of the river. Then among the maidens spoke goodly Odysseus: "Maidens, stand yonder apart, that by myself I may wash the brine from my shoulders, and anoint myself with olive oil; for of a truth it is long since oil came near my skin. But in your presence will I not bathe, for I am ashamed to make me naked in the midst of fair-tressed maidens."

So he said, and they went apart and told the princess. But with water from the river goodly Odysseus washed from his skin the brine which clothed his back and broad shoulders, and from his head he wiped the scurf of the unresting sea. But when he had washed his whole body and anointed himself with oil, and had put on him the raiment which the unwedded maid had given him, then Athene, the daughter of Zeus, made him taller to look upon and mightier, and from his head she made the locks to flow in curls like unto the hyacinth flower. And as when a man overlays silver with gold, a cunning workman whom Hephaestus and Pallas Athene have taught all manner of craft, and full of grace is the work he produces, even so the goddess shed grace upon his head and shoulders. Then he went apart and sat down on the shore of the sea, gleaming with beauty and grace; and the damsel marvelled at him, and spoke to her fair-tressed handmaids, saying:

"Listen, white-armed maidens, that I may say somewhat. Not without the will of all the gods who hold Olympus does this man come among the

223

Φαιήκεσσ᾽ ὅδ᾽ ἀνὴρ ἐπιμίσγεται ἀντιθέοισι·
πρόσθεν μὲν γὰρ δή μοι ἀεικέλιος δέατ᾽ εἶναι,
νῦν δὲ θεοῖσιν ἔοικε, τοὶ οὐρανὸν εὐρὺν ἔχουσιν.
αἲ γὰρ ἐμοὶ τοιόσδε πόσις κεκλημένος εἴη
ἐνθάδε ναιετάων, καί οἱ ἅδοι αὐτόθι μίμνειν.   2
ἀλλὰ δότ᾽, ἀμφίπολοι, ξείνῳ βρῶσίν τε πόσιν τε."
  ῝Ως ἔφαθ᾽, αἱ δ᾽ ἄρα τῆς μάλα μὲν κλύον ἠδ᾽ ἐπίθον
πὰρ δ᾽ ἄρ᾽ Ὀδυσσῆι ἔθεσαν βρῶσίν τε πόσιν τε.
ἦ τοι ὁ πῖνε καὶ ἦσθε πολύτλας δῖος Ὀδυσσεὺς
ἁρπαλέως· δηρὸν γὰρ ἐδητύος ἦεν ἄπαστος.   2
  Αὐτὰρ Ναυσικάα λευκώλενος ἄλλ᾽ ἐνόησεν·
εἵματ᾽ ἄρα πτύξασα τίθει καλῆς ἐπ᾽ ἀπήνης,
ζεῦξεν δ᾽ ἡμιόνους κρατερώνυχας, ἂν δ᾽ ἔβη αὐτή,
ὤτρυνεν δ᾽ Ὀδυσῆα, ἔπος τ᾽ ἔφατ᾽ ἔκ τ᾽ ὀνόμαζεν·
"῎Ορσεο δὴ νῦν, ξεῖνε, πόλινδ᾽ ἴμεν, ὄφρα σε πέμψω
πατρὸς ἐμοῦ πρὸς δῶμα δαΐφρονος, ἔνθα σέ φημι   2
πάντων Φαιήκων εἰδησέμεν ὅσσοι ἄριστοι.
ἀλλὰ μάλ᾽ ὧδ᾽ ἔρδειν, δοκέεις δέ μοι οὐκ ἀπινύσσειν·
ὄφρ᾽ ἂν μέν κ᾽ ἀγροὺς ἴομεν καὶ ἔργ᾽ ἀνθρώπων,
τόφρα σὺν ἀμφιπόλοισι μεθ᾽ ἡμιόνους καὶ ἄμαξαν   2
καρπαλίμως ἔρχεσθαι· ἐγὼ δ᾽ ὁδὸν ἡγεμονεύσω.
αὐτὰρ ἐπὴν πόλιος ἐπιβήομεν, ἣν πέρι πύργος
ὑψηλός, καλὸς δὲ λιμὴν ἑκάτερθε πόληος,
λεπτὴ δ᾽ εἰσίθμη· νῆες δ᾽ ὁδὸν ἀμφιέλισσαι
εἰρύαται· πᾶσιν γὰρ ἐπίστιόν ἐστιν ἑκάστῳ.   2
ἔνθα δέ τέ σφ᾽ ἀγορὴ καλὸν Ποσιδήιον ἀμφίς,
ῥυτοῖσιν λάεσσι κατωρυχέεσσ᾽ ἀραρυῖα.
ἔνθα δὲ νηῶν ὅπλα μελαινάων ἀλέγουσι,

godlike Phaeacians. Before he seemed to me un-
couth, but now he is like the gods, who hold broad
heaven. Would that a man such as he might be
called my husband, dwelling here, and that it might
please him here to remain. But come, my maidens;
give to the stranger food and drink."

So she spoke, and they readily hearkened and
obeyed, and set before Odysseus food and drink.
Then verily did the much-enduring goodly Odysseus
drink and eat, ravenously; for long had he been
without taste of food.

But the white-armed Nausicaa took other counsel.
She folded the raiment and put it in the fair waggon,
and yoked the stout-hoofed mules, and mounted the
car herself. Then she hailed Odysseus, and spoke
and addressed him : " Rouse thee now, stranger, to
go to the city, that I may escort thee to the house
of my wise father, where, I tell thee, thou shalt
come to know all the noblest of the Phaeacians.
Only do thou thus, and, methinks, thou dost not
lack understanding : so long as we are passing
through the country and the tilled fields of men
go thou quickly with the handmaids behind the
mules and the waggon, and I will lead the way.
But when we are about to enter the city, around
which runs a lofty wall,—a fair harbour lies on either
side of the city and the entrance is narrow, and
curved ships are drawn up along the road, for they
all have stations for their ships, each man one for
himself. There, too, is their place of assembly about
the fair temple of Poseidon, fitted with huge [1] stones
set deep in the earth. Here the men are busied

---

[1] Lit. "drawn thither," or, according to others, "quarried."
cf. xiv. 10.

πείσματα καὶ σπεῖρα, καὶ ἀποξύνουσιν ἐρετμά.
οὐ γὰρ Φαιήκεσσι μέλει βιὸς οὐδὲ φαρέτρη,
ἀλλ᾽ ἱστοὶ καὶ ἐρετμὰ νεῶν καὶ νῆες ἐῖσαι,
ᾗσιν ἀγαλλόμενοι πολιὴν περόωσι θάλασσαν.
τῶν ἀλεείνω φῆμιν ἀδευκέα, μή τις ὀπίσσω
μωμεύῃ· μάλα δ᾽ εἰσὶν ὑπερφίαλοι κατὰ δῆμον·
καί νύ τις ὧδ᾽ εἴπῃσι κακώτερος ἀντιβολήσας·
῾Τίς δ᾽ ὅδε Ναυσικάᾳ ἕπεται καλός τε μέγας τε
ξεῖνος; ποῦ δέ μιν εὗρε; πόσις νύ οἱ ἔσσεται αὐτῇ.
ἦ τινά που πλαγχθέντα κομίσσατο ἧς ἀπὸ νηὸς
ἀνδρῶν τηλεδαπῶν, ἐπεὶ οὔ τινες ἐγγύθεν εἰσίν·
ἤ τίς οἱ εὐξαμένῃ πολυάρητος θεὸς ἦλθεν
οὐρανόθεν καταβάς, ἕξει δέ μιν ἤματα πάντα.
βέλτερον, εἰ καὐτή περ ἐποιχομένη πόσιν εὗρεν
ἄλλοθεν· ἦ γὰρ τούσδε γ᾽ ἀτιμάζει κατὰ δῆμον
Φαίηκας, τοί μιν μνῶνται πολέες τε καὶ ἐσθλοί.᾽
ὣς ἐρέουσιν, ἐμοὶ δέ κ᾽ ὀνείδεα ταῦτα γένοιτο.
καὶ δ᾽ ἄλλῃ νεμεσῶ, ἥ τις τοιαῦτά γε ῥέζοι,
ἥ τ᾽ ἀέκητι φίλων πατρὸς καὶ μητρὸς ἐόντων,
ἀνδράσι μίσγηται, πρίν γ᾽ ἀμφάδιον γάμον ἐλθεῖν.
ξεῖνε, σὺ δ᾽ ὧκ᾽[1] ἐμέθεν ξυνίει ἔπος, ὄφρα τάχιστα
πομπῆς καὶ νόστοιο τύχῃς παρὰ πατρὸς ἐμοῖο.
δήεις ἀγλαὸν ἄλσος Ἀθήνης ἄγχι κελεύθου
αἰγείρων· ἐν δὲ κρήνη νάει, ἀμφὶ δὲ λειμών·
ἔνθα δὲ πατρὸς ἐμοῦ τέμενος τεθαλυῖά τ᾽ ἀλωή,
τόσσον ἀπὸ πτόλιος, ὅσσον τε γέγωνε βοήσας.
ἔνθα καθεζόμενος μεῖναι χρόνον, εἰς ὅ κεν ἡμεῖς

_____
[1] ὧκ᾽ Aristarchus : ὧδ᾽ MSS.

with the tackle of their black ships, with cables and
sails, and here they shape the thin oar-blades.   For
the Phaeacians care not for bow or quiver, but for
masts and oars of ships, and for the shapely ships,
rejoicing in which they cross over the grey sea.   It
is their ungentle speech that I shun, lest hereafter
some man should taunt me, for indeed there are
insolent folk in the land, and thus might some
baser fellow say, shall he meet us: 'Who is this
that follows Nausicaa, a comely man and tall, a
stranger? Where did she find him? He will
doubtless be a husband for her. Haply she has
brought from his ship some wanderer of a folk that
dwell afar—for none are near us—or some god,
long prayed-for, has come down from heaven in
answer to her prayers, and she will have him as her
husband all her days. Better so, even if she has
herself gone forth and found a husband from another
people; for of a truth she scorns the Phaeacians here
in the land, where she has wooers many and noble!'
So will they say, and this would become a reproach
to me.   Yea, I would myself blame another maiden
who should do such thing, and in despite of her
dear father and mother, while yet they live, should
consort with men before the day of open marriage.
Nay, stranger, do thou quickly hearken to my words,
that with all speed thou mayest win from my father
an escort and a return to thy land.   Thou wilt find
a goodly grove of Athene hard by the road, a grove
of poplar trees.   In it a spring wells up, and round
about is a meadow.   There is my father's park and
fruitful vineyard, as far from the city as a man's
voice carries when he shouts.   Sit thou down there,
and wait for a time, until we come to the city and

ἄστυδε ἔλθωμεν καὶ ἱκώμεθα δώματα πατρός.
αὐτὰρ ἐπὴν ἡμέας ἔλπῃ ποτὶ δώματ' ἀφῖχθαι,
καὶ τότε Φαιήκων ἴμεν ἐς πόλιν ἠδ' ἐρέεσθαι
δώματα πατρὸς ἐμοῦ μεγαλήτορος Ἀλκινόοιο.
ῥεῖα δ' ἀρίγνωτ' ἐστί, καὶ ἂν πάϊς ἡγήσαιτο   30
νήπιος· οὐ μὲν γάρ τι ἐοικότα τοῖσι τέτυκται
δώματα Φαιήκων, οἷος δόμος Ἀλκινόοιο
ἥρωος.   ἀλλ' ὁπότ' ἄν σε δόμοι κεκύθωσι καὶ αὐλή,
ὦκα μάλα μεγάροιο διελθέμεν, ὄφρ' ἂν ἵκηαι
μητέρ' ἐμήν· ἡ δ' ἧσται ἐπ' ἐσχάρῃ ἐν πυρὸς αὐγῇ, 30
ἠλάκατα στρωφῶσ' ἀλιπόρφυρα, θαῦμα ἰδέσθαι,
κίονι κεκλιμένη· δμωαὶ δέ οἱ εἵατ' ὄπισθεν.
ἔνθα δὲ πατρὸς ἐμοῖο θρόνος ποτικέκλιται αὐτῇ,
τῷ ὅ γε οἰνοποτάζει ἐφήμενος ἀθάνατος ὥς.
τὸν παραμειψάμενος μητρὸς περὶ γούνασι χεῖρας   31
βάλλειν ἡμετέρης, ἵνα νόστιμον ἦμαρ ἴδηαι
χαίρων καρπαλίμως, εἰ καὶ μάλα τηλόθεν ἐσσί.
εἴ κέν τοι κείνη γε φίλα φρονέῃσ' ἐνὶ θυμῷ,
ἐλπωρή τοι ἔπειτα φίλους τ' ἰδέειν καὶ ἱκέσθαι
οἶκον ἐϋκτίμενον καὶ σὴν ἐς πατρίδα γαῖαν." ¹   31

   Ὡς ἄρα φωνήσασ' ἵμασεν μάστιγι φαεινῇ
ἡμιόνους· αἱ δ' ὦκα λίπον ποταμοῖο ῥέεθρα.
αἱ δ' ἐϋ μὲν τρώχων, ἐϋ δὲ πλίσσοντο πόδεσσιν·
ἡ δὲ μάλ' ἡνιόχευεν, ὅπως ἅμ' ἑποίατο πεζοὶ
ἀμφίπολοί τ' Ὀδυσεύς τε, νόῳ δ' ἐπέβαλλεν ἱμάσθλη·
δύσετό τ' ἠέλιος καὶ τοὶ κλυτὸν ἄλσος ἵκοντο   32
ἱρὸν Ἀθηναίης, ἵν' ἄρ' ἕζετο δῖος Ὀδυσσεύς.
αὐτίκ' ἔπειτ' ἠρᾶτο Διὸς κούρῃ μεγάλοιο·
   "Κλῦθί μευ, αἰγιόχοιο Διὸς τέκος, ἀτρυτώνη·
νῦν δή πέρ μευ ἄκουσον, ἐπεὶ πάρος οὔ ποτ' ἄκουσας 32

---

¹ Lines 313-5 are omitted in many MSS.; cf. vii. 75-7.

reach the house of my father. But when thou
thinkest that we have reached the house, then do
thou go to the city of the Phaeacians and ask for
the house of my father, great-hearted Alcinous.
Easily may it be known, and a child could guide
thee, a mere babe; for the houses of the Phaeacians
are no wise built of such sort as is the palace of the
lord Alcinous. But when the house and the court
enclose thee, pass quickly through the great hall,
till thou comest to my mother, who sits at the hearth
in the light of the fire, spinning the purple yarn, a
wonder to behold, leaning against a pillar, and her
handmaids sit behind her. There, too, leaning against
the selfsame pillar, is set the throne of my father,
whereon he sits and quaffs his wine, like unto an
immortal. Him pass thou by, and cast thy hands
about my mother's knees, that thou mayest quickly
see with rejoicing the day of thy return, though
thou art come from never so far. If in her sight
thou dost win favour, then there is hope that thou
wilt see thy friends, and return to thy well-built house
and unto thy native land."

So saying, she smote the mules with the shining
whip, and they quickly left the streams of the river.
Well did they trot, well did they ply their ambling
feet,[1] and she drove with care that the maidens and
Odysseus might follow on foot, and with judgment
did she ply the lash. Then the sun set, and they
came to the glorious grove, sacred to Athene. There
Odysseus sat him down, and straightway prayed to
the daughter of great Zeus: " Hear me, child of aegis-
bearing Zeus, unwearied one. Hearken now to my
prayer, since aforetime thou didst not hearken when

---

[1] The word πλίσσοντο is doubtless connected with πλέκω,
but the rendering should not be made too specific.

ῥαιομένου, ὅτε μ' ἔρραιε κλυτὸς ἐννοσίγαιος.
δός μ' ἐς Φαίηκας φίλον ἐλθεῖν ἠδ' ἐλεεινόν."
    Ὣς ἔφατ' εὐχόμενος, τοῦ δ' ἔκλυε Παλλὰς Ἀθήνη·
αὐτῷ δ' οὔ πω φαίνετ' ἐναντίη· αἴδετο γάρ ῥα
πατροκασίγνητον· ὁ δ' ἐπιζαφελῶς μενέαινεν
ἀντιθέῳ Ὀδυσῆι πάρος ἣν γαῖαν ἱκέσθαι.

I was smitten, what time the glorious Earth-shaker smote me. Grant that I may come to the Phaeacians as one to be welcomed and to be pitied."

So he spoke in prayer, and Pallas Athene heard him; but she did not yet appear to him face to face, for she feared her father's brother; but he furiously raged against godlike Odysseus, until at length he reached his own land.

Η

Ὣς ὁ μὲν ἔνθ᾽ ἠρᾶτο πολύτλας δῖος Ὀδυσσεύς,
κούρην δὲ προτὶ ἄστυ φέρεν μένος ἡμιόνοιιν.
ἡ δ᾽ ὅτε δὴ οὗ πατρὸς ἀγακλυτὰ δώμαθ᾽ ἵκανε,
στῆσεν ἄρ᾽ ἐν προθύροισι, κασίγνητοι δέ μιν ἀμφὶς
ἵσταντ᾽ ἀθανάτοις ἐναλίγκιοι, οἵ ῥ᾽ ὑπ᾽ ἀπήνης
ἡμιόνους ἔλυον ἐσθῆτά τε ἔσφερον εἴσω.
αὐτὴ δ᾽ ἐς θάλαμον ἐὸν ἤιε· δαῖε δέ οἱ πῦρ
γρῆυς Ἀπειραίη, θαλαμηπόλος Εὐρυμέδουσα,
τήν ποτ᾽ Ἀπείρηθεν νέες ἤγαγον ἀμφιέλισσαι·
Ἀλκινόῳ δ᾽ αὐτὴν γέρας ἔξελον, οὕνεκα πᾶσιν   10
Φαιήκεσσιν ἄνασσε, θεοῦ δ᾽ ὣς δῆμος ἄκουεν·
ἣ τρέφε Ναυσικάαν λευκώλενον ἐν μεγάροισιν.
ἥ οἱ πῦρ ἀνέκαιε καὶ εἴσω δόρπον ἐκόσμει.

Καὶ τότ᾽ Ὀδυσσεὺς ὦρτο πόλινδ᾽ ἴμεν· ἀμφὶ δ᾽ Ἀθήνη
πολλὴν ἠέρα χεῦε φίλα φρονέουσ᾽ Ὀδυσῆι,   15
μή τις Φαιήκων μεγαθύμων ἀντιβολήσας
κερτομέοι τ᾽ ἐπέεσσι καὶ ἐξερέοιθ᾽ ὅτις εἴη.
ἀλλ᾽ ὅτε δὴ ἄρ᾽ ἔμελλε πόλιν δύσεσθαι ἐραννήν,
ἔνθα οἱ ἀντεβόλησε θεά, γλαυκῶπις Ἀθήνη,
παρθενικῇ ἐικυῖα νεήνιδι, κάλπιν ἐχούσῃ.   20
στῆ δὲ πρόσθ᾽ αὐτοῦ, ὁ δ᾽ ἀνείρετο δῖος Ὀδυσσεύς·

BOOK VII

So he prayed there, the much-enduring goodly
Odysseus, while the two strong mules bore the
maiden to the city. But when she had come to
the glorious palace of her father, she halted the
mules at the outer gate, and her brothers thronged
about her, men like the immortals, and loosed the
mules from the waggon, and bore the raiment
within; and she herself went to her chamber. There
a fire was kindled for her by her waiting-woman,
Eurymedusa, an aged dame from Apeirê. Long ago
the curved ships had brought her from Apeirê, and
men had chosen her from the spoil as a gift of
honour for Alcinous, for that he was king over all
the Phaeacians, and the people hearkened to him
as to a god. She it was who had reared the white-
armed Nausicaa in the palace, and she it was who
kindled the fire for her, and made ready her supper
in the chamber.

Then Odysseus roused himself to go to the city,
and Athene, with kindly purpose, cast about him
a thick mist, that no one of the great-hearted
Phaeacians, meeting him, should speak mockingly
to him, and ask him who he was. But when he
was about to enter the lovely city, then the goddess,
flashing-eyed Athene, met him in the guise of a
young maiden carrying a pitcher, and she stood before
him; and goodly Odysseus questioned her, saying:

"'Ω τέκος, οὐκ ἄν μοι δόμον ἀνέρος ἡγήσαιο
'Αλκινόου, ὃς τοῖσδε μετ' ἀνθρώποισι ἀνάσσει;
καὶ γὰρ ἐγὼ ξεῖνος ταλαπείριος ἐνθάδ' ἱκάνω
τηλόθεν ἐξ ἀπίης γαίης· τῷ οὔ τινα οἶδα
ἀνθρώπων, οἳ τήνδε πόλιν καὶ γαῖαν ἔχουσιν." [1]
   Τὸν δ' αὖτε προσέειπε θεά, γλαυκῶπις 'Αθήνη·
" Τοιγὰρ ἐγώ τοι, ξεῖνε πάτερ, δόμον, ὅν με κελεύεις,
δείξω, ἐπεί μοι πατρὸς ἀμύμονος ἐγγύθι ναίει.
ἀλλ' ἴθι σιγῇ τοῖον, ἐγὼ δ' ὁδὸν ἡγεμονεύσω,
μηδέ τιν' ἀνθρώπων προτιόσσεο μηδ' ἐρέεινε.
οὐ γὰρ ξείνους οἵδε μάλ' ἀνθρώπους ἀνέχονται,
οὐδ' ἀγαπαζόμενοι φιλέουσ' ὅς κ' ἄλλοθεν ἔλθῃ.
νηυσὶ θοῇσιν τοί γε πεποιθότες ὠκείῃσι
λαῖτμα μέγ' ἐκπερόωσιν, ἐπεί σφισι δῶκ' ἐνοσίχθων·
τῶν νέες ὠκεῖαι ὡς εἰ πτερὸν ἠὲ νόημα."
   'Ως ἄρα φωνήσασ' ἡγήσατο Παλλὰς 'Αθήνη
καρπαλίμως· ὁ δ' ἔπειτα μετ' ἴχνια βαῖνε θεοῖο.
τὸν δ' ἄρα Φαίηκες ναυσικλυτοὶ οὐκ ἐνόησαν
ἐρχόμενον κατὰ ἄστυ διὰ σφέας· οὐ γὰρ 'Αθήνη
εἴα ἐυπλόκαμος, δεινὴ θεός, ἥ ῥά οἱ ἀχλὺν
θεσπεσίην κατέχευε φίλα φρονέουσ' ἐνὶ θυμῷ.
θαύμαζεν δ' 'Οδυσεὺς λιμένας καὶ νῆας ἐίσας
αὐτῶν θ' ἡρώων ἀγορὰς καὶ τείχεα μακρὰ
ὑψηλά, σκολόπεσσιν ἀρηρότα, θαῦμα ἰδέσθαι.
ἀλλ' ὅτε δὴ βασιλῆος ἀγακλυτὰ δώμαθ' ἵκοντο,
τοῖσι δὲ μύθων ἦρχε θεά, γλαυκῶπις 'Αθήνη·
" Οὗτος δή τοι, ξεῖνε πάτερ, δόμος, ὅν με κελεύεις

─────────
[1] γαῖαν ἔχουσιν : ἔργα νέμονται.

" My child, couldst thou not guide me to the
house of him they call Alcinous, who is lord among
the people here ? For I am come hither a stranger
sore-tried from afar, from a distant country ; where-
fore I know no one of the people who possess this
city and land."

Then the goddess, flashing-eyed Athene, answered
him : " Then verily, Sir stranger, I will shew thee
the palace as thou dost bid me, for it lies hard
by the house of my own noble father. Only go
thou quietly, and I will lead the way. But turn not
thine eyes upon any man nor question any, for the
men here endure not stranger-folk, nor do they give
kindly welcome to him who comes from another
land. They, indeed, trusting in the speed of their
swift ships, cross over the great gulf of the sea,
for this the Earth-shaker has granted them ; and
their ships are swift as a bird on the wing or as
a thought."

So speaking, Pallas Athene led the way quickly,
and he followed in the footsteps of the goddess.
And as he went through the city in the midst of
them, the Phaeacians, famed for their ships, took
no heed of him, for fair-tressed Athene, the dread
goddess, would not suffer it, but shed about him
a wondrous mist, for her heart was kind toward him.
And Odysseus marvelled at the harbours and the
stately ships, at the meeting-places where the heroes
themselves gathered, and the walls, long and high
and crowned with palisades, a wonder to behold.
But when they had come to the glorious palace of
the king, the goddess, flashing-eyed Athene, was
the first to speak, saying :

" Here, Sir stranger, is the house which thou

πεφραδέμεν· δήεις δὲ διοτρεφέας βασιλῆας
δαίτην δαινυμένους· σὺ δ' ἔσω κίε, μηδέ τι θυμῷ
τάρβει· θαρσαλέος γὰρ ἀνὴρ ἐν πᾶσιν ἀμείνων
ἔργοισιν τελέθει, εἰ καί ποθεν ἄλλοθεν ἔλθοι.
δέσποιναν μὲν πρῶτα κιχήσεαι ἐν μεγάροισιν·
Ἀρήτη δ' ὄνομ' ἐστὶν ἐπώνυμον, ἐκ δὲ τοκήων
τῶν αὐτῶν οἵ περ τέκον Ἀλκίνοον βασιλῆα.
Ναυσίθοον μὲν πρῶτα Ποσειδάων ἐνοσίχθων
γείνατο καὶ Περίβοια, γυναικῶν εἶδος ἀρίστη,
ὁπλοτάτη θυγάτηρ μεγαλήτορος Εὐρυμέδοντος,
ὅς ποθ' ὑπερθύμοισι Γιγάντεσσιν βασίλευεν.
ἀλλ' ὁ μὲν ὤλεσε λαὸν ἀτάσθαλον, ὤλετο δ' αὐτός·
τῇ δὲ Ποσειδάων ἐμίγη καὶ ἐγείνατο παῖδα
Ναυσίθοον μεγάθυμον, ὃς ἐν Φαίηξιν ἄνασσε·
Ναυσίθοος δ' ἔτεκεν Ῥηξήνορά τ' Ἀλκίνοόν τε.
τὸν μὲν ἄκουρον ἐόντα βάλ' ἀργυρότοξος Ἀπόλλων
νυμφίον ἐν μεγάρῳ, μίαν οἴην παῖδα λιπόντα
Ἀρήτην· τὴν δ' Ἀλκίνοος ποιήσατ' ἄκοιτιν,
καί μιν ἔτισ', ὡς οὔ τις ἐπὶ χθονὶ τίεται ἄλλη,
ὅσσαι νῦν γε γυναῖκες ὑπ' ἀνδράσιν οἶκον ἔχουσιν.
ὣς κείνη περὶ κῆρι τετίμηταί τε καὶ ἔστιν
ἔκ τε φίλων παίδων ἔκ τ' αὐτοῦ Ἀλκινόοιο
καὶ λαῶν, οἵ μίν ῥα θεὸν ὣς εἰσορόωντες
δειδέχαται μύθοισιν, ὅτε στείχῃσ' ἀνὰ ἄστυ.
οὐ μὲν γάρ τι νόου γε καὶ αὐτὴ δεύεται ἐσθλοῦ·
ᾗσί τ' [1] ἐὺ φρονέῃσι καὶ ἀνδράσι νείκεα λύει.
εἴ κέν τοι κείνη γε φίλα φρονέῃσ' ἐνὶ θυμῷ,
ἐλπωρή τοι ἔπειτα φίλους τ' ἰδέειν καὶ ἱκέσθαι
οἶκον ἐς ὑψόροφον καὶ σὴν ἐς πατρίδα γαῖαν."

----

[1] ᾗσί τ': οἷσί(ν) τ'.

didst bid me shew to thee, and thou wilt find the kings, fostered of Zeus, feasting at the banquet. Go thou within, and let thy heart fear nothing; for a bold man is better in all things, though he ·be a stranger from another land. The queen shalt thou approach first in the palace; Arete is the name by which she is called, and she is sprung from the same line as is the king Alcinous. Nausithous at the first was born from the earth-shaker Poseidon and Periboea, the comeliest of women, youngest daughter of great-hearted Eurymedon, who once was king over the insolent Giants. But he brought destruction on his froward people, and was himself destroyed. But with Periboea lay Poseidon and begat a son, great-hearted Nausithous, who ruled over the Phaeacians; and Nausithous begat Rhexenor and Alcinous. Rhexenor, when as yet he had no son, Apollo of the silver bow smote in his hall, a bridegroom though he was, and he left only one daughter, Arete. Her Alcinous made his wife, and honoured her as no other woman on earth is honoured, of all those who in these days direct their households in subjection to their husbands; so heartily is she honoured, and has ever been, by her children and by Alcinous himself and by the people, who look upon her as upon a goddess, and greet her as she goes through the city. For she of herself is no wise lacking in good understanding, and for the women [1] to whom she has good will she makes an end of strife even among their husbands. If in her sight thou dost win favour, then there is hope that thou wilt see thy friends, and return to thy high-roofed house and unto thy native land."

[1] Or, reading οἷσι, "settles the quarrels of those to whom she has good will, even though they be men."

Ὣς ἄρα φωνήσασ' ἀπέβη γλαυκῶπις Ἀθήνη
πόντον ἐπ' ἀτρύγετον, λίπε δὲ Σχερίην ἐρατεινήν,
ἵκετο δ' ἐς Μαραθῶνα καὶ εὐρυάγυιαν Ἀθήνην,
δῦνε δ' Ἐρεχθῆος πυκινὸν δόμον. αὐτὰρ Ὀδυσσεὺς
Ἀλκινόου πρὸς δώματ' ἴε κλυτά· πολλὰ δέ οἱ κῆρ
ὥρμαιν' ἱσταμένῳ, πρὶν χάλκεον οὐδὸν ἱκέσθαι.
ὥς τε γὰρ ἠελίου αἴγλη πέλεν ἠὲ σελήνης
δῶμα καθ' ὑψερεφὲς μεγαλήτορος Ἀλκινόοιο.
χάλκεοι μὲν γὰρ τοῖχοι ἐληλέδατ' ἔνθα καὶ ἔνθα,
ἐς μυχὸν ἐξ οὐδοῦ, περὶ δὲ θριγκὸς κυάνοιο·
χρύσειαι δὲ θύραι πυκινὸν δόμον ἐντὸς ἔεργον·
σταθμοὶ δ' ἀργύρεοι ἐν χαλκέῳ ἕστασαν οὐδῷ,
ἀργύρεον δ' ἐφ' ὑπερθύριον, χρυσέη δὲ κορώνη.
χρύσειοι δ' ἑκάτερθε καὶ ἀργύρεοι κύνες ἦσαν,
οὓς Ἥφαιστος ἔτευξεν ἰδυίῃσι πραπίδεσσι
δῶμα φυλασσέμεναι μεγαλήτορος Ἀλκινόοιο,
ἀθανάτους ὄντας καὶ ἀγήρως ἤματα πάντα.
ἐν δὲ θρόνοι περὶ τοῖχον ἐρηρέδατ' ἔνθα καὶ ἔνθα,
ἐς μυχὸν ἐξ οὐδοῖο διαμπερές, ἔνθ' ἐνὶ πέπλοι
λεπτοὶ ἐΰννητοι βεβλήατο, ἔργα γυναικῶν.
ἔνθα δὲ Φαιήκων ἡγήτορες ἑδριόωντο
πίνοντες καὶ ἔδοντες· ἐπηετανὸν γὰρ ἔχεσκον.
χρύσειοι δ' ἄρα κοῦροι ἐϋδμήτων ἐπὶ βωμῶν   1
ἕστασαν αἰθομένας δαΐδας μετὰ χερσὶν ἔχοντες,
φαίνοντες νύκτας κατὰ δώματα δαιτυμόνεσσι.
πεντήκοντα δέ οἱ δμωαὶ κατὰ δῶμα γυναῖκες
αἱ μὲν ἀλετρεύουσι μύλῃς ἔπι μήλοπα καρπόν,
αἱ δ' ἱστοὺς ὑφόωσι καὶ ἠλάκατα στρωφῶσιν   1

---

1 There stood upon the Acropolis of Athens in very ancient
days a temple dedicated jointly to Athene and Erectheus.
2 A blue enamel, or glass paste, imitating *lapis lazuli*.
Fragments of this have been found at Tiryns.

So saying, flashing-eyed Athene departed over the unresting sea, and left lovely Scheria. She came to Marathon and broad-wayed Athens, and entered the well-built house of Erectheus;[1] but Odysseus went to the glorious palace of Alcinous. There he stood, and his heart pondered much before he reached the threshold of bronze; for there was a gleam as of sun or moon over the high-roofed house of great-hearted Alcinous. Of bronze were the walls that stretched this way and that from the threshold to the innermost chamber, and around was a cornice of cyanus.[2] Golden were the doors that shut in the well-built house, and doorposts of silver were set in a threshold of bronze. Of silver was the lintel above, and of gold the handle. On either side of the door there stood gold and silver dogs, which Hephaestus had fashioned with cunning skill to guard the palace of great-hearted Alcinous; immortal were they and ageless all their days.[3] Within, seats were fixed along the wall on either hand, from the threshold to the innermost chamber, and on them were thrown robes of soft fabric, cunningly woven, the handiwork of women. On these the leaders of the Phaeacians were wont to sit drinking and eating, for they had unfailing store. And golden youths stood on well-built pedestals, holding lighted torches in their hands to give light by night to the banqueters in the hall. And fifty slave-women he had in the house, of whom some grind the yellow grain on the millstone, and others weave webs, or, as they sit, twirl

---

[3] The dogs, though wrought of gold and silver, are thought of as alive. The Phaeacians dwell in fairyland.

ἤμεναι, οἷά τε φύλλα μακεδνῆς αἰγείροιο·
καιρουσσέων δ' ὀθονέων ἀπολείβεται ὑγρὸν ἔλαιον.
ὅσσον Φαίηκες περὶ πάντων ἴδριες ἀνδρῶν
νῆα θοὴν ἐνὶ πόντῳ ἐλαυνέμεν, ὣς δὲ γυναῖκες
ἱστῶν τεχνῆσσαι· πέρι γάρ σφισι δῶκεν Ἀθήνη   110
ἔργα τ' ἐπίστασθαι περικαλλέα καὶ φρένας ἐσθλάς.
ἔκτοσθεν δ' αὐλῆς μέγας ὄρχατος ἄγχι θυράων
τετράγυος· περὶ δ' ἕρκος ἐλήλαται ἀμφοτέρωθεν.
ἔνθα δὲ δένδρεα μακρὰ πεφύκασι τηλεθόωντα,
ὄγχναι καὶ ῥοιαὶ καὶ μηλέαι ἀγλαόκαρποι   115
συκέαι τε γλυκεραὶ καὶ ἐλαῖαι τηλεθόωσαι.
τάων οὔ ποτε καρπὸς ἀπόλλυται οὐδ' ἀπολείπει
χείματος οὐδὲ θέρευς, ἐπετήσιος· ἀλλὰ μάλ' αἰεὶ
Ζεφυρίη πνείουσα τὰ μὲν φύει, ἄλλα δὲ πέσσει.
ὄγχνη ἐπ' ὄγχνῃ γηράσκει, μῆλον δ' ἐπὶ μήλῳ,   120
αὐτὰρ ἐπὶ σταφυλῇ σταφυλή, σῦκον δ' ἐπὶ σύκῳ.
ἔνθα δέ οἱ πολύκαρπος ἀλωὴ ἐρρίζωται,
τῆς ἕτερον μὲν θειλόπεδον λευρῷ ἐνὶ χώρῳ
τέρσεται ἠελίῳ, ἑτέρας δ' ἄρα τε τρυγόωσιν,
ἄλλας δὲ τραπέουσι· πάροιθε δέ τ' ὄμφακές εἰσιν   125
ἄνθος ἀφιεῖσαι, ἕτεραι δ' ὑποπερκάζουσιν.
ἔνθα δὲ κοσμηταὶ πρασιαὶ παρὰ νείατον ὄρχον
παντοῖαι πεφύασιν, ἐπηετανὸν γανόωσαι·
ἐν δὲ δύω κρῆναι ἡ μέν τ' ἀνὰ κῆπον ἅπαντα
σκίδναται, ἡ δ' ἑτέρωθεν ὑπ' αὐλῆς οὐδὸν ἵησι   130
πρὸς δόμον ὑψηλόν, ὅθεν ὑδρεύοντο πολῖται.
τοῖ' ἄρ' ἐν Ἀλκινόοιο θεῶν ἔσαν ἀγλαὰ δῶρα.

---

[1] Said with reference to their restless activity.
[2] The reference is probably to the use of a wash to give a

the yarn, like unto the leaves [1] of a tall poplar tree;
and from the closely-woven linen the soft olive oil
drips down.[2] For as the Phaeacian men are skilled
above all others in speeding a swift ship upon the sea,
so are the women cunning workers at the loom, for
Athene has given to them above all others skill
in fair handiwork, and an understanding· heart.
But without the courtyard, hard by the door, is a
great orchard of four acres,[3] and a hedge runs about
it on either side. Therein grow trees, tall and
luxuriant, pears and pomegranates and apple-trees
with their bright fruit, and sweet figs, and luxuriant
olives. Of these the fruit perishes not nor fails in
winter or in summer, but lasts throughout the year;
and ever does the west wind, as it blows, quicken to
life some fruits, and ripen others; pear upon pear
waxes ripe, apple upon apple, cluster upon cluster,
and fig upon fig. There, too, is his fruitful vine-
yard planted, one part of which, a warm spot on
level ground, is being dried in the sun, while other
grapes men are gathering, and others, too, they are
treading; but in front are unripe grapes that are
shedding the blossom, and others that are turning
purple. There again, by the last row of the vines,
grow trim garden beds of every sort, blooming the
year through, and therein are two springs, one of
which sends its water throughout all the garden,
while the other, over against it, flows beneath the
threshold of the court toward the high house; from
this the townsfolk drew their water. Such were the
glorious gifts of the gods in the palace of Alcinous.

gloss to the linen. Others assume the meaning to be that
the linen is so closely woven that oil will not soak through it.
[3] The word appears to mean a stretch of four days'
(mornings') ploughing.

Ἔνθα στὰς θηεῖτο πολύτλας δῖος Ὀδυσσεύς.
αὐτὰρ ἐπεὶ δὴ πάντα ἑῷ θηήσατο θυμῷ,
καρπαλίμως ὑπὲρ οὐδὸν ἐβήσετο δώματος εἴσω.   1
εὗρε δὲ Φαιήκων ἡγήτορας ἠδὲ μέδοντας
σπένδοντας δεπάεσσιν ἐϋσκόπῳ ἀργεϊφόντῃ,
ᾧ πυμάτῳ σπένδεσκον, ὅτε μνησαίατο κοίτου.
αὐτὰρ ὁ βῆ διὰ δῶμα πολύτλας δῖος Ὀδυσσεὺς
πολλὴν ἠέρ᾽ ἔχων, ἥν οἱ περίχευεν Ἀθήνη,   1
ὄφρ᾽ ἵκετ᾽ Ἀρήτην τε καὶ Ἀλκίνοον βασιλῆα.
ἀμφὶ δ᾽ ἄρ᾽ Ἀρήτης βάλε γούνασι χεῖρας Ὀδυσσεύς,
καὶ τότε δή ῥ᾽ αὐτοῖο πάλιν χύτο θέσφατος ἀήρ.
οἱ δ᾽ ἄνεῳ ἐγένοντο, δόμον κάτα φῶτα ἰδόντες·
θαύμαζον δ᾽ ὁρόωντες. ὁ δὲ λιτάνευεν Ὀδυσσεύς·   1
   "Ἀρήτη, θύγατερ Ῥηξήνορος ἀντιθέοιο,
σόν τε πόσιν σά τε γούναθ᾽ ἱκάνω πολλὰ μογήσας
τούσδε τε δαιτυμόνας· τοῖσιν θεοὶ ὄλβια δοῖεν
ζωέμεναι, καὶ παισὶν ἐπιτρέψειεν ἕκαστος
κτήματ᾽ ἐνὶ μεγάροισι γέρας θ᾽ ὅ τι δῆμος ἔδωκεν·
αὐτὰρ ἐμοὶ πομπὴν ὀτρύνετε πατρίδ᾽ ἱκέσθαι
θᾶσσον, ἐπεὶ δὴ δηθὰ φίλων ἄπο πήματα πάσχω."
   Ὣς εἰπὼν κατ᾽ ἄρ᾽ ἕζετ᾽ ἐπ᾽ ἐσχάρῃ ἐν κονίῃσιν
πὰρ πυρί· οἱ δ᾽ ἄρα πάντες ἀκὴν ἐγένοντο σιωπῇ.
ὀψὲ δὲ δὴ μετέειπε γέρων ἥρως Ἐχένηος,
ὃς δὴ Φαιήκων ἀνδρῶν προγενέστερος ἦεν
καὶ μύθοισι κέκαστο, παλαιά τε πολλά τε εἰδώς·
ὅ σφιν ἐϋ φρονέων ἀγορήσατο καὶ μετέειπεν·
   "Ἀλκίνο᾽, οὐ μέν τοι τόδε κάλλιον, οὐδὲ ἔοικε,

There the much-enduring goodly Odysseus stood and gazed. But when he had marvelled in his heart at all things, he passed quickly over the threshold into the house. There he found the leaders and counsellors of the Phaeacians pouring libations from their cups to the keen-sighted Argeïphontes, to whom they were wont to pour the wine last of all, when they were minded to go to their rest. But the much-enduring goodly Odysseus went through the hall, wrapped in the thick mist which Athene had shed about him, till he came to Arete and to Alcinous the king. About the knees of Arete Odysseus cast his hands, and straightway the wondrous mist melted from him, and a hush fell upon all that were in the room at sight of the man, and they marvelled as they looked upon him. But Odysseus made his prayer:

" Arete, daughter of godlike Rhexenor, to thy husband and to thy knees am I come after many toils,—aye and to these banqueters, to whom may the gods grant happiness in life, and may each of them hand down to his children the wealth in his halls, and the dues of honour which the people have given him. But for me do ye speed my sending, that I may come to my native land, and that quickly; for long time have I been suffering woes far from my friends."

So saying he sat down on the hearth in the ashes by the fire, and they were all hushed in silence. But at length there spoke among them the old lord Echeneüs, who was an elder among the Phaeacians, well skilled in speech, and understanding all the wisdom of old. He with good intent addressed the assembly, and said: " Alcinous, lo, this is not the

ξεῖνον μὲν χαμαὶ ἦσθαι ἐπ' ἐσχάρῃ ἐν κονίῃσιν,　　1
οἵδε δὲ σὸν μῦθον ποτιδέγμενοι ἰσχανόωνται.
ἀλλ' ἄγε δὴ ξεῖνον μὲν ἐπὶ θρόνου ἀργυροήλου
εἷσον ἀναστήσας, σὺ δὲ κηρύκεσσι κέλευσον
οἶνον ἐπικρῆσαι, ἵνα καὶ Διὶ τερπικεραύνῳ
σπείσομεν, ὅς θ' ἱκέτῃσιν ἅμ' αἰδοίοισιν ὀπηδεῖ·　　1
δόρπον δὲ ξείνῳ ταμίη δότω ἔνδον ἐόντων."
　　Αὐτὰρ ἐπεὶ τό γ' ἄκουσ' ἱερὸν μένος Ἀλκινόοιο,
χειρὸς ἑλὼν Ὀδυσῆα δαΐφρονα ποικιλομήτην
ὦρσεν ἀπ' ἐσχαρόφιν καὶ ἐπὶ θρόνου εἷσε φαεινοῦ,
υἱὸν ἀναστήσας ἀγαπήνορα Λαοδάμαντα,　　1
ὅς οἱ πλησίον ἷζε, μάλιστα δέ μιν φιλέεσκεν.
χέρνιβα δ' ἀμφίπολος προχόῳ ἐπέχευε φέρουσα
καλῇ χρυσείῃ ὑπὲρ ἀργυρέοιο λέβητος,
νίψασθαι· παρὰ δὲ ξεστὴν ἐτάνυσσε τράπεζαν.
σῖτον δ' αἰδοίη ταμίη παρέθηκε φέρουσα,　　1
εἴδατα πόλλ' ἐπιθεῖσα, χαριζομένη παρεόντων.
αὐτὰρ ὁ πῖνε καὶ ἦσθε πολύτλας δῖος Ὀδυσσεύς.
καὶ τότε κήρυκα προσέφη μένος Ἀλκινόοιο·
　　"Ποντόνοε, κρητῆρα κερασσάμενος μέθυ νεῖμον
πᾶσιν ἀνὰ μέγαρον, ἵνα καὶ Διὶ τερπικεραύνῳ　　18
σπείσομεν, ὅς θ' ἱκέτῃσιν ἅμ' αἰδοίοισιν ὀπηδεῖ."
　　Ὣς φάτο, Ποντόνοος δὲ μελίφρονα οἶνον ἐκίρνα,
νώμησεν δ' ἄρα πᾶσιν ἐπαρξάμενος δεπάεσσιν.
αὐτὰρ ἐπεὶ σπεῖσάν τ' ἔπιόν θ', ὅσον ἤθελε θυμός,
τοῖσιν δ' Ἀλκίνοος ἀγορήσατο καὶ μετέειπε·　　18

better way, nor is it seemly, that a stranger should sit upon the ground on the hearth in the ashes; but these others hold back waiting for thy word. Come, make the stranger to arise, and set him upon a silver-studded chair, and bid the heralds mix wine, that we may pour libations also to Zeus, who hurls the thunderbolt; for he ever attends upon reverend suppliants. And let the housewife give supper to the stranger of the store that is in the house."

When the strong and mighty Alcinous heard this, he took by the hand Odysseus, the wise and crafty-minded, and raised him from the hearth, and set him upon a bright chair from which he bade his son, the kindly[1] Laodamas, to rise; for he sat next to him, and was his best beloved. Then a handmaid brought water for the hands in a fair pitcher of gold, and poured it over a silver basin, for him to wash, and beside him drew up a polished table. And the grave housewife brought and set before him bread, and therewith dainties in abundance, giving freely of her store. So the much-enduring goodly Odysseus drank and ate; and then the mighty Alcinous spoke to the herald, and said:

"Pontonous, mix the bowl, and serve wine to all in the hall, that we may pour libations also to Zeus, who hurls the thunderbolt; for he ever attends upon reverend suppliants."

He spoke, and Pontonous mixed the honey-hearted wine, and served out to all, pouring first drops for libation into the cups. But when they had poured libations, and had drunk to their heart's content, Alcinous addressed the assembly, and spoke among them:

[1] The word is commonly rendered "valiant."

" Κέκλυτε, Φαιήκων ἡγήτορες ἠδὲ μέδοντες
ὄφρ' εἴπω τά με θυμὸς ἐνὶ στήθεσσι κελεύει.
νῦν μὲν δαισάμενοι κατακείετε οἴκαδ' ἰόντες·
ἠῶθεν δὲ γέροντας ἐπὶ πλέονας καλέσαντες
ξεῖνον ἐνὶ μεγάροις ξεινίσσομεν ἠδὲ θεοῖσιν
ῥέξομεν ἱερὰ καλά, ἔπειτα δὲ καὶ περὶ πομπῆς
μνησόμεθ', ὥς χ' ὁ ξεῖνος ἄνευθε πόνου καὶ ἀνίης
πομπῇ ὑφ' ἡμετέρῃ ἣν πατρίδα γαῖαν ἵκηται
χαίρων καρπαλίμως, εἰ καὶ μάλα τηλόθεν ἐστί,
μηδέ τι μεσσηγύς γε κακὸν καὶ πῆμα πάθῃσι,
πρίν γε τὸν ἧς γαίης ἐπιβήμεναι· ἔνθα δ' ἔπειτα
πείσεται, ἅσσα οἱ αἶσα κατὰ κλῶθές τε βαρεῖαι
γιγνομένῳ νήσαντο λίνῳ, ὅτε μιν τέκε μήτηρ.
εἰ δέ τις ἀθανάτων γε κατ' οὐρανοῦ εἰλήλουθεν,
ἄλλο τι δὴ τόδ' ἔπειτα θεοὶ περιμηχανόωνται.
αἰεὶ γὰρ τὸ πάρος γε θεοὶ φαίνονται ἐναργεῖς
ἡμῖν, εὖτ' ἔρδωμεν ἀγακλειτὰς ἑκατόμβας,
δαίνυνταί τε παρ' ἄμμι καθήμενοι ἔνθα περ ἡμεῖς.
εἰ δ' ἄρα τις καὶ μοῦνος ἰὼν ξύμβληται ὁδίτης,
οὔ τι κατακρύπτουσιν, ἐπεί σφισιν ἐγγύθεν εἰμέν,
ὥς περ Κύκλωπές τε καὶ ἄγρια φῦλα Γιγάντων."
    Τὸν δ' ἀπαμειβόμενος προσέφη πολύμητις Ὀδυσσ
" 'Αλκίνο', ἄλλο τί τοι μελέτω φρεσίν· οὐ γὰρ ἐγώ
ἀθανάτοισιν ἔοικα, τοὶ οὐρανὸν εὐρὺν ἔχουσιν,
οὐ δέμας οὐδὲ φυήν, ἀλλὰ θνητοῖσι βροτοῖσιν.
οὕς τινας ὑμεῖς ἴστε μάλιστ' ὀχέοντας ὀιζὺν
ἀνθρώπων, τοῖσίν κεν ἐν ἄλγεσιν ἰσωσαίμην.
καὶ δ' ἔτι κεν καὶ μᾶλλον[1] ἐγὼ κακὰ μυθησαίμην,
ὅσσα γε δὴ ξύμπαντα θεῶν ἰότητι μόγησα.
ἀλλ' ἐμὲ μὲν δορπῆσαι ἐάσατε κηδόμενόν περ·
οὐ γάρ τι στυγερῇ ἐπὶ γαστέρι κύντερον ἄλλο

---

[1] μᾶλλον : πλείον.

" Hearken to me, leaders and counsellors of the Phaeacians, that I may say what the heart in my breast bids me. Now that ye have finished your feast, go each of you to his house to rest. But in the morning we will call more of the elders together, and will entertain the stranger in our halls and offer goodly victims to the gods. After that we will take thought also of his sending, that without toil or pain yon stranger may under our sending, come to his native land speedily and with rejoicing, though he come from never so far. Nor shall he meanwhile suffer any evil or harm, until he sets foot upon his own land ; but thereafter he shall suffer whatever Fate and the dread Spinners spun with their thread for him at his birth, when his mother bore him. But if he is one of the immortals come down from heaven, then is this some new thing which the gods are planning ; for ever heretofore have they been wont to appear to us in manifest form, when we sacrifice to them glorious hecatombs, and they feast among us, sitting even where we sit. Aye, and if one of us as a lone wayfarer meets them, they use no concealment, for we are of near kin to them, as are the Cyclopes and the wild tribes of the Giants."

Then Odysseus of many wiles answered him, and said : " Alcinous, far from thee be that thought ; for I am not like the immortals, who hold broad heaven, either in stature or in form, but like mortal men. Whomsoever ye know among men who bear greatest burden of woe, to them might I liken myself in my sorrows. Yea, and I could tell a yet longer tale of all the evils which I have endured by the will of the gods. But as for me, suffer me now to eat, despite my grief ; for there is nothing more

ἔπλετο, ἥ τ' ἐκέλευσεν ἕο μνήσασθαι ἀνάγκῃ
καὶ μάλα τειρόμενον καὶ ἐνὶ φρεσὶ πένθος ἔχοντα,
ὡς καὶ ἐγὼ πένθος μὲν ἔχω φρεσίν, ἡ δὲ μάλ' αἰεὶ
ἐσθέμεναι κέλεται καὶ πινέμεν, ἐκ δέ με πάντων   22
ληθάνει ὅσσ' ἔπαθον, καὶ ἐνιπλησθῆναι ἀνώγει.
ὑμεῖς δ' ὀτρύνεσθαι ἅμ' ἠοῖ φαινομένηφιν,
ὥς κ' ἐμὲ τὸν δύστηνον ἐμῆς ἐπιβήσετε πάτρης
καί περ πολλὰ παθόντα· ἰδόντα με καὶ λίποι αἰὼν
κτῆσιν ἐμήν, δμῶάς τε καὶ ὑψερεφὲς μέγα δῶμα."   22

  Ὡς ἔφαθ', οἱ δ' ἄρα πάντες ἐπήνεον ἠδ' ἐκέλευον
πεμπέμεναι τὸν ξεῖνον, ἐπεὶ κατὰ μοῖραν ἔειπεν.
αὐτὰρ ἐπεὶ σπεῖσάν τ' ἔπιον θ' ὅσον ἤθελε θυμός,
οἱ μὲν κακκείοντες ἔβαν οἰκόνδε ἕκαστος,
αὐτὰρ ὁ ἐν μεγάρῳ ὑπελείπετο δῖος Ὀδυσσεύς,   23
πὰρ δέ οἱ Ἀρήτη τε καὶ Ἀλκίνοος θεοειδὴς
ἥσθην· ἀμφίπολοι δ' ἀπεκόσμεον ἔντεα δαιτός.
τοῖσιν δ' Ἀρήτη λευκώλενος ἤρχετο μύθων·
ἔγνω γὰρ φᾶρός τε χιτῶνά τε εἵματ' ἰδοῦσα
καλά, τά ῥ' αὐτὴ τεῦξε σὺν ἀμφιπόλοισι γυναιξί·   23
καί μιν φωνήσασ' ἔπεα πτερόεντα προσηύδα·

  " Ξεῖνε, τὸ μέν σε πρῶτον ἐγὼν εἰρήσομαι αὐτή·
τίς, πόθεν εἰς ἀνδρῶν; τίς τοι τάδε εἵματ' ἔδωκεν;
οὐ δὴ φῂς ἐπὶ πόντον ἀλώμενος ἐνθάδ' ἱκέσθαι;"

  Τὴν δ' ἀπαμειβόμενος προσέφη πολύμητις Ὀδυσσεὺ
" Ἀργαλέον, βασίλεια, διηνεκέως ἀγορεῦσαι   24
κήδε', ἐπεί μοι πολλὰ δόσαν θεοὶ Οὐρανίωνες·
τοῦτο δέ τοι ἐρέω ὅ μ' ἀνείρεαι ἠδὲ μεταλλᾷς.
248

shameless than a hateful belly, which bids a man perforce take thought thereof, be he never so sore distressed and laden with grief at heart, even as I, too, am laden with grief at heart, yet ever does my belly bid me eat and drink, and makes me forget all that I have suffered, and commands me to eat my fill. But do ye make haste at break of day, that ye may set me, hapless one, on the soil of my native land, even after my many woes. Yea, let life leave me, when I have seen once more my possessions, my slaves, and my great high-roofed house."

So he spoke, and they all praised his words, and bade send the stranger on his way, since he had spoken fittingly. Then when they had poured libations, and had drunk to their heart's content, they went each man to his home, to take their rest, and goodly Odysseus was left behind in the hall, and beside him sat Arete and godlike Alcinous; and the handmaids cleared away the dishes of the feast. Then white-armed Arete was the first to speak; for, as she saw it, she knew his fair raiment, the mantle and tunic, which she herself had wrought with her handmaids. And she spoke, and addressed him with winged words:

"Stranger, this question will I myself ask thee first. Who art thou among men, and from whence? Who gave thee this raiment? Didst thou not say that thou camest hither wandering over the sea?"

Then Odysseus of many wiles answered her, and said: "Hard were it, O queen, to tell to the end the tale of my woes, since full many have the heavenly gods given me. But this will I tell thee, of which thou dost ask and enquire. There is an

'Ωγυγίη τις νῆσος ἀπόπροθεν εἰν ἁλὶ κεῖται·
ἔνθα μὲν Ἄτλαντος θυγάτηρ, δολόεσσα Καλυψὼ
ναίει ἐυπλόκαμος, δεινὴ θεός· οὐδέ τις αὐτῇ
μίσγεται οὔτε θεῶν οὔτε θνητῶν ἀνθρώπων.
ἀλλ' ἐμὲ τὸν δύστηνον ἐφέστιον ἤγαγε δαίμων
οἶον, ἐπεί μοι νῆα θοὴν ἀργῆτι κεραυνῷ
Ζεὺς ἔλσας¹ ἐκέασσε μέσῳ ἐνὶ οἴνοπι πόντῳ.
ἔνθ' ἄλλοι μὲν πάντες ἀπέφθιθεν ἐσθλοὶ ἑταῖροι,
αὐτὰρ ἐγὼ τρόπιν ἀγκὰς ἑλὼν νεὸς ἀμφιελίσσης
ἐννῆμαρ φερόμην· δεκάτῃ δέ με νυκτὶ μελαίνῃ
νῆσον ἐς 'Ωγυγίην πέλασαν θεοί, ἔνθα Καλυψὼ
ναίει ἐυπλόκαμος, δεινὴ θεός, ἥ με λαβοῦσα
ἐνδυκέως ἐφίλει τε καὶ ἔτρεφεν ἠδὲ ἔφασκε
θήσειν ἀθάνατον καὶ ἀγήραον ἤματα πάντα·
ἀλλ' ἐμὸν οὔ ποτε θυμὸν ἐνὶ στήθεσσιν ἔπειθεν.²
ἔνθα μὲν ἑπτάετες μένον ἔμπεδον, εἵματα δ' αἰεὶ
δάκρυσι δεύεσκον, τά μοι ἄμβροτα δῶκε Καλυψώ·
ἀλλ' ὅτε δὴ ὀγδόατόν μοι ἐπιπλόμενον ἔτος ἦλθεν,
καὶ τότε δή μ' ἐκέλευσεν ἐποτρύνουσα νέεσθαι
Ζηνὸς ὑπ' ἀγγελίης, ἦ καὶ νόος ἐτράπετ' αὐτῆς.
πέμπε δ' ἐπὶ σχεδίης πολυδέσμου, πολλὰ δ' ἔδωκε,
σῖτον καὶ μέθυ ἡδύ, καὶ ἄμβροτα εἵματα ἕσσεν,
οὖρον δὲ προέηκεν ἀπήμονά τε λιαρόν τε.
ἑπτὰ δὲ καὶ δέκα μὲν πλέον ἤματα ποντοπορεύων,
ὀκτωκαιδεκάτῃ δ' ἐφάνη ὄρεα σκιόεντα
γαίης ὑμετέρης, γήθησε δέ μοι φίλον ἦτορ
δυσμόρῳ· ἦ γὰρ ἔμελλον ἔτι ξυνέσεσθαι ὀιζυῖ
πολλῇ, τήν μοι ἐπῶρσε Ποσειδάων ἐνοσίχθων,
ὅς μοι ἐφορμήσας ἀνέμους κατέδησε κέλευθον,
ὤρινεν δὲ θάλασσαν ἀθέσφατον, οὐδέ τι κῦμα

---

¹ ἔλσας : ἐλάσας ; cf. v. 132.
² Lines 251-8 were rejected by Aristarchus.

isle, Ogygia, which lies far off in the sea. Therein
dwells the fair-tressed daughter of Atlas, guileful
Calypso, a dread goddess, and with her no one either
of gods or mortals hath aught to do ; but me in my
wretchedness did fate bring to her hearth alone,
for Zeus had smitten my swift ship with his bright
thunderbolt, and had shattered it in the midst of
the wine-dark sea. There all the rest of my trusty
comrades perished, but I clasped in my arms the
keel of my curved ship and was borne drifting for
nine days, and on the tenth black night the gods
brought me to the isle, Ogygia, where the fair-
tressed Calypso dwells, a dread goddess. She took
me to her home with kindly welcome, and gave me
food, and said that she would make me immortal
and ageless all my days ; but she could never per-
suade the heart in my breast. There for seven years'
space I remained continually, and ever with my tears
would I wet the immortal raiment which Calypso
gave me. But when the eighth year came in circling
course, then she roused me and bade me go, either be-
cause of some message from Zeus, or because her own
mind was turned. And she sent me on my way on
a raft, stoutly bound, and gave me abundant store of
bread and sweet wine, and clad me in immortal
raiment, and sent forth a gentle wind and warm.
So for seventeen days I sailed over the sea, and on
the eighteenth appeared the shadowy mountains of
your land ; and my heart was glad, ill-starred that I
was ; for verily I was yet to have fellowship with
great woe, which Poseidon, the earth-shaker, sent
upon me. For he stirred up the winds against me and
stayed my course, and wondrously roused the sea,

εἶα ἐπὶ σχεδίης ἀδινὰ στενάχοντα φέρεσθαι.
τὴν μὲν ἔπειτα θύελλα διεσκέδασ'· αὐτὰρ ἐγώ γε
νηχόμενος τόδε λαῖτμα διέτμαγον, ὄφρα με γαίῃ
ὑμετέρῃ ἐπέλασσε φέρων ἄνεμός τε καὶ ὕδωρ.
ἔνθα κέ μ' ἐκβαίνοντα βιήσατο κῦμ' ἐπὶ χέρσου,
πέτρῃς πρὸς μεγάλῃσι βαλὸν καὶ ἀτερπέι χώρῳ·
ἀλλ' ἀναχασσάμενος νῆχον πάλιν, ἧος ἐπῆλθον
ἐς ποταμόν, τῇ δή μοι ἐείσατο χῶρος ἄριστος,
λεῖος πετράων, καὶ ἐπὶ σκέπας ἦν ἀνέμοιο.
ἐκ δ' ἔπεσον θυμηγερέων, ἐπὶ δ' ἀμβροσίη νὺξ
ἤλυθ'. ἐγὼ δ' ἀπάνευθε διιπετέος ποταμοῖο
ἐκβὰς ἐν θάμνοισι κατέδραθον, ἀμφὶ δὲ φύλλα
ἠφυσάμην· ὕπνον δὲ θεὸς κατ' ἀπείρονα χεῦεν.
ἔνθα μὲν ἐν φύλλοισι φίλον τετιημένος ἦτορ
εὗδον παννύχιος καὶ ἐπ' ἠῶ καὶ μέσον ἦμαρ.
δείλετό[1] τ' ἠέλιος καί με γλυκὺς ὕπνος ἀνῆκεν.
ἀμφιπόλους δ' ἐπὶ θινὶ τεῆς ἐνόησα θυγατρὸς
παιζούσας, ἐν δ' αὐτὴ ἔην εἰκυῖα θεῇσι·
τὴν ἱκέτευσ'· ἡ δ' οὔ τι νοήματος ἤμβροτεν ἐσθλοῦ,
ὡς οὐκ ἂν ἔλποιο νεώτερον ἀντιάσαντα
ἐρξέμεν· αἰεὶ γάρ τε νεώτεροι ἀφραδέουσιν.
ἥ μοι σῖτον ἔδωκεν ἅλις ἠδ' αἴθοπα οἶνον
καὶ λοῦσ' ἐν ποταμῷ καί μοι τάδε εἵματ' ἔδωκε.
ταῦτά τοι ἀχνύμενός περ ἀληθείην κατέλεξα."
  Τὸν δ' αὖτ' Ἀλκίνοος ἀπαμείβετο φώνησέν τε·
" Ξεῖν', ἦ τοι μὲν τοῦτό γ' ἐναίσιμον οὐκ ἐνόησε

2

2

2

2

2

---

[1] δείλετο Aristarchus : δύσετο.

nor would the wave suffer me to be borne upon my raft, as I groaned ceaselessly. My raft indeed the storm shattered, but by swimming I clove my way through yon gulf of the sea, until the wind and the waves, as they bore me, brought me to your shores. There, had I sought to land, the waves would have hurled me upon the shore, and dashed me against the great crags and a cheerless place, but I gave way, and swam back until I came to a river, where seemed to me the best place, since it was smooth of rocks, and besides there was shelter from the wind. Forth then I staggered, and sank down, gasping for breath, and immortal night came on. Then I went forth from the heaven-fed river, and lay down to sleep in the bushes, gathering leaves about me ; and a god shed over me infinite sleep. So there among the leaves I slept, my heart sore stricken, the whole night through, until the morning and until midday ; and the sun turned to his setting[1] ere sweet sleep released me. Then I saw the handmaids of thy daughter on the shore at play, and amid them was she, fair as the goddesses. To her I made my prayer ; and she in no wise failed in good understanding, to do as thou wouldst not deem that one of younger years would do on meeting thee ; for younger folk are ever thoughtless. She gave bread in plenty and sparkling wine, and bathed me in the river, and gave me this raiment. In this, for all my sorrows, have I told thee the truth.''

Then in turn Alcinous answered him, and said : " Stranger, verily my daughter was not minded

---

[1] In thus rendering δείλετο I have attempted to meet the difficulty that most of the events recorded in Book VI. occur in the interval between the waking of Odysseus and the actual setting of the sun. Hence δύσετο is impossible.

παῖς ἐμή, οὕνεκά σ' οὔ τι μετ' ἀμφιπόλοισι γυναιξὶν
ἦγεν ἐς ἡμέτερον, σὺ δ' ἄρα πρώτην ἱκέτευσας."
   Τὸν δ' ἀπαμειβόμενος προσέφη πολύμητις Ὀδυσσε
"Ἥρως, μή τοι τούνεκ' ἀμύμονα νείκεε κούρην·
ἡ μὲν γάρ μ' ἐκέλευε σὺν ἀμφιπόλοισιν ἕπεσθαι,
ἀλλ' ἐγὼ οὐκ ἔθελον δείσας αἰσχυνόμενός τε,
μή πως καὶ σοὶ θυμὸς ἐπισκύσσαιτο ἰδόντι·
δύσζηλοι γάρ τ' εἰμὲν ἐπὶ χθονὶ φῦλ' ἀνθρώπων."
   Τὸν δ' αὖτ' Ἀλκίνοος ἀπαμείβετο φώνησέν τε·
" Ξεῖν', οὔ μοι τοιοῦτον ἐνὶ στήθεσσι φίλον κῆρ
μαψιδίως κεχολῶσθαι· ἀμείνω δ' αἴσιμα πάντα.
αἲ γάρ, Ζεῦ τε πάτερ καὶ Ἀθηναίη καὶ Ἄπολλον,
τοῖος ἐὼν οἷός ἐσσι, τά τε φρονέων ἅ τ' ἐγώ περ,
παῖδά τ' ἐμὴν ἐχέμεν καὶ ἐμὸς γαμβρὸς καλέεσθαι
αὖθι μένων· οἶκον δέ κ' ἐγὼ καὶ κτήματα δοίην,
εἴ κ' ἐθέλων γε μένοις· ἀέκοντα δέ σ' οὔ τις ἐρύξει
Φαιήκων· μὴ τοῦτο φίλον Διὶ πατρὶ γένοιτο.
πομπὴν δ' ἐς τόδ' ἐγὼ τεκμαίρομαι, ὄφρ' ἐὺ εἰδῇς,
αὔριον ἔς· τῆμος δὲ σὺ μὲν δεδμημένος ὕπνῳ
λέξεαι, οἱ δ' ἐλόωσι γαλήνην, ὄφρ' ἂν ἵκηαι
πατρίδα σὴν καὶ δῶμα, καὶ εἴ πού τοι φίλον ἐστίν,
εἴ περ καὶ μάλα πολλὸν ἑκαστέρω ἔστ' Εὐβοίης,
τήν περ τηλοτάτω φάσ' ἔμμεναι, οἵ μιν ἴδοντο
λαῶν ἡμετέρων, ὅτε τε ξανθὸν Ῥαδάμανθυν
ἦγον ἐποψόμενον Τιτυὸν Γαιήιον υἱόν.
καὶ μὲν οἱ ἔνθ' ἦλθον καὶ ἄτερ καμάτοιο τέλεσσαν
ἤματι τῷ αὐτῷ καὶ ἀπήνυσαν οἴκαδ' ὀπίσσω.
εἰδήσεις δὲ καὶ αὐτὸς ἐνὶ φρεσὶν ὅσσον ἄρισται
νῆες ἐμαὶ καὶ κοῦροι ἀναρρίπτειν ἅλα πηδῷ."

aright in this, that she did not bring thee to our house with her maidens. Yet it was to her first that thou didst make thy prayer."

Then Odysseus of many wiles answered him, and said : " Prince, rebuke not for this, I pray thee, thy blameless daughter. She did indeed bid me follow with her maidens, but I would not for fear and shame, lest haply thy heart should darken with wrath as thou sawest it ; for we are quick to anger, we tribes of men upon the earth."

And again Alcinous answered him, and said : " Stranger, not such is the heart in my breast, to be filled with wrath without a cause. Better is due measure in all things. I would, O father Zeus, and Athene and Apollo, that thou, so goodly a man, and like-minded with me, wouldst have my daughter to wife, and be called my son, and abide here ; a house and possessions would I give thee, if thou shouldst choose to remain, but against thy will shall no one of the Phaeacians keep thee ; let not that be the will of father Zeus. But as for thy sending, that thou mayest know it surely, I appoint a time thereto, even the morrow. Then shalt thou lie down, over-come by sleep, and they shall row thee over the calm sea until thou comest to thy country and thy house, or to whatsoever place thou wilt, aye though it be even far beyond Euboea, which those of our people who saw it, when they carried fair-haired Rhadamanthus to visit Tityus, the son of Gaea, say is the furthest of lands. Thither they went, and without toil accomplished their journey, and on the selfsame day came back home. So shalt thou, too, know for thyself how far my ships are the best, and my youths at tossing the brine with the oar-blade."

Ὣς φάτο, γήθησεν δὲ πολύτλας δῖος Ὀδυσσεύς,
εὐχόμενος δ' ἄρα εἶπεν, ἔπος τ' ἔφατ' ἔκ τ' ὀνόμαζεν·[1] 3
" Ζεῦ πάτερ, αἴθ' ὅσα εἶπε τελευτήσειεν ἅπαντα
Ἀλκίνοος· τοῦ μέν κεν ἐπὶ ζείδωρον ἄρουραν
ἄσβεστον κλέος εἴη, ἐγὼ δέ κε πατρίδ' ἱκοίμην."
Ὣς οἱ μὲν τοιαῦτα πρὸς ἀλλήλους ἀγόρευον·
κέκλετο δ' Ἀρήτη λευκώλενος ἀμφιπόλοισιν   3⟨⟩
δέμνι' ὑπ' αἰθούσῃ θέμεναι καὶ ῥήγεα καλὰ
πορφύρε' ἐμβαλέειν, στορέσαι τ' ἐφύπερθε τάπητας
χλαίνας τ' ἐνθέμεναι οὔλας καθύπερθεν ἕσασθαι.
αἱ δ' ἴσαν ἐκ μεγάροιο δάος μετὰ χερσὶν ἔχουσαι·
αὐτὰρ ἐπεὶ στόρεσαν πυκινὸν λέχος ἐγκονέουσαι,   3⟨⟩
ὤτρυνον δ' Ὀδυσῆα παριστάμεναι ἐπέεσσιν·
" Ὄρσο κέων, ὦ ξεῖνε· πεποίηται δέ τοι εὐνή."
Ὣς φάν, τῷ δ' ἀσπαστὸν ἐείσατο κοιμηθῆναι.
ὣς ὁ μὲν ἔνθα καθεῦδε πολύτλας δῖος Ὀδυσσεὺς
τρητοῖς ἐν λεχέεσσιν ὑπ' αἰθούσῃ ἐριδούπῳ·   3⟨⟩
Ἀλκίνοος δ' ἄρα λέκτο μυχῷ δόμου ὑψηλοῖο,
πὰρ δὲ γυνὴ δέσποινα λέχος πόρσυνε καὶ εὐνήν.

1 ἔπος ... ὀνόμαζεν: πρὸς ὃν μεγαλήτορα θυμόν.

So said he, and the much-enduring goodly Odysseus was glad; and he spoke in prayer, and said: " Father Zeus, grant that Alcinous may bring to pass all that he has said. So shall his fame be unquenchable over the earth, the giver of grain, and I shall reach my native land."

Thus they spoke to one another, and white-armed Arete bade her maidens place a bedstead under cover of the portico, and to lay on it fair blankets of purple, and to spread thereover coverlets, and on these to put fleecy cloaks for clothing. So they went forth from the hall with torches in their hands. But when they had busily spread the stout-built bedstead, they came to Odysseus, and called to him, and said: " Rouse thee now, stranger, to go to thy rest; thy bed is made."

Thus they spoke, and welcome did it seem to him to lay him down to sleep. So there he slept, the much-enduring goodly Odysseus, on the corded bedstead under the echoing portico. But Alcinous lay down in the inmost chamber of the lofty house, and beside him lay the lady his wife, who had strewn the couch.

Ἦμος δ' ἠριγένεια φάνη ῥοδοδάκτυλος Ἠώς,
ὤρνυτ' ἄρ' ἐξ εὐνῆς ἱερὸν μένος Ἀλκινόοιο,
ἂν δ' ἄρα διογενὴς ὦρτο πτολίπορθος Ὀδυσσεύς.
τοῖσιν δ' ἡγεμόνευ' ἱερὸν μένος Ἀλκινόοιο
Φαιήκων ἀγορήνδ', ἥ σφιν παρὰ νηυσὶ τέτυκτο.
ἐλθόντες δὲ καθῖζον ἐπὶ ξεστοῖσι λίθοισι
πλησίον.   ἡ δ' ἀνὰ ἄστυ μετῴχετο Παλλὰς Ἀθήνη
εἰδομένη κήρυκι δαΐφρονος Ἀλκινόοιο,
νόστον Ὀδυσσῆι μεγαλήτορι μητιόωσα,
καί ῥα ἑκάστῳ φωτὶ παρισταμένη φάτο μῦθον·   1

" Δεῦτ' ἄγε, Φαιήκων ἡγήτορες ἠδὲ μέδοντες,
εἰς ἀγορὴν ἰέναι, ὄφρα ξείνοιο πύθησθε,
ὃς νέον Ἀλκινόοιο δαΐφρονος ἵκετο δῶμα
πόντον ἐπιπλαγχθείς, δέμας ἀθανάτοισιν ὁμοῖος."

Ὣς εἰποῦσ' ὤτρυνε μένος καὶ θυμὸν ἑκάστου.   1
καρπαλίμως δ' ἔμπληντο βροτῶν ἀγοραί τε καὶ ἕδραι
ἀγρομένων· πολλοὶ δ' ἄρ' ἐθηήσαντο ἰδόντες
υἱὸν Λαέρταο δαΐφρονα· τῷ δ' ἄρ' Ἀθήνη
θεσπεσίην κατέχευε χάριν κεφαλῇ τε καὶ ὤμοις
καί μιν μακρότερον καὶ πάσσονα θῆκεν ἰδέσθαι,   2
ὥς κεν Φαιήκεσσι φίλος πάντεσσι γένοιτο
δεινός τ' αἰδοῖός τε καὶ ἐκτελέσειεν ἀέθλους
πολλούς, τοὺς Φαίηκες ἐπειρήσαντ' Ὀδυσῆος.

BOOK VIII

As soon as early Dawn appeared, the rosy-fingered, the strong and mighty Alcinous rose from his couch, and up rose also Zeus-born Odysseus, the sacker of cities. And the strong and mighty Alcinous led the way to the place of assembly of the Phaeacians, which was builded for them hard by their ships. Thither they came and sat down on the polished stones close by one another; and Pallas Athene went throughout the city, in the likeness of the herald of wise Alcinous, devising a return for great-hearted Odysseus. To each man's side she came, and spoke and said:

"Hither now, leaders and counsellors of the Phaeacians, come to the place of assembly, that you may learn of the stranger who has newly come to the palace of wise Alcinous after his wanderings over the sea, and in form is like unto the immortals."

So saying she roused the spirit and heart of each man, and speedily the place of assembly and the seats were filled with men that gathered. And many marvelled at the sight of the wise son of Laertes, for wondrous was the grace that Athene shed upon his head and shoulders; and she made him taller and sturdier to behold, that he might be welcomed by all the Phaeacians, and win awe and reverence, and might accomplish the many feats wherein the Phaeacians made trial of Odysseus. Now when they were

αὐτὰρ ἐπεί ῥ' ἤγερθεν ὁμηγερέες τ' ἐγένοντο,
τοῖσιν δ' Ἀλκίνοος ἀγορήσατο καὶ μετέειπε·   25
" Κέκλυτε, Φαιήκων ἡγήτορες ἠδὲ μέδοντες,
ὄφρ' εἴπω τά με θυμὸς ἐνὶ στήθεσσι κελεύει.
ξεῖνος ὅδ', οὐκ οἶδ' ὅς τις, ἀλώμενος ἵκετ' ἐμὸν δῶ,
ἠὲ πρὸς ἠοίων ἢ ἑσπερίων ἀνθρώπων·
πομπὴν δ' ὀτρύνει, καὶ λίσσεται ἔμπεδον εἶναι.   30
ἡμεῖς δ', ὡς τὸ πάρος περ, ἐποτρυνώμεθα πομπήν.
οὐδὲ γὰρ οὐδέ τις ἄλλος, ὅτις κ' ἐμὰ δώμαθ' ἵκηται,
ἐνθάδ' ὀδυρόμενος δηρὸν μένει εἵνεκα πομπῆς.
ἀλλ' ἄγε νῆα μέλαιναν ἐρύσσομεν εἰς ἅλα δῖαν
πρωτόπλοον, κούρω δὲ δύω καὶ πεντήκοντα   35
κρινάσθων κατὰ δῆμον, ὅσοι πάρος εἰσὶν ἄριστοι.
δησάμενοι δ' εὖ πάντες ἐπὶ κληῖσιν ἐρετμὰ
ἔκβητ'· αὐτὰρ ἔπειτα θοὴν ἀλεγύνετε δαῖτα
ἡμετερόνδ' ἐλθόντες· ἐγὼ δ' εὖ πᾶσι παρέξω.
κούροισιν μὲν ταῦτ' ἐπιτέλλομαι· αὐτὰρ οἱ ἄλλοι   40
σκηπτοῦχοι βασιλῆες ἐμὰ πρὸς δώματα καλὰ
ἔρχεσθ', ὄφρα ξεῖνον ἐνὶ μεγάροισι φιλέωμεν,
μηδέ τις ἀρνείσθω. καλέσασθε δὲ θεῖον ἀοιδὸν
Δημόδοκον· τῷ γάρ ῥα θεὸς πέρι δῶκεν ἀοιδὴν
τέρπειν, ὅππῃ θυμὸς ἐποτρύνῃσιν ἀείδειν."   45
Ὣς ἄρα φωνήσας ἡγήσατο, τοὶ δ' ἅμ' ἕποντο
σκηπτοῦχοι· κῆρυξ δὲ μετῴχετο θεῖον ἀοιδόν.
κούρω δὲ κρινθέντε δύω καὶ πεντήκοντα
βήτην, ὡς ἐκέλευσ', ἐπὶ θῖν' ἁλὸς ἀτρυγέτοιο.
αὐτὰρ ἐπεί ῥ' ἐπὶ νῆα κατήλυθον ἠδὲ θάλασσαν,   50
νῆα μὲν οἵ γε μέλαιναν ἁλὸς βένθοσδε ἔρυσσαν,
ἐν δ' ἱστόν τ' ἐτίθεντο καὶ ἱστία νηὶ μελαίνῃ,

assembled and met together, Alcinous addressed their assembly and spoke among them :

"Hearken to me, leaders and counsellors of the Phaeacians, that I may speak what the heart in my breast bids me. This stranger—I know not who he is—has come to my house in his wanderings, whether from men of the east or of the west. He urges that he be sent on his way, and prays for assurance, and let us on our part, as of old we were wont, speed on his sending ; for verily no man soever who comes to my house, abides here long in sorrow for lack of sending. Nay come, let us draw a black ship down to the bright sea for her first voyage, and let men choose two and fifty youths from out the people, even those that have heretofore been the best. And when you have all duly lashed the oars to the thole-pins,[1] go ashore, and then go your way to my house, and prepare a feast with speed ; and I will provide bountifully for all. To the youths this is my command, but do you others, the sceptred kings, come to my fair palace, that we may entertain yon stranger in the halls ; and let no man say me nay. And summon hither the divine minstrel, Demodocus ; for to him above all others has the god granted skill in song, to give delight in whatever way his spirit prompts him to sing."

So saying, he led the way, and the sceptred kings followed him, while a herald went for the divine minstrel. And chosen youths, two and fifty, went, as he bade, to the shore of the unresting sea. And when they had come down to the ship and to the sea, they drew the black ship down to the deep water, and placed the mast and sail in the black

---

[1] Or "rowing-benches," as commonly.

ἠρτύναντο δ' ἐρετμὰ τροποῖς ἐν δερματίνοισι,
πάντα κατὰ μοῖραν, ἀνά θ' ἱστία λευκὰ πέτασσαν.
ὑψοῦ δ' ἐν νοτίῳ τήν γ' ὥρμισαν· αὐτὰρ ἔπειτα   5
βάν ῥ' ἴμεν Ἀλκινόοιο δαΐφρονος ἐς μέγα δῶμα.
πλῆντο δ' ἄρ' αἴθουσαί τε καὶ ἔρκεα καὶ δόμοι ἀνδρῶν
ἀγρομένων· πολλοὶ δ' ἄρ' ἔσαν, νέοι ἠδὲ παλαιοί.[1]
τοῖσιν δ' Ἀλκίνοος δυοκαίδεκα μῆλ' ἱέρευσεν,
ὀκτὼ δ' ἀργιόδοντας ὗας, δύο δ' εἰλίποδας βοῦς·   6
τοὺς δέρον ἀμφί θ' ἕπον, τετύκοντό τε δαῖτ' ἐρατεινήν.

Κῆρυξ δ' ἐγγύθεν ἦλθεν ἄγων ἐρίηρον ἀοιδόν,
τὸν πέρι μοῦσ' ἐφίλησε, δίδου δ' ἀγαθόν τε κακόν τε·
ὀφθαλμῶν μὲν ἄμερσε, δίδου δ' ἡδεῖαν ἀοιδήν.
τῷ δ' ἄρα Ποντόνοος θῆκε θρόνον ἀργυρόηλον   6
μέσσῳ δαιτυμόνων, πρὸς κίονα μακρὸν ἐρείσας·
κὰδ δ' ἐκ πασσαλόφι κρέμασεν φόρμιγγα λίγειαν
αὐτοῦ ὑπὲρ κεφαλῆς καὶ ἐπέφραδε χερσὶν ἑλέσθαι
κῆρυξ· πὰρ δ' ἐτίθει κάνεον καλήν τε τράπεζαν,
πὰρ δὲ δέπας οἴνοιο, πιεῖν ὅτε θυμὸς ἀνώγοι.   7
οἱ δ' ἐπ' ὀνείαθ' ἑτοῖμα προκείμενα χεῖρας ἴαλλον.
αὐτὰρ ἐπεὶ πόσιος καὶ ἐδητύος ἐξ ἔρον ἕντο,
μοῦσ' ἄρ' ἀοιδὸν ἀνῆκεν ἀειδέμεναι κλέα ἀνδρῶν,
οἴμης τῆς τότ' ἄρα κλέος οὐρανὸν εὐρὺν ἵκανε,
νεῖκος Ὀδυσσῆος καὶ Πηλεΐδεω Ἀχιλῆος,   7
ὥς ποτε δηρίσαντο θεῶν ἐν δαιτὶ θαλείῃ
ἐκπάγλοις ἐπέεσσιν, ἄναξ δ' ἀνδρῶν Ἀγαμέμνων
χαῖρε νόῳ, ὅ τ' ἄριστοι Ἀχαιῶν δηριόωντο.
ὣς γάρ οἱ χρείων μυθήσατο Φοῖβος Ἀπόλλων
Πυθοῖ ἐν ἠγαθέῃ, ὅθ' ὑπέρβη λάινον οὐδὸν   8

---

[1] Line 58 is omitted in most MSS.

ship, and fitted the oars in the leathern thole-straps, all in due order, and spread the white sail. Well out in the roadstead they moored the ship, and then went their way to the great palace of the wise Alcinous. Filled were the porticoes and courts and rooms with the men that gathered, for many there were, both young and old. For them Alcinous slaughtered twelve sheep, and eight white-tusked boars, and two oxen of shambling gait. These they flayed and dressed, and made ready a goodly feast.

Then the herald drew near, leading the good minstrel, whom the Muse loved above all other men, and gave him both good and evil; of his sight she deprived him, but gave him the gift of sweet song. For him Pontonous, the herald, set a silver-studded chair in the midst of the banqueters, leaning it against a tall pillar, and he hung the clear-toned lyre from a peg close above his head, and showed him how to reach it with his hands. And beside him he placed a basket and a beautiful table, and a cup of wine, to drink when his heart should bid him. So they put forth their hands to the good cheer lying ready before them. But when they had put from them the desire of food and drink, the Muse moved the minstrel to sing of the glorious deeds of warriors, from that lay the fame whereof had then reached broad heaven, even the quarrel of Odysseus and Achilles, son of Peleus, how once they strove with furious words at a rich feast of the gods, and Agamemnon, king of men, was glad at heart that the best of the Achaeans were quarrelling; for thus Phoebus Apollo, in giving his response, had told him that it should be, in sacred Pytho, when he passed over the threshold of stone to enquire of the oracle.

χρησόμενος· τότε γάρ ρα κυλίνδετο πήματος ἀρχὴ
Τρωσί τε καὶ Δαναοῖσι Διὸς μεγάλου διὰ βουλάς.

Ταῦτ' ἄρ' ἀοιδὸς ἄειδε περικλυτός· αὐτὰρ Ὀδυσσεὺς
πορφύρεον μέγα φᾶρος ἑλὼν χερσὶ στιβαρῇσι
κὰκ κεφαλῆς εἴρυσσε, κάλυψε δὲ καλὰ πρόσωπα· 85
αἴδετο γὰρ Φαίηκας ὑπ' ὀφρύσι δάκρυα λείβων.
ἦ τοι ὅτε λήξειεν ἀείδων θεῖος ἀοιδός,
δάκρυ ὀμορξάμενος κεφαλῆς ἄπο φᾶρος ἔλεσκε
καὶ δέπας ἀμφικύπελλον ἑλὼν σπείσασκε θεοῖσιν·
αὐτὰρ ὅτ' ἂψ ἄρχοιτο καὶ ὀτρύνειαν ἀείδειν 90
Φαιήκων οἱ ἄριστοι, ἐπεὶ τέρποντ' ἐπέεσσιν,
ἂψ Ὀδυσεὺς κατὰ κρᾶτα καλυψάμενος γοάασκεν.
ἔνθ' ἄλλους μὲν πάντας ἐλάνθανε δάκρυα λείβων,
Ἀλκίνοος δέ μιν οἶος ἐπεφράσατ' ἠδ' ἐνόησεν
ἥμενος ἄγχ' αὐτοῦ, βαρὺ δὲ στενάχοντος ἄκουσεν. 95
αἶψα δὲ Φαιήκεσσι φιληρέτμοισι μετηύδα·

"Κέκλυτε, Φαιήκων ἡγήτορες ἠδὲ μέδοντες.
ἤδη μὲν δαιτὸς κεκορήμεθα θυμὸν εἴσης
φόρμιγγός θ', ἣ δαιτὶ συνήορός ἐστι θαλείῃ·
νῦν δ' ἐξέλθωμεν καὶ ἀέθλων πειρηθῶμεν 100
πάντων, ὥς χ' ὁ ξεῖνος ἐνίσπῃ οἷσι φίλοισιν
οἴκαδε νοστήσας, ὅσσον περιγιγνόμεθ' ἄλλων
πύξ τε παλαιμοσύνῃ τε καὶ ἅλμασιν ἠδὲ πόδεσσιν."

Ὣς ἄρα φωνήσας ἡγήσατο, τοὶ δ' ἅμ' ἕποντο.
κὰδ δ' ἐκ πασσαλόφι κρέμασεν φόρμιγγα λίγειαν, 105
Δημοδόκου δ' ἕλε χεῖρα καὶ ἔξαγεν ἐκ μεγάροιο
κῆρυξ· ἦρχε δὲ τῷ αὐτὴν ὁδὸν ἥν περ οἱ ἄλλοι
Φαιήκων οἱ ἄριστοι, ἀέθλια θαυμανέοντες.
βὰν δ' ἴμεν εἰς ἀγορήν, ἅμα δ' ἕσπετο πουλὺς ὅμιλος,

For then the beginning of woe was rolling upon Trojans and Danaans through the will of great Zeus.

This song the famous minstrel sang; but Odysseus grasped his great purple cloak with his stout hands, and drew it down over his head, and hid his comely face; for he had shame of the Phaeacians as he let fall tears from beneath his eyebrows. Yea, and as often as the divine minstrel ceased his singing, Odysseus would wipe away his tears and draw the cloak from off his head, and taking the two-handled cup would pour libations to the gods. But as often as he began again, and the nobles of the Phaeacians bade him sing, because they took pleasure in his lay, Odysseus would again cover his head and moan. Now from all the rest he concealed the tears that he shed, but Alcinous alone marked him and took heed, for he sat by him, and heard him groaning heavily. And straightway he spoke among the Phaeacians, lovers of the oar:

" Hear me, ye leaders and counsellors of the Phaeacians, already have we satisfied our hearts with the equal banquet and with the lyre, which is the companion of the rich feast. But now let us go forth, and make trial of all manner of games, that yon stranger may tell his friends, when he returns home, how far we excel other men in boxing and wrestling and leaping and in speed of foot."

So saying, he led the way, and they followed him. From the peg the herald hung the clear-toned lyre, and took Demodocus by the hand, and led him forth from the hall, guiding him by the self-same road by which the others, the nobles of the Phaeacians, had gone to gaze upon the games. They went their way to the place of assembly, and with them went a

μυρίοι· ἂν δ᾽ ἵσταντο νέοι πολλοί τε καὶ ἐσθλοί.　110

ὦρτο μὲν Ἀκρόνεώς τε καὶ Ὠκύαλος καὶ Ἐλατρεύς,
Ναυτεύς τε Πρυμνεύς τε καὶ Ἀγχίαλος καὶ Ἐρετμεύς,
Ποντεύς τε Πρωρεύς τε, Θόων Ἀναβησίνεώς τε
Ἀμφίαλός θ᾽, υἱὸς Πολυνήου Τεκτονίδαο·
ἂν δὲ καὶ Εὐρύαλος, βροτολοιγῷ ἶσος Ἄρηι,　115
Ναυβολίδης, ὃς ἄριστος ἔην εἶδός τε δέμας τε
πάντων Φαιήκων μετ᾽ ἀμύμονα Λαοδάμαντα.
ἂν δ᾽ ἔσταν τρεῖς παῖδες ἀμύμονος Ἀλκινόοιο,
Λαοδάμας θ᾽ Ἅλιός τε καὶ ἀντίθεος Κλυτόνηος.
οἱ δ᾽ ἦ τοι πρῶτον μὲν ἐπειρήσαντο πόδεσσι.　120
τοῖσι δ᾽ ἀπὸ νύσσης τέτατο δρόμος· οἱ δ᾽ ἅμα πάντες
καρπαλίμως ἐπέτοντο κονίοντες πεδίοιο·
τῶν δὲ θέειν ὄχ᾽ ἄριστος ἔην Κλυτόνηος ἀμύμων·
ὅσσον τ᾽ ἐν νειῷ οὖρον πέλει ἡμιόνοιιν,
τόσσον ὑπεκπροθέων λαοὺς ἵκεθ᾽, οἱ δ᾽ ἐλίποντο.　125
οἱ δὲ παλαιμοσύνης ἀλεγεινῆς πειρήσαντο·
τῇ δ᾽ αὖτ᾽ Εὐρύαλος ἀπεκαίνυτο πάντας ἀρίστους.
ἅλματι δ᾽ Ἀμφίαλος πάντων προφερέστατος ἦεν·
δίσκῳ δ᾽ αὖ πάντων πολὺ φέρτατος ἦεν Ἐλατρεύς,
πὺξ δ᾽ αὖ Λαοδάμας, ἀγαθὸς πάις Ἀλκινόοιο.　130
αὐτὰρ ἐπεὶ δὴ πάντες ἐτέρφθησαν φρέν᾽ ἀέθλοις,
τοῖς ἄρα Λαοδάμας μετέφη πάις Ἀλκινόοιο·

   "Δεῦτε, φίλοι, τὸν ξεῖνον ἐρώμεθα εἴ τιν᾽ ἄεθλον
οἶδέ τε καὶ δεδάηκε. φυήν γε μὲν οὐ κακός ἐστι,
μηρούς τε κνήμας τε καὶ ἄμφω χεῖρας ὕπερθεν　135
αὐχένα τε στιβαρὸν μέγα τε σθένος· οὐδέ τι ἥβης
δεύεται, ἀλλὰ κακοῖσι συνέρρηκται πολέεσσιν·

---

¹ This rendering of νύσσα is given by Agar (*Homerica*,
pp. 115 ff.). The word is generally taken to denote the
"scratch," not the turning-point, and the line is then
rendered: "The course was stretched (laid out) from the

great throng, past counting; and up rose many noble
youths. There rose Acroneüs, and Ocyalus, and Ela-
treus, and Nauteus, and Prymneus, and Anchialus,
and Eretmeus, and Ponteus, and Proreus, Thoon and
Anabesineüs, and Amphialus, son of Polyneüs, son of
Tecton; and up rose also Euryalus, the peer of man-
destroying Ares, the son of Naubolus, who in come-
liness and form was the best of all the Phaeacians
after peerless Laodamas; and up rose the three sons
of noble Alcinous, Laodamas, and Halius, and god-
like Clytoneüs. These then first made trial in the
foot-race: a course was marked out for them from
the turning point,[1] and they all sped swiftly, raising
the dust of the plain; but among them noble Clyto-
neüs was far the best at running, and by as far as is
the range[2] of a team of mules in fallow land, by so
far he shot to the front and reached the host, and
the others were left behind. Then they made trial
of toilsome wrestling, and here in turn Euryalus
excelled all the princes. And in leaping Amphialus
was best of all, and with the discus again far the
best of all was Elatreus, and in boxing Laodamas,
the good son of Alcinous. But when the hearts of
all had taken pleasure in the contests, Laodamas,
the son of Alcinous, spoke among them:

"Come, friends, let us ask yon stranger whether
he knows and has learned any contests. In build,
surely, he is no mean man, in thighs and calves, and
in his two arms above, his stout neck, and his great
might. In no wise does he lack aught of the
strength of youth, but he has been broken by many

starting-point," or "From the start their running was
strained to the utmost."
[2] The word probably denotes the length of the furrow cut
before a turn was made.

οὐ γὰρ ἐγώ γέ τί φημι κακώτερον ἄλλο θαλάσσης
ἄνδρα γε συγχεῦαι, εἰ καὶ μάλα καρτερὸς εἴη."
   Τὸν δ' αὖτ' Εὐρύαλος ἀπαμείβετο φώνησέν τε   1
" Λαοδάμα, μάλα τοῦτο ἔπος κατὰ μοῖραν ἔειπες.
αὐτὸς νῦν προκάλεσσαι ἰὼν καὶ πέφραδε μῦθον." [1]
   Αὐτὰρ ἐπεὶ τό γ' ἄκουσ' ἀγαθὸς πάις Ἀλκινόοιο,
στῆ ῥ' ἐς μέσσον ἰὼν καὶ Ὀδυσσῆα προσέειπε·
" Δεῦρ' ἄγε καὶ σύ, ξεῖνε πάτερ, πείρησαι ἀέθλων,   1
εἴ τινά που δεδάηκας· ἔοικε δέ σ' ἴδμεν ἀέθλους·
οὐ μὲν γὰρ μεῖζον κλέος ἀνέρος ὄφρα κ' ἔῃσιν,
ἢ ὅ τι ποσσίν τε ῥέξῃ καὶ χερσὶν ἑῇσιν.
ἀλλ' ἄγε πείρησαι, σκέδασον δ' ἀπὸ κήδεα θυμοῦ.
σοὶ δ' ὁδὸς οὐκέτι δηρὸν ἀπέσσεται, ἀλλά τοι ἤδη   1.
νηῦς τε κατείρυσται καὶ ἐπαρτέες εἰσὶν ἑταῖροι."
   Τὸν δ' ἀπαμειβόμενος προσέφη πολύμητις Ὀδυσσε[υ]
" Λαοδάμα, τί με ταῦτα κελεύετε κερτομέοντες;
κήδεά μοι καὶ μᾶλλον ἐνὶ φρεσὶν ἤ περ ἄεθλοι,
ὃς πρὶν μὲν μάλα πολλὰ πάθον καὶ πολλὰ μόγησα, 1.
νῦν δὲ μεθ' ὑμετέρῃ ἀγορῇ νόστοιο χατίζων
ἧμαι, λισσόμενος βασιλῆά τε πάντα τε δῆμον."
   Τὸν δ' αὖτ' Εὐρύαλος ἀπαμείβετο νείκεσέ τ' ἄντην·
" Οὐ γάρ σ' οὐδέ, ξεῖνε, δαήμονι φωτὶ ἐΐσκω
ἄθλων, οἷά τε πολλὰ μετ' ἀνθρώποισι πέλονται,   1[.]
ἀλλὰ τῷ, ὅς θ' ἅμα νηὶ πολυκληΐδι θαμίζων,
ἀρχὸς ναυτάων οἵ τε πρηκτῆρες ἔασιν,
φόρτου τε μνήμων καὶ ἐπίσκοπος ᾖσιν ὁδαίων
κερδέων θ' ἁρπαλέων· οὐδ' ἀθλητῆρι ἔοικας."

   [1] Line 142 was unknown to Alexandrian critics.

troubles. For to my mind there is naught worse than the sea to confound a man, be he never so strong."

And Euryalus in turn answered him, and said: "Laodamas, this word of thine is right fitly spoken. Go now thyself and challenge him, and make known thy word."

Now when the good son of Alcinous heard this he came and took his stand in the midst and spoke to Odysseus: "Come, Sir stranger, do thou, too, make trial of the contests, if thou knowest any; and it must be that thou knowest contests, for there is no greater glory for a man so long as he lives than that which he achieves by his own hands and his feet. Nay, come, make trial, and cast away care from thy heart. Thy journey shall no more be long delayed, nay, even now thy ship is launched and the crew is ready."

Then Odysseus of many wiles answered him, and said: "Laodamas, why do ye mock me with this challenge? Sorrow is in my mind far more than contests, seeing that in time past I have suffered much and toiled much, and now I sit in the midst of your assembly, longing for my return home, and making my prayer to the king and to all the people."

Then again Euryalus made answer and taunted him to his face: "Nay verily, stranger, for I do not liken thee to a man that is skilled in contests, such as abound among men, but to one who, faring to and fro with his benched ship, is a captain of sailors who are merchantmen, one who is mindful of his freight, and has charge of a home-borne cargo, and the gains of his greed. Thou dost not look like an athlete."

Τὸν δ' ἄρ' ὑπόδρα ἰδὼν προσέφη πολύμητις Ὀδυσσεὺ
" Ξεῖν', οὐ καλὸν ἔειπες· ἀτασθάλῳ ἀνδρὶ ἔοικας.   1
οὕτως οὐ πάντεσσι θεοὶ χαρίεντα διδοῦσιν
ἀνδράσιν, οὔτε φυὴν οὔτ' ἂρ φρένας οὔτ' ἀγορητύν.
ἄλλος μὲν γάρ τ' εἶδος ἀκιδνότερος πέλει ἀνήρ,
ἀλλὰ θεὸς μορφὴν ἔπεσι στέφει, οἱ δέ τ' ἐς αὐτὸν   1
τερπόμενοι λεύσσουσιν· ὁ δ' ἀσφαλέως ἀγορεύει
αἰδοῖ μειλιχίῃ, μετὰ δὲ πρέπει ἀγρομένοισιν,
ἐρχόμενον δ' ἀνὰ ἄστυ θεὸν ὣς εἰσορόωσιν.
ἄλλος δ' αὖ εἶδος μὲν ἀλίγκιος ἀθανάτοισιν,
ἀλλ' οὔ οἱ χάρις ἀμφιπεριστέφεται ἐπέεσσιν,   1
ὣς καὶ σοὶ εἶδος μὲν ἀριπρεπές, οὐδέ κεν ἄλλως
οὐδὲ θεὸς τεύξειε, νόον δ' ἀποφώλιός ἐσσι.
ὤρινάς μοι θυμὸν ἐνὶ στήθεσσι φίλοισιν
εἰπὼν οὐ κατὰ κόσμον. ἐγὼ δ' οὐ νῆις ἀέθλων,
ὡς σύ γε μυθεῖαι, ἀλλ' ἐν πρώτοισιν ὀίω   1
ἔμμεναι, ὄφρ' ἥβῃ τε πεποίθεα χερσί τ' ἐμῇσι.
νῦν δ' ἔχομαι κακότητι καὶ ἄλγεσι· πολλὰ γὰρ ἔτλην
ἀνδρῶν τε πτολέμους ἀλεγεινά τε κύματα πείρων.
ἀλλὰ καὶ ὥς, κακὰ πολλὰ παθών, πειρήσομ' ἀέθλων·
θυμοδακὴς γὰρ μῦθος, ἐπώτρυνας δέ με εἰπών."   1
Ἦ ῥα καὶ αὐτῷ φάρει ἀναΐξας λάβε δίσκον
μείζονα καὶ πάχετον, στιβαρώτερον οὐκ ὀλίγον περ
ἢ οἵῳ Φαίηκες ἐδίσκεον ἀλλήλοισι.
τόν ῥα περιστρέψας ἧκε στιβαρῆς ἀπὸ χειρός,
βόμβησεν δὲ λίθος· κατὰ δ' ἔπτηξαν ποτὶ γαίῃ   1

Then with an angry glance from beneath his brows Odysseus of many wiles answered him: "Stranger, thou hast not spoken well; thou art as one blind with folly. So true is it that the gods do not give gracious gifts to all alike, not form nor mind nor eloquence. For one man is inferior in comeliness, but the god sets a crown[1] of beauty upon his words, and men look upon him with delight, and he speaks on unfalteringly with sweet modesty, and is conspicuous among the gathered people, and as he goes through the city men gaze upon him as upon a god. Another again is in comeliness like the immortals, but no crown of grace is set about his words. So, in thy case, thy comeliness is preëminent, nor could a god himself mend it, but in mind thou art stunted. Thou hast stirred the spirit in my breast by speaking thus unmannerly. I am not unskilled in sports as thou pratest, nay, methinks I was among the first so long as I trusted in my youth and in my hands. But now I am bound by suffering and pains; for much have I endured in passing through wars of men and the grievous waves. But even so, though I have suffered much, I will make trial of the contests, for thy word has stung me to the heart, and thou hast provoked me with thy speech."

He spoke, and, leaping up with his cloak about him as it was, seized a discus larger than the rest and thick, no little heavier than those with which the Phaeacians were wont to contend one with another. This with a whirl he sent from his stout hand, and the stone hummed as it flew; and down they crouched to the earth, the Phaeacians of the

---

[1] στέφω does not of itself mean "crown," but the meaning here is fixed by vs. 175.

Φαίηκες δολιχήρετμοι, ναυσίκλυτοι ἄνδρες,
λαὸς ὑπὸ ῥιπῆς· ὁ δ' ὑπέρπτατο σήματα πάντων
ῥίμφα θέων ἀπὸ χειρός. ἔθηκε δὲ τέρματ' Ἀθήνη
ἀνδρὶ δέμας εἰκυῖα, ἔπος τ' ἔφατ' ἔκ τ' ὀνόμαζεν·

"Καί κ' ἀλαός τοι, ξεῖνε, διακρίνειε τὸ σῆμα   19
ἀμφαφόων, ἐπεὶ οὔ τι μεμιγμένον ἐστὶν ὁμίλῳ,
ἀλλὰ πολὺ πρῶτον. σὺ δὲ θάρσει τόνδε γ' ἄεθλον·
οὔ τις Φαιήκων τόδε γ' ἵξεται, οὐδ' ὑπερήσει."

Ὣς φάτο, γήθησεν δὲ πολύτλας δῖος Ὀδυσσεύς,
χαίρων, οὕνεχ' ἑταῖρον ἐνηέα λεῦσσ' ἐν ἀγῶνι.   20
καὶ τότε κουφότερον μετεφώνεε Φαιήκεσσιν·

"Τοῦτον νῦν ἀφίκεσθε, νέοι. τάχα δ' ὕστερον ἄλλον
ἥσειν ἢ τοσσοῦτον ὀΐομαι ἢ ἔτι μᾶσσον.
τῶν δ' ἄλλων ὅτινα κραδίη θυμός τε κελεύει,
δεῦρ' ἄγε πειρηθήτω, ἐπεί μ' ἐχολώσατε λίην,   20
ἢ πὺξ ἠὲ πάλῃ ἢ καὶ ποσίν, οὔ τι μεγαίρω,
πάντων Φαιήκων, πλήν γ' αὐτοῦ Λαοδάμαντος.
ξεῖνος γάρ μοι ὅδ' ἐστί· τίς ἂν φιλέοντι μάχοιτο;
ἄφρων δὴ κεῖνός γε καὶ οὐτιδανὸς πέλει ἀνήρ,
ὅς τις ξεινοδόκῳ ἔριδα προφέρηται ἀέθλων   2?
δήμῳ ἐν ἀλλοδαπῷ· ἕο δ' αὐτοῦ πάντα κολούει.
τῶν δ' ἄλλων οὔ πέρ τιν' ἀναίνομαι οὐδ' ἀθερίζω,
ἀλλ' ἐθέλω ἴδμεν καὶ πειρηθήμεναι ἄντην.
πάντα γὰρ οὐ κακός εἰμι, μετ' ἀνδράσιν ὅσσοι ἄεθλοι·
εὖ μὲν τόξον οἶδα ἐΰξοον ἀμφαφάασθαι·   2?
πρῶτός κ' ἄνδρα βάλοιμι ὀϊστεύσας ἐν ὁμίλῳ
ἀνδρῶν δυσμενέων, εἰ καὶ μάλα πολλοὶ ἑταῖροι
ἄγχι παρασταῖεν καὶ τοξαζοίατο φωτῶν.

long oars, men famed for their ships, beneath the rush of the stone. Past the marks of all it flew, speeding lightly from his hand, and Athene, in the likeness of a man, set the mark, and she spoke and addressed him:

"Even a blind man, stranger, could distinguish this mark, groping for it with his hands, for it is in no wise confused with the throng of the others, but is far the first. Be thou of good cheer for this bout at least: no one of the Phaeacians will reach this, or cast beyond it."

So she spoke, and the much-enduring goodly Odysseus was glad, rejoicing that he saw a true friend in the lists. Then with a lighter heart he spoke among the Phaeacians:

"Reach this now, young men; and presently, methinks, I will send another after it, as far or even further. Of the rest, if any man's heart and spirit bid him, let him come hither and make trial—for ye have greatly angered me—be it in boxing or in wrestling, aye, or in running, I care not; let any one come of all the Phaeacians, save Laodamas alone. For he is my host, and who would quarrel with one that entertains him? Foolish is that man and worthless, who challenges to a contest the host who receives him in a strange land; he does but mar his own fortunes. But of all the rest I refuse none, and make light of none, but am fain to know them, and make trial of them man to man. For in all things I am no weakling, even in all the contests that are practised among men. Well do I know how to handle the polished bow, and ever would I be the first to shoot and smite my man in the throng of the foe, even though many comrades stood by me and

οἷος δή με Φιλοκτήτης ἀπεκαίνυτο τόξῳ
δήμῳ ἔνι Τρώων, ὅτε τοξαζοίμεθ᾽ Ἀχαιοί.   2
τῶν δ᾽ ἄλλων ἐμέ φημι πολὺ προφερέστερον εἶναι,
ὅσσοι νῦν βροτοί εἰσιν ἐπὶ χθονὶ σῖτον ἔδοντες.
ἀνδράσι δὲ προτέροισιν ἐριζέμεν οὐκ ἐθελήσω,
οὔθ᾽ Ἡρακλῆι οὔτ᾽ Εὐρύτῳ Οἰχαλιῆι,
οἵ ῥα καὶ ἀθανάτοισιν ἐρίζεσκον περὶ τόξων.   2
τῷ ῥα καὶ αἶψ᾽ ἔθανεν μέγας Εὔρυτος, οὐδ᾽ ἐπὶ γῆρας
ἵκετ᾽ ἐνὶ μεγάροισι· χολωσάμενος γὰρ Ἀπόλλων
ἔκτανεν, οὕνεκά μιν προκαλίζετο τοξάζεσθαι.
δουρὶ δ᾽ ἀκοντίζω ὅσον οὐκ ἄλλος τις ὀιστῷ.
οἴοισιν δείδοικα ποσὶν μή τίς με παρέλθῃ   2
Φαιήκων· λίην γὰρ ἀεικελίως ἐδαμάσθην
κύμασιν ἐν πολλοῖς, ἐπεὶ οὐ κομιδὴ κατὰ νῆα
ἦεν ἐπηετανός· τῷ μοι φίλα γυῖα λέλυνται."
Ὣς ἔφαθ᾽, οἱ δ᾽ ἄρα πάντες ἀκὴν ἐγένοντο σιωπῇ.
Ἀλκίνοος δέ μιν οἶος ἀμειβόμενος προσέειπεν·   2
"Ξεῖν᾽, ἐπεὶ οὐκ ἀχάριστα μεθ᾽ ἡμῖν ταῦτ᾽ ἀγορεύεις,
ἀλλ᾽ ἐθέλεις ἀρετὴν σὴν φαινέμεν, ἥ τοι ὀπηδεῖ,
χωόμενος ὅτι σ᾽ οὗτος ἀνὴρ ἐν ἀγῶνι παραστὰς
νείκεσεν, ὡς ἂν σὴν ἀρετὴν βροτὸς οὔ τις ὄνοιτο,
ὅς τις ἐπίσταιτο ᾗσι φρεσὶν ἄρτια βάζειν·   2
ἀλλ᾽ ἄγε νῦν ἐμέθεν ξυνίει ἔπος, ὄφρα καὶ ἄλλῳ
εἴπῃς ἡρώων, ὅτε κεν σοῖς ἐν μεγάροισι
δαινύῃ παρὰ σῇ τ᾽ ἀλόχῳ καὶ σοῖσι τέκεσσιν,
ἡμετέρης ἀρετῆς μεμνημένος, οἷα καὶ ἡμῖν
Ζεὺς ἐπὶ ἔργα τίθησι διαμπερὲς ἐξ ἔτι πατρῶν.   2
οὐ γὰρ πυγμάχοι εἰμὲν ἀμύμονες οὐδὲ παλαισταί,
ἀλλὰ ποσὶ κραιπνῶς θέομεν καὶ νηυσὶν ἄριστοι,
αἰεὶ δ᾽ ἡμῖν δαίς τε φίλη κίθαρίς τε χοροί τε
εἵματά τ᾽ ἐξημοιβὰ λοετρά τε θερμὰ καὶ εὐναί.

were shooting at the men. Only Philoctetes excelled me with the bow in the land of the Trojans, when we Achaeans shot. But of all others I declare that I am best by far, of all mortals that are now upon the earth and eat bread. Yet with men of former days I will not seek to vie, with Heracles or with Eurytus of Oechalia, who strove even with the immortals in archery. Wherefore great Eurytus died soon, nor did old age come upon him in his halls, for Apollo waxed wroth and slew him, because he had challenged him to a contest with the bow. And with the spear I throw farther than any other man can shoot with an arrow. In the foot race alone I fear that someone of the Phaeacians may outstrip me, for cruelly have I been broken amid the many waves, since there was in my ship no lasting store of provisions; therefore my limbs are loosened."

So he spoke and they were all hushed in silence; but Alcinous alone answered him and said:

"Stranger, since not ungraciously dost thou speak thus in our midst, but art minded to shew forth the prowess which waits upon thee, in anger that yonder man came up to thee in the lists and taunted thee in a way in which no mortal would make light of thy prowess, who knew in his heart how to speak fitly; come, now, hearken to my words, that thou mayest tell to another hero, when in thy halls thou art feasting with thy wife and children, and rememberest our skill, what feats Zeus has vouchsafed to us from our fathers' days even until now. For we are not faultless boxers or wrestlers, but in the foot race we run swiftly, and we are the best seamen; and ever to us is the banquet dear, and the lyre, and the dance, and changes of raiment, and warm baths, and the couch.

ἀλλ' ἄγε, Φαιήκων βητάρμονες ὅσσοι ἄριστοι,　　25⟨
παίσατε, ὥς χ' ὁ ξεῖνος ἐνίσπῃ οἷσι φίλοισιν
οἴκαδε νοστήσας, ὅσσον περιγιγνόμεθ' ἄλλων
ναυτιλίῃ καὶ ποσσὶ καὶ ὀρχηστυῖ καὶ ἀοιδῇ.
Δημοδόκῳ δέ τις αἶψα κιὼν φόρμιγγα λίγειαν
οἰσέτω, ἥ που κεῖται ἐν ἡμετέροισι δόμοισιν."　　25⟨

῝Ως ἔφατ' Ἀλκίνοος θεοείκελος, ὦρτο δὲ κῆρυξ
οἴσων φόρμιγγα γλαφυρὴν δόμου ἐκ βασιλῆος.
αἰσυμνῆται δὲ κριτοὶ ἐννέα πάντες ἀνέσταν
δήμιοι, οἳ κατ' ἀγῶνας ἐῢ πρήσσεσκον ἕκαστα,
λείηναν δὲ χορόν, καλὸν δ' εὔρυναν ἀγῶνα.　　26⟨
κῆρυξ δ' ἐγγύθεν ἦλθε φέρων φόρμιγγα λίγειαν
Δημοδόκῳ· ὁ δ' ἔπειτα κί' ἐς μέσον· ἀμφὶ δὲ κοῦροι
πρωθῆβαι ἵσταντο, δαήμονες ὀρχηθμοῖο,
πέπληγον δὲ χορὸν θεῖον ποσίν. αὐτὰρ Ὀδυσσεὺς
μαρμαρυγὰς θηεῖτο ποδῶν, θαύμαζε δὲ θυμῷ.　　26⟨

Αὐτὰρ [1] ὁ φορμίζων ἀνεβάλλετο καλὸν ἀείδειν
ἀμφ' Ἄρεος φιλότητος εὐστεφάνου τ' Ἀφροδίτης,
ὡς τὰ πρῶτα μίγησαν ἐν Ἡφαίστοιο δόμοισι
λάθρῃ, πολλὰ δ' ἔδωκε, λέχος δ' ᾔσχυνε καὶ εὐνὴν
Ἡφαίστοιο ἄνακτος. ἄφαρ δέ οἱ ἄγγελος ἦλθεν　　27⟨
Ἥλιος, ὅ σφ' ἐνόησε μιγαζομένους φιλότητι.
Ἥφαιστος δ' ὡς οὖν θυμαλγέα μῦθον ἄκουσε,
βῆ ῥ' ἴμεν ἐς χαλκεῶνα κακὰ φρεσὶ βυσσοδομεύων,
ἐν δ' ἔθετ' ἀκμοθέτῳ μέγαν ἄκμονα, κόπτε δὲ δεσμοὺς
ἀρρήκτους ἀλύτους, ὄφρ' ἔμπεδον αὖθι μένοιεν.　　27⟨
αὐτὰρ ἐπεὶ δὴ τεῦξε δόλον κεχολωμένος Ἄρει,

---

[1] The whole passage 266–369 (or 267–366) was on moral
grounds rejected by some ancient critics.

But come now, all ye that are the best dancers of
the Phaeacians, make sport, that the stranger may
tell his friends on reaching home how far we surpass
others in seamanship and in fleetness of foot, and
in the dance and in song. And let one go straight-
way and fetch for Demodocus the clear-toned lyre
which lies somewhere in our halls."

So spoke Alcinous the godlike, and the herald
rose to fetch the hollow lyre from the palace of the
king. Then stood up masters of the lists, nine in all,
men chosen from out the people, who in their gather-
ings were wont to order all things aright. They
levelled a place for the dance, and marked out a fair
wide ring, and the herald came near, bearing the
clear-toned lyre for Demodocus. He then moved
into the midst, and around him stood boys in the
first bloom of youth, well skilled in the dance, and
they smote the goodly dancing floor with their feet.
And Odysseus gazed at the twinklings of their feet
and marvelled in spirit.

But the minstrel struck the chords in prelude to his
sweet lay and sang of the love of Ares and Aphrodite
of the fair crown, how first they lay together in the
house of Hephaestus secretly; and Ares gave her
many gifts, and shamed the bed of the lord Hephaes-
tus. But straightway one came to him with tidings,
even Helius, who had marked them as they lay
together in love. And when Hephaestus heard the
grievous tale, he went his way to his smithy, ponder-
ing evil in the deep of his heart, and set on the
anvil block the great anvil and forged bonds which
might not be broken or loosed, that the lovers[1]
might bide fast where they were. But when he had
fashioned the snare in his wrath against Ares, he

---

[1] Or the subject of μένοιεν may be the bonds.

βῆ ῥ' ἴμεν ἐς θάλαμον, ὅθι οἱ φίλα δέμνι' ἔκειτο,
ἀμφὶ δ' ἄρ' ἑρμῖσιν χέε δέσματα κύκλῳ ἁπάντῃ·
πολλὰ δὲ καὶ καθύπερθε μελαθρόφιν ἐξεκέχυντο,
ἠΰτ' ἀράχνια λεπτά, τά γ' οὔ κέ τις οὐδὲ ἴδοιτο,   28
οὐδὲ θεῶν μακάρων· πέρι γὰρ δολόεντα τέτυκτο.
αὐτὰρ ἐπεὶ δὴ πάντα δόλον πέρι δέμνια χεῦεν,
εἴσατ' ἴμεν ἐς Λῆμνον, ἐϋκτίμενον πτολίεθρον,
ἥ οἱ γαιάων πολὺ φιλτάτη ἐστὶν ἁπασέων.
οὐδ' ἀλαοσκοπιὴν εἶχε χρυσήνιος Ἄρης,   2
ὡς ἴδεν Ἥφαιστον κλυτοτέχνην νόσφι κιόντα·
βῆ δ' ἰέναι πρὸς δῶμα περικλυτοῦ Ἡφαίστοιο
ἰσχανόων φιλότητος ἐϋστεφάνου Κυθερείης.
ἡ δὲ νέον παρὰ πατρὸς ἐρισθενέος Κρονίωνος
ἐρχομένη κατ' ἄρ' ἕζεθ'· ὁ δ' εἴσω δώματος ᾔει,   2
ἔν τ' ἄρα οἱ φῦ χειρί, ἔπος τ' ἔφατ' ἔκ τ' ὀνόμαζε·

  " Δεῦρο, φίλη, λέκτρονδε τραπείομεν εὐνηθέντες·
οὐ γὰρ ἔθ' Ἥφαιστος μεταδήμιος, ἀλλά που ἤδη
οἴχεται ἐς Λῆμνον μετὰ Σίντιας ἀγριοφώνους."

  Ὣς φάτο, τῇ δ' ἀσπαστὸν ἐείσατο κοιμηθῆναι.   2
τὼ δ' ἐς δέμνια βάντε κατέδραθον· ἀμφὶ δὲ δεσμοὶ
τεχνήεντες ἔχυντο πολύφρονος Ἡφαίστοιο,
οὐδέ τι κινῆσαι μελέων ἦν οὐδ' ἀναεῖραι.
καὶ τότε δὴ γίγνωσκον, ὅ τ' οὐκέτι φυκτὰ πέλοντο.
ἀγχίμολον δέ σφ' ἦλθε περικλυτὸς ἀμφιγυήεις,   3
αὖτις ὑποστρέψας πρὶν Λήμνου γαῖαν ἱκέσθαι·
Ἥέλιος γάρ οἱ σκοπιὴν ἔχεν εἶπέ τε μῦθον.
βῆ δ' ἴμεναι πρὸς δῶμα φίλον τετιημένος ἦτορ·[1]

---

[1] Line 303 is omitted in most MSS.; *cf.* ii. 298.

went to his chamber where lay his bed, and everywhere round about the bed-posts he spread the bonds, and many too were hung from above, from the roof-beams, fine as spiders' webs, so that no one even of the blessed gods could see them, so exceeding craftily were they fashioned. But when he had spread all his snare about the couch, he made as though he would go to Lemnos, that well-built citadel, which is in his eyes far the dearest of all lands. And no blind watch did Ares of the golden rein keep, when he saw Hephaestus, famed for his handicraft, departing, but he went his way to the house of famous Hephaestus, eager for the love of Cytherea of the fair crown. Now she had but newly come from the presence of her father, the mighty son of Cronos, and had sat her down. And Ares came into the house and clasped her hand and spoke and addressed her:

"Come, love, let us to bed and take our joy, couched together. For Hephaestus is no longer here in the land, but has now gone, I ween, to Lemnos, to visit the Sintians of savage speech."

So he spoke, and a welcome thing it seemed to her to lie with him. So they two went to the couch, and lay them down to sleep, and about them clung the cunning bonds of the wise Hephaestus, nor could they in any wise stir their limbs or raise them up. Then at length they learned that there was no more escaping. And near to them came the famous god of the two strong arms,[1] having turned back before he reached the land of Lemnos; for Helius had kept watch for him and had brought him word. So he went to his house with a heavy heart, and stood at

---

[1] Others render "lame in both limbs."

ἔστη δ' ἐν προθύροισι, χόλος δέ μιν ἄγριος ᾕρει·
σμερδαλέον δ' ἐβόησε, γέγωνέ τε πᾶσι θεοῖσιν·   30

  "Ζεῦ πάτερ ἠδ' ἄλλοι μάκαρες θεοὶ αἰὲν ἐόντες,
δεῦθ', ἵνα ἔργα γελαστὰ καὶ οὐκ ἐπιεικτὰ ἴδησθε,
ὡς ἐμὲ χωλὸν ἐόντα Διὸς θυγάτηρ Ἀφροδίτη
αἰὲν ἀτιμάζει, φιλέει δ' ἀίδηλον Ἄρηα,
οὕνεχ' ὁ μὲν καλός τε καὶ ἀρτίπος, αὐτὰρ ἐγώ γε   31
ἠπεδανὸς γενόμην. ἀτὰρ οὔ τί μοι αἴτιος ἄλλος,
ἀλλὰ τοκῆε δύω, τὼ μὴ γείνασθαι ὄφελλον.
ἀλλ' ὄψεσθ', ἵνα τώ γε καθεύδετον ἐν φιλότητι
εἰς ἐμὰ δέμνια βάντες, ἐγὼ δ' ὁρόων ἀκάχημαι.
οὐ μέν σφεας ἔτ' ἔολπα μίνυνθά γε κείεμεν οὕτως   31
καὶ μάλα περ φιλέοντε· τάχ' οὐκ ἐθελήσετον ἄμφω
εὕδειν· ἀλλά σφωε δόλος καὶ δεσμὸς ἐρύξει,
εἰς ὅ κέ μοι μάλα πάντα πατὴρ ἀποδῷσιν ἔεδνα,
ὅσσα οἱ ἐγγυάλιξα κυνώπιδος εἵνεκα κούρης,
οὕνεκά οἱ καλὴ θυγάτηρ, ἀτὰρ οὐκ ἐχέθυμος."   32

  Ὣς ἔφαθ', οἱ δ' ἀγέροντο θεοὶ ποτὶ χαλκοβατὲς δῶ·
ἦλθε Ποσειδάων γαιήοχος, ἦλθ' ἐριούνης
Ἑρμείας, ἦλθεν δὲ ἄναξ ἑκάεργος Ἀπόλλων.
θηλύτεραι δὲ θεαὶ μένον αἰδοῖ οἴκοι ἑκάστη.
ἔσταν δ' ἐν προθύροισι θεοί, δωτῆρες ἐάων·   32
ἄσβεστος δ' ἄρ' ἐνῶρτο γέλως μακάρεσσι θεοῖσι
τέχνας εἰσορόωσι πολύφρονος Ἡφαίστοιο.
ὧδε δέ τις εἴπεσκεν ἰδὼν ἐς πλησίον ἄλλον·

  "Οὐκ ἀρετᾷ κακὰ ἔργα· κιχάνει τοι βραδὺς ὠκύν,
ὡς καὶ νῦν Ἥφαιστος ἐὼν βραδὺς εἷλεν Ἄρηα   33

the gateway, and fierce anger seized him. And terribly he cried out and called to all the gods:

"Father Zeus, and ye other blessed gods that are forever, come hither that ye may see a laughable matter and a monstrous,[1] even how Aphrodite, daughter of Zeus, scorns me for that I am lame and loves destructive Ares because he is comely and strong of limb, whereas I was born misshapen. Yet for this is none other to blame but my two parents—would they had never begotten me! But ye shall see where these two have gone up into my bed and sleep together in love; and I am troubled at the sight. Yet, methinks, they will not wish to lie longer thus, no, not for a moment, how loving soever they are. Soon shall both lose their desire to sleep; but the snare and the bonds shall hold them until her father pays back to me all the gifts of wooing that I gave him for the sake of his shameless girl; for his daughter is fair but bridles not her passion."[2]

So he spoke and the gods gathered to the house of the brazen floor.[3] Poseidon came, the earth-enfolder, and the helper Hermes came, and the lord Apollo, the archer god.[4] Now the goddesses abode for shame each in her own house, but the gods, the givers of good things, stood in the gateway; and unquenchable laughter arose among the blessed gods as they saw the craft of wise Hephaestus. And thus would one speak, with a glance at his neighbour:

"Ill deeds thrive not. The slow catches the swift; even as now Hephaestus, slow though he is, has out-

---

[1] Lit. "hard," "unyielding."
[2] Others render simply, "lacking in discretion."
[3] Or, "with threshold of brass."
[4] Or, possibly, "the averter of ills." The word means literally, "he who works afar."

ὠκύτατόν περ ἐόντα θεῶν οἳ Ὄλυμπον ἔχουσιν,
χωλὸς ἐὼν τέχνῃσι· τὸ καὶ μοιχάγρι᾽ ὀφέλλει."
    Ὣς οἱ μὲν τοιαῦτα πρὸς ἀλλήλους ἀγόρευον·
Ἑρμῆν δὲ προσέειπεν ἄναξ Διὸς υἱὸς Ἀπόλλων·
    "Ἑρμεία, Διὸς υἱέ, διάκτορε, δῶτορ ἐάων,   3
ἦ ῥά κεν ἐν δεσμοῖς ἐθέλοις κρατεροῖσι πιεσθεὶς
εὕδειν ἐν λέκτροισι παρὰ χρυσέῃ Ἀφροδίτῃ;"
    Τὸν δ᾽ ἠμείβετ᾽ ἔπειτα διάκτορος ἀργεϊφόντης·
"Αἲ γὰρ τοῦτο γένοιτο, ἄναξ ἑκατηβόλ᾽ Ἄπολλον·
δεσμοὶ μὲν τρὶς τόσσοι ἀπείρονες ἀμφὶς ἔχοιεν,   3
ὑμεῖς δ᾽ εἰσορόῳτε θεοὶ πᾶσαί τε θέαιναι,
αὐτὰρ ἐγὼν εὕδοιμι παρὰ χρυσέῃ Ἀφροδίτῃ."
    Ὣς ἔφατ᾽, ἐν δὲ γέλως ὦρτ᾽ ἀθανάτοισι θεοῖσιν.
οὐδὲ Ποσειδάωνα γέλως ἔχε, λίσσετο δ᾽ αἰεὶ
Ἥφαιστον κλυτοεργὸν ὅπως λύσειεν Ἄρηα.   3
καί μιν φωνήσας ἔπεα πτερόεντα προσηύδα·
    "Λῦσον· ἐγὼ δέ τοι αὐτὸν ὑπίσχομαι, ὡς σὺ κελεύει
τίσειν αἴσιμα πάντα μετ᾽ ἀθανάτοισι θεοῖσιν."
    Τὸν δ᾽ αὖτε προσέειπε περικλυτὸς ἀμφιγυήεις·
"Μή με, Ποσείδαον γαιήοχε, ταῦτα κέλευε·   3
δειλαί τοι δειλῶν γε καὶ ἐγγύαι ἐγγυάασθαι.
πῶς ἂν ἐγώ σε δέοιμι μετ᾽ ἀθανάτοισι θεοῖσιν,
εἴ κεν Ἄρης οἴχοιτο χρέος καὶ δεσμὸν ἀλύξας;"
    Τὸν δ᾽ αὖτε προσέειπε Ποσειδάων ἐνοσίχθων·
"Ἥφαιστ᾽, εἴ περ γάρ κεν Ἄρης χρεῖος ὑπαλύξας   3
οἴχηται φεύγων, αὐτός τοι ἐγὼ τάδε τίσω."
    Τὸν δ᾽ ἠμείβετ᾽ ἔπειτα περικλυτὸς ἀμφιγυήεις·
"Οὐκ ἔστ᾽ οὐδὲ ἔοικε τεὸν ἔπος ἀρνήσασθαι."

stripped Ares for all that he is the swiftest of the gods who hold Olympus. Lame though he is, he has caught him by craft, wherefore Ares owes the fine of the adulterer."

Thus they spoke to one another. But to Hermes the lord Apollo, son of Zeus, said:

"Hermes, son of Zeus, messenger, giver of good things, wouldst thou in sooth be willing, even though ensnared with strong bonds, to lie on a couch by the side of golden Aphrodite?"

Then the messenger, Argeïphontes, answered him: "Would that this might befall, lord Apollo, thou archer god—that thrice as many bonds inextricable might clasp me about and ye gods, aye, and all the goddesses too might be looking on, but that I might sleep by the side of golden Aphrodite."

So he spoke and laughter arose among the immortal gods. Yet Poseidon laughed not, but ever besought Hephaestus, the famous craftsman, to set Ares free; and he spoke, and addressed him with winged words:

"Loose him, and I promise, as thou biddest me, that he shall himself pay thee all that is right in the presence of the immortal gods."

Then the famous god of the two strong arms answered him: "Ask not this of me, Poseidon, thou earth-enfolder. A sorry thing to be sure of is the surety for a sorry knave. How could I put thee in bonds among the immortal gods, if Ares should avoid both the debt and the bonds and depart?"

Then again Poseidon, the earth-shaker, answered him: "Hephaestus, even if Ares shall avoid the debt and flee away, I will myself pay thee this."

Then the famous god of the two strong arms answered him: "It may not be that I should say thee nay, nor were it seemly."

Ὣς εἰπὼν δεσμὸν ἀνίει μένος Ἡφαίστοιο.
τὼ δ' ἐπεὶ ἐκ δεσμοῖο λύθεν, κρατεροῦ περ ἐόντος,   3[
αὐτίκ' ἀναΐξαντε ὁ μὲν Θρήκηνδε βεβήκει,
ἡ δ' ἄρα Κύπρον ἵκανε φιλομμειδὴς Ἀφροδίτη,
ἐς Πάφον· ἔνθα δέ οἱ τέμενος βωμός τε θυήεις.
ἔνθα δέ μιν Χάριτες λοῦσαν καὶ χρῖσαν ἐλαίῳ
ἀμβρότῳ, οἷα θεοὺς ἐπενήνοθεν αἰὲν ἐόντας,   3[
ἀμφὶ δὲ εἵματα ἕσσαν ἐπήρατα, θαῦμα ἰδέσθαι.

Ταῦτ' ἄρ' ἀοιδὸς ἄειδε περικλυτός· αὐτὰρ Ὀδυσσεὺς
τέρπετ' ἐνὶ φρεσὶν ᾗσιν ἀκούων ἠδὲ καὶ ἄλλοι
Φαίηκες δολιχήρετμοι, ναυσίκλυτοι ἄνδρες.

Ἀλκίνοος δ' Ἅλιον καὶ Λαοδάμαντα κέλευσεν   3'
μουνὰξ ὀρχήσασθαι, ἐπεί σφισιν οὔ τις ἔριζεν.
οἱ δ' ἐπεὶ οὖν σφαῖραν καλὴν μετὰ χερσὶν ἕλοντο,
πορφυρέην, τήν σφιν Πόλυβος ποίησε δαΐφρων,
τὴν ἕτερος ῥίπτασκε ποτὶ νέφεα σκιόεντα
ἰδνωθεὶς ὀπίσω, ὁ δ' ἀπὸ χθονὸς ὑψόσ' ἀερθεὶς   3
ῥηιδίως μεθέλεσκε, πάρος ποσὶν οὖδας ἱκέσθαι.
αὐτὰρ ἐπεὶ δὴ σφαίρῃ ἀν' ἰθὺν πειρήσαντο,
ὠρχείσθην δὴ ἔπειτα ποτὶ χθονὶ πουλυβοτείρῃ
ταρφέ' ἀμειβομένω· κοῦροι δ' ἐπελήκεον ἄλλοι
ἑσταότες κατ' ἀγῶνα, πολὺς δ' ὑπὸ κόμπος ὀρώρει. 3

Δὴ τότ' ἄρ' Ἀλκίνοον προσεφώνεε δῖος Ὀδυσσεύς·
" Ἀλκίνοε κρεῖον, πάντων ἀριδείκετε λαῶν,
ἠμὲν ἀπείλησας βητάρμονας εἶναι ἀρίστους,
ἠδ' ἄρ' ἑτοῖμα τέτυκτο· σέβας μ' ἔχει εἰσορόωντα."

Ὣς φάτο, γήθησεν δ' ἱερὸν μένος Ἀλκινόοιο,   3[
αἶψα δὲ Φαιήκεσσι φιληρέτμοισι μετηύδα·

So saying the mighty Hephaestus loosed the bonds and the two, when they were freed from that bond so strong, sprang up straightway. And Ares departed to Thrace, but she, the laughter-loving Aphrodite, went to Cyprus, to Paphos, where is her demesne and fragrant altar. There the Graces bathed her and anointed her with immortal oil, such as gleams [1] upon the gods that are forever. And they clothed her in lovely raiment, a wonder to behold.

This song the famous minstrel sang; and Odysseus was glad at heart as he listened, and so too were the Phaeacians of the long oars, men famed for their ships.

Then Alcinous bade Halius and Laodamas dance alone, for no one could vie with them. And when they had taken in their hands the beautiful ball of purple, which wise Polybus had made for them, the one would lean backward and toss it toward the shadowy clouds, and the other would leap up from the earth and skilfully catch it before his feet touched the ground again. But when they had tried their skill in throwing the ball straight up, the two fell to dancing on the bounteous earth, ever tossing the ball to and fro, and the other youths stood in the lists and beat time, and thereat a great din arose.

Then to Alcinous spoke goodly Odysseus: "Lord Alcinous, renowned above all men,[2] thou didst boast that thy dancers were the best, and lo, thy words are made good; amazement holds me as I look on them."

So he spoke, and the strong and mighty Alcinous was glad; and straightway he spoke among the Phaeacians, lovers of the oar:

[1] Or, simply, "decks," "covers."
[2] Or, "above all the people."

HOMER

" Κέκλυτε, Φαιήκων ἡγήτορες ἠδὲ μέδοντες.
ὁ ξεῖνος μάλα μοι δοκέει πεπνυμένος εἶναι.
ἀλλ' ἄγε οἱ δῶμεν ξεινήιον, ὡς ἐπιεικές.
δώδεκα γὰρ κατὰ δῆμον ἀριπρεπέες βασιλῆες   3?
ἀρχοὶ κραίνουσι, τρισκαιδέκατος δ' ἐγὼ αὐτός·
τῶν οἱ ἕκαστος φᾶρος ἐυπλυνὲς ἠδὲ χιτῶνα
καὶ χρυσοῖο τάλαντον ἐνείκατε τιμήεντος.
αἶψα δὲ πάντα φέρωμεν ἀολλέα, ὄφρ' ἐνὶ χερσὶν
ξεῖνος ἔχων ἐπὶ δόρπον ἴῃ χαίρων ἐνὶ θυμῷ.   3?
Εὐρύαλος δέ ἑ αὐτὸν ἀρεσσάσθω ἐπέεσσι
καὶ δώρῳ, ἐπεὶ οὔ τι ἔπος κατὰ μοῖραν ἔειπεν."

    Ὣς ἔφαθ', οἱ δ' ἄρα πάντες ἐπήνεον ἠδ' ἐκέλευον,
δῶρα δ' ἄρ' οἰσέμεναι πρόεσαν κήρυκα ἕκαστος.
τὸν δ' αὖτ' Εὐρύαλος ἀπαμείβετο φώνησέν τε·   4?

    " Ἀλκίνοε κρεῖον, πάντων ἀριδείκετε λαῶν,
τοιγὰρ ἐγὼ τὸν ξεῖνον ἀρέσσομαι, ὡς σὺ κελεύεις.
δώσω οἱ τόδ' ἄορ παγχάλκεον, ᾧ ἔπι κώπη
ἀργυρέη, κολεὸν δὲ νεοπρίστου ἐλέφαντος
ἀμφιδεδίνηται· πολέος δέ οἱ ἄξιον ἔσται."   4?

    Ὣς εἰπὼν ἐν χερσὶ τίθει ξίφος ἀργυρόηλον
καί μιν φωνήσας ἔπεα πτερόεντα προσηύδα·
" Χαῖρε, πάτερ ὦ ξεῖνε· ἔπος δ' εἴ πέρ τι βέβακται
δεινόν, ἄφαρ τὸ φέροιεν ἀναρπάξασαι ἄελλαι.
σοὶ δὲ θεοὶ ἄλοχόν τ' ἰδέειν καὶ πατρίδ' ἱκέσθαι   4?
δοῖεν, ἐπεὶ δὴ δηθὰ φίλων ἄπο πήματα πάσχεις."

    Τὸν δ' ἀπαμειβόμενος προσέφη πολύμητις Ὀδυσσε?
" Καὶ σὺ φίλος μάλα χαῖρε, θεοὶ δέ τοι ὄλβια δοῖεν.

" Hear me, leaders and counsellors of the Phaeacians. This stranger verily seems to me a man of understanding. Come then, let us give him a gift of friendship, as is fitting; for twelve glorious kings bear sway in our land as rulers, and I myself am the thirteenth. Now do you, each of the twelve, bring a newly washed cloak and tunic, and a talent of precious gold, and let us straightway bring all together, that the stranger with our gifts in his hands may go to his supper glad at heart. And let Euryalus make amends to the stranger himself with words and with a gift, for the word that he spoke was in no wise seemly."

So he spoke, and they all praised his words and bade that so it should be, and sent forth every man a herald to fetch the gifts. And Euryalus in turn made answer, and said:

" Lord Alcinous, renowned above all men, I will indeed make amends to the stranger, as thou biddest me. I will give him this sword, all of bronze, whereon is a hilt of silver, and a scabbard of new-sawn ivory is wrought about it; and it shall be to him a thing of great worth."

So saying, he put into his hands the silver-studded sword, and spoke, and addressed him with winged words: " Hail, Sir stranger; but if any word has been spoken that was harsh, may the storm-winds straightway snatch it and bear it away. And for thyself, may the gods grant thee to see thy wife, and to come to thy native land, for long time hast thou been suffering woes far from thy friends."

And Odysseus of many wiles answered him : " All hail to thee, too, friend; and may the gods grant

μηδέ τί τοι ξίφεός γε ποθὴ μετόπισθε γένοιτο
τούτου, ὃ δή μοι δῶκας ἀρεσσάμενος ἐπέεσσιν." 4**0**

Ἦ ῥα καὶ ἀμφ' ὤμοισι θέτο ξίφος ἀργυρόηλον.
δύσετό τ' ἠέλιος, καὶ τῷ κλυτὰ δῶρα παρῆεν.
καὶ τά γ' ἐς Ἀλκινόοιο φέρον κήρυκες ἀγανοί·
δεξάμενοι δ' ἄρα παῖδες ἀμύμονος Ἀλκινόοιο
μητρὶ παρ' αἰδοίη ἔθεσαν περικαλλέα δῶρα. 4**2**0
τοῖσιν δ' ἡγεμόνευ' ἱερὸν μένος Ἀλκινόοιο,
ἐλθόντες δὲ καθῖζον ἐν ὑψηλοῖσι θρόνοισι.
δή ῥα τότ' Ἀρήτην προσέφη μένος Ἀλκινόοιο·

" Δεῦρο, γύναι, φέρε χηλὸν ἀριπρεπέ', ἥ τις ἀρίστη·
ἐν δ' αὐτὴ θὲς φᾶρος ἐϋπλυνὲς ἠδὲ χιτῶνα. 4**2**5
ἀμφὶ δέ οἱ πυρὶ χαλκὸν ἰήνατε, θέρμετε δ' ὕδωρ,
ὄφρα λοεσσάμενός τε ἰδών τ' ἐῢ κείμενα πάντα
δῶρα, τά οἱ Φαίηκες ἀμύμονες ἐνθάδ' ἔνεικαν,
δαιτί τε τέρπηται καὶ ἀοιδῆς ὕμνον ἀκούων.
καί οἱ ἐγὼ τόδ' ἄλεισον ἐμὸν περικαλλὲς ὀπάσσω, 4**3**0
χρύσεον, ὄφρ' ἐμέθεν μεμνημένος ἤματα πάντα
σπένδῃ ἐνὶ μεγάρῳ Διί τ' ἄλλοισίν τε θεοῖσιν."

Ὣς ἔφατ', Ἀρήτη δὲ μετὰ δμῳῆσιν ἔειπεν
ἀμφὶ πυρὶ στῆσαι τρίποδα μέγαν ὅττι τάχιστα.
αἱ δὲ λοετροχόον τρίποδ' ἵστασαν ἐν πυρὶ κηλέῳ, 4**3**5
ἔν δ' ἄρ' ὕδωρ ἔχεαν, ὑπὸ δὲ ξύλα δαῖον ἑλοῦσαι.
γάστρην μὲν τρίποδος πῦρ ἄμφεπε, θέρμετο δ' ὕδωρ·
τόφρα δ' ἄρ' Ἀρήτη ξείνῳ περικαλλέα χηλὸν
ἐξέφερεν θαλάμοιο, τίθει δ' ἐνὶ κάλλιμα δῶρα,
ἐσθῆτα χρυσόν τε, τά οἱ Φαίηκες ἔδωκαν· 4**4**0

thee happiness, and mayest thou never hereafter miss this sword which thou hast given me, making amends with gentle speech."

He spoke, and about his shoulders hung the silver-studded sword. And the sun set, and the glorious gifts were brought him. These the lordly heralds bore to the palace of Alcinous, and the sons of peerless Alcinous took the beautiful gifts and set them before their honoured mother. And the strong and mighty Alcinous led the way, and they came in and sat down on the high seats. Then to Arete spoke the mighty Alcinous :

"Bring hither, wife, a goodly chest, the best thou hast, and thyself place in it a newly-washed cloak and tunic ; and do ye heat for the stranger a cauldron on the fire, and warm water, that when he has bathed and has seen well bestowed all the gifts which the noble Phaeacians have brought hither, he may take pleasure in the feast, and in hearing the strains of the song. And I will give him this beautiful cup of mine, wrought of gold, that he may remember me all his days as he pours libations in his halls to Zeus and to the other gods."

So he spoke, and Arete bade her handmaids to set a great cauldron on the fire with all speed. And they set on the blazing fire the cauldron for filling the bath, and poured in water, and took billets of wood and kindled them beneath it. Then the fire played about the belly of the cauldron, and the water grew warm ; but meanwhile Arete brought forth for the stranger a beautiful chest from the treasure chamber, and placed in it the goodly gifts, the raiment and the gold, which the Phaeacians

ἐν δ᾽ αὐτῇ φᾶρος θῆκεν καλόν τε χιτῶνα,
καί μιν φωνήσασ᾽ ἔπεα πτερόεντα προσηύδα·

" Αὐτὸς νῦν ἴδε πῶμα, θοῶς δ᾽ ἐπὶ δεσμὸν ἴηλον,
μή τίς τοι καθ᾽ ὁδὸν δηλήσεται, ὁππότ᾽ ἂν αὖτε
εὕδῃσθα γλυκὺν ὕπνον ἰὼν ἐν νηὶ μελαίνῃ."   4

Αὐτὰρ ἐπεὶ τό γ᾽ ἄκουσε πολύτλας δῖος Ὀδυσσεύς,
αὐτίκ᾽ ἐπήρτυε πῶμα, θοῶς δ᾽ ἐπὶ δεσμὸν ἴηλεν
ποικίλον, ὅν ποτέ μιν δέδαε φρεσὶ πότνια Κίρκη.
αὐτόδιον δ᾽ ἄρα μιν ταμίη λούσασθαι ἀνώγει
ἔς ῥ᾽ ἀσάμινθον βάνθ᾽· ὁ δ᾽ ἄρ᾽ ἀσπασίως ἴδε θυμῷ   4
θερμὰ λοέτρ᾽, ἐπεὶ οὔ τι κομιζόμενός γε θάμιζεν,
ἐπεὶ δὴ λίπε δῶμα Καλυψοῦς ἠυκόμοιο.
τόφρα δέ οἱ κομιδή γε θεῷ ὣς ἔμπεδος ἦεν.

Τὸν δ᾽ ἐπεὶ οὖν δμωαὶ λοῦσαν καὶ χρῖσαν ἐλαίῳ,
ἀμφὶ δέ μιν χλαῖναν καλὴν βάλον ἠδὲ χιτῶνα,   4
ἔκ ῥ᾽ ἀσαμίνθου βὰς ἄνδρας μέτα οἰνοποτῆρας
ἤιε· Ναυσικάα δὲ θεῶν ἄπο κάλλος ἔχουσα
στῆ ῥα παρὰ σταθμὸν τέγεος πύκα ποιητοῖο,
θαύμαζεν δ᾽ Ὀδυσῆα ἐν ὀφθαλμοῖσιν ὁρῶσα,
καί μιν φωνήσασ᾽ ἔπεα πτερόεντα προσηύδα·   4

" Χαῖρε, ξεῖν᾽, ἵνα καί ποτ᾽ ἐὼν ἐν πατρίδι γαίῃ
μνήσῃ ἐμεῦ, ὅτι μοι πρώτῃ ζωάγρι᾽ ὀφέλλεις."

Τὴν δ᾽ ἀπαμειβόμενος προσέφη πολύμητις Ὀδυσσε
" Ναυσικάα θύγατερ μεγαλήτορος Ἀλκινόοιο,
οὕτω νῦν Ζεὺς θείη, ἐρίγδουπος πόσις Ἥρης,   4
οἴκαδέ τ᾽ ἐλθέμεναι καὶ νόστιμον ἦμαρ ἰδέσθαι·

gave. And therein she herself placed a cloak and a fair tunic; and she spoke and addressed Odysseus with winged words:

"Look now thyself to the lid, and quickly cast a cord upon it, lest some one despoil thee of thy goods on the way, when later on[1] thou art lying in sweet sleep, as thou farest in the black ship."

Now when the much-enduring goodly Odysseus heard these words, he straightway fitted on the lid, and quickly cast a cord upon it—a cunning knot, which queenly Circe once had taught him. Then forthwith the housewife bade him go to the bath and bathe; and his heart was glad when he saw the warm bath, for he had not been wont to have such tendance from the time that he left the house of faired-haired Calypso, but until then he had tendance continually as a god.

Now when the handmaids had bathed him and anointed him with oil, and had cast about him a fair cloak and a tunic, he came forth from the bath, and went to join the men at their wine. And Nausicaa, gifted with beauty by the gods, stood by the door-post of the well-built hall, and she marvelled at Odysseus, as her eyes beheld him, and she spoke, and addressed him with winged words:

"Farewell, stranger, and hereafter even in thy own native land mayest thou remember me, for to me first thou owest the price of thy life."

Then Odysseus of many wiles answered her: "Nausicaa, daughter of great-hearted Alcinous, so may Zeus grant, the loud-thundering lord of Here, that I may reach my home and see the day of

[1] See Merry and Riddell *ad loc.*

τῷ κέν τοι καὶ κεῖθι θεῷ ὣς εὐχετοῴμην
αἰεὶ ἤματα πάντα· σὺ γάρ μ' ἐβιώσαο, κούρη."

Ἦ ῥα καὶ ἐς θρόνον ἷζε παρ' Ἀλκίνοον βασιλῆα·
οἱ δ' ἤδη μοίρας τ' ἔνεμον κερόωντό τε οἶνον.   47(
κῆρυξ δ' ἐγγύθεν ἦλθεν ἄγων ἐρίηρον ἀοιδόν,
Δημόδοκον λαοῖσι τετιμένον· εἷσε δ' ἄρ' αὐτὸν
μέσσῳ δαιτυμόνων, πρὸς κίονα μακρὸν ἐρείσας.
δὴ τότε κήρυκα προσέφη πολύμητις Ὀδυσσεύς,
νώτου ἀποπροταμών, ἐπὶ δὲ πλεῖον ἐλέλειπτο,   47(
ἀργιόδοντος ὑός, θαλερὴ δ' ἦν ἀμφὶς ἀλοιφή·

"Κῆρυξ, τῇ δή, τοῦτο πόρε κρέας, ὄφρα φάγῃσιν,
Δημοδόκῳ· καί μιν προσπτύξομαι ἀχνύμενός περ·
πᾶσι γὰρ ἀνθρώποισιν ἐπιχθονίοισιν ἀοιδοὶ
τιμῆς ἔμμοροί εἰσι καὶ αἰδοῦς, οὕνεκ' ἄρα σφέας   48(
οἴμας μοῦσ' ἐδίδαξε, φίλησε δὲ φῦλον ἀοιδῶν."

Ὣς ἄρ' ἔφη, κῆρυξ δὲ φέρων ἐν χερσὶν ἔθηκεν
ἥρῳ Δημοδόκῳ· ὁ δ' ἐδέξατο, χαῖρε δὲ θυμῷ.
οἱ δ' ἐπ' ὀνείαθ' ἑτοῖμα προκείμενα χεῖρας ἴαλλον.
αὐτὰρ ἐπεὶ πόσιος καὶ ἐδητύος ἐξ ἔρον ἕντο,   48(
δὴ τότε Δημόδοκον προσέφη πολύμητις Ὀδυσσεύς·

"Δημόδοκ', ἔξοχα δή σε βροτῶν αἰνίζομ' ἁπάντων.
ἢ σέ γε μοῦσ' ἐδίδαξε, Διὸς πάις, ἢ σέ γ' Ἀπόλλων·
λίην γὰρ κατὰ κόσμον Ἀχαιῶν οἶτον ἀείδεις,
ὅσσ' ἔρξαν τ' ἔπαθόν τε καὶ ὅσσ' ἐμόγησαν Ἀχαιοί,   49(
ὥς τέ που ἢ αὐτὸς παρεὼν ἢ ἄλλου ἀκούσας.
ἀλλ' ἄγε δὴ μετάβηθι καὶ ἵππου κόσμον ἄεισον

my returning. Then will I even there pray to thee as to a god all my days, for thou, maiden, hast given me life."

He spoke, and sat down on a chair beside king Alcinous. And now they were serving out portions and mixing the wine. Then the herald came near, leading the good minstrel, Demodocus, held in honour by the people, and seated him in the midst of the banqueters, leaning his chair against a high pillar. Then to the herald said Odysseus of many wiles, cutting off a portion of the chine of a white-tusked boar, whereof yet more was left, and there was rich fat on either side:

"Herald, take and give this portion to Demodocus, that he may eat, and I will greet him, despite my grief. For among all men that are upon the earth minstrels win honour and reverence, for that the Muse has taught them the paths of song, and loves the tribe of minstrels."

So he spoke, and the herald bore the portion and placed it in the hands of the lord Demodocus, and he took it and was glad at heart. So they put forth their hands to the good cheer lying ready before them. But when they had put from them the desire of food and drink, then to Demodocus said Odysseus of many wiles:

"Demodocus, verily above all mortal men do I praise thee, whether it was the Muse, the daughter of Zeus, that taught thee, or Apollo; for well and truly dost thou sing of the fate of the Achaeans, all that they wrought and suffered, and all the toils they endured, as though haply thou hadst thyself been present, or hadst heard the tale from another. But come now, change thy theme, and

δουρατέου, τὸν Ἐπειὸς ἐποίησεν σὺν Ἀθήνῃ,
ὅν ποτ' ἐς ἀκρόπολιν δόλον ἤγαγε δῖος Ὀδυσσεὺς
ἀνδρῶν ἐμπλήσας οἵ ῥ' Ἴλιον ἐξαλάπαξαν.   49
αἵ κεν δή μοι ταῦτα κατὰ μοῖραν καταλέξῃς,
αὐτίκ' ἐγὼ πᾶσιν μυθήσομαι ἀνθρώποισιν,
ὡς ἄρα τοι πρόφρων θεὸς ὤπασε θέσπιν ἀοιδήν."

Ὣς φάθ', ὁ δ' ὁρμηθεὶς θεοῦ ἤρχετο, φαῖνε δ' ἀοιδήν
ἔνθεν ἑλὼν ὡς οἱ μὲν ἐυσσέλμων ἐπὶ νηῶν   50
βάντες ἀπέπλειον, πῦρ ἐν κλισίῃσι βαλόντες,
Ἀργεῖοι, τοὶ δ' ἤδη ἀγακλυτὸν ἀμφ' Ὀδυσῆα
ἧατ' ἐνὶ Τρώων ἀγορῇ κεκαλυμμένοι ἵππῳ·
αὐτοὶ γάρ μιν Τρῶες ἐς ἀκρόπολιν ἐρύσαντο.
ὡς ὁ μὲν ἑστήκει, τοὶ δ' ἄκριτα πόλλ' ἀγόρευον   50
ἥμενοι ἀμφ' αὐτόν· τρίχα δέ σφισιν ἥνδανε βουλή,
ἠὲ διαπλῆξαι¹ κοῖλον δόρυ νηλέι χαλκῷ,
ἢ κατὰ πετράων βαλέειν ἐρύσαντας ἐπ' ἄκρης,
ἢ ἐάαν μέγ' ἄγαλμα θεῶν θελκτήριον εἶναι,
τῇ περ δὴ καὶ ἔπειτα τελευτήσεσθαι ἔμελλεν·   51
αἶσα γὰρ ἦν ἀπολέσθαι, ἐπὴν πόλις ἀμφικαλύψῃ
δουράτεον μέγαν ἵππον, ὅθ' ἥατο πάντες ἄριστοι
Ἀργείων Τρώεσσι φόνον καὶ κῆρα φέροντες.
ἤειδεν δ' ὡς ἄστυ διέπραθον υἷες Ἀχαιῶν
ἱππόθεν ἐκχύμενοι, κοῖλον λόχον ἐκπρολιπόντες.   51
ἄλλον δ' ἄλλῃ ἄειδε πόλιν κεραϊζέμεν αἰπήν,
αὐτὰρ Ὀδυσσῆα προτὶ δώματα Δηιφόβοιο
βήμεναι, ἠύτ' Ἄρηα σὺν ἀντιθέῳ Μενελάῳ.
κεῖθι δὴ αἰνότατον πόλεμον φάτο τολμήσαντα
νικῆσαι καὶ ἔπειτα διὰ μεγάθυμον Ἀθήνην.   52

¹ διαπλῆξαι Aristarchus : διατμῆξαι MSS.

sing of the building of the horse of wood, which Epeius made with Athene's help, the horse which once Odysseus led up into the citadel as a thing of guile, when he had filled it with the men who sacked Ilios. If thou dost indeed tell me this tale aright, I will declare to all mankind that the god has of a ready heart granted thee the gift of divine song."

So he spoke, and the minstrel, moved by the god, began, and let his song be heard, taking up the tale where the Argives had embarked on their benched ships and were sailing away, after casting fire on their huts, while those others led by glorious Odysseus were now sitting in the place of assembly of the Trojans, hidden in the horse; for the Trojans had themselves dragged it to the citadel. So there it stood, while the people talked long as they sat about it, and could form no resolve. Nay, in three ways did counsel find favour in their minds: either to cleave the hollow timber with the pitiless bronze, or to drag it to the height and cast it down the rocks, or to let it stand as a great offering to propitiate the gods, even as in the end it was to be brought to pass; for it was their fate to perish when their city should enclose the great horse of wood, wherein were sitting all the best of the Argives, bearing to the Trojans death and fate. And he sang how the sons of the Achaeans poured forth from the horse and, leaving their hollow ambush, sacked the city. Of the others he sang how in divers ways they wasted the lofty city, but of Odysseus, how he went like Ares to the house of Deiphobus together with godlike Menelaus. There it was, he said, that Odysseus braved the most terrible fight and in the end conquered by the aid of greathearted Athene.

Ταῦτ' ἄρ' ἀοιδὸς ἄειδε περικλυτός· αὐτὰρ Ὀδυσσεὺ
τήκετο, δάκρυ δ' ἔδευεν ὑπὸ βλεφάροισι παρειάς.
ὡς δὲ γυνὴ κλαίῃσι φίλον πόσιν ἀμφιπεσοῦσα,
ὅς τε ἑῆς πρόσθεν πόλιος λαῶν τε πέσῃσιν,
ἄστεϊ καὶ τεκέεσσιν ἀμύνων νηλεὲς ἦμαρ·   52
ἡ μὲν τὸν θνῄσκοντα καὶ ἀσπαίροντα ἰδοῦσα
ἀμφ' αὐτῷ χυμένη λίγα κωκύει· οἱ δέ τ' ὄπισθε
κόπτοντες δούρεσσι μετάφρενον ἠδὲ καὶ ὤμους
εἴρερον εἰσανάγουσι, πόνον τ' ἐχέμεν καὶ ὀιζύν·
τῆς δ' ἐλεεινοτάτῳ ἄχεϊ φθινύθουσι παρειαί·   530
ὣς Ὀδυσεὺς ἐλεεινὸν ὑπ' ὀφρύσι δάκρυον εἶβεν.
ἔνθ' ἄλλους μὲν πάντας ἐλάνθανε δάκρυα λείβων,
Ἀλκίνοος δέ μιν οἶος ἐπεφράσατ' ἠδ' ἐνόησεν,
ἥμενος ἄγχ' αὐτοῦ, βαρὺ δὲ στενάχοντος ἄκουσεν.
αἶψα δὲ Φαιήκεσσι φιληρέτμοισι μετηύδα·   535
    "Κέκλυτε, Φαιήκων ἡγήτορες ἠδὲ μέδοντες,
Δημόδοκος δ' ἤδη σχεθέτω φόρμιγγα λίγειαν·
οὐ γάρ πως πάντεσσι χαριζόμενος τάδ' ἀείδει.
ἐξ οὗ δορπέομέν τε καὶ ὦρορε θεῖος ἀοιδός,
ἐκ τοῦ δ' οὔ πω παύσατ' ὀιζυροῖο γόοιο   540
ὁ ξεῖνος· μάλα πού μιν ἄχος φρένας ἀμφιβέβηκεν.
ἀλλ' ἄγ' ὁ μὲν σχεθέτω, ἵν' ὁμῶς τερπώμεθα πάντες,
ξεινοδόκοι καὶ ξεῖνος, ἐπεὶ πολὺ κάλλιον οὕτως·
εἵνεκα γὰρ ξείνοιο τάδ' αἰδοίοιο τέτυκται,
πομπὴ καὶ φίλα δῶρα, τά οἱ δίδομεν φιλέοντες.   54
ἀντὶ κασιγνήτου ξεῖνός θ' ἱκέτης τε τέτυκται
ἀνέρι, ὅς τ' ὀλίγον περ ἐπιψαύῃ πραπίδεσσι.
τῶ νῦν μηδὲ σὺ κεῦθε νοήμασι κερδαλέοισιν
ὅττι κέ σ' εἴρωμαι· φάσθαι δέ σε κάλλιόν ἐστιν.

This song the famous minstrel sang. But the heart of Odysseus was melted and tears wet his cheeks beneath his eyelids. And as a woman wails and flings herself about her dear husband, who has fallen in front of his city and his people, seeking to ward off from his city and his children the pitiless day; and as she beholds him dying and gasping for breath, she clings to him and shrieks aloud, while the foe behind her smite her back and shoulders with their spears, and lead her away to captivity to bear toil and woe, while with most pitiful grief her cheeks are wasted: even so did Odysseus let fall pitiful tears from beneath his brows. Now from all the rest he concealed the tears that he shed, but Alcinous alone marked him and took heed, for he sat by him and heard him groaning heavily. And straightway he spoke among the Phaeacians, lovers of the oar:

"Hear me, leaders and counsellors of the Phaeacians, and let Demodocus now check his clear-toned lyre, for in no wise to all alike does he give pleasure with this song. Ever since we began to sup and the divine minstrel was moved to sing, from that time yon stranger has never ceased from sorrowful lamentation; surely, methinks, grief has encompassed his heart. Nay, let the minstrel cease, that we may all make merry, hosts and guest alike, since it is better thus. Lo, for the sake of the honoured stranger all these things have been made ready, his sending and the gifts of friendship which we give him of our love. Dear as a brother is the stranger and the suppliant to a man whose wits have never so short a range. Therefore do not thou longer hide with crafty thought whatever I shall ask thee; to speak out plainly is

εἴπ' ὄνομ' ὅττι σε κεῖθι κάλεον μήτηρ τε πατήρ τε   55
ἄλλοι θ' οἳ κατὰ ἄστυ καὶ οἳ περιναιετάουσιν.
οὐ μὲν γάρ τις πάμπαν ἀνώνυμός ἐστ' ἀνθρώπων,
οὐ κακὸς οὐδὲ μὲν ἐσθλός, ἐπὴν τὰ πρῶτα γένηται,
ἀλλ' ἐπὶ πᾶσι τίθενται, ἐπεί κε τέκωσι, τοκῆες.
εἰπὲ δέ μοι γαῖάν τε τεὴν δῆμόν τε πόλιν τε,   55
ὄφρα σε τῇ πέμπωσι τιτυσκόμεναι φρεσὶ νῆες·
οὐ γὰρ Φαιήκεσσι κυβερνητῆρες ἔασιν,
οὐδέ τι πηδάλι' ἔστι, τά τ' ἄλλαι νῆες ἔχουσιν·
ἀλλ' αὐταὶ ἴσασι νοήματα καὶ φρένας ἀνδρῶν,
καὶ πάντων ἴσασι πόλιας καὶ πίονας ἀγροὺς   56
ἀνθρώπων, καὶ λαῖτμα τάχισθ' ἁλὸς ἐκπερόωσιν
ἠέρι καὶ νεφέλῃ κεκαλυμμέναι· οὐδέ ποτέ σφιν
οὔτε τι πημανθῆναι ἔπι δέος οὔτ' ἀπολέσθαι.
ἀλλὰ τόδ' ὥς ποτε πατρὸς ἐγὼν εἰπόντος ἄκουσα
Ναυσιθόου, ὃς ἔφασκε Ποσειδάων' ἀγάσασθαι   56
ἡμῖν, οὕνεκα πομποὶ ἀπήμονές εἰμεν ἁπάντων.
φῆ ποτὲ Φαιήκων ἀνδρῶν εὐεργέα νῆα
ἐκ πομπῆς ἀνιοῦσαν ἐν ἠεροειδέι πόντῳ
ῥαισέμεναι, μέγα δ' ἧμιν ὄρος πόλει ἀμφικαλύψειν.
ὣς ἀγόρευ' ὁ γέρων· τὰ δέ κεν θεὸς ἢ τελέσειεν   57
ἤ κ' ἀτέλεστ' εἴη, ὥς οἱ φίλον ἔπλετο θυμῷ·
ἀλλ' ἄγε μοι τόδε εἰπὲ καὶ ἀτρεκέως κατάλεξον,
ὅππῃ ἀπεπλάγχθης τε καὶ ἅς τινας ἵκεο χώρας
ἀνθρώπων, αὐτούς τε πόλιάς τ' ἐὺ ναιετοώσας,
ἠμὲν ὅσοι χαλεποί τε καὶ ἄγριοι οὐδὲ δίκαιοι,   57
οἵ τε φιλόξεινοι, καί σφιν νόος ἐστὶ θεουδής.
εἰπὲ δ' ὅ τι κλαίεις καὶ ὀδύρεαι ἔνδοθι θυμῷ
Ἀργείων Δαναῶν ἠδ' Ἰλίου οἶτον ἀκούων.

the better course. Tell me the name by which they were wont to call thee in thy home, even thy mother and thy father and other folk besides, thy townsmen and the dwellers round about. For there is no one of all mankind who is nameless, be he base man or noble, when once he has been born, but parents bestow names on all when they give them birth. And tell me thy country, thy people, and thy city, that our ships may convey thee thither, discerning the course by their wits. For the Phaeacians have no pilots, nor steering-oars such as other ships have, but their ships of themselves understand the thoughts and minds of men, and they know the cities and rich fields of all peoples, and most swiftly do they cross over the gulf of the sea, hidden in mist and cloud, nor ever have they fear of harm or ruin. Yet this story I once heard thus told by my father Nausithous, who was wont to say that Poseidon was wroth with us because we give safe convoy to all men. He said that some day, as a well-built ship of the Phaeacians was return-ing from a convoy over the misty deep, Poseidon would smite her and would fling a great mountain about our city.[1] So that old man spoke, and these things the god will haply bring to pass, or will leave unfulfilled, as may be his good pleasure. But come, now, tell me this and declare it truly : whither thou hast wandered and to what countries of men thou hast come ; tell me of the people and of their well-built cities, both of those who are cruel and wild and unjust, and of those who love strangers and fear the gods in their thoughts. And tell me why thou dost weep and wail in spirit as thou hearest the doom of the Argive Danaans and of Ilios. This the gods

---

[1] That is, so as to cut them off from the sea.

τὸν δὲ θεοὶ μὲν τεῦξαν, ἐπεκλώσαντο δ' ὄλεθρον
ἀνθρώποις, ἵνα ᾖσι καὶ ἐσσομένοισιν ἀοιδή.   5
ἢ τίς τοι καὶ πηὸς ἀπέφθιτο Ἰλιόθι πρὸ
ἐσθλὸς ἐών, γαμβρὸς ἢ πενθερός, οἵ τε μάλιστα
κήδιστοι τελέθουσι μεθ' αἷμά τε καὶ γένος αὐτῶν;
ἢ τίς που καὶ ἑταῖρος ἀνὴρ κεχαρισμένα εἰδώς,
ἐσθλός; ἐπεὶ οὐ μέν τι κασιγνήτοιο χερείων   5
γίγνεται, ὅς κεν ἑταῖρος ἐὼν πεπνυμένα εἰδῇ."

wrought, and spun the skein of ruin for men, that there might be a song for those yet to be born. Did some kinsman of thine fall before Ilios, some good, true man, thy daughter's husband or thy wife's father, such as are nearest to one after one's own kin and blood? Or was it haply some comrade dear to thy heart, some good, true man? For no whit worse than a brother is a comrade who has an understanding heart."

I

Τὸν δ' ἀπαμειβόμενος προσέφη πολύμητις Ὀδυσσεί·
" Ἀλκίνοε κρεῖον, πάντων ἀριδείκετε λαῶν,
ἦ τοι μὲν τόδε καλὸν ἀκουέμεν ἐστὶν ἀοιδοῦ
τοιοῦδ' οἷος ὅδ' ἐστί, θεοῖς ἐναλίγκιος αὐδήν.
οὐ γὰρ ἐγώ γέ τί φημι τέλος χαριέστερον εἶναι
ἢ ὅτ' ἐυφροσύνη μὲν ἔχῃ κάτα δῆμον ἅπαντα,
δαιτυμόνες δ' ἀνὰ δώματ' ἀκουάζωνται ἀοιδοῦ
ἥμενοι ἑξείης, παρὰ δὲ πλήθωσι τράπεζαι
σίτου καὶ κρειῶν, μέθυ δ' ἐκ κρητῆρος ἀφύσσων
οἰνοχόος φορέῃσι καὶ ἐγχείῃ δεπάεσσι·
τοῦτό τί μοι κάλλιστον ἐνὶ φρεσὶν εἴδεται εἶναι.
σοὶ δ' ἐμὰ κήδεα θυμὸς ἐπετράπετο στονόεντα
εἴρεσθ', ὄφρ' ἔτι μᾶλλον ὀδυρόμενος στεναχίζω·
τί πρῶτόν τοι ἔπειτα, τί δ' ὑστάτιον καταλέξω;
κήδε' ἐπεί μοι πολλὰ δόσαν θεοὶ Οὐρανίωνες.
νῦν δ' ὄνομα πρῶτον μυθήσομαι, ὄφρα καὶ ὑμεῖς
εἴδετ', ἐγὼ δ' ἂν ἔπειτα φυγὼν ὕπο νηλεὲς ἦμαρ
ὑμῖν ξεῖνος ἔω καὶ ἀπόπροθι δώματα ναίων.
εἴμ' Ὀδυσεὺς Λαερτιάδης, ὃς πᾶσι δόλοισιν
ἀνθρώποισι μέλω, καί μευ κλέος οὐρανὸν ἵκει.
ναιετάω δ' Ἰθάκην ἐυδείελον· ἐν δ' ὄρος αὐτῇ
Νήριτον εἰνοσίφυλλον, ἀριπρεπές· ἀμφὶ δὲ νῆσοι
πολλαὶ ναιετάουσι μάλα σχεδὸν ἀλλήλῃσι,
Δουλίχιόν τε Σάμη τε καὶ ὑλήεσσα Ζάκυνθος.

BOOK IX

THEN Odysseus, of many wiles, answered him, and said: " Lord Alcinous, renowned above all men, verily this is a good thing, to listen to a minstrel such as this man is, like unto the gods in voice. For myself I declare that there is no greater fulfilment of delight than when joy possesses a whole people, and banqueters in the halls listen to a minstrel as they sit in order due, and by them tables are laden with bread and meat, and the cup-bearer draws wine from the bowl and bears it round and pours it into the cups. This seems to my mind the fairest thing there is. But thy heart is turned to ask of my grievous woes, that I may weep and groan the more. What, then, shall I tell thee first, what last ? for woes full many have the heavenly gods given me. First now will I tell my name, that ye, too, may know it, and that I hereafter, when I have escaped from the pitiless day of doom, may be your host, though I dwell in a home that is afar. I am Odysseus, son of Laertes, who am known among men for all manner of wiles,[1] and my fame reaches unto heaven. But I dwell in clear-seen Ithaca, wherein is a mountain, Neriton, covered with waving forests, conspicuous from afar ; and round it lie many isles hard by one another, Dulichium, and Same, and wooded Zacynthus.

[1] Or, "who am known among all men for my wiles."

αὐτὴ δὲ χθαμαλὴ πανυπερτάτη εἰν ἁλὶ κεῖται   2
πρὸς ζόφον, αἱ δέ τ' ἄνευθε πρὸς ἠῶ τ' ἠέλιόν τε,
τρηχεῖ', ἀλλ' ἀγαθὴ κουροτρόφος· οὔ τοι ἐγώ γε
ἧς γαίης δύναμαι γλυκερώτερον ἄλλο ἰδέσθαι.
ἦ μέν μ' αὐτόθ' ἔρυκε Καλυψώ, δῖα θεάων,
ἐν σπέσσι γλαφυροῖσι, λιλαιομένη πόσιν εἶναι·[1]   3
ὣς δ' αὔτως Κίρκη κατερήτυεν ἐν μεγάροισιν
Αἰαίη δολόεσσα, λιλαιομένη πόσιν εἶναι·
ἀλλ' ἐμὸν οὔ ποτε θυμὸν ἐνὶ στήθεσσιν ἔπειθον.
ὣς οὐδὲν γλύκιον ἧς πατρίδος οὐδὲ τοκήων
γίγνεται, εἴ περ καί τις ἀπόπροθι πίονα οἶκον   3
γαίῃ ἐν ἀλλοδαπῇ ναίει ἀπάνευθε τοκήων.
εἰ δ' ἄγε τοι καὶ νόστον ἐμὸν πολυκηδέ' ἐνίσπω,
ὅν μοι Ζεὺς ἐφέηκεν ἀπὸ Τροίηθεν ἰόντι.

" Ἰλιόθεν με φέρων ἄνεμος Κικόνεσσι πέλασσεν,
Ἰσμάρῳ. ἔνθα δ' ἐγὼ πόλιν ἔπραθον, ὤλεσα δ' αὐτούς·   4
ἐκ πόλιος δ' ἀλόχους καὶ κτήματα πολλὰ λαβόντες
δασσάμεθ', ὡς μή τίς μοι ἀτεμβόμενος κίοι ἴσης.
ἔνθ' ἦ τοι μὲν ἐγὼ διερῷ ποδὶ φευγέμεν ἡμέας
ἠνώγεα, τοὶ δὲ μέγα νήπιοι οὐκ ἐπίθοντο.
ἔνθα δὲ πολλὸν μὲν μέθυ πίνετο, πολλὰ δὲ μῆλα   4
ἔσφαζον παρὰ θῖνα καὶ εἰλίποδας ἕλικας βοῦς·
τόφρα δ' ἄρ' οἰχόμενοι Κίκονες Κικόνεσσι γεγώνευν,

----

[1] Line 30 is omitted in most MSS.

----

[1] This rendering of χθαμαλή is justified by Strabo x. ii. 12
and by modern Greek usage. The ordinary meaning "low"
cannot be right here. The translation given of this whole
passage brings Homer's description into agreement with the

Ithaca itself lies close in to the mainland[1] the furthest toward the gloom,[2] but the others lie apart toward the Dawn and the sun—a rugged isle, but a good nurse of young men; and for myself no other thing can I see sweeter than one's own land. Of a truth Calypso, the beautiful goddess, sought to keep me by her in her hollow caves, yearning that I should be her husband; and in like manner Circe would fain have held me back in her halls, the guileful lady of Aeaea, yearning that I should be her husband; but they could never persuade the heart within my breast. So true is it that naught is sweeter than a man's own land and his parents, even though it be in a rich house that he dwells afar in a foreign land away from his parents. But come, let me tell thee also of my woeful home-coming, which Zeus laid upon me as I came from Troy.

"From Ilios the wind bore me and brought me to the Cicones, to Ismarus. There I sacked the city and slew the men; and from the city we took their wives and great store of treasure, and divided them among us, that so far as lay in me no man might go defrauded of an equal share. Then verily I gave command that we should flee with swift foot, but the others in their great folly did not hearken. But there much wine was drunk, and many sheep they slew by the shore, and sleek kine of shambling gait. Meanwhile the Cicones went and called to other

actual facts. It accepts the view that Homer's Ithaca is to be identified, not with Thiaki, but with Leucas. As commonly rendered, the lines convict the poet of an utter ignorance of the geography of western Greece.

[2] That is, from the standpoint of a sailor making his way up the coast toward the dark and unknown region of the north and west.

οἵ σφιν γείτονες ἦσαν, ἅμα πλέονες καὶ ἀρείους,
ἤπειρον ναίοντες, ἐπιστάμενοι μὲν ἀφ' ἵππων
ἀνδράσι μάρνασθαι καὶ ὅθι χρὴ πεζὸν ἐόντα.
ἦλθον ἔπειθ' ὅσα φύλλα καὶ ἄνθεα γίγνεται ὥρῃ,
ἠέριοι· τότε δή ῥα κακὴ Διὸς αἶσα παρέστη
ἡμῖν αἰνομόροισιν, ἵν' ἄλγεα πολλὰ πάθοιμεν.
στησάμενοι δ' ἐμάχοντο μάχην παρὰ νηυσὶ θοῇσι,
βάλλον   ἀλλήλους χαλκήρεσιν ἐγχείῃσιν.
ὄφρα μὲν ἠὼς ἦν καὶ ἀέξετο ἱερὸν ἦμαρ,
τόφρα δ' ἀλεξόμενοι μένομεν πλέονάς περ ἐόντας.
ἦμος δ' ἠέλιος μετενίσσετο βουλυτόνδε,
καὶ τότε δὴ Κίκονες κλίναν δαμάσαντες Ἀχαιούς.
ἐξ δ' ἀφ' ἑκάστης νηὸς ἐυκνήμιδες ἑταῖροι
ὤλονθ'· οἱ δ' ἄλλοι φύγομεν θάνατόν τε μόρον τε.

"Ἔνθεν δὲ προτέρω πλέομεν ἀκαχήμενοι ἦτορ,
ἄσμενοι ἐκ θανάτοιο, φίλους ὀλέσαντες ἑταίρους.
οὐδ' ἄρα μοι προτέρω νῆες κίον ἀμφιέλισσαι,
πρίν τινα τῶν δειλῶν ἑτάρων τρὶς ἕκαστον ἀῦσαι,
οἳ θάνον ἐν πεδίῳ Κικόνων ὕπο δῃωθέντες.
νηυσὶ δ' ἐπῶρσ' ἄνεμον Βορέην νεφεληγερέτα Ζεὺς
λαίλαπι θεσπεσίῃ, σὺν δὲ νεφέεσσι κάλυψε
γαῖαν ὁμοῦ καὶ πόντον· ὀρώρει δ' οὐρανόθεν νύξ.
αἱ μὲν ἔπειτ' ἐφέροντ' ἐπικάρσιαι, ἱστία δέ σφιν
τριχθά τε καὶ τετραχθὰ διέσχισεν ἲς ἀνέμοιο.
καὶ τὰ μὲν ἐς νῆας κάθεμεν, δείσαντες ὄλεθρον,
αὐτὰς δ' ἐσσυμένως προερέσσαμεν ἠπειρόνδε.
ἔνθα δύω νύκτας δύο τ' ἤματα συνεχὲς αἰεὶ
κείμεθ', ὁμοῦ καμάτῳ τε καὶ ἄλγεσι θυμὸν ἔδοντες.

Cicones who were their neighbours, at once more numerous and braver than they—men that dwelt inland and were skilled at fighting with their foes from chariots, and, if need were, on foot. So they came in the morning, as thick as leaves or flowers spring up in their season; and then it was that an evil fate from Zeus beset us luckless men, that we might suffer woes full many. They set their battle in array and fought by the swift ships, and each side hurled at the other with bronze-tipped spears. Now as long as it was morn and the sacred day was waxing, so long we held our ground and beat them off, though they were more than we. But when the sun turned to the time for the unyoking of oxen, then the Cicones prevailed and routed the Achaeans, and six of my well-greaved comrades perished from each ship; but the rest of us escaped death and fate.

" Thence we sailed on, grieved at heart, glad to have escaped from death, though we had lost our dear comrades; nor did I let my curved ships pass on till we had called thrice on each of those hapless comrades of ours who died on the plain, cut down by the Cicones. But against our ships Zeus, the cloud-gatherer, roused the North Wind with a wondrous tempest, and hid with clouds the land and the sea alike, and night rushed down from heaven. Then the ships were driven headlong, and their sails were torn to shreds by the violence of the wind. So we lowered the sails and stowed them aboard, in fear of death, and rowed the ships hurriedly toward the land. There for two nights and two days continuously we lay, eating our hearts for weariness and sorrow. But

ἀλλ' ὅτε δὴ τρίτον ἦμαρ ἐυπλόκαμος τέλεσ' Ἠώς,
ἱστοὺς στησάμενοι ἀνά θ' ἱστία λεύκ' ἐρύσαντες
ἥμεθα, τὰς δ' ἄνεμός τε κυβερνῆταί τ' ἴθυνον.
καί νύ κεν ἀσκηθὴς ἱκόμην ἐς πατρίδα γαῖαν·
ἀλλά με κῦμα ῥόος τε περιγνάμπτοντα Μάλειαν   8
καὶ Βορέης ἀπέωσε, παρέπλαγξεν δὲ Κυθήρων.

"Ἔνθεν δ' ἐννῆμαρ φερόμην ὀλοοῖς ἀνέμοισιν
πόντον ἐπ' ἰχθυόεντα· ἀτὰρ δεκάτῃ ἐπέβημεν
γαίης Λωτοφάγων, οἵ τ' ἄνθινον εἶδαρ ἔδουσιν.
ἔνθα δ' ἐπ' ἠπείρου βῆμεν καὶ ἀφυσσάμεθ' ὕδωρ,   8
αἶψα δὲ δεῖπνον ἕλοντο θοῇς παρὰ νηυσὶν ἑταῖροι.
αὐτὰρ ἐπεὶ σίτοιό τ' ἐπασσάμεθ' ἠδὲ ποτῆτος,
δὴ τότ' ἐγὼν ἑτάρους προΐειν πεύθεσθαι ἰόντας,
οἵ τινες ἀνέρες εἶεν ἐπὶ χθονὶ σῖτον ἔδοντες
ἄνδρε δύω κρίνας, τρίτατον κήρυχ' ἅμ' ὀπάσσας.[1] 9
οἱ δ' αἶψ' οἰχόμενοι μίγεν ἀνδράσι Λωτοφάγοισιν·
οὐδ' ἄρα Λωτοφάγοι μήδονθ' ἑτάροισιν ὄλεθρον
ἡμετέροις, ἀλλά σφι δόσαν λωτοῖο πάσασθαι.
τῶν δ' ὅς τις λωτοῖο φάγοι μελιηδέα καρπόν,
οὐκέτ' ἀπαγγεῖλαι πάλιν ἤθελεν οὐδὲ νέεσθαι,   9
ἀλλ' αὐτοῦ βούλοντο μετ' ἀνδράσι Λωτοφάγοισι
λωτὸν ἐρεπτόμενοι μενέμεν νόστου τε λαθέσθαι.
τοὺς μὲν ἐγὼν ἐπὶ νῆας ἄγον κλαίοντας ἀνάγκῃ,
νηυσὶ δ' ἐνὶ γλαφυρῇσιν ὑπὸ ζυγὰ δῆσα ἐρύσσας.
αὐτὰρ τοὺς ἄλλους κελόμην ἐρίηρας ἑταίρους   10
σπερχομένους νηῶν ἐπιβαινέμεν ὠκειάων,
μή πώς τις λωτοῖο φαγὼν νόστοιο λάθηται.
οἱ δ' αἶψ' εἴσβαινον καὶ ἐπὶ κληῖσι καθῖζον,
ἑξῆς δ' ἑζόμενοι πολιὴν ἅλα τύπτον ἐρετμοῖς.

---

[1] Line 90 (= x. 102) is placed before 89 in most MSS. It seems inconsistent with 94.

when now fair-tressed Dawn brought to its birth the third day, we set up the masts and hoisted the white sails, and took our seats, and the wind and the helmsmen steered the ships. And now all unscathed should I have reached my native land, but the wave and the current and the North Wind beat me back as I was rounding Malea, and drove me from my course past Cythera.

"Thence for nine days' space I was borne by direful winds over the teeming deep; but on the tenth we set foot on the land of the Lotus-eaters, who eat a flowery food. There we went on shore and drew water, and straightway my comrades took their meal by the swift ships. But when we had tasted food and drink, I sent forth some of my comrades to go and learn who the men were, who here ate bread upon the earth; two men I chose, sending with them a third as a herald. So they went straightway and mingled with the Lotus-eaters, and the Lotus-eaters did not plan death for my comrades, but gave them of the lotus to taste. And whosoever of them ate of the honey-sweet fruit of the lotus, had no longer any wish to bring back word or to return, but there they were fain to abide among the Lotus-eaters, feeding on the lotus, and forgetful of their homeward way. These men, therefore, I brought back perforce to the ships, weeping, and dragged them beneath the benches and bound them fast in the hollow ships; and I bade the rest of my trusty comrades to embark with speed on the swift ships, lest perchance anyone should eat of the lotus and forget his homeward way. So they went on board straightway and sat down upon the benches, and sitting well in order smote the grey sea with their oars.

"Ἔνθεν δὲ προτέρω πλέομεν ἀκαχήμενοι ἦτορ· 10
Κυκλώπων δ' ἐς γαῖαν ὑπερφιάλων ἀθεμίστων
ἱκόμεθ', οἵ ῥα θεοῖσι πεποιθότες ἀθανάτοισιν
οὔτε φυτεύουσιν χερσὶν φυτὸν οὔτ' ἀρόωσιν,
ἀλλὰ τά γ' ἄσπαρτα καὶ ἀνήροτα πάντα φύονται,
πυροὶ καὶ κριθαὶ ἠδ' ἄμπελοι, αἵ τε φέρουσιν 11
οἶνον ἐρισταφύλον, καί σφιν Διὸς ὄμβρος ἀέξει.
τοῖσιν δ' οὔτ' ἀγοραὶ βουληφόροι οὔτε θέμιστες,
ἀλλ' οἵ γ' ὑψηλῶν ὀρέων ναίουσι κάρηνα
ἐν σπέσσι γλαφυροῖσι, θεμιστεύει δὲ ἕκαστος
παίδων ἠδ' ἀλόχων, οὐδ' ἀλλήλων ἀλέγουσιν. 11

" Νῆσος ἔπειτα λάχεια¹ παρὲκ λιμένος τετάνυσται
γαίης Κυκλώπων οὔτε σχεδὸν οὔτ' ἀποτηλοῦ,
ὑλήεσσ'· ἐν δ' αἶγες ἀπειρέσιαι γεγάασιν
ἄγριαι· οὐ μὲν γὰρ πάτος ἀνθρώπων ἀπερύκει,
οὐδέ μιν εἰσοιχνεῦσι κυνηγέται, οἵ τε καθ' ὕλην 12
ἄλγεα πάσχουσιν κορυφὰς ὀρέων ἐφέποντες.
οὔτ' ἄρα ποίμνῃσιν καταΐσχεται οὔτ' ἀρότοισιν,
ἀλλ' ἥ γ' ἄσπαρτος καὶ ἀνήροτος ἤματα πάντα
ἀνδρῶν χηρεύει, βόσκει δέ τε μηκάδας αἶγας.
οὐ γὰρ Κυκλώπεσσι νέες πάρα μιλτοπάρῃοι, 12
οὐδ' ἄνδρες νηῶν ἔνι τέκτονες, οἵ κε κάμοιεν
νῆας ἐυσσέλμους, αἵ κεν τελέοιεν ἕκαστα
ἄστε' ἐπ' ἀνθρώπων ἱκνεύμεναι, οἷά τε πολλὰ
ἄνδρες ἐπ' ἀλλήλους νηυσὶν περόωσι θάλασσαν·
οἵ κέ σφιν καὶ νῆσον ἐυκτιμένην ἐκάμοντο. 13
οὐ μὲν γάρ τι κακή γε, φέροι δέ κεν ὥρια πάντα·

¹ ἔπειτα λάχεια : ἔπειτ' ἐλάχεια Zenodotus ; cf. x. 509.

"Thence we sailed on, grieved at heart, and we came to the land of the Cyclopes, an overweening and lawless folk, who, trusting in the immortal gods, plant nothing with their hands nor plough; but all these things spring up for them without sowing or ploughing, wheat, and barley, and vines, which bear the rich clusters of wine, and the rain of Zeus gives them increase. Neither assemblies for council have they, nor appointed laws, but they dwell on the peaks of lofty mountains in hollow caves, and each one is lawgiver to his children and his wives, and they reck nothing one of another.

"Now there is a level[1] isle that stretches aslant outside the harbour, neither close to the shore of the land of the Cyclopes, nor yet far off, a wooded isle. Therein live wild goats innumerable, for the tread of men scares them not away, nor are hunters wont to come thither, men who endure toils in the woodland as they course over the peaks of the mountains. Neither with flocks is it held, nor with ploughed lands, but unsown and untilled all the days it knows naught of men, but feeds the bleating goats. For the Cyclopes have at hand no ships with vermilion cheeks,[2] nor are there shipwrights in their land who might build them well-benched ships, which should perform all their wants, passing to the cities of other folk, as men often cross the sea in ships to visit one another—craftsmen, who would have made of this isle also a fair settlement. For the isle is nowise poor, but would bear

---

[1] The word is a doubtful one. Others render, "deep-soiled," and still others, "overgrown with brush," *i.e.* "waste."

[2] That is, with bows painted red.

ἐν μὲν γὰρ λειμῶνες ἁλὸς πολιοῖο παρ' ὄχθας
ὑδρηλοὶ μαλακοί· μάλα κ' ἄφθιτοι ἄμπελοι εἶεν.
ἐν δ' ἄροσις λείη· μάλα κεν βαθὺ λήιον αἰεὶ
εἰς ὥρας ἀμῷεν, ἐπεὶ μάλα πῖαρ ὑπ' οὖδας.   1
ἐν δὲ λιμὴν εὔορμος, ἵν' οὐ χρεὼ πείσματός ἐστιν,
οὔτ' εὐνὰς βαλέειν οὔτε πρυμνήσι' ἀνάψαι,
ἀλλ' ἐπικέλσαντας μεῖναι χρόνον εἰς ὅ κε ναυτέων
θυμὸς ἐποτρύνῃ καὶ ἐπιπνεύσωσιν ἀῆται.
αὐτὰρ ἐπὶ κρατὸς λιμένος ῥέει ἀγλαὸν ὕδωρ,   1
κρήνη ὑπὸ σπείους· περὶ δ' αἴγειροι πεφύασιν.
ἔνθα κατεπλέομεν, καί τις θεὸς ἡγεμόνευεν
νύκτα δι' ὀρφναίην, οὐδὲ προυφαίνετ' ἰδέσθαι·
ἀὴρ γὰρ περὶ νηυσὶ βαθεῖ' ἦν, οὐδὲ σελήνη
οὐρανόθεν προύφαινε, κατείχετο δὲ νεφέεσσιν.
ἔνθ' οὔ τις τὴν νῆσον ἐσέδρακεν ὀφθαλμοῖσιν,
οὔτ' οὖν κύματα μακρὰ κυλινδόμενα προτὶ χέρσον
εἰσίδομεν, πρὶν νῆας ἐυσσέλμους ἐπικέλσαι.
κελσάσῃσι δὲ νηυσὶ καθείλομεν ἱστία πάντα,
ἐκ δὲ καὶ αὐτοὶ βῆμεν ἐπὶ ῥηγμῖνι θαλάσσης·   1
ἔνθα δ' ἀποβρίξαντες ἐμείναμεν Ἠῶ δῖαν.

"Ἦμος δ' ἠριγένεια φάνη ῥοδοδάκτυλος Ἠώς,
νῆσον θαυμάζοντες ἐδινεόμεσθα κατ' αὐτήν.
ὦρσαν δὲ νύμφαι, κοῦραι Διὸς αἰγιόχοιο,
αἶγας ὀρεσκῴους, ἵνα δειπνήσειαν ἑταῖροι.   1
αὐτίκα καμπύλα τόξα καὶ αἰγανέας δολιχαύλους
εἱλόμεθ' ἐκ νηῶν, διὰ δὲ τρίχα κοσμηθέντες
βάλλομεν· αἶψα δ' ἔδωκε θεὸς μενοεικέα θήρην.
νῆες μέν μοι ἕποντο δυώδεκα, ἐς δὲ ἑκάστην
ἐννέα λάγχανον αἶγες· ἐμοὶ δὲ δέκ' ἔξελον οἴῳ.   1

all things in season. In it are meadows by the shores of the grey sea, well-watered meadows and soft, where vines would never fail, and in it level plough-land, whence they might reap from season to season harvests exceeding deep, so rich is the soil beneath ; and in it, too, is a harbour giving safe anchorage, where there is no need of moorings, either to throw out anchor-stones or to make fast stern cables, but one may beach one's ship and wait until the sailors' minds bid them put out, and the breezes blow fair. Now at the head of the harbour a spring of bright water flows forth from beneath a cave, and round about it poplars grow. Thither we sailed in, and some god guided us through the murky night; for there was no light to see, but a mist lay deep about the ships and the moon showed no light from heaven, but was shut in by clouds. Then no man's eyes beheld that island, nor did we see the long waves rolling on the beach, until we ran our well-benched ships on shore. And when we had beached the ships we lowered all the sails and ourselves went forth on the shore of the sea, and there we fell asleep and waited for the bright Dawn.

"As soon as early Dawn appeared, the rosy-fingered, we roamed throughout the isle marvelling at it ; and the nymphs, the daughters of Zeus who bears the aegis, roused the mountain goats, that my comrades might have whereof to make their meal. Straightway we took from the ships our curved bows and long javelins, and arrayed in three bands we fell to smiting ; and the god soon gave us game to satisfy our hearts. The ships that followed me were twelve, and to each nine goats fell by lot, but for me alone they chose out ten.

313

"'Ὣς τότε μὲν πρόπαν ἦμαρ ἐς ἠέλιον καταδύντα
ἥμεθα δαινύμενοι κρέα τ' ἄσπετα καὶ μέθυ ἡδύ·
οὐ γάρ πω νηῶν ἐξέφθιτο οἶνος ἐρυθρός,
ἀλλ' ἐνέην· πολλὸν γὰρ ἐν ἀμφιφορεῦσιν ἕκαστοι
ἠφύσαμεν Κικόνων. ἱερὸν πτολίεθρον ἑλόντες.   1
Κυκλώπων δ' ἐς γαῖαν ἐλεύσσομεν ἐγγὺς ἐόντων,
καπνόν τ' αὐτῶν τε φθογγὴν ὀίων τε καὶ αἰγῶν.
ἦμος δ' ἠέλιος κατέδυ καὶ ἐπὶ κνέφας ἦλθε,
δὴ τότε κοιμήθημεν ἐπὶ ῥηγμῖνι θαλάσσης.
ἦμος δ' ἠριγένεια φάνη ῥοδοδάκτυλος Ἠώς,   1
καὶ τότ' ἐγὼν ἀγορὴν θέμενος μετὰ πᾶσιν ἔειπον·

" '"Ἄλλοι μὲν νῦν μίμνετ', ἐμοὶ ἐρίηρες ἑταῖροι·
αὐτὰρ ἐγὼ σὺν νηί τ' ἐμῇ καὶ ἐμοῖς ἑτάροισιν
ἐλθὼν τῶνδ' ἀνδρῶν πειρήσομαι, οἵ τινές εἰσιν,
ἦ ῥ' οἵ γ' ὑβρισταί τε καὶ ἄγριοι οὐδὲ δίκαιοι,   1
ἦε φιλόξεινοι, καί σφιν νόος ἐστὶ θεουδής.'

"'Ὣς εἰπὼν ἀνὰ νηὸς ἔβην, ἐκέλευσα δ' ἑταίρους
αὐτούς τ' ἀμβαίνειν ἀνά τε πρυμνήσια λῦσαι.
οἱ δ' αἶψ' εἴσβαινον καὶ ἐπὶ κληῖσι καθῖζον,
ἑξῆς δ' ἑζόμενοι πολιὴν ἅλα τύπτον ἐρετμοῖς.   1
ἀλλ' ὅτε δὴ τὸν χῶρον ἀφικόμεθ' ἐγγὺς ἐόντα,
ἔνθα δ' ἐπ' ἐσχατιῇ σπέος εἴδομεν ἄγχι θαλάσσης,
ὑψηλόν, δάφνῃσι κατηρεφές. ἔνθα δὲ πολλὰ
μῆλ', ὄιές τε καὶ αἶγες, ἰαύεσκον· περὶ δ' αὐλὴ
ὑψηλὴ δέδμητο κατωρυχέεσσι λίθοισι   1
μακρῇσίν τε πίτυσσιν ἰδὲ δρυσὶν ὑψικόμοισιν.
ἔνθα δ' ἀνὴρ ἐνίαυε πελώριος, ὅς ῥα τὰ μῆλα
οἶος ποιμαίνεσκεν ἀπόπροθεν· οὐδὲ μετ' ἄλλους
πωλεῖτ', ἀλλ' ἀπάνευθεν ἐὼν ἀθεμίστια ᾔδη.

"So then all day long till set of sun we sat feasting on abundant flesh and sweet wine. For not yet was the red wine spent from out our ships, but some was still left; for abundant store had we drawn in jars for each crew when we took the sacred citadel of the Cicones. And we looked across to the land of the Cyclopes, who dwelt close at hand, and marked the smoke, and the voice of men, and of the sheep, and of the goats. But when the sun set and darkness came on, then we lay down to rest on the shore of the sea. And as soon as early Dawn appeared, the rosy-fingered, I called my men together and spoke among them all :

"'Remain here now, all the rest of you, my trusty comrades, but I with my own ship and my own company will go and make trial of yonder men, to learn who they are, whether they are cruel, and wild, and unjust, or whether they love strangers and fear the gods in their thoughts.'

"So saying, I went on board the ship and bade my comrades themselves to embark, and to loose the stern cables. So they went on board straightway and sat down upon the benches, and sitting well in order smote the grey sea with their oars. But when we had reached the place, which lay close at hand, there on the land's edge hard by the sea we saw a high cave, roofed over with laurels, and there many flocks, sheep and goats alike, were wont to sleep. Round about it a high court was built with stones set deep in the earth, and with tall pines and high-crested oaks. There a monstrous man was wont to sleep, who shepherded his flocks alone and afar, and mingled not with others, but lived apart, with his

καὶ γὰρ θαῦμ᾽ ἐτέτυκτο πελώριον, οὐδὲ ἐῴκει
ἀνδρί γε σιτοφάγῳ, ἀλλὰ ῥίῳ ὑλήεντι
ὑψηλῶν ὀρέων, ὅ τε φαίνεται οἷον ἀπ᾽ ἄλλων.

  " Δὴ τότε τοὺς ἄλλους κελόμην ἐρίηρας ἑταίρους
αὐτοῦ πὰρ νηί τε μένειν καὶ νῆα ἔρυσθαι,
αὐτὰρ ἐγὼ κρίνας ἑτάρων δυοκαίδεκ᾽ ἀρίστους
βῆν· ἀτὰρ αἴγεον ἀσκὸν ἔχον μέλανος οἴνοιο
ἡδέος, ὅν μοι ἔδωκε Μάρων, Εὐάνθεος υἱός,
ἱρεὺς Ἀπόλλωνος, ὃς Ἴσμαρον ἀμφιβεβήκει,
οὕνεκά μιν σὺν παιδὶ περισχόμεθ᾽ ἠδὲ γυναικὶ
ἁζόμενοι· ᾤκει γὰρ ἐν ἄλσεϊ δενδρήεντι
Φοίβου Ἀπόλλωνος. ὁ δέ μοι πόρεν ἀγλαὰ δῶρα·
χρυσοῦ μέν μοι ἔδωκ᾽ ἐυεργέος ἑπτὰ τάλαντα,
δῶκε δέ μοι κρητῆρα πανάργυρον, αὐτὰρ ἔπειτα
οἶνον ἐν ἀμφιφορεῦσι δυώδεκα πᾶσιν ἀφύσσας
ἡδὺν ἀκηράσιον, θεῖον ποτόν· οὐδέ τις αὐτὸν
ἠείδη δμώων οὐδ᾽ ἀμφιπόλων ἐνὶ οἴκῳ,
ἀλλ᾽ αὐτὸς ἄλοχός τε φίλη ταμίη τε μῖ᾽ οἴη.
τὸν δ᾽ ὅτε πίνοιεν μελιηδέα οἶνον ἐρυθρόν,
ἓν δέπας ἐμπλήσας ὕδατος ἀνὰ εἴκοσι μέτρα
χεῦ᾽, ὀδμὴ δ᾽ ἡδεῖα ἀπὸ κρητῆρος ὀδώδει
θεσπεσίη· τότ᾽ ἂν οὔ τοι ἀποσχέσθαι φίλον ἦεν.
τοῦ φέρον ἐμπλήσας ἀσκὸν μέγαν, ἐν δὲ καὶ ᾖα
κωρύκῳ· αὐτίκα γάρ μοι ὀίσατο θυμὸς ἀγήνωρ
ἄνδρ᾽ ἐπελεύσεσθαι μεγάλην ἐπιειμένον ἀλκήν,
ἄγριον, οὔτε δίκας ἐὺ εἰδότα οὔτε θέμιστας.

  "Καρπαλίμως δ᾽ εἰς ἄντρον ἀφικόμεθ᾽, οὐδέ μιν ἔνδο

heart set on lawlessness. For he was fashioned a wondrous monster, and was not like a man that lives by bread, but like a wooded peak of lofty mountains, which stands out to view alone, apart from the rest.

"Then I bade the rest of my trusty comrades to remain there by the ship and to guard the ship, but I chose twelve of the best of my comrades and went my way. With me I had a goat-skin of the dark, sweet wine, which Maro, son of Euanthes, had given me, the priest of Apollo, the god who used to watch over Ismarus. And he had given it me because we had protected him with his child and wife out of reverence; for he dwelt in a wooded grove of Phoebus Apollo. And he gave me splendid gifts: of well-wrought gold he gave me seven talents, and he gave me a mixing-bowl all of silver; and besides these, wine, wherewith he filled twelve jars in all, wine sweet and unmixed, a drink divine. Not one of his slaves nor of the maids in his halls knew thereof, but himself and his dear wife, and one house-dame only. And as often as they drank that honey-sweet red wine he would fill one cup and pour it into twenty measures of water, and a smell would rise from the mixing-bowl marvellously sweet; then verily would one not choose to hold back. With this wine I filled and took with me a great skin, and also provision in a scrip; for my proud spirit had a foreboding that presently a man would come to me clothed in great might, a savage man that knew naught of justice or of law.[1]

"Speedily we came to the cave, nor did we find

---

[1] In the Greek both words are plural. The idea is therefore not abstract, but concrete, and suggests that "law" was to the speaker a body of traditional decrees, or dooms.

εὕρομεν, ἀλλ' ἐνόμευε νομὸν κάτα πίονα μῆλα.
ἐλθόντες δ' εἰς ἄντρον ἐθηεύμεσθα ἕκαστα.
ταρσοὶ μὲν τυρῶν βρῖθον, στείνοντο δὲ σηκοὶ
ἀρνῶν ἠδ' ἐρίφων· διακεκριμέναι δὲ ἕκασται   22
ἔρχατο, χωρὶς μὲν πρόγονοι, χωρὶς δὲ μέτασσαι,
χωρὶς δ' αὖθ' ἕρσαι.   ναῖον δ' ὀρῷ ἄγγεα πάντα,
γαυλοί τε σκαφίδες τε, τετυγμένα, τοῖς ἐνάμελγεν.
ἔνθ' ἐμὲ μὲν πρώτισθ' ἕταροι λίσσοντ' ἐπέεσσιν
τυρῶν αἰνυμένους ἰέναι πάλιν, αὐτὰρ ἔπειτα   22
καρπαλίμως ἐπὶ νῆα θοὴν ἐρίφους τε καὶ ἄρνας
σηκῶν ἐξελάσαντας ἐπιπλεῖν ἁλμυρὸν ὕδωρ·
ἀλλ' ἐγὼ οὐ πιθόμην, ἦ τ' ἂν πολὺ κέρδιον ἦεν,
ὄφρ' αὐτόν τε ἴδοιμι, καὶ εἴ μοι ξείνια δοίη·
οὐδ' ἄρ' ἔμελλ' ἑτάροισι φανεὶς ἐρατεινὸς ἔσεσθαι.   23

   " Ἔνθα δὲ πῦρ κήαντες ἐθύσαμεν ἠδὲ καὶ αὐτοὶ
τυρῶν αἰνύμενοι φάγομεν, μένομέν τέ μιν ἔνδον
ἥμενοι, ἧος ἐπῆλθε νέμων.   φέρε δ' ὄβριμον ἄχθος
ὕλης ἀζαλέης, ἵνα οἱ ποτιδόρπιον εἴη,
ἔντοσθεν[1] δ' ἄντροιο βαλὼν ὀρυμαγδὸν ἔθηκεν·   23
ἡμεῖς δὲ δείσαντες ἀπεσσύμεθ' ἐς μυχὸν ἄντρου.
αὐτὰρ ὅ γ' εἰς εὐρὺ σπέος ἤλασε πίονα μῆλα
πάντα μάλ' ὅσσ' ἤμελγε, τὰ δ' ἄρσενα λεῖπε θύρηφιν,
ἀρνειούς τε τράγους τε, βαθείης ἔκτοθεν[2] αὐλῆς.
αὐτὰρ ἔπειτ' ἐπέθηκε θυρεὸν μέγαν ὑψόσ' ἀείρας,   24
ὄβριμον· οὐκ ἂν τόν γε δύω καὶ εἴκοσ' ἄμαξαι
ἐσθλαὶ τετράκυκλοι ἀπ' οὔδεος ὀχλίσσειαν·

---

[1] ἔντοσθεν : ἔκτοσθεν.
[2] ἔκτοθεν : ἔντοθεν most editors ; cf. 338.

him within, but he was pasturing his fat flocks in the
fields.   So we entered the cave and gazed in wonder
at all things there.   The crates were laden with
cheeses, and the pens were crowded with lambs and
kids.   Each kind was penned separately : by them-
selves the firstlings, by themselves the later lambs,
and by themselves again the newly yeaned.   And
with whey were swimming all the well-wrought
vessels, the milk-pails and the bowls into which he
milked.   Then my comrades spoke and besought me
first of all to take of the cheeses and depart, and
thereafter speedily to drive to the swift ship the kids
and lambs from out the pens, and to sail over the
salt water.   But I did not listen to them—verily it
would have been better far—to the end that I might
see the man himself, and whether he would give me
gifts of entertainment.   Yet, as it fell, his appearing
was not to prove a joy to my comrades.

"Then we kindled a fire and offered sacrifice, and
ourselves, too, took of the cheeses and ate, and thus
we sat in the cave and waited for him until he came
back, herding his flocks.   He bore a mighty weight
of dry wood to serve him at supper time, and flung
it down with a crash inside the cave, but we, seized
with terror, shrank back into a recess of the cave.
But he drove his fat flocks into the wide cavern—all
those that he milked ; but the males—the rams and
the goats—he left without in the deep court.[1]   Then
he lifted on high and set in place the great door-
stone, a mighty rock ; two and twenty stout four-
wheeled waggons could not lift it from the ground,

[1] This rendering takes ἔκτοθεν as an adverb, and βαθείης
αὐλῆς as a local genitive (see Monro, *Homeric Grammar*,
§ 149). Otherwise we must change the text here and in 338.

τόσσην ἠλίβατον πέτρην ἐπέθηκε θύρῃσιν.
ἑζόμενος δ' ἤμελγεν ὄις καὶ μηκάδας αἶγας,
πάντα κατὰ μοῖραν, καὶ ὑπ' ἔμβρυον ἧκεν ἑκάστῃ.   24
αὐτίκα δ' ἥμισυ μὲν θρέψας λευκοῖο γάλακτος
πλεκτοῖς ἐν ταλάροισιν ἀμησάμενος κατέθηκεν,
ἥμισυ δ' αὖτ' ἔστησεν ἐν ἄγγεσιν, ὄφρα οἱ εἴη
πίνειν αἰνυμένῳ καί οἱ ποτιδόρπιον εἴη.
αὐτὰρ ἐπεὶ δὴ σπεῦσε πονησάμενος τὰ ἃ ἔργα,   25
καὶ τότε πῦρ ἀνέκαιε καὶ εἴσιδεν, εἴρετο δ' ἡμέας·
    "'Ὦ ξεῖνοι, τίνες ἐστέ; πόθεν πλεῖθ' ὑγρὰ κέλευθα
ἦ τι κατὰ πρῆξιν ἦ μαψιδίως ἀλάλησθε,
οἷά τε ληιστῆρες, ὑπεὶρ ἅλα, τοί τ' ἀλόωνται
ψυχὰς παρθέμενοι κακὸν ἀλλοδαποῖσι φέροντες;'   25
    "Ὣς ἔφαθ', ἡμῖν δ' αὖτε κατεκλάσθη φίλον ἦτορ,
δεισάντων φθόγγον τε βαρὺν αὐτόν τε πέλωρον.
ἀλλὰ καὶ ὣς μιν ἔπεσσιν ἀμειβόμενος προσέειπον·
    "'Ἡμεῖς τοι Τροίηθεν ἀποπλαγχθέντες Ἀχαιοὶ
παντοίοις ἀνέμοισιν ὑπὲρ μέγα λαῖτμα θαλάσσης,   26
οἴκαδε ἱέμενοι, ἄλλην ὁδὸν ἄλλα κέλευθα
ἤλθομεν· οὕτω που Ζεὺς ἤθελε μητίσασθαι.
λαοὶ δ' Ἀτρεΐδεω Ἀγαμέμνονος εὐχόμεθ' εἶναι,
τοῦ δὴ νῦν γε μέγιστον ὑπουράνιον κλέος ἐστί·
τόσσην γὰρ διέπερσε πόλιν καὶ ἀπώλεσε λαοὺς   26
πολλούς. ἡμεῖς δ' αὖτε κιχανόμενοι τὰ σὰ γοῦνα
ἱκόμεθ', εἴ τι πόροις ξεινήιον ἠὲ καὶ ἄλλως
δοίης δωτίνην, ἥ τε ξείνων θέμις ἐστίν.
ἀλλ' αἰδεῖο, φέριστε, θεούς· ἱκέται δέ τοί εἰμεν,
Ζεὺς δ' ἐπιτιμήτωρ ἱκετάων τε ξείνων τε,   27
ξείνιος, ὃς ξείνοισιν ἅμ' αἰδοίοισιν ὀπηδεῖ.'

such a towering mass of rock he set in the doorway. Thereafter he sat down and milked the ewes and bleating goats all in turn, and beneath each dam he placed her young. Then presently he curdled half the white milk, and gathered it in wicker baskets and laid it away, and the other half he set in vessels that he might have it to take and drink, and that it might serve him for supper. But when he had busily performed his tasks, then he rekindled the fire, and caught sight of us, and asked:

" 'Strangers, who are ye? Whence do ye sail over the watery ways? Is it on some business, or do ye wander at random over the sea, even as pirates, who wander, hazarding their lives and bringing evil to men of other lands?'

"So he spoke, and in our breasts our spirit was broken for terror of his deep voice and monstrous self; yet even so I made answer and spoke to him, saying:

" 'We, thou must know, are from Troy, Achaeans, driven wandering by all manner of winds over the great gulf of the sea. Seeking our home, we have come by another way, by other paths; so, I ween, Zeus was pleased to devise. And we declare that we are the men of Agamemnon, son of Atreus, whose fame is now mightiest under heaven, so great a city did he sack, and slew many people; but we on our part, thus visiting thee, have come as suppliants to thy knees, in the hope that thou wilt give us entertainment, or in other wise make some present, as is the due of strangers. Nay, mightiest one, reverence the gods; we are thy suppliants; and Zeus is the avenger of suppliants and strangers—Zeus, the strangers' god—who ever attends upon reverend strangers.'

"Ὣς ἐφάμην, ὁ δέ μ' αὐτίκ' ἀμείβετο νηλέι θυμῷ·
'Νήπιός εἰς, ὦ ξεῖν', ἢ τηλόθεν εἰλήλουθας,
ὅς με θεοὺς κέλεαι ἢ δειδίμεν ἢ ἀλέασθαι·
οὐ γὰρ Κύκλωπες Διὸς αἰγιόχου ἀλέγουσιν   2
οὐδὲ θεῶν μακάρων, ἐπεὶ ἦ πολὺ φέρτεροί εἰμεν·
οὐδ' ἂν ἐγὼ Διὸς ἔχθος ἀλευάμενος πεφιδοίμην
οὔτε σεῦ οὔθ' ἑτάρων, εἰ μὴ θυμός με κελεύοι.
ἀλλά μοι εἴφ' ὅπῃ ἔσχες ἰὼν ἐνεργέα νῆα,
ἤ που ἐπ' ἐσχατιῆς, ἦ καὶ σχεδόν, ὄφρα δαείω.'   2

"Ὣς φάτο πειράζων, ἐμὲ δ' οὐ λάθεν εἰδότα πολλά,
ἀλλά μιν ἄψορρον προσέφην δολίοις ἐπέεσσι·

"'Νέα μέν μοι κατέαξε Ποσειδάων ἐνοσίχθων
πρὸς πέτρῃσι βαλὼν ὑμῆς ἐπὶ πείρασι γαίης,
ἄκρῃ προσπελάσας· ἄνεμος δ' ἐκ πόντου ἔνεικεν·   2
αὐτὰρ ἐγὼ σὺν τοῖσδε ὑπέκφυγον αἰπὺν ὄλεθρον.'

"Ὣς ἐφάμην, ὁ δέ μ' οὐδὲν ἀμείβετο νηλέι θυμῷ,
ἀλλ' ὅ γ' ἀναΐξας ἑτάροις ἐπὶ χεῖρας ἴαλλε,
σὺν δὲ δύω μάρψας ὥς τε σκύλακας ποτὶ γαίῃ
κόπτ'· ἐκ δ' ἐγκέφαλος χαμάδις ῥέε, δεῦε δὲ γαῖαν.   2
τοὺς δὲ διὰ μελεϊστὶ ταμὼν ὡπλίσσατο δόρπον·
ἤσθιε δ' ὥς τε λέων ὀρεσίτροφος, οὐδ' ἀπέλειπεν,
ἔγκατά τε σάρκας τε καὶ ὀστέα μυελόεντα.
ἡμεῖς δὲ κλαίοντες ἀνεσχέθομεν Διὶ χεῖρας,
σχέτλια ἔργ' ὁρόωντες, ἀμηχανίη δ' ἔχε θυμόν.   2
αὐτὰρ ἐπεὶ Κύκλωψ μεγάλην ἐμπλήσατο νηδὺν
ἀνδρόμεα κρέ' ἔδων καὶ ἐπ' ἄκρητον γάλα πίνων,
κεῖτ' ἔντοσθ' ἄντροιο τανυσσάμενος διὰ μήλων.
τὸν μὲν ἐγὼ βούλευσα κατὰ μεγαλήτορα θυμὸν

" So I spoke, and he straightway made answer with pitiless heart: ' A fool art thou, stranger, or art come from afar, seeing that thou biddest me either to fear or to shun the gods. For the Cyclopes reck not of Zeus, who bears the aegis, nor of the blessed gods, since verily we are better far than they. Nor would I, to shun the wrath of Zeus, spare either thee or thy comrades, unless my own heart should bid me. But tell me where thou didst moor thy well-wrought ship on thy coming. Was it haply at a remote part of the land, or close by? I fain would know.'

" So he spoke, tempting me, but he trapped me not because of my great cunning; and I made answer again in crafty words:

" ' My ship Poseidon, the earth-shaker, dashed to pieces, casting her upon the rocks at the border of your land; for he brought her close to the headland, and the wind drove her in from the sea. But I, with these men here, escaped utter destruction.'

" So I spoke, but from his pitiless heart he made no answer, but sprang up and put forth his hands upon my comrades. Two of them at once he seized and dashed to the earth like puppies, and the brain flowed forth upon the ground and wetted the earth. Then he cut them limb from limb and made ready his supper, and ate them as a mountain-nurtured lion, leaving naught—ate the entrails, and the flesh, and the marrowy bones. And we with wailing held up our hands to Zeus, beholding his cruel deeds; and helplessness possessed our souls. But when the Cyclops had filled his huge maw by eating human flesh and thereafter drinking pure milk, he lay down within the cave, stretched out among the sheep. And I formed a plan in my great heart to steal near

ἆσσον ἰών, ξίφος ὀξὺ ἐρυσσάμενος παρὰ μηροῦ,　3

οὐτάμεναι πρὸς στῆθος, ὅθι φρένες ἧπαρ ἔχουσι,

χείρ᾽ ἐπιμασσάμενος· ἕτερος δέ με θυμὸς ἔρυκεν.

αὐτοῦ γάρ κε καὶ ἄμμες ἀπωλόμεθ᾽ αἰπὺν ὄλεθρον·

οὐ γάρ κεν δυνάμεσθα θυράων ὑψηλάων

χερσὶν ἀπώσασθαι λίθον ὄβριμον, ὃν προσέθηκεν.　3●

ὣς τότε μὲν στενάχοντες ἐμείναμεν Ἠῶ δῖαν.

" Ἦμος δ᾽ ἠριγένεια φάνη ῥοδοδάκτυλος Ἠώς,

καὶ τότε πῦρ ἀνέκαιε καὶ ἤμελγε κλυτὰ μῆλα,

πάντα κατὰ μοῖραν, καὶ ὑπ᾽ ἔμβρυον ἧκεν ἑκάστῃ.

αὐτὰρ ἐπεὶ δὴ σπεῦσε πονησάμενος τὰ ἃ ἔργα,　3●

σὺν δ᾽ ὅ γε δὴ αὖτε δύω μάρψας ὡπλίσσατο δεῖπνον.

δειπνήσας δ᾽ ἄντρου ἐξήλασε πίονα μῆλα,

ῥηιδίως ἀφελὼν θυρεὸν μέγαν· αὐτὰρ ἔπειτα

ἂψ ἐπέθηχ᾽, ὡς εἴ τε φαρέτρῃ πῶμ᾽ ἐπιθείη.

πολλῇ δὲ ῥοίζῳ πρὸς ὄρος τρέπε πίονα μῆλα　31

Κύκλωψ· αὐτὰρ ἐγὼ λιπόμην κακὰ βυσσοδομεύων,

εἴ πως τισαίμην, δοίη δέ μοι εὖχος Ἀθήνη.

" Ἥδε δέ μοι κατὰ θυμὸν ἀρίστη φαίνετο βουλή.

Κύκλωπος γὰρ ἔκειτο μέγα ῥόπαλον παρὰ σηκῷ,

χλωρὸν ἐλαΐνεον· τὸ μὲν ἔκταμεν, ὄφρα φοροίη　32

αὐανθέν. τὸ μὲν ἄμμες ἐίσκομεν εἰσορόωντες

ὅσσον θ᾽ ἱστὸν νηὸς ἐεικοσόροιο μελαίνης,

φορτίδος εὐρείης, ἥ τ᾽ ἐκπεράᾳ μέγα λαῖτμα·

τόσσον ἔην μῆκος, τόσσον πάχος εἰσοράασθαι.

τοῦ μὲν ὅσον τ᾽ ὄργυιαν ἐγὼν ἀπέκοψα παραστὰς　32

καὶ παρέθηχ᾽ ἑτάροισιν, ἀποξῦναι δ᾽ ἐκέλευσα·

οἱ δ᾽ ὁμαλὸν ποίησαν· ἐγὼ δ᾽ ἐθόωσα παραστὰς

him, and draw my sharp sword from beside my thigh and smite him in the breast, where the midriff holds the liver, feeling for the place with my hand. But a second thought checked me, for right there should we, too, have perished in utter ruin. For we should not have been able to thrust back with our hands from the high door the mighty stone which he had set there. So then, with wailing, we waited for the bright Dawn.

"As soon as early Dawn appeared, the rosy-fingered, he rekindled the fire and milked his goodly flocks all in turn, and beneath each dam placed her young. Then, when he had busily performed his tasks, again he seized two men at once and made ready his meal. And when he had made his meal he drove his fat flocks forth from the cave, easily moving away the great door-stone; and then he put it in place again, as one might set the lid upon a quiver. Then with loud whistling the Cyclops turned his fat flocks toward the mountain, and I was left there, devising evil in the deep of my heart, if in any way I might take vengeance on him, and Athene grant me glory.

"Now this seemed to my mind the best plan. There lay beside a sheep-pen a great club of the Cyclops, a staff of green olive-wood, which he had cut to carry with him when dry; and as we looked at it we thought it as large as is the mast of a black ship of twenty oars, a merchantman, broad of beam, which crosses over the great gulf; so huge it was in length and in breadth to look upon. To this I came, and cut off therefrom about a fathom's length and handed it to my comrades, bidding them dress it down; and they made it smooth, and I, standing by, sharpened it at the point, and then straightway took

ἄκρον, ἄφαρ δὲ λαβὼν ἐπυράκτεον ἐν πυρὶ κηλέῳ.
καὶ τὸ μὲν εὖ κατέθηκα κατακρύψας ὑπὸ κόπρῳ,
ἥ ῥα κατὰ σπείους κέχυτο μεγάλ᾽ ἤλιθα πολλή·   3⬚
αὐτὰρ τοὺς ἄλλους κλήρῳ πεπαλάσθαι [1] ἄνωγον,
ὅς τις τολμήσειεν ἐμοὶ σὺν μοχλὸν ἀείρας
τρῖψαι ἐν ὀφθαλμῷ, ὅτε τὸν γλυκὺς ὕπνος ἱκάνοι.
οἱ δ᾽ ἔλαχον τοὺς ἄν κε καὶ ἤθελον αὐτὸς ἑλέσθαι,
τέσσαρες, αὐτὰρ ἐγὼ πέμπτος μετὰ τοῖσιν ἐλέγμην.   3⬚
ἑσπέριος δ᾽ ἦλθεν καλλίτριχα μῆλα νομεύων.
αὐτίκα δ᾽ εἰς εὐρὺ σπέος ἤλασε πίονα μῆλα
πάντα μάλ᾽, οὐδέ τι λεῖπε βαθείης ἔκτοθεν [2] αὐλῆς,
ἤ τι ὀισάμενος, ἢ καὶ θεὸς ὣς ἐκέλευσεν.
αὐτὰρ ἔπειτ᾽ ἐπέθηκε θυρεὸν μέγαν ὑψόσ᾽ ἀείρας,   34
ἑζόμενος δ᾽ ἤμελγεν ὄις καὶ μηκάδας αἶγας,
πάντα κατὰ μοῖραν, καὶ ὑπ᾽ ἔμβρυον ἦκεν ἑκάστῃ.
αὐτὰρ ἐπεὶ δὴ σπεῦσε πονησάμενος τὰ ἃ ἔργα,
σὺν δ᾽ ὅ γε δὴ αὖτε δύω μάρψας ὡπλίσσατο δόρπον.
καὶ τότ᾽ ἐγὼ Κύκλωπα προσηύδων ἄγχι παραστάς,   3⬚
κισσύβιον μετὰ χερσὶν ἔχων μέλανος οἴνοιο·
   "᾽Κύκλωψ, τῆ, πίε οἶνον, ἐπεὶ φάγες ἀνδρόμεα κρέα
ὄφρ᾽ εἰδῇς οἷόν τι ποτὸν τόδε νηῦς ἐκεκεύθει
ἡμετέρη.   σοὶ δ᾽ αὖ λοιβὴν φέρον, εἴ μ᾽ ἐλεήσας
οἴκαδε πέμψειας· σὺ δὲ μαίνεαι οὐκέτ᾽ ἀνεκτῶς.   3⬚
σχέτλιε, πῶς κέν τίς σε καὶ ὕστερον ἄλλος ἵκοιτο
ἀνθρώπων πολέων, ἐπεὶ οὐ κατὰ μοῖραν ἔρεξας;"
   "῝Ως ἐφάμην, ὁ δ᾽ ἔδεκτο καὶ ἔκπιεν· ἥσατο δ᾽ αἰνῶς
ἡδὺ ποτὸν πίνων καί μ᾽ ᾔτεε δεύτερον αὖτις·

---

[1] πεπαλάσθαι Aristarchus, πεπαλάχθαι.
[2] ἔκτοθεν : ἔντοθεν most editors ; cf. 239.

it and hardened it in the blazing fire. Then I laid
it carefully away, hiding it beneath the dung, which
lay in great heaps throughout the cave. And I bade
my comrades cast lots among them, which of them
should have the hardihood with me to lift the stake
and grind it into his eye when sweet sleep should
come upon him. And the lot fell upon those whom
I myself would fain have chosen; four they were,
and I was numbered with them as the fifth. At even
then he came, herding his flocks of goodly fleece,
and straightway drove into the wide cave his fat
flocks one and all, and left not one without in the
deep court, either from some foreboding or because a
god so bade him. Then he lifted on high and set in
place the great door-stone, and sitting down he milked
the ewes and bleating goats all in turn, and beneath
each dam he placed her young. But when he had
busily performed his tasks, again he seized two men
at once and made ready his supper. Then I drew
near and spoke to the Cyclops, holding in my hands
an ivy [1] bowl of the dark wine:

"'Cyclops, take and drink wine after thy meal of
human flesh, that thou mayest know what manner of
drink this is which our ship contained. It was to
thee that I was bringing it as a drink offering, in the
hope that, touched with pity, thou mightest send me
on my way home; but thou ragest in a way that is
past all bearing. Cruel man, how shall any one of all
the multitudes of men ever come to thee again here-
after, seeing that thou hast wrought lawlessness?'

"So I spoke, and he took the cup and drained it,
and was wondrously pleased as he drank the sweet
draught, and asked me for it again a second time:

---

[1] That is, made of ivy wood.

" ' Δός μοι ἔτι πρόφρων, καί μοι τεὸν οὔνομα εἰπὲ   35
αὐτίκα νῦν, ἵνα τοι δῶ ξείνιον, ᾧ κε σὺ χαίρῃς.
καὶ γὰρ Κυκλώπεσσι φέρει ζείδωρος ἄρουρα
οἶνον ἐρισταφυλον, καί σφιν Διὸς ὄμβρος ἀέξει·
ἀλλὰ τόδ' ἀμβροσίης καὶ νέκταρός ἐστιν ἀπορρώξ.'
" '῝Ως φάτ', ἀτάρ οἱ αὖτις ἐγὼ πόρον αἴθοπα οἶνον. 30
τρὶς μὲν ἔδωκα φέρων, τρὶς δ' ἔκπιεν ἀφραδίῃσιν.
αὐτὰρ ἐπεὶ Κύκλωπα περὶ φρένας ἤλυθεν οἶνος,
καὶ τότε δή μιν ἔπεσσι προσηύδων μειλιχίοισι·
" ' Κύκλωψ, εἰρωτᾷς μ' ὄνομα κλυτόν, αὐτὰρ ἐγώ το
ἐξερέω· σὺ δέ μοι δὸς ξείνιον, ὥς περ ὑπέστης. 30
Οὖτις ἐμοί γ' ὄνομα· Οὖτιν δέ με κικλήσκουσι
μήτηρ ἠδὲ πατὴρ ἠδ' ἄλλοι πάντες ἑταῖροι.'
" '῝Ως ἐφάμην, ὁ δέ μ' αὐτίκ' ἀμείβετο νηλέι θυμῷ·
' Οὖτιν ἐγὼ πύματον ἔδομαι μετὰ οἷς ἑτάροισιν,
τοὺς δ' ἄλλους πρόσθεν· τὸ δέ τοι ξεινήιον ἔσται. 37
" '῏Η καὶ ἀνακλινθεὶς πέσεν ὕπτιος, αὐτὰρ ἔπειτα
κεῖτ' ἀποδοχμώσας παχὺν αὐχένα, κὰδ δέ μιν ὕπνος
ᾕρει πανδαμάτωρ· φάρυγος δ' ἐξέσσυτο οἶνος
ψωμοί τ' ἀνδρόμεοι· ὁ δ' ἐρεύγετο οἰνοβαρείων.
καὶ τότ' ἐγὼ τὸν μοχλὸν ὑπὸ σποδοῦ ἤλασα πολλῆς, 37
ἧος θερμαίνοιτο· ἔπεσσι δὲ πάντας ἑταίρους
θάρσυνον, μή τίς μοι ὑποδείσας ἀναδύη.
ἀλλ' ὅτε δὴ τάχ' ὁ μοχλὸς ἐλάινος ἐν πυρὶ μέλλεν
ἅψεσθαι, χλωρός περ ἐών, διεφαίνετο δ' αἰνῶς,
καὶ τότ' ἐγὼν ἆσσον φέρον ἐκ πυρός, ἀμφὶ δ' ἑταῖροι 38
ἵσταντ'· αὐτὰρ θάρσος ἐνέπνευσεν μέγα δαίμων.

328

"'Give it me again with a ready heart, and tell me thy name straightway, that I may give thee a stranger's gift· whereat thou mayest be glad. For among the Cyclopes the earth, the giver of grain, bears the rich clusters of wine, and the rain of Zeus gives them increase; but this is a streamlet of ambrosia and nectar.'

"So he spoke, and again I handed him the flaming wine. Thrice I brought and gave it him, and thrice he drained it in his folly. But when the wine had stolen about the wits of the Cyclops, then I spoke to him with gentle words:

"'Cyclops, thou askest me of my glorious name, and I will tell it thee; and do thou give me a stranger's gift, even as thou didst promise. Noman is my name, Noman do they call me—my mother and my father, and all my comrades as well.'

"So I spoke, and he straightway answered me with pitiless heart: 'Noman will I eat last among his comrades, and the others before him; this shall be thy gift.'

"He spoke, and reeling fell upon his back, and lay there with his thick neck bent aslant, and sleep, that conquers all, laid hold on him. And from his gullet came forth wine and bits of human flesh, and he vomited in his drunken sleep. Then verily I thrust in the stake under the deep ashes until it should grow hot, and heartened all my comrades with cheering words, that I might see no man flinch through fear. But when presently that stake of olive-wood was about to catch fire, green though it was, and began to glow terribly, then verily I drew nigh, bringing the stake from the fire, and my comrades stood round me and a god breathed into us

329

οἱ μὲν μοχλὸν ἑλόντες ἐλάινον, ὀξὺν ἐπ' ἄκρῳ,
ὀφθαλμῷ ἐνέρεισαν· ἐγὼ δ' ἐφύπερθεν ἐρεισθεὶς [1]
δίνεον, ὡς ὅτε τις τρυπῷ δόρυ νήιον ἀνὴρ
τρυπάνῳ, οἱ δέ τ' ἔνερθεν ὑποσσείουσιν ἱμάντι   385
ἁψάμενοι ἑκάτερθε, τὸ δὲ τρέχει ἐμμενὲς αἰεί.
ὣς τοῦ ἐν ὀφθαλμῷ πυρίηκεα μοχλὸν ἑλόντες
δινέομεν, τὸν δ' αἷμα περίρρεε θερμὸν ἐόντα.
πάντα δέ οἱ βλέφαρ' ἀμφὶ καὶ ὀφρύας εὗσεν ἀυτμὴ
γλήνης καιομένης, σφαραγεῦντο δέ οἱ πυρὶ ῥίζαι.   390
ὡς δ' ὅτ' ἀνὴρ χαλκεὺς πέλεκυν μέγαν ἠὲ σκέπαρνον
εἰν ὕδατι ψυχρῷ βάπτῃ μεγάλα ἰάχοντα
φαρμάσσων· τὸ γὰρ αὖτε σιδήρου γε κράτος ἐστίν·
ὣς τοῦ σίζ' ὀφθαλμὸς ἐλαϊνέῳ περὶ μοχλῷ.
σμερδαλέον δὲ μέγ' ᾤμωξεν, περὶ δ' ἴαχε πέτρη,   395
ἡμεῖς δὲ δείσαντες ἀπεσσύμεθ'· αὐτὰρ ὁ μοχλὸν
ἐξέρυσ' ὀφθαλμοῖο πεφυρμένον αἵματι πολλῷ.
τὸν μὲν ἔπειτ' ἔρριψεν ἀπὸ ἕο χερσὶν ἀλύων,
αὐτὰρ ὁ Κύκλωπας μεγάλ' ἤπυεν, οἵ ῥά μιν ἀμφὶς
ᾤκεον ἐν σπήεσσι δι' ἄκριας ἠνεμοέσσας.   400
οἱ δὲ βοῆς ἀίοντες ἐφοίτων ἄλλοθεν ἄλλος,
ἱστάμενοι δ' εἴροντο περὶ σπέος ὅττι ἑ κήδοι·
    " ' Τίπτε τόσον, Πολύφημ', ἀρημένος ὧδ' ἐβόησας
νύκτα δι' ἀμβροσίην καὶ ἀύπνους ἄμμε τίθησθα;
ἦ μή τίς σευ μῆλα βροτῶν ἀέκοντος ἐλαύνει;   405
ἦ μή τίς σ' αὐτὸν κτείνει δόλῳ ἠὲ βίηφιν;'
    " Τοὺς δ' αὖτ' ἐξ ἄντρου προσέφη κρατερὸς Πολύ-
        φημος·
'Ὦ φίλοι, Οὖτίς με κτείνει δόλῳ οὐδὲ βίηφιν.'
    " Οἱ δ' ἀπαμειβόμενοι ἔπεα πτερόεντ' ἀγόρευον·
' Εἰ μὲν δὴ μή τίς σε βιάζεται οἶον ἐόντα,   410

---

[1] ἐρεισθεὶς Aristarchus : ἀερθείς.

great courage. They took the stake of olive-wood, sharp at the point, and thrust it into his eye, while I, throwing my weight upon it from above, whirled it round, as when a man bores a ship's timber with a drill, while those below keep it spinning with the thong, which they lay hold of by either end, and the drill runs around unceasingly. Even so we took the fiery-pointed stake and whirled it around in his eye, and the blood flowed around the heated thing. And his eyelids wholly and his brows round about did the flame singe as the eyeball burned, and its roots crackled in the fire. And as when a smith dips a great axe or an adze in cold water amid loud hissing to temper it—for therefrom comes the strength of iron—even so did his eye hiss round the stake of olive-wood. Terribly then did he cry aloud, and the rock rang around; and we, seized with terror, shrank back, while he wrenched from his eye the stake, all befouled with blood, and flung it from him, wildly waving his arms. Then he called aloud to the Cyclopes, who dwelt round about him in caves among the windy heights, and they heard his cry and came thronging from every side, and standing around the cave asked him what ailed him:

" 'What so sore distress is thine, Polyphemus, that thou criest out thus through the immortal night, and makest us sleepless? Can it be that some mortal man is driving off thy flocks against thy will, or slaying thee thyself by guile or by might?'

"Then from out the cave the mighty Polyphemus answered them: 'My friends, it is Noman that is slaying me by guile and not by force.'

"And they made answer and addressed him with winged words: 'If, then, no man does violence to

νοῦσόν γ' οὔ πως ἔστι Διὸς μεγάλου ἀλέασθαι,
ἀλλὰ σύ γ' εὔχεο πατρὶ Ποσειδάωνι ἄνακτι.'
  "Ὣς ἄρ' ἔφαν ἀπιόντες, ἐμὸν δ' ἐγέλασσε φίλον κῆρ
ὡς ὄνομ' ἐξαπάτησεν ἐμὸν καὶ μῆτις ἀμύμων.
Κύκλωψ δὲ στενάχων τε καὶ ὠδίνων ὀδύνῃσι   4
χερσὶ ψηλαφόων ἀπὸ μὲν λίθον εἷλε θυράων,
αὐτὸς δ' εἰνὶ θύρῃσι καθέζετο χεῖρε πετάσσας,
εἴ τινά που μετ' ὄεσσι λάβοι στείχοντα θύραζε·
οὕτω γάρ πού μ' ἤλπετ' ἐνὶ φρεσὶ νήπιον εἶναι.
αὐτὰρ ἐγὼ βούλευον, ὅπως ὄχ' ἄριστα γένοιτο,   4
εἴ τιν' ἑταίροισιν θανάτου λύσιν ἠδ' ἐμοὶ αὐτῷ
εὑροίμην· πάντας δὲ δόλους καὶ μῆτιν ὕφαινον
ὥς τε περὶ ψυχῆς· μέγα γὰρ κακὸν ἐγγύθεν ἦεν.
ἥδε δέ μοι κατὰ θυμὸν ἀρίστη φαίνετο βουλή.
ἄρσενες ὄιες ἦσαν ἐυτρεφέες, δασύμαλλοι,   4
καλοί τε μεγάλοι τε, ἰοδνεφὲς εἶρος ἔχοντες·
τοὺς ἀκέων συνέεργον ἐυστρεφέεσσι λύγοισιν,
τῆς ἔπι Κύκλωψ εὗδε πέλωρ, ἀθεμίστια εἰδώς,
σύντρεις αἰνύμενος· ὁ μὲν ἐν μέσῳ ἄνδρα φέρεσκε,
τὼ δ' ἑτέρω ἑκάτερθεν ἴτην σώοντες ἑταίρους.   4
τρεῖς δὲ ἕκαστον φῶτ' ὄιες φέρον· αὐτὰρ ἐγώ γε —
ἀρνειὸς γὰρ ἔην μήλων ὄχ' ἄριστος ἁπάντων,
τοῦ κατὰ νῶτα λαβών, λασίην ὑπὸ γαστέρ' ἐλυσθεὶς
κείμην· αὐτὰρ χερσὶν ἀώτου θεσπεσίοιο
νωλεμέως στρεφθεὶς ἐχόμην τετληότι θυμῷ.   4
ὣς τότε μὲν στενάχοντες ἐμείναμεν Ἠῶ δῖαν.
  "Ἦμος δ' ἠριγένεια φάνη ῥοδοδάκτυλος Ἠώς,
καὶ τότ' ἔπειτα νομόνδ' ἐξέσσυτο ἄρσενα μῆλα,
θήλειαι δὲ μέμηκον ἀνήμελκτοι περὶ σηκούς·

332

thee in thy loneliness, sickness which comes from great Zeus thou mayest in no wise escape. Nay, do thou pray to our father, the lord Poseidon.'

"So they spoke and went their way; and my heart laughed within me that my name and cunning device had so beguiled. But the Cyclops, groaning and travailing in anguish, groped with his hands and took away the stone from the door, and himself sat in the doorway with arms outstretched in the hope of catching anyone who sought to go forth with the sheep—so witless, forsooth, he thought in his heart to find me. But I took counsel how all might be the very best, if I might haply find some way of escape from death for my comrades and for myself. And I wove all manner of wiles and counsel, as a man will in a matter of life and death; for great was the evil that was nigh us. And this seemed to my mind the best plan. Rams there were, well-fed and thick of fleece, fine beasts and large, with wool dark as the violet. These I silently bound together with twisted withes on which the Cyclops, that monster with his heart set on lawlessness, was wont to sleep. Three at a time I took. The one in the middle in each case bore a man, and the other two went, one on either side, saving my comrades. Thus every three sheep bore a man. But as for me—there was a ram, far the best of all the flock; him I grasped by the back, and curled beneath his shaggy belly, lay there face upwards with steadfast heart, clinging fast with my hands to his wondrous fleece. So then, with wailing, we waited for the bright dawn.

"As soon as early Dawn appeared, the rosy-fingered, then the males of the flock hastened forth to pasture and the females bleated unmilked about the pens,

οὔθατα γὰρ σφαραγεῦντο. ἄναξ δ' ὀδύνῃσι κακῇσι 4·
τειρόμενος πάντων οἴων ἐπεμαίετο νῶτα
ὀρθῶν ἑσταότων· τὸ δὲ νήπιος οὐκ ἐνόησεν,
ὥς οἱ ὑπ' εἰροπόκων οἴων στέρνοισι δέδεντο.
ὕστατος ἀρνειὸς μήλων ἔστειχε θύραζε
λάχνῳ στεινόμενος καὶ ἐμοὶ πυκινὰ φρονέοντι.   4·
τὸν δ' ἐπιμασσάμενος προσέφη κρατερὸς Πολύφημος·
   "'Κριὲ πέπον, τί μοι ὧδε διὰ σπέος ἔσσυο μήλων
ὕστατος; οὔ τι πάρος γε λελειμμένος ἔρχεαι οἰῶν,
ἀλλὰ πολὺ πρῶτος νέμεαι τέρεν' ἄνθεα ποίης
μακρὰ βιβάς, πρῶτος δὲ ῥοὰς ποταμῶν ἀφικάνεις,   4·
πρῶτος δὲ σταθμόνδε λιλαίεαι ἀπονέεσθαι
ἑσπέριος· νῦν αὖτε πανύστατος. ἦ σύ γ' ἄνακτος
ὀφθαλμὸν ποθέεις, τὸν ἀνὴρ κακὸς ἐξαλάωσε
σὺν λυγροῖς ἑτάροισι δαμασσάμενος φρένας οἴνῳ,
Οὖτις, ὃν οὔ πώ φημι πεφυγμένον εἶναι ὄλεθρον.   4·
εἰ δὴ ὁμοφρονέοις ποτιφωνήεις τε γένοιο
εἰπεῖν ὅππῃ κεῖνος ἐμὸν μένος ἠλασκάζει·
τῷ κέ οἱ ἐγκέφαλός γε διὰ σπέος ἄλλυδις ἄλλῃ
θεινομένου ῥαίοιτο πρὸς οὔδεϊ, κὰδ δέ κ' ἐμὸν κῆρ
λωφήσειε κακῶν, τά μοι οὐτιδανὸς πόρεν Οὖτις.'   46
   "Ὣς εἰπὼν τὸν κριὸν ἀπὸ ἕο πέμπε θύραζε.
ἐλθόντες δ' ἠβαιὸν ἀπὸ σπείους τε καὶ αὐλῆς
πρῶτος ὑπ' ἀρνειοῦ λυόμην, ὑπέλυσα δ' ἑταίρους.
καρπαλίμως δὲ τὰ μῆλα ταναύποδα, πίονα δημῷ,
πολλὰ περιτροπέοντες ἐλαύνομεν, ὄφρ' ἐπὶ νῆα   46

for their udders were bursting. And their master, distressed with grievous pains, felt along the backs of all the sheep as they stood up before him, but in his folly he marked not this, that my men were bound beneath the breasts of his fleecy sheep. Last of all the flock the ram went forth, burdened with the weight of his fleece and my cunning self. And mighty Polyphemus, as he felt along his back, spoke to him, saying:

"'Good ram, why pray is it that thou goest forth thus through the cave the last of the flock? Thou hast not heretofore been wont to lag behind the sheep, but wast ever far the first to feed on the tender bloom of the grass, moving with long strides, and ever the first didst reach the streams of the river, and the first didst long to return to the fold at evening. But now thou art last of all. Surely thou art sorrowing for the eye of thy master, which an evil man blinded along with his miserable fellows, when he had overpowered my wits with wine, even Noman, who, I tell thee, has not yet escaped destruction. If only thou couldst feel as I do, and couldst get thee power of speech to tell me where he skulks away from my wrath, then should his brains be dashed on the ground here and there throughout the cave, when I had smitten him, and my heart should be lightened of the woes which good-for-naught Noman has brought me.'

"So saying, he sent the ram forth from him. And when we had gone a little way from the cave and the court, I first loosed myself from under the ram and set my comrades free. Speedily then we drove off those long-shanked sheep, rich with fat, turning full often to look about until we came to the ship.

ἱκόμεθ᾽. ἀσπάσιοι δὲ φίλοις ἑτάροισι φάνημεν,
οἳ φύγομεν θάνατον, τοὺς δὲ στενάχοντο γοῶντες.
ἀλλ᾽ ἐγὼ οὐκ εἴων, ἀνὰ δ᾽ ὀφρύσι νεῦον ἑκάστῳ,
κλαίειν, ἀλλ᾽ ἐκέλευσα θοῶς καλλίτριχα μῆλα
πόλλ᾽ ἐν νηὶ βαλόντας ἐπιπλεῖν ἁλμυρὸν ὕδωρ.   47
οἱ δ᾽ αἶψ᾽ εἴσβαινον καὶ ἐπὶ κληῖσι καθῖζον,
ἑξῆς δ᾽ ἑζόμενοι πολιὴν ἅλα τύπτον ἐρετμοῖς.
ἀλλ᾽ ὅτε τόσσον ἀπῆν, ὅσσον τε γέγωνε βοήσας,
καὶ τότ᾽ ἐγὼ Κύκλωπα προσηύδων κερτομίοισι·
  "᾽ Κύκλωψ, οὐκ ἄρ᾽ ἔμελλες ἀνάλκιδος ἀνδρὸς
        ἑταίρους   47
ἔδμεναι ἐν σπῆι γλαφυρῷ κρατερῆφι βίηφι.
καὶ λίην σέ γ᾽ ἔμελλε κιχήσεσθαι κακὰ ἔργα,
σχέτλι᾽, ἐπεὶ ξείνους οὐχ ἄζεο σῷ ἐνὶ οἴκῳ
ἐσθέμεναι· τῷ σε Ζεὺς τίσατο καὶ θεοὶ ἄλλοι.᾽
  "Ὣς ἐφάμην, ὁ δ᾽ ἔπειτα χολώσατο κηρόθι
        μᾶλλον,   48
ἧκε δ᾽ ἀπορρήξας κορυφὴν ὄρεος μεγάλοιο,
κὰδ δ᾽ ἔβαλε προπάροιθε νεὸς κυανοπρώροιο.[1]
ἐκλύσθη δὲ θάλασσα κατερχομένης ὑπὸ πέτρης·
τὴν δ᾽ αἶψ᾽ ἠπειρόνδε παλιρρόθιον φέρε κῦμα,   48
πλημυρὶς ἐκ πόντοιο, θέμωσε δὲ χέρσον ἱκέσθαι.
αὐτὰρ ἐγὼ χείρεσσι λαβὼν περιμήκεα κοντὸν
ὦσα παρέξ, ἑτάροισι δ᾽ ἐποτρύνας ἐκέλευσα
ἐμβαλέειν κώπῃς, ἵν᾽ ὑπὲκ κακότητα φύγοιμεν,
κρατὶ κατανεύων· οἱ δὲ προπεσόντες ἔρεσσον.   49
ἀλλ᾽ ὅτε δὴ δὶς τόσσον ἅλα πρήσσοντες ἀπῆμεν,

---

[1] Line 483 (=540), τυτθόν, ἐδεύησεν δ᾽ οἰήιον ἄκρον ἱκέσθαι,
was rejected by Aristarchus.

And welcome to our dear comrades was the sight of us who had escaped death, but for the others they wept and wailed; yet I would not suffer them to weep, but with a frown forbade each man. Rather I bade them to fling on board with speed the many sheep of goodly fleece, and sail over the salt water. So they went on board straightway and sat down upon the benches, and sitting well in order smote the grey sea with their oars. But when I was as far away as a man's voice carries when he shouts, then I spoke to the Cyclops with mocking words:

"'Cyclops, that man, it seems, was no weakling, whose comrades thou wast minded to devour by brutal strength in thy hollow cave. Full surely were thy evil deeds to fall on thine own head, thou cruel wretch, who didst not shrink from eating thy guests in thine own house. Therefore has Zeus taken vengeance on thee, and the other gods.'

"So I spoke, and he waxed the more wroth at heart, and broke off the peak of a high mountain and hurled it at us, and cast it in front of the dark-prowed ship.[1] And the sea surged beneath the stone as it fell, and the backward flow, like a flood from the deep, bore the ship swiftly landwards and drove it upon the shore. But I seized a long pole in my hands and shoved the ship off and along the shore, and with a nod of my head I roused my comrades, and bade them fall to their oars that we might escape out of our evil plight. And they bent to their oars and rowed. But when, as we fared over the sea, we were twice as far distant, then was I fain to call

---

[1] The spurious verse 483 has been omitted in the translation as ruinous to the sense. It has made its way into the text from 540, where it is in place.

καὶ τότε δὴ Κύκλωπα προσηύδων· ἀμφὶ δ' ἑταῖροι
μειλιχίοις ἐπέεσσιν ἐρήτυον ἄλλοθεν ἄλλος·

" ' Σχέτλιε, τίπτ' ἐθέλεις ἐρεθιζέμεν ἄγριον ἄνδρα;
ὃς καὶ νῦν πόντονδε βαλὼν βέλος ἤγαγε νῆα
αὖτις ἐς ἤπειρον, καὶ δὴ φάμεν αὐτόθ' ὀλέσθαι.
εἰ δὲ φθεγξαμένου τευ ἢ αὐδήσαντος ἄκουσε,
σύν κεν ἄραξ' ἡμέων κεφαλὰς καὶ νήια δοῦρα
μαρμάρῳ ὀκριόεντι βαλών· τόσσον γὰρ ἵησιν.'

" Ὣς φάσαν, ἀλλ' οὐ πεῖθον ἐμὸν μεγαλήτορα
θυμόν,
ἀλλά μιν ἄψορρον προσέφην κεκοτηότι θυμῷ·

" ' Κύκλωψ, αἴ κέν τίς σε καταθνητῶν ἀνθρώπων
ὀφθαλμοῦ εἴρηται ἀεικελίην ἀλαωτύν,
φάσθαι 'Οδυσσῆα πτολιπόρθιον ἐξαλαῶσαι,
υἱὸν Λαέρτεω, 'Ιθάκῃ ἔνι οἰκί' ἔχοντα.'

" Ὣς ἐφάμην, ὁ δέ μ' οἰμώξας ἠμείβετο μύθῳ·
' Ὢ πόποι, ἦ μάλα δή με παλαίφατα θέσφαθ' ἱκάνει.
ἔσκε τις ἐνθάδε μάντις ἀνὴρ ἠΰς τε μέγας τε,
Τήλεμος Εὐρυμίδης, ὃς μαντοσύνῃ ἐκέκαστο
καὶ μαντευόμενος κατεγήρα Κυκλώπεσσιν·
ὅς μοι ἔφη τάδε πάντα τελευτήσεσθαι ὀπίσσω,
χειρῶν ἐξ 'Οδυσῆος ἁμαρτήσεσθαι ὀπωπῆς.
ἀλλ' αἰεί τινα φῶτα μέγαν καὶ καλὸν ἐδέγμην
ἐνθάδ' ἐλεύσεσθαι, μεγάλην ἐπιειμένον ἀλκήν·
νῦν δέ μ' ἐὼν ὀλίγος τε καὶ οὐτιδανὸς καὶ ἄκικυς
ὀφθαλμοῦ ἀλάωσεν, ἐπεί μ' ἐδαμάσσατο οἴνῳ.
ἀλλ' ἄγε δεῦρ', 'Οδυσεῦ, ἵνα τοι πὰρ ξείνια θείω
πομπήν τ' ὀτρύνω δόμεναι κλυτὸν ἐννοσίγαιον·
τοῦ γὰρ ἐγὼ πάις εἰμί, πατὴρ δ' ἐμὸς εὔχεται εἶναι.

to the Cyclops, though round about me my comrades, one after another, sought to check me with gentle words :

" ' Reckless one, why wilt thou provoke to wrath a savage man, who but now hurled his missile into the deep and drove our ship back to the land, and verily we thought that we had perished there ? And had he heard one of us uttering a sound or speaking, he would have hurled a jagged rock and crushed our heads and the timbers of our ship, so mightily does he throw.'

" So they spoke, but they could not persuade my great-hearted spirit ; and I answered him again with angry heart :

" ' Cyclops, if any one of mortal men shall ask thee about the shameful blinding of thine eye, say that Odysseus, the sacker of cities, blinded it, even the son of Laertes, whose home is in Ithaca.'

" So I spoke, and he groaned and said in answer : ' Lo now, verily a prophecy uttered long ago is come upon me. There lived here a soothsayer, a good man and tall, Telemus, son of Eurymus, who excelled all men in soothsaying, and grew old as a seer among the Cyclopes. He told me that all these things should be brought to pass in days to come, that by the hands of Odysseus I should lose my sight. But I ever looked for some tall and comely man to come hither, clothed in great might, but now one that is puny, a man of naught and a weakling, has blinded me of my eye when he had overpowered me with wine. Yet come hither, Odysseus, that I may set before thee gifts of entertainment, and may speed thy sending hence, that the glorious Earth-shaker may grant it thee. For I am his son, and he declares him-

αὐτὸς δ᾽, αἴ κ᾽ ἐθέλῃσ᾽, ἰήσεται, οὐδέ τις ἄλλος   520
οὔτε θεῶν μακάρων οὔτε θνητῶν ἀνθρώπων.᾽
   "῝Ως ἔφατ᾽, αὐτὰρ ἐγώ μιν ἀμειβόμενος προσέειπον·
Αἲ γὰρ δὴ ψυχῆς τε καὶ αἰῶνός σε δυναίμην
εὖνιν ποιήσας πέμψαι δόμον ῝Αιδος εἴσω,
ὡς οὐκ ὀφθαλμόν γ᾽ ἰήσεται οὐδ᾽ ἐνοσίχθων.᾽   525
   "῝Ως ἐφάμην, ὁ δ᾽ ἔπειτα Ποσειδάωνι ἄνακτι
εὔχετο χεῖρ᾽ ὀρέγων εἰς οὐρανὸν ἀστερόεντα·
῾Κλῦθι, Ποσείδαον γαιήοχε κυανοχαῖτα,
εἰ ἐτεόν γε σός εἰμι, πατὴρ δ᾽ ἐμὸς εὔχεαι εἶναι,
δὸς μὴ ᾽Οδυσσῆα πτολιπόρθιον οἴκαδ᾽ ἱκέσθαι   530
υἱὸν Λαέρτεω, ᾽Ιθάκῃ ἔνι οἰκί᾽ ἔχοντα.[1]
ἀλλ᾽ εἴ οἱ μοῖρ᾽ ἐστὶ φίλους τ᾽ ἰδέειν καὶ ἱκέσθαι
οἶκον ἐυκτίμενον καὶ ἑὴν ἐς πατρίδα γαῖαν,
ὀψὲ κακῶς ἔλθοι, ὀλέσας ἄπο πάντας ἑταίρους,
νηὸς ἐπ᾽ ἀλλοτρίης, εὕροι δ᾽ ἐν πήματα οἴκῳ.᾽   535
   "῝Ως ἔφατ᾽ εὐχόμενος, τοῦ δ᾽ ἔκλυε κυανοχαίτης.
αὐτὰρ ὅ γ᾽ ἐξαῦτις πολὺ μείζονα λᾶαν ἀείρας
ἧκ᾽ ἐπιδινήσας, ἐπέρεισε δὲ ἶν᾽ ἀπέλεθρον,
κὰδ δ᾽ ἔβαλεν μετόπισθε νεὸς κυανοπρώροιο
τυτθόν, ἐδεύησεν δ᾽ οἰήιον ἄκρον ἱκέσθαι.   540
ἐκλύσθη δὲ θάλασσα κατερχομένης ὑπὸ πέτρης·
τὴν δὲ πρόσω φέρε κῦμα, θέμωσε δὲ χέρσον ἱκέσθαι.
   "᾽Αλλ᾽ ὅτε δὴ τὴν νῆσον ἀφικόμεθ᾽, ἔνθα περ ἄλλαι
νῆες ἐύσσελμοι μένον ἀθρόαι, ἀμφὶ δ᾽ ἑταῖροι
ἥατ᾽ ὀδυρόμενοι, ἡμέας ποτιδέγμενοι αἰεί,   545
νῆα μὲν ἔνθ᾽ ἐλθόντες ἐκέλσαμεν ἐν ψαμάθοισιν,
ἐκ δὲ καὶ αὐτοὶ βῆμεν ἐπὶ ῥηγμῖνι θαλάσσης.

[1] Line 531 is omitted in most MSS.

self my father; and he himself will heal me, if it be his good pleasure, but none other either of the blessed gods or of mortal men.'

"So he spoke, and I answered him and said: 'Would that I were able to rob thee of soul and life, and to send thee to the house of Hades, as surely as not even the Earth-shaker shall heal thine eye.'

"So I spoke, and he then prayed to the lord Poseidon, stretching out both his hands to the starry heaven: 'Hear me, Poseidon, earth-enfolder, thou dark-haired god, if indeed I am thy son and thou declarest thyself my father; grant that Odysseus, the sacker of cities, may never reach his home, even the son of Laertes, whose home is in Ithaca; but if it is his fate to see his friends and to reach his well-built house and his native land, late may he come and in evil case, after losing all his comrades, in a ship that is another's; and may he find woes in his house.'

"So he spoke in prayer, and the dark-haired god heard him. But the Cyclops lifted on high again a far greater stone, and swung and hurled it, putting into the throw measureless strength. He cast it a little behind the dark-prowed ship, and barely missed the end of the steering-oar. And the sea surged beneath the stone as it fell, and the wave bore the ship onward and drove it to the shore.

"Now when we had come to the island, where our other well-benched ships lay all together, and round about them our comrades, ever expecting us, sat weeping, then, on coming thither, we beached our ship on the sands, and ourselves went forth upon the shore

341

μῆλα δὲ Κύκλωπος γλαφυρῆς ἐκ νηὸς ἑλόντες
δασσάμεθ', ὡς μή τίς μοι ἀτεμβόμενος κίοι ἴσης.
ἀρνειὸν δ' ἐμοὶ οἴῳ ἐυκνήμιδες ἑταῖροι   5⁵
μήλων δαιομένων δόσαν ἔξοχα· τὸν δ' ἐπὶ θινὶ
Ζηνὶ κελαινεφέι Κρονίδῃ, ὃς πᾶσιν ἀνάσσει,
ῥέξας μηρί' ἔκαιον· ὁ δ' οὐκ ἐμπάζετο ἱρῶν,
ἀλλ' ὅ γε μερμήριζεν ὅπως ἀπολοίατο πᾶσαι
νῆες ἐύσσελμοι καὶ ἐμοὶ ἐρίηρες ἑταῖροι.   5⁵

    "Ὣς τότε μὲν πρόπαν ἦμαρ ἐς ἠέλιον καταδύντα
ἥμεθα δαινύμενοι κρέα τ' ἄσπετα καὶ μέθυ ἡδύ·
ἦμος δ' ἠέλιος κατέδυ καὶ ἐπὶ κνέφας ἦλθε,
δὴ τότε κοιμήθημεν ἐπὶ ῥηγμῖνι θαλάσσης.
ἦμος δ' ἠριγένεια φάνη ῥοδοδάκτυλος Ἠώς,   5⁰
δὴ τότ' ἐγὼν ἑτάροισιν ἐποτρύνας ἐκέλευσα
αὐτούς τ' ἀμβαίνειν ἀνά τε πρυμνήσια λῦσαι·
οἱ δ' αἶψ' εἴσβαινον καὶ ἐπὶ κληῖσι καθῖζον,
ἑξῆς δ' ἑζόμενοι πολιὴν ἅλα τύπτον ἐρετμοῖς.

    "Ἔνθεν δὲ προτέρω πλέομεν ἀκαχήμενοι ἦτορ,   5⁰
ἄσμενοι ἐκ θανάτοιο, φίλους ὀλέσαντες ἑταίρους.

of the sea. Then we took from out the hollow ship the flocks of the Cyclops, and divided them, that so far as in me lay no man might go defrauded of an equal share. But the ram my well-greaved comrades gave to me alone, when the flocks were divided, as a gift apart; and on the shore I sacrificed him to Zeus, son of Cronos, god of the dark clouds, who is lord of all, and burned the thigh-pieces. Howbeit he heeded not my sacrifice, but was planning how all my well-benched ships might perish and my trusty comrades.

"So, then, all day long till set of sun we sat feasting on abundant flesh and sweet wine; but when the sun set and darkness came on, then we lay down to rest on the shore of the sea. And as soon as early Dawn appeared, the rosy-fingered, I roused my comrades, and bade them themselves to embark and to loose the stern cables. So they went on board straightway and sat down upon the benches, and sitting well in order smote the grey sea with their oars.

"Thence we sailed on, grieved at heart, glad to have escaped death, though we had lost our dear comrades.

K

" Αἰολίην δ' ἐς νῆσον ἀφικόμεθ'· ἔνθα δ' ἔναιεν
Αἴολος Ἱπποτάδης, φίλος ἀθανάτοισι θεοῖσιν,
πλωτῇ ἐνὶ νήσῳ· πᾶσαν δέ τέ μιν πέρι τεῖχος
χάλκεον ἄρρηκτον, λισσὴ δ' ἀναδέδρομε πέτρη.
τοῦ καὶ δώδεκα παῖδες ἐνὶ μεγάροις γεγάασιν,
ἐξ μὲν θυγατέρες, ἐξ δ' υἱέες ἡβώοντες·
ἔνθ' ὅ γε θυγατέρας πόρεν υἱάσιν εἶναι ἀκοίτις.
οἱ δ' αἰεὶ παρὰ πατρὶ φίλῳ καὶ μητέρι κεδνῇ
δαίνυνται, παρὰ δέ σφιν ὀνείατα μυρία κεῖται,
κνισῆεν δέ τε δῶμα περιστεναχίζεται αὐλῇ
ἤματα· νύκτας δ' αὖτε παρ' αἰδοίης ἀλόχοισιν
εὕδουσ' ἔν τε τάπησι καὶ ἐν τρητοῖσι λέχεσσι.
καὶ μὲν τῶν ἱκόμεσθα πόλιν καὶ δώματα καλά.
μῆνα δὲ πάντα φίλει με καὶ ἐξερέεινεν ἕκαστα,
Ἴλιον Ἀργείων τε νέας καὶ νόστον Ἀχαιῶν·
καὶ μὲν ἐγὼ τῷ πάντα κατὰ μοῖραν κατέλεξα.
ἀλλ' ὅτε δὴ καὶ ἐγὼν ὁδὸν ᾔτεον ἠδ' ἐκέλευον
πεμπέμεν, οὐδέ τι κεῖνος ἀνήνατο, τεῦχε δὲ πομπήν.
δῶκε δέ μ' ἐκδείρας ἀσκὸν βοὸς ἐννεώροιο,
ἔνθα δὲ βυκτάων ἀνέμων κατέδησε κέλευθα·
κεῖνον γὰρ ταμίην ἀνέμων ποίησε Κρονίων,

---

[1] The meaning is that the savour and the sound of feasting
may be noticed even before one enters the house proper.
[2] The word is a doubtful one. The rendering here given
seems demanded by xi. 311, and fits all passages, though it

344

BOOK X

"THEN to the Aeolian isle we came, where dwelt
Aeolus, son of Hippotas, dear to the immortal gods,
in a floating island, and all around it is a wall of
unbreakable bronze, and the cliff runs up sheer.
Twelve children of his, too, there are in the halls,
six daughters and six sturdy sons, and he gave his
daughters to his sons to wife. These, then, feast
continually by their dear father and good mother,
and before them lies boundless good cheer. And
the house, filled with the savour of feasting, re-
sounds all about even in the outer court by day,[1]
and by night again they sleep beside their chaste
wives on blankets and on corded bedsteads. To
their city, then, and fair palace did we come, and for
a full month he made me welcome and questioned
me about each thing, about Ilios, and the ships of
the Argives, and the return of the Achaeans. And
I told him all the tale in due order. But when I, on
my part, asked him that I might depart and bade
him send me on my way, he, too, denied me nothing,
but furthered my sending. He gave me a wallet,
made of the hide of an ox nine years old,[2] which he
flayed, and therein he bound the paths of the blus-
tering winds; for the son of Cronos had made him

cannot be said to be appropriate in x. 390. Possibly nine
was felt merely as a round number, or the age of nine taken
merely to denote full maturity.

ἠμὲν παυέμεναι ἠδ' ὀρνύμεν, ὅν κ' ἐθέλῃσι.
νηὶ δ' ἐνὶ γλαφυρῇ κατέδει μέρμιθι φαεινῇ
ἀργυρέῃ, ἵνα μή τι παραπνεύσῃ ὀλίγον περ·
αὐτὰρ ἐμοὶ πνοιὴν Ζεφύρου προέηκεν ἀῆναι,   2
ὄφρα φέροι νῆάς τε καὶ αὐτούς· οὐδ' ἄρ' ἔμελλεν
ἐκτελέειν· αὐτῶν γὰρ ἀπωλόμεθ' ἀφραδίῃσιν.

  "'Εννῆμαρ μὲν ὁμῶς πλέομεν νύκτας τε καὶ ἦμαρ,
τῇ δεκάτῃ δ' ἤδη ἀνεφαίνετο πατρὶς ἄρουρα,
καὶ δὴ πυρπολέοντας ἐλεύσσομεν ἐγγὺς ἐόντες·[1]   3
ἔνθ' ἐμὲ μὲν γλυκὺς ὕπνος ἐπήλυθε κεκμηῶτα,
αἰεὶ γὰρ πόδα νηὸς ἐνώμων, οὐδέ τῳ ἄλλῳ
δῶχ' ἑτάρων, ἵνα θᾶσσον ἱκοίμεθα πατρίδα γαῖαν·
οἱ δ' ἕταροι ἐπέεσσι πρὸς ἀλλήλους ἀγόρευον,
καί μ' ἔφασαν χρυσόν τε καὶ ἄργυρον οἴκαδ' ἄγεσθαι 3
δῶρα παρ' Αἰόλου μεγαλήτορος Ἱπποτάδαο.
ὧδε δέ τις εἴπεσκεν ἰδὼν ἐς πλησίον ἄλλον·

  "''Ω πόποι, ὡς ὅδε πᾶσι φίλος καὶ τίμιός ἐστιν
ἀνθρώποις, ὁτεῶν τε πόλιν καὶ γαῖαν ἵκηται.
πολλὰ μὲν ἐκ Τροίης ἄγεται κειμήλια καλὰ   4
ληίδος, ἡμεῖς δ' αὖτε ὁμὴν ὁδὸν ἐκτελέσαντες
οἴκαδε νισσόμεθα κενεὰς σὺν χεῖρας ἔχοντες·
καὶ νῦν οἱ τάδ' ἔδωκε χαριζόμενος φιλότητι
Αἴολος. ἀλλ' ἄγε θᾶσσον ἰδώμεθα ὅττι τάδ' ἐστίν,
ὅσσος τις χρυσός τε καὶ ἄργυρος ἀσκῷ ἔνεστιν.'   4

  "Ὡς ἔφασαν, βουλὴ δὲ κακὴ νίκησεν ἑταίρων·
ἀσκὸν μὲν λῦσαν, ἄνεμοι δ' ἐκ πάντες ὄρουσαν.
τοὺς δ' αἶψ' ἁρπάξασα φέρεν πόντονδε θύελλα

_____
[1] ἐόντες : ἐόντας.

keeper of the winds, both to still and to rouse whatever one he will. And in my hollow ship he bound it fast with a bright cord of silver, that not a breath might escape, were it never so slight. But for my furtherance he sent forth the breath of the West Wind to blow, that it might bear on their way both ships and men. Yet this he was not to bring to pass, for we were lost through our own folly.

" For nine days we sailed, night and day alike, and now on the tenth our native land came in sight, and lo, we were so near that we saw men tending the beacon fires.[1] Then upon me came sweet sleep in my weariness, for I had ever kept in hand the sheet of the ship, and had yielded it to none other of my comrades, that we might the sooner come to our native land. But my comrades meanwhile began to speak one to another, and said that I was bringing home for myself gold and silver as gifts from Aeolus, the great-hearted son of Hippotas. And thus would one speak, with a glance at his neighbour :

" ' Out on it, how beloved and honoured this man is by all men, to whose city and land soever he comes ! Much goodly treasure is he carrying with him from the land of Troy from out the spoil, while we, who have accomplished the same journey as he, are returning, bearing with us empty hands. And now Aeolus has given him these gifts, granting them freely of his love. Nay, come, let us quickly see what is here, what store of gold and silver is in the wallet.'

" So they spoke, and the evil counsel of my comrades prevailed. They loosed the wallet, and all the winds leapt forth, and swiftly the storm-wind seized them

[1] Or the allusion may be to the fires of the herdsmen.

κλαίοντας, γαίης ἄπο πατρίδος. αὐτὰρ ἐγώ γε
ἐγρόμενος κατὰ θυμὸν ἀμύμονα μερμήριξα,   5
ἠὲ πεσὼν ἐκ νηὸς ἀποφθίμην ἐνὶ πόντῳ,
ἦ ἀκέων τλαίην καὶ ἔτι ζωοῖσι μετείην.
ἀλλ' ἔτλην καὶ ἔμεινα, καλυψάμενος δ' ἐνὶ νηὶ
κείμην. αἱ δ' ἐφέροντο κακῇ ἀνέμοιο θυέλλῃ
αὖτις ἐπ' Αἰολίην νῆσον, στενάχοντο δ' ἑταῖροι.   5

  " "Ἔνθα δ' ἐπ' ἠπείρου βῆμεν καὶ ἀφυσσάμεθ' ὕδωρ,
αἶψα δὲ δεῖπνον ἕλοντο θοῆς παρὰ νηυσὶν ἑταῖροι.
αὐτὰρ ἐπεὶ σίτοιό τ' ἐπασσάμεθ' ἠδὲ ποτῆτος,
δὴ τότ' ἐγὼ κήρυκά τ' ὀπασσάμενος καὶ ἑταῖρον
βῆν εἰς Αἰόλου κλυτὰ δώματα· τὸν δ' ἐκίχανον   6
δαινύμενον παρὰ ᾗ τ' ἀλόχῳ καὶ οἷσι τέκεσσιν.
ἐλθόντες δ' ἐς δῶμα παρὰ σταθμοῖσιν ἐπ' οὐδοῦ
ἑζόμεθ'· οἱ δ' ἀνὰ θυμὸν ἐθάμβεον ἔκ τ' ἐρέοντο·

  " 'Πῶς ἦλθες, Ὀδυσεῦ; τίς τοι κακὸς ἔχραε δαίμων;
ἦ μέν σ' ἐνδυκέως ἀπεπέμπομεν, ὄφρ' ἀφίκοιο   6
πατρίδα σὴν καὶ δῶμα καὶ εἴ πού τοι φίλον ἐστίν.'

  " "Ὣς φάσαν, αὐτὰρ ἐγὼ μετεφώνεον ἀχνύμενος κῆρ·
'Ἄασάν μ' ἕταροί τε κακοὶ πρὸς τοῖσί τε ὕπνος
σχέτλιος. ἀλλ' ἀκέσασθε, φίλοι· δύναμις γὰρ ἐν ὑμῖ

  " "Ὣς ἐφάμην μαλακοῖσι καθαπτόμενος ἐπέεσσιν,   7
οἱ δ' ἄνεῳ ἐγένοντο· πατὴρ δ' ἠμείβετο μύθῳ·

  " "'Ἔρρ' ἐκ νήσου θᾶσσον, ἐλέγχιστε ζωόντων·
οὐ γάρ μοι θέμις ἐστὶ κομιζέμεν οὐδ' ἀποπέμπειν
ἄνδρα τόν, ὅς κε θεοῖσιν ἀπέχθηται μακάρεσσιν·
ἔρρε, ἐπεὶ ἄρα θεοῖσιν ἀπεχθόμενος τόδ' ἱκάνεις.'   7
348

and bore them weeping out to sea away from their native land; but as for me, I awoke, and pondered in my goodly heart whether I should fling myself from the ship and perish in the sea, or endure in silence and still remain among the living. However, I endured and abode, and covering my head lay down in the ship. But the ships were borne by an evil blast of wind back to the Aeolian isle; and my comrades groaned.

"There we went ashore and drew water, and straightway my comrades took their meal by the swift ships. But when we had tasted of food and drink, I took with me a herald and one companion and went to the glorious palace of Aeolus, and I found him feasting beside his wife and his children. So we entered the house and sat down by the door-posts on the threshold, and they were amazed at heart, and questioned us:

"'How hast thou come hither, Odysseus? What cruel god assailed thee? Surely we sent thee forth with kindly care, that thou mightest reach thy native land and thy home, and whatever place thou wouldest.'

"So said they, but I with a sorrowing heart spoke among them and said: 'Bane did my evil comrades work me, and therewith sleep accursed; but bring ye healing, my friends, for with you is the power.'

"So I spoke and addressed them with gentle words, but they were silent. Then their father answered and said:

"'Begone from our island with speed, thou vilest of all that live. In no wise may I help or send upon his way that man who is hated of the blessed gods. Begone, for thou comest hither as one hated of the immortals.'

" Ὡς εἰπὼν ἀπέπεμπε δόμων βαρέα στενάχοντα.
ἔνθεν δὲ προτέρω πλέομεν ἀκαχήμενοι ἦτορ.
τείρετο δ' ἀνδρῶν θυμὸς ὑπ' εἰρεσίης ἀλεγεινῆς
ἡμετέρῃ ματίῃ, ἐπεὶ οὐκέτι φαίνετο πομπή.
ἑξῆμαρ μὲν ὁμῶς πλέομεν νύκτας τε καὶ ἦμαρ,   8
ἑβδομάτῃ δ' ἱκόμεσθα Λάμου αἰπὺ πτολίεθρον,
Τηλέπυλον Λαιστρυγονίην, ὅθι ποιμένα ποιμὴν
ἠπύει εἰσελάων, ὁ δέ τ' ἐξελάων ὑπακούει.
ἔνθα κ' ἄϋπνος ἀνὴρ δοιοὺς ἐξήρατο μισθούς,
τὸν μὲν βουκολέων, τὸν δ' ἄργυφα μῆλα νομεύων·   8
ἐγγὺς γὰρ νυκτός τε καὶ ἤματός εἰσι κέλευθοι.
ἐνθ' ἐπεὶ ἐς λιμένα κλυτὸν ἤλθομεν, ὃν πέρι πέτρη
ἠλίβατος τετύχηκε διαμπερὲς ἀμφοτέρωθεν,
ἀκταὶ δὲ προβλῆτες ἐναντίαι ἀλλήλῃσιν
ἐν στόματι προύχουσιν, ἀραιὴ δ' εἴσοδός ἐστιν,   9
ἔνθ' οἵ γ' εἴσω πάντες ἔχον νέας ἀμφιελίσσας.
αἱ μὲν ἄρ' ἔντοσθεν λιμένος κοίλοιο δέδεντο
πλησίαι· οὐ μὲν γάρ ποτ' ἀέξετο κῦμά γ' ἐν αὐτῷ,
οὔτε μέγ' οὔτ' ὀλίγον, λευκὴ δ' ἦν ἀμφὶ γαλήνη·
αὐτὰρ ἐγὼν οἶος σχέθον ἔξω νῆα μέλαιναν,   9
αὐτοῦ ἐπ' ἐσχατιῇ, πέτρης ἐκ πείσματα δήσας·
ἔστην δὲ σκοπιὴν ἐς παιπαλόεσσαν ἀνελθών.
ἔνθα μὲν οὔτε βοῶν οὔτ' ἀνδρῶν φαίνετο ἔργα,
καπνὸν δ' οἶον ὁρῶμεν ἀπὸ χθονὸς ἀΐσσοντα.
δὴ τότ' ἐγὼν ἑτάρους προΐειν πεύθεσθαι ἰόντας,   10
οἵ τινες ἀνέρες εἶεν ἐπὶ χθονὶ σῖτον ἔδοντες,

---

[1] The meaning appears to be that the interval between
nightfall and daybreak is so short that a herdsman return-
ing from his day's task meets his fellow already driving his

"So saying, he sent me forth from the house, groaning heavily. Thence we sailed on, grieved at heart. And worn was the spirit of the men by the grievous rowing, because of our own folly, for no longer appeared any breeze to bear us on our way. So for six days we sailed, night and day alike, and on the seventh we came to the lofty citadel of Lamus, even to Telepylus of the Laestrygonians, where herdsman calls to herdsman as he drives in his flock, and the other answers as he drives his forth. There a man who never slept could have earned a double wage, one by herding cattle, and one by pasturing white sheep; for the outgoings of the night and of the day are close together.[1] When we had come thither into the goodly harbour, about which on both sides a sheer cliff runs continuously, and projecting headlands opposite to one another stretch out at the mouth, and the entrance is narrow, then all the rest steered their curved ships in, and the ships were moored within the hollow harbour close together; for therein no wave ever swelled, great or small, but all about was a bright calm. But I alone moored my black ship outside, there on the border of the land, making the cables fast to the rock. Then I climbed to a rugged height, a point of outlook, and there took my stand; from thence no works of oxen or of men appeared; smoke alone we saw springing up from the land. So then I sent forth some of my comrades to go and learn who the men were, who here ate bread upon

---

flock forth for the following day. Thus a man who could do without sleep could earn a double wage. The passage is plainly due to some vague knowledge of the land of the midnight sun.

ἄνδρε δύω κρίνας, τρίτατον κήρυχ' ἅμ' ὀπάσσας.
οἱ δ' ἴσαν ἐκβάντες λείην ὁδόν, ᾗ περ ἄμαξαι
ἄστυδ' ἀφ' ὑψηλῶν ὀρέων καταγίνεον ὕλην,
κούρῃ δὲ ξύμβληντο πρὸ ἄστεος ὑδρευούσῃ,   10
θυγατέρ' ἰφθίμῃ Λαιστρυγόνος Ἀντιφάταο.
ἡ μὲν ἄρ' ἐς κρήνην κατεβήσετο καλλιρέεθρον
Ἀρτακίην· ἔνθεν γὰρ ὕδωρ προτὶ ἄστυ φέρεσκον·
οἱ δὲ παριστάμενοι προσεφώνεον ἔκ τ' ἐρέοντο
ὅς τις τῶνδ' εἴη βασιλεὺς καὶ οἷσιν ἀνάσσοι·   15
ἡ δὲ μάλ' αὐτίκα πατρὸς ἐπέφραδεν ὑψερεφὲς δῶ.
οἱ δ' ἐπεὶ εἰσῆλθον κλυτὰ δώματα, τὴν δὲ γυναῖκα
εὗρον, ὅσην τ' ὄρεος κορυφήν, κατὰ δ' ἔστυγον αὐτήν.
ἡ δ' αἶψ' ἐξ ἀγορῆς ἐκάλει κλυτὸν Ἀντιφατῆα,
ὃν πόσιν, ὃς δὴ τοῖσιν ἐμήσατο λυγρὸν ὄλεθρον.   11
αὐτίχ' ἕνα μάρψας ἑτάρων ὡπλίσσατο δεῖπνον·
τὼ δὲ δύ' ἀίξαντε φυγῇ ἐπὶ νῆας ἱκέσθην.
αὐτὰρ ὁ τεῦχε βοὴν διὰ ἄστεος· οἱ δ' ἀίοντες
φοίτων ἴφθιμοι Λαιστρυγόνες ἄλλοθεν ἄλλος,
μυρίοι, οὐκ ἄνδρεσσιν ἐοικότες, ἀλλὰ Γίγασιν.   1
οἵ ῥ' ἀπὸ πετράων ἀνδραχθέσι χερμαδίοισιν
βάλλον· ἄφαρ δὲ κακὸς κόναβος κατὰ νῆας ὀρώρει
ἀνδρῶν τ' ὀλλυμένων νηῶν θ' ἅμα ἀγνυμενάων·
ἰχθῦς δ' ὣς πείροντες ἀτερπέα δαῖτα φέροντο.[1]
ὄφρ' οἱ τοὺς ὄλεκον λιμένος πολυβενθέος ἐντός,   1

----

[1] φέροντο Zenodotus, Aristarchus : πένοντο.

---

[1] The word ἰφθίμη might in this context naturally be
taken to mean " stalwart," or even " huge " (cf. 113), but as

the earth—two men I chose, and sent with them a third as a herald. Now when they had gone ashore, they went along a smooth road by which waggons were wont to bring wood down to the city from the high mountains. And before the city they met a maiden drawing water, the goodly [1] daughter of Laestrygonian Antiphates, who had come down to the fair-flowing spring Artacia, from whence they were wont to bear water to the town. So they came up to her and spoke to her, and asked her who was king of this folk, and who they were of whom he was lord. And she showed them forthwith the high-roofed house of her father. Now when they had entered the glorious house, they found there his wife, huge as the peak of a mountain, and they were aghast at her. At once she called from the place of assembly the glorious Antiphates, her husband, and he devised for them woeful destruction. Straightway he seized one of my comrades and made ready his meal, but the other two sprang up and came in flight to the ships. Then he raised a cry throughout the city, and as they heard it the mighty Laestrygonians came thronging from all sides, a host past counting, not like men but like the Giants. They hurled at us from the cliffs with rocks huge as a man could lift, and at once there rose throughout the ships a dreadful din, alike from men that were dying and from ships that were being crushed. And spearing them like fishes they bore them home, a loathly meal. Now while they were slaying those within the deep harbour, I mean-

it is used twice of Penelope, and more than once of other women, in which cases no such connotation is to be thought of, I have preferred to give a more general rendering.

τόφρα δ' ἐγὼ ξίφος ὀξὺ ἐρυσσάμενος παρὰ μηροῦ
τῷ ἀπὸ πείσματ' ἔκοψα νεὸς κυανοπρώροιο.
αἶψα δ' ἐμοῖς ἑτάροισιν ἐποτρύνας ἐκέλευσα
ἐμβαλέειν κώπῃς, ἵν' ὑπὲκ κακότητα φύγοιμεν·
οἱ δ' ἄλα[1] πάντες ἀνέρριψαν, δείσαντες ὄλεθρον.   1?
ἀσπασίως δ' ἐς πόντον ἐπηρεφέας φύγε πέτρας
νηῦς ἐμή· αὐτὰρ αἱ ἄλλαι ἀολλέες αὐτόθ' ὄλοντο.

"Ἔνθεν δὲ προτέρω πλέομεν ἀκαχήμενοι ἦτορ,
ἄσμενοι ἐκ θανάτοιο, φίλους ὀλέσαντες ἑταίρους.
Αἰαίην δ' ἐς νῆσον ἀφίκομεθ'· ἔνθα δ' ἔναιε   1?
Κίρκη ἐυπλόκαμος, δεινὴ θεὸς αὐδήεσσα,
αὐτοκασιγνήτη ὀλοόφρονος Αἰήταο·
ἄμφω δ' ἐκγεγάτην φαεσιμβρότου Ἠελίοιο
μητρός τ' ἐκ Πέρσης, τὴν Ὠκεανὸς τέκε παῖδα.
ἔνθα δ' ἐπ' ἀκτῆς νηὶ κατηγαγόμεσθα σιωπῇ   14?
ναύλοχον ἐς λιμένα, καί τις θεὸς ἡγεμόνευεν.
ἔνθα τότ' ἐκβάντες δύο τ' ἤματα καὶ δύο νύκτας
κείμεθ' ὁμοῦ καμάτῳ τε καὶ ἄλγεσι θυμὸν ἔδοντες.
ἀλλ' ὅτε δὴ τρίτον ἦμαρ ἐυπλόκαμος τέλεσ' Ἠώς,
καὶ τότ' ἐγὼν ἐμὸν ἔγχος ἑλὼν καὶ φάσγανον ὀξὺ   14?
καρπαλίμως παρὰ νηὸς ἀνήιον ἐς περιωπήν,
εἴ πως ἔργα ἴδοιμι βροτῶν ἐνοπήν τε πυθοίμην.
ἔστην δὲ σκοπιὴν ἐς παιπαλόεσσαν ἀνελθών,
καί μοι ἐείσατο καπνὸς ἀπὸ χθονὸς εὐρυοδείης,
Κίρκης ἐν μεγάροισι, διὰ δρυμὰ πυκνὰ καὶ ὕλην.   1?
μερμήριξα δ' ἔπειτα κατὰ φρένα καὶ κατὰ θυμὸν
ἐλθεῖν ἠδὲ πυθέσθαι, ἐπεὶ ἴδον αἴθοπα καπνόν.
ὧδε δέ μοι φρονέοντι δοάσσατο κέρδιον εἶναι,

[1] ἄλα Rhianus, Callistratus : ἅμα Aristarchus : ἄρα.

while drew my sharp sword from beside my thigh, and cut therewith the cables of my dark-prowed ship; and quickly calling to my comrades bade them fall to their oars, that we might escape from out our evil plight. And they all tossed the sea with their oar-blades in fear of death, and joyfully seaward, away from the beetling cliffs, my ship sped on; but all those other ships were lost together there.

"Thence we sailed on, grieved at heart, glad to have escaped death, though we had lost our dear comrades; and we came to the isle of Aeaea, where dwelt fair-tressed Circe, a dread goddess of human speech, own sister to Aeetes of baneful mind; and both are sprung from Helius, who gives light to mortals, and from Perse, their mother, whom Oceanus begot. Here we put in to shore with our ship in silence, into a harbour where ships may lie, and some god guided us. Then we disembarked, and lay there for two days and two nights, eating our hearts for weariness and sorrow. But when fair-tressed Dawn brought to its birth the third day, then I took my spear and my sharp sword, and quickly went up from the ship to a place of wide prospect, in the hope that I might see the works of men, and hear their voice. So I climbed to a rugged height, a place of outlook, and there took my stand, and I saw smoke rising from the broad-wayed earth in the halls of Circe, through the thick brush and the wood. And I debated in mind and heart, whether I should go and make search, when I had seen the flaming smoke. And as I pondered, this seemed to me to be the better way, to go first

πρῶτ' ἐλθόντ' ἐπὶ νῆα θοὴν καὶ θῖνα θαλάσσης
δεῖπνον ἑταίροισιν δόμεναι προέμεν τε πυθέσθαι.   15
ἀλλ' ὅτε δὴ σχεδὸν ἦα κιὼν νεὸς ἀμφιελίσσης,
καὶ τότε τίς με θεῶν ὀλοφύρατο μοῦνον ἐόντα,
ὅς ῥά μοι ὑψίκερων ἔλαφον μέγαν εἰς ὁδὸν αὐτὴν
ἧκεν.   ὁ μὲν ποταμόνδε κατήιεν ἐκ νομοῦ ὕλης
πιόμενος· δὴ γάρ μιν ἔχεν μένος ἠελίοιο.   16
τὸν δ' ἐγὼ ἐκβαίνοντα κατ' ἄκνηστιν μέσα νῶτα
πλῆξα· τὸ δ' ἀντικρὺ δόρυ χάλκεον ἐξεπέρησε,
κὰδ δ' ἔπεσ' ἐν κονίῃσι μακών, ἀπὸ δ' ἔπτατο θυμός.
τῷ δ' ἐγὼ ἐμβαίνων δόρυ χάλκεον ἐξ ὠτειλῆς
εἰρυσάμην· τὸ μὲν αὖθι κατακλίνας ἐπὶ γαίῃ   16
εἴασ'· αὐτὰρ ἐγὼ σπασάμην ῥῶπάς τε λύγους τε,
πεῖσμα δ', ὅσον τ' ὄργυιαν, ἐυστρεφὲς ἀμφοτέρωθεν
πλεξάμενος συνέδησα πόδας δεινοῖο πελώρου,
βῆν δὲ καταλοφάδεια φέρων ἐπὶ νῆα μέλαιναν
ἔγχει ἐρειδόμενος, ἐπεὶ οὔ πως ἦεν ἐπ' ὤμου   17
χειρὶ φέρειν ἑτέρῃ· μάλα γὰρ μέγα θηρίον ἦεν.
κὰδ δ' ἔβαλον προπάροιθε νεός, ἀνέγειρα δ' ἑταίρους
μειλιχίοις ἐπέεσσι παρασταδὸν ἄνδρα ἕκαστον·

    " 'Ὦ φίλοι, οὐ γάρ πω καταδυσόμεθ' ἀχνύμενοί περ
εἰς Ἀίδαο δόμους, πρὶν μόρσιμον ἦμαρ ἐπέλθῃ·   17
ἀλλ' ἄγετ', ὄφρ' ἐν νηὶ θοῇ βρῶσίς τε πόσις τε,
μνησόμεθα βρώμης, μηδὲ τρυχώμεθα λιμῷ.'

    " Ὣς ἐφάμην, οἱ δ' ὦκα ἐμοῖς ἐπέεσσι πίθοντο,
ἐκ δὲ καλυψάμενοι παρὰ θῖν' ἁλὸς ἀτρυγέτοιο
θηήσαντ' ἔλαφον· μάλα γὰρ μέγα θηρίον ἦεν.   18

to the swift ship and the shore of the sea, and give my comrades their meal, and send them forth to make search. But when, as I went, I was near to the curved ship, then some god took pity on me in my loneliness, and sent a great, high-horned stag into my very path. He was coming down to the river from his pasture in the wood to drink, for the might of the sun oppressed him; and as he came out I struck him on the spine in the middle of the back, and the bronze spear passed right through him, and down he fell in the dust with a moan, and his spirit flew from him. Then I planted my foot upon him, and drew the bronze spear forth from the wound, and left it there to lie on the ground. But for myself, I plucked twigs and osiers, and weaving a rope as it were a fathom in length, well twisted from end to end, I bound together the feet of the monstrous beast, and went my way to the black ship, bearing him across my back and leaning on my spear, since in no wise could I hold him on my shoulder with one hand, for he was a very mighty beast. Down I flung him before the ship, and heartened my comrades with gentle words, coming up to each man in turn:

"'Friends, not yet shall we go down to the house of Hades, despite our sorrows, before the day of fate comes upon us. Nay, come, while there is yet food and drink in our swift ship, let us bethink us of food, that we pine not with hunger.'

"So I spoke, and they quickly hearkened to my words. From their faces they drew their cloaks,[1] and marvelled at the stag on the shore of the unresting sea, for he was a very mighty beast. But

[1] The Greek veiled his face under stress of despairing sorrow.

αὐτὰρ ἐπεὶ τάρπησαν ὁρώμενοι ὀφθαλμοῖσιν,
χεῖρας νιψάμενοι τεύχοντ᾽ ἐρικυδέα δαῖτα.
ὣς τότε μὲν πρόπαν ἦμαρ ἐς ἠέλιον καταδύντα
ἥμεθα δαινύμενοι κρέα τ᾽ ἄσπετα καὶ μέθυ ἡδύ·
ἦμος δ᾽ ἠέλιος κατέδυ καὶ ἐπὶ κνέφας ἦλθε,   185
δὴ τότε κοιμήθημεν ἐπὶ ῥηγμῖνι θαλάσσης.
ἦμος δ᾽ ἠριγένεια φάνη ῥοδοδάκτυλος Ἠώς,
καὶ τότ᾽ ἐγὼν ἀγορὴν θέμενος μετὰ πᾶσιν ἔειπον·
    " ' Κέκλυτέ μευ μύθων, κακά περ πάσχοντες ἑταῖροι
ὦ φίλοι, οὐ γάρ τ᾽ ἴδμεν, ὅπῃ ζόφος οὐδ᾽ ὅπῃ ἠώς,   190
οὐδ᾽ ὅπῃ ἠέλιος φαεσίμβροτος εἶσ᾽ ὑπὸ γαῖαν,
οὐδ᾽ ὅπῃ ἀννεῖται· ἀλλὰ φραζώμεθα θᾶσσον
εἴ τις ἔτ᾽ ἔσται μῆτις. ἐγὼ δ᾽ οὐκ οἴομαι εἶναι.
εἶδον γὰρ σκοπιὴν ἐς παιπαλόεσσαν ἀνελθὼν
νῆσον, τὴν πέρι πόντος ἀπείριτος ἐστεφάνωται·   195
αὐτὴ δὲ χθαμαλὴ κεῖται· καπνὸν δ᾽ ἐνὶ μέσσῃ
ἔδρακον ὀφθαλμοῖσι διὰ δρυμὰ πυκνὰ καὶ ὕλην.'
    " Ὣς ἐφάμην, τοῖσιν δὲ κατεκλάσθη φίλον ἦτορ
μνησαμένοις ἔργων Λαιστρυγόνος Ἀντιφάταο
Κύκλωπός τε βίης μεγαλήτορος, ἀνδροφάγοιο.   200
κλαῖον δὲ λιγέως θαλερὸν κατὰ δάκρυ χέοντες·
ἀλλ᾽ οὐ γάρ τις πρῆξις ἐγίγνετο μυρομένοισιν.
    " Αὐτὰρ ἐγὼ δίχα πάντας ἐυκνήμιδας ἑταίρους
ἠρίθμεον, ἀρχὸν δὲ μετ᾽ ἀμφοτέροισιν ὄπασσα·
τῶν μὲν ἐγὼν ἦρχον, τῶν δ᾽ Εὐρύλοχος θεοειδής.   205
κλήρους δ᾽ ἐν κυνέῃ χαλκήρεϊ πάλλομεν ὦκα·
ἐκ δ᾽ ἔθορε κλῆρος μεγαλήτορος Εὐρυλόχοιο.
βῆ δ᾽ ἰέναι, ἅμα τῷ γε δύω καὶ εἴκοσ᾽ ἑταῖροι
κλαίοντες· κατὰ δ᾽ ἄμμε λίπον γοόωντας ὄπισθεν.
εὗρον δ᾽ ἐν βήσσῃσι τετυγμένα δώματα Κίρκης   210

---

¹ Line 189 was rejected in antiquity.

when they had satisfied their eyes with gazing, they
washed their hands, and made ready a glorious feast.
So then all day long till set of sun we sat feasting
on abundant flesh and sweet wine. But when the
sun set and darkness came on, then we lay down
to rest on the shore of the sea. And as soon as
early Dawn appeared, the rosy-fingered, I called my
men together, and spoke among them all :

" ' Hearken to my words, comrades, for all your
evil plight. My friends, we know not where the
darkness is or where the dawn, neither where the
sun, who gives light to mortals, goes beneath
the earth, nor where he rises ; but let us straightway
take thought if any device be still left us. As for me
I think not that there is. For I climbed to a rugged
point of outlook, and beheld the island, about which
is set as a crown the boundless deep. The isle
itself lies low, and in the midst of it my eyes saw
smoke through the thick brush and the wood.'

" So I spoke, and their spirit was broken within
them, as they remembered the deeds of the Laes-
trygonian, Antiphates, and the violence of the
great-hearted Cyclops, the man-eater. And they
wailed aloud, and shed big tears. But no good
came of their mourning.

" Then I told off in two bands all my well-greaved
comrades, and appointed a leader for each band.
Of the one I took command, and of the other
godlike Eurylochus. Quickly then we shook lots
in a brazen helmet, and out leapt the lot of great-
hearted Eurylochus. So he set out, and with
him went two-and-twenty comrades, all weeping ;
and they left us behind, lamenting. Within the
forest glades they found the house of Circe, built

ξεστοῖσιν λάεσσι, περισκέπτῳ ἐνὶ χώρῳ·
ἀμφὶ δέ μιν λύκοι ἦσαν ὀρέστεροι ἠδὲ λέοντες,
τοὺς αὐτὴ κατέθελξεν, ἐπεὶ κακὰ φάρμακ' ἔδωκεν.
οὐδ' οἵ γ' ὡρμήθησαν ἐπ' ἀνδράσιν, ἀλλ' ἄρα τοί γε
οὐρῆσιν μακρῇσι περισσαίνοντες ἀνέσταν.   21
ὡς δ' ὅτ' ἂν ἀμφὶ ἄνακτα κύνες δαίτηθεν ἰόντα
σαίνωσ', αἰεὶ γάρ τε φέρει μειλίγματα θυμοῦ,
ὣς τοὺς ἀμφὶ λύκοι κρατερώνυχες ἠδὲ λέοντες
σαῖνον· τοὶ δ' ἔδεισαν, ἐπεὶ ἴδον αἰνὰ πέλωρα.
ἔσταν δ' ἐν προθύροισι θεᾶς καλλιπλοκάμοιο,   22
Κίρκης δ' ἔνδον ἄκουον ἀειδούσης ὀπὶ καλῇ,
ἱστὸν ἐποιχομένης μέγαν ἄμβροτον, οἷα θεάων
λεπτά τε καὶ χαρίεντα καὶ ἀγλαὰ ἔργα πέλονται.
τοῖσι δὲ μύθων ἦρχε Πολίτης ὄρχαμος ἀνδρῶν,
ὅς μοι κήδιστος ἑτάρων ἦν κεδνότατός τε·   22
   " 'Ὦ φίλοι, ἔνδον γάρ τις ἐποιχομένη μέγαν ἱστὸν
καλὸν ἀοιδιάει, δάπεδον δ' ἅπαν ἀμφιμέμυκεν,
ἢ θεὸς ἠὲ γυνή· ἀλλὰ φθεγγώμεθα θᾶσσον.'
   " Ὡς ἄρ' ἐφώνησεν, τοὶ δὲ φθέγγοντο καλεῦντες.
ἡ δ' αἶψ' ἐξελθοῦσα θύρας ὤιξε φαεινὰς   23
καὶ κάλει· οἱ δ' ἅμα πάντες ἀιδρείῃσιν ἕποντο·
Εὐρύλοχος δ' ὑπέμεινεν, ὀισάμενος δόλον εἶναι.
εἷσεν δ' εἰσαγαγοῦσα κατὰ κλισμούς τε θρόνους τε,
ἐν δέ σφιν τυρόν τε καὶ ἄλφιτα καὶ μέλι χλωρὸν
οἴνῳ Πραμνείῳ ἐκύκα· ἀνέμισγε δὲ σίτῳ   23
φάρμακα λύγρ', ἵνα πάγχυ λαθοίατο πατρίδος αἴης.

---

1 The phrase, used in line 426 and in xiv. 6 of high ground,
need here mean no more than that the palace of Circe was

of polished stone in a place of wide outlook,[1] and round about it were mountain wolves and lions, whom Circe herself had bewitched; for she gave them evil drugs. Yet these beasts did not rush upon my men, but pranced about them fawningly, wagging their long tails. And as when hounds fawn around their master as he comes from a feast, for he ever brings them bits to soothe their temper, so about them fawned the stout-clawed wolves and lions; but they were seized with fear, as they saw the dread monsters. So they stood in the gateway of the fair-tressed goddess, and within they heard Circe singing with sweet voice, as she went to and fro before a great imperishable web, such as is the handiwork of goddesses, finely-woven and beautiful, and glorious. Then among them spoke Polites, a leader of men, dearest to me of my comrades, and trustiest:

" ' Friends, within someone goes to and fro before a great web, singing sweetly, so that all the floor echoes; some goddess it is, or some woman. Come, let us quickly call to her.'

" So he spoke, and they cried aloud, and called to her. And she straightway came forth and opened the bright doors, and bade them in; and all went with her in their folly. Only Eurylochus remained behind, for he suspected that there was a snare. She brought them in and made them sit on chairs and seats, and made for them a potion of cheese and barley meal and yellow honey with Pramnian wine; but in the food she mixed baneful drugs, that they might utterly forget their native land. Now

situated in an open glade or clearing. The isle itself was low (line 196).

αὐτὰρ ἐπεὶ δῶκέν τε καὶ ἔκπιον, αὐτίκ' ἔπειτα
ῥάβδῳ πεπληγυῖα κατὰ συφεοῖσιν ἐέργνυ.
οἱ δὲ συῶν μὲν ἔχον κεφαλὰς φωνήν τε τρίχας τε
καὶ δέμας, αὐτὰρ νοῦς ἦν ἔμπεδος, ὡς τὸ πάρος περ.
ὣς οἱ μὲν κλαίοντες ἐέρχατο, τοῖσι δὲ Κίρκη   24
πάρ ῥ' ἄκυλον βάλανόν τε βάλεν καρπόν τε κρανείης
ἔδμεναι, οἷα σύες χαμαιευνάδες αἰὲν ἔδουσιν.

   " Εὐρύλοχος δ' αἶψ' ἦλθε θοὴν ἐπὶ νῆα μέλαιναν
ἀγγελίην ἑτάρων ἐρέων καὶ ἀδευκέα πότμον.   24
οὐδέ τι ἐκφάσθαι δύνατο ἔπος ἱέμενός περ,
κῆρ ἄχεϊ μεγάλῳ βεβολημένος· ἐν δέ οἱ ὄσσε
δακρυόφιν πίμπλαντο, γόον δ' ὠίετο θυμός.
ἀλλ' ὅτε δή μιν πάντες ἀγασσάμεθ' ἐξερέοντες,
καὶ τότε τῶν ἄλλων ἑτάρων κατέλεξεν ὄλεθρον·   25

   " ' Ἤιομεν, ὡς ἐκέλευες, ἀνὰ δρυμά, φαίδιμ' Ὀδυσσεῦ·
εὕρομεν ἐν βήσσῃσι τετυγμένα δώματα καλὰ
ξεστοῖσιν λάεσσι, περισκέπτῳ ἐνὶ χώρῳ.[1]
ἔνθα δέ τις μέγαν ἱστὸν ἐποιχομένη λίγ' ἄειδεν,
ἢ θεὸς ἠὲ γυνή· τοὶ δὲ φθέγγοντο καλεῦντες.   25
ἡ δ' αἶψ' ἐξελθοῦσα θύρας ὤιξε φαεινὰς
καὶ κάλει· οἱ δ' ἅμα πάντες ἀιδρείῃσιν ἕποντο·
αὐτὰρ ἐγὼν ὑπέμεινα, ὀισάμενος δόλον εἶναι.
οἱ δ' ἅμ' ἀιστώθησαν ἀολλέες, οὐδέ τις αὐτῶν
ἐξεφάνη· δηρὸν δὲ καθήμενος ἐσκοπίαζον.'   26

   " Ὣς ἔφατ', αὐτὰρ ἐγὼ περὶ μὲν ξίφος ἀργυρόηλον
ὤμοιιν βαλόμην, μέγα χάλκεον, ἀμφὶ δὲ τόξα·
τὸν δ' ἂψ ἠνώγεα αὐτὴν ὁδὸν ἡγήσασθαι.

---

[1] Line 253 is omitted in most MSS.

when she had given them the potion, and they
had drunk it off, then she presently smote them
with her wand, and penned them in the sties.
And they had the heads, and voice, and bristles,
and shape of swine, but their minds remained
unchanged even as before. So they were penned
there weeping, and before them Circe flung mast
and acorns, and the fruit of the cornel tree, to
eat, such things as wallowing swine are wont to
feed upon.

"But Eurylochus came back straightway to the
swift, black ship, to bring tiding of his comrades
and their shameful doom. Not a word could he
utter, for all his desire, so stricken to the heart
was he with great distress, and his eyes were filled
with tears, and his spirit was set on lamentation.
But when we questioned him in amazement, then
he told the fate of the others, his comrades.

"'We went through the thickets, as thou badest,
noble Odysseus. We found in the forest glades a
fair palace, built of polished stones, in a place of
wide outlook. There someone was going to and
fro before a great web, and singing with clear voice,
some goddess or some woman, and they cried aloud,
and called to her. And she came forth straightway,
and opened the bright doors, and bade them in;
and they all went with her in their folly. But I
remained behind, for I suspected that there was
a snare. Then they all vanished together, nor did
one of them appear again, though I sat long and
watched.'

"So he spoke, and I cast my silver-studded sword
about my shoulders, a great sword of bronze, and
slung my bow about me, and bade him lead me

αὐτὰρ ὅ γ᾽ ἀμφοτέρῃσι λαβὼν ἐλλίσσετο γούνων
καί μ᾽ ὀλοφυρόμενος ἔπεα πτερόεντα προσηύδα·[1] 26⟨

"'Μή μ᾽ ἄγε κεῖσ᾽ ἀέκοντα, διοτρεφές, ἀλλὰ λίπ᾽
αὐτοῦ.
οἶδα γάρ, ὡς οὔτ᾽ αὐτὸς ἐλεύσεαι οὔτε τιν᾽ ἄλλον
ἄξεις σῶν ἑτάρων. ἀλλὰ ξὺν τοίσδεσι θᾶσσον
φεύγωμεν· ἔτι γάρ κεν ἀλύξαιμεν κακὸν ἦμαρ.'

"'Ὡς ἔφατ᾽, αὐτὰρ ἐγώ μιν ἀμειβόμενος προσέειπον·
'Εὐρύλοχ᾽, ἦ τοι μὲν σὺ μέν᾽ αὐτοῦ τῷδ᾽ ἐνὶ χώρῳ 27⟨
ἔσθων καὶ πίνων κοίλῃ παρὰ νηὶ μελαίνῃ·
αὐτὰρ ἐγὼν εἶμι, κρατερὴ δέ μοι ἔπλετ᾽ ἀνάγκη.'

"'Ὡς εἰπὼν παρὰ νηὸς ἀνήιον ἠδὲ θαλάσσης.
ἀλλ᾽ ὅτε δὴ ἄρ᾽ ἔμελλον ἰὼν ἱερὰς ἀνὰ βήσσας 27⟨
Κίρκης ἵξεσθαι πολυφαρμάκου ἐς μέγα δῶμα,
ἔνθα μοι Ἑρμείας χρυσόρραπις ἀντεβόλησεν
ἐρχομένῳ πρὸς δῶμα, νεηνίῃ ἀνδρὶ ἐοικώς,
πρῶτον ὑπηνήτῃ, τοῦ περ χαριεστάτη ἥβη·
ἔν τ᾽ ἄρα μοι φῦ χειρί, ἔπος τ᾽ ἔφατ᾽ ἔκ τ᾽ ὀνόμαζε· 280

"'Πῇ δὴ αὖτ᾽, ὦ δύστηνε, δι᾽ ἄκριας ἔρχεαι οἶος,
χώρου ἄιδρις ἐών; ἕταροι δέ τοι οἵδ᾽ ἐνὶ Κίρκης
ἔρχαται ὥς τε σύες πυκινοὺς κευθμῶνας ἔχοντες.
ἦ τοὺς λυσόμενος δεῦρ᾽ ἔρχεαι; οὐδέ σέ φημι
αὐτὸν νοστήσειν, μενέεις δὲ σύ γ᾽, ἔνθα περ ἄλλοι. 28⟨
ἀλλ᾽ ἄγε δή σε κακῶν ἐκλύσομαι ἠδὲ σαώσω.
τῆ, τόδε φάρμακον ἐσθλὸν ἔχων ἐς δώματα Κίρκης
ἔρχευ, ὅ κέν τοι κρατὸς ἀλάλκῃσιν κακὸν ἦμαρ.
πάντα δέ τοι ἐρέω ὀλοφώια δήνεα Κίρκης.
τεύξει τοι κυκεῶ, βαλέει δ᾽ ἐν φάρμακα σίτῳ. 29⟨

[1] Line 265 is omitted in most MSS.

back by the self-same road. But he clasped me with both hands, and besought me by my knees, and with wailing he spoke to me winged words:

"'Lead me not thither against my will, O thou fostered of Zeus, but leave me here. For I know that thou wilt neither come back thyself, nor bring anyone of thy comrades. Nay, with these that are here let us flee with all speed, for still we may haply escape the evil day.'

"So he spoke, but I answered him, and said: 'Eurylochus, do thou stay here in this place, eating and drinking by the hollow, black ship; but I will go, for strong necessity is laid upon me.'

"So saying, I went up from the ship and the sea. But when, as I went through the sacred glades, I was about to come to the great house of the sorceress, Circe, then Hermes, of the golden wand, met me as I went toward the house, in the likeness of a young man with the first down upon his lip, in whom the charm of youth is fairest. He clasped my hand, and spoke, and addressed me:

"'Whither now again, hapless man, dost thou go alone through the hills, knowing naught of the country? Lo, thy comrades yonder in the house of Circe are penned like swine in close-barred sties. And art thou come to release them? Nay, I tell thee, thou shalt not thyself return, but shalt remain there with the others. But come, I will free thee from harm, and save thee. Here, take this potent herb, and go to the house of Circe, and it shall ward off from thy head the evil day. And I will tell thee all the baneful wiles of Circe. She will mix thee a potion, and cast drugs into the food; but

ἀλλ' οὐδ' ὣς θέλξαι σε δυνήσεται· οὐ γὰρ ἐάσει
φάρμακον ἐσθλόν, ὅ τοι δώσω, ἐρέω δὲ ἕκαστα.
ὁππότε κεν Κίρκη σ' ἐλάσῃ περιμήκεϊ ῥάβδῳ,
δὴ τότε σὺ ξίφος ὀξὺ ἐρυσσάμενος παρὰ μηροῦ
Κίρκῃ ἐπαῖξαι, ὥς τε κτάμεναι μενεαίνων.   29
ἡ δέ σ' ὑποδείσασα κελήσεται εὐνηθῆναι·
ἔνθα σὺ μηκέτ' ἔπειτ' ἀπανήνασθαι θεοῦ εὐνήν,
ὄφρα κέ τοι λύσῃ θ' ἑτάρους αὐτόν τε κομίσσῃ·
ἀλλὰ κέλεσθαί μιν μακάρων μέγαν ὅρκον ὀμόσσαι,
μή τί τοι αὐτῷ πῆμα κακὸν βουλευσέμεν ἄλλο,   30
μή σ' ἀπογυμνωθέντα κακὸν καὶ ἀνήνορα θήῃ.'
   "῝Ως ἄρα φωνήσας πόρε φάρμακον ἀργεϊφόντης
ἐκ γαίης ἐρύσας, καί μοι φύσιν αὐτοῦ ἔδειξε.
ῥίζῃ μὲν μέλαν ἔσκε, γάλακτι δὲ εἴκελον ἄνθος·
μῶλυ δέ μιν καλέουσι θεοί· χαλεπὸν δέ τ' ὀρύσσειν   30
ἀνδράσι γε θνητοῖσι, θεοὶ δέ τε πάντα δύνανται.[1]
Ἑρμείας μὲν ἔπειτ' ἀπέβη πρὸς μακρὸν Ὄλυμπον
νῆσον ἀν' ὑλήεσσαν, ἐγὼ δ' ἐς δώματα Κίρκης
ἦια, πολλὰ δέ μοι κραδίη πόρφυρε κιόντι.
ἔστην δ' εἰνὶ θύρῃσι θεᾶς καλλιπλοκάμοιο·   31
ἔνθα στὰς ἐβόησα, θεὰ δέ μευ ἔκλυεν αὐδῆς.
ἡ δ' αἶψ' ἐξελθοῦσα θύρας ὤιξε φαεινὰς
καὶ κάλει· αὐτὰρ ἐγὼν ἑπόμην ἀκαχήμενος ἦτορ.
εἷσε δέ μ' εἰσαγαγοῦσα ἐπὶ θρόνου ἀργυροήλου
καλοῦ δαιδαλέου· ὑπὸ δὲ θρῆνυς ποσὶν ἦεν·   31
τεῦχε δέ μοι κυκεῶ χρυσέῳ δέπαϊ, ὄφρα πίοιμι,
ἐν δέ τε φάρμακον ἧκε, κακὰ φρονέουσ' ἐνὶ θυμῷ.

---

[1] δύνανται : ἴσασιν ; cf. iv. 379.

even so she shall not be able to bewitch thee, for the potent herb that I shall give thee will not suffer it. And I will tell thee all. When Circe shall smite thee with her long wand, then do thou draw thy sharp sword from beside thy thigh, and rush upon Circe, as though thou wouldst slay her. And she will be seized with fear, and will bid thee lie with her. Then do not thou thereafter refuse the couch of the goddess, that she may set free thy comrades, and give entertainment to thee. But bid her swear a great oath by the blessed gods, that she will not plot against thee any fresh mischief to thy hurt, lest when she has thee stripped she may render thee a weakling and unmanned.'

"So saying, Argeïphontes gave me the herb, drawing it from the ground, and showed me its nature. At the root it was black, but its flower was like milk. Moly the gods call it, and it is hard for mortal men to dig; but with the gods all things are possible. Hermes then departed to high Olympus through the wooded isle, and I went my way to the house of Circe, and many things did my heart darkly ponder as I went. So I stood at the gates of the fair-tressed goddess. There I stood and called, and the goddess heard my voice. Straightway then she came forth, and opened the bright doors, and bade me in; and I went with her, my heart sore troubled. She brought me in and made me sit on a silver-studded chair, a beautiful chair, richly wrought, and beneath was a foot-stool for the feet. And she prepared me a potion in a golden cup, that I might drink, and put therein a drug, with evil purpose in her heart.

αὐτὰρ ἐπεὶ δῶκέν τε καὶ ἔκπιον, οὐδέ μ᾽ ἔθελξε,
ῥάβδῳ πεπληγυῖα ἔπος τ᾽ ἔφατ᾽ ἔκ τ᾽ ὀνόμαζεν·
‘Ἔρχεο νῦν συφεόνδε, μετ᾽ ἄλλων λέξο ἑταίρων.’   320

   “ Ὣς φάτ᾽, ἐγὼ δ᾽ ἄορ ὀξὺ ἐρυσσάμενος παρὰ μηροῦ
Κίρκῃ ἐπήϊξα ὥς τε κτάμεναι μενεαίνων.
ἡ δὲ μέγα ἰάχουσα ὑπέδραμε καὶ λάβε γούνων,
καί μ᾽ ὀλοφυρομένη ἔπεα πτερόεντα προσηύδα·   324

   “ ‘ Τίς, πόθεν εἰς ἀνδρῶν; πόθι τοι πόλις ἠδὲ τοκῆες;
θαῦμά μ᾽ ἔχει ὡς οὔ τι πιὼν τάδε φάρμακ᾽ ἐθέλχθης·
οὐδὲ γὰρ οὐδέ τις ἄλλος ἀνὴρ τάδε φάρμακ᾽ ἀνέτλη,
ὅς κε πίῃ καὶ πρῶτον ἀμείψεται ἕρκος ὀδόντων.
σοὶ δέ τις ἐν στήθεσσιν ἀκήλητος νόος ἐστίν.
ἦ σύ γ᾽ Ὀδυσσεύς ἐσσι πολύτροπος, ὅν τέ μοι αἰεὶ   330
φάσκεν ἐλεύσεσθαι χρυσόρραπις ἀργειφόντης,
ἐκ Τροίης ἀνιόντα θοῇ σὺν νηὶ μελαίνῃ.
ἀλλ᾽ ἄγε δὴ κολεῷ μὲν ἄορ θέο, νῶϊ δ᾽ ἔπειτα
εὐνῆς ἡμετέρης ἐπιβείομεν, ὄφρα μιγέντε
εὐνῇ καὶ φιλότητι πεποίθομεν ἀλλήλοισιν.’   335

   “ Ὣς ἔφατ᾽, αὐτὰρ ἐγώ μιν ἀμειβόμενος προσέειπον·
‘ Ὦ Κίρκη, πῶς γάρ με κέλεαι σοὶ ἤπιον εἶναι,
ἥ μοι σῦς μὲν ἔθηκας ἐνὶ μεγάροισιν ἑταίρους,
αὐτὸν δ᾽ ἐνθάδ᾽ ἔχουσα δολοφρονέουσα κελεύεις
ἐς θάλαμόν τ᾽ ἰέναι καὶ σῆς ἐπιβήμεναι εὐνῆς,   340
ὄφρα με γυμνωθέντα κακὸν καὶ ἀνήνορα θήῃς.
οὐδ᾽ ἂν ἐγώ γ᾽ ἐθέλοιμι τεῆς ἐπιβήμεναι εὐνῆς,
εἰ μή μοι τλαίης γε, θεά, μέγαν ὅρκον ὀμόσσαι
μή τί μοι αὐτῷ πῆμα κακὸν βουλευσέμεν ἄλλο.’

But when she had given it me, and I had drunk
it off, yet was not bewitched, she smote me with her
wand, and spoke, and addressed me: ' Begone now
to the sty, and lie with the rest of thy comrades.'

"So she spoke, but I, drawing my sharp sword
from beside my thigh, rushed upon Circe, as
though I would slay her. But she, with a loud
cry, ran beneath, and clasped my knees, and
with wailing she spoke to me winged words:

" 'Who art thou among men, and from whence?
Where is thy city, and where thy parents? Amaze-
ment holds me that thou hast drunk this charm
and wast in no wise bewitched. For no man
else soever hath withstood this charm, when once
he has drunk it, and it has passed the barrier
of his teeth. Nay, but the mind in thy breast
is one not to be beguiled. Surely thou art
Odysseus, the man of ready device, who Argeï-
phontes of the golden wand ever said to me would
come hither on his way home from Troy with his
swift, black ship. Nay, come, put up thy sword in
its sheath, and let us two then go up into my bed,
that couched together in love we may put trust in
each other.'

"So she spoke, but I answered her, and said:
' Circe, how canst thou bid me be gentle to thee,
who hast turned my comrades into swine in thy
halls, and now keepest me here, and with guileful
purpose biddest me go to thy chamber, and go
up into thy bed, that when thou hast me stripped
thou mayest render me a weakling and unmanned?
Nay, verily, it is not I that shall be fain to go
up into thy bed, unless thou, goddess, wilt consent
to swear a mighty oath that thou wilt not plot
against me any fresh mischief to my hurt.'

369

"Ὣς ἐφάμην, ἡ δ' αὐτίκ' ἀπώμνυεν, ὡς ἐκέλευον. 34

αὐτὰρ ἐπεί ῥ' ὄμοσέν τε τελεύτησέν τε τὸν ὅρκον,

καὶ τότ' ἐγὼ Κίρκης ἐπέβην περικαλλέος εὐνῆς.

"'Αμφίπολοι δ' ἄρα τέως μὲν ἐνὶ μεγάροισι πένοντο

τέσσαρες, αἵ οἱ δῶμα κάτα δρήστειραι ἔασι·

γίγνονται δ' ἄρα ταί γ' ἔκ τε κρηνέων ἀπό τ' ἀλσέων 35

ἔκ θ' ἱερῶν ποταμῶν, οἵ τ' εἰς ἅλαδε προρέουσι.

τάων ἡ μὲν ἔβαλλε θρόνοις ἔνι ῥήγεα καλὰ

πορφύρεα καθύπερθ', ὑπένερθε δὲ λῖθ' ὑπέβαλλεν·

ἡ δ' ἑτέρη προπάροιθε θρόνων ἐτίταινε τραπέζας

ἀργυρέας, ἐπὶ δέ σφι τίθει χρύσεια κάνεια·   35

ἡ δὲ τρίτη κρητῆρι μελίφρονα οἶνον ἐκίρνα

ἡδὺν ἐν ἀργυρέῳ, νέμε δὲ χρύσεια κύπελλα·

ἡ δὲ τετάρτη ὕδωρ ἐφόρει καὶ πῦρ ἀνέκαιε

πολλὸν ὑπὸ τρίποδι μεγάλῳ· ἰαίνετο δ' ὕδωρ.

αὐτὰρ ἐπεὶ δὴ ζέσσεν ὕδωρ ἐνὶ ἤνοπι χαλκῷ,   36

ἔς ῥ' ἀσάμινθον ἕσασα λό' ἐκ τρίποδος μεγάλοιο,

θυμῆρες κεράσασα, κατὰ κρατός τε καὶ ὤμων,

ὄφρα μοι ἐκ κάματον θυμοφθόρον εἵλετο γυίων.

αὐτὰρ ἐπεὶ λοῦσέν τε καὶ ἔχρισεν λίπ' ἐλαίῳ,

ἀμφὶ δέ με χλαῖναν καλὴν βάλεν ἠδὲ χιτῶνα,   36

εἷσε δέ μ' εἰσαγαγοῦσα ἐπὶ θρόνου ἀργυροήλου

καλοῦ δαιδαλέου, ὑπὸ δὲ θρῆνυς ποσὶν ἦεν·

χέρνιβα δ' ἀμφίπολος προχόῳ ἐπέχευε φέρουσα

καλῇ χρυσείῃ, ὑπὲρ ἀργυρέοιο λέβητος,

νίψασθαι· παρὰ δὲ ξεστὴν ἐτάνυσσε τράπεζαν.   37

σῖτον δ' αἰδοίη ταμίη παρέθηκε φέρουσα,

εἴδατα πόλλ' ἐπιθεῖσα, χαριζομένη παρεόντων.[1]

ἐσθέμεναι δ' ἐκέλευεν· ἐμῷ δ' οὐχ ἥνδανε θυμῷ,

ἀλλ' ἤμην ἀλλοφρονέων, κακὰ δ' ὄσσετο θυμός.

---

[1] Lines 368–72 are omitted in most MSS.

"So I spoke, and she straightway swore the oath to do me no harm, as I bade her. But when she had sworn, and made an end of the oath, then I went up to the beautiful bed of Circe.

"But her handmaids meanwhile were busied in the halls, four maidens who are her serving-women in the house. Children are they of the springs and groves, and of the sacred rivers that flow forth to the sea, and of them one threw upon chairs fair rugs of purple above, and spread beneath them a linen cloth; another drew up before the chairs tables of silver, and set upon them golden baskets; and the third mixed sweet, honey-hearted wine in a bowl of silver, and served out golden cups; and the fourth brought water, and kindled a great fire beneath a large cauldron, and the water grew warm. But when the water boiled in the bright bronze, she set me in a bath, and bathed me with water from out the great cauldron, mixing it to my liking, and pouring it over my head and shoulders, till she took from my limbs soul-consuming weariness. But when she had bathed me, and anointed me richly with oil, and had cast about me a fair cloak and a tunic, she brought me into the hall, and made me sit upon a silver-studded chair—a beautiful chair, richly wrought, and beneath was a foot-stool for the feet. Then a handmaid brought water for the hands in a fair pitcher of gold, and poured it over a silver basin for me to wash, and beside me drew up a polished table. And the grave housewife brought and set before me bread, and therewith meats in abundance, granting freely of her store. Then she bade me eat, but my heart inclined not thereto. Rather, I sat with other thoughts, and my spirit boded ill.

" Κίρκη δ' ὡς ἐνόησεν ἔμ' ἥμενον οὐδ' ἐπὶ σίτῳ   37
χεῖρας ἰάλλοντα, κρατερὸν[1] δέ με πένθος ἔχοντα,
ἄγχι παρισταμένη ἔπεα πτερόεντα προσηύδα·
    " ' Τίφθ' οὕτως, 'Οδυσεῦ, κατ' ἄρ' ἔζεαι ἶσος ἀναύδῳ,
θυμὸν ἔδων, βρώμης δ' οὐχ ἅπτεαι οὐδὲ ποτῆτος;
ἦ τινά που δόλον ἄλλον ὀίεαι· οὐδέ τί σε χρὴ   38
δειδίμεν· ἤδη γάρ τοι ἀπώμοσα καρτερὸν ὅρκον.'
    " ' Ὣς ἔφατ', αὐτὰρ ἐγώ μιν ἀμειβόμενος προσέειπον
' Ὦ Κίρκη, τίς γάρ κεν ἀνήρ, ὃς ἐναίσιμος εἴη,
πρὶν τλαίη πάσσασθαι ἐδητύος ἠδὲ ποτῆτος,
πρὶν λύσασθ' ἑτάρους καὶ ἐν ὀφθαλμοῖσιν ἰδέσθαι;   38
ἀλλ' εἰ δὴ πρόφρασσα πιεῖν φαγέμεν τε κελεύεις,
λῦσον, ἵν' ὀφθαλμοῖσιν ἴδω ἐρίηρας ἑταίρους.'
    " ' Ὣς ἐφάμην, Κίρκη δὲ διὲκ μεγάροιο βεβήκει
ῥάβδον ἔχουσ' ἐν χειρί, θύρας δ' ἀνέῳξε συφειοῦ,
ἐκ δ' ἔλασεν σιάλοισιν ἐοικότας ἐννεώροισιν.   39
οἱ μὲν ἔπειτ' ἔστησαν ἐναντίοι, ἡ δὲ δι' αὐτῶν
ἐρχομένη προσάλειφεν ἑκάστῳ φάρμακον ἄλλο.
τῶν δ' ἐκ μὲν μελέων τρίχες ἔρρεον, ἃς πρὶν ἔφυσε
φάρμακον οὐλόμενον, τό σφιν πόρε πότνια Κίρκη·
ἄνδρες δ' ἂψ ἐγένοντο νεώτεροι ἢ πάρος ἦσαν,   39
καὶ πολὺ καλλίονες καὶ μείζονες εἰσοράασθαι.
ἔγνωσαν δέ μ' ἐκεῖνοι ἔφυν τ' ἐν χερσὶν ἕκαστος.
πᾶσιν δ' ἱμερόεις ὑπέδυ γόος, ἀμφὶ δὲ δῶμα
σμερδαλέον κονάβιζε· θεὰ δ' ἐλέαιρε καὶ αὐτή.
    " ' Ἡ δέ μευ ἄγχι στᾶσα προσηύδα δῖα θεάων·   40
' Διογενὲς Λαερτιάδη, πολυμήχαν' 'Οδυσσεῦ,

[1] κρατερὸν : στυγερόν.

"Now when Circe noted that I sat thus, and did not put forth my hands to the food, but was burdened with sore grief, she came close to me, and spoke winged words:

"'Why, Odysseus, dost thou sit thus like one that is dumb, eating thy heart, and dost not touch food or drink? Dost thou haply forbode some other guile? Nay, thou needest in no wise fear, for already have I sworn a mighty oath to do thee no harm.'

"So she spoke, but I answered her, and said: 'Circe, what man that is right-minded could bring himself to taste of food or drink, ere yet he had won freedom for his comrades, and beheld them before his face? But if thou of a ready heart dost bid me eat and drink, set them free, that mine eyes may behold my trusty comrades.'

"So I spoke, and Circe went forth through the hall holding her wand in her hand, and opened the doors of the sty, and drove them out in the form of swine of nine years old. So they stood there before her, and she went through the midst of them, and anointed each man with another charm. Then from their limbs the bristles fell away which the baneful drug that queenly Circe gave them had before made to grow, and they became men again, younger than they were before, and far comelier and taller to look upon. They knew me, and clung to my hands, each man of them, and upon them all came a passionate sobbing, and the house about them rang wondrously, and the goddess herself was moved to pity.

"Then the beautiful goddess drew near me, and said: 'Son of Laertes, sprung from Zeus, Odysseus

ἔρχεο νῦν ἐπὶ νῆα θοὴν καὶ θῖνα θαλάσσης.
νῆα μὲν ἀρ πάμπρωτον ἐρύσσατε ἠπειρόνδε,
κτήματα δ᾽ ἐν σπήεσσι πελάσσατε ὅπλα τε πάντα·
αὐτὸς δ᾽ ἂψ ἰέναι καὶ ἄγειν ἐρίηρας ἑταίρους.᾽   405
    "Ὣς ἔφατ᾽, αὐτὰρ ἐμοί γ᾽ ἐπεπείθετο θυμὸς ἀγήνωρ,
βῆν δ᾽ ἰέναι ἐπὶ νῆα θοὴν καὶ θῖνα θαλάσσης.
εὗρον ἔπειτ᾽ ἐπὶ νηὶ θοῇ ἐρίηρας ἑταίρους
οἴκτρ᾽ ὀλοφυρομένους, θαλερὸν κατὰ δάκρυ χέοντας.
ὡς δ᾽ ὅτ᾽ ἂν ἄγραυλοι πόριες περὶ βοῦς ἀγελαίας,   410
ἐλθούσας ἐς κόπρον, ἐπὴν βοτάνης κορέσωνται,
πᾶσαι ἅμα σκαίρουσιν ἐναντίαι· οὐδ᾽ ἔτι σηκοὶ
ἴσχουσ᾽, ἀλλ᾽ ἁδινὸν μυκώμεναι ἀμφιθέουσι
μητέρας· ὣς ἔμ᾽ ἐκεῖνοι ἐπεὶ ἴδον ὀφθαλμοῖσι,
δακρυόεντες ἔχυντο· δόκησε δ᾽ ἄρα σφίσι θυμὸς   415
ὣς ἔμεν, ὡς εἰ πατρίδ᾽ ἱκοίατο καὶ πόλιν αὐτὴν
τρηχείης Ἰθάκης, ἵνα τ᾽ ἔτραφεν ἠδ᾽ ἐγένοντο.
καί μ᾽ ὀλοφυρόμενοι ἔπεα πτερόεντα προσηύδων·
    "'Σοὶ μὲν νοστήσαντι, διοτρεφές, ὡς ἐχάρημεν,
ὡς εἴ τ᾽ εἰς Ἰθάκην ἀφικοίμεθα πατρίδα γαῖαν·   420
ἀλλ᾽ ἄγε, τῶν ἄλλων ἑτάρων κατάλεξον ὄλεθρον.᾽
    "Ὣς ἔφαν, αὐτὰρ ἐγὼ προσέφην μαλακοῖς ἐπέεσσι·
'Νῆα μὲν ἀρ πάμπρωτον ἐρύσσομεν ἠπειρόνδε,
κτήματα δ᾽ ἐν σπήεσσι πελάσσομεν ὅπλα τε πάντα·
αὐτοὶ δ᾽ ὀτρύνεσθε ἐμοὶ ἅμα πάντες ἕπεσθαι,   425
ὄφρα ἴδηθ᾽ ἑτάρους ἱεροῖς ἐν δώμασι Κίρκης
πίνοντας καὶ ἔδοντας· ἐπηετανὸν γὰρ ἔχουσιν.᾽
    "Ὣς ἐφάμην, οἱ δ᾽ ὦκα ἐμοῖς ἐπέεσσι πίθοντο.
Εὐρύλοχος δέ μοι οἶος ἐρύκανε πάντας ἑταίρους·
καί σφεας φωνήσας ἔπεα πτερόεντα προσηύδα·[1]   430

---

[1] Line 430 is omitted in many MSS.

of many devices, go now to thy swift ship and to
the shore of the sea. First of all do ye draw the
ship up on the land, and store your goods and
all the tackling in caves. Then come back thyself,
and bring thy trusty comrades.'

"So she spoke, and my proud heart consented.
I went my way to the swift ship and the shore
of the sea, and there I found my trusty comrades
by the swift ship, wailing piteously, shedding big
tears. And as when calves in a farmstead sport
about the droves of cows returning to the yard,
when they have had their fill of grazing—all
together they frisk before them, and the pens no
longer hold them, but with constant lowing they
run about their mothers—so those men, when their
eyes beheld me, thronged about me weeping, and
it seemed to their hearts as though they had got
to their native land, and the very city of rugged
Ithaca, where they were bred and born. And with
wailing they spoke to me winged words:

"'At thy return, O thou fostered of Zeus, we
are as glad as though we had returned to Ithaca, our
native land. But come, tell the fate of the others,
our comrades.'

"So they spoke, and I answered them with gentle
words: 'First of all let us draw the ship up on the
land, and store our goods and all the tackling in caves.
Then haste you, one and all, to go with me that you
may see your comrades in the sacred halls of Circe,
drinking and eating, for they have unfailing store.'

"So I spoke, and they quickly hearkened to my
words. Eurylochus alone sought to hold back all
my comrades, and he spoke, and addressed them
with winged words:

" '᾿Α δειλοί, πόσ' ἴμεν; τί κακῶν ἱμείρετε τούτων;
Κίρκης ἐς μέγαρον καταβήμεναι, ἥ κεν ἅπαντας
ἢ σῦς ἠὲ λύκους ποιήσεται ἠὲ λέοντας,
οἵ κέν οἱ μέγα δῶμα φυλάσσοιμεν καὶ ἀνάγκῃ,
ὥς περ Κύκλωψ ἔρξ', ὅτε οἱ μέσσαυλον ἵκοντο   4
ἡμέτεροι ἕταροι, σὺν δ' ὁ θρασὺς εἵπετ' Ὀδυσσεύς·
τούτου γὰρ καὶ κεῖνοι ἀτασθαλίῃσιν ὄλοντο.'

" '῍Ως ἔφατ', αὐτὰρ ἐγώ γε μετὰ φρεσὶ μερμήριξα,
σπασσάμενος τανύηκες ἄορ παχέος παρὰ μηροῦ,
τῷ οἱ ἀποπλήξας[1] κεφαλὴν οὐδάσδε πελάσσαι,   4
καὶ πηῷ περ ἐόντι μάλα σχεδόν· ἀλλά μ' ἑταῖροι
μειλιχίοις ἐπέεσσιν ἐρήτυον ἄλλοθεν ἄλλος·

" ' Διογενές, τοῦτον μὲν ἐάσομεν, εἰ σὺ κελεύεις,
αὐτοῦ πὰρ νηΐ τε μένειν καὶ νῆα ἔρυσθαι·
ἡμῖν δ' ἡγεμόνευ' ἱερὰ πρὸς δώματα Κίρκης.'   4

" '῍Ως φάμενοι παρὰ νηὸς ἀνήιον ἠδὲ θαλάσσης.
οὐδὲ μὲν Εὐρύλοχος κοίλῃ παρὰ νηΐ λέλειπτο,
ἀλλ' ἕπετ'· ἔδεισεν γὰρ ἐμὴν ἔκπαγλον ἐνιπήν.

" Τόφρα δὲ τοὺς ἄλλους ἑτάρους ἐν δώμασι Κίρκη
ἐνδυκέως λοῦσέν τε καὶ ἔχρισεν λίπ' ἐλαίῳ,   4
ἀμφὶ δ' ἄρα χλαίνας οὔλας βάλεν ἠδὲ χιτῶνας·
δαινυμένους δ' ἐὺ πάντας ἐφεύρομεν ἐν μεγάροισιν.
οἱ δ' ἐπεὶ ἀλλήλους εἶδον φράσσαντό τ' ἐσάντα,
κλαῖον ὀδυρόμενοι, περὶ δὲ στεναχίζετο δῶμα.
ἡ δέ μευ ἄγχι στᾶσα προσηύδα δῖα θεάων·[2]   4

" 'Μηκέτι νῦν θαλερὸν γόον ὄρνυτε· οἶδα καὶ αὐτὴ
ἡμὲν ὅσ' ἐν πόντῳ πάθετ' ἄλγεα ἰχθυόεντι,
ἠδ' ὅσ' ἀνάρσιοι ἄνδρες ἐδηλήσαντ' ἐπὶ χέρσου.

---

[1] ἀποπλήξας Aristarchus (?) : ἀποτμήξας.
[2] After 455 the line Διογενὲς Λαερτιάδη, πολυμήχαν' Ὀδυσσεῦ, occurs in some MSS.

" ' Ah, wretched men, whither are we going? Why are you so enamoured of these woes, as to go down to the house of Circe, who will change us all to swine, or wolves, or lions, that so we may guard her great house perforce? Even so did the Cyclops, when our comrades went to his fold, and with them went this reckless Odysseus. For it was through this man's folly that they too perished.'

" So he spoke, and I pondered in heart, whether to draw my long sword from beside my stout thigh, and therewith strike off his head, and bring it to the ground, near kinsman of mine by marriage though he was; but my comrades one after another sought to check me with gentle words:

" ' O thou sprung from Zeus, as for this man, we will leave him, if thou so biddest, to abide here by the ship, and to guard the ship, but as for us, do thou lead us to the sacred house of Circe.'

" So saying, they went up from the ship and the sea. Nor was Eurylochus left beside the hollow ship, but he went with us, for he feared my dread reproof.

" Meanwhile in her halls Circe bathed the rest of my comrades with kindly care, and anointed them richly with oil, and cast about them fleecy cloaks and tunics; and we found them all feasting bountifully in the halls. But when they saw and recognized one another, face to face, they wept and wailed, and the house rang around. Then the beautiful goddess drew near me, and said:

" ' No longer now do ye rouse this plenteous lamenting. Of myself I know both all the woes you have suffered on the teeming deep, and all the wrong that cruel men have done you on the

ἀλλ' ἄγετ' ἐσθίετε βρώμην καὶ πίνετε οἶνον,　40
εἰς ὅ κεν αὖτις θυμὸν ἐνὶ στήθεσσι λάβητε,
οἷον ὅτε πρώτιστον ἐλείπετε πατρίδα γαῖαν
τρηχείης 'Ιθάκης. νῦν δ' ἀσκελέες καὶ ἄθυμοι,
αἰὲν ἄλης χαλεπῆς μεμνημένοι, οὐδέ ποθ' ὑμῖν
θυμὸς ἐν εὐφροσύνῃ, ἐπεὶ ἦ μάλα πολλὰ πέποσθε.'　40

"'Ὣς ἔφαθ', ἡμῖν δ' αὖτ' ἐπεπείθετο θυμὸς ἀγήνωρ.
ἔνθα μὲν ἤματα πάντα τελεσφόρον εἰς ἐνιαυτὸν
ἥμεθα δαινύμενοι κρέα τ' ἄσπετα καὶ μέθυ ἡδύ·
ἀλλ' ὅτε δή ῥ' ἐνιαυτὸς ἔην, περὶ δ' ἔτραπον ὧραι
μηνῶν φθινόντων, περὶ δ' ἤματα μακρὰ τελέσθη,[1]　47
καὶ τότε μ' ἐκκαλέσαντες ἔφαν ἐρίηρες ἑταῖροι·

"'Δαιμόνι', ἤδη νῦν μιμνήσκεο πατρίδος αἴης,
εἴ τοι θέσφατόν ἐστι σαωθῆναι καὶ ἱκέσθαι
οἶκον ἐς ὑψόροφον[2] καὶ σὴν ἐς πατρίδα γαῖαν.'

"'Ὣς ἔφαν, αὐτὰρ ἐμοί γ' ἐπεπείθετο θυμὸς ἀγήνωρ.
ὣς τότε μὲν πρόπαν ἦμαρ ἐς ἠέλιον καταδύντα　4
ἥμεθα, δαινύμενοι κρέα τ' ἄσπετα καὶ μέθυ ἡδύ·
ἦμος δ' ἠέλιος κατέδυ καὶ ἐπὶ κνέφας ἦλθεν,
οἱ μὲν κοιμήσαντο κατὰ μέγαρα σκιόεντα.
αὐτὰρ ἐγὼ Κίρκης ἐπιβὰς περικαλλέος εὐνῆς　4
γούνων ἐλλιτάνευσα, θεὰ δέ μευ ἔκλυεν αὐδῆς·
καί μιν φωνήσας ἔπεα πτερόεντα προσηύδων·

"'Ὦ Κίρκη, τέλεσόν μοι ὑπόσχεσιν ἥν περ ὑπέστης
οἴκαδε πεμψέμεναι· θυμὸς δέ μοι ἔσσυται ἤδη,
ἠδ' ἄλλων ἑτάρων, οἵ μευ φθινύθουσι φίλον κῆρ　4
ἀμφ' ἔμ' ὀδυρόμενοι, ὅτε που σύ γε νόσφι γένηαι.'

"'Ὣς ἐφάμην, ἡ δ' αὐτίκ' ἀμείβετο δῖα θεάων·
'Διογενὲς Λαερτιάδη, πολυμήχαν' 'Οδυσσεῦ,
μηκέτι νῦν ἀέκοντες ἐμῷ ἐνὶ μίμνετε οἴκῳ.

---

[1] Line 470 is omitted in many MSS.
[2] ἐς ὑψόροφον : ἐϋκτίμενον.

land. Nay, come, eat food and drink wine, until
you once more get spirit in your breasts such as
when at the first you left your native land of rugged
Ithaca; but now ye are withered and spiritless, ever
thinking of your weary wanderings, nor are your
hearts ever joyful, for verily ye have suffered
much.'

" So she spoke, and our proud hearts consented.
So there day after day for a full year we abode,
feasting on abundant flesh and sweet wine. But
when a year was gone and the seasons turned, as
the months waned and the long days were brought
in their course, then my trusty comrades called me
forth, and said:

" 'Strange man, bethink thee now at last of thy
native land, if it is fated for thee to be saved,
and to reach thy high-roofed house and thy native
land.'

" So they spoke, and my proud heart consented.
So then all day long till set of sun we sat feasting
on abundant flesh and sweet wine. But when
the sun set and darkness came on, they lay down
to sleep throughout the shadowy halls, but I went
up to the beautiful bed of Circe, and besought
her by her knees; and the goddess heard my voice,
and I spoke, and addressed her with winged words:

" ' Circe, fulfil for me the promise which thou gavest
to send me home; for my spirit is now eager to be
gone, and the spirit of my comrades, who make
my heart to pine, as they sit about me mourning,
whensoever thou haply art not at hand.'

" So I spoke, and the beautiful goddess straightway
made answer: 'Son of Laertes, sprung from Zeus,
Odysseus of many devices, abide ye now no longer

379

ἀλλ' ἄλλην χρὴ πρῶτον ὁδὸν τελέσαι καὶ ἱκέσθαι   49
εἰς Ἀίδαο δόμους καὶ ἐπαινῆς Περσεφονείης,
ψυχῇ χρησομένους Θηβαίου Τειρεσίαο,
μάντηος ἀλαοῦ, τοῦ τε φρένες ἔμπεδοί εἰσι·
τῷ καὶ τεθνηῶτι νόον πόρε Περσεφόνεια,
οἴῳ πεπνῦσθαι, τοὶ δὲ σκιαὶ ἀίσσουσιν.'   49

   "Ὣς ἔφατ', αὐτὰρ ἐμοί γε κατεκλάσθη φίλον ἦτορ·
κλαῖον δ' ἐν λεχέεσσι καθήμενος, οὐδέ νύ μοι κῆρ [1]
ἤθελ' ἔτι ζώειν καὶ ὁρᾶν φάος ἠελίοιο.
αὐτὰρ ἐπεὶ κλαίων τε κυλινδόμενός τ' ἐκορέσθην,
καὶ τότε δή μιν ἔπεσσιν ἀμειβόμενος προσέειπον·   50

   " 'Ὦ Κίρκη, τίς γὰρ ταύτην ὁδὸν ἡγεμονεύσει;
εἰς Ἀίδος δ' οὔ πώ τις ἀφίκετο νηὶ μελαίνῃ.'

   "Ὣς ἐφάμην, ἡ δ' αὐτίκ' ἀμείβετο δῖα θεάων·
' Διογενὲς Λαερτιάδη, πολυμήχαν' Ὀδυσσεῦ,
μή τί τοι ἡγεμόνος γε ποθὴ παρὰ νηὶ μελέσθω,   50
ἱστὸν δὲ στήσας ἀνά θ' ἱστία λευκὰ πετάσσας
ἧσθαι· τὴν δέ κέ τοι πνοιὴ Βορέαο φέρῃσιν.
ἀλλ' ὁπότ' ἂν δὴ νηὶ δι' Ὠκεανοῖο περήσῃς,
ἔνθ' ἀκτή τε λάχεια [2] καὶ ἄλσεα Περσεφονείης,
μακραί τ' αἴγειροι καὶ ἰτέαι ὠλεσίκαρποι,   51
νῆα μὲν αὐτοῦ κέλσαι ἐπ' Ὠκεανῷ βαθυδίνῃ,
αὐτὸς δ' εἰς Ἀίδεω ἰέναι δόμον εὐρώεντα.
ἔνθα μὲν εἰς Ἀχέροντα Πυριφλεγέθων τε ῥέουσιν
Κώκυτός θ', ὃς δὴ Στυγὸς ὕδατός ἐστιν ἀπορρώξ,
πέτρη τε ξύνεσίς τε δύω ποταμῶν ἐριδούπων·   51
ἔνθα δ' ἔπειθ', ἥρως, χριμφθεὶς πέλας, ὥς σε κελεύω,
βόθρον ὀρύξαι, ὅσον τε πυγούσιον ἔνθα καὶ ἔνθα,

---

[1] οὐδέ νύ μοι κῆρ : οὐδέ τι θυμὸς.
[2] τε λάχεια : τ' ἐλάχεια : τ' ἐλαχεῖα ; cf. ix. 116.

in my house against your will ; but you must first complete another. journey, and come to the house of Hades and dread Persephone, to seek soothsaying of the spirit of Theban Teiresias, the blind seer, whose mind abides steadfast. To him even in death Persephone has granted reason, that he alone should have understanding ; but the others flit about as shadows.'

"So she spoke, and my spirit was broken within me, and I wept as I sat on the bed, nor had my heart any longer desire to live and behold the light of the sun. But when I had had my fill of weeping and writhing, then I made answer, and addressed her, saying :

"'O Circe, who will guide us on this journey ? To Hades no man ever yet went in a black ship.'

"So I spoke, and the beautiful goddess straightway made answer : 'Son of Laertes, sprung from Zeus, Odysseus of many devices, let there be in thy mind no concern for a pilot to guide thy ship,[1] but set up thy mast, and spread the white sail, and sit thee down ; and the breath of the North Wind will bear her onward. But when in thy ship thou hast now crossed the stream of Oceanus, where is a level shore and the groves of Persephone—tall poplars, and willows that shed their fruit—there do thou beach thy ship by the deep eddying Oceanus, but go thyself to the dank house of Hades. There into Acheron flow Periphlegethon and Cocytus, which is a branch of the water of the Styx ; and there is a rock, and the meeting place of the two roaring rivers. Thither, prince, do thou draw nigh, as I bid thee, and dig a pit of a cubit's length this way and that, and around

[1] Or, "as thou tarriest by thy ship."

ἀμφ' αὐτῷ δὲ χοὴν χεῖσθαι πᾶσιν νεκύεσσιν,
πρῶτα μελικρήτῳ, μετέπειτα δὲ ἡδέι οἴνῳ,
τὸ τρίτον αὖθ' ὕδατι· ἐπὶ δ' ἄλφιτα λευκὰ παλύνειν. 52
πολλὰ δὲ γουνοῦσθαι νεκύων ἀμενηνὰ κάρηνα,
ἐλθὼν εἰς Ἰθάκην στεῖραν βοῦν, ἥ τις ἀρίστη,
ῥέξειν ἐν μεγάροισι πυρήν τ' ἐμπλησέμεν ἐσθλῶν,
Τειρεσίῃ δ' ἀπάνευθεν ὄιν ἱερευσέμεν οἴῳ
παμμέλαν', ὃς μήλοισι μεταπρέπει ὑμετέροισιν.   52
αὐτὰρ ἐπὴν εὐχῇσι λίσῃ κλυτὰ ἔθνεα νεκρῶν,
ἔνθ' ὄιν ἀρνειὸν ῥέξειν θῆλύν τε μέλαιναν
εἰς Ἔρεβος στρέψας, αὐτὸς δ' ἀπονόσφι τραπέσθαι
ἱέμενος ποταμοῖο ῥοάων· ἔνθα δὲ πολλαὶ
ψυχαὶ ἐλεύσονται νεκύων κατατεθνηώτων.   53
δὴ τότ' ἔπειθ' ἑτάροισιν ἐποτρῦναι καὶ ἀνῶξαι
μῆλα, τὰ δὴ κατάκειτ' ἐσφαγμένα νηλέι χαλκῷ,
δείραντας κατακῆαι, ἐπεύξασθαι δὲ θεοῖσιν,
ἰφθίμῳ τ' Ἀίδῃ καὶ ἐπαινῇ Περσεφονείῃ·
αὐτὸς δὲ ξίφος ὀξὺ ἐρυσσάμενος παρὰ μηροῦ   53
ἧσθαι, μηδὲ ἐᾶν νεκύων ἀμενηνὰ κάρηνα
αἵματος ἆσσον ἴμεν, πρὶν Τειρεσίαο πυθέσθαι.
ἔνθα τοι αὐτίκα μάντις ἐλεύσεται, ὄρχαμε λαῶν,
ὅς κέν τοι εἴπῃσιν ὁδὸν καὶ μέτρα κελεύθου
νόστον θ', ὡς ἐπὶ πόντον ἐλεύσεαι ἰχθυόεντα.'   54

  "Ὣς ἔφατ', αὐτίκα δὲ χρυσόθρονος ἤλυθεν Ἠώς.
ἀμφὶ δέ με χλαῖνάν τε χιτῶνά τε εἵματα ἕσσεν·
αὐτὴ δ' ἀργύφεον φᾶρος μέγα ἕννυτο νύμφη,
λεπτὸν καὶ χαρίεν, περὶ δὲ ζώνην βάλετ' ἰξυῖ
καλὴν χρυσείην, κεφαλῇ δ' ἐπέθηκε καλύπτρην.   54

it pour a libation to all the dead, first with milk
and honey, thereafter with sweet wine, and in
the third place with water, and sprinkle thereon
white barley meal.   And do thou earnestly entreat
the powerless heads of the dead, vowing that when
thou comest to Ithaca thou wilt sacrifice in thy
halls a barren heifer, the best thou hast, and wilt
fill the altar with rich gifts; and that to Teiresias
alone thou wilt sacrifice separately a ram, wholly
black, the goodliest of thy flock.   But when with
prayers thou hast made supplication to the glorious
tribes of the dead, then sacrifice a ram and a
black ewe, turning their heads toward Erebus
but thyself turning backward, and setting thy face
towards the streams of the river.   Then many
ghosts of men that are dead will come forth.
But do thou thereafter call to thy comrades, and
bid them flay and burn the sheep that lie there,
slain by the pitiless bronze, and make prayer to
the gods, to mighty Hades and to dread Perse-
phone.   And do thou thyself draw thy sharp sword
from beside thy thigh, and sit there, not suffering
the powerless heads of the dead to draw near to
the blood, till thou hast enquired of Teiresias.
Then the seer will presently come to thee, leader
of men, and he will tell thee thy way and the
measures of thy path, and of thy return, how thou
mayest go over the teeming deep.'

"So she spoke, and straightway came golden-
throned Dawn.   Round about me then she cast
a cloak and tunic as raiment, and the nymph
clothed herself in a long white robe, finely-woven
and beautiful, and about her waist she cast a fair
girdle of gold, and upon her head she put a veil.

αὐτὰρ ἐγὼ διὰ δώματ᾽ ἰὼν ὤτρυνον ἑταίρους
μειλιχίοις ἐπέεσσι παρασταδὸν ἄνδρα ἕκαστον·
"᾽ Μηκέτι νῦν εὕδοντες ἀωτεῖτε γλυκὺν ὕπνον,
ἀλλ᾽ ἴομεν· δὴ γάρ μοι ἐπέφραδε πότνια Κίρκη.'
"Ὣς ἐφάμην, τοῖσιν δ᾽ ἐπεπείθετο θυμὸς ἀγήνωρ. 55
οὐδὲ μὲν οὐδ᾽ ἔνθεν περ ἀπήμονας ἦγον ἑταίρους.
Ἐλπήνωρ δέ τις ἔσκε νεώτατος, οὔτε τι λίην
ἄλκιμος ἐν πολέμῳ οὔτε φρεσὶν ᾗσιν ἀρηρώς·
ὅς μοι ἄνευθ᾽ ἑτάρων ἱεροῖς ἐν δώμασι Κίρκης,
ψύχεος ἱμείρων, κατελέξατο οἰνοβαρείων. 55
κινυμένων δ᾽ ἑτάρων ὅμαδον καὶ δοῦπον ἀκούσας
ἐξαπίνης ἀνόρουσε καὶ ἐκλάθετο φρεσὶν ᾗσιν
ἄψορρον καταβῆναι ἰὼν ἐς κλίμακα μακρήν,
ἀλλὰ καταντικρὺ τέγεος πέσεν· ἐκ δέ οἱ αὐχὴν
ἀστραγάλων ἐάγη, ψυχὴ δ᾽ Ἄιδόσδε κατῆλθεν. 56

"Ἐρχομένοισι δὲ τοῖσιν ἐγὼ μετὰ μῦθον ἔειπον·
'Φάσθε νύ που οἴκόνδε φίλην ἐς πατρίδα γαῖαν
ἔρχεσθ᾽· ἄλλην δ᾽ ἧμιν ὁδὸν τεκμήρατο Κίρκη,
εἰς Ἀίδαο δόμους καὶ ἐπαινῆς Περσεφονείης
ψυχῇ χρησομένους Θηβαίου Τειρεσίαο.' 56

"Ὣς ἐφάμην, τοῖσιν δὲ κατεκλάσθη φίλον ἦτορ,
ἑζόμενοι δὲ κατ᾽ αὖθι γόων τίλλοντό τε χαίτας·
ἀλλ᾽ οὐ γάρ τις πρῆξις ἐγίγνετο μυρομένοισιν.

"Ἀλλ᾽ ὅτε δή ῥ᾽ ἐπὶ νῆα θοὴν καὶ θῖνα θαλάσσης
ᾔομεν ἀχνύμενοι θαλερὸν κατὰ δάκρυ χέοντες, 57
τόφρα δ᾽ ἄρ᾽ οἰχομένη Κίρκη παρὰ νηὶ μελαίνῃ
ἀρνειὸν κατέδησεν ὄιν θῆλύν τε μέλαιναν,
ῥεῖα παρεξελθοῦσα· τίς ἂν θεὸν οὐκ ἐθέλοντα
ὀφθαλμοῖσιν ἴδοιτ᾽ ἢ ἔνθ᾽ ἢ ἔνθα κιόντα;

But I went through the halls, and roused my men with gentle words, coming up to each man in turn ·

" ' No longer now sleep ye, and drowse in sweet slumber, but let us go; lo! queenly Circe has told me all.'

" So I spoke, and their proud hearts consented. But not even from thence could I lead my men unscathed. There was one, Elpenor, the youngest of all, not over valiant in war nor sound of understanding, who had laid him down apart from his comrades in the sacred house of Circe, seeking the cool air, for he was heavy with wine. He heard the noise and the bustle of his comrades as they moved about, and suddenly sprang up, and forgot to go to the long ladder that he might come down again, but fell headlong from the roof, and his neck was broken away from the spine, and his spirit went down to the house of Hades.

" But as my men were going on their way I spoke among them, saying: ' Ye think, forsooth, that ye are going to your dear native land; but Circe has pointed out for us another journey, even to the house of Hades and dread Persephone, to consult the spirit of Theban Teiresias.'

" So I spoke, and their spirit was broken within them, and sitting down right where they were, they wept and tore their hair. But no good came of their lamenting.

" But when we were on our way to the swift ship and the shore of the sea, sorrowing and shedding big tears, meanwhile Circe had gone forth and made fast beside the black ship a ram and a black ewe, for easily had she passed us by. Who with his eyes could behold a god against his will, whether going to or fro ?

385

Λ

"Αὐτὰρ ἐπεί ῥ' ἐπὶ νῆα κατήλθομεν ἠδὲ θάλασσαν,
νῆα μὲν ἂρ πάμπρωτον ἐρύσσαμεν εἰς ἅλα δῖαν,
ἐν δ' ἱστὸν τιθέμεσθα καὶ ἱστία νηὶ μελαίνῃ,
ἐν δὲ τὰ μῆλα λαβόντες ἐβήσαμεν, ἂν δὲ καὶ αὐτοὶ
βαίνομεν ἀχνύμενοι θαλερὸν κατὰ δάκρυ χέοντες.
ἡμῖν δ' αὖ κατόπισθε νεὸς κυανοπρῴροιο
ἴκμενον οὖρον ἵει πλησίστιον, ἐσθλὸν ἑταῖρον,
Κίρκη εὐπλόκαμος, δεινὴ θεὸς αὐδήεσσα.
ἡμεῖς δ' ὅπλα ἕκαστα πονησάμενοι κατὰ νῆα
ἥμεθα· τὴν δ' ἄνεμός τε κυβερνήτης τ' ἴθυνε.   1
τῆς δὲ πανημερίης τέταθ' ἱστία ποντοπορούσης·
δύσετό τ' ἠέλιος σκιόωντό τε πᾶσαι ἀγυιαί.

"Ἡ δ' ἐς πείραθ' ἵκανε βαθυρρόου Ὠκεανοῖο.
ἔνθα δὲ Κιμμερίων ἀνδρῶν δῆμός τε πόλις τε,
ἠέρι καὶ νεφέλῃ κεκαλυμμένοι· οὐδέ ποτ' αὐτοὺς   1
ἠέλιος φαέθων καταδέρκεται ἀκτίνεσσιν,
οὔθ' ὁπότ' ἂν στείχῃσι πρὸς οὐρανὸν ἀστερόεντα,
οὔθ' ὅτ' ἂν ἂψ ἐπὶ γαῖαν ἀπ' οὐρανόθεν προτράπηται,
ἀλλ' ἐπὶ νὺξ ὀλοὴ τέταται δειλοῖσι βροτοῖσι.
νῆα μὲν ἔνθ' ἐλθόντες ἐκέλσαμεν, ἐκ δὲ τὰ μῆλα   2
εἱλόμεθ'· αὐτοὶ δ' αὖτε παρὰ ῥόον Ὠκεανοῖο
ᾔομεν, ὄφρ' ἐς χῶρον ἀφικόμεθ', ὃν φράσε Κίρκη.

"Ἔνθ' ἱερήια μὲν Περιμήδης Εὐρύλοχός τε
ἔσχον· ἐγὼ δ' ἄορ ὀξὺ ἐρυσσάμενος παρὰ μηροῦ

BOOK XI

"BUT when we had come down to the ship and to the sea, first of all we drew the ship down to the bright sea, and set the mast and sail in the black ship, and took the sheep and put them aboard, and ourselves embarked, sorrowing, and shedding big tears. And for our aid in the wake of our dark-prowed ship a fair wind that filled the sail, a goodly comrade, was sent by fair-tressed Circe, dread goddess of human speech. So when we had made fast all the tackling throughout the ship, we sat down, and the wind and the helmsman made straight her course. All the day long her sail was stretched as she sped over the sea; and the sun set and all the ways grew dark.

"She came to deep-flowing Oceanus, that bounds the Earth,[1] where is the land and city of the Cimmerians, wrapped in mist and cloud. Never does the bright sun look down on them with his rays either when he mounts the starry heaven or when he turns again to earth from heaven, but baneful night is spread over wretched mortals. Thither we came and beached our ship, and took out the sheep, and ourselves went beside the stream of Oceanus until we came to the place of which Circe had told us.

"Here Perimedes and Eurylochus held the victims, while I drew my sharp sword from beside my thigh,

[1] Or, possibly, "to Ocean's further marge."

387

βόθρον ὄρυξ' ὅσσον τε πυγούσιον ἔνθα καὶ ἔνθα,   2⁵
ἀμφ' αὐτῷ δὲ χοὴν χεόμην πᾶσιν νεκύεσσι,
πρῶτα μελικρήτῳ, μετέπειτα δὲ ἡδέι οἴνῳ,
τὸ τρίτον αὖθ' ὕδατι· ἐπὶ δ' ἄλφιτα λευκὰ πάλυνον.
πολλὰ δὲ γουνούμην νεκύων ἀμενηνὰ κάρηνα,
ἐλθὼν εἰς Ἰθάκην στεῖραν βοῦν, ἥ τις ἀρίστη,   3⁰
ῥέξειν ἐν μεγάροισι πυρήν τ' ἐμπλησέμεν ἐσθλῶν,
Τειρεσίῃ δ' ἀπάνευθεν ὄιν ἱερευσέμεν οἴῳ
παμμέλαν', ὃς μήλοισι μεταπρέπει ἡμετέροισι.
τοὺς δ' ἐπεὶ εὐχωλῇσι λιτῇσί τε, ἔθνεα νεκρῶν,
ἐλλισάμην, τὰ δὲ μῆλα λαβὼν ἀπεδειροτόμησα   3⁵
ἐς βόθρον, ῥέε δ' αἷμα κελαινεφές· αἱ δ' ἀγέροντο
ψυχαὶ ὑπὲξ Ἐρέβευς νεκύων κατατεθνηώτων.
νύμφαι τ' ἠίθεοί τε πολύτλητοί τε γέροντες
παρθενικαί τ' ἀταλαὶ νεοπενθέα θυμὸν ἔχουσαι,
πολλοὶ δ' οὐτάμενοι χαλκήρεσιν ἐγχείῃσιν,   4⁰
ἄνδρες ἀρηίφατοι βεβροτωμένα τεύχε' ἔχοντες·
οἳ πολλοὶ περὶ βόθρον ἐφοίτων ἄλλοθεν ἄλλος
θεσπεσίῃ ἰαχῇ· ἐμὲ δὲ χλωρὸν δέος ᾕρει.¹
δὴ τότ' ἔπειθ' ἑτάροισιν ἐποτρύνας ἐκέλευσα
μῆλα, τὰ δὴ κατέκειτ' ἐσφαγμένα νηλέι χαλκῷ,   4⁵
δείραντας κατακῆαι, ἐπεύξασθαι δὲ θεοῖσιν,
ἰφθίμῳ τ' Ἀιδῃ καὶ ἐπαινῇ Περσεφονείῃ·
αὐτὸς δὲ ξίφος ὀξὺ ἐρυσσάμενος παρὰ μηροῦ
ἥμην, οὐδ' εἴων νεκύων ἀμενηνὰ κάρηνα
αἵματος ἆσσον ἴμεν, πρὶν Τειρεσίαο πυθέσθαι.   5⁰

"Πρώτη δὲ ψυχὴ Ἐλπήνορος ἦλθεν ἑταίρου·
οὐ γάρ πω ἐτέθαπτο ὑπὸ χθονὸς εὐρυοδείης·
σῶμα γὰρ ἐν Κίρκης μεγάρῳ κατελείπομεν ἡμεῖς
ἄκλαυτον καὶ ἄθαπτον, ἐπεὶ πόνος ἄλλος ἔπειγε.

¹ Lines 38–43 were rejected by Zenodotus, Aristophanes,
Aristarchus.

and dug a pit of a cubit's length this way and that, and around it poured a libation to all the dead, first with milk and honey, thereafter with sweet wine, and in the third place with water, and I sprinkled thereon white barley meal. And I earnestly entreated the powerless heads of the dead, vowing that when I came to Ithaca I would sacrifice in my halls a barren heifer, the best I had, and pile the altar with goodly gifts, and to Teiresias alone would sacrifice separately a ram, wholly black, the goodliest of my flocks. But when with vows and prayers I had made supplication to the tribes of the dead, I took the sheep and cut their throats over the pit, and the dark blood ran forth. Then there gathered from out of Erebus the spirits of those that are dead, brides, and unwedded youths, and toil-worn old men, and tender maidens with hearts yet new to sorrow, and many, too, that had been wounded with bronze-tipped spears, men slain in fight, wearing their blood-stained armour. These came thronging in crowds about the pit from every side, with a wondrous cry; and pale fear seized me. Then I called to my comrades and bade them flay and burn the sheep that lay there slain with the pitiless bronze, and to make prayer to the gods, to mighty Hades and dread Persephone. And I myself drew my sharp sword from beside my thigh and sat there, and would not suffer the powerless heads of the dead to draw near to the blood until I had enquired of Teiresias.

"The first to come was the spirit of my comrade Elpenor. Not yet had he been buried beneath the broad-wayed earth, for we had left his corpse behind us in the hall of Circe, unwept and unburied, since another task was then urging us on. When I saw him

τὸν μὲν ἐγὼ δάκρυσα ἰδὼν ἐλέησά τε θυμῷ,　　55
καί μιν φωνήσας ἔπεα πτερόεντα προσηύδων·
　" ' Ἐλπῆνορ, πῶς ἦλθες ὑπὸ ζόφον ἠερόεντα;
ἔφθης πεζὸς ἰὼν[1] ἢ ἐγὼ σὺν νηὶ μελαίνῃ.'
　" Ὣς ἐφάμην, ὁ δέ μ' οἰμώξας ἡμείβετο μύθῳ·
' Διογενὲς Λαερτιάδη, πολυμήχαν' Ὀδυσσεῦ,[2]　　60
ἆσέ με δαίμονος αἶσα κακὴ καὶ ἀθέσφατος οἶνος.
Κίρκης δ' ἐν μεγάρῳ καταλέγμενος οὐκ ἐνόησα
ἄψορρον καταβῆναι ἰὼν ἐς κλίμακα μακρήν,
ἀλλὰ καταντικρὺ τέγεος πέσον· ἐκ δέ μοι αὐχὴν
ἀστραγάλων ἐάγη, ψυχὴ δ' Ἄϊδόσδε κατῆλθε.　　65
νῦν δέ σε τῶν ὄπιθεν γουνάζομαι, οὐ παρεόντων,
πρός τ' ἀλόχου καὶ πατρός, ὅ σ' ἔτρεφε τυτθὸν ἐόντα,
Τηλεμάχου θ', ὃν μοῦνον ἐνὶ μεγάροισιν ἔλειπες·
οἶδα γὰρ ὡς ἐνθένδε κιὼν δόμου ἐξ Ἀίδαο
νῆσον ἐς Αἰαίην σχήσεις ἐυεργέα νῆα·　　70
ἔνθα σ' ἔπειτα, ἄναξ, κέλομαι μνήσασθαι ἐμεῖο.
μή μ' ἄκλαυτον ἄθαπτον ἰὼν ὄπιθεν καταλείπειν
νοσφισθείς, μή τοί τι θεῶν μήνιμα γένωμαι,
ἀλλά με κακκῆαι σὺν τεύχεσιν, ἄσσα μοι ἔστιν,
σῆμά τέ μοι χεῦαι πολιῆς ἐπὶ θινὶ θαλάσσης,　　75
ἀνδρὸς δυστήνοιο καὶ ἐσσομένοισι πυθέσθαι.
ταῦτά τέ μοι τελέσαι πῆξαί τ' ἐπὶ τύμβῳ ἐρετμόν,
τῷ καὶ ζωὸς ἔρεσσον ἐὼν μετ' ἐμοῖς ἑτάροισιν.'
　" Ὣς ἔφατ', αὐτὰρ ἐγώ μιν ἀμειβόμενος προσέειπον
' Ταῦτά τοι, ὦ δύστηνε, τελευτήσω τε καὶ ἔρξω.'　　80
　" Νῶι μὲν ὣς ἐπέεσσιν ἀμειβομένω στυγεροῖσιν

---

[1] ἰὼν Aristarchus : ἐὼν.
[2] Line 60 is omitted in most MSS.

I wept, and my heart had compassion on him; and I spoke and addressed him with winged words:

"'Elpenor, how didst thou come beneath the murky darkness? Thou coming on foot hast outstripped me in my black ship.'

"So I spoke, and with a groan he answered me and said: 'Son of Laertes, sprung from Zeus, Odysseus of many devices, an evil doom of some god was my undoing, and measureless wine. When I had lain down to sleep in the house of Circe I did not think to go to the long ladder that I might come down again, but fell headlong from the roof, and my neck was broken away from the spine and my spirit went down to the house of Hades. Now I beseech thee by those whom we left behind, who are not present with us, by thy wife and thy father who reared thee when a babe, and by Telemachus whom thou didst leave an only son in thy halls; for I know that as thou goest hence from the house of Hades thou wilt touch at the Aeaean isle with thy well-built ship. There, then, O prince, I bid thee remember me. Leave me not behind thee unwept and unburied as thou goest thence, and turn not away from me, lest haply I bring the wrath of the gods upon thee. Nay, burn me with my armour, all that is mine, and heap up a mound for me on the shore of the grey sea, in memory of an unhappy man, that men yet to be may learn of me. Fulfil this my prayer, and fix upon the mound my oar wherewith I rowed in life when I was among my comrades.'

"So he spoke, and I made answer and said: 'All this, unhappy man, will I perform and do.'

"Thus we two sat and held sad converse one with

ἥμεθ', ἐγὼ μὲν ἄνευθεν ἐφ' αἵματι φάσγανον ἴσχων,
εἴδωλον δ' ἑτέρωθεν ἑταίρου πόλλ' ἀγόρευεν·

" Ἦλθε δ' ἐπὶ ψυχὴ μητρὸς κατατεθνηυίης,
Αὐτολύκου θυγάτηρ μεγαλήτορος Ἀντίκλεια,   8
τὴν ζωὴν κατέλειπον ἰὼν εἰς Ἴλιον ἰρήν.
τὴν μὲν ἐγὼ δάκρυσα ἰδὼν ἐλέησά τε θυμῷ·
ἀλλ' οὐδ' ὣς εἴων προτέρην, πυκινόν περ ἀχεύων,
αἵματος ἆσσον ἴμεν, πρὶν Τειρεσίαο πυθέσθαι.

" Ἦλθε δ' ἐπὶ ψυχὴ Θηβαίου Τειρεσίαο   9
χρύσεον σκῆπτρον ἔχων, ἐμὲ δ' ἔγνω καὶ προσέειπεν·
' Διογενὲς Λαερτιάδη, πολυμήχαν' Ὀδυσσεῦ,[1]
τίπτ' αὖτ', ὦ δύστηνε, λιπὼν φάος ἠελίοιο
ἤλυθες, ὄφρα ἴδῃ νέκυας καὶ ἀτερπέα χῶρον;
ἀλλ' ἀποχάζεο βόθρου, ἄπισχε δὲ φάσγανον ὀξύ,   9
αἵματος ὄφρα πίω καί τοι νημερτέα εἴπω.'

" Ὥς φάτ', ἐγὼ δ' ἀναχασσάμενος ξίφος ἀργυρόηλον
κουλεῷ ἐγκατέπηξ'. ὁ δ' ἐπεὶ πίεν αἷμα κελαινόν,
καὶ τότε δή μ' ἐπέεσσι προσηύδα μάντις ἀμύμων·

" ' Νόστον δίζηαι μελιηδέα, φαίδιμ' Ὀδυσσεῦ·   10
τὸν δέ τοι ἀργαλέον θήσει θεός· οὐ γὰρ ὀίω
λήσειν ἐννοσίγαιον, ὅ τοι κότον ἔνθετο θυμῷ
χωόμενος ὅτι οἱ υἱὸν φίλον ἐξαλάωσας.
ἀλλ' ἔτι μέν κε καὶ ὣς κακά περ πάσχοντες ἵκοισθε,
αἴ κ' ἐθέλῃς σὸν θυμὸν ἐρυκακέειν καὶ ἑταίρων,   10
ὁππότε κε πρῶτον πελάσῃς ἐυεργέα νῆα
Θρινακίῃ νήσῳ, προφυγὼν ἰοειδέα πόντον,
βοσκομένας δ' εὕρητε βόας καὶ ἴφια μῆλα

---

[1] Line 92 is omitted in most MSS.

the other, I on one side holding my sword over the blood, while on the other side the phantom of my comrade spoke at large.

"Then there came up the spirit of my dead mother, Anticleia, the daughter of great-hearted Autolycus, whom I had left alive when I departed for sacred Ilios. At sight of her I wept, and my heart had compassion on her, but even so I would not suffer her to come near the blood, for all my great sorrow, until I had enquired of Teiresias.

"Then there came up the spirit of the Theban Teiresias, bearing his golden staff in his hand, and he knew me and spoke to me: 'Son of Laertes, sprung from Zeus, Odysseus of many devices, what now, hapless man? Why hast thou left the light of the sun and come hither to behold the dead and a region where is no joy? Nay, give place from the pit and draw back thy sharp sword, that I may drink of the blood and tell thee sooth.'

"So he spoke, and I gave place and thrust my silver-studded sword into its sheath, and when he had drunk the dark blood, then the blameless seer spoke to me and said:

"'Thou askest of thy honey-sweet return, glorious Odysseus, but this shall a god make grievous unto thee; for I think not that thou shalt elude the Earth-shaker, seeing that he has laid up wrath in his heart against thee, angered that thou didst blind his dear son. Yet even so ye may reach home, though in evil plight, if thou wilt curb thine own spirit and that of thy comrades, as soon as thou shalt bring thy well-built ship to the island Thrinacia, escaping from the violet sea, and ye find grazing there the kine and goodly flocks of Helios, who

Ἠελίου, ὃς πάντ' ἐφορᾷ καὶ πάντ' ἐπακούει.
τὰς εἰ μέν κ' ἀσινέας ἐάᾳς νόστου τε μέδηαι,   110
καί κεν ἔτ' εἰς Ἰθάκην κακά περ πάσχοντες ἵκοισθε·
εἰ δέ κε σίνηαι, τότε τοι τεκμαίρομ' ὄλεθρον,
νηί τε καὶ ἑτάροις. αὐτὸς δ' εἴ πέρ κεν ἀλύξῃς,
ὀψὲ κακῶς νεῖαι, ὀλέσας ἄπο πάντας ἑταίρους,
νηὸς ἐπ' ἀλλοτρίης· δήεις δ' ἐν πήματα οἴκῳ,   115
ἄνδρας ὑπερφιάλους, οἵ τοι βίοτον κατέδουσι
μνώμενοι ἀντιθέην ἄλοχον καὶ ἔδνα διδόντες.
ἀλλ' ἦ τοι κείνων γε βίας ἀποτίσεαι ἐλθών·
αὐτὰρ ἐπὴν μνηστῆρας ἐνὶ μεγάροισι τεοῖσι
κτείνῃς ἠὲ δόλῳ ἢ ἀμφαδὸν ὀξέι χαλκῷ,   120
ἔρχεσθαι δὴ ἔπειτα λαβὼν εὐῆρες ἐρετμόν,
εἰς ὅ κε τοὺς ἀφίκηαι οἳ οὐκ ἴσασι θάλασσαν
ἀνέρες, οὐδέ θ' ἅλεσσι μεμιγμένον εἶδαρ ἔδουσιν·
οὐδ' ἄρα τοί γ' ἴσασι νέας φοινικοπαρῄους
οὐδ' εὐήρε' ἐρετμά, τά τε πτερὰ νηυσὶ πέλονται.   125
σῆμα δέ τοι ἐρέω μάλ' ἀριφραδές, οὐδέ σε λήσει·
ὁππότε κεν δή τοι συμβλήμενος ἄλλος ὁδίτης
φήῃ ἀθηρηλοιγὸν ἔχειν ἀνὰ φαιδίμῳ ὤμῳ,
καὶ τότε δὴ γαίῃ πήξας εὐῆρες ἐρετμόν,
ῥέξας ἱερὰ καλὰ Ποσειδάωνι ἄνακτι,   130
ἀρνειὸν ταῦρόν τε συῶν τ' ἐπιβήτορα κάπρον,
οἴκαδ' ἀποστείχειν ἔρδειν θ' ἱερὰς ἑκατόμβας
ἀθανάτοισι θεοῖσι, τοὶ οὐρανὸν εὐρὺν ἔχουσι,
πᾶσι μάλ' ἑξείης. θάνατος δέ τοι ἐξ ἁλὸς αὐτῷ
ἀβληχρὸς μάλα τοῖος ἐλεύσεται, ὅς κέ σε πέφνῃ   135

---

¹ Or, more naturally, "from out the sea." The latter rendering assumes, however, a reference to the story of the *Tele-*

oversees and overhears all things. If thou leavest
these unharmed and heedest thy homeward way,
verily ye may yet reach Ithaca, though in evil plight.
But if thou harmest them, then I foresee ruin for
thy ship and thy comrades, and even if thou shalt
thyself escape, late shalt thou come home and in
evil case, after losing all thy comrades, in a ship that
is another's, and thou shalt find woes in thy house—
proud men that devour thy livelihood, wooing thy
godlike wife, and offering wooers' gifts. Yet verily
on their violent deeds shalt thou take vengeance
when thou comest. But when thou hast slain the
wooers in thy halls, whether by guile or openly with
the sharp sword, then do thou go forth, taking a
shapely oar, until thou comest to men that know
naught of the sea and eat not of food mingled with
salt, aye, and they know naught of ships with purple
cheeks, or of shapely oars that are as wings unto
ships. And I will tell thee a sign right manifest,
which will not escape thee. When another wayfarer,
on meeting thee, shall say that thou hast a winnowing-
fan on thy stout shoulder, then do thou fix in the
earth thy shapely oar and make goodly offerings to
lord Poseidon—a ram, and a bull, and a boar that
mates with sows—and depart for thy home and offer
sacred hecatombs to the immortal gods who hold
broad heaven, to each one in due order. And death
shall come to thee thyself far from the sea,[1] a death
so gentle, that shall lay thee low when thou art over-

gony, a "cyclic" poem, attributed to Eugammon of Cyrene,
in which Odysseus was killed by Telegonus, his son by Circe,
with a spear tipped with the bone of a sea-fish. This story
has no foundation in the *Odyssey,* and those who adopt the
rendering "from out the sea" assume that these lines are a
late interpolation.

γήραι ὕπο λιπαρῷ ἀρημένον· ἀμφὶ δὲ λαοὶ
ὄλβιοι ἔσσονται. τὰ δέ τοι νημερτέα εἴρω.'

"῝Ως ἔφατ', αὐτὰρ ἐγώ μιν ἀμειβόμενος προσέειπον
'Τειρεσίη, τὰ μὲν ἄρ που ἐπέκλωσαν θεοὶ αὐτοί.
ἀλλ' ἄγε μοι τόδε εἰπὲ καὶ ἀτρεκέως κατάλεξον·   14
μητρὸς τήνδ' ὁρόω ψυχὴν κατατεθνηυίης·
ἡ δ' ἀκέουσ' ἧσται σχεδὸν αἵματος, οὐδ' ἑὸν υἱὸν
ἔτλη ἐσάντα ἰδεῖν οὐδὲ προτιμυθήσασθαι.
εἰπέ, ἄναξ, πῶς κέν με ἀναγνοίη τὸν ἐόντα;'

"῝Ως ἐφάμην, ὁ δέ μ' αὐτίκ' ἀμειβόμενος προσέειπεν
'Ρηίδιόν τοι ἔπος ἐρέω καὶ ἐπὶ φρεσὶ θήσω.   14
ὅν τινα μέν κεν ἐᾷς νεκύων κατατεθνηώτων
αἵματος ἆσσον ἴμεν, ὁ δέ τοι νημερτὲς ἐνίψει·
ᾧ δέ κ' ἐπιφθονέῃς, ὁ δέ τοι πάλιν εἶσιν ὀπίσσω.'

"῝Ως φαμένη ψυχὴ μὲν ἔβη δόμον ῎Αιδος εἴσω   15
Τειρεσίαο ἄνακτος, ἐπεὶ κατὰ θέσφατ' ἔλεξεν·
αὐτὰρ ἐγὼν αὐτοῦ μένον ἔμπεδον, ὄφρ' ἐπὶ μήτηρ
ἤλυθε καὶ πίεν αἷμα κελαινεφές· αὐτίκα δ' ἔγνω,
καί μ' ὀλοφυρομένη ἔπεα πτερόεντα προσηύδα·

"'Τέκνον ἐμόν, πῶς ἦλθες ὑπὸ ζόφον ἠερόεντα   15
ζωὸς ἐών; χαλεπὸν δὲ τάδε ζωοῖσιν ὁρᾶσθαι.
μέσσῳ γὰρ μεγάλοι ποταμοὶ καὶ δεινὰ ῥέεθρα,
᾽Ωκεανὸς μὲν πρῶτα, τὸν οὔ πως ἔστι περῆσαι
πεζὸν ἐόντ', ἢν μή τις ἔχῃ εὐεργέα νῆα.[1]
ἢ νῦν δὴ Τροίηθεν ἀλώμενος ἐνθάδ' ἱκάνεις   16
νηί τε καὶ ἑτάροισι πολὺν χρόνον; οὐδέ πω ἦλθες
εἰς ᾽Ιθάκην, οὐδ' εἶδες ἐνὶ μεγάροισι γυναῖκα;'

[1] Lines 157-9 were rejected by Aristarchus.

come with sleek [1] old age, and thy people shall dwell in prosperity around thee. In this have I told thee sooth.'

"So he spoke, and I made answer and said : 'Teiresias, of all this, I ween, the gods themselves have spun the thread. But come, tell me this, and declare it truly. I see here the spirit of my dead mother ; she sits in silence near the blood, and deigns not to look upon the face of her own son or to speak to him. Tell me, prince, how she may recognize that I am he?'

"So I spoke, and he straightway made answer, and said : 'Easy is the word that I shall say and put in thy mind. Whomsoever of those that are dead and gone thou shalt suffer to draw near the blood, he will tell thee sooth ; but whomsoever thou refusest, he surely will go back again.'

"So saying the spirit of the prince, Teiresias, went back into the house of Hades, when he had declared his prophecies ; but I remained there steadfastly until my mother came up and drank the dark blood. At once then she knew me, and with wailing she spoke to me winged words :

"'My child, how didst thou come beneath the murky darkness, being still alive ? Hard is it for those that live to behold these realms, for between are great rivers and dread streams ; Oceanus first, which one may in no wise cross on foot, but only if one have a well-built ship. Art thou but now come hither from Troy after long wanderings with thy ship and thy companions? and hast thou not yet reached Ithaca, nor seen thy wife in thy halls?'

[1] That is, "in the midst of wealth and comfort."

"Ὣς ἔφατ', αὐτὰρ ἐγώ μιν ἀμειβόμενος προσέειπον·
' Μῆτερ ἐμή, χρειώ με κατήγαγεν εἰς Ἀίδαο
ψυχῇ χρησόμενον Θηβαίου Τειρεσίαο·   165
οὐ γάρ πω σχεδὸν ἦλθον Ἀχαιίδος, οὐδέ πω ἁμῆς
γῆς ἐπέβην, ἀλλ' αἰὲν ἔχων ἀλάλημαι ὀιζύν,
ἐξ οὗ τὰ πρώτισθ' ἑπόμην Ἀγαμέμνονι δίῳ
Ἴλιον εἰς εὔπωλον, ἵνα Τρώεσσι μαχοίμην.
ἀλλ' ἄγε μοι τόδε εἰπὲ καὶ ἀτρεκέως κατάλεξον·   170
τίς νύ σε κὴρ ἐδάμασσε τανηλεγέος θανάτοιο;
ἦ δολιχὴ νοῦσος, ἦ Ἄρτεμις ἰοχέαιρα
οἷς ἀγανοῖς βελέεσσιν ἐποιχομένη κατέπεφνεν;
εἰπὲ δέ μοι πατρός τε καὶ υἱέος, ὃν κατέλειπον,
ἦ ἔτι πὰρ κείνοισιν ἐμὸν γέρας, ἦέ τις ἤδη   175
ἀνδρῶν ἄλλος ἔχει, ἐμὲ δ' οὐκέτι φασὶ νέεσθαι.
εἰπὲ δέ μοι μνηστῆς ἀλόχου βουλήν τε νόον τε,
ἠὲ μένει παρὰ παιδὶ καὶ ἔμπεδα πάντα φυλάσσει
ἦ ἤδη μιν ἔγημεν Ἀχαιῶν ὅς τις ἄριστος.'
"Ὣς ἐφάμην, ἡ δ' αὐτίκ' ἀμείβετο πότνια μήτηρ·   180
' Καὶ λίην κείνη γε μένει τετληότι θυμῷ
σοῖσιν ἐνὶ μεγάροισιν· ὀιζυραὶ δέ οἱ αἰεὶ
φθίνουσιν νύκτες τε καὶ ἤματα δάκρυ χεούσῃ.
σὸν δ' οὔ πώ τις ἔχει καλὸν γέρας, ἀλλὰ ἕκηλος
Τηλέμαχος τεμένεα νέμεται καὶ δαῖτας ἐίσας   185
δαίνυται, ἃς ἐπέοικε δικασπόλον ἄνδρ' ἀλεγύνειν·
πάντες γὰρ καλέουσι. πατὴρ δὲ σὸς αὐτόθι μίμνει
ἀγρῷ, οὐδὲ πόλινδε κατέρχεται. οὐδέ οἱ εὐναὶ
δέμνια καὶ χλαῖναι καὶ ῥήγεα σιγαλόεντα,
ἀλλ' ὅ γε χεῖμα μὲν εὕδει ὅθι δμῶες ἐνὶ οἴκῳ,   190
ἐν κόνι ἄγχι πυρός, κακὰ δὲ χροὶ εἵματα εἶται·

"So she spoke, and I made answer and said : ' My mother, necessity brought me down to the house of Hades, to seek soothsaying of the spirit of Theban Teiresias. For not yet have I come near to the shore of Achaea, nor have I as yet set foot on my own land, but have ever been wandering, laden with woe, from the day when first I went with goodly Agamemnon to Ilios, famed for its horses, to fight with the Trojans. But come, tell me this, and declare it truly. What fate of grievous death overcame thee? Was it long disease, or did the archer, Artemis, assail thee with her gentle shafts, and slay thee? And tell me of my father and my son, whom I left behind me. Does the honour that was mine still abide with them, or does some other man now possess it, and do they say that I shall no more return? And tell me of my wedded wife, of her purpose and of her mind. Does she abide with her son, and keep all things safe? or has one already wedded her, whosoever is best of the Achaeans?'

"So I spoke, and my honoured mother straightway answered : 'Aye verily she abides with steadfast heart in thy halls, and ever sorrowfully for her do the nights and the days wane, as she weeps. But the fair honour that was thine no man yet possesses, but Telemachus holds thy demesne unharassed, and feasts at equal banquets, such as it is fitting that one who deals judgment should share, for all men invite him. But thy father abides there in the tilled land, and comes not to the city, nor has he, for bedding, bed and cloaks and bright coverlets, but through the winter he sleeps in the house, where the slaves sleep, in the ashes by the fire, and wears upon his body mean

αὐτὰρ ἐπὴν ἔλθῃσι θέρος τεθαλυῖά τ᾽ ὀπώρη,
πάντῃ οἱ κατὰ γουνὸν ἀλωῆς οἰνοπέδοιο
φύλλων κεκλιμένων χθαμαλαὶ βεβλήαται εὐναί.
ἔνθ᾽ ὅ γε κεῖτ᾽ ἀχέων, μέγα δὲ φρεσὶ πένθος ἀέξει   195
σὸν νόστον ποθέων,¹ χαλεπὸν δ᾽ ἐπὶ γῆρας ἱκάνει.
οὕτω γὰρ καὶ ἐγὼν ὀλόμην καὶ πότμον ἐπέσπον·
οὔτ᾽ ἐμέ γ᾽ ἐν μεγάροισιν ἐΰσκοπος ἰοχέαιρα
οἷς ἀγανοῖς βελέεσσιν ἐποιχομένη κατέπεφνεν,
οὔτε τις οὖν μοι νοῦσος ἐπήλυθεν, ἥ τε μάλιστα   200
τηκεδόνι στυγερῇ μελέων ἐξείλετο θυμόν·
ἀλλά με σός τε πόθος σά τε μήδεα, φαίδιμ᾽ Ὀδυσσεῦ,
σή τ᾽ ἀγανοφροσύνη μελιηδέα θυμὸν ἀπηύρα.᾽

‘“Ὣς ἔφατ᾽, αὐτὰρ ἐγώ γ᾽ ἔθελον φρεσὶ μερμηρίξας
μητρὸς ἐμῆς ψυχὴν ἑλέειν κατατεθνηυίης.   205
τρὶς μὲν ἐφωρμήθην, ἑλέειν τέ με θυμὸς ἀνώγει,
τρὶς δέ μοι ἐκ χειρῶν σκιῇ εἴκελον ἢ καὶ ὀνείρῳ
ἔπτατ᾽. ἐμοὶ δ᾽ ἄχος ὀξὺ γενέσκετο κηρόθι μᾶλλον,
καί μιν φωνήσας ἔπεα πτερόεντα προσηύδων·

‘“‘Μῆτερ ἐμή, τί νύ μ᾽ οὐ μίμνεις ἑλέειν μεμαῶτα,   210
ὄφρα καὶ εἰν Ἀΐδαο φίλας περὶ χεῖρε βαλόντε
ἀμφοτέρω κρυεροῖο τεταρπώμεσθα γόοιο;
ἦ τί μοι εἴδωλον τόδ᾽ ἀγανὴ Περσεφόνεια
ὤτρυν᾽, ὄφρ᾽ ἔτι μᾶλλον ὀδυρόμενος στεναχίζω;᾽

‘“Ὣς ἐφάμην, ἡ δ᾽ αὐτίκ᾽ ἀμείβετο πότνια μήτηρ·   215
‘Ὤ μοι, τέκνον ἐμόν, περὶ πάντων κάμμορε φωτῶν,
οὔ τί σε Περσεφόνεια Διὸς θυγάτηρ ἀπαφίσκει,
ἀλλ᾽ αὕτη δίκη ἐστὶ βροτῶν, ὅτε τίς κε θάνῃσιν·
οὐ γὰρ ἔτι σάρκας τε καὶ ὀστέα ἶνες ἔχουσιν,

¹ νόστον ποθέων : πότμον γοόων.

raiment. But when summer comes and rich autumn, then all about the slope of his vineyard plot are strewn his lowly beds of fallen leaves. There he lies sorrowing, and nurses his great grief in his heart, in longing for thy return, and heavy old age has come upon him. Even so did I too perish and meet my fate. Neither did the keen-sighted archer goddess assail me in my halls with her gentle shafts, and slay me, nor did any disease come upon me, such as oftenest through grievous wasting takes the spirit from the limbs; nay, it was longing for thee, and for thy counsels, glorious Odysseus, and for thy tender-heartedness, that robbed me of honey-sweet life.'

"So she spoke, and I pondered in heart, and was fain to clasp the spirit of my dead mother. Thrice I sprang towards her, and my heart bade me clasp her, and thrice she flitted from my arms like a shadow or a dream, and pain grew ever sharper at my heart. And I spoke and addressed her with winged words:

"'My mother, why dost thou not stay for me, who am eager to clasp thee, that even in the house of Hades we two may cast our arms each about the other, and take our fill of chill lamenting. Is this but a phantom that august Persephone has sent me, that I may lament and groan the more?'

"So I spoke, and my honoured mother straightway answered: 'Ah me, my child, ill-fated above all men, in no wise does Persephone, the daughter of Zeus, deceive thee, but this is the appointed way with mortals when one dies. For the sinews no longer hold the flesh and the bones together, but

ἀλλὰ τὰ μέν τε πυρὸς κρατερὸν μένος αἰθομένοιο   22
δαμνᾷ, ἐπεί κε πρῶτα λίπῃ λεύκ᾽ ὀστέα θυμός,
ψυχὴ δ᾽ ἠΰτ᾽ ὄνειρος ἀποπταμένη πεπότηται.
ἀλλὰ φόωσδε τάχιστα λιλαίεο· ταῦτα δὲ πάντα
ἴσθ᾽, ἵνα καὶ μετόπισθε τεῇ εἴπῃσθα γυναικί.᾽

   " Νῶι μὲν ὣς ἐπέεσσιν ἀμειβόμεθ᾽, αἱ δὲ γυναῖκες   22
ἤλυθον, ὤτρυνεν γὰρ ἀγαυὴ Περσεφόνεια,
ὅσσαι ἀριστήων ἄλοχοι ἔσαν ἠδὲ θύγατρες.
αἱ δ᾽ ἀμφ᾽ αἷμα κελαινὸν ἀολλέες ἠγερέθοντο,
αὐτὰρ ἐγὼ βούλευον ὅπως ἐρέοιμι ἑκάστην.
ἥδε δέ μοι κατὰ θυμὸν ἀρίστη φαίνετο βουλή·   23
σπασσάμενος τανύηκες ἄορ παχέος παρὰ μηροῦ
οὐκ εἴων πίνειν ἅμα πάσας αἷμα κελαινόν.
αἱ δὲ προμνηστῖναι ἐπήισαν, ἠδὲ ἑκάστη
ὃν γόνον ἐξαγόρευεν· ἐγὼ δ᾽ ἐρέεινον ἁπάσας.

   " Ἔνθ᾽ ἦ τοι πρώτην Τυρὼ ἴδον εὐπατέρειαν,   23
ἣ φάτο Σαλμωνῆος ἀμύμονος ἔκγονος εἶναι,
φῆ δὲ Κρηθῆος γυνὴ ἔμμεναι Αἰολίδαο·
ἣ ποταμοῦ ἠράσσατ᾽ Ἐνιπῆος θείοιο,
ὃς πολὺ κάλλιστος ποταμῶν ἐπὶ γαῖαν ἵησι,
καί ῥ᾽ ἐπ᾽ Ἐνιπῆος πωλέσκετο καλὰ ῥέεθρα.   24
τῷ δ᾽ ἄρα εἰσάμενος γαιήοχος ἐννοσίγαιος
ἐν προχοῇς ποταμοῦ παρελέξατο δινήεντος·
πορφύρεον δ᾽ ἄρα κῦμα περιστάθη, οὔρεϊ ἶσον,
κυρτωθέν, κρύψεν δὲ θεὸν θνητήν τε γυναῖκα.
λῦσε δὲ παρθενίην ζώνην, κατὰ δ᾽ ὕπνον ἔχευεν.¹   24
αὐτὰρ ἐπεί ῥ᾽ ἐτέλεσσε θεὸς φιλοτήσια ἔργα,
ἔν τ᾽ ἄρα οἱ φῦ χειρί, ἔπος τ᾽ ἔφατ᾽ ἔκ τ᾽ ὀνόμαζε·

   " ' Χαῖρε, γύναι, φιλότητι· περιπλομένου δ᾽ ἐνιαυτοῦ
τέξεις ἀγλαὰ τέκνα, ἐπεὶ οὐκ ἀποφώλιοι εὐναὶ

---

¹ Line 245, unknown to Zenodotus, was rejected by
Aristarchus.

the strong might of blazing fire destroys these, as soon as the life leaves the white bones, and the spirit, like a dream, flits away, and hovers to and fro. But haste thee to the light with what speed thou mayest, and bear all these things in mind, that thou mayest hereafter tell them to thy wife.'

"Thus we two talked with one another; and the women came, for august Persephone sent them forth, even all those that had been the wives and the daughters of chieftains. These flocked in throngs about the dark blood, and I considered how I might question each; and this seemed to my mind the best counsel. I drew my long sword from beside my stout thigh, and would not suffer them to drink of the dark blood all at one time. So they drew near, one after the other, and each declared her birth, and I questioned them all.

"Then verily the first that I saw was high-born Tyro, who said that she was the daughter of noble Salmoneus, and declared herself to be the wife of Cretheus, son of Aeolus. She became enamoured of the river, divine Enipeus, who is far the fairest of rivers that send forth their streams upon the earth, and she was wont to resort to the fair waters of Enipeus. But the Enfolder and Shaker of the earth took his form, and lay with her at the mouths of the eddying river. And the dark wave stood about them like a mountain, vaulted-over, and hid the god and the mortal woman. And he loosed her maiden girdle, and shed sleep upon her. But when the god had ended his work of love, he clasped her hand, and spoke, and addressed her:

"'Be glad, woman, in our love, and as the year goes on its course thou shalt bear glorious children,

403

ἀθανάτων· σὺ δὲ τοὺς κομέειν ἀτιταλλέμεναί τε.　250
νῦν δ' ἔρχευ πρὸς δῶμα, καὶ ἴσχεο μηδ' ὀνομήνῃς·
αὐτὰρ ἐγώ τοί εἰμι Ποσειδάων ἐνοσίχθων.'

"Ὣς εἰπὼν ὑπὸ πόντον ἐδύσετο κυμαίνοντα.
ἡ δ' ὑποκυσαμένη Πελίην τέκε καὶ Νηλῆα,
τὼ κρατερὼ θεράποντε Διὸς μεγάλοιο γενέσθην　255
ἀμφοτέρω· Πελίης μὲν ἐν εὐρυχόρῳ Ἰαωλκῷ
ναῖε πολύρρηνος, ὁ δ' ἄρ' ἐν Πύλῳ ἠμαθόεντι.
τοὺς δ' ἑτέρους Κρηθῆι τέκεν βασίλεια γυναικῶν,
Αἴσονά τ' ἠδὲ Φέρητ' Ἀμυθάονά θ' ἱππιοχάρμην.

"Τὴν δὲ μετ' Ἀντιόπην ἴδον, Ἀσωποῖο θύγατρα,　260
ἣ δὴ καὶ Διὸς εὔχετ' ἐν ἀγκοίνῃσιν ἰαῦσαι,
καί ῥ' ἔτεκεν δύο παῖδ', Ἀμφίονά τε Ζῆθόν τε,
οἳ πρῶτοι Θήβης ἕδος ἔκτισαν ἑπταπύλοιο,
πύργωσάν τ', ἐπεὶ οὐ μὲν ἀπύργωτόν γ' ἐδύναντο
ναιέμεν εὐρύχορον Θήβην, κρατερώ περ ἐόντε.　265

"Τὴν δὲ μετ' Ἀλκμήνην ἴδον, Ἀμφιτρύωνος ἄκοιτιν,
ἥ ῥ' Ἡρακλῆα θρασυμέμνονα θυμολέοντα
γείνατ' ἐν ἀγκοίνῃσι Διὸς μεγάλοιο μιγεῖσα·
καὶ Μεγάρην, Κρείοντος ὑπερθύμοιο θύγατρα,
τὴν ἔχεν Ἀμφιτρύωνος υἱὸς μένος αἰὲν ἀτειρής.　270

"Μητέρα τ' Οἰδιπόδαο ἴδον, καλὴν Ἐπικάστην,
ἣ μέγα ἔργον ἔρεξεν ἀιδρείῃσι νόοιο
γημαμένη ᾧ υἷι· ὁ δ' ὃν πατέρ' ἐξεναρίξας
γῆμεν· ἄφαρ δ' ἀνάπυστα θεοὶ θέσαν ἀνθρώποισιν.
ἀλλ' ὁ μὲν ἐν Θήβῃ πολυηράτῳ ἄλγεα πάσχων　275
Καδμείων ἤνασσε θεῶν ὀλοὰς διὰ βουλάς·

for not weak are the embraces of a god. These do thou tend and rear. But now go to thy house, and hold thy peace, and tell no man; but know that I am Poseidon, the shaker of the earth.'

"So saying, he plunged beneath the surging sea. But she conceived and bore Pelias and Neleus, who both became strong servants of great Zeus; and Pelias dwelt in spacious Iolcus, and was rich in flocks, and the other dwelt in sandy Pylos. But her other children she, the queenly among women, bore to Cretheus, even Aeson, and Pheres, and Amythaon, who fought from chariots.[1]

"And after her I saw Antiope, daughter of Asopus, who boasted that she had slept even in the arms of Zeus, and she bore two sons, Amphion and Zethus, who first established the seat of seven-gated Thebe, and fenced it in with walls, for they could not dwell in spacious Thebe unfenced, how mighty soever they were.

"And after her I saw Alcmene, wife of Amphitryon, who lay in the arms of great Zeus, and bore Heracles, staunch in fight, the lion-hearted. And Megara I saw, daughter of Creon, high-of-heart, whom the son of Amphitryon, ever stubborn in might, had to wife.

"And I saw the mother of Oedipodes, fair Epicaste, who wrought a monstrous deed in ignorance of mind, in that she wedded her own son, and he, when he had slain his own father, wedded her, and straightway the gods made these things known among men. Howbeit he abode as lord of the Cadmeans in lovely Thebe, suffering woes through the baneful counsels of the gods, but she

---

[1] Others render, "whose joy was in chariots." but it is not certain that χάρμη is connected with χαίρω.

ἡ δ' ἔβη εἰς Ἀίδαο πυλάρταο κρατεροῖο,
ἀψαμένη βρόχον αἰπὺν ἀφ' ὑψηλοῖο μελάθρου,
ᾧ ἄχεϊ σχομένη· τῷ δ' ἄλγεα κάλλιπ' ὀπίσσω
πολλὰ μάλ', ὅσσα τε μητρὸς Ἐρινύες ἐκτελέουσιν. 28

"Καὶ Χλῶριν εἶδον περικαλλέα, τήν ποτε Νηλεὺς
γῆμεν ἑὸν διὰ κάλλος, ἐπεὶ πόρε μυρία ἕδνα,
ὁπλοτάτην κούρην Ἀμφίονος Ἰασίδαο,
ὅς ποτ' ἐν Ὀρχομενῷ Μινυείῳ ἶφι ἄνασσεν·
ἡ δὲ Πύλου βασίλευε, τέκεν δέ οἱ ἀγλαὰ τέκνα, 28
Νέστορά τε Χρομίον τε Περικλύμενόν τ' ἀγέρωχον.
τοῖσι δ' ἐπ' ἰφθίμην Πηρὼ τέκε, θαῦμα βροτοῖσι,
τὴν πάντες μνώοντο περικτίται· οὐδ' ἄρα Νηλεὺς
τῷ ἐδίδου ὃς μὴ ἕλικας βόας εὐρυμετώπους
ἐκ Φυλάκης ἐλάσειε βίης Ἰφικληείης 29
ἀργαλέας· τὰς δ' οἶος ὑπέσχετο μάντις ἀμύμων
ἐξελάαν· χαλεπὴ δὲ θεοῦ κατὰ μοῖρα πέδησε,
δεσμοί τ' ἀργαλέοι καὶ βουκόλοι ἀγροιῶται.
ἀλλ' ὅτε δὴ μῆνές τε καὶ ἡμέραι ἐξετελεῦντο
ἂψ περιτελλομένου ἔτεος καὶ ἐπήλυθον ὧραι, 29
καὶ τότε δή μιν ἔλυσε βίη Ἰφικληείη,
θέσφατα πάντ' εἰπόντα· Διὸς δ' ἐτελείετο βουλή.

"Καὶ Λήδην εἶδον, τὴν Τυνδαρέου παράκοιτιν,
ἥ ῥ' ὑπὸ Τυνδαρέῳ κρατερόφρονε γείνατο παῖδε,
Κάστορά θ' ἱππόδαμον καὶ πὺξ ἀγαθὸν Πολυδεύκεα, 30
τοὺς ἄμφω ζωοὺς κατέχει φυσίζοος αἶα·
οἳ καὶ νέρθεν γῆς τιμὴν πρὸς Ζηνὸς ἔχοντες
ἄλλοτε μὲν ζώουσ' ἑτερήμεροι, ἄλλοτε δ' αὖτε
τεθνᾶσιν· τιμὴν δὲ λελόγχασιν ἶσα θεοῖσι.

went down to the house of Hades, the strong warder. She made fast a noose on high from a lofty beam, overpowered by her sorrow, but for him she left behind woes full many, even all that the Avengers of a mother bring to pass.

"And I saw beauteous Chloris, whom once Neleus wedded because of her beauty, when he had brought countless gifts of wooing. Youngest daughter was she of Amphion, son of Iasus, who once ruled mightily in Orchomenus of the Minyae. And she was queen of Pylos, and bore to her husband glorious children, Nestor, and Chromius, and lordly Periclymenus, and besides these she bore noble Pero, a wonder to men. Her all that dwelt about sought in marriage, but Neleus would give her to no man, save to him who should drive from Phylace the kine of mighty Iphicles, sleek and broad of brow; and hard they were to drive. These the blameless seer alone undertook to drive off; but a grievous fate of the gods ensnared him, even hard bonds and the herdsmen of the field. Howbeit when at length the months and the days were being brought to fulfilment, as the year rolled round, and the seasons came on, then verily mighty Iphicles released him, when he had told all the oracles; and the will of Zeus was fulfilled.

"And I saw Lede, the wife of Tyndareus, who bore to Tyndareus two sons, stout of heart, Castor the tamer of horses, and the boxer Polydeuces. These two the earth, the giver of life, covers, albeit alive, and even in the world below they have honour from Zeus. One day they live in turn, and one day they are dead; and they have won honour like unto that of the gods.

" Τὴν δὲ μετ' Ἰφιμέδειαν, Ἀλωῆος παράκοιτιν   30
εἴσιδον, ἣ δὴ φάσκε Ποσειδάωνι μιγῆναι,
καί ῥ' ἔτεκεν δύο παῖδε, μινυνθαδίω δ' ἐγενέσθην,
Ὦτόν τ' ἀντίθεον τηλεκλειτόν τ' Ἐφιάλτην,
οὓς δὴ μηκίστους θρέψε ζείδωρος ἄρουρα
καὶ πολὺ καλλίστους μετά γε κλυτὸν Ὠρίωνα·   31
ἐννέωροι γὰρ τοί γε καὶ ἐννεαπήχεες ἦσαν
εὖρος, ἀτὰρ μῆκός γε γενέσθην ἐννεόργυιοι.
οἵ ῥα καὶ ἀθανάτοισιν ἀπειλήτην ἐν Ὀλύμπῳ
φυλόπιδα στήσειν πολυάικος πολέμοιο.
Ὄσσαν ἐπ' Οὐλύμπῳ μέμασαν θέμεν, αὐτὰρ ἐπ' Ὄσσ
Πήλιον εἰνοσίφυλλον, ἵν' οὐρανὸς ἀμβατὸς εἴη.   31
καί νύ κεν ἐξετέλεσσαν, εἰ ἥβης μέτρον ἵκοντο·
ἀλλ' ὄλεσεν Διὸς υἱός, ὃν ἠύκομος τέκε Λητώ,
ἀμφοτέρω, πρὶν σφωιν ὑπὸ κροτάφοισιν ἰούλους
ἀνθῆσαι πυκάσαι τε γένυς ἐυανθέι λάχνῃ.   32
  " Φαίδρην τε Πρόκριν τε ἴδον καλήν τ' Ἀριάδνην,
κούρην Μίνωος ὀλοόφρονος, ἥν ποτε Θησεὺς
ἐκ Κρήτης ἐς γουνὸν Ἀθηνάων ἱεράων
ἦγε μέν, οὐδ' ἀπόνητο· πάρος δέ μιν Ἄρτεμις ἔκτα[1]
Δίῃ ἐν ἀμφιρύτῃ Διονύσου μαρτυρίῃσιν.   32
  " Μαῖράν τε Κλυμένην τε ἴδον στυγερήν τ' Ἐριφύλην
ἣ χρυσὸν φίλου ἀνδρὸς ἐδέξατο τιμήεντα.
πάσας δ' οὐκ ἂν ἐγὼ μυθήσομαι οὐδ' ὀνομήνω,
ὅσσας ἡρώων ἀλόχους ἴδον ἠδὲ θύγατρας·
πρὶν γάρ κεν καὶ νὺξ φθῖτ' ἄμβροτος. ἀλλὰ καὶ ὥρη   33
εὕδειν, ἢ ἐπὶ νῆα θοὴν ἐλθόντ' ἐς ἑταίρους
ἢ αὐτοῦ· πομπὴ δὲ θεοῖς ὑμῖν τε μελήσει."
  Ὣς ἔφαθ', οἱ δ' ἄρα πάντες ἀκὴν ἐγένοντο σιωπῇ,
κηληθμῷ δ' ἔσχοντο κατὰ μέγαρα σκιόεντα.
τοῖσιν δ' Ἀρήτη λευκώλενος ἤρχετο μύθων·   33

[1] ἔκτα: ἔσχεν.

"And after her I saw Iphimedeia, wife of Aloeus, who declared that she had lain with Poseidon. She bore two sons, but short of life were they, godlike Otus, and far-famed Ephialtes—men whom the earth, the giver of grain, reared as the tallest, and far the comeliest, after the famous Orion. For at nine years they were nine cubits in breadth and in height nine fathoms. Yea, and they threatened to raise the din of furious war against the immortals in Olympus. They were fain to pile Ossa on Olympus, and Pelion, with its waving forests, on Ossa, that so heaven might be scaled. And this they would have accomplished, if they had reached the measure of manhood; but the son of Zeus, whom fair-haired Leto bore, slew them both before the down blossomed beneath their temples and covered their chins with a full growth of beard.

"And Phaedra and Procris I saw, and fair Ariadne, the daughter of Minos of baneful mind, whom once Theseus was fain to bear from Crete to the hill of sacred Athens; but he had no joy of her, for ere that Artemis slew her in sea-girt Dia because of the witness of Dionysus.

"And Maera and Clymene I saw, and hateful Eriphyle, who took precious gold as the price of the life of her own lord. But I cannot tell or name all the wives and daughters of heroes that I saw; ere that immortal night would wane. Nay, it is now time to sleep, either when I have gone to the swift ship and the crew, or here. My sending shall rest with the gods, and with you."

So he spoke, and they were all hushed in silence, and were held spell-bound throughout the shadowy halls. Then among them white-armed Arete was the first to speak:

" Φαίηκες, πῶς ὕμμιν ἀνὴρ ὅδε φαίνεται εἶναι
εἶδός τε μέγεθός τε ἰδὲ φρένας ἔνδον ἐίσας;
ξεῖνος δ' αὖτ' ἐμός ἐστιν, ἕκαστος δ' ἔμμορε τιμῆς·
τῷ μὴ ἐπειγόμενοι ἀποπέμπετε, μηδὲ τὰ δῶρα
οὕτω χρηΐζοντι κολούετε· πολλὰ γὰρ ὑμῖν   34
κτήματ' ἐνὶ μεγάροισι θεῶν ἰότητι κέονται."
    Τοῖσι δὲ καὶ μετέειπε γέρων ἥρως Ἐχένηος,
ὃς δὴ Φαιήκων ἀνδρῶν προγενέστερος ἦεν·[1]
"Ὦ φίλοι, οὐ μὰν ἥμιν ἀπὸ σκοποῦ οὐδ' ἀπὸ δόξης
μυθεῖται βασίλεια περίφρων· ἀλλὰ πίθεσθε.   34
Ἀλκινόου δ' ἐκ τοῦδ' ἔχεται ἔργον τε ἔπος τε."
    Τὸν δ' αὖτ' Ἀλκίνοος ἀπαμείβετο φώνησέν τε·
" Τοῦτο μὲν οὕτω δὴ ἔσται ἔπος, αἴ κεν ἐγώ γε
ζωὸς Φαιήκεσσι φιληρέτμοισιν ἀνάσσω·
ξεῖνος δὲ τλήτω μάλα περ νόστοιο χατίζων   35
ἔμπης οὖν ἐπιμεῖναι ἐς αὔριον, εἰς ὅ κε πᾶσαν
δωτίνην τελέσω.   πομπὴ δ' ἄνδρεσσι μελήσει
πᾶσι, μάλιστα δ' ἐμοί· τοῦ γὰρ κράτος ἔστ' ἐνὶ δήμῳ.
    Τὸν δ' ἀπαμειβόμενος προσέφη πολύμητις Ὀδυσσεὺ
" Ἀλκίνοε κρεῖον, πάντων ἀριδείκετε λαῶν,   35
εἴ με καὶ εἰς ἐνιαυτὸν ἀνώγοιτ' αὐτόθι μίμνειν,
πομπὴν δ' ὀτρύνοιτε καὶ ἀγλαὰ δῶρα διδοῖτε,
καί κε τὸ βουλοίμην, καί κεν πολὺ κέρδιον εἴη,
πλειοτέρη σὺν χειρὶ φίλην ἐς πατρίδ' ἱκέσθαι·
καί κ' αἰδοιότερος καὶ φίλτερος ἀνδράσιν εἴην   36
πᾶσιν, ὅσοι μ' Ἰθάκηνδε ἰδοίατο νοστήσαντα."
    Τὸν δ' αὖτ' Ἀλκίνοος ἀπαμείβετο φώνησέν τε·
"Ὦ Ὀδυσεῦ, τὸ μὲν οὔ τί σ' ἐΐσκομεν εἰσορόωντες,

[1] Line 343 is omitted in many MSS.

" Phaeacians, how seems this man to you for come-
liness and stature, and for the balanced spirit within
him ? And moreover he is my guest, though each
of you has a share in this honour. Wherefore be
not in haste to send him away, nor stint your gifts
to one in such need ; for many are the treasures
which lie stored in your halls by the favour of the
gods."

Then among them spoke also the old lord Eche-
neus, who was an elder among the Phaeacians :
" Friends, verily not wide of the mark or of our
own thought are the words of our wise queen. Nay,
do you give heed to them. Yet it is on Alcinous
here that deed and word depend."

Then again Alcinous answered him and said :
" This word of hers shall verily hold, as surely as I
live and am lord over the Phaeacians, lovers of the
oar. But let our guest, for all his great longing
to return, nevertheless endure to remain until to-
morrow, till I shall make all our gift complete.
His sending shall rest with the men, with all, but
most of all with me ; for mine is the control in the
land."

Then Odysseus of many wiles answered him and
said : " Lord Alcinous, renowned above all men, if
you should bid me abide here even for a year, and
should further my sending, and give glorious gifts,
even that would I choose ; and it would be better
far to come with a fuller hand to my dear native
land. Aye, and I should win more respect and
love from all men who should see me when I had
returned to Ithaca."

Then again Alcinous made answer and said :
" Odysseus, in no wise as we look on thee do we

ἠπεροπῆά τ' ἔμεν καὶ ἐπίκλοπον, οἷά τε πολλοὺς
βόσκει γαῖα μέλαινα πολυσπερέας ἀνθρώπους,   365
ψεύδεά τ' ἀρτύνοντας ὅθεν κέ τις οὐδὲ ἴδοιτο·
σοὶ δ' ἔπι μὲν μορφὴ ἐπέων, ἔνι δὲ φρένες ἐσθλαί.
μῦθον δ' ὡς ὅτ' ἀοιδὸς ἐπισταμένως κατέλεξας,
πάντων τ' Ἀργείων σέο τ' αὐτοῦ κήδεα λυγρά.
ἀλλ' ἄγε μοι τόδε εἰπὲ καὶ ἀτρεκέως κατάλεξον,   370
εἴ τινας ἀντιθέων ἑτάρων ἴδες, οἵ τοι ἅμ' αὐτῷ
Ἴλιον εἰς ἅμ' ἕποντο καὶ αὐτοῦ πότμον ἐπέσπον.
νὺξ δ' ἥδε μάλα μακρή, ἀθέσφατος· οὐδέ πω ὥρη
εὕδειν ἐν μεγάρῳ, σὺ δέ μοι λέγε θέσκελα ἔργα.
καί κεν ἐς ἠῶ δῖαν ἀνασχοίμην, ὅτε μοι σὺ   375
τλαίης ἐν μεγάρῳ τὰ σὰ κήδεα μυθήσασθαι."

    Τὸν δ' ἀπαμειβόμενος προσέφη πολύμητις Ὀδυσσεύ·
" Ἀλκίνοε κρεῖον, πάντων ἀριδείκετε λαῶν,
ὥρη μὲν πολέων μύθων, ὥρη δὲ καὶ ὕπνου·
εἰ δ' ἔτ' ἀκουέμεναί γε λιλαίεαι, οὐκ ἂν ἐγώ γε[1]   380
τούτων σοι φθονέοιμι καὶ οἰκτρότερ' ἄλλ' ἀγορεύειν,
κήδε' ἐμῶν ἑτάρων, οἳ δὴ μετόπισθεν ὄλοντο,
οἳ Τρώων μὲν ὑπεξέφυγον στονόεσσαν ἀϋτήν,
ἐν νόστῳ δ' ἀπόλοντο κακῆς ἰότητι γυναικός.

    " Αὐτὰρ ἐπεὶ ψυχὰς μὲν ἀπεσκέδασ' ἄλλυδις ἄλλη   385
ἁγνὴ Περσεφόνεια γυναικῶν θηλυτεράων,
ἦλθε δ' ἐπὶ ψυχὴ Ἀγαμέμνονος Ἀτρεΐδαο
ἀχνυμένη· περὶ δ' ἄλλαι ἀγηγέραθ', ὅσσοι ἅμ' αὐτῷ
οἴκῳ ἐν Αἰγίσθοιο θάνον καὶ πότμον ἐπέσπον.
ἔγνω δ' αἶψ' ἔμ' ἐκεῖνος, ἐπεὶ πίεν αἷμα κελαινόν·   390
κλαῖε δ' ὅ γε λιγέως, θαλερὸν κατὰ δάκρυον εἴβων,

[1] ἐγώ γε : ἔπειτα.

412

deem this of thee, that thou art a cheat and a dissembler, such as are many whom the dark earth breeds scattered far and wide, men that fashion lies out of what no man can even see. But upon thee is grace of words, and within thee is a heart of wisdom, and thy tale thou hast told with skill, as doth a minstrel, even the grievous woes of all the Argives and of thine own self. But come, tell me this, and declare it truly, whether thou sawest any of thy godlike comrades, who went to Ilios together with thee, and there met their fate. The night is before us, long, aye, wondrous long, and it is not yet the time for sleep in the hall. Tell on, I pray thee, the tale of these wondrous deeds. Verily I could abide until bright dawn, so thou wouldest be willing to tell in the hall of these woes of thine."

Then Odysseus of many wiles answered him and said: "Lord Alcinous, renowned above all men, there is a time for many words and there is a time also for sleep. But if thou art fain still to listen, I would not begrudge to tell thee of other things more pitiful still than these, even the woes of my comrades, who perished afterward, who escaped from the dread battle-cry of the Trojans, but perished on their return through the will of an evil woman.

"When then holy Persephone had scattered this way and that the spirits of the women, there came up the spirit of Agamemnon, son of Atreus, sorrowing; and round about him others were gathered, spirits of all those who were slain with him in the house of Aegisthus, and met their fate. He knew me straightway, when he had drunk the dark blood, and he wept aloud, and shed big tears, and stretched

413

πιτνὰς εἰς ἐμὲ χεῖρας, ὀρέξασθαι μενεαίνων·
ἀλλ' οὐ γάρ οἱ ἔτ' ἦν ἲς ἔμπεδος οὐδέ τι κῖκυς,
οἵη περ πάρος ἔσκεν ἐνὶ γναμπτοῖσι μέλεσσι.
   " Τὸν μὲν ἐγὼ δάκρυσα ἰδὼν ἐλέησά τε θυμῷ,   395
καί μιν φωνήσας ἔπεα πτερόεντα προσηύδων·
' Ἀτρεΐδη κύδιστε, ἄναξ ἀνδρῶν Ἀγάμεμνον,
τίς νύ σε κὴρ ἐδάμασσε τανηλεγέος θανάτοιο;
ἦε σέ γ' ἐν νήεσσι Ποσειδάων ἐδάμασσεν
ὄρσας ἀργαλέων ἀνέμων ἀμέγαρτον ἀυτμήν;   400
ἦέ σ' ἀνάρσιοι ἄνδρες ἐδηλήσαντ' ἐπὶ χέρσου
βοῦς περιταμνόμενον ἠδ' οἰῶν πώεα καλά,
ἠὲ περὶ πτόλιος μαχεούμενον ἠδὲ γυναικῶν;'
   " Ὣς ἐφάμην, ὁ δέ μ' αὐτίκ' ἀμειβόμενος προσέειπε·
' Διογενὲς Λαερτιάδη, πολυμήχαν' Ὀδυσσεῦ,   405
οὔτ' ἐμέ γ' ἐν νήεσσι Ποσειδάων ἐδάμασσεν
ὄρσας ἀργαλέων ἀνέμων ἀμέγαρτον ἀυτμήν,[1]
οὔτε μ' ἀνάρσιοι ἄνδρες ἐδηλήσαντ' ἐπὶ χέρσου,
ἀλλά μοι Αἴγισθος τεύξας θάνατόν τε μόρον τε
ἔκτα σὺν οὐλομένῃ ἀλόχῳ, οἶκόνδε καλέσσας,   410
δειπνίσσας, ὥς τίς τε κατέκτανε βοῦν ἐπὶ φάτνῃ.
ὣς θάνον οἰκτίστῳ θανάτῳ· περὶ δ' ἄλλοι ἑταῖροι
νωλεμέως κτείνοντο σύες ὣς ἀργιόδοντες,
οἵ ῥά τ' ἐν ἀφνειοῦ ἀνδρὸς μέγα δυναμένοιο
ἢ γάμῳ ἢ ἐράνῳ ἢ εἰλαπίνῃ τεθαλυίῃ.   415
ἤδη μὲν πολέων φόνῳ ἀνδρῶν ἀντεβόλησας,
μουνὰξ κτεινομένων καὶ ἐνὶ κρατερῇ ὑσμίνῃ·
ἀλλά κε κεῖνα μάλιστα ἰδὼν ὀλοφύραο θυμῷ,
ὡς ἀμφὶ κρητῆρα τραπέζας τε πληθούσας
κείμεθ' ἐνὶ μεγάρῳ, δάπεδον δ' ἅπαν αἵματι θῦεν.   420
οἰκτροτάτην δ' ἤκουσα ὄπα Πριάμοιο θυγατρός,

---

[1] Line 407 is omitted in most MSS.

forth his hands toward me eager to reach me. But no longer had he aught of strength or might remaining such as of old was in his supple limbs.

"When I saw him I wept, and my heart had compassion on him, and I spoke, and addressed him with winged words: 'Most glorious son of Atreus, king of men, Agamemnon, what fate of grievous death overcame thee? Did Poseidon smite thee on board thy ships, when he had roused a furious blast of cruel winds? Or did foemen work thee harm on the land, while thou wast cutting off their cattle and fair flocks of sheep, or wast fighting to win their city and their women?'

"So I spoke, and he straightway made answer and said: 'Son of Laertes, sprung from Zeus, Odysseus of many devices, neither did Poseidon smite me on board my ships, when he had roused a furious blast of cruel winds, nor did foemen work me harm on the land, but Aegisthus wrought for me death and fate, and slew me with the aid of my accursed wife, when he had bidden me to his house and made me a feast, even as one slays an ox at the stall. So I died by a most pitiful death, and round about me the rest of my comrades were slain unceasingly like white-tusked swine, which are slaughtered in the house of a rich man of great might at a marriage feast, or a joint meal, or a rich drinking-bout. Ere now thou hast been present at the slaying of many men, killed in single combat or in the press of the fight, but in heart thou wouldst have felt most pity hadst thou seen that sight, how about the mixing bowl and the laden tables we lay in the hall, and the floor all swam with blood. But the most piteous cry that I heard was

Κασσάνδρης, τὴν κτεῖνε Κλυταιμνήστρη δολόμητις
ἀμφ' ἐμοί, αὐτὰρ ἐγὼ ποτὶ γαίῃ χεῖρας ἀείρων
βάλλον ἀποθνήσκων περὶ φασγάνῳ· ἡ δὲ κυνῶπις
νοσφίσατ', οὐδέ μοι ἔτλη ἰόντι περ εἰς 'Αίδαο   425
χερσὶ κατ' ὀφθαλμοὺς ἑλέειν σύν τε στόμ' ἐρεῖσαι.
ὡς οὐκ αἰνότερον καὶ κύντερον ἄλλο γυναικός,
ἥ τις δὴ τοιαῦτα μετὰ φρεσὶν ἔργα βάληται·
οἷον δὴ καὶ κείνη ἐμήσατο ἔργον ἀεικές,
κουριδίῳ τεύξασα πόσει φόνον. ἦ τοι ἔφην γε   430
ἀσπάσιος παίδεσσιν ἰδὲ δμώεσσιν ἐμοῖσιν
οἴκαδ' ἐλεύσεσθαι· ἡ δ' ἔξοχα λυγρὰ ἰδυῖα
οἷ τε κατ' αἶσχος ἔχευε καὶ ἐσσομένῃσιν ὀπίσσω
θηλυτέρῃσι γυναιξί, καὶ ἥ κ' ἐυεργὸς ἔῃσιν.'

    "῝Ως ἔφατ', αὐτὰρ ἐγώ μιν ἀμειβόμενος προσέειπον·
'῍Ω πόποι, ἦ μάλα δὴ γόνον 'Ατρέος εὐρύοπα Ζεὺς   436
ἐκπάγλως ἤχθηρε γυναικείας διὰ βουλὰς
ἐξ ἀρχῆς· 'Ελένης μὲν ἀπωλόμεθ' εἵνεκα πολλοί,
σοὶ δὲ Κλυταιμνήστρη δόλον ἤρτυε τηλόθ' ἐόντι.'

    "῝Ως ἐφάμην, ὁ δέ μ' αὐτίκ' ἀμειβόμενος προσέειπε·
' Τῷ νῦν μή ποτε καὶ σὺ γυναικί περ ἤπιος εἶναι·   441
μή οἱ μῦθον ἅπαντα πιφαυσκέμεν, ὅν κ' ἐὺ εἰδῇς,
ἀλλὰ τὸ μὲν φάσθαι, τὸ δὲ καὶ κεκρυμμένον εἶναι.
ἀλλ' οὐ σοί γ', 'Οδυσεῦ, φόνος ἔσσεται ἔκ γε γυναικός·
λίην γὰρ πινυτή τε καὶ ἐὺ φρεσὶ μήδεα οἶδε   445
κούρη 'Ικαρίοιο, περίφρων Πηνελόπεια.

---

[1] Or, "as she clung to me." The whole passage is one of
very doubtful interpretation. I have, in the main, followed

that of the daughter of Priam, Cassandra, whom
guileful Clytemnestra slew by my side.[1] And I
sought to raise my hands and smite down the
murderess, dying though I was, pierced through
with the sword. But she, the shameless one,
turned her back upon me, and even though I
was going to the house of Hades deigned neither
to draw down my eyelids with her fingers nor to
close my mouth. So true is it that there is nothing
more dread or more shameless than a woman who
puts into her heart such deeds, even as she too
devised a monstrous thing, contriving death for
her wedded husband. Verily I thought that I
should come home welcome to my children and to
my slaves; but she, with her heart set on utter
wickedness, has shed shame on herself and on
women yet to be, even upon her that doeth up-
rightly.'

"So he spoke, and I made answer and said: 'Ah,
verily has Zeus, whose voice is borne afar, visited
wondrous hatred on the race of Atreus from the first
because of the counsels of women. For Helen's sake
many of us perished, and against thee Clytemnestra
spread a snare whilst thou wast afar.'

"So I spoke, and he straightway made answer and
said: 'Wherefore in thine own case be thou never
gentle even to thy wife. Declare not to her all the
thoughts of thy heart, but tell her somewhat, and let
somewhat also be hidden. Yet not upon thee, Odys-
seus, shall death come from thy wife, for very prudent
and of an understanding heart is the daughter of

Agar, *Homerica*, 189 f.   Others take χεῖρας ἀείρων as indicat-
ing a gesture of supplication, and render βάλλον "let them
fall to the ground." But this is highly unsatisfactory.

ἦ μέν μιν νύμφην γε νέην κατελείπομεν ἡμεῖς
ἐρχόμενοι πόλεμόνδε· πάις δέ οἱ ἦν ἐπὶ μαζῷ
νήπιος, ὅς που νῦν γε μετ' ἀνδρῶν ἵζει ἀριθμῷ,
ὄλβιος· ἦ γὰρ τόν γε πατὴρ φίλος ὄψεται ἐλθών,   450
καὶ κεῖνος πατέρα προσπτύξεται, ἧ θέμις ἐστίν.
ἡ δ' ἐμὴ οὐδέ περ υἷος ἐνιπλησθῆναι ἄκοιτις
ὀφθαλμοῖσιν ἔασε· πάρος δέ με πέφνε καὶ αὐτόν.
ἄλλο δέ τοι ἐρέω, σὺ δ' ἐνὶ φρεσὶ βάλλεο σῇσιν·
κρύβδην, μηδ' ἀναφανδά, φίλην ἐς πατρίδα γαῖαν   455
νῆα κατισχέμεναι· ἐπεὶ οὐκέτι πιστὰ γυναιξίν.¹
ἀλλ' ἄγε μοι τόδε εἰπὲ καὶ ἀτρεκέως κατάλεξον,
εἴ που ἔτι ζώοντος ἀκούετε παιδὸς ἐμοῖο,
ἤ που ἐν Ὀρχομενῷ ἢ ἐν Πύλῳ ἠμαθόεντι,
ἤ που πὰρ Μενελάῳ ἐνὶ Σπάρτῃ εὐρείῃ·   460
οὐ γάρ πω τέθνηκεν ἐπὶ χθονὶ δῖος Ὀρέστης.'
    "῝Ως ἔφατ', αὐτὰρ ἐγώ μιν ἀμειβόμενος προσέειπον
'Ἀτρεΐδη, τί με ταῦτα διείρεαι; οὐδέ τι οἶδα,
ζώει ὅ γ' ἢ τέθνηκε· κακὸν δ' ἀνεμώλια βάζειν.'
    " Νῶι μὲν ὣς ἐπέεσσιν ἀμειβομένω στυγεροῖσιν   465
ἕσταμεν ἀχνύμενοι θαλερὸν κατὰ δάκρυ χέοντες·
ἦλθε δ' ἐπὶ ψυχὴ Πηληιάδεω Ἀχιλῆος
καὶ Πατροκλῆος καὶ ἀμύμονος Ἀντιλόχοιο
Αἴαντός θ', ὃς ἄριστος ἔην εἶδός τε δέμας τε
τῶν ἄλλων Δαναῶν μετ' ἀμύμονα Πηλεΐωνα.   470
ἔγνω δὲ ψυχή με ποδώκεος Αἰακίδαο
καί ῥ' ὀλοφυρομένη ἔπεα πτερόεντα προσηύδα·
    "'Διογενὲς Λαερτιάδη, πολυμήχαν' Ὀδυσσεῦ,
σχέτλιε, τίπτ' ἔτι μεῖζον ἐνὶ φρεσὶ μήσεαι ἔργον;
πῶς ἔτλης Ἄιδόσδε κατελθέμεν, ἔνθα τε νεκροὶ   475
ἀφραδέες ναίουσι, βροτῶν εἴδωλα καμόντων;'

---

¹ Lines 454-6 were lacking in most ancient editions.

Icarius, wise Penelope. Verily we left her a bride newly wed, when we went to the war, and a boy was at her breast, a babe, who now, I ween, sits in the ranks of men, happy in that his dear father will behold him when he comes, and he will greet his father as is meet. But my wife did not let me sate my eyes even with sight of my own son. Nay, ere that she slew even me, her husband. And another thing will I tell thee, and do thou lay it to heart: in secret and not openly do thou bring thy ship to the shore of thy dear native land; for no longer is there faith in women. But, come, tell me this, and declare it truly, whether haply ye hear of my son as yet alive in Orchomenus it may be, or in sandy Pylos, or yet with Menelaus in wide Sparta; for not yet has goodly Orestes perished on the earth.'

"So he spoke, and I made answer and said: 'Son of Atreus, wherefore dost thou question me of this? I know not at all whether he be alive or dead, and it is an ill thing to speak words vain as wind.'

"Thus we two stood and held sad converse with one another, sorrowing and shedding big tears; and there came up the spirit of Achilles, son of Peleus, and those of Patroclus and of peerless Antilochus and of Aias, who in comeliness and form was the goodliest of all the Danaans after the peerless son of Peleus. And the spirit of the swift-footed son of Aeacus recognized me, and weeping, spoke to me winged words:

"'Son of Laertes, sprung from Zeus, Odysseus of many devices, rash man, what deed yet greater than this wilt thou devise in thy heart? How didst thou dare to come down to Hades, where dwell the unheeding dead, the phantoms of men outworn.'[1]

---

[1] Or, perhaps, "who have done with (life's) toils."

"῍Ως ἔφατ', αὐτὰρ ἐγώ μιν ἀμειβόμενος προσέειπον·
'῏Ω 'Αχιλεῦ Πηλῆος υἱέ, μέγα φέρτατ' 'Αχαιῶν,
ἦλθον Τειρεσίαο κατὰ χρέος, εἴ τινα βουλὴν
εἴποι, ὅπως 'Ιθάκην ἐς παιπαλόεσσαν ἱκοίμην·   480
οὐ γάρ πω σχεδὸν ἦλθον 'Αχαιίδος, οὐδέ πω ἁμῆς
γῆς ἐπέβην, ἀλλ' αἰὲν ἔχω κακά. σεῖο δ', 'Αχιλλεῦ,
οὔ τις ἀνὴρ προπάροιθε μακάρτατος οὔτ' ἄρ' ὀπίσσω.
πρὶν μὲν γάρ σε ζωὸν ἐτίομεν ἶσα θεοῖσιν
'Αργεῖοι, νῦν αὖτε μέγα κρατέεις νεκύεσσιν   485
ἐνθάδ' ἐών· τῷ μή τι θανὼν ἀκαχίζευ, 'Αχιλλεῦ.'

"῍Ως ἐφάμην, ὁ δέ μ' αὐτίκ' ἀμειβόμενος προσέειπε
' Μὴ δή μοι θάνατόν γε παραύδα, φαίδιμ' 'Οδυσσεῦ.
βουλοίμην κ' ἐπάρουρος ἐὼν θητευέμεν ἄλλῳ,
ἀνδρὶ παρ' ἀκλήρῳ, ᾧ μὴ βίοτος πολὺς εἴη,   490
ἢ πᾶσιν νεκύεσσι καταφθιμένοισιν ἀνάσσειν.
ἀλλ' ἄγε μοι τοῦ παιδὸς ἀγαυοῦ μῦθον ἐνίσπες,
ἢ ἕπετ' ἐς πόλεμον πρόμος ἔμμεναι, ἦε καὶ οὐκί.
εἰπὲ δέ μοι Πηλῆος ἀμύμονος, εἴ τι πέπυσσαι,
ἢ ἔτ' ἔχει τιμὴν πολέσιν μετὰ Μυρμιδόνεσσιν,   495
ἢ μιν ἀτιμάζουσιν ἀν' 'Ελλάδα τε Φθίην τε,
οὕνεκά μιν κατὰ γῆρας ἔχει χεῖράς τε πόδας τε.
οὐ γὰρ ¹ ἐγὼν ἐπαρωγὸς ὑπ' αὐγὰς ἠελίοιο,
τοῖος ἐών, οἷός ποτ' ἐνὶ Τροίῃ εὐρείῃ
πέφνον λαὸν ἄριστον, ἀμύνων 'Αργείοισιν·   500
εἰ τοιόσδ' ἔλθοιμι μίνυνθά περ ἐς πατέρος δῶ·
τῷ κέ τεῳ στύξαιμι μένος καὶ χεῖρας ἀάπτους,
οἳ κεῖνον βιόωνται ἐέργουσίν τ' ἀπὸ τιμῆς.'

¹ οὐ γάρ: εἰ γάρ Zenodotus.

---

¹ Or, possibly, " to consult with Teiresias."

"'So he spoke, and I made answer and said:
'Achilles, son of Peleus, far the mightiest of the
Achaeans, I came through need of Teiresias,[1] if haply
he would tell me some plan whereby I might reach
rugged Ithaca. For not yet have I come near to
the land of Achaea, nor have I as yet set foot on my
own country, but am ever suffering woes; whereas
than thou, Achilles, no man aforetime was more
blessed nor shall ever be hereafter. For of old, when
thou wast alive, we Argives honoured thee even as
the gods, and now that thou art here, thou rulest
mightily among the dead. Wherefore grieve not at
all that thou art dead, Achilles.'

"So I spoke, and he straightway made answer and
said: 'Nay, seek not to speak soothingly to me of
death, glorious Odysseus. I should choose, so I
might live on earth,[2] to serve as the hireling of
another, of some portionless man whose livelihood
was but small, rather than to be lord over all the
dead that have perished. But come, tell me tidings
of my son, that lordly youth, whether or not he
followed to the war to be a leader. And tell
me of noble Peleus, if thou hast heard aught,
whether he still has honour among the host of
the Myrmidons, or whether men do him dishonour
throughout Hellas and Phthia, because old age binds
him hand and foot. For I am not there to bear him
aid beneath the rays of the sun in such strength as
once was mine in wide Troy, when I slew the best
of the host in defence of the Argives. If but in such
strength I could come, were it but for an hour, to
my father's house, I would give many a one of those
who do him violence and keep him from his honour,
cause to rue my strength and my invincible hands.'

---

[2] Some take ἐπάρουρος as "attached to the soil," "a serf."

"῝Ως ἔφατ᾽, αὐτὰρ ἐγώ μιν ἀμειβόμενος προσέειπον·
'῍Η τοι μὲν Πηλῆος ἀμύμονος οὔ τι πέπυσμαι,   505
αὐτάρ τοι παιδός γε Νεοπτολέμοιο φίλοιο
πᾶσαν ἀληθείην μυθήσομαι, ὥς με κελεύεις·
αὐτὸς γάρ μιν ἐγὼ κοίλης ἐπὶ νηὸς ἐΐσης
ἤγαγον ἐκ Σκύρου μετ᾽ ἐϋκνήμιδας Ἀχαιούς.
ἦ τοι ὅτ᾽ ἀμφὶ πόλιν Τροίην φραζοίμεθα βουλάς,   510
αἰεὶ πρῶτος ἔβαζε καὶ οὐχ ἡμάρτανε μύθων·
Νέστωρ ἀντίθεος καὶ ἐγὼ νικάσκομεν οἴω.
αὐτὰρ ὅτ᾽ ἐν πεδίῳ Τρώων μαρναίμεθα χαλκῷ,[1]
οὔ ποτ᾽ ἐνὶ πληθυῖ μένεν ἀνδρῶν οὐδ᾽ ἐν ὁμίλῳ,
ἀλλὰ πολὺ προθέεσκε τὸ ὃν μένος οὐδενὶ εἴκων,   515
πολλοὺς δ᾽ ἄνδρας ἔπεφνεν ἐν αἰνῇ δηϊοτῆτι.
πάντας δ᾽ οὐκ ἂν ἐγὼ μυθήσομαι οὐδ᾽ ὀνομήνω,
ὅσσον λαὸν ἔπεφνεν ἀμύνων Ἀργείοισιν,
ἀλλ᾽ οἷον τὸν Τηλεφίδην κατενήρατο χαλκῷ,
ἥρω᾽ Εὐρύπυλον, πολλοὶ δ᾽ ἀμφ᾽ αὐτὸν ἑταῖροι   520
Κήτειοι κτείνοντο γυναίων εἵνεκα δώρων.
κεῖνον δὴ κάλλιστον ἴδον μετὰ Μέμνονα δῖον.
αὐτὰρ ὅτ᾽ εἰς ἵππον κατεβαίνομεν, ὃν κάμ᾽ Ἐπειός,
Ἀργείων οἱ ἄριστοι, ἐμοὶ δ᾽ ἐπὶ πάντα τέταλτο,
ἠμὲν ἀνακλῖναι πυκινὸν λόχον ἠδ᾽ ἐπιθεῖναι,[2]   525
ἔνθ᾽ ἄλλοι Δαναῶν ἡγήτορες ἠδὲ μέδοντες
δάκρυά τ᾽ ὠμόργνυντο τρέμον θ᾽ ὑπὸ γυῖα ἑκάστου·
κεῖνον δ᾽ οὔ ποτε πάμπαν ἐγὼν ἴδον ὀφθαλμοῖσιν
οὔτ᾽ ὠχρήσαντα χρόα κάλλιμον οὔτε παρειῶν
δάκρυ ὀμορξάμενον· ὁ δέ με μάλα πόλλ᾽ ἱκέτευεν   530
ἱππόθεν ἐξέμεναι, ξίφεος δ᾽ ἐπεμαίετο κώπην
καὶ δόρυ χαλκοβαρές, κακὰ δὲ Τρώεσσι μενοίνα.

---

[1] μαρναίμεθα χαλκῷ : μαρναίμεθ᾽ Ἀχαιοί.
[2] Line 525 was unknown to Aristarchus.

"So he spoke, and I made answer and said:
'Verily of noble Peleus have I heard naught, but as
touching thy dear son, Neoptolemus, I will tell thee
all the truth, as thou biddest me. I it was, myself,
who brought him from Scyros in my shapely, hollow
ship to join the host of the well-greaved Achaeans.
And verily, as often as we took counsel around the
city of Troy, he was ever the first to speak, and made
no miss of words; godlike Nestor and I alone sur-
passed him. But as often as we fought with the
bronze on the Trojan plain, he would never remain
behind in the throng or press of men, but would ever
run forth far to the front, yielding to none in his
might; and many men he slew in dread combat. All
of them I could not tell or name, all the host that he
slew in defence of the Argives; but what a warrior
was that son of Telephus whom he slew with the
sword, the prince Eurypylus! Aye, and many of his
comrades, the Ceteians, were slain about him, because
of gifts a woman craved.[1] He verily was the come-
liest man I saw, next to goodly Memnon. And again,
when we, the best of the Argives, were about to go
down into the horse which Epeus made, and the
command of all was laid upon me, both to open and
to close the door of our stout-built ambush, then the
other leaders and counsellors of the Danaans would
wipe away tears from their eyes, and each man's
limbs shook beneath him, but never did my eyes see
his fair face grow pale at all, nor see him wiping tears
from his cheeks; but he earnestly besought me to
let him go forth from the horse, and kept handling
his sword-hilt and his spear heavy with bronze, and

[1] The reference is to the golden vine, given by Priam to
Astyoche, wife of Telephus, which gift led her to send her
son Eurypylus to the aid of the Trojans.

ἀλλ' ὅτε δὴ Πριάμοιο πόλιν διεπέρσαμεν αἰπήν,
μοῖραν καὶ γέρας ἐσθλὸν ἔχων ἐπὶ νηὸς ἔβαινεν
ἀσκηθής, οὔτ' ἄρ βεβλημένος ὀξέι χαλκῷ   535
οὔτ' αὐτοσχεδίην οὐτασμένος, οἷά τε πολλὰ
γίγνεται ἐν πολέμῳ· ἐπιμὶξ δέ τε μαίνεται Ἄρης.'

   "Ὡς ἐφάμην, ψυχὴ δὲ ποδώκεος Αἰακίδαο
φοίτα μακρὰ βιβᾶσα κατ' ἀσφοδελὸν λειμῶνα,
γηθοσύνη ὅ οἱ υἱὸν ἔφην ἀριδείκετον εἶναι.   540

   " Αἱ δ' ἄλλαι ψυχαὶ νεκύων κατατεθνηώτων
ἕστασαν ἀχνύμεναι, εἴροντο δὲ κήδε' ἑκάστη.
οἴη δ' Αἴαντος ψυχὴ Τελαμωνιάδαο
νόσφιν ἀφεστήκει, κεχολωμένη εἵνεκα νίκης,
τήν μιν ἐγὼ νίκησα δικαζόμενος παρὰ νηυσὶ   545
τεύχεσιν ἀμφ' Ἀχιλῆος· ἔθηκε δὲ πότνια μήτηρ.
παῖδες δὲ Τρώων δίκασαν καὶ Παλλὰς Ἀθήνη.
ὡς δὴ μὴ ὄφελον νικᾶν τοιῷδ' ἐπ' ἀέθλῳ·
τοίην γὰρ κεφαλὴν ἕνεκ' αὐτῶν γαῖα κατέσχεν,
Αἴανθ', ὃς πέρι μὲν εἶδος, πέρι δ' ἔργα τέτυκτο   550
τῶν ἄλλων Δαναῶν μετ' ἀμύμονα Πηλεΐωνα.
τὸν μὲν ἐγὼν ἐπέεσσι προσηύδων μειλιχίοισιν·

   " ' Αἶαν, παῖ Τελαμῶνος ἀμύμονος, οὐκ ἄρ' ἔμελλες
οὐδὲ θανὼν λήσεσθαι ἐμοὶ χόλου εἵνεκα τευχέων
οὐλομένων; τὰ δὲ πῆμα θεοὶ θέσαν Ἀργείοισι,   555
τοῖος γάρ σφιν πύργος ἀπώλεο· σεῖο δ' Ἀχαιοὶ
ἶσον Ἀχιλλῆος κεφαλῇ Πηληιάδαο
ἀχνύμεθα φθιμένοιο διαμπερές· οὐδέ τις ἄλλος
αἴτιος, ἀλλὰ Ζεὺς Δαναῶν στρατὸν αἰχμητάων
ἐκπάγλως ἤχθηρε, τεῒν δ' ἐπὶ μοῖραν ἔθηκεν.   560

was eager to work harm to the Trojans. But after we had sacked the lofty city of Priam, he went on board his ship with his share of the spoil and a goodly prize—all unscathed he was, neither smitten with the sharp spear nor wounded in close fight, as often befalls in war; for Ares rages confusedly.'

"So I spoke, and the spirit of the son of Aeacus departed with long strides over the field of asphodel, joyful in that I said that his son was preeminent.

"And other spirits of those dead and gone stood sorrowing, and each asked of those dear to him. Alone of them all the spirit of Aias, son of Telamon, stood apart, still full of wrath for the victory that I had won over him in the contest by the ships for the arms of Achilles, whose honoured mother had set them for a prize; and the judges were the sons of the Trojans and Pallas Athene. I would that I had never won in the contest for such a prize, over so noble a head did the earth close because of those arms, even over Aias, who in comeliness and in deeds of war was above all the other Achaeans, next to the peerless son of Peleus. To him I spoke with soothing words:

"'Aias, son of peerless Telamon, wast thou then not even in death to forget thy wrath against me because of those accursed arms? Surely the gods set them to be a bane to the Argives: such a tower of strength was lost to them in thee; and for thee in death we Achaeans sorrow unceasingly, even as for the life of Achilles, son of Peleus. Yet no other is to blame but Zeus, who bore terrible hatred against the host of Danaan spearmen, and brought

425

ἀλλ' ἄγε δεῦρο, ἄναξ, ἵν' ἔπος καὶ μῦθον ἀκούσῃς
ἡμέτερον· δάμασον δὲ μένος καὶ ἀγήνορα θυμόν.'

"Ὣς ἐφάμην, ὁ δέ μ' οὐδὲν ἀμείβετο, βῆ δὲ μετ' ἄλλα
ψυχὰς εἰς Ἔρεβος νεκύων κατατεθνηώτων.
ἔνθα χ' ὅμως προσέφη κεχολωμένος, ἤ κεν ἐγὼ τόν· 565
ἀλλά μοι ἤθελε θυμὸς ἐνὶ στήθεσσι φίλοισι
τῶν ἄλλων ψυχὰς ἰδέειν κατατεθνηώτων.

" Ἔνθ' ἦ τοι Μίνωα ἴδον, Διὸς ἀγλαὸν υἱόν,
χρύσεον σκῆπτρον ἔχοντα, θεμιστεύοντα νέκυσσιν,
ἥμενον, οἱ δέ μιν ἀμφὶ δίκας εἴροντο ἄνακτα, 570
ἥμενοι ἑσταότες τε κατ' εὐρυπυλὲς Ἄιδος δῶ.

" Τὸν δὲ μετ' Ὠρίωνα πελώριον εἰσενόησα
θῆρας ὁμοῦ εἰλεῦντα κατ' ἀσφοδελὸν λειμῶνα,
τοὺς αὐτὸς κατέπεφνεν ἐν οἰοπόλοισιν ὄρεσσι
χερσὶν ἔχων ῥόπαλον παγχάλκεον, αἰὲν ἀαγές. 575

" Καὶ Τιτυὸν εἶδον, Γαίης ἐρικυδέος υἱόν,
κείμενον ἐν δαπέδῳ· ὁ δ' ἐπ' ἐννέα κεῖτο πέλεθρα,
γῦπε δέ μιν ἑκάτερθε παρημένω ἧπαρ ἔκειρον,
δέρτρον ἔσω δύνοντες, ὁ δ' οὐκ ἀπαμύνετο χερσί·
Λητὼ γὰρ ἥλκησε, Διὸς κυδρὴν παράκοιτιν, 580
Πυθῶδ' ἐρχομένην διὰ καλλιχόρου Πανοπῆος.

" Καὶ μὴν Τάνταλον εἰσεῖδον κρατέρ' [1] ἄλγε' ἔχοντα
ἑστεῶτ' ἐν λίμνῃ· ἡ δὲ προσέπλαζε γενείῳ·
στεῦτο δὲ διψάων, πιέειν δ' οὐκ εἶχεν ἑλέσθαι·
ὁσσάκι γὰρ κύψει' ὁ γέρων πιέειν μενεαίνων, 585
τοσσάχ' ὕδωρ ἀπολέσκετ' ἀναβροχέν, ἀμφὶ δὲ ποσσὶ

---

[1] κρατέρ': χαλέπ'; cf. 593.

on thee thy doom. Nay, come hither, prince, that thou mayest hear my word and my speech; and subdue thy wrath and thy proud spirit.'

"So I spoke, but he answered me not a word, but went his way to Erebus to join the other spirits of those dead and gone. Then would he nevertheless have spoken to me for all his wrath, or I to him, but the heart in my breast was fain to see the spirits of those others that are dead.

"There then I saw Minos, the glorious son of Zeus, golden sceptre in hand, giving judgment to the dead from his seat, while they sat and stood about the king through the wide-gated house of Hades, and asked of him judgment.

"And after him I marked huge Orion driving together over the field of asphodel wild beasts which himself had slain on the lonely hills, and in his hands he held a club all of bronze, ever unbroken.

"And I saw Tityos, son of glorious Gaea, lying on the ground. Over nine roods[1] he stretched, and two vultures sat, one on either side, and tore his liver, plunging their beaks into his bowels, nor could he beat them off with his hands. For he had offered violence to Leto, the glorious wife of Zeus, as she went toward Pytho through Panopeus with its lovely lawns.

"Aye, and I saw Tantalus in violent torment, standing in a pool, and the water came nigh unto his chin. He seemed as one athirst, but could not take and drink; for as often as that old man stooped down, eager to drink, so often would the water be swallowed up and vanish away, and at

[1] Renderings of πέλεθρα can only be tentative.

γαῖα μέλαινα φάνεσκε, καταζήνασκε δὲ δαίμων.
δένδρεα δ' ὑψιπέτηλα κατὰ κρῆθεν χέε καρπόν,
ὄγχναι καὶ ῥοιαὶ καὶ μηλέαι ἀγλαόκαρποι
συκέαι τε γλυκεραὶ καὶ ἐλαῖαι τηλεθόωσαι·   590
τῶν ὁπότ' ἰθύσει' ὁ γέρων ἐπὶ χερσὶ μάσασθαι,
τὰς δ' ἄνεμος ῥίπτασκε ποτὶ νέφεα σκιόεντα.

    " Καὶ μὴν Σίσυφον εἰσεῖδον κρατέρ' [1] ἄλγε' ἔχοντα
λᾶαν βαστάζοντα πελώριον ἀμφοτέρῃσιν.
ἦ τοι ὁ μὲν σκηριπτόμενος χερσίν τε ποσίν τε   595
λᾶαν ἄνω ὤθεσκε ποτὶ λόφον· ἀλλ' ὅτε μέλλοι
ἄκρον ὑπερβαλέειν, τότ' ἀποστρέψασκε κραταιΐς·
αὖτις ἔπειτα πέδονδε κυλίνδετο λᾶας ἀναιδής.
αὐτὰρ ὅ γ' ἂψ ὤσασκε τιταινόμενος, κατὰ δ' ἱδρὼς
ἔρρεεν ἐκ μελέων, κονίη δ' ἐκ κρατὸς ὀρώρει.   600

    " Τὸν δὲ μετ' εἰσενόησα βίην Ἡρακληείην,
εἴδωλον· αὐτὸς δὲ μετ' ἀθανάτοισι θεοῖσι
τέρπεται ἐν θαλίῃς καὶ ἔχει καλλίσφυρον Ἥβην,
παῖδα Διὸς μεγάλοιο καὶ Ἥρης χρυσοπεδίλου.[2]
ἀμφὶ δέ μιν κλαγγὴ νεκύων ἦν οἰωνῶν ὥς,   605
πάντοσ' ἀτυζομένων· ὁ δ' ἐρεμνῇ νυκτὶ ἐοικώς,
γυμνὸν τόξον ἔχων καὶ ἐπὶ νευρῆφιν ὀιστόν,
δεινὸν παπταίνων, αἰεὶ βαλέοντι ἐοικώς.
σμερδαλέος δέ οἱ ἀμφὶ περὶ στήθεσσιν ἀορτὴρ
χρύσεος ἦν τελαμών, ἵνα θέσκελα ἔργα τέτυκτο,   610
ἄρκτοι τ' ἀγρότεροί τε σύες χαροποί τε λέοντες,
ὑσμῖναί τε μάχαι τε φόνοι τ' ἀνδροκτασίαι τε.
μὴ τεχνησάμενος μηδ' ἄλλο τι τεχνήσαιτο,

    [1] κρατέρ': χαλέπ'; cf. 582.
    [2] Lines 602-4 were rejected by some ancient critics as having been inserted in the text by Onomacritus.

428

his feet the black earth would appear, for some god made all dry. And trees, high and leafy, let stream their fruits above his head, pears, and pomegranates, and apple trees with their bright fruit, and sweet figs, and luxuriant olives. But as often as that old man would reach out toward these, to clutch them with his hands, the wind would toss them to the shadowy clouds.

"Aye, and I saw Sisyphus in violent torment, seeking to raise a monstrous stone with both his hands. Verily he would brace himself with hands and feet, and thrust the stone toward the crest of a hill, but as often as he was about to heave it over the top, the weight would turn it back, and then down again to the plain would come rolling the ruthless stone. But he would strain again and thrust it back, and the sweat flowed down from his limbs, and dust rose up from his head.

"And after him I marked the mighty Heracles— his phantom; for he himself among the immortal gods takes his joy in the feast, and has to wife Hebe, of the fair ankles, daughter of great Zeus and of Here, of the golden sandals. About him rose a clamour from the dead, as of birds flying everywhere in terror; and he like dark night, with his bow bare and with arrow on the string, glared about him terribly, like one in act to shoot. Awful was the belt about his breast, a baldric of gold, whereon wondrous things were fashioned, bears and wild boars, and lions with flashing eyes, and conflicts, and battles, and murders, and slayings of men. May he never have designed,[1] or hereafter

---

[1] Again, as in the similar passage, iv. 684, I follow Agar (*Homerica*, p. 199).

ὃς κεῖνον τελαμῶνα ἑῇ ἐγκάτθετο τέχνῃ.
ἔγνω δ' αὖτ' ἔμ' ἐκεῖνος, ἐπεὶ ἴδεν ὀφθαλμοῖσιν,　61
καί μ' ὀλοφυρόμενος ἔπεα πτερόεντα προσηύδα·
　"'Διογενὲς Λαερτιάδη, πολυμήχαν' Ὀδυσσεῦ,
ἆ δείλ', ἦ τινὰ καὶ σὺ κακὸν μόρον ἡγηλάζεις,
ὅν περ ἐγὼν ὀχέεσκον ὑπ' αὐγὰς ἠελίοιο.
Ζηνὸς μὲν πάϊς ἦα Κρονίονος, αὐτὰρ ὀιζὺν　62
εἶχον ἀπειρεσίην· μάλα γὰρ πολὺ χείρονι φωτὶ
δεδμήμην, ὁ δέ μοι χαλεποὺς ἐπετέλλετ' ἀέθλους.
καί ποτέ μ' ἐνθάδ' ἔπεμψε κύν' ἄξοντ'· οὐ γὰρ ἔτ' ἄλλ
φράζετο τοῦδέ γέ μοι κρατερώτερον[1] εἶναι ἄεθλον·
τὸν μὲν ἐγὼν ἀνένεικα καὶ ἤγαγον ἐξ Ἀίδαο·　62
Ἑρμείας δέ μ' ἔπεμψεν ἰδὲ γλαυκῶπις Ἀθήνη.'
　"Ὥς εἰπὼν ὁ μὲν αὖτις ἔβη δόμον Ἄιδος εἴσω,
αὐτὰρ ἐγὼν αὐτοῦ μένον ἔμπεδον, εἴ τις ἔτ' ἔλθοι
ἀνδρῶν ἡρώων, οἳ δὴ τὸ πρόσθεν ὄλοντο.
καί νύ κ' ἔτι προτέρους ἴδον ἀνέρας, οὓς ἔθελόν περ,　63
Θησέα Πειρίθοόν τε, θεῶν ἐρικυδέα τέκνα·[2]
ἀλλὰ πρὶν ἐπὶ ἔθνε' ἀγείρετο μυρία νεκρῶν
ἠχῇ θεσπεσίῃ· ἐμὲ δὲ χλωρὸν δέος ᾕρει,
μή μοι Γοργείην κεφαλὴν δεινοῖο πελώρου
ἐξ Ἀίδεω πέμψειεν ἀγαυὴ Περσεφόνεια.　63
　"Αὐτίκ' ἔπειτ' ἐπὶ νῆα κιὼν ἐκέλευον ἑταίρους
αὐτούς τ' ἀμβαίνειν ἀνά τε πρυμνήσια λῦσαι.
οἱ δ' αἶψ' εἴσβαινον καὶ ἐπὶ κληῖσι καθῖζον.
τὴν δὲ κατ' Ὠκεανὸν ποταμὸν φέρε κῦμα ῥόοιο,
πρῶτα μὲν εἰρεσίῃ, μετέπειτα δὲ κάλλιμος οὖρος.　64

---

[1] κρατερώτερον: χαλεπώτερον; cf. 582, 593.
[2] Line 631 was attributed to Pisistratus by Hereas of Megara (Plut. *Thes.* 20).

design such another, even he who stored up in his craft the device of that belt. He in turn knew me when his eyes beheld me, and weeping spoke to me winged words :

" 'Son of Laertes, sprung from Zeus, Odysseus of many devices, ah, wretched man, dost thou, too, drag out an evil lot such as I once bore beneath the rays of the sun? I was the son of Zeus, son of Cronos, but I had woe beyond measure; for to a man far worse than I was I made subject, and he laid on me hard labours. Yea, he once sent me hither to fetch the hound of Hades, for he could devise for me no other task mightier than this. The hound I carried off and led forth from the house of Hades; and Hermes was my guide, and flashing-eyed Athene.'

" So saying, he went his way again into the house of Hades, but I abode there steadfastly, in the hope that some other haply might still come forth of the warrior heroes who died in the days of old. And I should have seen yet others of the men of former time, whom I was fain to behold, even Theseus and Peirithous, glorious children of the gods, but ere that the myriad tribes of the dead came thronging up with a wondrous cry, and pale fear seized me, lest august Persephone might send forth upon me from out the house of Hades the head of the Gorgon, that awful monster.

" Straightway then I went to the ship and bade my comrades themselves to embark, and to loose the stern cables. So they went on board quickly and sat down upon the benches. And the ship was borne down the stream Oceanus by the swelling flood, first with our rowing, and afterwards the wind was fair.

M

" Αὐτὰρ ἐπεὶ ποταμοῖο λίπεν ῥόον Ὠκεανοῖο
νηῦς, ἀπὸ δ᾽ ἵκετο κῦμα θαλάσσης εὐρυπόροιο
νῆσόν τ᾽ Αἰαίην, ὅθι τ᾽ Ἠοῦς ἠριγενείης
οἰκία καὶ χοροί εἰσι καὶ ἀντολαὶ Ἠελίοιο,
νῆα μὲν ἔνθ᾽ ἐλθόντες ἐκέλσαμεν ἐν ψαμάθοισιν,
ἐκ δὲ καὶ αὐτοὶ βῆμεν ἐπὶ ῥηγμῖνι θαλάσσης· [1]
ἔνθα δ᾽ ἀποβρίξαντες ἐμείναμεν Ἠῶ δῖαν.
" Ἦμος δ᾽ ἠριγένεια φάνη ῥοδοδάκτυλος Ἠώς,
δὴ τότ᾽ ἐγὼν ἑτάρους προΐειν ἐς δώματα Κίρκης
οἰσέμεναι νεκρόν, Ἐλπήνορα τεθνηῶτα.
φιτροὺς δ᾽ αἶψα ταμόντες, ὅθ᾽ ἀκροτάτη πρόεχ᾽ ἀκτή,
θάπτομεν ἀχνύμενοι θαλερὸν κατὰ δάκρυ χέοντες.
αὐτὰρ ἐπεὶ νεκρός τ᾽ ἐκάη καὶ τεύχεα νεκροῦ,
τύμβον χεύαντες καὶ ἐπὶ στήλην ἐρύσαντες
πήξαμεν ἀκροτάτῳ τύμβῳ εὐῆρες ἐρετμόν.
" Ἡμεῖς μὲν τὰ ἕκαστα διείπομεν· οὐδ᾽ ἄρα Κίρκην
ἐξ Ἀΐδεω ἐλθόντες ἐλήθομεν, ἀλλὰ μάλ᾽ ὦκα
ἦλθ᾽ ἐντυναμένη· ἅμα δ᾽ ἀμφίπολοι φέρον αὐτῇ
σῖτον καὶ κρέα πολλὰ καὶ αἴθοπα οἶνον ἐρυθρόν.
ἡ δ᾽ ἐν μέσσῳ στᾶσα μετηύδα δῖα θεάων·
" ' Σχέτλιοι, οἳ ζώοντες ὑπήλθετε δῶμ᾽ Ἀΐδαο,
δισθανέες, ὅτε τ᾽ ἄλλοι ἅπαξ θνήσκουσ᾽ ἄνθρωποι.

[1] Line 6 is omitted in many MSS.

BOOK XII

" Now after our ship had left the stream of the river Oceanus and had come to the wave of the broad sea, and the Aeaean isle, where is the dwelling of early Dawn and her dancing-lawns, and the risings of the sun, there on our coming we beached our ship on the sands, and ourselves went forth upon the shore of the sea, and there we fell asleep, and waited for the bright Dawn.

" As soon as early Dawn appeared, the rosy-fingered, then I sent forth my comrades to the house of Circe to fetch the body of the dead Elpenor. Straightway then we cut billets of wood and gave him burial where the headland runs furthest out to sea, sorrowing and shedding big tears. But when the dead man was burned, and the armour of the dead, we heaped up a mound and dragged on to it a pillar, and on the top of the mound we planted his shapely oar.

" We then were busied with these several tasks, howbeit Circe was not unaware of our coming forth from the house of Hades, but speedily she arrayed herself and came, and her handmaids brought with her bread and meat in abundance and flaming red wine. And the beautiful goddess stood in our midst, and spoke among us, saying :

" ' Rash men, who have gone down alive to the house of Hades to meet death twice, while other

433

ἀλλ' ἄγετ' ἐσθίετε βρώμην καὶ πίνετε οἶνον
αὖθι πανημέριοι· ἅμα δ' ἠοῖ φαινομένηφι
πλεύσεσθ'· αὐτὰρ ἐγὼ δείξω ὁδὸν ἠδὲ ἕκαστα   2
σημανέω, ἵνα μή τι κακορραφίῃ ἀλεγεινῇ
ἢ ἁλὸς ἢ ἐπὶ γῆς ἀλγήσετε πῆμα παθόντες.'

   "'Ὣς ἔφαθ', ἡμῖν δ' αὖτ' ἐπεπείθετο θυμὸς ἀγήνωρ.
ὣς τότε μὲν πρόπαν ἦμαρ ἐς ἠέλιον καταδύντα
ἤμεθα δαινύμενοι κρέα τ' ἄσπετα καὶ μέθυ ἡδύ·   3
ἦμος δ' ἠέλιος κατέδυ καὶ ἐπὶ κνέφας ἦλθεν,
οἱ μὲν κοιμήσαντο παρὰ πρυμνήσια νηός,
ἡ δ' ἐμὲ χειρὸς ἑλοῦσα φίλων ἀπονόσφιν ἑταίρων
εἷσέ τε καὶ προσέλεκτο καὶ ἐξερέεινεν ἕκαστα·
αὐτὰρ ἐγὼ τῇ πάντα κατὰ μοῖραν κατέλεξα.   3
καὶ τότε δή μ' ἐπέεσσι προσηύδα πότνια Κίρκη·

   "'Ταῦτα μὲν οὕτω πάντα πεπείρανται, σὺ δ' ἄκουσον
ὥς τοι ἐγὼν ἐρέω, μνήσει δέ σε καὶ θεὸς αὐτός.
Σειρῆνας μὲν πρῶτον ἀφίξεαι, αἵ ῥά τε πάντας
ἀνθρώπους θέλγουσιν, ὅτις σφεας εἰσαφίκηται.   4
ὅς τις ἀιδρείῃ πελάσῃ καὶ φθόγγον ἀκούσῃ
Σειρήνων, τῷ δ' οὔ τι γυνὴ καὶ νήπια τέκνα
οἴκαδε νοστήσαντι παρίσταται οὐδὲ γάνυνται,
ἀλλά τε Σειρῆνες λιγυρῇ θέλγουσιν ἀοιδῇ
ἥμεναι ἐν λειμῶνι, πολὺς δ' ἀμφ' ὀστεόφιν θὶς   4
ἀνδρῶν πυθομένων, περὶ δὲ ῥινοὶ μινύθουσι.
ἀλλὰ παρεξελάαν, ἐπὶ δ' οὔατ' ἀλεῖψαι ἑταίρων
κηρὸν δεψήσας μελιηδέα, μή τις ἀκούσῃ
τῶν ἄλλων· ἀτὰρ αὐτὸς ἀκουέμεν αἴ κ' ἐθέλῃσθα,
δησάντων σ' ἐν νηὶ θοῇ χεῖράς τε πόδας τε   5
ὀρθὸν ἐν ἱστοπέδῃ, ἐκ δ' αὐτοῦ πείρατ' ἀνήφθω,

men die but once. Nay, come, eat food and drink
wine here this whole day through; but at the
coming of Dawn ye shall set sail, and I will point
out the way and declare to you each thing, in
order that ye may not suffer pain and woes through
wretched ill-contriving either by sea or on land.'

"So she spoke, and our proud hearts consented.
So then all day long till set of sun we sat feasting
on abundant flesh and sweet wine. But when
the sun set and darkness came on, they lay down
to rest beside the stern cables of the ship; but Circe
took me by the hand, and leading me apart from
my dear comrades, made me to sit, and herself
lay down close at hand and asked me all the tale.
And I told her all in due order. Then queenly
Circe spoke to me and said:

"'All these things have thus found an end;
but do thou hearken as I shall tell thee, and a god
shall himself bring it to thy mind. To the Sirens
first shalt thou come, who beguile all men whoso-
ever comes to them. Whoso in ignorance draws
near to them and hears the Sirens' voice, he never-
more returns, that his wife and little children may
stand at his side rejoicing, but the Sirens beguile
him with their clear-toned song, as they sit in a
meadow, and about them is a great heap of bones
of mouldering men, and round the bones the skin
is shrivelling. But do thou row past them, and
anoint the ears of thy comrades with sweet wax,
which thou hast kneaded, lest any of the rest
may hear. But if thou thyself hast a will to listen,
let them bind thee in the swift ship hand and
foot upright in the step of the mast, and let the
ropes be made fast at the ends to the mast itself,

ὄφρα κε τερπόμενος ὄπ' ἀκούσῃς Σειρήνοιιν.
εἰ δέ κε λίσσηαι ἑτάρους λῦσαί τε κελεύῃς,
οἱ δέ σ' ἔτι πλεόνεσσι τότ' ἐν δεσμοῖσι διδέντων.
αὐτὰρ ἐπὴν δὴ τάς γε παρὲξ ἐλάσωσιν ἑταῖροι,   55
ἔνθα τοι οὐκέτ' ἔπειτα διηνεκέως ἀγορεύσω,
ὁπποτέρη δή τοι ὁδὸς ἔσσεται, ἀλλὰ καὶ αὐτὸς
θυμῷ βουλεύειν· ἐρέω δέ τοι ἀμφοτέρωθεν.
ἔνθεν μὲν γὰρ πέτραι ἐπηρεφέες, προτὶ δ' αὐτὰς
κῦμα μέγα ῥοχθεῖ κυανώπιδος Ἀμφιτρίτης·   60
Πλαγκτὰς δή τοι τάς γε θεοὶ μάκαρες καλέουσι.
τῇ μέν τ' οὐδὲ ποτητὰ παρέρχεται οὐδὲ πέλειαι
τρήρωνες, ταί τ' ἀμβροσίην Διὶ πατρὶ φέρουσιν,
ἀλλά τε καὶ τῶν αἰὲν ἀφαιρεῖται λὶς πέτρη·
ἀλλ' ἄλλην ἐνίησι πατὴρ ἐναρίθμιον εἶναι.   65
τῇ δ' οὔ πώ τις νηῦς φύγεν ἀνδρῶν, ἥ τις ἵκηται,
ἀλλά θ' ὁμοῦ πίνακάς τε νεῶν καὶ σώματα φωτῶν
κύμαθ' ἁλὸς φορέουσι πυρός τ' ὀλοοῖο θύελλαι.
οἴη δὴ κείνη γε παρέπλω ποντοπόρος νηῦς,
Ἀργὼ πᾶσι μέλουσα, παρ' Αἰήταο πλέουσα.   70
καί νύ κε τὴν ἔνθ' ὦκα βάλεν μεγάλας ποτὶ πέτρας,
ἀλλ' Ἥρη παρέπεμψεν, ἐπεὶ φίλος ἦεν Ἰήσων.
    "'Οἱ δὲ δύω σκόπελοι ὁ μὲν οὐρανὸν εὐρὺν ἱκάνει
ὀξείῃ κορυφῇ, νεφέλη δέ μιν ἀμφιβέβηκε
κυανέη· τὸ μὲν οὔ ποτ' ἐρωεῖ, οὐδέ ποτ' αἴθρη   75
κείνου ἔχει κορυφὴν οὔτ' ἐν θέρει οὔτ' ἐν ὀπώρῃ.
οὐδέ κεν ἀμβαίη βροτὸς ἀνὴρ οὐδ' ἐπιβαίη,
οὐδ' εἴ οἱ χεῖρές τε ἐείκοσι καὶ πόδες εἶεν·
πέτρη γὰρ λὶς ἐστι, περιξεστῇ ἐικυῖα.

that with delight thou mayest listen to the voice of the two Sirens. And if thou shalt implore and bid thy comrades to loose thee, then let them bind thee with yet more bonds. But when thy comrades shall have rowed past these, thereafter I shall not fully say on which side thy course is to lie, but do thou thyself ponder it in mind, and I will tell thee of both ways. For on the one hand are beetling crags, and against them roars the great wave of dark-eyed Amphitrite; the Planctae[1] do the blessed gods call these. Thereby not even winged things may pass, no, not the timorous doves that bear ambrosia to father Zeus, but the smooth rock ever snatches away one even of these, and the father sends in another to make up the tale. And thereby has no ship of men ever yet escaped that has come thither, but the planks of ships and bodies of men are whirled confusedly by the waves of the sea and the blasts of baneful fire. One seafaring ship alone has passed thereby, that Argo famed of all, on her voyage from Aeetes, and even her the wave would speedily have dashed there against the great crags, had not Here sent her through, for that Jason was dear to her.

"'Now on the other path are two cliffs, one of which reaches with its sharp peak to the broad heaven, and a dark cloud surrounds it. This never melts away, nor does clear sky ever surround that peak in summer or in harvest time. No mortal man could scale it or set foot upon the top, not though he had twenty hands and feet; for the rock is smooth, as if it were polished. And in

---

[1] *i.e.* "the wandering," or, perhaps, "the clashing, rocks."

μέσσῳ δ' ἐν σκοπέλῳ ἔστι σπέος ἠεροειδές,　　　　8⟨
πρὸς ζόφον εἰς Ἔρεβος τετραμμένον, ᾗ περ ἂν ὑμεῖς
νῆα παρὰ γλαφυρὴν ἰθύνετε, φαίδιμ' Ὀδυσσεῦ.
οὐδέ κεν ἐκ νηὸς γλαφυρῆς αἰζήιος ἀνὴρ
τόξῳ οἰστεύσας κοῖλον σπέος εἰσαφίκοιτο.
ἔνθα δ' ἐνὶ Σκύλλη ναίει δεινὸν λελακυῖα.　　　　8⟨
τῆς ἦ τοι φωνὴ μὲν ὅση σκύλακος νεογιλῆς
γίγνεται, αὐτὴ δ' αὖτε πέλωρ κακόν· οὐδέ κέ τίς μιν
γηθήσειεν ἰδών, οὐδ' εἰ θεὸς ἀντιάσειεν.
τῆς ἦ τοι πόδες εἰσὶ δυώδεκα πάντες ἄωροι,
ἐξ δέ τέ οἱ δειραὶ περιμήκεες, ἐν δὲ ἑκάστῃ　　　　9⟨
σμερδαλέη κεφαλή, ἐν δὲ τρίστοιχοι ὀδόντες
πυκνοὶ καὶ θαμέες, πλεῖοι μέλανος θανάτοιο.
μέσση μέν τε κατὰ σπείους κοίλοιο δέδυκεν,
ἔξω δ' ἐξίσχει κεφαλὰς δεινοῖο βερέθρου,
αὐτοῦ δ' ἰχθυάᾳ, σκόπελον περιμαιμώωσα,　　　　9⟨
δελφῖνάς τε κύνας τε, καὶ εἴ ποθι μεῖζον ἕλῃσι
κῆτος, ἃ μυρία βόσκει ἀγάστονος Ἀμφιτρίτη.
τῇ δ' οὔ πώ ποτε ναῦται ἀκήριοι εὐχετόωνται
παρφυγέειν σὺν νηί· φέρει δέ τε κρατὶ ἑκάστῳ
φῶτ' ἐξαρπάξασα νεὸς κυανοπρώροιο.　　　　　　10⟨
　"'Τὸν δ' ἕτερον σκόπελον χθαμαλώτερον ὄψει,
Ὀδυσσεῦ.
πλησίον ἀλλήλων· καί κεν διοϊστεύσειας.
τῷ δ' ἐν ἐρινεὸς ἔστι μέγας, φύλλοισι τεθηλώς·
τῷ δ' ὑπὸ δῖα Χάρυβδις ἀναρροιβδεῖ μέλαν ὕδωρ.
τρὶς μὲν γάρ τ' ἀνίησιν ἐπ' ἤματι, τρὶς δ' ἀναροιβδεῖ 10⟨
δεινόν· μὴ σύ γε κεῖθι τύχοις, ὅτε ῥοιβδήσειεν·
οὐ γάρ κεν ῥύσαιτό σ' ὑπὲκ κακοῦ οὐδ' ἐνοσίχθων.
ἀλλὰ μάλα Σκύλλης σκοπέλῳ πεπλημένος ὦκα

the midst of the cliff is a dim cave, turned to the West, toward Erebus, even where you shall steer your hollow ship, glorious Odysseus. Not even a man of might could shoot an arrow from the hollow ship so as to reach into that vaulted cave. Therein dwells Scylla, yelping terribly. Her voice is indeed but as the voice of a new-born whelp, but she herself is an evil monster, nor would anyone be glad at sight of her, no, not though it were a god that met her. Verily she has twelve feet, all misshapen,[1] and six necks, exceeding long, and on each one an awful head, and therein three rows of teeth, thick and close, and full of black death. Up to her middle she is hidden in the hollow cave, but she holds her head out beyond the dread chasm, and fishes there, eagerly searching around the rock for dolphins and sea-dogs and whatever greater beast she may haply catch, such creatures as deep-moaning Amphitrite rears in multitudes past counting. By her no sailors yet may boast that they have fled unscathed in their ship, for with each head she carries off a man, snatching him from the dark-prowed ship.

"'But the other cliff, thou wilt note, Odysseus, is lower—they are close to each other; thou couldst even shoot an arrow across—and on it is a great fig tree with rich foliage, but beneath this divine Charybdis sucks down the black water. Thrice a day she belches it forth, and thrice she sucks it down terribly. Mayest thou not be there when she sucks it down, for no one could save thee from ruin, no, not the Earth-shaker. Nay, draw

---

[1] The word is a doubtful one. Others render, "dangling down."

νῆα παρὲξ ἐλάαν, ἐπεὶ ἦ πολὺ φέρτερόν ἐστιν
ἐξ ἑτάρους ἐν νηὶ ποθήμεναι ἢ ἅμα πάντας.'   11
  "'Ὣς ἔφατ', αὐτὰρ ἐγώ μιν ἀμειβόμενος [1] προσέειπον·
' Εἰ δ' ἄγε δή μοι τοῦτο, θεά, νημερτὲς ἐνίσπες,
εἴ πως τὴν ὀλοὴν μὲν ὑπεκπροφύγοιμι Χάρυβδιν,
τὴν δέ κ' ἀμυναίμην, ὅτε μοι σίνοιτό γ' ἑταίρους.'
  "'Ὣς ἐφάμην, ἡ δ' αὐτίκ' ἀμείβετο δῖα θεάων·   11
' Σχέτλιε, καὶ δὴ αὖ τοι πολεμήια ἔργα μέμηλε
καὶ πόνος· οὐδὲ θεοῖσιν ὑπείξεαι ἀθανάτοισιν;
ἡ δέ τοι οὐ θνητή, ἀλλ' ἀθάνατον κακόν ἐστι,
δεινόν τ' ἀργαλέον τε καὶ ἄγριον οὐδὲ μαχητόν·
οὐδέ τις ἔστ' ἀλκή· φυγέειν κάρτιστον ἀπ' αὐτῆς.   12
ἢν γὰρ δηθύνησθα κορυσσόμενος παρὰ πέτρῃ,
δείδω, μή σ' ἐξαῦτις ἐφορμηθεῖσα κίχῃσι
τόσσῃσιν κεφαλῇσι, τόσους δ' ἐκ φῶτας ἕληται.
ἀλλὰ μάλα σφοδρῶς ἐλάαν, βωστρεῖν δὲ Κράταιιν,
μητέρα τῆς Σκύλλης, ἥ μιν τέκε πῆμα βροτοῖσιν·   12
ἥ μιν ἔπειτ' ἀποπαύσει ἐς ὕστερον ὁρμηθῆναι.
  "'Θρινακίην δ' ἐς νῆσον ἀφίξεαι· ἔνθα δὲ πολλαὶ
βόσκοντ' Ἠελίοιο βόες καὶ ἴφια μῆλα,
ἑπτὰ βοῶν ἀγέλαι, τόσα δ' οἰῶν πώεα καλά,
πεντήκοντα δ' ἕκαστα. γόνος δ' οὐ γίγνεται αὐτῶν,   13
οὐδέ ποτε φθινύθουσι. θεαὶ δ' ἐπιποιμένες εἰσίν,
νύμφαι ἐυπλόκαμοι, Φαέθουσά τε Λαμπετίη τε,
ἃς τέκεν Ἠελίῳ Ὑπερίονι δῖα Νέαιρα.
τὰς μὲν ἄρα θρέψασα τεκοῦσά τε πότνια μήτηρ
Θρινακίην ἐς νῆσον ἀπῴκισε τηλόθι ναίειν,   13
μῆλα φυλασσέμεναι πατρώια καὶ ἕλικας βοῦς.
τὰς εἰ μέν κ' ἀσινέας ἐάᾳς νόστου τε μέδηαι,
ἦ τ' ἂν ἔτ' εἰς Ἰθάκην κακά περ πάσχοντες ἵκοισθε·

----

[1] ἀμειβόμενος : ἀτυζόμενος.

440

very close to Scylla s cliff, and drive thy ship past quickly; for it is better far to mourn six comrades in thy ship than all together.'

"So she spoke, but I made answer and said: 'Come, I pray thee, goddess, tell me this thing truly, if in any wise I might escape from fell Charybdis, and ward off that other, when she works harm to my comrades.'

"So I spoke, and the beautiful goddess answered and said: 'Rash man, lo, now again thy heart is set on the deeds of war and on toil. Wilt thou not yield even to the immortal gods? She is not mortal, but an immortal bane, dread, and dire, and fierce, and not to be fought with; there is no defence; to flee from her is bravest. For if thou tarriest to arm thyself by the cliff, I fear lest she may again dart forth and attack thee with as many heads and seize as many men as before. Nay, row past with all thy might, and call upon Crataiis, the mother of Scylla, who bore her for a bane to mortals. Then will she keep her from darting forth again.

"'And thou wilt come to the isle Thrinacia. There in great numbers feed the kine of Helios and his goodly flocks, seven herds of kine and as many fair flocks of sheep, and fifty in each. These bear no young, nor do they ever die, and goddesses are their shepherds, fair-tressed nymphs, Phaethusa and Lampetie, whom beautiful Neaera bore to Helios Hyperion. These their honoured mother, when she had borne and reared them, sent to the isle Thrinacia to dwell afar, and keep the flocks of their father and his sleek kine. If thou leavest these unharmed and heedest thy homeward way, verily ye may yet reach Ithaca, though in evil

εἰ δέ κε σίνηαι, τότε τοι τεκμαίρομ' ὄλεθρον,
νηΐ τε καὶ ἑτάροις· αὐτὸς δ' εἴ πέρ κεν ἀλύξῃς,   140
ὀψὲ κακῶς νεῖαι, ὀλέσας ἄπο πάντας ἑταίρους.'

   "Ὣς ἔφατ', αὐτίκα δὲ χρυσόθρονος ἤλυθεν Ἠώς.
ἡ μὲν ἔπειτ' ἀνὰ νῆσον ἀπέστιχε δῖα θεάων·
αὐτὰρ ἐγὼν ἐπὶ νῆα κιὼν ὤτρυνον ἑταίρους
αὐτούς τ' ἀμβαίνειν ἀνά τε πρυμνήσια λῦσαι·   145
οἱ δ' αἶψ' εἴσβαινον καὶ ἐπὶ κληῖσι καθῖζον.
ἑξῆς δ' ἑζόμενοι πολιὴν ἅλα τύπτον ἐρετμοῖς.[1]
ἡμῖν δ' αὖ κατόπισθε νεὸς κυανοπρώροιο
ἴκμενον οὖρον ἵει πλησίστιον, ἐσθλὸν ἑταῖρον,
Κίρκη ἐυπλόκαμος, δεινὴ θεὸς αὐδήεσσα.   150
αὐτίκα δ' ὅπλα ἕκαστα πονησάμενοι κατὰ νῆα
ἥμεθα· τὴν δ' ἄνεμός τε κυβερνήτης τ' ἴθυνε.

   "Δὴ τότ' ἐγὼν ἑτάροισι μετηύδων ἀχνύμενος κῆρ·
'Ὦ φίλοι, οὐ γὰρ χρὴ ἕνα ἴδμεναι οὐδὲ δύ' οἴους
θέσφαθ' ἅ μοι Κίρκη μυθήσατο, δῖα θεάων·   155
ἀλλ' ἐρέω μὲν ἐγών, ἵνα εἰδότες ἤ κε θάνωμεν
ἤ κεν ἀλευάμενοι θάνατον καὶ κῆρα φύγοιμεν.
Σειρήνων μὲν πρῶτον ἀνώγει θεσπεσιάων
φθόγγον ἀλεύασθαι καὶ λειμῶν' ἀνθεμόεντα.
οἶον ἔμ' ἠνώγει ὄπ' ἀκουέμεν· ἀλλά με δεσμῷ   160
δήσατ' ἐν ἀργαλέῳ, ὄφρ' ἔμπεδον αὐτόθι μίμνω,
ὀρθὸν ἐν ἱστοπέδῃ, ἐκ δ' αὐτοῦ πείρατ' ἀνήφθω.
εἰ δέ κε λίσσωμαι ὑμέας λῦσαί τε κελεύω,
ὑμεῖς δὲ πλεόνεσσι τότ' ἐν δεσμοῖσι πιέζειν.'

---

[1] Line 147 is omitted in most MSS.

plight. But if thou harmest them, then I foretell
ruin for thy ship and for thy comrades, and even
if thou shalt thyself escape, late shalt thou come
home and in evil case, after losing all thy com-
rades.'

"So she spoke, and presently came golden-
throned Dawn. Then the beautiful goddess de-
parted up the island, but I went to the ship and
roused my comrades themselves to embark and to
loose the stern cables. So they went on board
straightway and sat down upon the benches, and
sitting well in order smote the grey sea with their
oars. And for our aid in the wake of our dark-
prowed ship a fair wind that filled the sail, a
goodly comrade, was sent by fair-tressed Circe,
dread goddess of human speech. So when we had
straightway made fast all the tackling throughout
the ship we sat down, but the wind and the helms-
man guided the ship.

"Then verily I spoke among my comrades,
grieved at heart: 'Friends, since it is not right
that one or two alone should know the oracles
that Circe, the beautiful goddess, told me, there-
fore will I tell them, in order that knowing them
we may either die or, shunning death and fate,
escape. First she bade us avoid the voice of the
wondrous Sirens, and their flowery meadow. Me
alone she bade to listen to their voice; but do
ye bind me with grievous bonds, that I may abide
fast where I am, upright in the step of the mast,
and let the ropes be made fast at the ends to
the mast itself; and if I implore and bid you to
loose me, then do ye tie me fast with yet more
bonds.'

443

" Ἦ τοι ἐγὼ τὰ ἕκαστα λέγων ἑτάροισι πίφαυσκον·
τόφρα δὲ καρπαλίμως ἐξίκετο νηῦς ἐνεργὴς   166
νῆσον Σειρήνοιιν· ἔπειγε γὰρ οὖρος ἀπήμων.
αὐτίκ' ἔπειτ' ἄνεμος μὲν ἐπαύσατο ἠδὲ γαλήνη
ἔπλετο νηνεμίη, κοίμησε δὲ κύματα δαίμων.
ἀνστάντες δ' ἕταροι νεὸς ἱστία μηρύσαντο   170
καὶ τὰ μὲν ἐν νηὶ γλαφυρῇ θέσαν,[1] οἱ δ' ἐπ' ἐρετμὰ
ἑζόμενοι λεύκαινον ὕδωρ ξεστῇς ἐλάτῃσιν.
αὐτὰρ ἐγὼ κηροῖο μέγαν τροχὸν ὀξέι χαλκῷ
τυτθὰ διατμήξας χερσὶ στιβαρῇσι πίεζον·
αἶψα δ' ἰαίνετο κηρός, ἐπεὶ κέλετο μεγάλη ἲς   175
Ἠελίου τ' αὐγὴ Ὑπεριονίδαο ἄνακτος·
ἐξείης δ' ἑτάροισιν ἐπ' οὔατα πᾶσιν ἄλειψα.
οἱ δ' ἐν νηί μ' ἔδησαν ὁμοῦ χεῖράς τε πόδας τε
ὀρθὸν ἐν ἱστοπέδῃ, ἐκ δ' αὐτοῦ πείρατ' ἀνῆπτον·
αὐτοὶ δ' ἑζόμενοι πολιὴν ἅλα τύπτον ἐρετμοῖς.   180
ἀλλ' ὅτε τόσσον ἀπῆμεν ὅσον[2] τε γέγωνε βοήσας,
ῥίμφα διώκοντες, τὰς δ' οὐ λάθεν ὠκύαλος νηῦς
ἐγγύθεν ὀρνυμένη, λιγυρὴν δ' ἔντυνον ἀοιδήν·

" ' Δεῦρ' ἄγ' ἰών, πολύαιν' Ὀδυσεῦ, μέγα κῦδος Ἀχαιῶν,
νῆα κατάστησον, ἵνα νωιτέρην ὄπ' ἀκούσῃς.   185
οὐ γάρ πώ τις τῇδε παρήλασε νηὶ μελαίνῃ,
πρίν γ' ἡμέων μελίγηρυν ἀπὸ στομάτων ὄπ' ἀκοῦσαι,
ἀλλ' ὅ γε τερψάμενος νεῖται καὶ πλείονα εἰδώς.
ἴδμεν γάρ τοι πάνθ' ὅσ' ἐνὶ Τροίῃ εὐρείῃ

---

[1] θέσαν : βάλον.
[2] ἀπῆμεν ὅσον : ἀπὴν ὅσσον.

" Thus I rehearsed all these things and told them to my comrades. Meanwhile the well-built ship speedily came to the isle of the two Sirens, for a fair and gentle wind bore her on. Then presently the wind ceased and there was a windless calm, and a god lulled the waves to sleep. But my comrades rose up and furled the sail and stowed it in the hollow ship, and thereafter sat at the oars and made the water white with their polished oars of fir. But I with my sharp sword cut into small bits a great round cake of wax, and kneaded it with my strong hands, and soon the wax grew warm, forced by the strong pressure and the rays of the lord Helios Hyperion.[1] Then I anointed with this the ears of all my comrades in turn; and they bound me in the ship hand and foot, upright in the step of the mast, and made the ropes fast at the ends to the mast itself; and themselves sitting down smote the grey sea with their oars. But when we were as far distant as a man can make himself heard when he shouts, driving swiftly on our way, the Sirens failed not to note the swift ship as it drew near, and they raised their clear-toned song:

" ' Come hither, as thou farest, renowned Odysseus, great glory of the Achaeans ; stay thy ship that thou mayest listen to the voice of us two. For never yet has any man rowed past this isle in his black ship until he has heard the sweet voice from our lips. Nay, he has joy of it, and goes his way a wiser man. For we know all the toils that in wide Troy the

---

[1] This rendering takes Ὑπεριονίδης to be an equivalent of Ὑπερίων. If it be regarded as a patronymic, this passage is out of harmony with others.

Ἀργεῖοι Τρῶές τε θεῶν ἰότητι μόγησαν,　　　　　　190
ἴδμεν δ᾽, ὅσσα γένηται ἐπὶ χθονὶ πουλυβοτείρῃ.᾽

　　"῝Ως φάσαν ἱεῖσαι ὄπα κάλλιμον· αὐτὰρ ἐμὸν κῆρ
ἤθελ᾽ ἀκουέμεναι, λῦσαί τ᾽ ἐκέλευον ἑταίρους
ὀφρύσι νευστάζων· οἱ δὲ προπεσόντες ἔρεσσον.
αὐτίκα δ᾽ ἀνστάντες Περιμήδης Εὐρύλοχός τε　　195
πλείοσί μ᾽ ἐν δεσμοῖσι δέον μᾶλλόν τε πίεζον.
αὐτὰρ ἐπεὶ δὴ τάς γε παρήλασαν, οὐδ᾽ ἔτ᾽ ἔπειτα
φθογγῆς Σειρήνων ἠκούομεν οὐδέ τ᾽ ἀοιδῆς,
αἶψ᾽ ἀπὸ κηρὸν ἕλοντο ἐμοὶ ἐρίηρες ἑταῖροι,
ὅν σφιν ἐπ᾽ ὠσὶν ἄλειψ᾽, ἐμέ τ᾽ ἐκ δεσμῶν ἀνέλυσαν.　200

　　"Ἀλλ᾽ ὅτε δὴ τὴν νῆσον ἐλείπομεν, αὐτίκ᾽ ἔπειτα
καπνὸν καὶ μέγα κῦμα ἴδον καὶ δοῦπον ἄκουσα.
τῶν δ᾽ ἄρα δεισάντων ἐκ χειρῶν ἔπτατ᾽ ἐρετμά,
βόμβησαν δ᾽ ἄρα πάντα κατὰ ῥόον· ἔσχετο δ᾽ αὐτοῦ
νηῦς, ἐπεὶ οὐκέτ᾽ ἐρετμὰ προήκεα χερσὶν ἔπειγον.　205
αὐτὰρ ἐγὼ διὰ νηὸς ἰὼν ὤτρυνον ἑταίρους
μειλιχίοις ἐπέεσσι παρασταδὸν ἄνδρα ἕκαστον·

　　"῏Ω φίλοι, οὐ γάρ πώ τι κακῶν ἀδαήμονές εἰμεν·
οὐ μὲν δὴ τόδε μεῖζον ἔπει [1] κακόν, ἢ ὅτε Κύκλωψ
εἴλει ἐνὶ σπῆι γλαφυρῷ κρατερῆφι βίηφιν·　　　210
ἀλλὰ καὶ ἔνθεν ἐμῇ ἀρετῇ, βουλῇ τε νόῳ τε,
ἐκφύγομεν, καί που τῶνδε μνήσεσθαι ὀίω.
νῦν δ᾽ ἄγεθ᾽, ὡς ἂν ἐγὼ εἴπω, πειθώμεθα πάντες.
ὑμεῖς μὲν κώπῃσιν ἁλὸς ῥηγμῖνα βαθεῖαν
τύπτετε κληίδεσσιν ἐφήμενοι, αἴ κέ ποθι Ζεὺς　215
δώῃ τόνδε γ᾽ ὄλεθρον ὑπεκφυγέειν καὶ ἀλύξαι·
σοὶ δέ, κυβερνῆθ᾽, ὧδ᾽ ἐπιτέλλομαι· ἀλλ᾽ ἐνὶ θυμῷ

---

[1] ἔπει : ἔπι : ἔχει Zenodotus.

Argives and Trojans endured through the will of the gods, and we know all things that come to pass upon the fruitful earth.'

"So they spoke, sending forth their beautiful voice, and my heart was fain to listen, and I bade my comrades loose me, nodding to them with my brows; but they fell to their oars and rowed on. And presently Perimedes and Eurylochus arose and bound me with yet more bonds and drew them tighter. But when they had rowed past the Sirens, and we could no more hear their voice or their song, then straightway my trusty comrades took away the wax with which I had anointed their ears and loosed me from my bonds.

"But when we had left the island, I presently saw smoke and a great billow, and heard a booming. Then from the hands of my men in their terror the oars flew, and splashed one and all in the swirl, and the ship stood still where it was, when they no longer plied with their hands the tapering oars. But I went through the ship and cheered my men with gentle words, coming up to each man in turn:

"'Friends, hitherto we have been in no wise ignorant of sorrow; surely this evil that besets us now is no greater than when the Cyclops penned us in his hollow cave by brutal strength; yet even thence we made our escape through my valour and counsel and wit; these dangers, too, methinks we shall some day remember. But now come, as I bid, let us all obey. Do you keep your seats on the benches and smite with your oars the deep surf of the sea, in the hope that Zeus may grant us to escape and avoid this death. And to thee, steersman, I give this command, and do thou lay it to

βάλλευ, ἐπεὶ νηὸς γλαφυρῆς οἰήια νωμᾷς.
τούτου μὲν καπνοῦ καὶ κύματος ἐκτὸς ἔεργε
νῆα, σὺ δὲ σκοπέλου ἐπιμαίεο, μή σε λάθῃσι   220
κεῖσ᾽ ἐξορμήσασα καὶ ἐς κακὸν ἄμμε βάλῃσθα.᾽

    "῞Ως ἐφάμην, οἱ δ᾽ ὦκα ἐμοῖς ἐπέεσσι πίθοντο.
Σκύλλην δ᾽ οὐκέτ᾽ ἐμυθεόμην, ἄπρηκτον ἀνίην,
μή πώς μοι δείσαντες ἀπολλήξειαν ἑταῖροι
εἰρεσίης, ἐντὸς δὲ πυκάζοιεν σφέας αὐτούς.   225
καὶ τότε δὴ Κίρκης μὲν ἐφημοσύνης ἀλεγεινῆς
λανθανόμην, ἐπεὶ οὔ τί μ᾽ ἀνώγει θωρήσσεσθαι·
αὐτὰρ ἐγὼ καταδὺς κλυτὰ τεύχεα καὶ δύο δοῦρε
μάκρ᾽ ἐν χερσὶν ἑλὼν εἰς ἴκρια νηὸς ἔβαινον
πρῴρης· ἔνθεν γάρ μιν ἐδέγμην πρῶτα φανεῖσθαι   230
Σκύλλην πετραίην, ἥ μοι φέρε πῆμ᾽ ἑτάροισιν.
οὐδέ πῃ ἀθρῆσαι δυνάμην, ἔκαμον δέ μοι ὄσσε
πάντῃ παπταίνοντι πρὸς ἠεροειδέα πέτρην.

    "Ἡμεῖς μὲν στεινωπὸν ἀνεπλέομεν γοόωντες·
ἔνθεν μὲν Σκύλλη, ἑτέρωθι δὲ δῖα Χάρυβδις   235
δεινὸν ἀνερροίβδησε θαλάσσης ἁλμυρὸν ὕδωρ.
ἦ τοι ὅτ᾽ ἐξεμέσειε, λέβης ὣς ἐν πυρὶ πολλῷ
πᾶσ᾽ ἀναμορμύρεσκε κυκωμένη, ὑψόσε δ᾽ ἄχνη
ἄκροισι σκοπέλοισιν ἐπ᾽ ἀμφοτέροισιν ἔπιπτεν·
ἀλλ᾽ ὅτ᾽ ἀναβρόξειε θαλάσσης ἁλμυρὸν ὕδωρ,   240
πᾶσ᾽ ἔντοσθε φάνεσκε κυκωμένη, ἀμφὶ δὲ πέτρῃ
δεινὸν ἐβεβρύχει, ὑπένερθε δὲ γαῖα φάνεσκε
ψάμμῳ κυανέη· τοὺς δὲ χλωρὸν δέος ᾕρει.
ἡμεῖς μὲν πρὸς τὴν ἴδομεν δείσαντες ὄλεθρον·
τόφρα δέ μοι Σκύλλη γλαφυρῆς ἐκ νηὸς ἑταίρους   245
ἐξ ἕλεθ᾽, οἳ χερσίν τε βίηφί τε φέρτατοι ἦσαν.

heart, since thou wieldest the steering oar of the hollow ship. From this smoke and surf keep the ship well away and hug the cliff, lest, ere thou know it, the ship swerve off to the other side and thou cast us into destruction.'

"So I spoke, and they quickly hearkened to my words. But of Scylla I went not on to speak, a cureless bane, lest haply my comrades, seized with fear, should cease from rowing and huddle together in the hold. Then verily I forgot the hard command of Circe, whereas she bade me in no wise to arm myself; but when I had put on my glorious armour and grasped in my hand two long spears, I went to the fore-deck of the ship, whence I deemed that Scylla of the rock would first be seen, who was to bring ruin upon my comrades. But nowhere could I descry her, and my eyes grew weary as I gazed everywhere toward the misty rock.

"We then sailed on up the narrow strait with wailing. For on one side lay Scylla and on the other divine Charybdis terribly sucked down the salt water of the sea. Verily whenever she belched it forth, like a cauldron on a great fire she would seethe and bubble in utter turmoil, and high over head the spray would fall on the tops of both the cliffs. But as often as she sucked down the salt water of the sea, within she could all be seen in utter turmoil, and round about the rock roared terribly, while beneath the earth appeared black with sand; and pale fear seized my men. So we looked toward her and feared destruction; but meanwhile Scylla seized from out the hollow ship six of my comrades who were the best in strength and in might. Turning my eyes to

σκεψάμενος δ' ἐς νῆα θοὴν ἅμα καὶ μεθ' ἑταίρους
ἤδη τῶν ἐνόησα πόδας καὶ χεῖρας ὕπερθεν
ὑψόσ' ἀειρομένων· ἐμὲ δὲ φθέγγοντο καλεῦντες
ἐξονομακλήδην, τότε γ' ὕστατον, ἀχνύμενοι κῆρ· 25⟨⟩
ὡς δ' ὅτ' ἐπὶ προβόλῳ ἁλιεὺς περιμήκεϊ ῥάβδῳ
ἰχθύσι τοῖς ὀλίγοισι δόλον κατὰ εἴδατα βάλλων
ἐς πόντον προΐησι βοὸς κέρας ἀγραύλοιο,
ἀσπαίροντα δ' ἔπειτα λαβὼν ἔρριψε θύραζε,
ὣς οἵ γ' ἀσπαίροντες ἀείροντο προτὶ πέτρας· 25⟨⟩
αὐτοῦ δ' εἰνὶ θύρῃσι κατήσθιε κεκληγῶτας
χεῖρας ἐμοὶ ὀρέγοντας ἐν αἰνῇ δηιοτῆτι·
οἴκτιστον δὴ κεῖνο ἐμοῖς ἴδον ὀφθαλμοῖσι
πάντων, ὅσσ' ἐμόγησα πόρους ἁλὸς ἐξερεείνων.

"Αὐτὰρ ἐπεὶ πέτρας φύγομεν δεινήν τε Χάρυβδιν 26⟨⟩
Σκύλλην τ', αὐτίκ' ἔπειτα θεοῦ ἐς ἀμύμονα νῆσον
ἱκόμεθ'· ἔνθα δ' ἔσαν καλαὶ βόες εὐρυμέτωποι,
πολλὰ δὲ ἴφια μῆλ' Ὑπερίονος Ἠελίοιο.
δὴ τότ' ἐγὼν ἔτι πόντῳ ἐὼν ἐν νηὶ μελαίνῃ
μυκηθμοῦ τ' ἤκουσα βοῶν αὐλιζομενάων 2⟨⟩
οἰῶν τε βληχήν· καί μοι ἔπος ἔμπεσε θυμῷ
μάντηος ἀλαοῦ, Θηβαίου Τειρεσίαο,
Κίρκης τ' Αἰαίης, ἥ μοι μάλα πόλλ' ἐπέτελλε
νῆσον ἀλεύασθαι τερψιμβρότου Ἠελίοιο.
δὴ τότ' ἐγὼν ἑτάροισι μετηύδων ἀχνύμενος κῆρ· 2⟨⟩

"'Κέκλυτέ μευ μύθων κακά περ πάσχοντες ἑταῖρο⟨⟩
ὄφρ' ὑμῖν εἴπω μαντήια Τειρεσίαο
Κίρκης τ' Αἰαίης, ἥ μοι μάλα πόλλ' ἐπέτελλε
νῆσον ἀλεύασθαι τερψιμβρότου Ἠελίοιο·

---

[1] Or, possibly, "to find my men."
[2] Three views are held regarding this obscure passage:
(1) that the poet refers to spearing, or "hooking," fish with

the swift ship and to the company of my men,[1] even then I noted above me their feet and hands as they were raised aloft. To me they cried aloud, calling upon me by name for that last time in anguish of heart. And as a fisher on a jutting rock, when he casts in his baits as a snare to the little fishes, with his long pole lets down into the sea the horn of an ox of the steading,[2] and then as he catches a fish flings it writhing ashore, even so were they drawn writhing up towards the cliffs. Then at her doors she devoured them shrieking and stretching out their hands toward me in their awful death-struggle. Most piteous did mine eyes behold that thing of all that I bore while I explored the paths of the sea.

"Now when we had escaped the rocks, and dread Charybdis and Scylla, presently then we came to the goodly island of the god, where were the fair kine, broad of brow, and the many goodly flocks of Helios Hyperion. Then while I was still out at sea in my black ship, I heard the lowing of the cattle that were being stalled and the bleating of the sheep, and upon my mind fell the words of the blind seer, Theban Teiresias, and of Aeaean Circe, who very straitly charged me to shun the island of Helios, who gives joy to mortals. Then verily I spoke among my comrades, grieved at heart :

"'Hear my words, comrades, for all your evil plight, that I may tell you the oracles of Teiresias and of Aeaean Circe, who very straitly charged me to shun the island of Helios, who gives joy to

a pole tipped with bone (it will be noticed that there is no mention of a line) ; (2) that a bit of hollow, tube-like bone was slipped over the line just above the hook to prevent its being bitten through : and (3) that the bone was really an artificial bait (see Haskins in *Journ. Philol.* xix. 238 ff.).

ἔνθα γὰρ αἰνότατον κακὸν ἔμμεναι ἄμμιν ἔφασκεν. 275
ἀλλὰ παρὲξ τὴν νῆσον ἐλαύνετε νῆα μέλαιναν.'

   "Ὣς ἐφάμην, τοῖσιν δὲ κατεκλάσθη φίλον ἦτορ.
αὐτίκα δ' Εὐρύλοχος στυγερῷ μ' ἠμείβετο μύθῳ·

   "'Σχέτλιός εἰς, Ὀδυσεῦ· περί τοι μένος, οὐδέ τι γυῖα
κάμνεις· ἦ ῥά νυ σοί γε σιδήρεα πάντα τέτυκται, 280
ὅς ῥ' ἑτάρους καμάτῳ ἀδηκότας ἠδὲ καὶ ὕπνῳ
οὐκ ἐάᾳς γαίης ἐπιβήμεναι, ἔνθα κεν αὖτε
νήσῳ ἐν ἀμφιρύτῃ λαρὸν τετυκοίμεθα δόρπον,
ἀλλ' αὔτως διὰ νύκτα θοὴν ἀλάλησθαι ἄνωγας
νήσου ἀποπλαγχθέντας ἐν ἠεροειδέι πόντῳ. 285
ἐκ νυκτῶν δ' ἄνεμοι χαλεποί, δηλήματα νηῶν,
γίγνονται· πῇ κέν τις ὑπεκφύγοι αἰπὺν ὄλεθρον,
ἤν πως ἐξαπίνης ἔλθῃ ἀνέμοιο θύελλα,
ἢ Νότου ἢ Ζεφύροιο δυσαέος, οἵ τε μάλιστα
νῆα διαρραίουσι θεῶν ἀέκητι ἀνάκτων. 290
ἀλλ' ἦ τοι νῦν μὲν πειθώμεθα νυκτὶ μελαίνῃ
δόρπον θ' ὁπλισόμεσθα θοῇ παρὰ νηὶ μένοντες,
ἠῶθεν δ' ἀναβάντες ἐνήσομεν εὐρέι πόντῳ.'

   "Ὣς ἔφατ' Εὐρύλοχος, ἐπὶ δ' ᾔνεον ἄλλοι ἑταῖροι.
καὶ τότε δὴ γίγνωσκον ὃ δὴ κακὰ μήδετο δαίμων, 295
καί μιν φωνήσας ἔπεα πτερόεντα προσηύδων·

   "'Εὐρύλοχ', ἦ μάλα δή με βιάζετε μοῦνον ἐόντα.
ἀλλ' ἄγε νῦν μοι πάντες ὀμόσσατε καρτερὸν ὅρκον·
εἴ κέ τιν' ἠὲ βοῶν ἀγέλην ἢ πῶυ μέγ' οἰῶν
εὕρωμεν, μή πού τις ἀτασθαλίῃσι κακῇσιν 300
ἢ βοῦν ἠέ τι μῆλον ἀποκτάνῃ· ἀλλὰ ἕκηλοι
ἐσθίετε βρώμην, τὴν ἀθανάτη πόρε Κίρκη.'

mortals; for there, she said, was our most terrible bane. Nay, row the black ship out past the island.'

"So I spoke, but their spirit was broken within them, and straightway Eurylochus answered me with hateful words:

"'Hardy art thou, Odysseus; thou hast strength beyond that of other men and thy limbs never grow weary. Verily thou art wholly wrought of iron, seeing that thou sufferest not thy comrades, worn out with toil and drowsiness, to set foot on shore, where on this sea-girt isle we might once more make ready a savoury supper; but thou biddest us even as we are to wander on through the swift night, driven away from the island over the misty deep. It is from the night that fierce winds are born, wreckers of ships. How could one escape utter destruction, if haply there should suddenly come a blast of the South Wind or the blustering West Wind, which oftenest wreck ships in despite of the sovereign gods? Nay, verily for this time let us yield to black night and make ready our supper, remaining by the swift ship, and in the morning we will go aboard, and put out into the broad sea.'

"So spoke Eurylochus, and the rest of my comrades gave assent. Then verily I knew that some god was assuredly devising ill, and I spoke and addressed him with winged words:

"'Eurylochus, verily ye constrain me, who stand alone. But come now, do ye all swear to me a mighty oath, to the end that, if we haply find a herd of kine or a great flock of sheep, no man may slay either cow or sheep in the blind folly of his mind; but be content to eat the food which immortal Circe gave.'

"'Ὡς ἐφάμην, οἱ δ' αὐτίκ' ἀπώμνυον, ὡς ἐκέλευεν.
αὐτὰρ ἐπεί ῥ' ὅμοσάν τε τελεύτησάν τε τὸν ὅρκον,
στήσαμεν ἐν λιμένι γλαφυρῷ ἐυεργέα νῆα   305
ἄγχ' ὕδατος γλυκεροῖο, καὶ ἐξαπέβησαν ἑταῖροι
νηός, ἔπειτα δὲ δόρπον ἐπισταμένως τετύκοντο.
αὐτὰρ ἐπεὶ πόσιος καὶ ἐδητύος ἐξ ἔρον ἔντο,
μνησάμενοι δὴ ἔπειτα φίλους ἔκλαιον ἑταίρους,
οὓς ἔφαγε Σκύλλη γλαφυρῆς ἐκ νηὸς ἑλοῦσα·   310
κλαιόντεσσι δὲ τοῖσιν ἐπήλυθε νήδυμος ὕπνος.
ἦμος δὲ τρίχα νυκτὸς ἔην, μετὰ δ' ἄστρα βεβήκει,
ὦρσεν ἔπι ζαὴν ἄνεμον νεφεληγερέτα Ζεὺς
λαίλαπι θεσπεσίῃ, σὺν δὲ νεφέεσσι κάλυψε
γαῖαν ὁμοῦ καὶ πόντον· ὀρώρει δ' οὐρανόθεν νύξ.   315
ἦμος δ' ἠριγένεια φάνη ῥοδοδάκτυλος Ἠώς,
νῆα μὲν ὡρμίσαμεν κοῖλον σπέος εἰσερύσαντες.
ἔνθα δ' ἔσαν νυμφέων καλοὶ χοροὶ ἠδὲ θόωκοι·
καὶ τότ' ἐγὼν ἀγορὴν θέμενος μετὰ μῦθον[1] ἔειπον·

"'Ὦ φίλοι, ἐν γὰρ νηὶ θοῇ βρῶσίς τε πόσις τε   320
ἔστιν, τῶν δὲ βοῶν ἀπεχώμεθα, μή τι πάθωμεν·
δεινοῦ γὰρ θεοῦ αἵδε βόες καὶ ἴφια μῆλα,
Ἠελίου, ὃς πάντ' ἐφορᾷ καὶ πάντ' ἐπακούει.'

"'Ὡς ἐφάμην, τοῖσιν δ' ἐπεπείθετο θυμὸς ἀγήνωρ.
μῆνα δὲ πάντ' ἄλληκτος ἄη Νότος, οὐδέ τις ἄλλος   325
γίγνετ' ἔπειτ' ἀνέμων εἰ μὴ Εὖρός τε Νότος τε.

" Οἱ δ' ἧος μὲν σῖτον ἔχον καὶ οἶνον ἐρυθρόν,
τόφρα βοῶν ἀπέχοντο λιλαιόμενοι βιότοιο.
ἀλλ' ὅτε δὴ νηὸς ἐξέφθιτο ἤια πάντα,

[1] μῦθον : πᾶσιν

"So I spoke; and they straightway swore that they would not, even as I bade them. But when they had sworn and made an end of the oath, we moored our well-built ship in the hollow harbour near a spring of sweet water, and my comrades went forth from the ship and skilfully made ready their supper. But when they had put from them the desire of food and drink, then they fell to weeping, as they remembered their dear comrades whom Scylla had snatched from out the hollow ship and devoured; and sweet sleep came upon them as they wept. But when it was the third watch of the night, and the stars had turned their course, Zeus, the cloud-gatherer, roused against us a fierce wind with a wondrous tempest, and hid with clouds the land and sea alike, and night rushed down from heaven. And as soon as early Dawn appeared, the rosy-fingered, we dragged our ship, and made her fast in a hollow cave, where were the fair dancing-floors and seats of the nymphs. Then I called my men together and spoke among them:

"'Friends, in our swift ship is meat and drink; let us therefore keep our hands from those kine lest we come to harm, for these are the cows and goodly sheep of a dread god, even of Helios, who oversees all things and overhears all things.'

"So I spoke, and their proud hearts consented. Then for a full month the South Wind blew unceasingly, nor did any other wind arise except the East and the South.

"Now so long as my men had grain and red wine they kept their hands from the kine, for they were eager to save their lives.[1] But when all the stores

---

[1] Some prefer to render "though pining for livelihood"; but the meaning seems fixed by xxiv. 534 f.

καὶ δὴ ἄγρην ἐφέπεσκον ἀλητεύοντες ἀνάγκῃ, 330
ἰχθῦς ὄρνιθάς τε, φίλας ὅ τι χεῖρας ἵκοιτο,
γναμπτοῖς ἀγκίστροισιν, ἔτειρε δὲ γαστέρα λιμός·
δὴ τότ' ἐγὼν ἀνὰ νῆσον ἀπέστιχον, ὄφρα θεοῖσιν
εὐξαίμην, εἴ τίς μοι ὁδὸν φήνειε νέεσθαι.
ἀλλ' ὅτε δὴ διὰ νήσου ἰὼν ἤλυξα ἑταίρους, 335
χεῖρας νιψάμενος, ὅθ' ἐπὶ σκέπας ἦν ἀνέμοιο,
ἠρώμην πάντεσσι θεοῖς οἳ Ὄλυμπον ἔχουσιν·
οἱ δ' ἄρα μοι γλυκὺν ὕπνον ἐπὶ βλεφάροισιν ἔχευαν.
Εὐρύλοχος δ' ἑτάροισι κακῆς ἐξῆρχετο βουλῆς·
"'Κέκλυτέ μευ μύθων κακά περ πάσχοντες ἑταῖροι.
πάντες μὲν στυγεροὶ θάνατοι δειλοῖσι βροτοῖσι, 341
λιμῷ δ' οἴκτιστον θανέειν καὶ πότμον ἐπισπεῖν.
ἀλλ' ἄγετ', Ἠελίοιο βοῶν ἐλάσαντες ἀρίστας
ῥέξομεν ἀθανάτοισι, τοὶ οὐρανὸν εὐρὺν ἔχουσιν·
εἰ δέ κεν εἰς Ἰθάκην ἀφικοίμεθα, πατρίδα γαῖαν, 345
αἶψά κεν Ἠελίῳ Ὑπερίονι πίονα νηὸν
τεύξομεν, ἐν δέ κε θεῖμεν ἀγάλματα πολλὰ καὶ ἐσθλά.
εἰ δὲ χολωσάμενός τι βοῶν ὀρθοκραιράων
νῆ' ἐθέλῃ ὀλέσαι, ἐπὶ δ' ἕσπωνται θεοὶ ἄλλοι,
βούλομ' ἅπαξ πρὸς κῦμα χανὼν ἀπὸ θυμὸν ὀλέσσαι, 350
ἢ δηθὰ στρεύγεσθαι ἐὼν ἐν νήσῳ ἐρήμῃ.'
"Ὣς ἔφατ' Εὐρύλοχος, ἐπὶ δ' ᾔνεον ἄλλοι ἑταῖροι.
αὐτίκα δ' Ἠελίοιο βοῶν ἐλάσαντες ἀρίστας
ἐγγύθεν, οὐ γὰρ τῆλε νεὸς κυανοπρώροιο
βοσκέσκονθ' ἕλικες καλαὶ βόες εὐρυμέτωποι, 355
τὰς δὲ περίστησάν τε[1] καὶ εὐχετόωντο θεοῖσιν,
φύλλα δρεψάμενοι τέρενα δρυὸς ὑψικόμοιο·

---

[1] περιστησάν τε Bekker : περιστήσαντο MSS.

456

had been consumed from out the ship, and now they must needs roam about in search of game, fishes, and fowl, and whatever might come to their hands —fishing with bent hooks, for hunger pinched their bellies—then I went apart up the island that I might pray to the gods in the hope that one of them might show me a way to go. And when, as I went through the island, I had got away from my comrades, I washed my hands in a place where there was shelter from the wind, and prayed to all the gods that hold Olympus; but they shed sweet sleep upon my eyelids. And meanwhile Eurylochus began to give evil counsel to my comrades:

" 'Hear my words, comrades, for all your evil plight. All forms of death are hateful to wretched mortals, but to die of hunger, and so meet one's doom, is the most pitiful. Nay, come, let us drive off the best of the kine of Helios and offer sacrifice to the immortals who hold broad heaven. And if we ever reach Ithaca, our native land, we will straightway build a rich temple to Helios Hyperion and put therein many goodly offerings. And if haply he be wroth at all because of his straight-horned kine, and be minded to destroy our ship, and the other gods consent, rather would I lose my life once for all with a gulp at the wave, than pine slowly away in a desert isle.'

"So spoke Eurylochus, and the rest of my comrades gave assent. Straightway they drove off the best of the kine of Helios from near at hand, for not far from the dark-prowed ship were grazing the fair, sleek kine, broad of brow. Around these, then, they stood and made prayer to the gods, plucking the tender leaves from off a high-crested oak;[1] for

[1] The green leaves were to serve as a substitute for the barley grains ordinarily used in sacrifice.

οὐ γὰρ ἔχον κρῖ λευκὸν ἐυσσέλμου ἐπὶ νηός.
αὐτὰρ ἐπεί ῥ' εὔξαντο καὶ ἔσφαξαν καὶ ἔδειραν,
μηρούς τ' ἐξέταμον κατά τε κνίσῃ ἐκάλυψαν   360
δίπτυχα ποιήσαντες, ἐπ' αὐτῶν δ' ὠμοθέτησαν.
οὐδ' εἶχον μέθυ λεῖψαι ἐπ' αἰθομένοις ἱεροῖσιν,
ἀλλ' ὕδατι σπένδοντες ἐπώπτων ἔγκατα πάντα.
αὐτὰρ ἐπεὶ κατὰ μῆρ' ἐκάη καὶ σπλάγχνα πάσαντο,
μίστυλλόν τ' ἄρα τἆλλα καὶ ἀμφ' ὀβελοῖσιν ἔπειραν. 365
καὶ τότε μοι βλεφάρων ἐξέσσυτο νήδυμος ὕπνος,
βῆν δ' ἰέναι ἐπὶ νῆα θοὴν καὶ θῖνα θαλάσσης.
ἀλλ' ὅτε δὴ σχεδὸν ἦα κιὼν νεὸς ἀμφιελίσσης,
καὶ τότε με κνίσης ἀμφήλυθεν ἡδὺς ἀυτμή.
οἰμώξας δὲ θεοῖσι μέγ' [1] ἀθανάτοισι γεγώνευν·   370
    "'Ζεῦ πάτερ ἠδ' ἄλλοι μάκαρες θεοὶ αἰὲν ἐόντες,
ἦ με μάλ' εἰς ἄτην κοιμήσατε νηλέι ὕπνῳ.
οἱ δ' ἕταροι μέγα ἔργον ἐμητίσαντο μένοντες.'
    "'Ὠκέα δ' Ἠελίῳ Ὑπερίονι ἄγγελος ἦλθε
Λαμπετίη τανύπεπλος, ὅ οἱ βόας ἔκταμεν ἡμεῖς.   375
αὐτίκα δ' ἀθανάτοισι μετηύδα χωόμενος κῆρ·
    "'Ζεῦ πάτερ ἠδ' ἄλλοι μάκαρες θεοὶ αἰὲν ἐόντες,
τῖσαι δὴ ἑτάρους Λαερτιάδεω Ὀδυσῆος,
οἵ μευ βοῦς ἔκτειναν ὑπέρβιον, ᾗσιν ἐγώ γε
χαίρεσκον μὲν ἰὼν εἰς οὐρανὸν ἀστερόεντα,   380
ἠδ' ὁπότ' ἂψ ἐπὶ γαῖαν ἀπ' οὐρανόθεν προτραποίμην.
εἰ δέ μοι οὐ τίσουσι βοῶν ἐπιεικέ' ἀμοιβήν,
δύσομαι εἰς Ἀίδαο καὶ ἐν νεκύεσσι φαείνω.'
    "Τὸν δ' ἀπαμειβόμενος προσέφη νεφεληγερέτα Ζεύς·
'Ἠέλι', ἦ τοι μὲν σὺ μετ' ἀθανάτοισι φάεινε   385

---

[1] μέγ' Bekker : μετ' MSS.